AN ANTHOLOGY OF Living
Religions

Editorial Director: Craig Campanella
Editor in Chief: Dickson Musslewhite
Publisher: Nancy Roberts
Project Manager: Nicole Conforti
Editorial Assistant: Nart Varoqua
Managing Editor: Ann Marie McCarthy
Operations Specialist: Christina Amato

10 9 8 7 6 5 4 3 2 1

This book was designed and produced by
Laurence King Publishing Ltd., London
www.laurenceking.com

Designed by Mark Holt
Production Manager: Simon Walsh
Editorial Manager: Kara Hattersley-Smith
Development Editor: Melanie White
Literary Permissions: Lucy Macmillan, Vimbai Shire

Credits and acknowledgments of material borrowed from other sources and reproduced, with permission, in this textbook appear on pages 375–377.

Every effort has been made to contact the copyright holders, but should there be any errors or omissions, Laurence King Publishing Ltd would be pleased to insert the appropriate acknowledgment in any subsequent printing of this publication.

Library of Congress Cataloging-in-Publication Data

An anthology of living religions / [edited by] Mary Pat Fisher, Lee W. Bailey. -- 3rd ed.
    p. cm.
  Includes index.
  ISBN-13: 978-0-205-24680-9 (pbk. : alk. paper)
  ISBN-10: 0-205-24680-X (pbk. : alk. paper)
  1. Religions. 2. Religions--History--Sources. I. Fisher, Mary Pat, 1943- II. Bailey, Lee Worth.
  BL74.A58 2012
  200--dc23

                                    2011024266

ISBN-10: 0-205-24680-X
ISBN-13: 978-0-205-24680-9

Front cover: © David Pearson / Alamy
People bathing and praying at the Ganges, Varanasi, India.

AN ANTHOLOGY OF Living Religions

THIRD EDITION

MARY PAT FISHER • LEE W. BAILEY

PEARSON

Boston Columbus Indianapolis New York San Francisco Upper Saddle River
Amsterdam Cape Town Dubai London Madrid Milan Munich Paris Montréal Toronto
Delhi Mexico City São Paulo Sydney Hong Kong Seoul Singapore Taipei Tokyo

CONTENTS

CHAPTER 2
INDIGENOUS SACRED WAYS 39

CHAPTER 3
HINDUISM 64

CHAPTER 9
CHRISTIANITY 235

CHAPTER 10
ISLAM 275

PREFACE

Religious points of view underlie the thinking and behavior of the majority of the world's citizens. As the twenty-first century evolves, a deeper understanding of these perspectives is a necessity in our increasingly interwoven, pluralistic cultures. To enhance understanding and perhaps appreciation of each religion, we offer an introductory chapter summarizing major overarching methods for studying religions worldwide, such as the sociology of religion. The following chapters contain a selection of interesting and significant texts explaining each religion from the inside, as its founders and practitioners have explained it and as people are trying to live by its precepts today. It is important to give the major world religions—as well as a sampling of local and new religions—the opportunity to explain themselves in their own terms.

We have tried to open many windows to understanding. We offer excerpts from each religion's original inspired writings or oral traditions, exemplary stories about the founders, significant later elaborations of the teachings, and recent articles showing each religion grappling with contemporary issues. These include globalization, environmental decay, women's issues, social injustice, the relation between religion and politics, and tensions between fundamentalist and liberal interpretations of the faith. We have included women's voices and histories throughout the anthology. We believe that these excerpts old and new illustrate that religions are dynamic and relevant in today's world.

To guide readers through this wealth of material, we first introduce the founder, history, and basic principles of each faith. Each excerpt or group of excerpts is preceded by a brief introduction to the context and significance of the material. Unfamiliar terms are defined in a glossary at the end of the chapter. For each religion, we also offer a list of holy days, a historical outline, questions for review, and a list of further resources including websites. Although this anthology thus stands on its own, it follows the organization of Mary Pat Fisher's bestselling textbook, *Living Religions*, and can be used with that text for deeper understanding.

Additions to the Third Edition
In this third edition we have added many new pieces to bring the book up to date and to meet reviewers' requests for both historical and contemporary materials. The improvements include reorganization to reflect changes in the eighth edition of *Living Religions*, revision of introductions and review questions, plus:

- Methodologies for the study of religions, including Ninian Smart's "Dimensions of the Sacred"
- Atheism, Irish myth and Zen koan
- "The Spiritual Idea of the 'Feminine'" from an Asian Indian scholar
- African, Maori, and Adivasi spiritual ways
- Buddhism in North America
- Chinese Religions as a whole, including goddesses and folk religion
- New chapter on Shinto
- Zoroastrianism and the Gatha texts
- Reform and Reconstructionist Judaism

- Elie Wiesel on indifference to the Nazi Holocaust
- Founding of the Pentecostal movement and Amish forgiveness
- Christian social justice, megachurches, environmental crises, and globalization in South Korea, Brazil, and Africa
- Outward and inward aspects of the Qur'an
- Ayatollah Khomeini on Islamic governance, plus contemporary articles on issues of jihad and just war
- The oneness of God by a feminist Sikh scholar
- The Church of Jesus Christ of Latter-day Saints, CaoDai, and Wicca
- The impact of globalization on religions
- Secularism versus exclusivism
- A Muslim scholar analyzing "demonizing" of the "Other"
- Authentic spirituality

We hope that these additions and changes will make the study of world religions more accessible in their historical context and more relevant to today's situations.

Acknowledgments

Many people around the world helped in gathering materials for the first and second editions and are gratefully acknowledged therein. For this new edition, the authors want to express special gratitude to David Peck, Harvey Sindima, Vijaya Ramaswamy, Tina Mehta, Neeraj Gupta, and Nikky Gunninder Kaur Singh for preparing and/or sharing new materials. The constructive criticisms of our reviewers have been of great help in preparing this third edition, and for this we want to thank Jon Brammer, Dr. Diana Dimitrova, Rahuldeep Singh Gill, Steven Leonard Jacobs, Bill Lanning, Michael A. O'Malley, Joseph L. Price, Santos Roman, David W. Suter, James W. Ward, and Mark Owen Webb.

At Laurence King Publishing, we thank our beloved editors Melanie White, Clare Double, and Kara Hattersley-Smith, who have been most patient and wise in guiding our process, Lucy Macmillan, very careful in seeking permissions for the extracts, and at Pearson Nicole Conforti, who has been wonderfully supportive.

Lee Bailey expresses his special thanks to the devoted scholars whose work helped revise this edition, including Charles Prebish, Ellen Umansky, and Min Qin Wang.

For Mary Pat Fisher, preparation of this anthology has been particularly inspired by the late Baba Virsa Singh, patron of the Gobind Sadan Institute for Advanced Studies in Comparative Religion, who generously shared his profound appreciation and understanding of the world's sacred scriptures with people of all faiths. May our readers also grow in understanding and appreciation, for the sake of us all.

Mary Pat Fisher, Gobind Sadan Institute for Advanced Studies in Comparative Religion, Delhi
Lee W. Bailey, Department of Philosophy and Religion, Ithaca College, New York (retired)

The predominant forms of religions in the world today

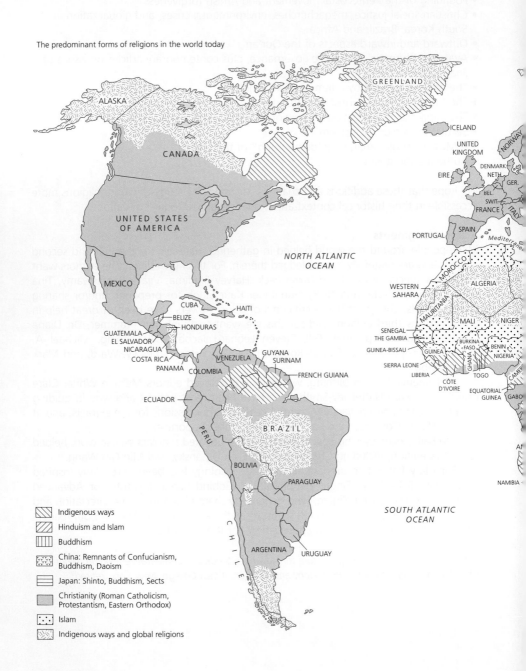

Indigenous ways

Hinduism and Islam

Buddhism

China: Remnants of Confucianism, Buddhism, Daoism

Japan: Shinto, Buddhism, Sects

Christianity (Roman Catholicism, Protestantism, Eastern Orthodox)

Islam

Indigenous ways and global religions

MAP xix

RUSSIAN FEDERATION

ND

TONIA
LATVIA
LITHUANIA
BELARUS

RAINE

MOLDOVA

GEORGIA

KAZAKHSTAN

UZBEKISTAN

MONGOLIA

ARMENIA

AZER.

TURKMENISTAN

KYRGYZSTAN

TAJIKISTAN

NORTH
KOREA

SOUTH
KOREA

JAPAN

TURKEY

ECE

SYRIA

LEB.

IRAQ

ISRAEL
Judaism

JORDAN

KUWAIT

IRAN

AFGHANISTAN

PAKISTAN

NEPAL

BANGLADESH

CHINA

TAIWAN

HONG KONG

NORTH PACIFIC
OCEAN

PT.

SAUDI
ARABIA

OMAN

Sikhism

INDIA

MYANMAR
(BURMA)

LAOS

PHILIPPINES

ERITREA

YEMEN

Parsism
(Zoroastrianism)

THAILAND

VIETNAM

AN

SRI LANKA

CAMBODIA

ETHIOPIA

KENYA

SOMALIA

MALAYSIA

SOUTH PACIFIC
OCEAN

TANZANIA

INDONESIA

PAPUA
NEW
GUINEA

MALAWI

MOZAMBIQUE

BWE

MADAGASCAR

INDIAN OCEAN

BOTSWANA

SWAZILAND

LESOTHO

TH
CA

AUSTRALIA

NEW ZEALAND

	←—2000 BCE	1500	1000	500	0	300 CE
Indigenous	Neolithic reverence for ←—nature, mother goddess, ancestors					
Hinduism	Indus River cultures with ←—goddess and indigenous religions c. 2500 BCE	Vedas first written c. 1500 BCE	Vyasa systematizes Upanishads c. 1000–500 BCE	*Ramayana* and *Mahabharata* in present form 400 BCE–200 CE	*The Laws of Manu* compiled by 100–300 CE	
				Patanjali systematizes *Yoga Sutras* by 200 BCE		
Jainism	23 Tirthankaras ←—before c. 777 BCE		Mahavira, last Tirthankara, c. 599–527 BCE	Some *Agam Sutras* written down c. 300 BCE Svetambaras and Digambaras diverge after 300 BCE		
Buddhism			Gautama Buddha c. 563–483 BCE	King Ashoka spreads Buddhism c. 258 BCE Theravada Buddhism develops 200 BCE–200 CE	Mahayana Buddhism develops c. 100 CE Asvagahosha writes *Acts of the Buddha* 2nd c. CE	
Chinese Religions			Laozi c. 600–300 BCE Confucius c. 551–479 BCE Liezi c. 475–221 BCE	Mencius c. 390–305 BCE Zhuangzi c. 365–290 BCE Educational system based on Confucian Classics from 206 BCE	Ge Hong on alchemy 200–300 CE Pure Land Buddhism enters China c. 100 CE	
Judaism	Abraham c. 1900–1700 BCE?	Exodus from Egypt led by Moses c. 1250 BCE King David c. 1010–970 BCE King Solomon builds First Temple c. 950 BCE	First Temple destroyed; Jews exiled 586 BCE	Jerusalem falls to Romans; Jewish Diaspora begins 70 CE Canon of Tanakh agreed c. 90 CE Rabbinical tradition develops 1st–4th c. CE	Mishnah c. 200 CE	
Christianity				Jesus c. 4 BCE–30 CE Letters of Paul 48–64 CE Gospels written down c. 70–95 CE	Athanasius 296–373 CE Council of Nicaea: divinity of Jesus 325 CE Augustine 354–430 CE Official religion of Roman Empire 392 CE	
Islam						
Sikhism						
New Religious Movements						

600	900	1200	1500	1800	2000
	Viking invasions carry Norse religion into northern Europe 800–1100		European colonialists invade indigenous cultures in Americas from 1492	Slave trade introduces African religions into Americas from 1550	Hopi Message to the U.N. General Assembly 1992
Puranas written down 500–1500					
Bhakti movement 600–1800				Mahatma Gandhi 1869–1948	
	Sankara organizes Vedanta school c. 788–820		Kabir c. 1440–1518	Paramahansa Yogananda 1893–1952	
			Mirabai c. 1500–50	V. D. Savarkar, "Hindutva" 1923	
Division of Svetambaras and Digambaras formalized c. 450			New orders under Mughal rule 1526–1818	Jain teaching spreads out from India from 1818	Jain monks establish centers outside India 1970s–80s
	Buddhism declared national religion of Tibet 700s	Chan Buddhism to Japan as Zen 13th c.			Buddhism spreads in the West 20th c.
	Persecution of Chinese Buddhists begins 845				
Emperor declares Daoism official religion c. 400–448	Song dynasty: Neo-Confucianism 960–1279			End of Confucianism as state ideology in China 1911	
Guanyin flourishes from c. 400	Zhou Dunyi 1017–73			Cultural Revolution attacks religions 1966–76	
Japan imports Confucianism c. 500–600	Zhang Zai 1020–77			Confucian and Daoist revival in East Asia from 1980s	
Chan Buddhism begins c. 600	Zhang Boduan, *Awakening to Perfection* 1075–8				
Jerusalem Talmud c. 500	Maimonides c. 1135–1204			Baal-Shem Tov begins Hasidism c 1700–60	Nazi Holocaust 1933–45
Babylonian Talmud c. 600			Mass expulsion of Jews from Spain 1492		Independent state of Israel 1948
					Six-Day War 1967
					Conflict between Hezbollah and Israel 2006+
Canon of Bible set c. 400	Consolidation of papal power 800–1300		Monastic orders proliferate 14th c.	Methodism: John Wesley 1707–88	Mother Teresa 1910–97
		Anselm of Canterbury 1033–1109	Spanish Inquisition established 1478		Martin Luther King 1929–68
		Western and Eastern churches split 1054	Protestantism begins with Martin Luther's "95 Theses" 1517		Vatican II 1962
			Council of Trent 1545–63		Pope Benedict XVI elected 2005
Muhammad 570–632	Islam's cultural peak under Abbasids 750–1258		Akbar becomes Mughal emperor 1556	Sufi Order of the West 1910	
Spread of Islam begins 633	*Sahih Bukhari* by 870	Al-Ghazali 1058–1111		Muslim-majority Pakistan separates from Hindu-majority India 1947	
Canon of Qur'an set 650	*Sahih Muslim* by 875	Ibn Rushd 1126–98			
	Ibn Sina 980–1037	Ibn 'Arabi 1165–1240		OPEC; Muslim resurgence 1970s	
		Turks conquer Constantinople 1453		9/11 attacks in U.S. 2001	
				U.S. and allies invade Iraq 2003	
		Guru Nanak 1469–1539	Guru Gobind Singh initiates Khalsa 1699	British massacre Sikhs in Amritsar 1919	
			Guru Granth Sahib installed as Guru 1708	Sikhs demand separate state 1984	
				Celebration of 300th anniversary of Khalsa 1999	
			Bahá'u'lláh 1817–92	Sun Myung Moon founds Unification Church 1954	
			Mormon Church founded 1822	Parliament of the World's Religions 1993, 1999, 2004	
			Jehovah's Witnesses established 1872		
			Theosophical Society starts 1875		

CHAPTER 1
RELIGIOUS RESPONSES

Religious affiliations are sources of both comfort and conflict. Religions provide important guides to meaning and consolation in difficult times. But globally increased religiously supported violence, coupled with powerful new weapons, has intensified the urgency of understanding others' beliefs. Global religions and new religious movements are vibrant in many regions, often playing a significant role in public events as well as people's personal lives. For great numbers of people around the world, religion is a central aspect of life's patterns and meanings. Religious experiences may inspire courage, patience, tolerance, charity, morality, acts of extreme altruism, and selfless love. They may have a healing, transformative effect. They may reveal unseen dimensions of existence. Religious experiences and training unfortunately may also frighten, oppress, and breed violence and hatred of others, if the teachings have been misunderstood or distorted by religious "authorities" acting in their own self-interest.

There is no one pattern that can be universally termed "religion." Many prophets, teachers, and gurus have offered what is understood by their followers as enlightened wisdom. Institutions have been built around their teachings and, with them, somewhat different understandings of life and different methods of approaching the truth of existence. To some people, religion refers to reverence for communications with the "supernatural" recorded in sacred texts, but other interpretations, such as some Buddhist traditions, focus on overcoming worldly sufferings through meditatively awakening to cosmic "emptiness" in the world.

In subsequent chapters, we will offer a wealth of primary source material giving intimate glimpses into each world of faith as the faithful understand it. However, before doing so, in this chapter we will approach religions from a distance, trying to gain a critical basis for understanding the many perspectives from which religious phenomena have been studied.

Some readers coming to the study of world religions from a traditional religious background may react with discomfort as they encounter new ideas and new religions. Others more skeptical or critical of traditional religions may be uncomfortable with certain practices, such as some authors' use of the masculine pronouns or expressions such as "man" meant to include both genders. We hope that readers will maintain both a sympathetic respect and a critical eye, and strive to understand the historical background and personal diversity for the colorful variety of human religious expressions. The best reasons for maintaining or changing religious practices come from understanding them.

The study of world religions

As the world shrinks with globalization, the potential for violent conflict increases unless people can gain tolerance by understanding each other's basic worldviews and religious traditions. The rise of technological society has also strengthened materialistic thinking and the problems associated with it. But spiritual sensitivity can go a long way towards combating tribalism, nationalism, suicide, greed, environmental destruction, and abuse. At its best, religion has a healing and peaceful effect.

Methodologies for Studying Religions by Lee W. Bailey

The academic study of religion, which seeks to understand various religions empathetically and without the claim that any one is true, uses different methods and is sometimes called "comparative religion." The study of these methods, or basic principles used for study in various academic fields, is known as **hermeneutics**. Awareness of these metaphysical or ontological frameworks and their foundational assumptions is critically important.[1]

First, can religion be defined globally? There are many possible broad definitions: simply the "way things are," belief in God or gods, creedal statements, the **ground of Being** (foundation of existence), obedience to laws, belonging to an institutional religion, what one does in one's private inwardness, social norms for ethical behavior, meditative experience of a nameless cosmic presence, participation in awesome natural wonders, gratefulness for existence itself, or belief that goodness ultimately overcomes suffering and evil. Religions are perhaps too deep and complex for a simple definition to include all.

In the nineteenth century, the comparison of world religions grew into an academic project in the West. F. Max Müller (1823–1900), at Oxford University in England, translated and collected numerous sacred texts for the first time later in the century. He prepared the 50-volume *Sacred Books of the East* in English, which included Hindu, Buddhist, Chinese, and Muslim texts. Müller advocated the "scientific" study of world religions through a detached understanding, seeking "objective" knowledge outside the lens of Western **monotheistic** categories. Müller analyzed **myths** as rationalizations of natural events, a "proto-science" in cultural evolution. He sought to explain

---

1 Metaphysics—the largely rational study of ultimate reality or Being. Ontology—the largely intuitive study of ultimate reality or Being.

Indo-European religions as a widespread family of linguistically related strands and reduced religion to natural evolutionary causes. In this era, "science" was not as rigorous as it is today; it was more "natural philosophy," especially when applied to culture. But philosophical assumptions, such as **reduction**, still play an important role in scientific thinking.

From 1890 to 1937 James Frazer (1854–1941) wrote *The Golden Bough*, an extensive, though not fully accurate, encyclopedia of world myths, **rituals**, and religions. He expanded new cross-cultural themes such as magic, divine kingship, and the dying and rising god or goddess of vegetation. He put them into the era's popular schema of an historical evolution from magic through religions, giving way to science. Religions were thus interpreted as backward, unsuccessful, primitive sciences—a theory which anthropologists disproved by observing, for example, South Pacific island cultures that could make large boats and navigate effectively.

Some early theories showed the strong influence of Darwinian theory, and its offspring cultural evolution, with its effort to schematize world cultures into a developmental pattern that ended up with Christianity or Western scientific cultures on top. The scientific method seemed to offer a neutral stance, but perhaps exaggerated its ability to transfer the scientific study of nature to religion. Comparative studies pulled the mantle of scientific authority over itself partly to defend against strong traditions of church influences that rejected the neutral stance. We no longer interpret religions as primitive science and newer scientific methods are used.

Today the scientific method has produced a generation of "New Atheists." Contemporary scientists, using a philosophy of reduction, argue that religions can be reduced to scientific categories, such as evolution. Richard Dawkins, for example, argues that religion is a scientific hypothesis, to be judged as such. So God's existence is a scientific question.[2]

As the social sciences developed their application of scientific methods to the study of society, many theories unfolded that interpreted religion as social rather than **transcendent**. The anthropologist Emile Durkheim (1858–1917) in France published the widely influential *Forms of the Religious Life* (1912). He saw religion as the most characteristic element of the collective mind of each society, the "glue" that holds it together, expressed in rituals about gods, totems, taboos, and ancestor spirits. He sought to explain away transcendence by reducing it to the level of a social force.

Max Weber (1864–1920) in Germany developed the **sociology of religion**, arguing that economic forces directly influence concepts of gods and demons. In his *Protestant Ethic and the Spirit of Capitalism* (1905), he stressed the affinity between the Puritan spirit and the rise of middle-class capitalism. Combined with increased rationalism, he argued, Protestant Christianity's work ethic—notably in Calvinism—promoted greed for profit (the "prosperity gospel"), as successful pursuit of gain was seen as God's

---

2 Richard Dawkins, *The Blind Watchmaker*. New York: W.W. Norton, 1996.

blessing. He also developed the notion of **charisma**, the dynamic, heroic personality type set apart with superhuman qualities.[3]

The **psychological** method for studying religion involves various approaches, such as the theory of developmental stages of faith, from infantile security, through mythic literalism, **anthropomorphism**, conventional religion, reflective, and universalizing types.[4]

Highly symbolic themes have been found in the study of the unconscious and in religious literature and experiences. Early in the twentieth century, Sigmund Freud (1856–1939) in Vienna, Austria showed through the interpretation of dreams, family dynamics, errors, and symptoms that the unconscious psyche is not random images but meaningful messages. He developed many theories which are still used, such as the **projection** of unconscious contents into the world, and interpreted God as a projected infantile father image. Freud also over-emphasized the role of sexuality and kept a nineteenth-century materialist view of religion as an illusion. His colleague, Carl Jung (1875–1961), developed the psychology of religion most compatible with religion.

Jung's psychotherapeutic (analytic) method interpreted dreams with both personal meanings and parallel images in the "collective unconscious" that appear in **archetypal** images throughout myth, folklore, religion, and in cultural images such as heroes, enemies, lovers, warriors, and gods. Joseph Campbell (1904–87) expanded upon Jung's theory of myth, emphasizing the "hero's journey" into the depths of the collective unconscious, encountering various archetypal figures and returning renewed and wiser. Jung showed that myths are not all just errors, but read non-literally, they can be important archetypal symbols of the spiritual quest, and thus provide a fresh approach to interpreting religions. Gods, devils, lovers, and enemies in sacred traditions emerge with very personal meanings, as well as collective significance.

The **historical** method of studying religion is the work of digging up the past and discovering important evidence through archaeology and ancient texts. For example, the buried funeral remains of the Chinese Emperor Qin (Chin) and his astonishing army of 7,000 life-sized terracotta army figures (210 BCE) show the power of the ancient belief in sacred kings and immortality. Textual analysis of uncovered texts, such as the *Nag Hammadi Library*, provides glimpses of the environment of ancient Judaism and emerging Christianity. Its "Thunder, Perfect Mind" and the "Gospel of Mary" show an expanded view of women and goddesses at that time.

Today, the major academic methodology for studying religion is called **phenomenology of religion**. It focuses on experience in world religions, rather than cognition. Theism, or having anthropomorphic gods, is not necessary. Somewhat different from other kinds of phenomenology, it

---

3 Max Weber, *The Theory of Social and Economic Organization*, trans. Henderson & Parsons. New York: Free Press, 1947.
4 James Fowler, *Stages of Faith*. San Francisco: Harper & Row, 1981.

stresses empathy for the spiritual qualities of a religion and does not adopt the metaphysics of the subject/object dualism, which tries to restrict feelings to internal realities. Nor does it apply reductionism, trying to explain religion by shrinking it to simpler, non-religious, natural entities or causes. Freud reduced religion to an illusory infantile Oedipal fixation, others to cognitive, evolutionary, or genetic causes.

Early phenomenology of religion sought to find the "essence" of a religious phenomenon, such as compassion or forgiveness, and to express the presence of Being and its various manifestations. It also emphasized neutrality concerning the truth of each particular tradition. In scholarship, the truth question is "bracketed", although personally one may or may not believe. This is distinct from science which usually practices "methodological atheism," or its opposite, theology, which assumes one religion to be true.

Rudolf Otto (1869–1937) in Germany wrote *The Idea of the Holy* (1917), arguing against the idea that the naturalistic sciences could reduce religion to a natural or social force. Otto advocated the *sui generis* nature of religion— religion as a category unto itself, not reducible to others. Behind **creeds, dogmas**, and religious institutions, Otto stressed the reality of the holy phenomena described as the awesome **numinous** experience of the sacred, essential to true religious understanding. Felt in the wonder of life in the cosmos, the numinous evokes the presence of a transcendent and present power outside oneself (*mysterium tremendum*).

From 1925 to 1950, Gerardus van der Leeuw (1890–1950) in the Netherlands was formative in shaping the phenomenology of religion. His influential work *Religion as Essence and Manifestation* (1933) explored the intuitive "essences" of many phenomena, such as sacred time, mysticism, compassion, obedience, art, and love, without reducing them to natural categories.

Mircea Eliade (1907–86) led the history and phenomenology of religion movement at the University of Chicago after World War II. Following study in India, he wrote classic books on many topics, such as yoga, myth, and shamanism. Although he welcomed the input of the social sciences, he did not reduce religion to conscious experience and the natural world. He stressed the *sui generis,* non-reducible quality of religious experiences, even if unconscious. His book *Patterns in Comparative Religion* (1958) outlines major phenomenological themes with historical examples from world religions. He developed a theory that myth and ritual are ways of re-experiencing the ultimate powers of existence expressed in past stories and events. For him sky, sun, stone, fertility, and temple all disclose sacred powers through the human thirst for primordial ultimate reality. He edited the first edition of the major *Encyclopedia of Religion* (1987, 2004).

Ninian Smart (1927–2001), at Lancaster University in England and University of California at Santa Barbara, refined the phenomenological method, in important books such as *Dimensions of the Sacred* (1996). Smart focused on a list of seven dimensions of the sacred—ritual, doctrinal, mythic, experiential, ethical, organizational, and materialistic—that can be found in world religions and which are valuable ways of exploring the phenomenology of each tradition.

Anthropologists criticized phenomenology of religion for trying to link too many divergent religious elements and for neglecting the specific historical details of various traditions. The growth of **postmodernist** thought (around 1980) raised criticisms of the phenomenological method. Postmodernists such as Jacques Derrida (1930–2004) and Michel Foucault (1926–84) rejected the authority of the "meta-narratives" of religious cosmic stories, such as creation and historical dramas of salvation, as well as the claims to rational certainty about the natural world of some scientific thinkers.

Feminists, such as Mary Daly, joined the deconstruction of sacred authorities such as patriarchy in religion. Phyllis Trible exposed the "texts of terror" in sacred books that seemingly justify the abuse of women. Other feminist scholars, such as Carol Christ, explored worship of the goddess and witchcraft.

Jonathan Z. Smith at the University of Chicago makes the contemporary argument that comparative religion lacks the necessary scientific method. He rejects the phenomenological effort to find the "essences" of religious patterns. He rejects any view of the sacred if it is not a theoretical, conscious object or term (such as "projection of subject onto object"). He welcomes statistical studies as more objective.

Many scholars of world religions still seek to find common ground. Examples include Huston Smith's *The Primordial Tradition* (1976), Matthew Fox's *One River, Many Wells* (2000), John Hick's *God has Many Names* (1980), Raimon Panikkar's *The Intra-religious Dialogue* (1978), and Thich Nhat Hanh's *Living Buddha, Living Christ* (1995).

Other religious scholars are now finding a middle ground between broad generalizations about common patterns and careful attention to local cultural differences. Diana Eck at Harvard, for example, says that we must be careful of over-generalizing in comparisons. In her study of Hinduism in Banares, for example, she found that the English term "worship" overlaps only slightly with the Hindu experience of *darshan* as "seeing" or "beholding" a divine presence. Also, she criticizes supposed "objectivity"—"the so-called scientific study of religion and its notions of purely 'objective' scholarship with no authorial viewpoint is increasingly understood to be intellectually naïve.... even the most 'secular' of social scientists write out of a set of premises..."[5]

Kimberly Patton, also at Harvard, stresses that postmodern scholars are themselves typically committed to meta-narratives, such as social justice, anti-racism, women's rights, and opposition to imperialism and colonialism.

Clearly there are a variety of approaches to the study of religion, and their various positions need examination. Many methods are represented

5 Kimberly Patton and Benjamin Ray, *A Magic Still Dwells: Comparative Religion in the Postmodern Age.* Berkeley, CA: University of California Press, 2000, p. 141.

within this volume. One can look at them independently side-by-side, or seek common themes and compare the way each tradition has developed them. Themes, such as transcendence, law, compassion, war, social justice, and inner peace, take innumerable local religious forms.

SOURCE: Original article for this book by Lee W. Bailey, 2011

The Sacredness of Nature and Cosmic Religion

by Mircea Eliade

Mircea Eliade (1907–86) of the University of Chicago was a pioneer in the historical and phenomenological approach to the study of religion. He blended two major methods in his approach: first, the history of religions, in order to clarify the factual side of religions, such as the dates, places, historical contexts, and texts; and second, the phenomenology of religions, in order to reflect intuitively and symbolically on the "essences" of religions by comparing archetypal themes such as the **sacred** and the **profane** in space, time, nature, and human existence. He was a major contributor to a renewed understanding of myth and ritual as worldwide religious phenomena, highly symbolic and meaningful. Eliade's multicultural analysis of the "sky gods" from his classic 1957 book *The Sacred and the Profane* is an example of this approach.

For religious man, nature is never only "natural"; it is always fraught with a religious value. This is easy to understand, for the cosmos is a divine creation; coming from the hands of the gods, the world is impregnated with sacredness. It is not simply a sacrality *communicated* by the gods, as is the case, for example, with a place or an object consecrated by the divine presence. The gods did more; *they manifested the different modalities of the sacred in the very structure of the world and of cosmic phenomena.*

The world stands displayed in such a manner that, in contemplating it, religious man discovers the many modalities of the sacred, and hence of being. Above all, the world exists, it is there, and it has a structure; it is not a chaos but a cosmos, hence it presents itself as creation, as work of the gods. This divine work always preserves its quality of transparency, that is, it spontaneously reveals the many aspects of the sacred. The sky directly, "naturally," reveals the infinite distance, the transcendence of the deity. The earth too is transparent; it presents itself as universal mother and nurse. The cosmic rhythms manifest order, harmony, permanence, fecundity. The cosmos as a whole is an organism at once *real, living,* and *sacred*; it simultaneously reveals the modalities of being and of sacrality. Ontophany[6] and hierophany meet.

In this chapter we shall try to understand how the world presents itself to the eyes of religious man—or, more precisely, how sacrality is revealed through the very structures of the world. We must not forget that for

---

6 Ontophany—a manifestation of being or sacred ultimate reality.

religious man the supernatural is indissolubly connected with the natural, that nature always expresses something that transcends it. As we said earlier: a sacred stone is venerated because it is *sacred*, not because it is a *stone*; it is the sacrality *manifested through the mode of being of the stone* that reveals its true essence. This is why we cannot speak of naturism or of natural religion in the sense that the nineteenth century gave to those terms; for it is "supernature" that the religious man apprehends through the natural aspects of the world.

The Celestial Sacred and the Uranian Gods Simple contemplation of the celestial vault already provokes a religious experience. The sky shows itself to be infinite, transcendent. It is pre-eminently the "wholly other" than the little represented by man and his environment. Transcendence is revealed by simple awareness of infinite height. "Most high" spontaneously becomes an attribute of divinity. The higher regions inaccessible to man, the sidereal zones, acquire the momentousness of the transcendent, of absolute reality, of eternity. There dwell the gods; there a few privileged mortals make their way by rites of ascent; there, in the conception of certain religions, mount the souls of the dead. The "most high" is a dimension inaccessible to man as man; it belongs to superhuman forces and beings. He who ascends by mounting the steps of a sanctuary or the ritual ladder that leads to the sky ceases to be a man; in one way or another, he shares in the divine condition.

All this is not arrived at by a logical, rational operation. The transcendental category of height, of the superterrestrial, of the infinite, is revealed to the whole man, to his intelligence and his soul. It is a total awareness on man's part; beholding the sky, he simultaneously discovers the divine incommensurability and his own situation in the cosmos. For the sky, *by its own mode of being*, reveals transcendence, force, eternity. It *exists absolutely because it is high, infinite, eternal, powerful.*

This is the true significance of the statement made above—that the gods manifested the different modalities of the sacred in the very structure of the world. In other words, the cosmos—paradigmatic work of the gods—is so constructed that a religious sense of the divine transcendence is aroused by the very existence of the sky. And since the sky *exists* absolutely, many of the supreme gods of primitive peoples are called by names designating height, the celestial vault, meteorological phenomena, or simply Owner of the Sky or Sky Dweller.

The supreme divinity of the Maori is named Iho; *iho* means elevated, high up. Uwoluwu, the supreme god of the Akposo [Africans], signifies what is on high, the upper regions. Among the Selk'nam of Tierra del Fuego God is called Dweller in the Sky or He Who is in the Sky. Puluga, the supreme being of the Andaman Islanders, dwells in the sky; the thunder is his voice, wind his breath, the storm is the sign of his anger, for with his lightning he punishes those who break his commandments.

SOURCE: Mircea Eliade, *The Sacred and the Profane: The Nature of Religion*, trans. W. R. Trask. New York and London: Harcourt Brace Jovanovich, 1959, pp. 116–20

Dimensions of the Sacred   by Ninian Smart

Ninian Smart (1927–2001), at Lancaster University in England and University of California, Santa Barbara, developed a typology of the "dimensions of the sacred." In seven categories, he explored the phenomenology of world religions and worldviews. These are not to be taken as "essences" of religion, since early phenomenologists wrongly hardened such suggestive categories. But they do help recognize and focus on similar themes in religions. Smart embraced the wider definition of religion to include "worldviews" as a way of exploring the religious-like dimensions of practices such as nationalism, rationalism, and Marxism, and also of other secular systems that have their own dogmas, myths, and rituals and which command strong commitments and social movements.

1. The ritual or practical dimension. This is the aspect of religion which involves such activities as worship, meditation, pilgrimage, sacrifice, sacramental rites and healing activities. We may note that meditation is often not regarded as a ritual, though it is often strictly patterned. This is partly why I also call this dimension the practical ...

2. The doctrinal or philosophical dimension. For different reasons religions evolve doctrines and philosophies. Thus the doctrine of impermanence is central to Buddhism. It also interacts dialectically with the ritual or practical dimension, since philosophical reflection of a certain kind aids meditation, and meditation in turn helps the individual to see existentially the force of the doctrine. Some traditions are keener on doctrinal rectitude than others: Catholicism more than Quakerism, Buddhism more than traditional African religions, Theraveda more than Zen. We may note that diverse traditions put differing weights on the differing dimensions. Religions are by no means equidimensional.

3. The mythic or narrative dimension. Every religion has its stories. The story of Christ's life, death and resurrection is clearly central to the Christian faith. The story of the Buddha's life, though somewhat less central to Buddhism, is still vital to Buddhist piety. In the case of secular worldviews and to an important degree in modernizing traditions, history is the narrative which takes the place of myth elsewhere. So the version of history taught in a nation's schools is not only a major ingredient in the national sense of identity, but enhances pride in 'our' ancestors, 'our' national heroes and heroines.

4. The experiential or emotional dimension. It is obvious that certain experiences can be important in religious history—the enlightenment of the Buddha, the prophetic visions of Muhammad, the conversion of Paul and so on. Again there are variations in the importance attached to visionary and meditative experiences: they are obviously vital to Zen and Native American classical religion (the vision quest); they are less important in Scottish Calvinism. But they or associated emotional

reactions to the world and to ritual are everywhere more or less dynamic, and have been studied extensively (e.g. Otto, 1917/1923).

5. The ethical or legal dimensions. A religious tradition or sub-tradition affirms not only a number of doctrines and myths but some ethical and often legal imperatives. The Torah as a set of injunctions is central to orthodox Judaism; the Shari'a is integral to Islam; Buddhism affirms the four great virtues (*brahmavih ras*); Confucianism lays down the desired attitudes of the gentleman; and so on. Again, the degree of investment in ideal human behaviour varies: it is central to Quakerism, less important in the Shinto tradition (though Shinto ritual was tied to the notion of the *kokutai* or national essence during the Meiji era and into the between-wars period). In modern national states certain norms of civil behaviour tend to be prescribed in schools.

6. The organizational or social component. Any tradition will manifest itself in society, either as a separate organization with priests or other religious specialists (gurus, lawyers, pastors, rabbis, imams, shamans and so on), or as coterminous with society. Embedded in a social context, a tradition will take on aspects of that context (thus the Church of England cleric begins to play a part in the English class system).

7. The material or artistic dimension. A religion or worldview will express itself typically in material creations, from chapels to cathedrals to temples to mosques, from icons and divine statuary to books and pulpits. Such concrete expressions are important in varying ways. If you only have to carry around a book (like an evangelical preacher in Communist Eastern Europe) you are freer than if you have a great monastery or convent to occupy.

SOURCE: Ninian Smart, *Dimensions of the Sacred: An Anatomy of the World's Beliefs*. Berkeley, CA: University of California Press, 1996, pp. 10–11

Materialistic perspectives on religion

In recent centuries, the point of view of people of faith has often given way to a more materialistic point of view, which suggests that only the quantifiable material world is real and the sacred reality which most people have not seen is just a figment of human imagination. The following excerpts give Sigmund Freud's and Karl Marx's interpretations that humans invented religion, Friedrich Nietzsche's charge that "God is Dead," and Emile Durkheim's thesis that "God is society."

The Future of an Illusion by Sigmund Freud

Sigmund Freud (1856–1939), a Viennese physician, founded the widely influential psychoanalytic movement. He demonstrated, through the interpretation of dreams, errors, and physical symptoms, the reality and meaningfulness of the unconscious mind. Sexuality and distorted relationships with one's parents, Freud thought, were the central dynamics of the unconscious psyche. Religion, he charged, is an infantile illusion, an unconscious search for security in a father figure, projected into the heavens.

When the growing individual finds that he is destined to remain a child forever, that he can never do without protection against strange superior powers, he lends these powers the features belonging to the figure of his father; he creates for himself the gods whom he dreads, whom he seeks to propitiate, and whom he nevertheless entrusts with his own protection. Thus his longing for a father is a motive identical with his need for protection against the consequences of his human weakness. ...

Religious ideas ... are not precipitates of experience or end-results of thinking: they are illusions, fulfillments of the oldest, strongest and most urgent wishes of mankind. The secret of their strength lies in the strength of those wishes. As we already know, the terrifying impression of helplessness in childhood aroused the need for protection—for protection through love— which was provided by the father; and the recognition that this helplessness lasts throughout life made it necessary to cling to the existence of a father, but this time a more powerful one. Thus the benevolent rule of a divine Providence[7] allays our fear of the dangers of life; the establishment of a moral world-order ensures the fulfillment of the demands of justice, which have so often remained unfulfilled in human civilization; and the promulgation of earthly existence in a future life provides the local and temporal framework in which these wish-fulfillments shall take place. Answers to the riddles that tempt the curiosity of man, such as how the universe began or what the relation is between body and mind, are developing in conformity with the underlying assumptions of this system. It is an enormous relief to the individual psyche if the conflicts of its childhood arising from the father-complex—conflicts which it has never wholly overcome—are removed from it and brought to a solution which is universally accepted.

An illusion is not the same thing as an error. ... What is characteristic of illusions is that they are derived from human wishes. In this respect they come near to psychiatric delusions ... For instance, a middle-class girl may have the illusion that a prince will come and marry her. This is possible; and a few such cases have occurred. That the Messiah will come and found a golden age is much less likely ... Thus we call a belief an illusion when a wish-fulfillment is a prominent factor in its motivation, and in so doing we disregard its relations to reality, just as the illusion sets no store by verification.

SOURCE: Sigmund Freud, *The Future of an Illusion*. New York: Doubleday, 1961, pp. 35–49

/ Providence—God's care and guidance through inward inspiration and outer events.

Religion as the Opium of the People   by Karl Marx

Karl Marx (1818–83) was a German philosopher who founded Communism. With Friedrich Engels (1820–95), he developed the theory that class struggle is the primary mover of history, and posited that the working class would lead society from democratic bourgeois capitalism to a socialist, then a communist state. His analyses of the alienation of workers from industrialism and of the unjust and destructive effects of capitalism still influence many thinkers. Marx proclaimed "dialectical materialism"—the material interchange between human economic arrangements and the natural world—to be the guiding force in history. His view of religion is similar to that of Ludwig Feuerbach (1804–72), who in 1841 charged that religion is an illusory psychological projection of human emotions into the heavens. Marx added that this process is more social than psychological, with religion sanctioning and blessing the unjust status quo.

For Germany the *criticism of religion* is in the main complete, and criticism of religion is the premise of all criticism.

The *profane* existence of error is discredited after its *heavenly* speech for the altars and hearths has been rejected. Man, who looked for a superman in the fantastic reality of heaven and found nothing there but the *reflexion* of himself, will no longer be disposed to find but the *semblance* of himself, the non-human where he seeks and must seek his true reality.

The basis of irreligious criticism is: *Man makes religion,* religion does not make man. In other words, religion is the self-consciousness and self-feeling of man who has either not yet found himself or has already lost himself again. But *man* is no abstract being squatting outside the world. Man is *the world of man,* the state, society. This state, this society, produce religion, *a reversed world-consciousness,* because they are a *reversed* world. Religion is the general theory of that world, its encyclopaedic compendium, its logic in a popular form, its spiritualistic point of honor, its enthusiasm, its moral sanction, its solemn completion, its universal ground for consolation and justification. It is *the fantastic realization* of the human essence, because the *human essence* has no true reality. The struggle against religion is therefore mediately the fight against *the other world* of which religion is the spiritual *aroma.*

Religious distress is at the same time the *expression* of real distress and the *protest* against real distress. Religion is the sigh of the oppressed creature, the heart of a heartless world, just as it is the spirit of a spiritless situation. It is the *opium* of the people.

The abolition of religion as the *illusory* happiness of the people is required for their real happiness. The demand to give up the illusions about its condition is the *demand to give up the condition which needs illusions.* The criticism of religion is therefore *in embryo the criticism of the vale of woe, the halo* of which is religion. ... Religion is only the illusory sun which revolves round man as long as he does not revolve round himself.

SOURCE: Karl Marx and Friedrich Engels, *On Religion*. Moscow: Foreign Languages Publishing House, 1955, pp. 41–2

God is Dead by Friedrich Nietzsche

The maverick German intellectual Friedrich Nietzsche (1844–1900) was one of the most influential of modern thinkers. Highly iconoclastic, he challenged many social and intellectual conventions. He said: "Morality is nothing else … than obedience to customs." He took the implications of industrial culture a step further than many dared, charging that "God is Dead," thereby strengthening modern atheism and clearing the way for science. Nietzsche also foreshadowed other important themes of the twentieth century, such as the Will to Power, soon unleashed in new wars of unimagined destruction, and in technologies applied with minimal ethical restraint. But Nietzsche did not cling to consistency. He was skeptical about the certainty of accepted truths, so his madman's proclamation of the death of God also expresses his fear of the consequences.

The Madman Have you not heard of the madman who lit a lantern in the bright morning hours, ran to the market-place and cried incessantly: "I seek God! I seek God!"—As many of those who did not believe in God were standing around just then, he provoked much laughter. Why, did he get lost? said one. Did he lose his way like a child? said another. Or is he hiding? Is he afraid of us? Has he gone on a voyage? or emigrated?—Thus they yelled and laughed. The madman jumped into their midst and pierced them with his glances.

"Whither is God?" he cried. "I shall tell you! *We have killed him,*—you and I. We are all his murderers! But how have we done this? How were we able to drink up the sea? Who gave us the sponge to wipe away the entire horizon? What did we do when we unchained this earth from its sun? Whither is it moving now? Whither are we moving now? Away from all suns? Are we not plunging continually? Backward, sideward, forward, in all directions? Is there any up or down left? Are we not straying as through an infinite nothing? Do we not feel the breath of empty space? Has it not become colder? Is not night and more night coming on all the while? Must not lanterns be lit in the morning? Do we not hear anything yet of the noise of the gravediggers who are burying God? Do we not smell anything yet of God's decomposition? Gods too decompose. God is Dead. God remains dead. And we have killed him. How shall we, the murderers of all murderers, comfort ourselves? What was holiest and most powerful of all that the world has yet owned has bled to death under our knives. Who will wipe this blood off us? … Must we not ourselves become gods simply to seem worthy of it?"

SOURCE: Friedrich Nietzsche, *The Gay Science*, repr. in *The Portable Nietzsche*, ed. and trans. Walter Kaufmann. New York: Viking Press, 1968, pp. 95–6

God is Society by Emile Durkheim

Emile Durkheim (1858–1917), together with Karl Marx and Max Weber, changed the direction of the study of world religions toward sociology by arguing that religion at base is not an individual psychological reality, nor a genetic biological function or an illusion, as rationalist skeptics think. They also argued that religion is not a supernatural reality, as believers think, nor is it a reaction to death that envisions an afterlife. They believed that religion, symbol, myth, Gods, mothers, saviors, behavioral rules, hopes and fears, and religious wars, are at base the emanations of a powerful social force, which is *sui generis*, a power in itself. This explains their endurance beyond criticism. Religion is real, but as an expression of society's collective consciousness, not as the revelation of a divine, supernatural force. One might ask why religiously inspired rebels against society arise, such as Martin Luther King Jr. (1929–68) or Mahatma Gandhi (1869–1948). But Durkheim says that even ideals above the norm arise from society. In his analysis of the collective image of the totem (e.g a king or cross), Durkheim writes:

Thus the totem is before all a symbol, a material expression of something else. But of what? From the analysis to which we have been giving our attention, it is evident that it expresses and symbolizes two different sorts of things. In the first place, it is the outward and visible form of what we have called the totemic principle or god. But it is also the symbol of the determined society called the clan. It is its flag; it is the sign by which each clan distinguishes itself from the other, the visible mark of its personality, a mark borne by everything which is a part of the clan under any title whatsoever, men, beasts or thing. So if it is at once the symbol of the [society's] god and of the society, is that not because the god and the society are only one? How could the emblem of the group have been able to become the figure of this quasi-divinity, if the group and the divinity were two distinct realities? The god of the clan, the totemic principle, can therefore be nothing else than the [projected image of the] clan itself, personified and represented to the imagination under the visible from of the animal or vegetable which serves as totem. ...

In a general way, it is unquestionable that a society has all that is necessary to arouse the sensation of the divine in minds, merely by the power that it has over them; for to its member it is what a god is to its worshippers. In fact, a god is, first of all, a being whom men think of as superior to themselves, and upon whom they feel that they depend. Whether it be a conscious personality, such as Zeus or Jahveh, or merely abstract forces such as those in play in totemism [or Laws], the worshipper, in the one case as in the other, believes himself held to certain manners of acting which are imposed upon him by the nature of the sacred principle with which he feels that he is in communion. Now society also gives us the sensation of a perpetual dependence.

Religion ceases to be an inexplicable hallucination and takes a foothold in reality. In fact, we can say that the believer is not deceived when he believes in the existence of a moral power upon which he depends and from which he receives all that is best in himself; this power exists, it is society. ... the god is only the imaginative expression of the society... Behind these figures and metaphors, be they gross or refined, there is a concrete and living reality..... Before all, it is a system of ideas with which the individuals represent to themselves the society of which they are members. ... [The practices of the cult] strengthen the bonds attaching the believer to his god, they at the same time really strengthen the bonds attaching the individual to the society of which he is a member, since the god is only a figurative expression of the society.

SOURCE: Emile Durkheim, *The Elementary Forms of the Religious Life*, French, 1912, trans. 1915 Joseph W. Swain. New York: The Free Press, pp. 236–7, 257–8

Ritual, symbol, and myth

Whereas some branches of every religion have interpreted their faith's stories, scriptures, and rituals as literally true, others have embraced them as symbols and metaphors for spiritual realities that cannot be described in literal language. Two leading figures in the study of religions from the latter point of view have been Carl Jung and Joseph Campbell.

Mandalas: Deity Unfolding in the World by Carl G. Jung

Carl Jung (1875–1961) was a Swiss psychologist who developed archetypal psychology, which is the psychology most open to religious understanding. Jung built on Freud's demonstration of the meaningfulness of the unconscious psyche, while rejecting his views on the centrality of sex and the illusory nature of religion. Jung saw images from all religions as meaningful expressions of the "collective unconscious" of humanity. He spoke of "archetypes," meaning unconscious collective psychological instincts or patterns. The "Self" for Jung is the central, regulating archetype, the "God within" that guides and heals. It may be symbolized in many ways, not just as a heavenly old man on a throne. In dreams and myths, rituals and theologies, the ineffable depth called "God" may appear as a crystal, a goddess, a star, a tree, an animal, or even a geometric form—most notably the **mandala**, a circular design, such as a cathedral's round "rose" window, focusing on the "center": the center of the universe, the center of one's life.

The Sanskrit word *mandala* means "circle" in the ordinary sense of the word. In the sphere of religious practices and in psychology it denotes circular images, which are drawn, painted, modeled, or danced. Plastic structures of this kind are to be found, for instance, in Tibetan Buddhism, and as dance figures these circular patterns occur also in Dervish monasteries. As psychological phenomena they appear spontaneously in dreams, in certain states of conflict, and in cases of schizophrenia. Very frequently they contain a quaternity or a multiple of four, in the form of a cross, a star, a square, an octagon, etc. ...

   In Tibetan Buddhism the figure has the significance of a ritual instrument (*yantra*), whose purpose is to assist meditation and concentration. ... Its spontaneous occurrence in modern individuals enables psychological research to make a closer investigation into its functional meaning. As a rule a mandala occurs in conditions of psychic dissociation or disorientation, for instance in the case of children between the ages of eight and eleven whose parents are about to be divorced, or in adults who, as the result of a neurosis[8] and its treatment, are confronted with the problem of opposites in human nature and are consequently disoriented; or again in schizophrenics whose view of the world has become confused, owing to the invasion of incomprehensible contents from the unconscious. In such cases it is easy to see how the severe pattern imposed by a circular image of this kind compensates the disorder and confusion of the psychic state— namely, through the construction of a central point to which everything is related, or by a concentric arrangement of the disordered multiplicity and of contradictory and irreconcilable elements. This is evidently an *attempt at self-healing* on the part of Nature, which does not spring from conscious reflection but from an instinctive impulse. Here, as comparative research has shown, a fundamental schema is made use of, an archetype which, so to speak, occurs everywhere and by no means owes its individual existence to tradition, any more than the instincts would need to be transmitted in that way. Instincts are given in the case of every newborn individual and belong to the inalienable stock of those qualities which characterize a species. What psychology designates as archetype is really a particular, frequently occurring, formal aspect of instinct, and is just as much an *a priori* factor as the latter. Therefore, despite external differences, we find a fundamental conformity in mandalas regardless of their origin in time and space.

The "squaring of the circle" is one of the many archetypal motifs which form the basic patterns of our dreams and fantasies. But it is distinguished by the fact that it is one of the most important of them from the functional point of view. Indeed, it could even be called the *archetype of wholeness*. Because of this significance, the "quaternity of the One" is the schema for all images of God, as depicted in the visions of Ezekiel, Daniel, and Enoch, and as the representation of Horus[9] with his four sons also shows. The latter suggests an interesting differentiation, inasmuch as there are occasionally representations in which three of the sons have animals' heads and only one a human head, in keeping with the Old Testament visions as well as with the emblems of the seraphim which were transferred to the evangelists, and—last but not least— with the nature of the Gospels themselves: three of which are synoptic and one "Gnostic."…

As is to be expected, individual mandalas display an enormous variety. The overwhelming majority are characterized by the circle and the quaternity. In a few, however, the three or the five predominates, for which there are usually special reasons.

---

8 Neurosis—a mild form of mental illness.
9 Horus—an ancient Egyptian divinity, son of Isis and Osiris.

Whereas ritual mandalas always display a definite style and a limited number of typical motifs as their content, individual mandalas make use of a well-nigh unlimited wealth of motifs and symbolic allusions, from which it can easily be seen that they are endeavouring to express either the totality of the individual in his inner or outer experience of the world, or its essential point of reference. Their object is the *self* in contradistinction to the *ego*, which is only the point of reference for consciousness, whereas the self comprises the totality of the psyche altogether, i.e., conscious *and* unconscious. It is therefore not unusual for individual mandalas to display a division into a light and a dark half, together with their typical symbols. An historical example of this kind is Jakob Böhme's mandala, in his treatise *XL Questions concerning the Soule*. It is at the same time an image of God and is designated as such. This is not a matter of chance, for Indian philosophy, which developed the idea of the self, Atman or Purusha, to the highest degree, makes no distinction in principle between the human essence and the divine. Correspondingly, in the Western mandala, the *scintilla* or soul-spark, the innermost divine essence of man, is characterized by symbols which can just as well express a God-image, namely the image of Deity unfolding in the world, in nature, and in man.

The fact that images of this kind have under certain circumstances a considerable therapeutic effect on their authors is empirically proved and also readily understandable, in that they often represent very bold attempts to see and put together apparently irreconcilable opposites and bridge over apparently hopeless splits.

SOURCE: Carl G. Jung, "Mandalas," in *The Archetypes and the Collective Unconscious*, vol. 9, part 1 of The *Collected Works of C. G. Jung*. 2nd ed. Princeton, NJ: Princeton University Press, 1968, pp. 387–90

The Hero with a Thousand Faces by Joseph Campbell

At Sarah Lawrence College, Joseph Campbell (1904–87) expanded Jung's archetypal theory of myth as a meaningful story, rather than a fictional error. He proposed a theory of the "monomyth," a pattern found, sometimes fragmentarily, in myths worldwide. The pattern follows the hero's journey into the mystical underworld, where various powers are met for struggles and learning. After the re-ascent to ordinary life, the hero can use the new powers to aid his or her people. As Campbell developed his theory of myth, he integrated more anthropological and historical themes.

Myth is the secret opening through which the inexhaustible energies of the cosmos pour into human cultural manifestation. Religions, philosophies, arts, the social forms of primitive and historic man, prime discoveries in science and technology, the very dreams that blister sleep, boil up from the basic, magic ring of myth. …

The bold and truly epoch-making writings of the psychoanalysts are indispensable to the student of mythology; for, whatever may be thought of the detailed and sometimes contradictory interpretations of specific cases and problems, Freud, Jung, and their followers have demonstrated irrefutably that the logic, the heroes, and the deeds of myth survive into modern times. In the absence of an effective general mythology, each of us has his private, unrecognized, rudimentary, yet secretly potent pantheon of dream.[10] The latest incarnation of Oedipus, the continued romance of Beauty and the Beast, stand this afternoon on the corner of Forty-second Street and Fifth Avenue[11] waiting for the traffic light to change. ...

The unconscious sends all sorts of vapors, odd beings, terrors, and deluding images up into the mind—whether in dream, broad daylight, or insanity; for the human kingdom, beneath the floor of the comparatively neat little dwelling that we call our consciousness, goes down into unsuspected Aladdin caves. There not only jewels but also dangerous jinn abide: the inconvenient or resisted psychological powers that we have not thought or dared to integrate into our lives. And they remain unsuspected, or, on the other hand, some chance word, the smell of a landscape, the taste of a cup of tea, or the glance of an eye may touch a magic spring, and then dangerous messengers begin to appear in the brain. These are dangerous because they threaten the fabric of the security into which we have built ourselves and our family. But they are fiendishly fascinating too, for they carry keys that open the whole realm of the desired and feared adventure of the discovery of the self. Destruction of the world that we have built and in which we live, and of ourselves within it; but then a wonderful reconstruction, of the bolder, cleaner, more spacious, and fully human life—that is the lure, the promise and terror, of these disturbing night visitants from the mythological realm that we carry within. ...

It has always been the prime function of mythology and rite to supply the symbols that carry the human spirit forward, in counteraction to those other constant human fantasies that tend to tie it back. In fact, it may well be that the very high incidence of neuroticism among ourselves follows from the decline among us of such effective spiritual aid. We remain fixated to the unexorcised images of our infancy, and hence disinclined to the necessary passages of our adulthood. ...

The first work of the hero is to retreat from the world scene of secondary effects to those causal zones of the psyche where the difficulties really reside, and there to clarify the difficulties, eradicate them in his own case (i.e., give battle to the nursery demons of his local culture) and break through to the undistorted, direct experience and assimilation of what C. G. Jung has called "the archetypal images." This is the process known to Hindu and Buddhist philosophy as *viveka*, "discrimination."

---

10 Campbell's 1940s masculine view has stimulated feminist and African versions of his theory of myth. See Maureen Murdock, *The Heroine's Journey*. Boston: Shambhala, 1990. Also, see Clyde Ford, *The Hero With an African Face*. New York: Bantam, 1999.
11 A central street crossing in New York City.

The archetypes to be discovered and assimilated are precisely those that have inspired, throughout the annals of human culture, the basic images of ritual, mythology, and vision.

Dream is the personalized myth, myth the depersonalized dream; both myth and dream are symbolic in the same general way of the dynamics of the psyche. But in the dream the forms are quirked by the peculiar troubles of the dreamer, whereas in myth the problems and solutions shown are directly valid for all mankind.

The hero, therefore, is the man or woman who has been able to battle past his personal and local historical limitations to the generally valid, normally human forms. Such a one's visions, ideas, and inspirations come pristine from the primary springs of human life and thought. Hence they are eloquent, not of the present, disintegrating society and psyche, but of the unquenched source through which society is reborn. The hero has died as a modern man; but as eternal man—perfected, unspecific, universal man—he has been reborn. His second solemn task and deed therefore … is to return then to us, transfigured, and teach the lesson he has learned of life renewed. …

Furthermore, we have not even to risk the adventure alone; for the heroes of all time have gone before us; the labyrinth is thoroughly known; we have only to follow the thread of the hero-path. And where we had thought to find an abomination, we shall find a god; where we had thought to slay another, we shall slay ourselves; where we had thought to travel outward, we shall come to the center of our own existence; where we had thought to be alone, we shall be with all the world. …

The standard path of the mythological adventure of the hero is a magnification of the formula represented in the rites of passage: *separation–initiation–return:* which might be named the nuclear unit of the monomyth.

> A hero ventures forth from the world of common day into a region of supernatural wonder: fabulous forces are there encountered and a decisive victory is won: the hero comes back from this mysterious adventure with the power to bestow boons on his fellow man.

Aeneas[12] went down into the underworld, crossed the dreadful river of the dead, threw a sop to the three-headed watchdog Cerberus, and conversed, at last, with the shade of his dead father. All things were unfolded to him: the destiny of souls, the destiny of Rome, which he was about to found, "and in what wise he might avoid or endure every burden." He returned through the ivory gate to his work in the world. …

A comparable vision is described in the apocryphal[13] Gospel of Eve. "I stood on a lofty mountain and saw a gigantic man and another a dwarf; and I heard as it were a voice of thunder, and drew nigh for to hear; and He spake unto me and said: I am thou, and thou art I; and wheresoever thou mayest

---

12 Aeneas—legendary founder of the Roman race, whose journey is described by Virgil in the *Aeneid*.
13 Apocryphal—relating to unofficial, uncanonical ancient texts considered sacred by some.

be I am there. In all am I scattered, and whensoever thou willest, thou gatherest Me; and gathering Me, thou gatherest Thyself."

The two—the hero and his ultimate god, the seeker and the found—are thus understood as the outside and inside of a single, self-mirrored mystery, which is identical with the mystery of the manifest world. The great deed of the supreme hero is to come to the knowledge of this unity in multiplicity and then to make it known.

SOURCE: Joseph Campbell, *The Hero with a Thousand Faces*. 2nd ed. Princeton, NJ: Princeton University Press, 1968, pp. 3–40

Myth and Religion: *The Irish Voyage of Bran*

This Irish Celtic legend "Immram Brain" illustrates many familiar mythic themes, such as the call to adventure, the ego/hero's journey to paradise beyond death, and the magical symbolic branch of crystal and silver (a sign from a transcendent realm, from an enchanting messenger who calls ordinary souls to the immortal mysteries beyond that heal life's pains). On his voyage Bran encounters divine figures such as the Lord of the sea. After visiting the land of everlasting life, innocence, and joy, Bran returns to his people and tells them of discoveries that expand earthly life into just a fragment of a greater immortal universe.

This myth was written down around the eighth century CE, most likely by monks because it has some obvious Christian additions. There are several manuscripts in Celtic, and a number of translations. This is a summary.

The Voyage of Bran to the Land of the Immortals

Prince Bran of Ireland walked alone outside his stronghold when he heard a strange, sweet music from nowhere. Then he fell asleep. When he awoke he picked up a silver branch with white blossoms. He took it into his royal house where he joined the courtiers, and they saw a strange woman. She chanted this lay:

"Crystal and silver the apple branch that to you I show; 'tis from a wondrous distant isle, known as the Isle of Joy, where no wailing or treachery is known, no sorrow, no sickness, no death, only sweet music. 'Tis a bright land of dragonstones and crystals, gold and silver chariots, wealth and treasure. At dawn a fair man and his companions glide across the sea to the conspicuous standing stone that sings many songs, swelling with the chorus of hundreds, women run along the beach, seeing neither decay nor death. There are thrice fifty such islands to the west, each two or three times the size of Ireland. He who rules heaven forever will be born after ages, he who will heal and purify with wisdom.

"Whoever to these islands comes, and hears that song, shall know all delight, all through the ages, lovers laughing with delight. This song is for you, Bran. Now arise and depart!"

After she disappeared, Bran was so captivated by this call from the beautiful, glowing woman with the magical branch that he prepared his ship and sailed with his brave companions over the sea horses, along with the jumping speckled salmon. They passed by the ship of the Lord of the Sea Moninnan, son of Ler, who would soon become a vigorous bed-fellow with the fair Irish lady Fiachna, who would give birth to the valiant hero Mongan. This divine son would delight on every fairy-knoll, and appear in the shape of animals on sea and land—a dragon, a wolf, a swan and a stag with silver horns—ruling for a hundred years, or perhaps only fifty, if killed by a dragonstone from the sea.

At sundown, Bran and his men approached the strange Island of Joy where appeared on the beach a group of people gaping amidst silver streams and gold steps, some lying man and woman together under a bush, without sin, without transgression, some laughing at Bran's boat. "We are from the beginning of creation," they called out, "without decay; the sin has not reached us." One of Bran's men rowed toward them, and stayed.

They sailed on to the Island of Women, where the Queen called out to Bran: "Come hither, Prince Bran, son of Febal, come ashore and find welcome here." Bran's ship was irresistibly drawn to the island's shore by a magical thread, and the men were embraced by the women. There was a bed for every couple. They ate food from dishes that never emptied. They stayed for many years, lacking no pleasure. But homesickness overcame one of the men, Nechtan, and the crew prayed to return home. The woman said they would regret returning to Ireland, and must never set foot on the shore. "Rather you must look from afar and then return to this Land of the Ever-living."

Bran led his men back to Ireland. As they approached their familiar green Ireland, they saw people on the shore who shouted out: "Who comes over the ocean?" Prince Bran replied that he and his men had returned home. But the people ashore replied: "We know of no such persons, except in legends of the fabled Prince Bran, who sailed afar in ages past." Bran and his men were agitated, and one man impatiently jumped into the sea and eagerly swam ashore. But as soon as he touched the sand, he collapsed into a heap of ashes, like a long-buried corpse.

Thereupon Bran spoke to the people of his wanderings. And he wrote these quatrains in Ogam, then bade them farewell. His wanderings remain a mystery.

SOURCE: A summary of the story taken from *The Voyage of Bran Son of Febal to the Land of the Living*, trans. Kuno Meyer, with an essay by Alfred Nutt. London: David Nutt, 1895

The Sound of One Hand: Ritual in Zen Buddhism

Ritual is a mysterious, dramatic individual or group ceremony that opens the soul to the transformative depths of Being. In Japanese Buddhism there are group rituals of chanting, speaking, and meditation (zazen). An advanced ritual is the monastic tradition of an adventure in self-awakening: the transmission of the **dharma** by a student meeting with a Zen master in *sanzen*, where the master gives the student a riddle or koan to solve. The answer must come from the student's unique experience of the deepest mystery, a flash of insight from the profound light of the Buddhamind. It may take years of repeated efforts. Paradox, poetry or a simple, profound observation are all forms of an answer – for the emergence of the Buddhamind is more than ordinary logic. This classic koan is typical.

The Sound of One Hand

The master of Kennin temple was Mokurai, Silent Thunder. He had a little protégé named Toyo who was only twelve years old. Toyo saw the older disciples visit the master's room each morning and evening to receive instruction in sanzen or personal guidance in which they were given koans to stop mind-wandering.

Toyo wished to do sanzen also.

"Wait a while," said Mokurai. "You are too young."

But the child insisted, so the teacher finally consented.

In the evening little Toyo went at the proper time to the threshold of Mokurai's sanzen room. He struck the gong to announce his presence, bowed respectfully three times outside the door, and went to sit before the master in respectful silence.

"You can hear the sound of two hands when they clap together," said Mokurai. "Now show me the sound of one hand."

Toyo bowed and went to his room to consider this problem. From his window he could hear the music of the geishas. "Ah, I have it!" he proclaimed.

The next evening, when his teacher asked him to illustrate the sound of one hand, Toyo began to play the music of the geishas.

"No, no," said Mokurai. "That will never do. That is not the sound of one hand. You've not got it at all."

Thinking that such music might interrupt, Toyo moved his abode to a quiet place. He meditated again. "What can the sound of one hand be?" He happened to hear some water dripping. "I have it," imagined Toyo.

When he next appeared before his teacher, Toyo imitated dripping water.

"What is that?" asked Mokurai. "That is the sound of dripping water, but not the sound of one hand. Try again."

In vain Toyo meditated to hear the sound of one hand. He heard the sighing of the wind. But the sound was rejected.

He heard the cry of an owl. This also was rejected.

The sound of one hand was not the locusts.

For more than ten times Toyo visited Mokurai with different sounds. All were wrong. For almost a year he pondered what the sound of one hand might be.

At last little Toyo entered true meditation and transcended all sounds. "I could collect no more," he explained later, "so I reached the soundless sound."

Toyo had realized the sound of one hand.

SOURCE: *Zen Flesh, Zen Bones: A Collection of Zen and Pre-Zen Writings* compiled by Paul Reps. New York: Doubleday & Company Inc., 1957, pp. 24–6

Religious points of view

Religious believers agree that the scientific method of explanatory reduction of nature to lesser scale events, such as atoms reduced to protons, is suitable for the material world. They reject, however, the application of reduction to spiritual events. In much of culture, they argue, "the greater cannot be explained by the lesser." The faithful go on to describe the "greater" in various ways.

In the following three extracts, we see contemporary statements of faith in the monotheistic oneness of divinity, in the **polytheistic** plurality of divinities, and in no-divinity, concentrating instead upon human consciousness as part of the ground of Being.

The Oneness of the Divine   by Abraham Heschel

Abraham Heschel (1907–72) was born into the Jewish mystical tradition of Hasidism in Warsaw, and educated in the mysticism of the Kabbalah. He studied in Berlin, but in 1938 he was forced out of Germany and escaped to England, then to New York, where he taught for many years at New York's Jewish Theological Seminary and wrote several influential books, including *Man is not Alone* (1951) and *The Prophets* (1962). He spoke for civil rights and interfaith co-operation. He blends the traditional Hasidic yearning for spirituality with the modern taste for free inquiry and impartial truth.

How do we identify the divine? … The notion of God as a perfect being is not of Biblical extraction. It is the product not of prophetic religion but of Greek philosophy; a postulate of reason rather than a direct, compelling, initial answer of man to His reality.[14] In the Decalogue,[15] God does not speak of His being perfect but of His having made free men out of slaves. Signifying a state of being without defect and lack, perfection is a term of praise which we may utter in pouring forth our emotion; yet for man to utter it as a name for His essence would mean to evaluate and to endorse Him.

There is, however, one idea that carries our thoughts beyond the horizon of our island; an idea which addresses itself to all minds and is tacitly accepted as an axiom by science and as a dogma by monotheistic religion. It is the idea of the one. All knowledge and understanding rest upon its validity. In spite of the profound differences in what it describes and means in the various realms of human thought, there is much that is common and much that is of mutual importance.

The perspective on which we depend in science and philosophy, notwithstanding all specialization and meticulousness in studying the details, is a view of the whole, without which our knowledge would be like a book composed exclusively of iotas. Accordingly, all sciences and philosophies

---

14 Heschel presented his position in a traditionally masculine voice. Jewish feminists (including Heschel's daughter Susan) have subsequently presented another view.
15 Decalogue—the Ten Commandments.

have one axiom in common—the axiom of *unity* of all that is, was and will be. They all assume that things are not entirely divorced from and indifferent to each other, but subject to universal laws, and that they form, by their interaction with one another or, as Lotze put it, by their "sympathetic rapport," a universe. However, the possibility of their interaction with each other is conditioned upon a unity that pervades all of them. The world could not exist at all except as one; deprived of unity, it would not be a cosmos but chaos, an agglomeration of countless possibilities. ...

Knowledge is at all possible because of the kinship of the knower and the known, because man's intelligence seems to correspond to the world's intelligibility. But over and above that there is another kinship: the kinship of being. We are all—men, stars, flowers, birds—assigned to the same cast, rehearsing for the same inexplicable drama. We all have a mystery in common—the mystery of being.

SOURCE: Abraham Heschel, *Between God and Man: An Interpretation of Judaism*. New York and London: Simon and Schuster, 1998, pp. 98–100

The New Polytheism by David Miller

David Miller is a comparative mythologist (emeritus) at Syracuse University whose book *The New Polytheism* (1974) showed the growing impact of the study of world religions. He argued that monotheism—a belief in only one deity—may suffer from industrial culture's critique, but under the surface, polytheism—belief in a plurality of deities—has always been at work.

The death of God was in fact the demise of a monotheistic way of thinking and speaking about God and a monotheistic way of thinking and speaking about human meaning and being generally. The announcement of the death of God was the obituary of a useless single-minded and one-dimensional norm of a civilization that has been predominantly monotheistic, not only in its religion, but also in its politics, its history, its social order, its ethics, and its psychology. When released from the tyrannical imperialism of monotheism by the death of God, man has the opportunity of discovering new dimensions hidden in the depths of reality's history. He may discover a new freedom to acknowledge variousness and many-sidedness. He may find, as if for the first time, a new potency to create imaginatively his hopes and desires, his laws and pleasures. ...

The death of God gives rise to the rebirth of the Gods. We are polytheists.

Polytheism is the name given to a specific religious situation. The situation is characterized by plurality, a plurality that manifests itself in many forms. Socially, polytheism is a situation in which there are various values, patterns of social organization, and principles by which man governs his political life. These values, patterns, and principles sometimes mesh harmoniously, but more often they war with one another to be elevated as the single center of normal social order. Such a situation would be sheer anarchy and chaos were it not possible to identify the many orders as each containing a coherence of its own. Socially understood, polytheism is eternally in unresolvable conflict with social monotheism, which in its worst form is fascism and in its less destructive forms is imperialism, capitalism, feudalism, and monarchy. There is an incipient polytheism always lurking in democracy. This polytheism will surface during the history of democracies if the civilization does not first succumb to anarchy. In calling our time polytheist, we are saying something about the state of democracy in our time.

Polytheism is not only a social reality; it is also a philosophical condition. It is that reality, experienced by men and women when Truth with a capital "T" cannot be articulated reflectively according to a single grammar, a single logic, or a single symbol-system. It is a situation that exists when metaphors, stories, anecdotes, aphorisms, puns, dramas, and movies, with all their mysterious ambiguity, seem more compelling than the rhetoric of political, religious, and philosophical systems. They seem more compelling than tightly argued and logically coherent explanations of self and society because they allow for multiple meanings to exist simultaneously, as if Truth, Goodness, and Beauty can never be contained in a logic that allows for only one of the following: good versus evil, light versus dark, truth versus fiction, reality versus illusion, being versus becoming. In a philosophically polytheistic situation the "new science" of the time will break forth with principles of relativism, indeterminacy, plural logic systems, irrational numbers; substances that do not have substance, such as quarks; double explanations for light; and black holes in the middle of actual realities. ...

Religiously, polytheism is the worship of many Gods and Goddesses. Though monotheism in its exclusive forms—say, in Christianity, Judaism, and Islam—rules out the possibility of polytheism in religion, polytheism, in a curious way, includes a monotheism of sorts. The great polytheist cultures—Greek, Hindu, Egyptian, Mesopotamian, American Indian—have in actual practice been composed of communities of men and women who worship one God or Goddess, or at least they worship one at a time—Athena, Vishnu, Ra, Baal, Wakan Tanka. The *theologies* of these peoples, however, affirm the reality and the worship of many. This implies that a polytheistic religion is actually a polytheistic theology, a system of symbolizing reality in a plural way in order to account for all experience, but that the religious practice is composed of consecutive monotheisms. Similarly, it would seem possible that one might profess a monotheistic faith, but need a polytheistic theology to account for all of one's experiences in the life-context of that faith. ...

What does this mean about theological explanations, about the nature of the Gods and Goddesses? It means that the Gods and Goddesses are the names of powers, of forces, which have autonomy and are not conditioned or affected by social and historical events, by human will or reason, or by personal and individual factors. This is one meaning of our use of the word "Immortal" as it is applied to divinities. The Gods are not contingent upon the conditions of mortality. Insofar as they manifest themselves in life they are felt to be informing powers that give shape to social, intellectual, and personal behavior. The Gods and Goddesses are the names of the plural patterns of our existence. Their stories are the paradigms[16] and symbols that allow us to account for, to express, and to celebrate those multiple aspects of our reality that otherwise would seem fragmented and anarchic.

SOURCE: David L. Miller, *The New Polytheism: Rebirth of the Gods and Goddesses*. New York and London: Harper and Row, 1974, pp. 3–7

The Ground of Being by Tarthang Tulku

Religion can exist without reference to any deity, as it does in some forms of Buddhism. Here the object of contemplation is consciousness itself. Tarthang Tulku is a contemporary Buddhist teacher in California, one of the first refugees from Tibet who began to explain to Westerners the insights of Tibetan Buddhism. In this selection from his book *Openness Mind* (1978), he discusses meditation as a process of discovering various levels of the workings of the mind in search of peace, the resolution of conflicting emotions, and, ultimately, the ground of Being. Is this "open ground" that which monotheists call God? This question is much debated today.

All of us are part of being; we *are* being. Our total life experience is this being, this ground, which embraces all of existence. Nirvana[17] and *samsara*[18] are both manifested within this ground level. The more we understand this, the more life becomes rich and fulfilling. We see that this ground of being is totally open; everything is manifest there. Nothing can destroy this openness.

Meditation enables us to remain at this ground state for long periods of time. Because it is a very peaceful state, free from desires and conflicting emotions, some of the Buddha's disciples stayed on this level for hundreds of years. However, this ground level is only an initial stage; nothing can actually be realized there. The mind naturally moves from this ground level to a second stage, which is a more conscious level, similar to recognition. This second stage is not actually sense perception, but rather an intuitive, seeing quality, a lightness and clarity. By very sensitively developing our awareness, we touch this intuitive second level directly.

The first stage of experience is like touching the ground, the second stage is like looking around, and then the third stage occurs, which is like surveying the horizon—observing with more precision and perceptivity. What we usually refer to as "experience" is produced on the second and third levels. We can learn to recognize these three levels of experience in each thought: first, the ground state; then we recognize the quality of the experience; finally we learn to extend the experience as long as possible.

As we become more familiar with the distinctions and qualities of each of these levels of experience, we are able to appreciate the subtle complexities and the more inward workings of the mind. Until our perception has

16 Paradigm—a model of reality, such as the materialistic or idealistic model.
17 Nirvana—in Buddhism, the cessation of suffering, attained through spiritual awakening.
18 *Samsara*—the endless round of bodily reincarnations in this world, with all its illusions.

developed in this way, we are like someone who has never eaten an apricot: we cannot imagine the taste. But once we are skilled at perceiving the arising and flowing of thought, we are able to go beyond this level of perception, to experience a level that is similar to the fresh perception of childhood. We are able to directly experience mind as a process. When we can soar, when we can transmute the quality of the mind, then we approach genuine freedom.

SOURCE: Tarthang Tulku, *Openness Mind*. Berkeley, CA: Dharma Publishing, 1978, pp. 92–4

Scientific perspectives on religion

After the eighteenth-century Enlightenment, science and religion seemed to go separate ways. Scientists placed their faith in that which could be observed and quantified, so leaving out explanations of reality which rest on the unseen and unquantifiable. However, twentieth-century scientific advances revealed that the universe is not as it appears on the surface, and that the tiny components of any apparently solid object seem to be racing through space behaving somewhat like energy and somewhat like matter.

From the study of Darwinian evolution developed the study of gene-centered evolution, which led to a "New Atheism." It is not really new, however, because while its science is strong, it adapts some classical arguments against religion. New Atheism led some scientists to expand into the philosophical realm and claim that the new views of evolution made divinity unnecessary, even illusory. Philosophical and religious thinkers have responded with several important arguments, such as the critique of scientific reductionism and the inadequate depth of evolutionary theory.

The Blind Watchmaker by Richard Dawkins

In 1976, Richard Dawkins at Oxford University in England led the popularization of the gene-centered view of evolution with his book *The Selfish Gene*. He later went on to argue in *The Blind Watchmaker* (1986) against the argument of intelligent design, saying that evolution by random selection is a mistaken concept. Rather, evolution is a long process of selection of the best genes which have proven their survival value. He argues against the 1802 position of the philosopher William Paley (1743–1805) that the existence of a watch implies the existence of a watchmaker – that the world must, therefore, have a divine creator. Dawkins replies that no such inference is necessary, that adaptive evolution is more like a blind watchmaker, not a god. Dawkins, like others, adopts some metaphysical assumptions, such as the mechanical nature of DNA, which go beyond strict scientific method.

Maybe, it is argued, the Creator does not control the day-to-day succession of evolutionary events, maybe he did not frame the tiger and the lamb, maybe he did not make a tree, but he did set up the original machinery of replication and replicator power, the original machinery of DNA and protein that made cumulative selection, and hence all of evolution, possible.

This is a transparently feeble argument, indeed it is obviously self-defeating. Organized complexity is the thing that we are having difficulty in explaining. Once we are allowed simply to *postulate* organized complexity, if only the organized complexity of the DNA/protein replicating engine, it is relatively easy to invoke it as a generator of yet more organized complexity. … But of course any God capable of intelligently designing something as complex as the DNA/protein replicating machine must have been at least as complex and organized as that machine itself. Far more so if we suppose him *additionally* capable of such advanced functions as listening to prayers and forgiving sins. To explain the origin of the DNA/protein machine by invoking a supernatural Designer is to explain precisely nothing, for it leaves unexplained the origin of the Designer. You have to say something like 'God was always there,' and if you allow yourself that kind of lazy way out, you might as well just say 'DNA was always there,' or 'Life was always there,' and be done with it.

The more we can get away from miracles, major improbabilities, fantastic coincidences, large chance events, and the more thoroughly we can break large chance events up into a cumulative series of small chance events, the more satisfying to rational minds our explanation will be. But in this chapter we are asking *how* improbable, how *miraculous*, a single event we are allowed to postulate. What is the largest single event of sheer naked coincidence, sheer unadulterated miraculous luck, that we are allowed to get away with in our theories, and still say that we have a satisfactory explanation of life? In order for a monkey to write 'Methinks it is like a weasel' by chance, it needs a very large amount of luck, but it is still measurable. We calculated the odds against it as about 10 thousand million million million million million million (10^{40}) to 1 against. Nobody can really comprehend or imagine such a large number, and we just think of this degree of improbability as synonymous with impossible. But although we can't comprehend these levels of improbability in our minds, we shouldn't just run away from them in terror. The number 10^{40} may be very large but we can still write it down, and we can still use it in calculations. There are, after all, even larger numbers: 10^{46}, for instance is not just larger; you must add 10^{40} to itself a million times in order to obtain 10^{46}. What if we could somehow must a gang of 10^{46} monkeys each with its own typewriter? Why, lo and behold, one of them would solemnly type 'Methinks it is like a weasel', and another would almost certainly type 'I think therefore I am'. The problem is, of course, that we couldn't assemble that many monkeys. If all the matter in the universe were turned into monkey flesh, we still couldn't get enough monkeys. The miracle of a monkey typing 'Methinks it is like a weasel' is quantitatively too great, *measurably* too great, for us to admit it to our theories about what actually happens. But we couldn't know this until we sat down and did the calculation.

So, there are some levels of sheer luck, not only too great for puny human imaginations but too great to be allowed in our hard-headed calculations about the origin of life. But, to repeat the question, how great a level of luck, how much of a miracle, *are* we allowed to postulate? Don't let's run away from this question just because large numbers are involved. It is a perfectly valid question, and we can at least write down what we would need to know in order to calculate the answer. ...

If we want to postulate a deity capable of engineering all the organized complexity in the world, either instantaneously or by guiding evolution, that deity must already have been vastly complex in the first place. The creationist, whether a naive Bible-thumper or an educated bishop, simply *postulates* an already existing being of prodigious intelligence and complexity. If we are going to allow ourselves the luxury of postulating organized complexity without offering an explanation, we might as well make a job of it and simply postulate the existence of life as we know it! In short, divine creation, whether instantaneous or in the form of guided evolution, joins the list of other theories we have considered in this chapter. All give some superficial appearance of being alternatives to Darwinism, whose merits might be tested by an appeal to evidence. All turn out, on closer inspection, not to be rivals of Darwinism at all. The theory of evolution by cumulative natural selection is the only theory we know of that is in principle *capable* of explaining the existence of organized complexity. Even if the evidence did not favour it, it would *still* be the best theory available! In fact the evidence does favour it. But that is another story.

Let us hear the conclusion of the whole matter. The essence of life is statistical improbability on a colossal scale. Whatever is the explanation for life, therefore, it cannot be chance. The true explanation for the existence of life must embody the very antithesis of chance. The antithesis of chance is nonrandom survival, properly understood. Nonrandom survival, improperly understood, is not the antithesis of chance, it is chance itself. There is a continuum connecting these two extremes, and it is the continuum from single-step selection to cumulative selection. Single-step selection is just another way of saying pure chance. This is what I mean by nonrandom survival improperly understood. *Cumulative selection*, by slow and gradual degrees, is the explanation, the only workable explanation that has ever been proposed, for the existence of life's complex design.

SOURCE: Richard Dawkins, *The Blind Watchmaker*. New York and London: W. W. Norton & Company, 1996, pp. 141–2, 316–17

Deeper than Darwin by John F. Haught

John F. Haught, at Georgetown University, argues in his 2003 book *Deeper than Darwin* that evolutionary theory as science is not qualified to expand beyond that and to make unscientific claims, such as the belief that science "goes all the way down," explaining everything in the universe, and thus denying the need for divinity or calling it illusory. While he accepts Richard Dawkins' science of adaptive evolution, he argues that scientific materialism ignores essential elements of life, such as the meanings of life and death. It does not go deep enough. It is the role of religion, he says, to explore the permanence beneath the changing world, which gives life hope, care, love, and beauty. These cannot be explained or cultivated by the scientific method. Haught argues that scientific logic and literalism, its reductivism and narrow scope, impose limits on its perception of the depth of Being.

... [E]volutionary discovery has taken us deep into nature, perhaps deeper than science had ever ventured before. Have we perhaps, through Darwinian eyes, stared into the very bottom of nature's well? Or may we look down even deeper?

The point of this book is to dig deeper than Darwin. I will assume here the fundamental correctness of evolutionary biology, but I want to question the nonscientific brief that evolutionary biology—or for that matter the cumulative body of natural sciences—amounts to an adequate explanation of living phenomena. Even though Darwinism is illuminating, it by no means tells us everything we need to know about life, even in principle. It certainly does not alone provide the space within which people, including the most devout Darwinians, can live their lives. Although evolutionary biology gives an enlightening account of some aspects of life, like all sciences it leaves out a lot. And although Darwinism concepts can even shed light on human existence, their explanatory power is easily exaggerated. To find the *deepest*, though certainly not the clearest, understandings of life and the universe, we may still profitably consult the religions of the world. ...

The arrival of literacy, as I have just noted, brings with it the possibility of literalism. And it is often scriptural literalism that leads religion into apparent conflict with science. However, in a parallel way, a literalist interpretation of nature—one that goes no deeper than Galileo's quantitative symbols or Darwin's idea of natural selection—can also lead scientists to dismiss religion for the shallowest of reasons. Scientific deciphering of nature has been the occasion for great gains in knowledge, but it has also permitted the emergence of a most soul-deadening "cosmic literalism." Our recently acquired scientific expertise in reading the text of nature has led us into such a trance-like fixation on surface codes and signifiers, and on life's evolutionary grammar, that we fail to look into the depth that lies beneath them. I hope in the following pages to burrow beneath both religious and cosmic literalism. Only in the depth beneath the texts of nature and holy writ shall we find a way to reconcile science and religion, evolution and the idea of God. ...

Of course, in its investigation of living phenomena, pure science legitimately employs a reductively physicalist or materialist method. There can be no justifiable objection to a "methodologist" materialism in biology, for example, as long as its practitioners remain aware that their abstract mechanical or atomistic models are leaving out most of what common sense and cumulative human wisdom understand as "life." But when this modeling is taken too literally, it becomes in effect a belief system of its own, one that not only arbitrarily opposes religion, but also ironically imprisons and diminishes science itself. Once materialist approaches attain the status of a general view of reality, that is, of metaphysics, they become an impediment to the kind of open inquiry that we rightly associate with science. The intellectual clarity that materialist interpretations of life and evolution seem to offer is purchased at a great price: The very depth of life and the universe becomes lost to consciousness. ...

In Darwinian perspective the *ultimate* reasons why ideas about the gods persist and religions continue to survive is because they are biologically adaptive. As vehicles of evolutionary cunning, religions motivate us to work hard, raise families and communicate a sprit of trust to our offspring. But now, with Darwin's help, we have found out what is *really* going on underneath our religious posturing. It is simply this: Our genes are seeing to get themselves into the next generation. All the rich layers of religious symbolism are, in the final analysis, nothing more than the consequence of our genetic endowment seeking out a circuitous path to immortality. Genes may not be the direct or immediate cause of our specific religious ideas, but they are the ultimate explanation.

By explaining religion, therefore, evolutionary ideas also seem to explain it away. In Darwinism, if we are to believe some of its adherents, the world is now finally handing itself over completely to human understanding. ...

[A]s it considers the large question of the possible "point" or purpose of the universe, theology may now reasonably conjecture that this same divine care takes into itself all of the suffering, discord, tragedy and enjoyment in biological evolution and cosmic unfolding, as well as in human history. If the permanence beneath process is endowed with the character of care, as theology is entitled to assume, it is not beyond reason to trust that this eternal care could also transform local cosmic contradictions into a wider harmony of contrasts, that is, into an unfathomable depth of beauty, and that our own destiny beyond death admits of conscious enjoyment of this beauty as well.

SOURCE: John F. Haught, *Deeper than Darwin*. Boulder, Colorado and London: Westview Press, 2003, pp. xi, xv, xiii, and 158

Women and the feminine in religion

During the twentieth century, extensive research was begun in order to discover and restore women's leadership in religions, to reconsider patriarchal language and assumptions found in scriptures, and to explore situations in which the deity is known as Goddess. In all religions, women are demanding access to religious education and opportunities to serve in significant roles, and the important spiritual contributions of individual women are being brought to light.

The Spiritual Idea of the "Feminine" by Vijaya Ramaswamy

Writing from an Asian Indian perspective, Vijaya Ramaswamy explores the "feminine" ideals of giving, self-surrender, and nurturing as being distinct from male-female dichotomies. In her book, *Walking Naked* (1997), she also explores spirituality as a path that has allowed some rare women to break free from patriarchal structures and be honored as saints, priestesses, or healers.

The notions of the "feminine" and "female" acquire a very different dimension in the spiritual sphere if one were to move out of patriarchal epistemological constructs. In spirituality patriarchal ideas of empowerment vis-à-vis disempowerment, dominance versus dependence, conquest as opposed to surrender do not have the same values as in the material realm. In fact in the spiritual realm all those notions are reversed. The values that get emphasized in the spiritual path are those of giving (very different from the patriarchal notion of "abject surrender"), and caring or nurturing, different again from the materialist values of hoarding and accumulating in the interests of oneself and one's immediate family. Both giving and nurturing arise from care and compassion and are qualities which acquire centrality in the spiritual sphere. This can be illustrated in terms of the Tamil legend of Manimekalai … in which the Buddhist renunciate Manimekalai receives the magic bowl. … Here, what would be the caring, nurturing qualities of the housewife turn into the begging bowl in the hands of a woman ascetic. The attributes of compassion and nurturing are used by the ascetic Manimekalai to feed thousands from the divine bowl and nurture and care for humanity at large. The qualities of caring and compassion which constitute striking features of the personality of the Buddha are to be found as much among spiritual/ humanistic men as among women. Therefore the qualities which command primacy in the spiritual field overflow gender constructs and lift the entire debate out of the contested terrain of male versus female epistemologies. …

Interestingly the root "ma" from where the terms for "mother" are derived in many languages means in Sanskrit *one who measures the needs of each and apportions their share accordingly.* Sharing which is so central to spirituality is very different from appropriation, which is essentially an attribute of a materialistic patriarchal society. The implications of gendered spirituality therefore effect a radical alteration of epistemological constructs. The giving of oneself … is no longer a sign of weakness or dependence which it would be within a patriarchal framework of values but a spiritually loaded term indicating the surrender of the individual ego and the expanding of the individual self into the infinite. …

The notion of service as an indispensable feature of love for the divine is also central to the concept of spirituality. The universal love immanent in true spirituality manifests itself in service to humanity. … It is significant that in the context of feudal relations … service signified inferiority, bondage and subordination. Service coupled with humility was the characteristic of females as well as low born males, especially untouchables. In the spiritual realm, however, these patriarchal ideas get reversed. Selfless service rendered with humility divested of its caste/gender pre-conceptions, becomes the hallmark of a truly spiritual person, irrespective and independent of whether one was male or female, high born or low born. …

Patriarchal values get subverted or rejected in the realm of female spirituality. A woman in the spiritual field may defy every social norm, reject marriage …, violate notions of "feminine modesty" as did Akka Mahadevi or Lallesvari by walking naked, and break ritual taboos like Kakrur Amma who insisted on worshipping the Linga while she was menstruating. Despite these blatant violations of social norms, these women enjoyed great respect and reverence, thus making gender behavioral patterns which would have been unacceptable in the social realm, acceptable and valorized in the spiritual realm. The spiritual path helped women to transcend all stereotypes, if they so desired. A spiritual woman could break free from tradition, orthodoxy and convention which attempted to control her and seek the godhead. …

SOURCE: Vijaya Ramaswamy, *Walking Naked: Women, Society, Spirituality in South India*. Shimla, India: Indian Institute of Advanced Study, 1997, pp. 15–19

The need for religion today

As the twenty-first century unfolds, many thoughtful people are asserting that religion is a necessity today, not just an historical artifact. However, they are redefining what is meant by "religion." The extract that follows from Paul Tillich is an example of fresh ways of thinking about religion and its place in modern life.

The Lost Dimension in Religion by Paul Tillich

Paul Tillich (1886–1965) was a German Protestant theologian who emigrated to the United States. He developed many original themes for twentieth-century religions, such as "ultimate concern" as a definition of religion, "the ground of Being" as a way of discussing "God," and "the new being" as a new way of viewing Christ. Religious institutions, he envisioned, are "emergency" institutions, only made necessary by our forgetfulness of Being. He urged industrial culture to overcome its anxiety and despair due to its estrangement from the depths, from the ground of Being.

Being religious means asking passionately the questions of the meaning of our existence and being willing to receive answers, even if the answers hurt. Such an idea of religion makes religion universally human, but it certainly differs from what is usually called religion. It does not describe religion as the belief in the existence of gods or one God, and as a set of activities and institutions for the sake of relating oneself to these beings in thought, devotion and obedience. No one can deny that the religions which have appeared in history are religions in this sense. Nevertheless, religion in its innermost nature is more than religion in this narrower sense. It is the state of being concerned about one's own being and being universally.

There are many people who are ultimately concerned in this way who feel far removed, however, from religion in the narrower sense, and therefore from every historical religion. It often happens that such people take the question of the meaning of their life infinitely seriously and reject any historical religion just for this reason. They feel that the concrete religions fail to express their profound concern adequately. They are religious while rejecting the religions. ...

If we define religion as the state of being grasped by an infinite concern we must say: Man [sic] in our time has lost such infinite concern. And the resurgence of religion is nothing but a desperate and mostly futile attempt to regain what has been lost.

How did the dimension of depth become lost?...

Modern man is neither more pious nor more impious than man in any other period. The loss of the dimension of depth is caused by the relation of man to his world and to himself in our period, the period in which nature is being subjected scientifically and technically to the control of man. In this period, life in the dimension of depth is replaced by life in the horizontal dimension. The driving forces of the industrial society of which we are a part go ahead horizontally and not vertically. In popular terms this is expressed in phrases like "better and better," "bigger and bigger," "more and more." One should not disparage the feeling which lies behind such speech. [Industrial society believes that] Man is right in feeling that he is able to know and transform the world he encounters without a foreseeable limit. He can go ahead in all directions without a definite boundary. ...

The predominance of the horizontal dimension over the dimension of depth has been immensely increased by the opening of the space beyond the space of earth.

If we now ask what does man do and seek if he goes ahead in the horizontal dimension, the answer is difficult. Sometimes one is inclined to say that the mere movement ahead without an end, the intoxication with speeding forward without limits, is what satisfies him. But this answer is by no means sufficient. ... He transforms everything he encounters into a tool; and in doing so he himself becomes a tool. But if he asks, a tool for what, there is no answer.

One does not need to look far beyond everyone's daily experience in order to find examples to describe this predicament. Indeed our daily life in office and home, in cars and airplanes, at parties and conferences, while reading magazines and watching television, while looking at advertisements and hearing radio, are in themselves continuous examples of a life which has lost the dimension of depth. It runs ahead, every moment is filled with something which must be done or seen or said or planned. But no one can experience depth without stopping and becoming aware of himself. Only if he has moments in which he does not care about what comes next can he experience the meaning of this moment here and now and ask himself about the meaning of his life. As long as the preliminary, transitory concerns are not silenced, no matter how interesting and valuable and important they may be, the voice of the ultimate concern cannot be heard. This is the deepest root of the loss of the dimension of depth in our period—the loss of religion in its basic and universal meaning.

When in this way man has deprived himself of the dimension of depth and the symbols expressing it, he then becomes a part of the horizontal plane. He loses his self and becomes a thing among things. He becomes an element in the process of manipulated production and manipulated consumption. This is now a matter of public knowledge. We have become aware of the degree to which everyone in our social structure is managed, even if one knows it and even if one belongs himself to the managing group. The influence of the gang mentality on adolescents, of the corporation's demands on the executives, of the conditioning of everyone by public communication, by propaganda and advertising under the guidance of motivation research, et cetera, have all been described in many books and articles.

Under these pressures, man can hardly escape the fate of becoming a thing among the things he produces, a bundle of conditioned reflexes without a free, deciding and responsible self. The immense mechanism, set up by man to produce objects for his use, transforms man himself into an object used by the same mechanism of production and consumption.

But man has not ceased to be man. He resists this fate anxiously, desperately, courageously. He asks the question, for what? And he realizes that there is no answer. He becomes aware of the emptiness which is covered by the continuous movement ahead and the production of means for ends which become means again without an ultimate end. Without knowing what has happened to him, he feels that he has lost the meaning of life, the dimension of depth. ...

What we need above all—and partly have—is the radical realization of our predicament, without trying to cover it up by secular or religious ideologies. The revival of religious interest would be a creative power in our culture if it would develop into a movement of search for the lost dimension of depth.

This does not mean that the traditional religious symbols should be dismissed. They certainly have lost their meaning in the literalistic form into which they have been distorted, thus producing the critical reaction against them. But they have not lost their genuine meaning, namely, of answering the question which is implied in man's very existence in powerful, revealing and saving symbols. If the resurgence of religion would produce a new understanding of the symbols of the past and their relevance for our situation, instead of premature and deceptive answers, it would become a creative factor in our culture and a saving factor for many who live in estrangement, anxiety and despair. The religious answer has always the character of "in spite of." In spite of the loss of dimension of depth, its power is present, and most present in those who are aware of the loss and are striving to regain it with ultimate seriousness.

SOURCE: Paul Tillich, "The Lost Dimension in Religion," in *The Essential Tillich*, ed. F. Forrester Church. New York: Macmillan, 1987, pp. 1–8

GLOSSARY

Anthropomorphism The expression of the divine in human form—king, child, goddess; a mythic image of a mysterious power that helps people relate to abstract Being through earthly images.

Archetypal Image Carl Jung's theory of a symbolic element of the collective unconscious—such as the hero, shadow evil, lover, or god—discovered in dreams and myths, whose stories shape the psyche and religions.

Being, ground of Being The absolute, the depth, the foundation of existence glimpsed in experience, paradox, and images, not just in cognition; symbolized in many ways—gods, nature, stars, compassion.

Charisma The dynamic, heroic personality type set apart with superhuman qualities, positive or negative.

Creed Confession of faith that identifies a religious group.

Dharma (or dhamma) The teachings of the Buddha.

Dogma A statement of beliefs considered authoritative or absolute truth.

Hermeneutics The study of methodologies of interpretation; originally of religious scriptures, now of any principle of interpretation, such as literalism.

History of religion The study of the historical dimension of religion—texts and timelines, for example—sometimes reducing it to sociocultural events.

Mandala A visual design, usually circular, symbolizing the divine.

Monotheism Belief in one supreme god only, in contrast with polytheism.

Myth Symbolic narrative or a literary or religious event. In religious studies, not considered inherently untrue, but can reveal the depths of Being.

Numinous From the Latin *numen*, the spiritual experience of awesome mystery.

Phenomenology The study of religious manifestations of Being that explore the general themes of spirituality, such as myth, ritual, initiation, compassion.

Polytheism Belief in many gods, in contrast with monotheism.

Postmodernism A wide-ranging critical approach to modern belief in the metaphysics of objective truth, technological progress, religious traditions, science, patriarchy; deconstructing cultural meta-narratives as social constructs, not rooted in absolute truth.

Profane Opposite of sacred, literally "outside the temple;" whatever is considered as impure or rejected by a group's sense of what is sacred.

Projection Theoretical concept of psychology; the externalization of unconscious material into the world, as in falling in love at first sight, or hating someone or something not really known. God in religious critique.

Psychology of religion The study of the role of psychology in religion, sometimes reducing it to a byproduct of psychology.

Reduction A method of explaining one domain as a product of a lower domain, such as saying that Gods are projections of the psyche, as Sigmund Freud did. Basic to science, also applied to culture.

Ritual Symbolic actions, individual or group, crude or refined, such as a fight, a funeral, wedding, meditation, or worship.

Sacred Opposite of profane, the realm of ultimate reality, appearance of the infinite, Being.

Sociology of religion The study of the role of religion in society, sometimes reducing it to a byproduct of society.

Transcendent Rising above common thought; exalted, mystical, ultimate.

REVIEW QUESTIONS

1   Outline the importance of hermeneutics and explain the difference between the hermeneutics of belief in one religion only and globalism.
2   Explain some major methodologies for studying world religions. Give an example of a scholar using each method.
3   What is the meaning of the religious term "Being"? Describe several of the ways it manifests itself in the world.

DISCUSSION QUESTIONS

1   Imagine a debate between representatives of the materialistic perspectives on religion and the phenomenologists. Outline the major arguments of each group and draw a conclusion.
2   Choose a major dimension of religions worldwide and explain, giving examples, how it functions and what it means for believers.
3   Contrast the use of literal language and symbolic language in religions. Give examples and discuss the advantages and disadvantages of each kind.

INFORMATION RESOURCES

Bailey, Lee W., general ed. *Introduction to the World's Major Religions*. 6 vols. Westport, CT: Greenwood Press, 2006.

Barua, Archana. *Phenomology of Religion*. Lanham, MD: Lexington, 2009.

Brasher, Brenda, ed. *Encyclopedia of Fundamentalism*. New York: Routledge, 2001.

Doniger, Wendy, ed. *Britannica Encyclopedia of World Religions*. Chicago, IL: Encyclopaedia Britannica, Inc., 2006.

Esposito, John, Darrell Fashing, Todd Lewis, eds. *Religion & Globalization: World Religions in Historical Perspective*. Oxford: Oxford University Press, 2008.

Films for the Humanities and Sciences/ World Religions
<http://ffh.films.com>

Internet Sacred Text Archive
<http://www.sacred-texts.com>

Jones, Lindsay, ed. *Encyclopedia of Religion*. 15 vols. 2nd ed. New York: Macmillan, 2005.

Leeming, David, Kathryn Madden, and Stanton Marlan, eds. *Encyclopedia of Psychology and Religion*, 2 vols. New York: Springer, 2010.

Palmer-Fernandez, Gabriel, ed. *Encyclopedia of Religion and War*. New York: Routledge, 2004.

Religion Facts
<http://www.religionfacts.com>

Religious Tolerance
<http://www.religioustolerance.org/var_rel.htm>

Smart, Ninian. *Atlas of the World's Religions*. Oxford: Oxford University Press, 1999.

Swatos, William, ed. *Encyclopedia of Religion and Society*. Walnut Creek, CA: Alta Mira Press, 1998.

Van Huytssteen, J., and Wentzel Vrede, eds. *Encyclopedia of Science and Religion*. New York: Macmillan, 2003.

The Virtual Religion Index
<http://virtualreligion.net/vri>

Wabash Center Guide to Internet Resources
<http://www.wabashcenter.wabash.edu/ resources/guide-headings.aspx/>

World Religions Photo Library
<http://www.worldreligions.co.uk>

Young, Serinity, ed. *Encyclopedia of Women and World Religion*. New York: Macmillan, 1999.

CHAPTER 2

INDIGENOUS SACRED WAYS

In pockets of the world remote from industrial culture, traditional small-scale societies still exist. Although they are increasingly being drawn into the global economy, some have managed to maintain part of their traditional religious ways. In these **indigenous** religions, the sacred and the profane are not separate; religious understanding pervades everyday life and every aspect of the environment.

Despite great differences from one indigenous culture to the next, certain common themes can be found. One is the concept of sacred relationship to all that exists. One's individuality is of less importance than one's kinship with the whole natural system. All beings are interrelated, and shaking the cosmic web at any point affects all things. Such relationships are described in myths and symbols.

Another common indigenous belief is that the natural world is pervaded by living, thinking presences, which should not be ignored even if one cannot see them. There are spirits in trees, in rocks, in rivers, in mountains, in the elements, and one should stay in proper spiritual relationship with them. The appropriate human attitude toward these spirits may be a certain fear or awe, and it may be necessary to make offerings to the spirits or carry out certain divinations or other rituals to keep them happy. Often these spirits are seen as the souls of dead ancestors. In addition to a plurality of spiritual beings, there may also be a belief in an underlying cosmic force which creates and sustains the natural world.

Although such awarenesses are incumbent on everyone in traditional indigenous cultures, there are also specialists who deal with the spirit worlds. By enduring great hardships, they develop communication with the spirits and thus can act as go-betweens on behalf of the people.

These ancient spiritual ways have typically been handed down and added to orally over the millennia within the local communities. But now that these small-scale societies have been marginalized, oppressed, or brought into industrial society, there are few people left to carry on the rituals and retell the stories. However, people both within and outside these ancient ways are learning to cherish them again as containing valuable instructions for living in harmony with the cosmos.

Understanding indigenous sacred ways

The spiritual lifeways of indigenous people may not be understood properly from the perspective of the major global religions. The spiritual and the sacred are not separate spheres, and in these largely **oral traditions**, music, dance, and storytelling play large roles in preserving and transmitting the traditions.

African Spiritual Tradition by Harvey J. Sindima

Rev. Dr. Harvey J. Sindima of Malawi, professor at Colgate University, explains the unity of sacred and secular in African traditional religions. This holistic worldview is common to most indigenous religions.

In African tradition the divine is infused with everything and every aspect or dimension of life so that there is no leaving this world for eternal bliss; there is no salvation, no liberation, and no enlightenment in African tradition. African tradition is a religion of structure, a contrast to religions of salvation of the Middle East and Asia.

... I have chosen to use the word tradition for religion. Tradition is a comprehensive term that includes modes of thinking and ways of being in the world that is fused with the divine to the degree that there is no department of life that is not sacred so that there is no bifurcation of the world into sacred and secular. Such a dichotomous world view does not exist in African cosmology. John Mbiti points out that no African language has a word for religion. Instead, other words such as worship, reverence, sacrifice, etc., are used. ... I prefer then to use the word tradition for religion because the term includes the philosophy, knowledge, ethical and ritual practises of African life. Tradition expresses much better the totality of African life by demonstrating that there is nothing that is not spiritual or has spiritual implication; nothing is secular. ...

The African is fiercely an earthly being, a creature whose whole being is oriented to fulfillment of life in this world. The African is not bound to heaven; the African glories in having his or her abode on this earth to realise the fulness of life as the creator intended it. The African takes earthly life seriously as a place for the totality of his or her being: body and spirit or soul. Africans reason that if the earth was not important, divinity would not have made humans and instruct them to live on it.

The whole cosmos is for the African a workshop for realising fulness of life, or personhood which Malawians call *umunthu*. This Malawian term for fulness of life, *umunthu*, derives from the word, *munthu*, person, whose ontology is grounded in Being itself, or divinity itself. This means *munthu* is not simply matter, flesh, and blood, but a being beyond matter who shares his or her essence with divinity, the divine Being. This does not mean that the African sees himself or herself as divine, but that his or her being partakes of and participates in divine essence, the being of divinity. This is to say, humans are divine albeit not to the status of divinity itself. ...

Many cosmogonies in African tradition maintain that once divinity dwelt on earth, but retreated into the heavens above because of human greed, or some other unbecoming human action. Nevertheless, Africans do not aspire to go to heaven to be with divinity. On the contrary, Africans want to realise their divine nature right here on earth and in this life. African orientation towards life is not to seek salvation, or flight from this life and the earth, rather to develop structures of life so infused with divine presence so that there is no human act that is outside the sphere of the divine, in which humans seek flight of their soul from the earth to heaven to be with divinity. Even in death, the African spirit does not go to heaven; it joins the ancestors here on earth and together they belong to a realm of spirits in which divinity is the head. The African wants body and soul to achieve their highest on earth. … The divinity who retreated to the heavens above, the transcendent divinity, is always eminent on earth.

SOURCE: Rev. Dr. Harvey J. Sindima, "Mysticism and Spirituality in African Tradition," for Mysticism in World Religions conference, February 17–18, 2010, co-convened by Jamia Milia University and Gobind Sadan Institute for the Advanced Study of Comparative Religion, New Delhi

The Talking Drum: African Sacred Liturgy
by Georges Niangoran-Bouah

Georges Niangoran-Bouah, who taught at the University of Abidjan in Ivory Coast, West Africa, brings to life the deeper meanings of the African drum's sacred messages. The drums' ancient poetry, carrying in rhythm far across African plains, praises God the Creator, Goddess Earth, and beautiful Moon. This primal discourse carries the sacred consciousness of ancient ways, he says, much as holy books do for other faiths.

Generally speaking, the outsider who comes to Africa for the first time is surprised by the omnipresence of the drum in both religious and profane ceremonies. The drum is an instrument that everybody hears and sees; it is the instrument of kings. …

The Sacred According to religious anthropology, the Sacred is that which is connected to religion and that which inspires respect and deep veneration. The Sacred is whatever goes beyond man and inspires his respect, his admiration. From the Sacred generally emanates a particular fervor, coupled with an element of fear of an absolute power and an element of mystery. The sacred being or object enjoys a fascinating power, often presented as being the locus of energy able to manifest itself at any moment and anywhere.

For the traditional African, the Sacred is an organized and hierarchized universe filled with invisible beings which include God, spirits, the spirits of the ancestors, myths, legends, ceremonies, elaborate rituals, and cult objects.

It is this universe of absolute power, of mystery, of fascinating might, that we are trying to reconstitute through what the African drums say. …

In black Africa, the talking drum is in fact a precious element of communication. In the highlands, with a favorable direction of the wind, the language of a drum can be heard at a distance of 40 kilometers.

For the Akan [tribe], the drummed documentation is serious; it is sacred and respected by the whole population. This is the reason that it is the preferred method of communication with gods, the spirits, and the ancestors. ...

Among the Akan in Côte d'Ivoire and Ghana, the drum defines its origin itself by saying:

> God in creating the world
> Has suffered to create.
> What did he create?
> He created the Drum.
> Divine Drum,
> Wherever you are
> In nature,
> We call upon you,
> Come.
> *(Abron[1] drum text)*

The drum is an animated being   In this chapter, the drum is no longer only perceived as a material object of human conception and fabrication but also as an animated being endowed with a vital force and spiritual principle.

> While organizing the world,
> God-the-Creator
> Has suffered to create.
> What did He create?
> He has created the Word
> And the Word-carrier,
> Has created the drum and
> The drummer. ...
> Divine drum,
> Wherever you be
> In nature,
> We call upon you, come!
> Divine drum,
> We shall wake you up
> And make you heard.
> *(Abron drum text)*
> I am coming from my dream
> And find myself
> In the hands
> Of the drummer.
> *(Abron drum)*

---

1 Abron—West African tribe in Ghana and Ivory Coast.

The Creation according to the drum

God-the-Creator
Has created Heaven,
And he has created the Earth.
He has created the night,
And has created the day,
Alone
Absolutely alone.
God has created the water
And has created the crocodile.
(Agni² drum)

Attitude and behavior of humans towards the Eternal One

Great God
Infinitely mighty
You who give us life
We glorify you,
Bless us!
(Agni drum)

SOURCE: Georges Niangoran-Bouah, "The Talking Drum: A Traditional African Instrument of Liturgy and of Mediation with the Sacred," in *African Traditional Religions in Contemporary Society*, ed. Jacob Ôlupona. New York: Paragon House, 1991, pp. 81–92

The Theft of Light by the Tsimshian Nation

This folktale is a traditional story from the Tsimshian people of the Northwest Coast of North America, where the year has a long period of dim Arctic night. Food was available in abundance in that lushly forested area, so there was plenty of leisure time during which the people evolved complex clan systems and spiritual traditions. The following story is one version of the myth explaining how light appeared in the world, with theft of light from the gods perhaps symbolizing the granting of clarity of conscious knowledge to uncomprehending humans. It includes reference to Raven, who was considered a shape-changing creature, a symbol of metamorphosis and change. In many stories, he is a trickster. In this story, even his skin has shape-changing power. The conception of a divine child by asexual means appears in stories from many religions.

The whole world was covered with darkness. The people were distressed by this. Then Giant remembered that there was light in heaven, whence he had come. On the following day Giant put on his raven skin, which his father the chief had given to him, and flew upward. Finally he found the hole in the sky, and he flew through it. He took off the raven skin and put it down near

2 Agni—West African tribe in Ivory Coast.

the hole in the sky. He went on, and came to a spring near the house of the chief of heaven.

Then the chief's daughter came out, carrying a small bucket in which she was about to fetch water. When Giant saw her coming along, he transformed himself into the leaf of a cedar and floated on the water. The chief's daughter dipped it up in her bucket and drank it. After a short time she was with child, and not long after she gave birth to a boy. Then the chief and the chieftainess were very glad.

Now the child was strong and crept about every day. He began to cry *"Hama, hama!"* The great chief was troubled, and called in some of his slaves to carry about the boy, but he kept on crying, *"Hama, hama!"* Therefore the chief invited all his wise men, and said to them that he did not know what the boy wanted and why he was crying. He wanted the box that was hanging in the chief's house. This box, in which the daylight was kept, was hanging in one corner of the house. Its name was *mā*. Giant had known it before he descended to our world.

One of the wise men, who understood him, said to the chief, "He is crying for the *mā*." Therefore the chief ordered it to be taken down. They put it down near the fire, and the boy sat down near it and ceased crying, for he was glad. Then he rolled the *mā* about inside the house. Sometimes he would carry it to the door. Now the great chief did not think of it. Then the boy really took up the *mā*, put it on his shoulders, and ran out with it. While he was running, someone said, "Giant is running away with the *mā*!" He ran away, and the hosts of heaven pursued him. He came to the hole of the sky, put on the skin of the raven, and flew down, carrying the *mā*.

At that time the world was still dark. Giant had come down near the mouth of Nass River. He went up the river in the dark. A little farther up he heard the noise of the people, who were catching *olachen* in bag nets in their canoes. Giant, who was sitting on the shore, said, "Throw ashore one of the things that you are catching, my dear people!" Those on the water scolded him, "Where did you come from, great liar...?" Then Giant said again, "Throw ashore one of the things that you are catching, or I shall break the *mā*."

Giant repeated his request four times, but those on the water refused what he had asked for. Therefore Giant broke the *mā*. It broke, and it was daylight. The north wind began to blow hard, and all the fishermen, the Frogs who had made fun of Giant, were driven away down river until they arrived at one of the large mild tenderness islands. Here the Frogs tried to climb up the rock; but they stuck to the rock, being frozen by the north wind, and became stone. They are still on the rock ... and all the world had the daylight.

SOURCE: Abridged from Tsimshian Nation, "The Theft of Light," a Raven's Adventure Story collected by Franz Boaz, in the Report of the Bureau of Ethnology of the Smithsonian Institution. Washington, DC: Smithsonian Institution, 1916, vol. 31, p. 60

The circle of right relationships

Since indigenous traditions perceive connections among all things within the cosmos, people are taught the necessity of staying in proper relationship with everything, lest the web of life be disturbed. The following are examples of this teaching from varying indigenous cultures.

That Mountain Has Spirit by Southwest Indigenous Peoples

In indigenous understanding, everything is alive.

You go out and get a certain piece of rock. It's not just a rock. It's got energy forces in it; it's a living thing, too. …

   You look at that mountain, that mountain has spirit, that mountain has holiness. There's a quiet there and yet there's a fervor there. And if you've ever seen clouds there you see that mountain like a hand grasping those clouds. There's life up there. That's why it's sacred. …

   Before you go hunting the important thing is that you are going to have a little prayer … to the Mother Nature, the nature of the sky, and then the animal, and then you more or less cry a little bit, and ask Mother Nature to spare you some meat. When you went into that forest, you had to be that deer. …

   We must try and worship the land, the ground and the stars and the skies, for they are the ones that have spirit. They are the mighty spirits which guide and direct us, which help us to survive.

SOURCE: Stephen Trimble, ed., *Our Voices, Our Land*: based on an audio-visual show created for the Heard Museum, Phoenix, Arizona. Courtesy Heard Museum. Flagstaff, AZ: Northland Press, © 1986, pp. 24–47

The Energy of Oya by Judith Gleason

The spirits who cannot be seen are properly regarded with awe, and perhaps fear, for they are so powerful. In this extract, priestess Judith Gleason describes the complexities of the African goddess Oya.

The goddess Oya, of African origin, manifests herself in various natural forms: the river Niger, tornadoes, strong winds generally, fire, lightning, and buffalo. She is also associated with certain cultural phenomena among the Yoruba people … notably with masquerades constructed of bulky, billowing cloth—ancestral apparitions—and with funerals. To the leader of the market women in Yoruba communities she offers special protection and encouragement in negotiation with civil authorities and arbitration of disputes. Thus, one may speak of Oya as patron of feminine leadership, of persuasive charm reinforced by *aje*—an efficacious gift usually translated as "witchcraft." Although Oya is associated with pointed speech, most of what she's about is highly secret. Always vanishing, she presents herself in concealment. More abstractly, Oya is the goddess of edges, of the dynamic interplay between surfaces, of transformation from one state of being to another. She is a jittery goddess, then, but with a keen sense of direction.

To describe and elaborate upon Oya's various manifestations is inevitably to present an idea not commonly thought of when the word "goddess" is mentioned. Oya's patterns, persisting through many media—from air to the human psyche—suggest something like a unified field theory of a certain type of energy that our culture certainly doesn't think of as feminine. …

Old women, the grandmothers are a strong, affecting presence in religious places all over the world. They light the candles. They arrange the flowers. They sew the altar cloths, the vestments, the shrouds. When speaking of the Yoruba system of belief, it is important to point to the predominance of feminine symbolism as well … a succession of opaque containers rounded about hidden matrices. The feminine is primary to the Yoruba imagination. Womankind, therefore, is regarded with ambivalence. Female passion, potentially overwhelming, in turn is contained by male structures of thought and language … which then by their own logic exclude women, except for occasional grandmothers, from enclaves and conclaves of authority. Even grandmothers are suspect. … A woman who has *aje* won't admit it. … In true womanly fashion, she'll contain it. Secrecy is feminine. …

What is especially interesting about Oya in human context is her refusal to stay out of the enclaves of cult and culture preempted by male authority. She has, potentially, a sharp tongue, which occasionally she wields like a sword. Now and again her mouth spits fire. Furthermore, though she's rounded, though she might stay for a time in her corner (which is where her altars are always placed), suddenly she's storming all over the place, a revolutionary. So she has to be made part of the picture. … If excluded altogether, Oya turns unimaginably violent. She has whirled her way into the Yoruba pantheon (she isn't natally Yoruba). She has even managed to set herself indispensably in the midst of the male ancestral cult. …

Oya is her simplest name. It is a verb form conveying her passage as an event with disastrous consequences. *O-ya*, meaning "She tore" in Yoruba. And what happened? A big tree … getting in the way of the storm, wildly agitated its branches. Perhaps its crown got lopped off. She tore. A river overflowed its banks. Whole cloth was ripped into shreds. Barriers were broken down. A tumultuous feeling suddenly destroyed one's peace of mind. "*Eeepa!*" one exclaims, by way of homage. "*Eeepa Heyi!*" What a goddess!

SOURCE: Judith Gleason, *Oya: In Praise of the Goddess*. Boston: Shambhala, 1987, pp. 1–11

Maori Environmental Ethics   by Manuka Henare

Maoris are the indigenous people of New Zealand, comprising 16 percent of the population. Most now live in cities, and many have become Christians because of missionary activity. But, according to Maori Manuka Henare, European colonialism, Christianity, and urbanization have not separated the people from their traditional relationships with the natural environment.

Philosophically, Māori people do not see themselves as separate from nature, humanity, and the natural world, being direct descendants of Earth Mother. Thus, the resources of the earth do not belong to humankind; rather, humans belong to the earth. While humans as well as animals, birds, fish and trees can harvest the bounty of Mother Earth's resources, they do not own them. Instead, humans have "user rights." Māori have recorded their user rights in their cosmic and genealogical relations with the natural world. ...

Māori history began in the time before creation progressed to the birth of the mythical and original homeland of Māori called Hawaiki, a place distant in time and space, which is the link with the spirit world. In this sense Hawaiki is a cosmic place. After the birth of Hawaiki, the gods were created. Rangi the Sky Father and Papa-tua-nuku the Earth Mother were lovers locked in an age-long embrace, during which they had many children. The offspring lived between them, becoming the spirit beings of the sea, winds, forests, wild foods, crops, and humanity. In fact, the children are the progenitors of the world and its environment as we know it. The growing children lived in continuous darkness and in the confined space were crushed by their parents. The children decided it was enough and that their circumstances had to change. They separated the parent lovers and created a world of light. One of the children, called Tane, the spirit being of forests, tore Sky Father from Earth Mother and so the New World, called Te Whenua Hawaiki, came into being. The earthly Hawaiki exists. It was light at last.

Like Tane, the other children were allocated domains of the natural world for which they were each responsible, and thus humanity and a diverse natural world was born. In an oratorical way the elder called confidently, triumphantly, "Tīhei mauriora!—Ah t'is life." According to the elder, affection for and attachment to the land and environment historically commenced.

Philosophically and metaphysically, the sundering of the parents and the concomitant burst of light into the cosmos was the spark that started life for plants, fish, birds, and people. Like a wind, it swept through the cosmos bringing freedom and renewal. Once established in the new milieu, the power could be called upon by humans and transmitted through ritual pathways into receptacles such as stones or people. According to Māori thought, the cosmos started with a burst of primal energy. ...

This spiritual, humanistic value of land and environment makes things vital, holy, and sacred in Māori understanding. ... *Tapu* is a cosmic power imbued in all things at the time of creation and would normally remain for the duration of a thing's existence, its being. In the Sky Father and Earth Mother account, each of the children were conceived with the *tapu* of the parents, and they in turn are the sources of the *tapu* of all the domains and things of creation ascribed to them. Persons, places, or objects are *tapu* and are therefore in a sacred state or condition. Philosophically, *tapu* is linked to the notion of *mana* and is "being with potentiality for power." In its primary meaning, *tapu* expressed the understanding that once a thing is, it has within itself a real potency, *mana*. Each being, material or non-material, from its first moment of existence, has this potentiality and its own power and authority. Coupled with the potential for power is the idea of awe and sacredness, which commands respect and separateness. It is in this sense that *tapu* can mean restrictions and prohibitions. However, *tapu*, a core part of Pacific belief systems, was glossed as taboo by earlier Western observers and recognized largely in terms of restrictions or prohibitions. Unfortunately, it is the limited and negative understanding that is used to explain *tapu*, but this is only one aspect of its meaning.

Mana is religious power, authority, and ancestral efficacy. Together with *tapu* it derives from the creation parents and children, and ultimately from Io. It is humanity's greatest possession. *Tapu* is traditionally applied to many things and there are, therefore, many types of *tapu*. All children are *tapu*, individuals and groups are *tapu*. Houses and gardens are *tapu*, trees and birds are *tapu*, as are rivers, lakes, and oceans. Ecosystems and the environment as a whole are therefore *tapu*. *Tapu* needs to be treated with respect, awe, and sometimes fear, but it depends on the relationship of one's own *tapu* to the *tapu* belonging to other persons and life systems in the environment. A respectful relationship ensures balance, health, and well-being, but a bad relationship of abuse often leads to disharmony and imbalance. This applies to the *tapu* of distinct features of ecosystems. They need to be protected, strengthened, and constantly confirmed so that balance, harmony, and potentialities can be fulfilled. …

Mauri is variously described as a unique power, a life essence, a life force, and a vital principle. *Mauri* refers to the vital spark, originally possessed by Io, the Primary Life Force and Supreme Cosmic Being. It is a force transmitted by Hauora, one of the children of the creation parents, who is responsible for *hau* and *mauri* and, therefore, life in all creation. It is intimately related to other metaphysical powers—*tapu, mana, hau,* and *wairua*—and all of these forces are essences of forms of life in persons, objects, and nonobjectified beings. They endow a thing with its special character, which must correspond to its nature. *Mauri* is a concentration of life itself, like the center of an energy source and, because of its power and energy, its purpose is to make it "possible for everything to move and live in accordance with the conditions and limits of its existence." Everything has its own *mauri*, its own nature—people, tribe, land, mountains, stones, fish, animals, birds, trees, rivers, lakes, oceans, thoughts, words, houses, factories—that permits these living things to exist within their own realm and sphere.

All *mauri* may be violated, abused, or diminished through neglect or attack. Thus, trees and plants, rivers, lakes, and oceans may not produce in limitless abundance. Fruits would be scarce, there would be fewer birds, animals, or fish. From a Māori perspective forests, rivers, and oceans can have their *mauri* restored through rituals of conservation accompanied by appropriate ritual prayer forms and ceremonies. The restored *mauri* would ensure that depleted food supplies, such as fish, shell fish, or birds, would be abundant again. …

Outlined below is what can best be described as a spiral of traditional ethics, which simultaneously presents Mäori worldview and acts as a check on that worldview. This ... constitutes a Pacific Polynesian view of holism and way of linking humanity and environment in a relationship of reciprocity and respect.

- ethic of wholeness, cosmos (*te ao märama*)
- ethic of life essences, vitalism, reverence for life (*mauri*)
- ethic of being and potentiality, the sacred (*tapu*)
- ethic of power, authority, and common good (*mana*)
- ethic of spiritual power of obligatory reciprocity in relationships with nature (*hau*)
- ethic of the spirit and sprituality (*wairuatanga*)
- ethic of the right way, of the quest for justice (*tika*)
- ethic of care and support, reverence for humanity (*manaaki-tanga*)
- ethic of belonging, reverence for the human person (*wha-naungatanga*)
- ethic of change and tradition (*te ao hurihuri*)
- ethic of solidarity (*kotahitanga*)
- ethic of guardianship of creation (*kaitiakitanga*)

SOURCE: Manuka Henare, "Tapu, Mana, Mauri, Hau, Wairua: A Maori Philosophy of Vitalism and Cosmos," in *Indigenous Traditions and Ecology: The Interbeing of Cosmology and Community*, ed. John A. Grim. Cambridge, MA: Harvard University Press, 2001, pp. 202–14

Spiritual specialists

Indigenous traditions often provide special roles for men and women with spiritual gifts. They may be storytellers, drummers, dancers, sacred clowns, members of secret societies, priests, priestesses, or intermediaries between the spirits and the people.

Calling of the Shaman by John A. Grim

Those spiritual specialists who are in touch with unseen forces and act as channels for their power may serve as healers and counselors for people in distress. Religious scholars refer to them by the generic term **shamans**. Shamans do not adopt their demanding role by their own choice; rather, in whatever culture they appear, they first receive what they experience as a divine call to serve. John Grim compares the calling of shamans from two geographically distinct areas—southwestern Siberia and the Ojibway Indians of North America.

The shaman's formation classifies him or her as a religious personality. It is during this period that he or she develops the special qualities and skills needed to be spiritually effective. The formation is a gradual process filled with grave challenges and fraught with enormous difficulties. Despite the spontaneous nature of the initial contact with cosmic forces, the shaman-to-be passes through extensive periods of solitary reflection or training with elder shamans. He or she must overcome all manner of doubts and fears to master the sacred craft. ...

Among the Sagay tribe of the Turkish region of Abakan in southwestern Siberia shamanic figures receive their vocational call in one of three ways: from the family-shaman spirits, by the will of a mountain spirit or from the spirit of some sickness. Shaman Kyzlasov received his vocational call in the most traditional manner. He was made ill by the family spirits for many years, and then, during a particular dream, he was taken by the family spirits to the ancestral spirit. He described the dream as follows:

> I have been sick and I have been dreaming. In my dreams I had been taken to the ancestor and cut into pieces on a black table. They chopped me up and then threw me into the kettle and I was boiled. There were some men there: two black and two fair ones. Their chieftain was there too. He issued the orders concerning me. I saw all this. While the pieces of my body were boiled, they found a bone around the ribs, which had a hole in the middle. This was the excess bone. This brought about my becoming a shaman. Because, only those men can become shaman in whose body such a bone can be found. One looks across the hole of this bone and begins to see all, to know all and, that is when one becomes a shaman. ... When I came to from this state, I woke up. This meant that my soul had returned. Then the shamans declared: "You are the sort of man who may become a shaman. You should become a shaman, you must begin to shamanize."

The mythological location of the ancestral spirit among these Turkish Siberian tribes is at the center of the cosmic tree. While Kyzlasov was sick and dreaming, he was led to that locus of cosmological power to be dismembered and reassembled with a new shamanic perception of reality. He witnessed the sacrificial death and rebirth through which he was called to his vocation. His new shamanic vision was identified with the "excess bone" across the opening of which he could look "to see all, to know all. ..."

> He came up to me where I lay. There was a light glowing all around him; it even looked as if the light shone right through his body. And his body was covered with hair from head to foot. I could not recognize the face because it was hidden behind the hair.

> I was not going to speak to him because I was overwhelmed with surprise and fear. I never thought I would see anyone like that before me. It is very hard for me to describe what I saw.

> When he first spoke to me his voice sounded like an echo from the sky above. I could not understand what he said, I was so afraid. ... Then my fear vanished and I calmed down. He spoke words of greeting to me:

> "Ke-koko-ta-chi-ken. Grandchild, be not afraid."

As he spoke he raised his arms in a friendly gesture. It was obvious he had not come to do me harm but teach me the things I had come there to learn. After a few moments he was so friendly my fears were gone. He spoke to me again:

"I know what you want without asking. I will help you as long as you live. Your future is clear and bright. If you follow my wisdom I will protect you from harm. ..."

The dream-calls Kyzlasov and Mis-quona-queb initiated them into the powerful world of cosmic forces. Both shamans directly experienced this mysterious region because of the mediation of spirits. Kyzlasov was carried in a dream by the spirits of his clan to the cosmic tree, while Mis-quona-queb apprehended the manitou of a traditional cosmic personality. While the specific manner of the shamanic call was different, these encounters with the numinous forces that cause a personal transformation were similar. Kyzlasov's and Mis-quona-queb's shamanic call were alike in their experiential quality, in their cosmic centredness, and in their capacity to direct the individual's life.

SOURCE: John A. Grim, *The Shaman: Patterns of Religious Healing among the Ojibway Indians*. Norman, OK: University of Oklahoma Press, 1983, pp. 169–72

Group observances

Many aspects of indigenous sacred lifeways occur in communal settings. Community rituals may be used to honor and invoke spiritual blessings for occasions such as seasonal changes, puberty, marriage, and death, or for special needs, such as healing. Here we sample ritual observances from indigenous groups in Africa and Australia.

An African Boy's Initiation by Malidoma Patrice Somé

Malidoma Somé, born in Burkina Faso, West Africa, is an initiated shaman in his Dagara culture. He also holds three master's degrees and two doctorates. This selection tells of his initiation into his tribal wisdom after several years in a French missionary school. It describes the ritually altered states of consciousness through which he grasped the transcendent mysteries of his ancient people's traditions.

"So my initiation begins tomorrow—and I am not the least prepared for it."
    "Your not knowing is your being prepared."...
    I walked out of my room into the inner yard, where Father was waiting for me. He held ash in one hand and a bowl of water in the other. He handed me the water and I followed him into the **medicine** room.
    We knelt down and he began. "*Walai!*" he said, saluting the spirits.
"To the rising of the sun, to the powers of life. To you who established the

directives and the meaning of crossing the bridge from nonperson to person through the hard road of knowledge. Here is another one who leaves his warm home and comes to you seeking the path of memory. The road is dangerous, the process uncertain, but with your protection, upon which we rely, he will return to us a man. Let him come back alive."

Father motioned to me to hand him the water, which he sprinkled onto the spirits, the statues of the male and female ancestors. He had already done the same with the ash in his hands. Then he continued, "Take this ash and give him the power of his ancestors. Take this water to seal the contract between us that he will return from his journey with a heart turned toward his tribe and a soul toward his ancestors."

He then turned to me and said, "The time has come. I will not have much to say to you again until … I may never say anything to you again unless you come back. I have done what a father should do, the rest is in your hands. Please come back to us."

The whole family was outside watching. When I followed Father out into the compound, everybody looked at me with sympathy. My younger brothers were staring at me as if I were going on a long journey with no specific time of return. I had no idea how long I was going to be absent. We all walked away from the house toward the outskirts of the village. As we neared the bush, more and more people joined us. There was a large group of young adolescents, maybe 13, maybe 14 years old packed together at the end of the bush. They looked so young that I felt out of place. They were all naked.

Nakedness is very common in the tribe. It is not a shameful thing; it is an expression of one's relationship with the spirit of nature. To be naked is to be open-hearted. …

The naked kids were singing. As I came closer I could hear their words.

> My little family I leave today.
> My great Family I meet tomorrow.
> Father, don't worry, I shall come back,
> Mother, don't cry, I am a man.
> As the sun rises and the sun sets
> My body into them shall melt,
> And one with you and them
> Forever and ever I shall be …

As the candidates for initiation passed through the crowd, they took off their shirts and shorts. Their families embraced them. Some family members grabbed their hands and sobbed with them; perhaps they were saying goodbye for the last time. There were so many young men that I could not count them all. Many of them were strangers to me. My father asked me to take my clothes off. I obeyed him, but I felt ashamed. No one paid any attention to my nakedness, however. In the village clothing attracts more attention than nakedness. My sister was weeping …

We sang as we walked into the belly of the bush, swallowed by the trees. ...

In the middle of the circle that we had instinctively formed, the coach was directing the singing. The song got inside of you, burning your heart like fire. I was quickly caught up with its rhythms, words, melody. We held each other's hands and swayed in cadence. It was intoxicating to sing in the middle of the bush at night—even on an empty stomach. ...

The elders chose this time to make a dramatic entrance. They looked like living skeletons, half naked and covered with white lines painted on their faces, necks, bellies, and backs. Each elder wore ritual cotton shorts. They were voluminous and looked from afar like bags. Their thin black bodies were not visible in the dark, just the white, almost phosphorescent lines painted on them. In addition each elder was carrying his medicine bag, made of feline skin. They walked in a line; slowly, quietly, and imperturbably. When shrouded in the darkness, far away from the fire, their bodies were luminescent, but as they came closer, into the light, the luminescence disappeared.

Their presence intensified the song. We sang more furiously as if the force of the elders, suddenly available, were a gift that flowed from the power of being old. Our teachers walked around the fireplace in the center of the circle—three times clockwise and three times counterclockwise. They did not sing with us. When they stopped their procession the song stopped as if by enchantment. Nobody asked us to stop singing—we simply lost the song. It departed from us as if a force had removed it from our lips as a calabash of water is removed from the thirsty lips of its drinker. The silence that followed was as thick as the darkness behind us in the bush.

One of the elders pulled something out of his bag, a pouch with an end like a tail. One could see long, mysterious, stiff hairs sprouting from the pouch as if they grew there. He brought the thing to his mouth and said something silently. Only his lips moved. Then he directed the tail end of the pouch toward the fire and uttered something in primal language. The color of the fire changed to violet and increased its roar. We still held each other's hands. The elder moved close to the fire, speaking again in primal tongue. With each of his movements, the fire grew taller and taller until the violet flame stood almost six meters in the air. From then on I heard nothing and thought nothing. ...

The fifth elder, the one responsible for the initial experience, still stood in the middle of the circle next to the fireplace. Walking slowly around the circle, he spoke incessantly and breathlessly. ...

What he said was this: The place where he was standing was the center. Each one of us possessed a center that he had grown away from after birth. To be born was to lose contact with our center, and to grow from childhood to adulthood was to walk away from it.

"The center is both within and without. It is everywhere. But we must realize it exists, find it, and be with it, for without the center we cannot tell who we are, where we come from, and where we are going."

He explained that the purpose of Baor[3] was to find our center. ...

All around me and underneath me I could feel life pulsating, down to the smallest piece of dirt on the ground. The way this life expressed itself was otherworldly: sounds were blue or green, colors were loud. I saw incandescent visions and apparitions, breathing color and persistent immobility. Everything seemed alive with meaning. Even the stonelike circle of people partook of the same cacophony of meaning. Each person was like the sum total of all the emanations taking place. The people, however, were not in charge of the operation of the universe around them—they were dependent on it and they were useful to it as well.

The elder in the center of the circle was the most intriguing to watch. He looked like an impalpable being in fusion, an amalgamation of colors, sounds of varying pitch, and innumerable forms. All of his smallest constituent parts—his cells and bacteria in his body, even the tiniest atomic particles of his being—had come alive. He was not moving, but the colors, the sounds, and the life forms were. Without being able to put it into words, I understood what was happening, for at that stage of consciousness there is no difference between meaning and being. Things had become their meaning and I knew that was the lesson for the evening. I also understood that this was the kind of knowledge I was going to become gradually acquainted with—not by going outside of myself, but by looking within myself and a few others. For now, all I could do was to feel and honor the effects of the subtle invisible world breaking through my own blindness and preempting my perceptions. How acquiescent one becomes when face to face with the pure universal energy! ...

I thought about the hardships of the day—the baking heat of the sun and my sweat falling into my eyes and burning them like pepper. I had lost all sense of chronology. I told myself that this is what the world looked like when one had first expired. I felt as if I were being quite reasonable. I could still think and respond to sensations around me, but I was no longer experiencing the biting heat of the sun or my restless mind trying to keep busy or ignoring my assignment. Where I was now was just plain real.

When I looked once more at the yila, I became aware that it was not a tree at all. How had I ever seen it as such? I do not know how this transformation occurred. Things were not happening logically, but as if this were a dream. Out of nowhere, in the place where the tree had stood, appeared a tall woman dressed in black from head to foot. She resembled a nun, although her outfit did not seem religious. Her tunic was silky and black as the night. She wore a veil over her face, but I could tell that behind this veil was an extremely beautiful and powerful entity. I could sense the intensity emanating from her, and that intensity exercised an irresistible magnetic pull. To give in to that pull was like drinking water after a day of wandering in the desert.

My body felt like it was floating, as if I were a small child being lulled by a nurturing presence that was trying to calm me by singing soothing lullabies

---

3 Baor—a boys' initiation into manhood ritual for the West African Dagora people.

and rocking me rhythmically. I felt as if I were floating weightless in a small body of water. My eyes locked on to the lady in the veil, and the feeling of being drawn toward her increased. For a moment I was overcome with shyness, uneasiness, and a feeling of inappropriateness, and I had to lower my eyes. When I looked again, she had lifted her veil, revealing an unearthly face. She was green, light green. Even her eyes were green, though very small and luminescent. She was smiling and her teeth were the color of violet and had light emanating from them. The greenness in her had nothing to do with the color of her skin. She was green from the inside out, as if her body was filled with green fluid. I do not know how I knew this, but this green was the expression of immeasurable love.

Never before had I felt so much love. I felt as if I had missed her all my life and was grateful to heaven for having finally released her back to me. We knew each other, but at the time I could not tell why, when, or how. I also could not tell the nature of our love. It was not romantic or filial; it was a love that surpassed any known classifications. Like two loved ones who had been apart for an unduly long period of time, we dashed toward each other and flung ourself into each other's arms. …

While she held me in her embrace, the green lady spoke to me for a long time in the softest voice that ever was. She was so much taller than I was that I felt like a small boy in her powerful arms. She placed her lips close to my left ear and she spoke so softly and tenderly to me that nothing escaped my attention. I cried abundantly the whole time, not because what she told me was sad, but because every word produced an indescribable sensation of nostalgia and longing in me. …

When I opened my eyes I realized I was desperately hugging the yila tree. It was the same as it had been before. Meanwhile, the elders had moved closer to me, obviously watching everything I had been doing. I heard one of them say, "They are always like this. First they resist and play dumb when there are a lot of things waiting to be done, and then when it happens, they won't let go either. Children are so full of contradictions. The very experience you rejected before with lies, you are now accepting without apology." …

Nature looks the way it looks because of the way we are. We could not live our whole lives on the ecstatic level of the sacred. Our senses would soon become exhausted and the daily business of living would never get done. There does, however, come a time when one must learn to move between the two ways of "seeing" reality in order to become a whole person. Traditional education consists of three parts: enlargement of one's ability to see, destabilization of the body's habit of being bound to one plane of being, and the ability to voyage transdimensionally and return. Enlarging one's vision and abilities has nothing supernatural about it, rather it is "natural" to be a part of nature and to participate in a wider understanding of reality.

SOURCE: Malidoma Patrice Somé, *Of Water and Spirit: Ritual, Magic, and Initiation in the Life of an African Shaman.* New York: Penguin Books, 1994, pp. 192–226

Women's Health Rituals   by Diane Bell

Only a century ago, hundreds of Aboriginal bands were scattered across great areas of Australia, sustaining themselves by ancient subsistence techniques. Now they no longer have access to such vast hunting grounds, and their traditional lives have been greatly changed by roads, towns, animal grazing, missionaries, and settlements.

Anthropologist Diane Bell lived on settlements in central Australia studying the rituals of women.

When we consider the wide range of women's involvement in the maintenance of health, it becomes impossible to discuss women's activities as merely "growing up" children and applying a few herbal remedies. Women, in order to maintain good health, are staging ceremonies which focus on health at the cosmic level of restoration of harmony and happiness. This is because women have rights in the country from which they derive power and for which they hold a sacred trust. ...

All women's group ritual curing activities have to do with giving—with the infusing of the body with strength. Women attempt to restore a person to health by the gift of blood, fat or bodily secretions from underarm or eyes. In giving, women are once again acting out their nurturance role where love, care and power are freely given. *Ngangkayi* [traditional healers'] practice on the other hand is essentially an individual activity concerned more with the removal of foreign objects and alien forces from a person.

The role of women in the domain of health in Aboriginal society has been rendered almost invisible by the focus upon the healer and not the healed, the disease and not the context of the ill health, the magico-religious practices and not the relationships of health to other aspects of the culture. However, I suggest that women are acutely aware of the decline in physical health and the breakdown in social relationships. Fighting and drunkenness now disrupt their lives in a fashion unknown several generations ago. Women are aware that in the shift from the hunter-gatherer mode of subsistence to settlement life they have suffered. Daily they are presented with tensions and sorcery accusations on a scale which could not have been sustained in the past. They have sought to repair and restore damaged bonds through their most powerful and spectacular rituals.

This resurgence in women's ritual activity has not been accompanied by a concomitant increase in the status of women: their autonomy has been fundamentally eroded and their relationship to land dislocated. Women's contribution to the maintenance of health in the past was within the small family group and focused upon life-crisis ceremonies. It was in these rituals that women stated their importance as the makers of adult women and in their control over their own bodies. Here, then, is the physiological basis for their nurturance roles: women do give birth, they do menstruate. This power and the nurturance roles associated with birth and growth are symbolized in *yawulyu* [women's ceremonies and designs] rituals.

SOURCE: Diane Bell, *Daughters of the Dreaming*. 2nd ed. Minneapolis, MN: University of Minnesota Press, 1993, pp. 160–1

Contemporary issues

Dispossessed of their ancestral lands and under oppression by majority groups, indigenous peoples are facing many problems in today's world. They worry about environmental destruction as well as spiritual deprivation.

The Hopi Message to the United Nations General Assembly
by Thomas Banyacya

In his historic 1992 speech to the United Nations in New York, this Hopi chief sketches an indigenous people's warnings about the dangers present in the current world.

My name is Banyacya of the Wolf, Fox and Coyote clan and I am a member of the Hopi sovereign nation. Hopi in our language means a peaceful, kind, gentle, truthful people. The traditional Hopi follows the spiritual path that was given to us by Massau'u the Great Spirit. We made a sacred covenant to follow his life plan at all times, which includes the responsibility of taking care of this land and life for his divine purpose. We have never made treaties with any foreign nation including the United States, but for many centuries we have honored this sacred agreement. Our goals are not to gain political control, monetary wealth nor military power, but rather to pray and to promote the welfare of all living beings and to preserve the world in a natural way. We still have our ancient sacred stone tablets and spiritual religious societies which are the foundations of the Hopi way of life. Our history says our white brother should have retained those same sacred objects and spiritual foundations. ...

Nature itself does not speak with a voice that we can easily understand. Neither can the animals and birds we are threatening with extinction talk to us. Who in this world can speak for nature and the spiritual energy that creates and flows through all life? In every continent are human beings who are like you but who have not separated themselves from the land and from nature. It is through their voice that Nature can speak to us. You have heard those voices and many messages from the four corners of the world today. I have studied comparative religion and I think in your own nations and cultures you have knowledge of the consequences of living out of balance with nature and spirit. The native peoples of the world have seen and spoken to you about the destruction of their lives and homelands, the ruination of nature and the desecration of their sacred sites. It is time the United Nations used its rules to investigate these occurrences and stop them now.

This rock drawing [he holds up picture] shows part of the Hopi prophecy. There are two paths. The first with high technology but separate from natural and spiritual law leads to these jagged lines representing chaos. The lower path is one that remains in harmony with natural law. Here we see a line that represents a choice like a bridge joining the paths. If we return to spiritual harmony and live from our hearts we can experience a paradise in this world. If we continue only on this upper path, we will come to destruction.

SOURCE: Thomas Banyacya, from "The Hopi Message to the United Nations General Assembly," Kykyotsmovi, Arizona, December 10, 1992
<http://banyacya.indigenousnative.org/un92.html>

Adivasis in India Encounter Modernity and Majority
by Smitu Kothari

Adivasis are the indigenous peoples of India. There are some 75 million of them in 414 main tribes, and they account for 23 percent of all the indigenous and tribal people in the world. All the central aspects of their traditions are under assault at present.

While any generalization is disrespectful of the vast diversity of traditions that has evolved in geographically diverse areas, there are clearly four elements that define the core of [Indian] tribal traditions, their ecological practices, and their assertion of identity.

1. *The centrality of forests, land, and place to their life sphere.* An overwhelming majority still live in forest areas, and the forest has historically been the primary source of their physical and cultural life, the host of their gods and goddesses and of the spirits of their ancestors. Dispersed throughout adivasi areas are numerous sacred groves, encompassing a relatively undisturbed space of pristine biodiversity, numerous spirits, and gods and goddesses.

   The forest has also been the center of private and state accumulation as colonial and post-independence governments have appropriated— legally and militaristically—most rights over the forests. ...

   Massive alienation of tribal lands continues in tribal regions in all parts of the country. Tribal land alienation is the most important manifestation of the pauperization as well as the growing insecurity and cultural erosion of tribal people. ...

   It is common that senior officials of the government rarely meet adivasi communities in their own villages; yet, they have accumulated a body of legislation that gives them the power to dominate almost every aspect of the adivasis' productive life. Often, officials visit communities only to bring the news that the people are to be displaced for a development project. In the case of the Narmada dams, for instance, these visits are all that communities, who will lose everything, get. For the Bhilalas and Bhils who reside in the area, the river is their mother, and the river, the valley, and the sphere of "life in place" are all an integral part of their identity. There are, for most of them, no boundaries between the cultural, the ecological, and the spiritual. To be compelled to leave, often with only a few weeks' notice, is tantamount to social and cultural violence. Several scholars have documented the enormous physiological and psychological pain that communities are subjected to when displaced from their sources of subsistence and meaning. The degree of attitudinal insensitivity to the importance of place, of spaces imbued with value, with spirit, and with livelihood, of the connection of place and the cosmos, raises critical questions for those concerned about the value of cultural pluralism in our world today. The inevitable justification, that "you are sacrificing for the larger good," or "for progress," or "in the national interest," has raised additional issues regarding who speaks on behalf of whom, who speaks for the nation— indeed, who comprises the nation? The dominant attitude is most sharply expressed in what a politician in the state of Gujarat said about tribals who were to be displaced by the reservoir of a proposed dam and who were resisting or seeking just and comprehensive resettlement: "they are rats who will be flushed out of their rat-holes when the water rise." ...

2. *The primacy of community and the collective.* The numerous creation myths and daily practices of the adivasis exhort the community to respect and nurture all life, communally. In the years after India became independent, Prime Minister Jawaharlal Nehru drafted a "policy," the *Panchsheel,* which pledged that the country would respect adivasis and allow them to nurture their own ways of being and come to terms with the "mainstream" in their own ways.

    It is not a coincidence that even when the state spoke a language of non-interference, it systematically sought to undermine and subvert the customary rights and the collective stewardship of the forests that adivasi communities enjoyed, that is, by the creation of individual (predominantly male-centered) titles to land. ...

3. *The defense and regeneration of language.* Every adivasi community's creation myths or epic verses and songs have been narrated and sung in their own language. They weave together an elaborate fabric of responsibilities within the natural world, often elaborately defining practices which regenerate life. The post-independence state organized and internally divided the country around dominant languages. All adivasi languages were neglected or consciously devalued. Additionally, the imposition of "national" or regional languages through the formal education system, including the privileging of English, has played havoc with most adivasi languages, many of which have become extinct in the last few decades. This process has contributed to the social and cultural fragmentation and the loss of self-confidence. ...

4. *The struggle for political and economic autonomy.* In the recent past, the sacred and natural worlds of the adivasis have been under an unprecedented threat, both from a developmentalist state that privileges national and transnational capital over its duties to nurture greater justice and equity and from a reductionist, distorted ideology of Hindutva [see Chapter 3, page 88] that is far removed from the essentially plural and tolerant Hindu ethos. A decline in, or retreat of, plural religious sensibilities, coupled with the degeneration of public morality, has fueled an aggressive, violent and fascistic ideology that is attempting to reconfigure India into a Hindu "kingdom".

The purveyors of this ideology seem comfortable with a marriage of convenience with the forces of economic globalization. This marriage has brought a new onslaught on adivasi areas and, as a related development, greater unrest and agitation among adivasi communities who are witnessing, like never before, the adverse impacts of economic development and the desacralized, aggressive, and instrumental use of religion. ...

Despite these relentless processes, from within the margins and spaces of exclusion, facing overt and covert efforts to subjugate and co-opt them, adivasis have crafted remarkable initiatives of resistance. Based on a profoundly simple demand—that their lives and life systems could only be nurtured in a legally sanctioned framework of self-rule, they have launched local and nationwide agitation, mobilizing in the process support from a diverse range of social and political forces. Self-rule is seen as an essential ingredient of sovereignty.

SOURCE: Smitu Kothari, "Sovereignty and Swaraj: Adivasi Encounters with Modernity and Majority," in *Indigenous Religions and Ecology: The Interbeing of Cosmology and Community*, ed. John A. Grim. Cambridge, MA: Harvard University Press, 2001, pp. 453–64

GLOSSARY

Indigenous First nations native to a region.

Medicine Since indigenous cultures participate fully in the environment, healing partakes of several factors: physiological, astronomical, behavioral, and spiritual. Good medicine may include herbal mixtures, songs to ancestors or divinities, art, good social co-operation, family counseling, or sacrificial offerings.

Oral tradition Storytelling and singing are the vehicles for teaching and passing on sacred knowledge among indigenous peoples with no books.

Shaman an indigenous people's medicine healer and leader of sacred ways; an inspired, ecstatic, and charismatic man or woman with the power to control spirits, often by incarnating them or making out-of-body journeys.

TYPICAL HOLY WAYS

Corroboree An Australian Aborigine dance festival held at special ceremonial grounds to celebrate events such as the gathering of clans, a battle victory, marriages, and initiations.

Divination An indigenous ritual for uncovering the spiritual cause of a problem and how to solve it, by indicators such as dreams, ordeals, reading bones, or animal behavior.

Kwanzaa An African-American and Pan-African holiday for family, community, and culture. Celebrated from December 26 through January 1, its origins are in the first harvest celebrations of Africa. The name Kwanzaa is derived from the phrase *matunda ya kwanza*, which means "first fruits" in Swahili, the most widely spoken African language. Kwanzaa was created by an African-American to introduce and reinforce the Nguzo Saba (the Seven Principles): *Umoja* (unity), *Kujichagulia* (self-determination), *Ujima* (collective work and responsibility), *Ujamaa* (co-operative economics), *Nia* (purpose), *Kuumba* (creativity), and *Imani* (faith).

Kwanzaa is a cultural holiday, not a religious one, thus available to and practiced by Africans of all religious faiths.

Sacred pipe ceremony As a ceremonial, long, wood stemmed pipe with a bowl made of pipestone, common in North American Plains tribes, is filled with sacred tobacco, all the world, including the ceremony's participants, identify with it as their own center and the center of the universe. Its smoke is an offering to the powers of the universe.

Sun dance A Lakota (Sioux) summer full-moon ceremony where men pierce their chest or back skin and dance around a central sacred tree or drag buffalo skulls until the skin rips, as an offering to the great sacred power, Wakan Tanka.

Sweat lodge A purification ceremony in a domed lodge of skins; a group of participants sit inside, while a central hole is filled with hot rocks and water is poured over them, making steam; prayers are offered to the powers of the universe present in the earth, stone, water, and all beings.

HISTORICAL OUTLINE

c. 5 million BCE—evolution of human ancestors in Africa

c. 200,000 BCE—*Homo sapiens* appears in Africa

c. 70,000 BCE—Neanderthals bury dead with red ocher, food, and tools, suggesting belief in afterlife

c. 30,000 BCE—migration of Aborigines from Asia to Australia

c. 22,000 BCE—possible date for migration of Native Americans across the Bering Strait from Asia

c. 1200–400 BCE—Olmec civilization in Meso-America

c. 1st century CE—hunter-gatherer Bantu people start migration to central and southern Africa

250–900 CE—Classic Maya civilization in Meso-America

5th century–1076—empire of Ghana in Africa

800–1100—Viking invasions carry Norse religion into northern Europe

from 12th century—Benin civilization in Nigeria

1100–1400—empire of Mali in West Africa

1300–1600—empire of Songhay in West Africa

1325–1521 Aztec Empire in Meso-America

early 15th century–1531—Inka Empire in South America

from 1492—European colonialists invade indigenous cultures in Americas

from 1550—slave trade introduces African religions into Americas

1992—Hopi Message to the U.N. General Assembly

REVIEW QUESTIONS

1 What do you think is meant by the Dagara song: "My little family I leave today / My great Family I meet tomorrow"?
2 Why does Sindima prefer the term "traditions" to "religions"? Write to convince one who disagrees with him.
3 Explain Maori environmental ethics and their implications for industrial societies.

DISCUSSION QUESTIONS

1 Describe how basic assumptions of industrial society's worldview differ from indigenous sacred ways worldviews.
2 Do you think visions such as those of Malidoma Somé are "real"?
3 Do the sacred ways of indigenous people have anything of value to offer to modern society?

INFORMATION RESOURCES

Aboriginal Studies WWW Virtual Library
<http://www.ciolek.com/
WWWVL-Aboriginal.html>

Allen, Paula Gunn. *The Sacred Hoop: Recovering the Feminine in American Indian Traditions*, Boston, MA: Beacon Press, 1992.

Bell, Diane. *Daughters of the Dreaming*, 2nd ed. Minneapolis, MN: University of Minnesota Press, 1993.

Berndt, R. M., and **C. H. Berndt**. *The Speaking Land: Myth and Story in Aboriginal Australia*. Ringwood, Victoria: Penguin Books, 1989.

Burger, Julian. *The Gaia Atlas of First Peoples*. New York: Anchor Doubleday, 1990.

Campbell, Joseph. *Historical Atlas of World Mythology*. 4 vols. San Francisco: Harper and Row, 1989.

Charlesworth, M., *et al.*, eds. *Religion in Aboriginal Australia*. St. Lucia, Queensland: University of Queensland Press, 1984.

Drury, Nevell. *Shamanism*. Shaftesbury, Dorset: Element Books, 1996.

Eliade, Mircea. *Australian Religions: An Introduction*. Ithaca, NY: Cornell University Press, 1973.

Eliade, Mircea. *Shamanism: Archaic Techniques of Ecstasy*. Princeton, NJ: Princeton University Press, 1951/1964.

Fergie, Deane, *et al.* "Australian Indigenous Religions," in *Encyclopedia of Religion*, ed. Lindsay Jones. 2nd ed. Vol. 2, pp. 634–92. New York: Macmillan, 2005.

Ford, Clyde W. *The Hero with an African Face: Mythic Wisdom of Traditional Africa*. New York: Bantam Books, 1999.

Gill, Sam D. *Native American Religions*. Belmont, CA: Wadsworth, 1982.

Grim, John A., ed. *Indigenous Traditions and Ecology: The Interbeing of Cosmology and Community*. Cambridge, MA: Harvard University Press, 2001.

Grim, John A. *The Shaman: Patterns of Religious Healing Among the Ojibway Indians*. Norman, OK: University of Oklahoma Press, 1983.

Halifax, Joan. *Shamanic Voices: A Survey of Visionary Narratives*. New York: Viking Penguin Arkana, 1979.

Harvey, Graham. *Indigenous Religions: A Companion*. London: Cassell, 2000.

Hirschfelder, Arlene, and **Paulette Molin**. *Encyclopedia of Native American Religions*. New York: Facts on File, 1992.

Hoxie, Frederick E., ed. *Encyclopedia of North American Indians*. Boston: Houghton Mifflin, 1996.

Hultkrantz, Åke, *et al.* "North American [Indian] Religions," in *Encyclopedia of Religion*, ed. Lindsay Jones. 2nd ed. Vol. 10, pp. 6658–730. New York: Macmillan, 2005.

Indians
<http://www.indians.org>

Isizoh, Chidi Denis, ed. "African Traditional Religion."
<http://www.afrikaworld.net>

Karenga, Maulana, ed. "Kwanzaa."
<http://www.officialkwanzaawebsite.org>

Kehoe, Alice. *North American Indians: A Comprehensive Account*. Upper Saddle River, NJ: Prentice-Hall, 1981.

Lambert, Johanna, ed. *Wise Women of the Dreamtime: Aboriginal Tales of the Ancestral Powers*. Rochester, VT: Inner Traditions, 1993.

Lawlor, Robert. *Voices of the First Day: Awakening in the Aboriginal Dreamtime*. Rochester, VT: Inner Traditions, 1991.

Lawson, E. Thomas. *Religions of Africa: Traditions in Transformation*. Prospect Heights, IL: Waveland Press, 1985.

Macdonald, Mary N., ed. *Experiences of Place*. Cambridge, MA: Harvard University Press, 2003.

Magesa, Laurenti. *African Religion: The Moral Traditions of Abundant Life*. Nairobi: Pauline Publications Africa, 1998.

Malinowski, Sharon, *et al.*, eds. *Encyclopedia of Native American Tribes*. Detroit: Gale Research, 1988.

Mann, Charles C. *1491: New Revelations of the Americas Before Columbus*. New York: Knopf, 2005.

Mbiti, John S. *African Religions and Philosophy*, 2nd edition. Oxford: Heinemann, 1990.

Murray, Larry, *et al.*, eds. *Encyclopedia of African American Religions*. New York: Garland, 1993.

Native America
<http://www.nativeweb.org>

Olupona, Jacob K., ed. *African Traditional Religions in Contemporary Society*. New York: Paragon House, 1991.

Ray, Ben C., *et al.*, eds. "African Religions," in *Encyclopedia of Religion*, ed. Lindsay Jones. 2nd ed. Vol. 1, pp. 83–119. New York: Macmillan, 2005.

Somé, Malidoma Patrice. *The Healing Wisdom of Africa*. New York: Jeremy Tarcher, 1999.

St. Pierre, Mark and **Tilda Long Soldier**. *Walking in the Sacred Manner: Healers, Dreamers, and Pipe Carriers—Medicine Women of the Plains Indians*. New York: Simion and Schuster, 1995.

Weatherford, Jack. *Native Roots: How the Indians Enriched America*. New York: Fawcett Columbine, 1991.

Wilson, Monica. "Southern African Religions," in *Encyclopedia of Religion*, ed. Lindsay Jones. 2nd ed. Vol. 13, pp. 8655–88. New York: Macmillan, 2005.

CHAPTER 3

HINDUISM

The label "Hinduism" has been applied to a great variety of practices, beliefs, and scriptures which seem to have originated in the Indian subcontinent at least five thousand years ago and which are continuing to evolve today. It encompasses ancient mystical texts referring to the formless and transcendent Self, abstract philosophical treatises that disagree with each other about the truth of existence, and a wealth of ascetic meditation practices for realization of the eternal. It also includes a large pantheon of deities, many of whom may be individually worshipped as the totality of divinity and yet may coexist with other deities, even in the same temples. Devotees are free to choose their own favorite manifestations of the Divine. Today, as from ancient times, deities are worshipped with offerings of grains and clarified butter placed in sacred fires, with the waving of oil lamps, with fragrances and flowers, and with song and chants. In addition, villagers worship their local goddesses and gods, many of whom are unknown elsewhere. The "Hindu way of life" also includes pilgrimages to a great number of places that are considered especially holy.

Despite its great diversity, "Hinduism" has certain underlying themes. One is a belief in **reincarnation**: the idea that we are born again and again. Our lives are molded by our **karma**: the positive or negative effects of our previous thoughts and actions. Human life should reflect the order of the cosmos, and thus one has social obligations and a certain social standing defined by one's hereditary **caste**. Through good actions, lofty thoughts, detachment from the illusory and ephemeral material world, and profound meditation on the Absolute or self-surrendering love for any one of its divine manifestations, one may gradually achieve enlightenment, merge with Ultimate Reality, and escape from the karmic wheel of rebirths.

"Hinduism" has spread far beyond India, initially carried by emigrants and more recently by growing Western interest in its ancient wisdom and spiritual practices. It is currently undergoing a vibrant renaissance, with many new temples being built around the world and staffed by a growing number of **brahman pandits** (those of the hereditary priestly caste who are learned in the ancient ways and scriptures). Issues that are being disputed today include the politicizing of "Hindu-ness," the status of women, and the traditional system of castes which is still deeply entrenched in India.

Sruti texts

According to orthodox Hindu scholarship, the ancient scriptures are divided into two categories. One is the sruti texts which were "heard" by ancient **rishis** (enlightened sages) in profound and ascetic meditation. The other category is the subsequent **smrti** texts, which explain the hidden meanings of the *sruti* texts for wider audiences in later, less enlightened ages.

The foundational *sruti* texts for most forms of Sanatana Dharma are the **Vedas.** Scholars think that they were written down by about 1500 BCE but represent a much older orally transmitted tradition. According to Hindu belief, the Vedas were heard by the rishis and then written down in 3102 BCE at the beginning of **Kali Yuga**, the current dark age, by the sage Vyasa. The language is terse poetic **Sanskrit**, whose sounds are said to evoke the realities to which they refer but whose deep meanings are not easily translated or fully understood.

Hymn to Agni, God of Fire from the Rig Vedas

The oldest of the Vedas are the Rig Vedas. They consist largely of invocations of different gods or goddesses, such as Usha, goddess of dawn, or Agni, the god of fire, which have been used since ancient times to carry offerings to the Unseen. These deities have also been understood metaphysically as abstract forces within the oneness of Creation. The extract below is from a hymn to Agni.

Your envoy who possesses all, Immortal, bearer of your gifts,
Best worshipper, I woo with song.
He, Mighty, knows the gift of wealth, he knows the deep recess of heaven:
He shall bring hitherward the Gods.
He knows, a God himself, to guide Gods to the righteous in his home:
He gives e'en treasures that we love.
He is the Herald: well-informed, he doth his errand to and fro,
Knowing the deep recess of heaven.
May we be they who gratify Agni with sacrificial gifts,
Who cherish and enkindle him.
Illustrious for wealth are they, and hero deeds, victorious,
Who have served Agni reverently.
So unto us, day after day, may riches craved by many come,
And power and might spring up for us.
That holy Singer in his strength shoots forth his arrows swifter than
The swift shafts of the tribes of men.

Hymn on Creation from the Rig Vedas

This hymn is from Book 10 of the Rig Vedas. It illustrates the philosophical sophistication of the realization of ancient rishis. They sat in profound meditation to explore the mysteries of primordial time before anything existed in the material universe. It is interesting to compare this passage with the theories of modern science about the origins of the cosmos.

Then was not non-existent nor existent: there was no realm of air, no sky
    beyond it.
What covered in, and where? and what gave shelter? Was water there,
    unfathomed depth of water?
Death was not then, nor was there aught immortal: no sign was there, the
    day's and night's divider.
That One Thing,[1] breathless, breathed by its own nature: apart from it was
    nothing whatsoever.
Darkness there was: at first concealed in darkness this All was
    indiscriminated chaos.
All that existed then was void and formless: by the great power of Warmth
    was born that Unit.
Thereafter rose Desire in the beginning, Desire, the primal seed and germ of
    Spirit.
Sages who searched with their heart's thought discovered the existent's
    kinship in the non-existent.
Transversely was their severing line[2] extended: what was above it then, and
    what below it?
There were begetters, there were mighty forces, free action here and energy
    up yonder.
Who verily knows and who can here declare it, whence it was born and
    whence comes this creation?
The Gods are later than this world's production. Who knows then whence it
    first came into being?
He, the first origin of this creation, whether he formed it all or did not form it,
Whose eye controls this world in highest heaven, he verily knows it, or
    perhaps he knows not.

SOURCE: *The Hymns of the Rigveda*, trans. Ralph T. H. Griffith. New rev. ed. Delhi: Motilal Banarsidass, 1973, pp. 206, 633–4.

Married Life from the Rig Vedas and Atharvaveda

The thousands of hymns in the Vedas include not only invocations and rituals involving the deities but also glimpses of the culture of the time. Ideals regarding married life continue today in Indian culture, including the preference for sons.

Dwell you two here, be not parted. Enjoy the full length of life, playing with son and grandsons and rejoicing in your own home. ...

    I am song, you are verse. I am heaven, you are earth. We two together will live here, becoming parents of children. ...

---

1 That One Thing—the single primordial substance out of which the universe was made.
2 Severing line—a line drawn by the rishis to divide the upper world from the lower, to bring duality out of unity.

May you two together enjoy prosperous fortune, acclaiming *Rita* [cosmic order] and conducting yourselves according to *Rita*. …

Hoping for love, children, fortune, and wealth, and by being always behind thy husband in his life's vocation, gird yourself for immortality. …

Husband and wife, being of one mind … with sons and daughters by their side, enjoy the full term of life. … They worship together for immortality.

Here may affection increase with your children and in this home be watchful in ruling the household. With this your husband completely unite yourself and then, both growing old, address the religious assembly.

SOURCE: Rig Veda 10.85.26, 42, Atharvaveda 14.2.64, Rig Veda 10.85.47, Atharvaveda 14.2.71, Atharvaveda 14.1.31, Atharvaveda 14.1. in *Thus Spake the Vedas*. Chennai, India: Sri Ramakrishna Math, pp. 81–5

The Brahman Taught by the Upanishads

from the Svetasvatara Upanishad

Probably the latest of the Vedas are the **Upanishads**. Scholars think that they were compiled around 600 to 100 BCE. They are profound and haunting reflections on ultimate truth as realized by the rishis and transmitted to their students. This passage from Svetasvatara Upanishad introduces the Brahman, the undifferentiated, nonmanifest Being, the essential underlying Reality.

That is full; this is full. This fullness has been projected from that fullness. When this fullness merges in that fullness, all that remains is fullness.

Om. Peace! Peace! Peace!

1. Rishis, discoursing on Brahman, ask: Is Brahman the cause? Whence are we born? By what do we live? Where do we dwell at the end? Please tell us, O ye who know Brahman, under whose guidance we abide, whether in pleasure or in pain.
2. Should time, or nature, or necessity, or chance, or the elements be regarded as the cause? Or he who is called the perusha[3], the living self?
3. The sages, absorbed in meditation through one—pointedness of mind, discovered the creative power, belonging to the Lord Himself and hidden in its own gunas[4]. That non-dual Lord rules over all those causes—time, the self and the rest …
7. It is the Supreme Brahman alone untouched by phenomena that is proclaimed in the Upanishads. In It is established the triad of the enjoyer, the object and the Lord who is the Controller. This Brahman is the immutable foundation; It is imperishable. The sages, having realized Brahman to be the essence of phenomena, become devoted to Him. Completely merged in Brahman, they attain freedom from rebirth. …

3 Perusha—according to the Upanishads, the cosmic Spirit, the eternal Self.
4 Gunas—three attributes whose interplay defines material existence: pure intelligence, energy, and inertia.

11. When the Lord is known all fetters fall off; with the cessation of miseries, birth and death come to an end. From meditation on Him there arises, after the dissolution of the body, the third state, that of universal lordship. And lastly, the aspirant, transcending that state also, abides in the complete Bliss of Brahman. ...

15–16. As oil exists in sesame seeds, butter in milk, water in river-beds and fire in wood, so the Self is realized as existing within the self, when a man looks for It by means of truthfulness and austerity—when he looks for the Self, which pervades all things as butter pervades milk and whose roots are Self-Knowledge and austerity. That is the Brahman taught by the Upanishad; yea, that is the Brahman taught by the Upanishads.

SOURCE: Svetasvatara Upanishad 1, verses 1–3, 7, 11, 15–16, *The Upanishads: A New Translation*, trans. Swami Nikhilananda
<http://www.sankaracharya.org/svetasvatara_upanishad.php>

Realise the Brahman from the Upanishads

The extract below is from chapter 2 of Mundaka Upanishad. It describes the method of attaining the goal of spiritual striving: the Brahman, the undifferentiated, nonmanifest Being, the essential underlying Reality. **Om** is considered the primordial sound vibration by which everything was created; the **atman** is the individual soul.

Realise the *Brahman* in whom can be found heaven, the earth, and the atmosphere. In him reside your senses and your heart. Forget everything else and attain the one and only *Brahman*. That is the way to salvation.

The spokes of a wheel surround the nave. Like that, the veins surround the heart. And in the heart is the being with many forms. He is the *Brahman*. Meditate on him, meditate on his symbol, the syllable *om*. May you be blessed so that you may cross the ocean of ignorance.

He is the fount of all wisdom; he is omniscient. The *Brahman* resides in the radiance of the heart. He rules over the mind and life. He is bliss. He is immortality. The learned ones are those who can visualise the *Brahman* in their own *atmans*.

He is the cause. He is action. When an individual visualises the *Brahman*, his heart is freed from all bondage. All his doubts are dispelled. He rises above the confines of mere action.

The *Brahman* is supreme and radiant. He has no form and he banishes all ignorance. He is like a sword in a scabbard. He is pure and full of energy. It is he who makes all objects shine. It is only the learned ones who know of the *Brahman*.

The sun cannot manifest the *Brahman*, nor can the moon or the stars. Lightning cannot make him manifest. How can the fire possibly manifest him? It is because the *Brahman* is radiant that the entire universe shines. All other objects draw their radiance from him.

The *Brahman* is in the forefront and he is everything. The *Brahman* is to the back, he is to the north and the south. He is above and below. This universe is nothing but the supreme *Brahman*.

SOURCE: Mundaka Upanishad, in *The Upanishads*, trans. Bibek Debroy and Dipavali Debroy. 2nd ed. Delhi: Books for All, 1995, chapter 2, pp. 64–6

The Soul Takes a New Body from the Brihadaranyaka Upanishad

It is taken for granted in Hinduism that the soul survives death of the body and takes birth again and again, in the process known as reincarnation, unless it is finally liberated from the cycle of birth and death. This process of reincarnation is described in some detail in Brihadaranyaka Upanishad.

Just as a heavily loaded cart moves along, creaking, even so the self identified with the body, being presided over by the Self which is all consciousness (the Supreme Self), moves along, groaning, when breathing becomes difficult at the approach of death.

When this body grows thin—becomes emaciated or diseased—then, as a mango or a fig or a fruit of the peepul tree becomes detached from its stalk, so does this infinite being completely detaching himself from the parts of the body, again move on, in the same way that he came, to another body for the remanifestation of his vital breath (*prana*). ...

Now, when that self becomes weak and unconscious, as it were, the organs gather around it. Having wholly seized these particles of light, the self comes to the heart. When the presiding deity of the eye turns back from all sides, the dying man fails to notice colour.

The eye becomes united with the subtle body; then people say: 'He does not see.' The nose becomes united with the subtle body; then they say: 'He does not smell.' The tongue becomes united with the subtle body; then they say: 'He does not taste.' The vocal organ becomes united with the subtle body; then they say: 'He does not speak.' The ear becomes united with the subtle body; then they say: 'He does not hear.' The mind becomes united with the subtle body; then they say: 'He does not think.' The skin becomes united with the subtle body; then they say: 'He does not touch.' The intellect becomes united with the subtle body; then they say: 'He does not know.'

The upper end of the heart lights up and by that light the self departs, either through the eye or through the head or through any other part (aperture) of the body.

And when the self departs, the vital breath follows and when the vital breath departs, all the organs follow.

Then the self becomes endowed with a particular consciousness and passes on to the body to be attained by that consciousness.

Knowledge, work and past experience follow the self.

And just as a leech moving on a blade of grass reaches its end, takes hold of another and draws itself together towards it, so does the self, after throwing off this body, that is to say, after making it unconscious, take hold of another support and draw itself together towards it.

And just as a goldsmith takes a small quantity of gold and fashions out of it another—a newer and better—form, so does the self, after throwing off this body, that is to say, after making it unconscious, fashion another—a newer and better—form.

SOURCE: Brihadaranyaka Upanishad, 4, chapter 3: 35–36, 4: 1–4. English translation of Holy Upanishads by Swami Nikhilananda taken from <http://sanatan.intnet.mu/>, in <http://www.ishwar.com/hinduism/holy_upanishads/brihadaranyaka_upanishad/part_04.html>

Smrti texts

According to classical Hindu thought, the sublime realizations recorded in the Upanishads cannot be understood by the masses. In the current long period of darkest ignorance and irreligion, Kali Yuga, more popular scriptures and forms of worship are needed. Thus great epic poems, lengthy descriptions of the gods and goddesses, and codes of moral conduct have been added to the scriptural treasury.

Worship Me with Love from the *Bhagavad Gita*

One of the two greatest Indian narratives is the *Mahabharata*, a lengthy semi-historical depiction of events thought to have taken place in approximately 1000 BCE, as two rival branches of a great family both laid claims to a kingdom near what is now Delhi. Its one hundred thousand verses depict all that is noble and ignoble in human nature. They include a major text of Hindu philosophy, the *Bhagavad Gita*. In it, Krishna, one of the major Hindu deities, gives spiritual instruction to Arjuna on the threshold of a great battle. Here, Krishna reveals the "most profound secret"—personal knowledge of God. In Hinduism, any one deity may be understood as the totality of divinity. Thus Krishna describes himself as all-pervasive creator of all that is, the "eternal source of all," and also as the One Being who can say, "I am what is and what is not."

Truly great souls seek my divine nature. They worship me with a one-pointed mind, having realized that I am the eternal source of all. Constantly striving, they make firm their resolve and worship me without wavering. Full of devotion, they sing of my divine glory.

Others follow the path of *jnana*,[5] spiritual wisdom. They see that where there is One, that One is me; where there are many, all are me; they see my face everywhere. …

I am the goal of life, the Lord and support of all, the inner witness, the abode of all. I am the only refuge, the one true friend; I am the beginning, the staying, and the end of creation; I am the womb and the eternal seed. …

5 *Jnana*—higher wisdom.

Those who worship other gods with faith and devotion also worship me, Arjuna, even if they do not observe the usual forms. I am the object of all worship, its enjoyer and Lord. ...

Whatever I am offered in devotion with a pure heart—a leaf, a flower, fruit, or water—I partake of that love offering. Whatever you do, make it an offering to me—the food you eat, the sacrifices you make, the help you give, even your suffering. In this way you will be freed from the bondage of *karma*, and from its results both pleasant and painful. Then, firm in renunciation and **yoga**, with your heart free, you will come to me.

I look upon all creatures equally; none are less dear to me and none more dear. But those who worship me with love live in me, and I come to life in them.

Even a sinner becomes holy when he worships me alone with firm resolve. Quickly his soul conforms to **dharma** and he attains to boundless peace. Never forget this, Arjuna: no one who is devoted to me will ever come to harm.

All those who take refuge in me, whatever their birth, race, sex, or caste, will attain the supreme goal; this realization can be attained even by those whom society scorns. Kings and sages too seek this goal with devotion. Therefore, having been born in this transient and forlorn world, give all your love to me. Fill your mind with me; love me; serve me; worship me always. Seeking me in your heart, you will at last be united with me.

SOURCE: *Bhagavad Gita*, chapter 9, trans. Eknath Easwaran. Tomales, CA: Nilgiri Press, 2007, pp. 173–7

Karma Yoga: Selfless Service from the *Bhagavad Gita*

In advising Arjuna, Krishna repeatedly stresses the value of service without any desire for the fruits of one's actions. Only service undertaken in this spirit is thought to clear one's karmic account.

Sri Krishna

At the beginning of time I declared two paths for the pure heart: *jnana yoga*, the contemplative path of spiritual wisdom, and *karma yoga*, the active part of selfless service.

He who shirks action does not attain freedom; no one can gain perfection by abstaining from work. Indeed, there is no one who rests for even an instant; every creature is driven to action by his own nature.

Those who abstain from action while allowing the mind to dwell on sensual pleasure cannot be called sincere spiritual aspirants. But they excel who control their senses through the mind, using them for selfless service.

Fulfill all your duties; action is better than inaction. Even to maintain your body, Arjuna, you are obliged to act. Selfish action imprisons the world. Act selflessly, without any thought of personal profit.

At the beginning, mankind and the obligation of selfless service were created together. "Through selfless service, you will always be fruitful and find the fulfillment of your desires": this is the promise of the Creator.

Honor and cherish the devas as they honor and cherish you; through this honor and love you will attain the supreme good. All human desires are fulfilled by the devas, who are pleased by selfless service. But anyone who enjoys the things given by the devas without offering selfless acts in return is a thief. ...

Every selfless act, Arjuna, is born from Brahman, the eternal, infinite Godhead. He is present in every act of service. All life turns on this law, O Arjuna. Whoever violates it, indulging his senses for his own pleasure and ignoring the needs of others, has wasted his life. But those who realize the Self are always satisfied. Having found the source of joy and fulfillment, they no longer seek happiness from the external world. They have nothing to gain or lose by any action: neither people nor things can affect their security.

Strive constantly to serve the welfare of the world; by devotion to selfless work one attains the supreme goal of life. Do your work with the welfare of others always in mind. ...

What the outstanding person does, others will try to do. The standards such people create will be followed by the whole world.

SOURCE: *Bhagavad Gita*, chapter 3, 3–26, trans. Eknath Easwaran. Tomales, CA: Nilgiri Press, 2007, pp. 104–9

Rama, Sita, and Lakshman Enter the Forest

from the *Ramayana*

The greatest examples of noble human conduct which continue to inspire Hindus today are Rama and his wife Sita. They are central characters in a long epic poem, the *Ramayana*, which was compiled in its present form approximately 400 BCE to 200 CE. In brief, Rama, noble son of King Dasaratha by one of his three wives, Kausalya, was about to be crowned king. But instead, Rama was banished to the forest for 14 years by the king, due to the machinations of an evil friend of his stepmother Kaikeyi. Rama's wife Sita and his stepbrother Lakshman, son of Kaikeyi, nobly insisted on accompanying him. During their sojourn in the forest, Sita was kidnapped by the king of the demons. A terrific battle ensued in which Rama was at last victorious, and he and Sita returned to the capital, Ayodhya. In some parts of India, Lord Rama is worshipped as the Lord Incarnate. The following excerpt (from chapter 19 of the *Ramayana*), in which Prince Rama first enters the forest to live as an ascetic, illustrates his exceptionally noble qualities.

The chariot reached the bank of the Ganga. They proceeded along the bank, admiring the beauty of the river. Finding a spot of surpassing charm, Raama [Rama] said: "We shall spend the night here."

Untying the horses, they sat under a tree. Guha, the chief of the region, having learnt already from his men that Raama would be coming there, came forward with his retinue to greet Raama and Lakshmana [Lakshman].

He had unbounded love for the Royal family and for Raama. Being the chieftain of the tribes who dwelt on the banks of Ganga, he was a man of great prestige and power. Raama and Lakshmana rose to greet Guha, even while the latter was still at some distance from them. Guha welcomed them with a hearty embrace, saying: "Regard this land as your own. This place is as much yours as is Ayodhya. Who can hope to have a guest like you? It is indeed my good fortune."

Guha had prepared a lavish entertainment. He said "Feel perfectly at home and happy in my kingdom. You may spend all the fourteen years with us here. You will not lack anything, I assure you. Looking after you will be a pleasure and privilege to me. Be gracious enough to accept my hospitality."

Warmly embracing Guha again, Raama said: "Brother, I know how deep is your love for me. Your wish is itself as good as hospitality rendered. I am bound by my vows and must refuse anything more. I have come to dwell in the forest and not to enjoy life as a chieftain's guest. These horses are my dear father's favourites. Pray feed them well. We shall be content with simple food and rest for the night."

They lay under the tree for the night. ...

Early next morning, Raama told Lakshmana: "We must now cross the river. Ask Guha to make ready a boat big enough for crossing this broad river." Guha ordered his men to get this done and informed Raama.

Sumantra bowed low and stood before Raama seeking his further commands.

Raama understood Sumantra's unuttered grief and, laying his hand on Sumantra's shoulders, said: "Sumantra, return to Ayodhya with all speed and be at the side of the King. Your duty is now to look after him."

"O Raama," exclaimed Sumantra, "rectitude, learning and culture seem to be of no value. You and your brother and Vaidehi are going to live in the forest. What is going to be our lot? How are we going to fare under Kaikeyi's rule?" He now wept like a child.

Wiping the tears from Sumantra's eyes, Raama said: "Our family has known no nobler friend than you. It will be your task to console my father. His heart is riven by grief. Whatever his commands, carry them out dutifully. Do not ask yourself whether he wants a thing for himself or with a view to pleasing Kaikeyi. Avoid giving him any pain of mind. Have no anxiety about us.

"You should say this on my behalf to my aged father who is stricken with a grief he never knew before. Clasp his feet as you have seen me do, and assure him from me that none of us—not I nor Lakshmana, nor Seeta [Sita]—feel injured or sorry at having been sent away from Ayodhya. We look forward to fourteen years of forest life which will speed on happy wings, and then surely we shall return to his feet for blessings. Give our love to my mother Kausalya, and tell her that protected by her blessings we are well and give a like message to my stepmothers, specially to Kaikeyi, lest she should think we have parted in anger. Tell the Mahaaraaja that it is my earnest prayer that he should hasten with the installation of Bharata, so that he may be a comfort to him in our absence."

But Sumantra, unable to restrain his grief, burst out: "How am I to return and with what words can I give comfort?" And when he looked at the empty chariot, he wept and said: "How shall I drive this chariot that stands desolate without you?"

Once again Raama spoke words of comfort and courage to Sumantra and urged on him the duty of patience, and sent him home.

"Guha," said Raama, "I could indeed spend fourteen years in your kingdom as you desire. But would that be fulfilling my vow? I have left Ayodhya to fulfil my father's pledge. I must therefore lead the life of a *tapasvi*.[6] I must not touch dishes daintily cooked and served. We have to live only on fruits, roots and permissible kinds of meat such as we offer in the sacrificial fire."

Comforting Guha thus, the brothers got their locks matted with the milk of the banyan. They helped Seeta into the boat and then got into it themselves. Guha bade the boatmen to row it across.

The boatmen took them quickly across the river. At midstream Seeta offered a prayer to the goddess of the river: "Devi, help us fulfil our vow and return safe to our homeland."

They talked as they went on. They reached the farther bank of Ganga. And there, for the first time, the three stood alone, unattended by friends!

"Lakshmana, you are my sole armed guard now," said Raama. "You will go first. Seeta will follow. And I shall walk behind you both. We must save Seeta as far as possible from the hardships of forest life. Hereafter there will be none to keep us company and no fun or amusement."

Raama's thoughts went to his mother Kausalya.

"Lakshmana," he said, "should you not go back to Ayodhya and look after mother Kausalya and Sumitra Devi? I shall manage my forest stay somehow."

Lakshmana replied: "Forgive me, brother; I am not going back to Ayodhya." Raama indeed expected no other answer.

SOURCE: *Ramayana*, trans. C. Rajagopalachari. 27th ed. Mumbai: Bharatiya Vidya Bhavan, 1990, pp. 86–9

Duties of the Four Castes from the *Manu smrti*

Hindu legal and social mores are codified in *The Laws of Manu*, or *Manu smrti*, compiled into 12 books by 100 to 300 CE. These codes are regarded by some as propaganda by the priestly Brahman caste, for they give divine authority for the division of humanity into four castes: the priestly Brahmans, the warrior Kshatriyas, the merchant Vaishyas, and the servant class, Sudras. The extract below, from *Manu smrti* chapter 1, describes how the castes were assigned different duties.

---

6 *Tapasvi*—renunciate.

For the sake of the preservation of this entire creation, [Purusha], the exceedingly resplendent one, assigned separate duties to the classes which had sprung from his mouth, arms, thighs, and feet.

Teaching, studying, performing sacrificial rites, so too making others perform sacrificial rites, and giving away and receiving gifts—these he assigned to the brāhmans.

Protection of the people, giving away of wealth, performance of sacrificial rites, study, and nonattachment to sensual pleasures—these are, in short, the duties of a kshatriya.

Tending of cattle, giving away of wealth, performance of sacrificial rites, study, trade and commerce, usury, and agriculture—these are the occupations of a vaishya.

The Lord has prescribed only one occupation for a shūdra, namely, service without malice of even these other three classes.

Man is stated to be purer above the navel than below it; hence his mouth has been declared to be the purest part by the Self-existent One.

On account of his origin from the best limb of the Cosmic Person, on account of his seniority, and on account of the preservation by him of the Veda—the brāhman is in respect of dharma the lord of this entire creation. ...

Of created beings, those which are animate are the best; of the animate, those who subsist by means of their intellect; of the intelligent, men are the best; and of men, the brāhmans are traditionally declared to be the best ...

The very birth of a brāhman is the eternal incarnation of dharma. For he is born for the sake of dharma and tends toward becoming one with the Brahman. ...

SOURCE: W. Theodore de Bary, ed., *Sources of Indian Tradition*. New York and London: Columbia University Press, 1958, vol. 1, pp. 220–1

The Faithful Wife from the *Manu smrti*

Manu smrti also justifies the subjugation of women to men. In this extract, from *Manu smrti* chapter 5, the virtues of the faithful wife are described.

The husband who wedded her with sacred texts, always gives happiness to his wife, both in season and out of season, in this world and in the next.

Though destitute of virtue, or seeking pleasure (elsewhere), or devoid of good qualities, (yet) a husband must be constantly worshipped as a god by a faithful wife.

No sacrifice, no vow, no fast must be performed by women apart (from their husbands); if a wife obeys her husband, she will for that (reason alone) be exalted in heaven.

A faithful wife, who desires to dwell (after death) with her husband, must never do anything that might displease him who took her hand, whether he be alive or dead.

At her pleasure let her emaciate her body by (living on) pure flowers, roots, and fruit; but she must never even mention the name of another man after her husband has died.

Until death let her be patient (of hardships), self-controlled, and chaste, and strive (to fulfil) that most excellent duty which (is prescribed) for wives who have one husband only.

SOURCE: Serinity Young, ed., *An Anthology of Sacred Texts by and about Women*. New York: Crossroad, 1995, p. 278

A Method of Enlightening the Disciple   by Sankara

The Vedas gave rise to a number of different schools of Hindu philosophy. One of the major ones was that of Sankhya, classically attributed to the sage Kapila, who made clear distinctions between spirit and matter. An opposing school is that of Advaita Vedanta, whose greatest teacher was the highly influential Sankara (c. 788–820 CE or earlier). In his nondualistic philosophy, the absolute ground of being is Brahman, the eternal and unchanging that lies within the world of changing appearances. Realization that only Brahman is real, and that the individual soul is not different from Brahman is the essence of Sankara's philosophy. All appearances of difference are considered illusions. This perspective became predominant in Hindu philosophy. Note that in imparting this teaching, the proper disciple is assumed to be a Brahmin male.

That means to liberation, viz., Knowledge, should be explained again and again until it is firmly grasped, to a pure Brahmana disciple who is indifferent to everything that is transitory and achievable through certain means, who has given up the desire for a son, for wealth and for this world and the next, who has adopted the life of a wandering monk and is endowed with control over the mind and senses, with compassion etc., as well as with the qualities of a disciple well-known in the scriptures and who has approached the teacher in the prescribed manner and has been examined in respect of his caste, profession, conduct, learning and parentage.

The Sruti also says, "A Brahmana after examining those worlds which are the result of Vedic actions should be indifferent to them seeing that nothing eternal can be achieved by means of those actions. Then, with fuel in his hands he should approach a teacher versed in the Vedas and established in Brahman in order to know the Eternal. The learned teacher should correctly explain to that disciple who has self-control and a tranquil mind and has approached him in the prescribed manner, the knowledge of Brahman revealing the imperishable and the eternal Being." For only when knowledge is firmly grasped, it conduces to one's own good and is capable of transmission. This transmission of knowledge is helpful to people, like a boat to one who wants to cross a river. ...

The disciple who has thus learnt the definition of the inner Self from the Srutis and the Smritis and is eager to cross the ocean of transmigratory existence is asked, "Who are you, my child?"

If he says, "I am the son of a Brahmana belonging to such and such a lineage; I was a student or a householder and am now a wandering monk anxious to cross the ocean of transmigratory existence infested with the terrible sharks of birth and death," the teacher should say, "My child, how do you desire to go beyond transmigratory existence as your body will be eaten up by birds or will turn into earth even here when you die? For, burnt to ashes on this side of the river, you cannot cross to the other side."

If he says, "I am different from the body. The body is born and it dies; it is eaten up by birds, is destroyed by weapons, fire etc., and suffers from diseases and the like. I have entered it, like a bird its nest, on account of merit and demerit accruing from acts done by myself and like a bird going to another nest when the previous one is destroyed I shall enter into different bodies again and again as a result of merits and demerits when the present body is gone. Thus in this beginningless world on account of my own actions I have been giving up successive bodies assumed among gods, men, animals and the denizens of hell and assuming ever new ones. I have in this way been made to go round and round in the cycle of endless births and deaths, as in a Persian wheel by my past actions and having in the course of time obtained the present body I have got tired of this going round and round in the wheel of transmigration and have come to you, Sir, to put an end to this rotation. I am, therefore, always different from the body. It is bodies that come and go, like clothes on a person," the teacher would reply, "You have spoken well. You see aright." ...

SOURCE: "A Method of Enlightening the Disciple" from *Upadesa Sahasri (A Thousand Teachings)*, chapter 1, by Adi Sankaracharya, trans. Swami Jagananda. Chennai: Sri Ramakrishna Math <http://www.shankaracharya.org>

Yoga Sutras by Patanjali

A third major philosophical system based on the Upanishads is the school of Yoga, traditionally thought to have been given organized form by the sage Patanjali by 200 BCE. The Yogic system combines ancient meditation practices with a philosophy which is similar to that of Sankhya, but asserts the existence of a supreme God. These excerpts are from Patanjali's *Yoga Sutras*, 196 sutras or sayings methodically delineating a system for attaining the highest state of consciousness.

Now, when a sincere seeker approaches an enlightened teacher, with the right attitude of discipleship and with the right spirit of enquiry, at the right time and the right place, communication of yoga takes place.

Yoga happens when there is stilling of the movement of thought— without expression or suppression—in the indivisible intelligence in which there is no movement.

In the light of non-volitional, non-moving and therefore spontaneous and choiceless awareness the undivided intelligence with its apparent and passing modifications or movements of thought within itself is not confused with nor confined to any of these. Then the seer or the homogeneous intelligence which is ignorantly regarded as the separate experiencer of sensations and emotions, and the separate performer of actions, is not split up into one or the other of the states or modifications of the mind, and exists by itself and as itself. ...

These apparent movements or states or moods of the mind, which are concepts, ideas or images in it, can all be grouped under five categories, irrespective of whether they are experienced as painful or non-painful, and whether or not they are covertly or clearly tainted by the five-fold afflictions described later.

These five categories of apparent movements of the mind are:

1. proven theory
2. unsound thinking or wrong knowledge
3. fancy or hallucination or imagination
4. a state of dullness or sleep
5. memory ...

The right understanding and the realisation of the real nature of these five categories of mental states, is gained by

1. right exertion, and
2. the simultaneous, effortless and wise avoidance of the distracting influences. ...

Any steady and continuous or persistent and vigilant endeavour to stand firm in the understanding of the truth of the indivisibility of cosmic intelligence is known as spiritual practice (right exertion).

But, when is one said to be well grounded in practice?

When this spontaneous awareness or cosmic consciousness continues without interruption, for a long time, and one is devoted to it with all one's being, in all sincerity and earnestness.

SOURCE: "Yoga Sutras" by Patanjali, chapter 1, from Swami Venkatesananda, copyright 2009 CYT <http://SwamiVenkatesananda.org>

In Praise of Durga from the *Siva Purana*

Whereas philosophical texts were for the highly learned, a much more widespread form of *smrti* scriptures are the **Puranas**. These are Sanskrit poetic texts which were probably set down in written form between 500 and 1500 CE, although they contain material which is much older. This popular devotional literature gives elaborate depictions of various gods and goddesses and their miraculous powers and exploits, as known to their devotees. Excerpted first here is a passage from the *Siva Purana*, in which the powers of the goddess Durga are briefly described. Seated on her lion, she defeated the demons who were threatening to overrun the world. She is also known as the consort and spiritual power of the god Siva.

I began a continuous laudatory prayer of the Goddess Durgā, the beloved of Śiva, the creator of the universe, of the nature of Vidyā and Avidyā[7] and identical with the pure supreme Brahman.

I salute the Goddess who is omnipresent, eternal, for whom there is no support, who is never distressed, who is the mother of the three deities, who is the grossest of the gross and yet has no form.

O Goddess of the devas, you are Perfect Knowledge, Supreme Bliss, identical with the supreme Soul. Be pleased. Grant me the fulfilment of my task. Obeisance to you.

O celestial sage, on being thus lauded Candikā[8] … appeared before me.

Her complexion had the glossy hue of collyrium. She had comely features. She had four divine arms. She was seated on a lion. She showed the mystic gesture of granting boons by one of her hands, and pearls adorned her dishevelled hair.

Her face shone like the autumnal moon, the crescent moon bedecked her forehead. She had three eyes, looked beautiful and the nails of her lotus-like feet glistened.

O sage, seeing her who was Śiva's Energy herself, directly in front of me, my lofty shoulders bent down with devotion and I eulogized her after due obeisance.

Obeisance, obeisance, to Thee, who art in the form of Pravṛti (Action) and Nivṛtti (Abstinence); who art in the form of creation and sustenance of the universe. Thou art the eternal Energy of the movable and the immovable beings capable of enchanting everyone.

Thou hast manifested thyself as Śrī, a garland round Keśava's form, who in the form of Earth holdest everything within, who art of yore the great Goddess causing creation and the destruction of the three worlds and art beyond the three Gunas.

Thou art present in everything even in the essential atom and who art charmingly honoured by Yogins;[9] who art perceivable in the hearts of the Yogins purified by restraints, as well as in the path of their meditation.

Thou art the Vidyā of diverse sorts. Thou art endowed with illumination, purity and detachment. Thou assumest Kūṭastha (perpetually immovable), Avyakta (unmanifest) and Ananta (infinite) form and Thou art the eternal time holding all the worlds.

SOURCE: *Śiva Purāna*, translated by Professor Jagdish Lal Shastri. Delhi: Motilal Banarsidass, 1970, pp. 320–1

The Way of Devotion   from the *Bhagavata Purana*

The *Puranas* also contain instructions for worship of the gods and goddesses, according to the growing **bhakti** tradition of ecstatic devotion to one's favorite incarnation of the Divine. The feeling is that the Divine takes on human form

7 Vidyā and Avidyā—knowledge and ignorance.
8 Candikā—another name for Durga.
9 Yogins—practitioners of yoga.

for the sake of helping humanity, but remains pure in the midst of material life. Most popular of the Puranas is the *Bhagavata Purana*, which describes the incarnations of the Lord in forms such as Krishna, the cowherding boy. This excerpt from the *Bhagavata Purana* describes ways of worship which are pleasing to the Lord incarnate.

One should therefore resort to a teacher, desiring to know what constitutes the supreme welfare. ... Taking the teacher as the deity, one should learn from him the practices characteristic of the Lord's devotees. ... First detachment from all undesirable associations, then association with the good souls, compassion, friendliness, and due humility toward all beings, purity, penance, forbearance, silence, study of sacred writings, straightforwardness, continence, nonviolence, equanimity, seeing one's own Self and the Lord everywhere, seeking solitude, freedom from home, wearing clean recluse robes, satisfying oneself with whatever comes to one, faith in the scriptures of devotion and refraining from censure of those of other schools, subjugation of mind, speech, and action, truthfulness, quietude, restraint, listening to accounts of the Lord's advents, exploits, and qualities, singing of the Lord, contemplation of the Lord of wonderful exploits, engaging in acts only for His sake, dedicating unto the Lord everything—the rites one does, gifts, penance, sacred recital, righteous conduct and whatever is dear to one like one's wife, son, house, and one's own life—cultivating friendship with those who consider the Lord as their soul and master, service to the Lord and to the world and especially to the great and good souls, sharing in the company of fellow devotees the sanctifying glory of the Lord, sharing with them one's delight, satisfaction and virtues of restraint, remembering oneself and reminding fellow-worshipers of the Lord who sweeps away all sin; bearing a body thrilled with devotion and ecstatic experience of the Lord, now in tears with some thought of the Lord, now laughing, now rejoicing, now speaking out, now dancing, now singing, now imitating the Lord's acts, and now becoming quiet with the blissful experience of the Supreme—such are the Lord's devotees, who behave like persons not of this world.

SOURCE: W. Theodore de Bary, ed., *Sources of Indian Tradition*. New York and London: Columbia University Press, 1958, vol. 1, pp. 333–4

Songs of the saints

Despite the wealth of ancient Sanskrit scriptures, Jainism and later Buddhism—Indian religions that were not based on the Vedas—gained many adherents. But with the flowering of the bhakti tradition, saintly devotees of the Hindu deities began to sing of their ecstatic realization of the Divine, in their own languages. The tremendous attraction of their songs in the vernacular[10] and the strength of

---

10 Vernacular—the language of the people, as opposed to a classical language such as Sanskrit which was not understood by everyone.

their love, which the common people could understand, brought an upsurge of devotional worship of the Hindu deities. These saints came from all classes and were both women and men, unlike those of the classical Sanskrit tradition, which was controlled by brahman men.

Ravi Das was a fourteenth- to fifteenth-century shoemaker, whose occupation meant that he was considered of extremely low caste. However, his poetry reveals the heights of his realization.

The World of Illusion by Ravi Das

There is but One God. He is obtained by the True Guru's[11] grace.
When there was egoism in me, Thou wert not with me.
Now that Thou art there, there is no egoism,
As huge waves are raised by the wind in the great ocean, but are only
     water in water.
O Lord of wealth, what should I say about this delusion?
What we deem a thing to be, in reality it is not like that.

It is like a king falling asleep on his throne and becoming a beggar in
     dream;
His kingdom is intact, but separating from it, he suffers pain. Such
     indeed, has been my condition. ...
Amidst all, the One Lord has assumed many forms
And He is enjoying within all hearts.
Says Ravi Das, the Lord is nearer to us than our hands and feet.
So let it happen as will naturally happen. ...

Tell: Of what account are kingly mansion and throne without devotional
     service of the Lord?
Thou hast not thought of the relish of the Lord King's Name, a relish in
     which all other relishes are forgotten.
We have become mad, we know not what we ought to know, and
     consider not what we ought to consider.
Like this our days are passing away. ...

Lord of wealth, if Thou breakest not with me, then I will not break with
     Thee.
For if I break with Thee, with whom else shall I join?
If Thou art an earthen lamp, then I am Thy wick.
If Thou art a place of pilgrimage, then I am Thy pilgrim.
In true love I have joined with Thee, O Lord.
Attaching myself to Thee, I have broken with all others.
Wherever I go, I perform Thy service.
There is no other lord like Thee, O God. ...

11 True Guru—a perfectly enlightened spiritual teacher who can lead one to God-realization.

The skeleton is of bones, flesh and veins; within it abides the poor soul
   bird.
O mortal, what is mine and what is thine?
As a bird perches on a tree, so does the soul in the body.
Thou layest foundations and buildest walls.
Three and a half cubit measure of place is for thee in the end.
Thou beautifully dressest thy hair and wearest slanting turban on thy
   head,
But this body shall be reduced to a heap of ashes.
Lofty are thy palaces and beauteous thy brides,
But without the Lord's Name, the game is lost.

My caste is low, my lineage is lowly, and mean is my birth.
I have entered Thy sanctuary O my Luminous Lord King, says the
   cobbler Ravi Das.

SOURCE: *Guru Granth Sahib*, pp. 657–9, adapted from English translation of Manmohan Singh. 3rd ed.
Amritsar, Punjab: Shiromani Gurdwara Parbandhak Committee, 1989, pp. 2157–62

Without Krishna I Cannot Sleep   by Mirabai

Mirabai (c. 1500–50) was a princess of Rajasthan, but she was far more devoted to
Lord Krishna than to her husband. When her husband died, she defied her in-laws'
desire that she immolate herself along with her husband (throw herself on his
funeral pyre), and instead became a wandering mendicant (beggar).

Without Krishna I cannot sleep.
Tortured by longing, I cannot sleep,
And the fire of love
Drives me to wander hither and thither.
Without the light of the Beloved
My house is dark,
And lamps do not please me.
Without the Beloved my bed is uninviting,
And I pass the nights awake.
When will my Beloved return home?
The frogs are croaking, the peacock's cry
And the cuckoo's song are heard.
Low black clouds are gathering,
Lightning flashes, stirring fear in the heart.
My eyes fill with tears.
What shall I do? Where shall I go?
Who can quench my pain?
My body has been bitten
By the snake of "absence,"
And my life is ebbing away
With every beat of the heart.

Fetch the herb quickly.
Which of my companions
Will come bringing the Beloved to meet me?
My Lord when will you come
To meet your Mīrā?
Manamohan [a generic term meaning "one who attracts minds"], the
    Charmer of Hearts,
Fills me with delight. When, my Lord,
Will you come to laugh and talk with me?

SOURCE: *The Devotional Poems of Mīrābī*, trans. A. J. Alston. Delhi: Motilal Banarsidass, 1980, pp. 64–5

Two Poems by Kabir

Kabir (c. 1440–1518) was a Muslim-born weaver with a Hindu guru. His hymns are still greatly loved today by Muslims and Sikhs as well as Hindus, for they describe inner experiences that are common to mystics of all religions.

I.13 *mo ko kahāṉ ḍhūṉṛo bande*

O servant, where dost thou seek me?
Lo! I am beside thee.
I am neither in temple nor in mosque: I am neither in Kaaba[12] nor in
    Kailash:[13]
Neither am I in rites and ceremonies, nor in Yoga and renunciation.
If thou art a true seeker, thou shalt at once see Me: thou shalt meet Me
    in a moment of time.
Kabir says, "O Sadhu![14] God is the breath of all breath."

I.36 *sūr parkāś, tanh rain kahā pāïye*

Lay hold on your sword, and join in the fight. Fight, O my brother, as
    long as life lasts.
Strike off your enemy's head, and there make an end of him quickly:
    then come, and bow your head at your King's Durbar.[15]
He who is brave, never forsakes the battle: he who flies from it is no true
    fighter.
In the field of this body a great war goes forward, against passion, anger,
    pride, and greed:
It is in the kingdom of truth, contentment and purity, that this battle is
    raging; and the sword that rings forth most loudly is the sword of His
    Name.

Kabir says: "When a brave knight takes the field, a host of cowards is put
    to flight.

---

12 Kaaba—holiest of Muslim shrines, at Mecca.
13 Kailash—legendary mountain abode of Lord Siva.
14 Sadhu—Hindu ascetic.
15 Durbar—court.

It is a hard fight and a weary one, this fight of the truth-seeker: for the
   vow of the truth-seeker is more hard than that of the warrior, or of
   the widowed wife who would follow her husband.
For the warrior fights for a few hours, and the widow's struggle with
   death is soon ended:
But the truth-seeker's battle goes on day and night, as long as life lasts it
   never ceases."

SOURCE: *Songs of Kabir*, trans. Rabindranath Tagore. New York: Samuel Weiser, 1977, pp. 45–86

Modern texts

Vision of the Mother by Paramahansa Yogananda

One of the modern saints who has contributed to the global spread of Hindu principles and practices is Paramahansa Yogananda (1893–1952). His *Autobiography of a Yogi*, first published in 1946, has awakened keen interest in the miraculous aspects of Hinduism among people outside India.

I proceeded alone to the portico that fronts the large temple of Kali (God in the aspect of Mother Nature). Selecting a shady spot near one of the pillars, I sat down and assumed the lotus posture. Although it was only about seven o'clock, the morning sun would soon be oppressive.

The world receded as I became devotionally entranced. My mind was concentrated on Goddess Kali. Her statue in this very temple in Dakshineswar had been the special object of adoration by the great master, Sri Ramakrishna Paramahansa. In answer to his anguished demands, the stone image had often taken a living form and conversed with him.

"Silent Mother of stone," I prayed, "Thou didst become filled with life at the plea of Thy beloved devotee Ramakrishna; why dost Thou not also heed the wails of this yearning son of Thine?"

My aspiring zeal increased boundlessly, accompanied by a divine peace. Yet, when five hours had passed, and the Goddess whom I was inwardly visualizing had made no response, I felt slightly disheartened. Sometimes it is a test by God to delay the fulfilment of prayers. But He eventually appears to the persistent devotee in whatever form he holds dear. A devout Christian sees Jesus; a Hindu beholds Krishna, or the Goddess Kali, or an expanding Light if his worship takes an impersonal turn.

Reluctantly I opened my eyes, and saw that the temple doors were being locked by a priest, in conformance with a noon-hour custom. I rose from my secluded seat on the portico and stepped into the courtyard. Its stone surface was scorched by the midday sun; my bare feet were painfully burned.

"Divine Mother," I silently remonstrated, "Thou didst not come to me in vision, and now Thou art hidden in the temple behind closed doors. I wanted to offer a special prayer to Thee today on behalf of my brother-in-law."

My inward petition was instantly acknowledged. First, a delightful cold wave descended over my back and under my feet, banishing all discomfort. Then, to my amazement, the temple became greatly magnified. Its large door slowly opened, revealing the stone figure of Goddess Kali. Gradually the statue changed into a living form, smilingly nodding in greeting, thrilling me with joy indescribable. As if by a mystic syringe, the breath was withdrawn from my lungs; my body became very still, though not inert.

An ecstatic enlargement of consciousness followed. I could see clearly for several miles over the Ganges River to my left, and beyond the temple into the entire Dakshineswar precincts. The walls of all buildings glimmered transparently; through them I observed people walking to and fro over distant acres.

Though I was breathless and though my body remained in a strangely quiet state, I was able to move my hands and feet freely. For several minutes I experimented in closing and opening my eyes; in either state I saw distinctly the whole Dakshineswar panorama.

Spiritual sight, X-ray-like, penetrates into all matter; the divine eye is centre everywhere, circumference nowhere. I realized anew, standing there in the sunny courtyard, that when a man ceases to be a prodigal child of God, engrossed in a physical world indeed dream, baseless as a bubble, he reinherits his eternal realms. If escapism be a need of man, cramped in his narrow personality, can any other escape compare with that of omnipresence?

SOURCE: Paramahansa Yogananda, *Autobiography of a Yogi*. 2nd ed. Mumbai: Jaico Publishing House, 1975, pp. 207–9

The Hindu way of life

Pilgrimage to the City of Light by Diana Eck

Pilgrimage to sacred sites is for faithful Hindus a spiritual desire that must be fulfilled, no matter how great the effort. Thus people of all ages undertake arduous voyages, often by foot, to be specially blessed at those places. In India's sacred geography, some pilgrimage sites are places of the deities in the mountains, some at holy rivers, some in areas made famous by the great epics. At the end of their lives, many people aspire to reach the sacred city of Varanasi, also known as "Kashi" or "Benares," because dying there is believed to be a direct path to liberation of the soul. One of many spiritual traditions associated with Kashi is its fame as the "City of Light."

In the *Kāshī Rahasya*, the time is recalled when the earth has sunk into the waters of the flood, as it does at the end of each cycle of ages. The great sages, from their vantage point in the heaven of the sages, look out and see that the earth has sunk, and they call upon Vishnu to assume his boar incarnation, to dive into the water and raise the earth up again. Scanning the waters, the sages see something astounding: a great shaft of light, rising and fanning out over the waters like an umbrella. 'What is this light which shines above the waters of destruction,' they ask, 'and why does it not sink when everything else is submerged in the ocean?' Vishnu tells them, 'This is the supreme light, famous in the scriptures as Kāshī.'

In telling the sages about Kāshī, Vishnu contrasts Kāshī with everything else on earth. Everything else is created, but Kāshī is not. Everything else is, in the end, too dense and heavy to float in the ocean of the *pralaya*, and so it sinks. Kāshī, however, is made of luminous wisdom and does not sink. When the earth sinks, Kāshī floats above the waters of destruction. And when Vishnu retrieves the earth from the bottom of the sea, he brings it up and places it as *terra firma* beneath Kāshī. But Kāshī is not attached to the earth as other places are.

The City of Light transcends the cycles of time and the eternal evolution and dissolution of space. This is the light that Brahmā and Vishnu saw. They tried to discover its source and its top, but they could not. It was called a *linga*[16] of light—the 'partless' (*nishkala*) form of the Supreme Shiva, Sadā Shiva, an unfathomable brilliance, transcending the three worlds.

The word *'linga'* ordinarily refers to the image of the Supreme Shiva, either established by human hands or self-manifest, as the focal point of worship in a temple. The word 'Kāshī' ordinarily refers to a city, sacred as it is. Here, however, we have an extraordinary statement: the city is a *linga*. The whole of the sacred zone of Kāshī … is an enormous *linga* of light, the focal point of worship in the sanctum of the entire universe.

The city is the embodiment of the Supreme Shiva. The sages ask, innocently, 'Why does Kāshī have a feminine name if it is a *linga*?' Shiva tells them that 'he' is both Shakti[17] and Shiva, both the manifest and visible energy of life and the unmanifest, invisible spiritual essence. Taking form in the world, active and luminous in the world, is Shakti. Kāshī is Shakti as a goddess, with a *mūrti* or 'image' form. She is also a city, with a *kshetra* or geographical form. And she is the embodiment of *chit*, 'luminous wisdom', which is always feminine.

Sometimes Kāshī is said to be the very body of Shiva. For instance, 'This city is my body—measuring five *kroshas*, with wealth of unfractured magnitude, the very cause of *nirvāna*.' Since the body is a primary symbol of the whole it is an appropriate image for Kāshī, which is the whole. The rivers Asi and Varanā are the two great arteries of Shiva's mystical body here. In the language of *yogis*, they are called *idā* and *pingalā*, and the third artery, *sushumnā*, where duality is transcended and *moksha*[18] achieved, is identified with Matsyodarī River or with Brahma Nāla. The various *tīrthas*[19] and *lingas* here are said to correspond to the parts of the body of God.

16 *Linga or lingam*—symbol of generative energy.
17 Shakti—a spiritual power, often understood as a feminine force.
18 *Moksha*—liberation from the cycle of birth and death and rebirth.
19 *Tīrtha*—place of pilgrimage.

Whether Kāshī is spoken of as Shiva's *linga*, Shiva's *shakti*, or Shiva's body, this is a visible and earthly ford for the crossing to the far shore of liberation.

SOURCE: Diana Eck, "Pilgrimage to the City of Light," from "Kashi: City of All India," in *Religion in India*, ed. T. N. Madan. Delhi: Oxford University Press, 1991–92, pp. 138–55

Contemporary issues

Hinduism has given birth to many reformers who warned against practicing the ancient rituals without inner engagement, or who protested what they regarded as social injustices institutionalized by Brahmanic Hinduism. Among these are the deeply embedded caste system and the subordination and abuse of women (which persists side by side with worship of the goddess).

Untouchability by Mahatma Gandhi

The father of the Indian independence movement, Mahatma Gandhi (1869–1948), was a vehement critic of the caste system, which causes some people to be considered "untouchable" by those of higher castes. He also fought against Hindu exclusivism[20] in a country that is home to large numbers of people from other faiths, trying to establish the principle of secularism,[21] meaning that the government would not favor any one religion and all would enjoy equal privileges.

There is an ineffaceable blot that Hinduism today carries with it. I have declined to believe that it has been handed down to us from immemorial times. I think that this miserable, wretched, enslaving spirit of "untouchableness" must have come to us when we were at our lowest ebb. This evil has stuck to us and still remains with us. ...

Untouchability as it is practised in Hinduism today is, in my opinion, a sin against God and man and is, therefore, like a poison slowly eating into the very vitals of Hinduism. In my opinion, it has no sanction whatsoever in the Hindu *Shastras*[22] taken as a whole. ... It has degraded both the untouchables and the touchables. It has stunted the growth of nearly 40 million human beings. They are denied even the ordinary amenities of life. The sooner, therefore, it is ended, the better for Hinduism, the better for India, and perhaps better for mankind in general.

So far as I am concerned with the untouchability question it is one of life and death for Hinduism. As I have said repeatedly, if untouchability lives, Hinduism perishes, and even India perishes; but if untouchability is eradicated from the Hindu heart, root and branch, then Hinduism has a definite message for the world. I have said the first thing to hundreds of audiences but not the latter part. Now that is the utterance of a man who accepts Truth as God. It is

20 Exclusivism—belief in the validity of only one religion.
21 Secularism—although usually meaning a non-sacred perspective, in modern India "secularism" means governmental non-preference for any religion.
22 *Shastras*—Hindu law books, such as *Manu smrti*.

therefore no exaggeration. If untouchability is an integral part of Hinduism, the latter is a spent bullet. But untouchability is a hideous untruth. My motive in launching the anti-untouchability campaign is clear. What I am aiming at is not every Hindu touching an "untouchable," but every touchable Hindu driving untouchability from his heart, going through a complete change of heart.

It is bad enough when dictated by selfish motives to consider ourselves high and other people low. But it is not only worse but a double wrong when we tack religion to an evil like untouchability. It, therefore, grieves me when learned pundits come forward and invoke the authority of *Shastras* for a patent evil like untouchability. I have said, and I repeat today, that we, Hindus, are undergoing a period of probation. Whether we desire it or not, untouchability is going. But if during this period of probation we repent for the sin, if we reform and purify ourselves, history will record that one act as a supreme act of purification on the part of the Hindus. But if, through the working of the time spirit, we are compelled to do things against our will and Harijans come into their own, it will be no credit to the Hindus or to Hinduism. But I go a step further and say that if we fail in this trial, Hinduism and Hindus will perish.

Harijan means "a man of God." All the religions of the world describe God preeminently as the Friend of the friendless, Help of the helpless, and Protector of the weak. The rest of the world apart, in India who can be more friendless, helpless or weaker than the 40 million or more Hindus of India who are classified as "untouchables"? If, therefore, any body of people can be fitly described as men of God, they are surely these helpless, friendless and despised people. Hence ... I have always adopted Harijan as the name signifying "untouchables." Not that the change of name brings about any change of status but one may at least be spared the use of a term which is itself one of reproach. When caste Hindus have of their own inner conviction and, therefore, voluntarily, got rid of the present-day untouchability we shall all be called Harijans, for, according to my humble opinion, caste Hindus will then have found favour with God and may, therefore, be fitly described as His men.

SOURCE: Mahatma Gandhi, "For the Well-Being of the Nation," in *The Message of Mahatma Gandhi*, ed. U. S. Mohan Rao. Delhi: Ministry of Information and Broadcasting, 1968, pp. 90–2

Hindu-ness by V. D. Savarkar

The exclusivist movement has increased in recent times and has gained considerable political power. A major document encouraging Hindu exclusivism and nationalism was written in 1923 by V. D. Savarkar (1883–1966), who was opposed to harmonious coexistence with Muslims and to Gandhian principles. Many contemporary scholars, however, refute the idea that Hinduism supports any exclusive claims to truth. They argue that "Hindu-ness" is being used as a political rallying point, for there is no single Hindu religion but rather a multiplicity of ways to the Truth. This essay, "Hindutva" ("Hindu-ness"), and Savarkar's subsequent ideas have considerably influenced those who have promoted Hinduism as the national tradition of India in opposition to the claims of the non-Hindu minorities in India.

A country, a common home, is the first important essential of stable strong nationality: and as of all countries in the world our country can hardly be surpassed by any in its capacity to afford a soil so specially fitted for the growth of a great nation; we Hindus, whose very first article of faith is the love we bear to the common Fatherland, have in that love the strongest talismanic tie that can bind close and keep a nation firm and enthuse and enable it to accomplish things greater than ever.

The second essential of *Hindutva* puts the estimate of our latent powers of national cohesion and greatness yet higher. No country in the world, with the exception of China again, is peopled by a race so homogeneous, yet so ancient and yet so strong both numerically and vitally. ... Mohammedans are no race nor are the Christians. They are a religious unit, yet neither a racial nor a national one. But we Hindus, if possible, are all the three put together and live under our ancient and common roof. The numerical strength of our race is an asset that cannot be too highly prized. ...

The ideal conditions, therefore, under which a nation can attain perfect solidarity and cohesion would, other things being equal, be found in the case of those people who inhabit the land they adore, the land of whose forefathers is also the land of their Gods and Angels, of Seers and Prophets; the scenes of whose history are also the scenes of their mythology.

The Hindus are about the only people who are blessed with these ideal conditions that are at the same time incentive to national solidarity, cohesion, and greatness. ...

Thus the actual essentials of *Hindutva* are, as this running sketch reveals, also the ideal essentials of nationality. If we would we can build on this foundation of *Hindutva*, a future greater than what any other people on earth can dream of—greater even than our own past; provided we are able to utilize our opportunities! ...

Thirty crores[23] of people, with India for their basis of operation, for their Fatherland and for their Holyland, with such a history behind them, bound together by ties of a common blood and common culture, can dictate their terms to the whole world. A day will come when mankind will have to face the force.

Equally certain it is that whenever the Hindus come to hold such a position whence they could dictate terms to the whole world—those terms cannot be very different from the terms which [the] *Gītā* dictates or the Buddha lays down. A Hindu is most intensely so, when he ceases to be a Hindu; and with a Kabir claims the whole earth for a Benares[24] ... or with a Tukaram[25] exclaims: "My country? Oh brothers, the limits of the Universe— there the frontiers of my country lie."

SOURCE: V. D. Savarkar, "Hindutva" (1923), in *Sources of Indian Tradition,* ed. S. Hay. New York: Columbia University Press, 1988, vol. 2, pp. 292–5

23 Crore—10 million.
24 Benares—Varanasi or Kashi, a sacred place of pilgrimage.
25 Tukaram—seventeenth-century Hindu poet who believed in the equality of all humankind.

The Secular Face of Hinduism   by Joseph Vellaringatt

According to the Indian Constitution, India is to be a secular country, meaning that no particular religion is to be favored by the government. However, the ideals of Hindutva have been promoted by some political groups in the name of Hinduism, creating an exclusivist, fundamentalist approach that many observers feel is alien to Indian traditions. Joseph Vellaringatt, a Jesuit scholar, explains the tolerance, flexibility, and sense of the sacredness of everything that many feel is the true face of Hinduism.

Hindu fundamentalism of the present day has to be looked upon as the cumulative effect of various historical, socio-political and economic factors. In itself, the Hindutva ideology is a deviation from the true spirit of Hinduism. Such deviations have, from time to time, made their appearance in Christianity and Islam and other major religions of the world. The essentially liberal and secular core of Hinduism is, in course of time, bound to re-assert itself and disown its fundamentalist and ugly caricature. ...

Tolerance and Flexibility   Hinduism allows the widest freedom in matters of faith and worship. Therefore we come across a wide variety of beliefs and practices, various philosophical systems dealing with the nature of God, man and the world, and various ways to God-realization. "Let good thoughts come from all sides" has always been the guiding principle. In India a prophet or a religious teacher never lacked a receptive audience. Even though some of the medieval saints came from the lower strata of society, they too found respectability and following among people of all castes. This spirit of openness has been of great help to Hinduism in withstanding the onslaughts of other religions and keeping its own separate identity. Hinduism has stood its ground by accepting and assimilating some of the positive elements found in them. ...

The concept of Hinduism as a separate religion is a latter-day development. In the Hindu religious scriptures we do not come across the use of the term Hindu *dharma* to designate a separate religious identity. *Dharma* generally stood for moral conduct or the performance of each one's duty following the prescribed socio-ethical norms. It is only with the advent of religions of foreign origin that Hinduism came to assume a separate identity. It will not, therefore, be far from the truth to assert that "Hinduism" as a concept is largely the invention of foreigners, which gradually came to be accepted by Indians themselves. Hinduism does not have one single founder, or one single date and place of origin, or one single Scripture which is considered authoritative and binding on all. What we call Hinduism today is in fact the meeting point of various religious traditions that took birth and developed in various parts of India in different epochs of its history. ...

Since the Hindu religion did not have a stereotyped form to which all were bound to conform, people could pick and choose according to each one's likes and temperaments. ... One's understanding of God and the choice of one or other of the various ways of worshipping God are by and large determined by one's aptitudes, learning, level of enlightenment and personal preference. Thus, for instance, a man of intellectual and mystical bend of mind might find it easy to conceptualize and enjoy union with a God who is without name or form. Such a person may not feel the need of temples, rituals and symbols in worship. Another person might feel at home with a God whom he can lovingly call Rama or Krishna and one whom he can touch and see in the form of an idol. For such a person religious rituals and symbols are a great help in expressing the inner sentiments of the heart. Hinduism gives due respect and recognition to both forms of worship. ...

Sense of the Sacred or the Divine This whole universe is the dwelling place of God. The Transcendent One, who is greater than the greatest ... is also smaller than the smallest ... as he is intimately present in the heart of every being. ... There is the touch of the divine in every fibre of being. Creation is a theophany, a revelation, a presence of God. Every thing in creation, every flower, every leaf, is charged with the grandeur of God and can, therefore, lead us to communion with him. ...

Sacredness of the Human Being If every thing is sacred and divine, the most sacred of all God's creatures is undoubtedly the human being who is created in the very image and likeness of God. Both God and the human being are in essence spirit (atman), pure awareness. ... Not only are they of the same nature, but there is also an intimate relationship between them.

The affirmation of the fundamental divinity of the human being makes it the object of special reverence and respect. All forms of violence towards human beings, therefore, go against the true spirit of Hinduism. Fundamentalism and religious intolerance, leading to atrocities committed against others in the name of God and religion, thus are a negation of one of the cardinal principles of Hindu religion.

SOURCE: Joseph Vellaringatt, "The Secular Face of Hinduism," in *Vidyajyoti Journal of Theological Reflection*, September 2001, vol. 65, no. 9, pp. 645–50

Awakening of Universal Motherhood by Mata Amritanandamayi

In traditional Indian society, women are secondary to men. However, there are now strong movements supporting women's liberation from oppression. The contemporary guru Mata Amritanandamayi ordains women as priests, contrary to Brahmin male domination of religion, and she argues for more recognition for women's important contributions even within the context of the traditional division of labor, in which the woman's place is in the home, defined by family relationships. "Amma" herself is considered a divine mother by her many followers around the world.

Woman is the creator of the human race. She is the first Guru, the first guide and mentor of humanity. Think of the tremendous forces, either positive or negative, that one human being can unleash into the world. Each one of us has a far-reaching effect on others, whether we are aware of it or not. The responsibility of a mother, when it comes to influencing and inspiring her children, cannot be underestimated. ... Wherever you see happy, peaceful individuals; wherever you see children endowed with noble qualities and good dispositions; wherever you see men who have immense strength when faced with failure and adverse situations; wherever you see people who possess a great measure of understanding, sympathy, love, and compassion towards the suffering, and who give of themselves to others—you will usually find a great mother who has inspired them to become what they are.

Mothers are the ones who are most able to sow the seeds of love, universal kinship, and patience in the minds of human beings. There is a special bond between a mother and child. The mother's inner qualities are transmitted to the child even through her breast milk. The mother understands the heart of her child; she pours her love into the child, teaches him or her the positive lessons of life, and corrects the child's mistakes. If you walk through a field of soft, green grass a few times, you will easily make a path. The good thoughts and positive values we cultivate in our children will stay with them forever. It is easy to mold a child's character when he or she is very young, and much more difficult to do so when the child grows up.

It is thus, through the influence she has on her child, that a mother influences the future of the world. A woman who has awakened her innate motherhood brings heaven to earth wherever she is. ... And so it is that the one who rocks the cradle of the babe is the one who holds up the lamp, shedding light upon the world. ...

The essence of motherhood is not restricted to women who have given birth; it is a principle inherent in both women and men. It is the attitude of the mind. It is love—and that love is the very breath of life. No one would say, "I will breathe only when I am with my family and friends; I won't breathe in front of my enemies." Similarly, for those in whom motherhood has awakened, love and compassion for everyone is as much part of their being as breathing.

Real leadership is not to dominate or to control, but to serve others with love and compassion, and to inspire women and men alike through the example of our lives. Amma feels that the forthcoming age should be dedicated to reawakening the healing power of motherhood. This is crucial. May all nations, all people, and their leaders realize that we do not have a choice. It is vitally important that we restore the lost balance in our world for the sake of humanity and Mother Earth, who sustains us all.

SOURCE: Mata Amritanandamayi, from "The Awakening of Universal Motherhood," an address to A Global Peace Initiative of Women Religious and Spiritual Leaders, Geneva, October 7, 2002

GLOSSARY

Atman In Hinduism, the soul.

Bhakti Popular devotion to a god/goddess or guru, with love and adoration.

Brahman The impersonal ultimate principle; also, one of the priestly, aristocratic caste.

Caste A social organization by hierarchy of occupations, sanctified by Hinduism.

Dharma In Hinduism, the universal cosmic law, duty; in Buddhism, cosmic law, the teachings of the Buddha, and the realization and practice of truth (the second of the Three Jewels: Buddha, dharma, sangha).

Kali Yuga The contemporary era, a dark age, one of many cycles (yugas) of a vast cosmic time.

Karma In Hinduism, the cosmic moral law of consequences for ethical actions and their effects on social and personal well-being or suffering that are seen as rewards and punishments for prior incarnations; the goal of religion is liberation from karmic cycles.

Om In Hinduism, the primordial sound vibration.

Pandit One of the hereditary priestly caste learned in ancient texts, customs, and rituals.

Puranas Mythological texts of ancient days; popular devotional texts.

Reincarnation After death, rebirth in a new body higher or lower in the caste system, according to one's karma.

Rishi (seer) A poetic sage; rishis are visionary authors of Vedic hymns heard within in meditation.

Sanskrit The ancient language of the holy scriptures.

Smrti texts Great epic poems, descriptions of gods and goddesses, codes of moral conduct, such as the *Mahabharata*.

Sruti texts "Heard" by ancient sages in meditation, mostly the Vedas.

Upanishads Philosophical reflections on ultimate reality, a oneness in which we all participate.

Vedas Foundational scriptures for Hindu tradition, written down c. 1500 BCE; oldest are the Rig Vedas.

Yoga (yoking [to divinity]) Techniques for transforming consciousness and attaining liberation; there are many forms, such as guru yoga, devotion, work, study, asceticism, physical exercises, mantra repetition, visualization, meditation.

HOLY DAYS

Hindu holy days are numerous and varied across India. Times are calculated variously by region, astrological sign, sun, and moon. Most communal religious celebrations are held during the bright half of the lunar months, for the full moon is sacred.

Domestic rites Conception, wishing for a son, and birth are surrounded with rituals (pujas) using food, fire, and prayers. Between the ages of 8 and 12 an upper-caste boy can be initiated into being a "twice-born." At weddings the bride and groom walk around the sacrificial fire in seven stages, solemnizing their union.

Fall renewals Gods' birthdays are celebrated as overcoming the hot summer (monsoons included). The birthdays of Krishna, avatar of Vishnu, and Vamana, dwarf avatar of Vishnu, signal a restored, auspicious time of year. The goddess Durga kills a buffalo demon in fall. In some parts of India late fall is seen as the time of the awakening of Vishnu, who has been asleep on the cobra Ananta for four months. Divali is a celebration of Lakshmi, the goddess of prosperity, and the victory of gods over evil forces.

Pilgrimages These usually take place in summer, especially to sacred rivers such as the Ganges, where bathing (despite its current physical pollution) is ritually purifying. The dying are taken to Benares to be cremated.

Other pilgrimages are taken to temples, for the sake of ancestors and worldly rewards, or for spiritual purification and rebirth in Heaven instead of earth.

Spring Holi For the lower castes a boisterous celebration, throwing colored powder and water and celebrating Kama, god of sexual desire; the past year's evils are symbolically thrown into bonfires. In Bengal, associated with Krishna.

Spring New Year Soon after Holi the New Year is celebrated near the spring equinox, a time of cosmic balance and beginning/ending.

HISTORICAL OUTLINE

c. 2500 BCE—Harappan city civilization with goddess and indigenous religions in Indus valley, now in Pakistan

c. 2000–900 BCE—Aryan invasions of northern India

c. 1000–500 BCE—Upanishads systematized by Vyasa

c. 900–700 BCE—*Brahmanas* recorded

200 BCE—*Yoga Sutras* organized by Patanjali

400 BCE–200 CE—*Ramayana* recorded

400 BCE–400 CE—*Mahabharata* recorded

100–300 CE—*The Laws of Manu* compiled

c. 300 CE—Tantric texts recorded

500–1500 CE—*Puranas* recorded

600–1800 CE—*bhakti* movement strong

711 CE—Muslim invasions begin

c. 788–820—Vedanta school organized by Sankara

1556–1707—Muslim Mughal Empire

1836–86—Ramakrishna

1857–1947—British rule in India

1893–1952—Paramahansa Yogananda

1947—formation of Pakistan and East Pakistan (now Bangladesh)

1948—assassination of Mahatma Gandhi

1992—destruction of Babri mosque by extremist Hindus

REVIEW QUESTIONS

1   Contrast the dualistic philosophy of Sankhya versus the monistic philosophy of Advaita Vedanta, and explain how they affect what is considered to be ultimately real.
2   How would a believer respond to the monotheistic charge of idolatry for worshipping statues?
3   How did Yogananda's meditation "reinherit his eternal realm" at the temple of the goddess Kali?
4   How did Gandhi argue against untouchability, against Hindu tradition and law? What did he rename untouchables and why?

DISCUSSION QUESTIONS

1   What in human nature makes possible Hinduism's refined, universalist spirituality and simultaneously, its caste system, treatment of women, and exclusivist nationalism?
2   How can Hinduism embrace the extremes of severe sadhu asceticism and elaborate, imaginative, sensuous images of gods and goddesses?
3   What themes in Hinduism do you think might offer positive alternatives for monotheism's insistence on one god, which leaves out women, nature, and other areas?

INFORMATION RESOURCES

Alston, A. J. *The Devotional Poems of Mirabai.* Delhi: Motilal Banarsidass, 1980.

Classic texts in English translation
<http://www.hinduwebsite.com>

De Bary, W. Theodore. *Sources of Indian Tradition.* New York: Columbia University Press, 1958.

Fuller, C. J. *The Camphor Flame: Popular Hinduism and Society in India.* Princeton, NJ: Princeton University Press, 2004.

Gandhi, Mahatma. *The Message of Mahatma Gandhi,* ed. U. S. Mohan Rao. Delhi: Ministry of Information, Government of India, 1990.

Hawley, John S., *et al.* "Hinduism" in *Encyclopedia of Religion,* ed. Lindsay Jones. 2nd ed. Vol. 6, pp. 3988–4021. New York: Macmillan, 2005.

Hindu temples
<http://www.sacred-destinations.com/categories/hindu-temples>

The Hindu Universe
<http://www.hindunet.org>

Hinduism Today magazine
<http://www.hinduismtoday.com>

Kabir. *Songs of Kabir,* trans. R. Tagore. New York: Weiser, 1981.

Kinsley, David. *Hindu Goddesses.* Delhi: Motilal Banarsidass, 1986.

Prabhupada, A. C. B., Swami. *Bhagavad-Gita As It Is.* Los Angeles, London, Mumbai: Bhaktivedanta Book Trust, 1976.

Purohit, Shree, Swami, and **W. B. Yeats,** trans. *The Ten Principal Upanishads.* Calcutta: Rupa & Co., 1992.

Rajagopalachari, C., trans. *Mahabharata.* Mumbai: Bharatiya Vidya Bhavan, 1994.

——. *Ramayana.* Mumbai: Bharatiya Vidya Bhavan, 1990.

——. *The Siva Purana.* Delhi: Motilal Banarsidass, 1990.

Rinehart, Robin, ed. *Contemporary Hinduism: Ritual, Culture, and Practice.* Santa Barbara, CA: ABC-CLIO, 2004.

Sankara texts and Advaita Vedanta
<http://www.sankaracharya.org>

Shastri, J. L., ed. *Hymns of the Rigveda,* trans. Ralph T. H. Griffith. Delhi: Motilal Banarsidass, 1986.

Vivekananda, Swami. *Karma-Yoga and Bhakti-Yoga.* New York: Ramakrishna-Vivekananada Center, 1982.

Yogananada, Paramahansa, *Autobiography of a Yogi.* Los Angeles, CA: Self-Realization Fellowship/ Mumbai: Jaico Publishing House, 1974.

CHAPTER 4

JAINISM

In addition to the Vedic religions of ancient India, another path evolved independently. This is Jainism (from *jina*, winner over passions), an extremely ascetic path. Its goal is liberation from the soul-tarnishing negative effects of one's actions, thoughts, and speech—one's **karma**. In Jain teaching, this liberation comes only through one's own strenuous and mindful efforts not to do wrong in any way. Jains reject the Hindu caste system and the idea of a creator God, but, like Hindus and Buddhists, believe in reincarnation.

The teachers of this path are called **Tirthankaras** ("bridgebuilders"). According to tradition, there have been 24 Tirthankaras during the current era. There is historic evidence of the existence of the three most recent teachers. The last is the best known: Mahavir (c. 559–527 BCE), who had been a prince but renounced his life of pleasure and power at the age of 30 to become a homeless ascetic. His austerities were so extreme that people thought him mad and tormented him. But he endured all hardships with equanimity, achieved perfect liberation, and taught others the way to liberation from karma. In order to increase sensitivity toward non-human life forms, he made detailed studies and gave insights into the categories and qualities of all that exists. A large community of monks, nuns, and laypeople gathered around him, and he gave them minute instructions on how to live without accumulating negative karma.

Today there is renewed interest in this ascetic way of life, for its basic principles are antidotes to modern problems. For example, Mahatma Gandhi's assertion of the power of non-violent resistance to oppression was strongly influenced by the Jain principle of **ahimsa**, or non-violence, based on reverence for all life. Jain precepts of non-violence, the interdependence of all life forms, compassion, non-acquisitiveness, and relativity are also being invoked as correctives to environmentally destructive modern lifestyles and to conflicts of dogma.

Teachings of Mahavir

The teachings of Mahavir did not necessarily originate with him but are part of a much more ancient tradition. They were transmitted orally by his followers for several centuries, along with the commentaries of learned teachers. The literature to be remembered was quite vast, and during 12 years of famine about 300 BCE, many monks died who had been carrying the teachings in their memory. Little had been written down, for books were considered possessions and causes for attachment, and were renounced by Jain ascetics like other possessions. At that time, books were written out by hand and were rare in any case.

The compilation of teachings and commentaries formed a **canon** called the *Agam Sutras*. After the famine, one group of Jain ascetics, the **Svetambara** sect, maintained that they had managed to remember most of the major texts. They held three conferences to compile and preserve what was available. Another even more ascetic sect, the **Digambara**, claimed that the entire canon had been lost. Today, the sects still disagree about the validity of the Jain Agamic scriptures. The Digambaras use scriptures written by great teachers from 100 to 800 CE which are thought to have been based on the earlier texts.

Mahavir's Stoicism from the *Akaranga Sutra*

Mahavir's own life is cited as a perfect example of the Jain teaching of self-mastery and non-aggressiveness toward all beings. The ideal is to bear both pleasure and pain with equanimity and compassion for other beings. Many stories of the torments endured by Mahavir with great **stoicism** appear in the classic *Akaranga Sutra*, an excerpt from which is here retold by Shashi Ahluwalia. Before his liberation, Mahavir is referred to by his worldly name, Vardhaman.

Vardhaman left the palace and started his long journey like an ascetic. He had only a piece of cloth on his body and gave even that to a beggar. He became completely naked—*Digambara*. As Vardhaman was about to start from the Jnatri-sanda park on a wandering career, a Brahman named Soma approached him with a prayer for help. But Vardhaman had hardly anything worthwhile to give. So he shared half of his garment with the beggar and placed the other half on his shoulder.

The Brahman took the garment to a tailor to have the hem bound. The tailor advised him to get the other half, so that the two pieces together, duly repaired, would fetch him a handsome amount in the market. So the Brahman started at once and followed Vardhaman like his shadow, and waiting for a chance to get it. The chance came after 13 months. When Vardhaman was going from South Vacala to the North Vacala the piece on his shoulder was caught in a thorny bush and remained there. It was picked up by Brahman Soma.

At this point, Vardhaman took five resolutions which were

1. I shall not stay at an uncongenial place;
2. I shall meditate all the time in a statuesque posture;
3. I shall generally maintain silence;
4. I shall use the hollow on my palm as begging bowl; and
5. I shall not humble myself to any householder.

These resolutions became his guidelines throughout his life.

The famous "Ohana-Sutra" in the *Akaranga* contains the following account of his soul-stirring *sadhana*:[1]

Many living beings gathered on his body, crawled about it, and caused pain. Then he meditated, walking with his eye fixed on a square space before him of the length of a man. Many people who were shocked at the sight struck him and cried. He shunned the company of the female sex and of all householders. Asked, he gave no reply. He did not even answer those who saluted him. He was beaten with sticks and struck by sinful people. He wandered about disregarding all slights, not being attracted by any worldly amusement.

For more than a couple of years he went without using cold water. He realized singleness, guarded his body, obtained intuition and became calm. He carefully avoided doing injury to the meanest form of life. He did not use what was specially prepared for him. He used to eat only clean food. He did not use another man's robe, nor did he eat out of another man's vessel. He observed moderation in eating and drinking. He neither rubbed his eyes nor scratched his body.

He sometimes took shelter in workshops, sometimes in factories, sometimes in garden houses, sometimes in a cemetery, in deserted houses, or at the foot of a tree. In such places he sought shelter for 13 years. He meditated day and night, undisturbed, unperturbed, exerting himself strenuously. He never cared for sleep for the sake of pleasure. He waked up himself and slept only a little, free from cares and desires. Waking up again, going outside for once in a night, he walked about for an hour.

At his resting places, crawling or flying animals attacked him. Bad people, the guard of the village, or lance-bearers attacked him. Well-controlled, he bore all dreadful calamities and different kinds of feelings and he wandered about, speaking but little. Ill-treated, he engaged himself in his meditations, free from resentment. He endured all hardships in calmness. Well-guarded, he bore the pains caused by grass, cold, heat, flies and gnats.

He travelled in the pathless country of *Radha*—in *Vajrabhumi* and *Svabhrabhumi*, where he used miserable beds and seats. The rude natives of the place attacked him and set dogs to bite him. But he never used the stick to keep off the dogs. He endured the abusive language of the rustics, being perfectly enlightened. The inhabitants of the place caused him all sorts of tortures. Abandoning the care of his body, he bore pain, free from desire.

He abstained from indulgence of the flesh, though he was never attacked by diseases. Whether wounded or not, he did not desire medical treatment. In the cold season he meditated in the shade. In summer he exposed himself to the heat. He lived on rough food like rice, pounded jujube [wild fruit], and jujube. Using these three kinds of food, he sustained himself for eight months. Sometimes he did not drink for half a month or even for a month. Sometimes he did not drink for more than two months, or even six months. Sometimes he ate only the sixth meal, or the eighth, the tenth, the

---

1 *Sadhana*—spiritual practice.

twelfth. Sometimes he ate stale food. He committed no sin himself, nor did he induce others to do so, nor did he consent to the sin of others.

He meditated persevering in some posture, without the smallest motion. He meditated in mental concentration on the things above, below, beside. He meditated free from sin and desire, not attached to sounds and colours, and never acted carelessly.

Thus, as a hero at the head of a battle, he bore all hardships, and remaining undisturbed, proceeded on the road to deliverance. Understanding the truth and restraining the impulses for the purification of soul, he was finally liberated.

SOURCE: "Ohana Sutra, Akaranga," in Shashi Ahluwalia, *Spiritual Masters from India*. Delhi: Manas Publications, 1987, pp. 4–6

Harmlessness

Whatever their historicity, the Jain scriptures comprise a vast body of wisdom. Some of the literature concerns intricate systems for classifying all aspects of living and non-living beings, space, and time. Minute sentient life-forms are said to exist in the earth, in fire, in air, and in water, in addition to the more visible plants and "movable beings." Many Jain sutras concern precepts for doing as little harm as possible to other beings.

On Non-Violence from the *Jain Sutras*

Know other creatures' love for life, for they are like you. Kill them not: save their life from fear and enmity.

All living beings desire happiness, and have revulsion from pain and suffering. They are fond of life, they love to live, long to live, and they feel repulsed at the idea of hurt and injury to or destruction of their life. Hence, no living being should be hurt, injured, or killed.

All things breathing, all things existing, all things living, all beings whatsoever, should not be slain, or treated with violence, or insulted, or tortured, or driven away.

He who hurts living beings himself, or gets them hurt by others, or approves of hurt caused by others, augments the world's hostility toward himself.

He who views all living beings as his own self, and sees them all as being alike, has stopped all influx of karma; he is self-restrained, and incurs no sin.

On Self-Restraint from the *Jain Sutras*

The painful condition of the self is the result of its own action; it has not been brought about by any other cause.

The soul is the maker and the unmaker, the doer and undoer; it is itself responsible for its own happiness and misery, is its own friend and its own foe; it itself decides its own conditions, good or evil.

Wealth and property, movable or immovable, cannot save a person from the sufferings he or she undergoes on account of the fruition of his or her own karma.

Greater is the victory of one who conquers his own self than that of him who conquers thousands of thousands of formidable foes in a valiant fight.

Fight with yourself; why fight with external foes? Happy is he who conquers his self by his self.

Conquer yourself, for difficult it is to conquer the self. If the self is conquered, you shall be happy in this world and hereafter.

All the creatures of the earth look for happiness outside of themselves, but real happiness must be sought inside the depths of their own hearts.

SOURCE: *Jain Sutras*, trans. Dr. Jyoti Prasad Jain, in *Religion and Culture of the Jains*. 3rd ed. Delhi: Bharatiya Jnanpith, 1983, pp. 187–8

Respect for Life from the *Akaranga Sutra*

Earth is afflicted and wretched, it is hard to teach, it has no discrimination. Unenlightened men, who suffer from the effects of past deeds, cause great pain in a world full of pain already, for in earth souls are individually embodied. If, thinking to gain praise, honor, or respect, ... or to achieve a good rebirth, ... or to win salvation, or to escape pain, a man sins against earth or causes or permits others to do so, ... he will not gain joy or wisdom. ... Injury to the earth is like striking, cutting, maiming, or killing a blind man. ... Knowing this a man should not sin against earth or cause or permit others to do so. He who understands the nature of sin against earth is called a true sage who understands karma. ...

And there are many souls embodied in water. Truly water ... is alive. ... He who injures the lives in water does not understand the nature of sin or renounce it. ... Knowing this, a man should not sin against water, or cause or permit others to do so. He who understands the nature of sin against water is called a true sage who understands karma. ...

By wicked or careless acts one may destroy fire-beings and, moreover, harm other beings by means of fire. ... For there are creatures living in earth, grass, leaves, wood, cowdung, or dustheaps, and jumping creatures which ... fall into a fire if they come near it. If touched by fire, they shrivel up, ... lose their senses, and die. ... He who understands the nature of sin in respect of fire is called a true sage who understands karma.

And just as it is the nature of a man to be born and grow old, so is it the nature of a plant to be born and grow old. ... One is endowed with reason, and so is the other; one is sick, if injured, and so is the other; one grows larger, and so does the other; one changes with time, and so does the other. ... He who understands the nature of sin against plants is called a true sage who understands karma....

All beings with two, three, four, or five senses, ... in fact all creation, know individually pleasure and displeasure, pain, terror, and sorrow. All are full of fears which come from all directions. And yet there exist people who would cause greater pain to them. ... Some kill animals for sacrifice, some for their skin, flesh, blood, ... feathers, teeth, or tusks; ... some kill them intentionally and some unintentionally; some kill because they have been previously injured by them, ... and some because they expect to be injured. He who harms animals has not understood or renounced deeds of sin. ... He who understands the nature of sin against animals is called a true sage who understands karma. ...

A man who is averse from harming even the wind knows the sorrow of all things living. ... He who knows what is bad for himself knows what is bad for others, and he who knows what is bad for others knows what is bad for himself. This reciprocity should always be borne in mind. Those whose minds are at peace and who are free from passions do not desire to live [at the expense of others]. ... He who understands the nature of sin against wind is called a true sage who understands karma.

In short he who understands the nature of sin in respect of all the six types of living beings is called a true sage who understands karma.

SOURCE: *Akaranga Sutra*, in *Sources of Indian Tradition*, ed. W. Theodore de Bary. New York: Columbia University Press, 1958, vol. 1, pp. 59–60

Perfection of the soul

If one compassionately avoids harming all forms of life, one may gradually free the soul or **jiva** from its karmic accretions and entanglements with material things, thereby achieving perfection and liberation of the *jiva*. The **Five Jain Vows** are made to help achieve this aim.

The Five Great Vows from the *Akaranga Sutra*

The first great vow, Sir, runs thus:

I renounce all killing of living beings, whether subtle or gross, whether movable or immovable. Nor shall I myself kill living beings. As long as I live, I confess and blame, repent and exempt myself of these sins, in the thrice threefold way [acting, commanding, consenting, either in the past or the present or the future], in mind, speech, and body.

There are five clauses:

A Nirgrantha[2] is careful in his walk, not careless. The Kevalin[3] assigns as the reason, that a Nirgrantha, careless in his walk, might hurt or displace or injure or kill living beings.

A Nirgrantha searches into his mind. If his mind is sinful, blamable, intent on works, acting on impulses, produces division and dissension, quarrels, faults, and pains, injures living beings, or kills creatures, he should not employ such a mind in action.

2 Nirgrantha—a person without attachments, impurities, or possessiveness.
3 Kevalin—omniscient one.

A Nirgrantha searches into his speech; if his speech is sinful, blamable, intent on works, acting on impulses, produces division and dissension, quarrels, faults, and pains, injures living beings, or kills creatures, he should not utter that speech.

A Nirgrantha is careful in laying down his utensils of begging; he is not careless in it. The Kevalin says: A Nirgrantha who is careless in laying down his utensils of begging might hurt or displace or injure all sorts of living beings.

A Nirgrantha eats and drinks after inspecting his food and drink; he does not eat and drink without inspecting his food and drink. The Kevalin says: If a Nirgrantha would eat and drink without inspecting his food and drink, he might hurt and displace or injure or kill all sorts of living beings.

The second great vow runs thus:

I renounce all vices of lying speech from anger or greed or fear or mirth. I shall neither myself speak lies, nor cause others to speak lies, nor consent to the speaking of lies by others. I confess and blame, repent and exempt myself of these sins in the thrice threefold way, in mind, speech, and body. ...

The third great vow runs thus:

I renounce all taking of anything not given, either in a village or a town or a wood, either of little or much, of small or great, of living or lifeless things. I shall neither take myself what is not given, nor cause others to take it, nor consent to their taking it. ...

The fourth great vow runs thus:

I renounce all sexual pleasures, either with gods or men or animals. I shall not give way to sensuality. As long as I live, I confess and blame, repent and exempt myself of these sins, in the thrice threefold way, in mind, speech, and body. ...

The fifth great vow runs thus:

I renounce all attachments, whether little or much, small or great, living or lifeless; neither shall I myself form such attachments, nor cause others to do so, nor consent to their doing so. As long as I live, I confess and blame, repent and exempt myself of these sins, in the thrice threefold way, in mind, speech, and body.

There are five clauses:

If a creature with ears hears agreeable and disagreeable sounds, it should not be attached to, nor delighted with, nor desiring of, nor infatuated by, nor covetous of, nor disturbed by the agreeable or disagreeable sounds.

If a creature with eyes sees agreeable and disagreeable forms, it should not be attached to, nor delighted with, nor desiring of, nor infatuated by, nor covetous of, nor disturbed by them.

If a creature with an organ of smell smells agreeable or disagreeable smells, it should not be attached to them. ...

If a creature with a tongue tastes agreeable or disagreeable tastes, it should not be attached to them. ...

If a creature with an organ of feeling feels agreeable or disagreeable touches, it should not be attached to them. ...

He who is well provided with these great vows and their 25 clauses is really Houseless, if he, according to the sacred lore, the precepts, and the way correctly practices, follows, executes, explains, establishes, and according to the precept, effects them.

SOURCE: *Akaranga Sutra*, Book II, Lecture 15, trans. Hermann Jacobi in *The Sacred Books of the East*, ed. F. Max Müller. Delhi: Motilal Banarsidass, 1964, vol. 22, pp. 202–10 (first published by OUP, 1884)

The principles of anekantavada and syadvada

A central Jain principle is that of the multiplicity (**anekantavada**) and relativity (**syadvada**) of all points of view. The total of all perspectives can only be seen by the perfected soul whose clear vision encompasses the entire universe. If we grasp this teaching, we are less likely to fight to defend our own point of view, and thus we will be less violent and more tolerant in our relationships with others. This important teaching was explained by L. M. Singhvi, former Ambassador of India to England, as part of a statement about Jain principles presented to Prince Philip in 1990, marking the entry of the Jain faith into the Network on Conservation and Religion of the World Wide Fund for Nature.

Anekantavada (The Doctrine of Manifold Aspects)
by L. M. Singhvi

The concept of universal interdependence underpins the Jain theory of knowledge, known as *anekantavada* or the doctrine of **manifold aspects**. *Anekantavada* describes the world as a multifaceted, everchanging reality with an infinity of viewpoints depending on the time, place, nature and state of the one who is the viewer and that which is viewed.

This leads to the doctrine of *syadvada* or relativity, which states that truth is relative to different viewpoints. What is true from one point of view is open to question from another. Absolute truth cannot be grasped from any particular viewpoint alone because absolute truth is the sum total of all the different viewpoints that make up the universe.

Because it is rooted in the doctrines of *anekantavada* and *syadvada*, Jainism does not look upon the universe from an anthropocentric, ethnocentric or egocentric viewpoint. It takes into account the viewpoints of other species, other communities and nations and other human beings.

SOURCE: L. M. Singhvi, "The Jain Declaration on Nature," pamphlet published privately and presented to Prince Philip on October 23, 1990, at Buckingham Palace, London

The Blind Men and the Elephant A traditional Jain fable

The principle of relativity of viewpoints is so important to Jain understanding that it is explained by way of numerous fables, such as the traditional Indian story of the blind men and the elephant. Not only Jains but also Hindus and Buddhists use this story as a moral fable.

As a joke, a king sent six blind men to feel an elephant and describe its nature. Each approached the elephant from a different direction, seized a different part, and, being blind, assumed that what he perceived was the whole elephant. One grasped the ear and declared, "Elephant is like a large fan." Another grasped a leg and declared, "Elephant is like a great pillar." Another blind man found the trunk, and feeling it, proclaimed, "Elephant is like the branch of a tree." Another grasped the tail and declared, "Elephant is like a rope hanging from the sky." A fifth encountered the side of the elephant and maintained, "Elephant is like a wall." The sixth insisted that the others were all wrong, for he had grasped the tusk. He proclaimed, "Elephant is not any of those; elephant is like a spear." Each being certain of the truth of his own experience, they began to fight.

  A person who could see chanced to come by and found them quarreling. After listening to their individual perceptions from their different points of view, he gently explained that there was no need for fighting over the issue, for each was partially right. But to have complete knowledge of the nature of the elephant, he said, one would have to be able to be aware of and combine all the different aspects of the creature.

Renunciation

Another major Jain principle is that of **renunciation:** one should reduce one's desires and keep consumption to a minimum, thus freeing the soul from karmic entanglements with the material world and minimizing one's destruction of the planet. To overconsume, to misuse or pollute natural resources, are considered acts of violence.

  There are degrees of harmfulness, corresponding to the karmic density of the soul. An example often used is ways of obtaining fruit. The most densely stained black soul uproots the whole tree to get its fruits. The blue-stained soul cuts the tree down for its fruit. The grey-stained soul cuts off a fruit-bearing branch. These three types of souls are all heavily karmically laden. Three other categories represent successively lighter karmic burdens. The yellow-stained soul cuts off a bunch of fruit. The lotus-pink soul picks ripe fruit from the tree. The sixth and most pure, the luminous white soul, simply picks up ripe fruit that has fallen to the ground.

  Today voluntary simplicity and abstinence are being widely hailed as necessary for preservation of the environment. But Jains have always tried to live thus.

The Righteous Path for Laity and Ascetics
by Acharya Kund-Kund

Acharya Kund-Kund was a revered ascetic and teacher from approximately the second century CE.

Conduct of laymen is eleven-fold, and of ascetics, ten-fold
Lord Jinendra who enjoys Supreme Bliss ordains an eleven-fold code
of conduct for laymen and ten-fold for ascetics. This is based on right
perception.

Code for the laity The stage of the right view, of vows, of attaining
equanimity, of fasting on certain holy days, of purity of nourishment, of not
consuming food at night, of celibacy or absolute continence, of giving up
occupation, of giving up possessions, abstinence from approving household
activities, and renunciation of specially prepared food or lodging: These are
the eleven stages of the conduct of renunciation for laymen.

The ascetic's code of conduct Supreme forgiveness, humility, uprightness,
truthfulness, purity, restraint, austerity, renunciation, non-attachment, and
celibacy: These are the ten forms of righteousness of the ascetics.

Supreme forgiveness One who does not feel angry in the least, even while
there are direct extraneous reasons for provocations to anger, observes the
virtue of forgiveness.

Supreme humility The ascetic who does not in the least feel proud about
his ancestry, appearance, birth, wisdom, austerity, scriptural learning, and
conduct, observes the virtue of humility.

Supreme uprightness An ascetic, who abstaining from thoughts of deceit
follows the code of conduct with a pure heart, observes the virtue of
uprightness as enjoined.

Supreme truthfulness An ascetic who abstains from speech that torments
others and speaks what does good both to oneself and to others observes the
fourth virtue of truthfulness.

Supreme purity An ascetic in the highest stage who has freed himself of
desires and conducts himself with aversion for them is endowed with the
virtue of purity.

Supreme restraint An ascetic who gives up the afflictions of mind, speech,
and body, overcomes all sensual desires, and evolves himself by observing
the vows and regulations, is endowed with the virtue of restraint.

Supreme austerity A saint who through meditation and scriptural study
realizes the consummation of the subjugation of sensual desires and passions
and is devoted to contemplation of Self, truly practices the virtue of austerity.

Supreme renunciation The ascetic who has abjured the desire for all objects
and is imbued with the three-fold detachment (from the mundane world,
his own body, and pleasures) is endowed with the virtue of renunciation;
so have the Jinendras declared.

Supreme non-attachment The homeless ascetic who has forsaken all possessions, has subdued his thought impulses for pleasure and pain and acts with equanimity, is endowed with the virtue of non-attachment.

Supreme celibacy The ascetic who on seeing all parts of women's body refrains from excitement with passion about them is really able to practice the rigorous virtue of celibacy.

[Explanation: Sex, in fact, has no meaning to a saint, who views the physical body as inert and extraneous matter.]

Only those who observe the ascetic's code attain liberation The soul that discontinues the laymen's path to follow the ascetic's righteous path cannot fail to attain emancipation. This ought to be the incessant contemplation on righteousness.

Contemplation of Self with equanimity From the real standpoint, the soul stands distinct from the vows of both the householder and the ascetic. The pure soul should therefore be contemplated upon constantly with equanimity.

[Explanation: With due consideration of practical norms, different codes of conduct have been prescribed for the pious householders and the ascetic. But this distinction is purely conventional.

From the strictly real standpoint, it is the pristine purity of the Soul that is to be contemplated upon. Self-realization is the ultimate goal of the householder and the ascetic alike. The layman in his spiritual quest adopts the ascetic's vows as he advances spiritually. His aim is to liberate himself from the karmic bondage.]

SOURCE: Acharya Kund-Kund, *Barasa Anuvekkha*. Delhi: Kund-Kund Bharati, 1990, pp. 76–86

The Renunciate Life of Sādhvi Vicakṣaṇa by N. Shanta

Although all Jains follow a path of renunciation and austerity, monks and nuns do so to an extreme degree. They have only a few possessions, which they carry with them, including a broom to sweep insects aside before inadvertently treading on them as they walk. Many wear a cloth over their mouth to avoid inadvertently inhaling any minute living beings. In winter they tolerate cold without heavy blankets; Digambara monks in fact never wear any clothing. In summer the monks and nuns tolerate intense heat without fans. This life is so arduous that one might imagine few would undertake it, but in fact there are large communities of Jain monks and nuns in India, even today. Many of them radiate an inner happiness which is the paradoxical result of extreme self-discipline.

The following story of a Jain nun who lived from 1912 to 1980 illustrates the particular difficulties for a woman choosing the path of renunciation, and also the liberating effects of doing so. It is noteworthy that Svetambara Jains have long believed that women are capable of a strict renunciate life, capable of fully understanding the teachings, and capable of helping both men and women to find the way to liberation.

... The horoscope of the child revealed, so it was said, an unusual degree of courage and predicted that she would become an ascetic of great renown. In the meantime, she was an affectionate, friendly and intelligent child. They called her Dākhi, from *drākṣā*, bunch of grapes. In accordance with the custom of the day, she was affianced in childhood and up to the age of eight she knew the life of a happy family. The sudden death of her father was a terrible shock for her, for not only did she now lack his parental affection, but she began to ask the reason for her father's being so abruptly snatched from her. Life changed for her. Having neither brothers nor sisters, she remained alone with her mother, a young widow who was obliged to yield to the customs of her community. After many enquiries, this latter managed to trace the whereabouts of her cousin Sādhvi Suvaraṇa and, taking Dākhi with her, stayed with her several times. Thus Dākhi came into contact with the *sādhvis*[4] whom she proceeded to astonish by the liveliness of her intelligence. The mother of Dākhi had decided to receive *dikṣā*[5] when[ever] her daughter married the young man to whom she had been betrothed. This, however, was not Dākhi's desire. She felt an attraction for the ascetic life and to fulfil this aspiration, she carried on a tenacious struggle with her paternal grandfather, who loved her dearly and refused to give his consent to the *dikṣā*. The young man's family, perturbed and unhappy, also applied pressure. Dākhi struggled alone with a grandfather whom, at the same time, she loved—alone, as neither could her mother or the *sādhvis* help her in any way, for the grandfather would have accused them of bringing influence to bear upon the child.

Dākhi was kept at home and forbidden to go out to visit the temple or the *upāśrayā*.[6] Dākhi replied that she would obey, [but] as she was being forbidden to go to the temple, she would fast. This, then, is what she did. In the evening of the first day of the fast, her grandfather, softened at heart, offered her a cup of milk, but Dākhi refused. Softened still further, the grandfather gave her permission to attend the temple, but re-affirmed stoutly that he would never give his consent to her receiving *dikṣā* and that Dākhi must needs get married. To this she replied that she would not disobey, so, said she, she would wait for *dikṣā* but would never on any account marry! Confrontations of this sort continued for one week. The grandfather, realizing his powerlessness to persuade Dākhi and despairing of the affair, lodged an appeal with the civil authorities. He informed them that the *sādhvis* had brought pressure to bear upon his 13-year-old granddaughter and were desirous of admitting her to *dikṣā* against the will of her guardian (himself); that they should be so good as to help him prevent Dākhi from joining the *sādhvis*. A *ṭhākura*, a type of magistrate of the district, was appointed to study the case and administer justice.

Here, now, are her chief replies in her dialogue with the magistrate:

4 *Sādhvi*—a Jain nun.
5 *Dikṣā*—consecration as a member of an ascetic Jain order.
6 *Upāśrayā*—community of renunciates.

Ṭhākura: "Do you really, my child, desire to embrace the ascetic life?"
Dākhi: "Yes, sir."
Ṭhākura: "Why?"
Dākhi: "It is an inner call."
Ṭhākura: "Why do you not wish to marry?"
Dākhi: "I have no desire for it."
Ṭhākura: "Do you know what the ascetic life means?"
Dākhi: "Without a knowledge of the ascetic life it is not possible to experience its attraction. I do know what is meant by both life in the world and by asceticism."
Ṭhākura: "Is not obedience to one's parents also part of the _dharma_?"
Dākhi: "Yes, indeed, but if it is clear that one's parents' demands are an obstacle to the full realization of human life and of the _ātman_, respectfully to oppose these demands is not contrary to the _dharma_."
Ṭhākura: "Do you see, my child, what is in front of you?"
Dākhi: "Yes, it is a rifle."
Ṭhākura: (to test her) "Leave aside all these arguments of yours and do as your grandfather tells you. If not, I'm going to use this rifle."—and with that he grasped the rifle.
Dākhi: "If it is your duty to do so, use the rifle. I have no fear of death; one must die some day. It's all the same, whether I die today from a gunshot or tomorrow from some illness. It is a great thing to die for one's ideal."...

Finally, after all these painful contretemps, the mother and her daughter received _dikṣā_; Rūpāmadevi became Sādhvi Vijñāna Śri and Dākhi, Sādhvi Vicakṣaṇa Śri, _vicakṣaṇa_ meaning the one who is farsighted, wise, intelligent, who has discernment. ...

After [7] years of training in Delhi, Sādhvi Vicakṣaṇa began her _vihāras_[7] up and down the country. We find her in the North, in the West, in the Centre and in the South. Her ardour is diminished by no obstacle or difficulty.

Of what does Sādhvi Vicakṣaṇa speak? Why do the crowds flock to hear her? The answer is simple: her language is direct, without pomposity or the slightest affectation; she goes straight to the essentials. It is her deep sincerity, her love for all living beings and the clarity with which she expresses herself that not only captivate all hearts, but transform them, removing both barriers and prejudices and lessening or even completely obliterating all enmities. ...

In the presence of Digambaras, Sādhvi Vicakṣaṇa, herself a Śvetāmbara, attacks neither party, but rather seeks that which may unite them. At Hastināpura, a pilgrimage-place venerated by both traditions, but where the Digambaras are more numerous and more firmly entrenched, she broached the subject of the principal causes of dispute between them: can women attain _mokṣā_?[8] Do the _kevalins_ take nourishment or not? The Digambaras

---

7 _Vihāra_—movement from one location to another.
8 _Mokṣā_—liberation of the soul from accumulated karma.

answer both questions in the negative, the Śvetāmbara in the affirmative. Addressing the whole assembly, she told them: "Do we not believe, you and I, that the *ātman*[9] is neither male nor female, that it is subject to no change and that male-ness and female-ness are due to the mode of *karman* relative to the body? But is *mokṣā* attained in the *ātman* or in the body? ..." In the same vein, she said: "Do the *kevalins* take nourishment or not? Does that really affect the state of *kevāla-jñāna*? *Jñāna*[10] appertains to the *ātman*; nourishment is for the body. It is of little concern to us whether the *kevalins* take nourishment or not. Our aim is to believe in the state of being of the *kevalin* and to strive towards it. These useless quarrels are damaging and lead nowhere." Thus she exhorts them all, as disciples of Mahāvira, to drop these scholastic disputes inherited from the past, to come to a brotherly understanding and demonstrate *viśvamaitri*[11] instead of reviling one another.

SOURCE: "The Renunciate Life of Sādhvi Vicakṣaṇa," in N. Shanta, *The Unknown Pilgrims: The Voice of the Sādhvis: The History, Spirituality and Life of the Jaina Women Ascetics*, trans. from French by Mary Rogers. Delhi: Sri Satguru Publications, 1997, pp. 585–96

Jain ethics today

Remembering our own First Principles by Michael Tobias

Jains are a highly respected and economically successful community within India and in other countries where they have settled. It seems that their success has something to do with their strict principles. Michael Tobias, a global ecologist, author of 35 books, filmmaker, professor of environmental studies, and president of the Dancing Star Foundation in California, which is dedicated to animal and habitat preservation, has done research into Jain ethics and finds them a viable basis for a sustainable future.

Jainism is a momentous example to all of us that there can, and does, exist a successful, ecologically responsible way of life which is abundantly non-violent in thought, action and deed. We might misread our history, go forward confusedly to perpetrate other follies, but we will do so knowing that there is a viable alternative. ...

According to Jainism, animals will eventually be reborn as human animals, at which time they will have to choose: empathy, peace, compassion—*ahimsa*—or perpetual degrees of violence. Humanity is the launching site for this choice. We have it in our power to reverse an evolutionary masterplan that is brutal, that needs fixing. The Jains have modeled themselves after a vision of nature that favors peace and love over war and hatred, and they have envisioned—indeed, realized—a major world religion whose guiding tenet is this heartfelt aspiration. The reader is likely

---

9 *Ātman*—soul.
10 *Jñāna*—knowledge.
11 *Viśvamaitri*—universal friendship.

to stop here and declare, "But all religions—or certainly most of them—are about love. What's the big deal?" Jainism departs from this theoretical norm in one striking and all-important manner: it has never deviated from its original pledge. If we can understand how an ancient, seemingly uncomplicated ethical position can continue to flourish in a more complex modernity, we will have accomplished a critical hurdle. ...

Contrary to evolutionary expectation, the elephant, the gorilla, the rhino, the hippo, the megamouth shark (the largest shark in the world) are all vegetarians, in spite of their size and the human presumption that the mighty need meat ... Others will argue that they simply *crave* the taste of a hamburger once in a while. And since there's no law preventing it, and nobody's looking over their shoulder, they can afford to ignore their conscience for the few minutes that it takes to devour a fast-food lunch. Jains have analyzed those "few minutes" and worked out various meditations and disciplines to avoid such temptation. ... Killing, directly or indirectly, is the worst of all toxins. Not only does it kill a living being, but it inflicts enormous damage on one's own soul, which is the quintessence of all life. The soul itself, say the Jains, is not the one eating the hamburger. The soul is pure. But the physical body and its complex of desires and neuroses attach themselves to the soul, weaken it, obscure its nascent purity, and this process thickens with each needless moment of oblivion, until the soul is virtually snuffed out, mumbling in perdurable [eternal] darkness, with no one to hear it, and no hope of ever making beautiful music.

Those "few minutes" of psychological impasse, passion, disinterest, oblivion, appetite, are the same few moments that it takes to vent rage, to murder someone, to inflict every pain known to the human arsenal. Those few moments—repeated in so many variations—caused World War I—with its 20 million dead, 50 million injured; and nearly every other violent tantrum and disorder known to the brain. To temper that killer in man, and the subsequent killing fields, is to grope with those few moments where conflict begins.

Two minutes of unthinking, unfeeling behavior: Whether in the eating of a hamburger, the casting of a fishing line, or, more subtly, the habit of taking one's children to a circus to view animals who in fact have been reduced to insanity and pain. Two minutes of our own insanity, in the breeding of captive animals who were meant to be free, or worse—the abandoning of those pets to certain death; in the reining, or worse, the racing of horses; the killing of bugs in a frenzy of vindictiveness, as opposed to more patiently removing them without injury. The litany of transgressions cascades with numbing ubiquity. And it all comes down to the collaboration—mindful or not—with atrocity carried out by, or on behalf of, humans, and committed against other living creatures—whether around the dinner table, on the job, on the farm, the ranch, in the street, at the grocery store, in one's financial investments, in the donations one makes (many medical foundations, for example, put their charity dollars towards animal research—animal torture, in other words), in the clothes one wears, and so on. ...

Jains are accountable to nature, and thus to themselves, to their families, their community, and to the vast menageries of life forms which co-inhabit this planet with them. Jainism's accessible genius is this total embrace of the earth—so ancient, so contemporary. ...

Everyone I have ever known who has taken the time to learn about Jainism has become something of a Jain. I truly believe such conversion is unavoidable, not because the Jains teach anything we don't already intimately understand, at least in our hearts, but precisely because they remind us of our own first principles in such a way that we can no longer deny the urgency and beauty of such remembrance.

SOURCE: Michael Tobias, *Life Force: The World of Jainism*. Berkeley, CA: Asian Humanities Press, 1991, pp. 5–16

GLOSSARY

Ahimsa Principle of non-violence, based on reverence for all life.

Anekantavada The principle of manifold aspects, or the relativity of knowledge.

Canon The official list of books with authority in a religion, either because they are believed to be inspired or revealed, or have been so designated.

Digambara (atmosphere-clad) A nude Jain sect.

Five Jain Vows Non-violence, truthfulness, non-stealing, continence, and non-possessiveness.

Jiva Soul; every soul is potentially divine, and greatly influenced by karma.

Karma In Jainism, the cosmic moral law of consequences for ethical actions and their effects from prior incarnations; it appears as subtle particles that accumulate on the soul as a result of one's thoughts and actions, and is to be avoided by ascetic self-restraint.

Manifold aspects The multiplicity and relativity of all points of view, visible to perfected souls, promoting tolerance and non-violence.

Renunciation Reducing desires and minimizing consumption to free the soul from karmic entanglements and lessen earthly pollution.

Stoicism Impassive indifference to pleasure or pain (Greek word).

Svetambara (white-clad) A Jain sect that wears white clothing.

Syadvada The relativity of truth to different points of view.

Tirthankara (bridgebuilder) The 24 great enlightened Jain teachers.

HOLY DAYS

Most Jain festivals celebrate events in the lives of the Tirthankaras. Scriptures about their lives are read during the festivals.

Diwali For Jains, a celebration to commemorate Mahavira's attainment of liberation.

Paryushana The custom of wandering monks staying in one place during the rainy season, when they meditate and teach local Jain householders the principles of dharma.

Pratikramana A meditation for reflecting on one's spiritual journey and renewing the faith; it may be daily, monthly, or annual.

Samet Sikhar Yatra A popular pilgrimage to Samet Sikhar in Bihar, India, where 20 Tirthankaras attained nirvana.

HISTORICAL OUTLINE

c. 900 BCE—life of 22nd Tirthankara, Arishtameni, who renounced the cruelty of society to become a wandering ascetic

c. 900–800 BCE—life of 23rd Tirthankara, "Beloved Parshva," a saintly teacher for 70 years

c. 599–527 BCE—life of Mahavira, greatest Jain saint and 24th Tirthankara

c. 300 BCE—some *Agam Sutras* written down

after 300 BCE—division of Jains into Svetambara (white-clad) and Digambara (atmosphere-clad, i.e. naked) sects

c. 450 CE—division of Svetambaras and Digambaras formalized

1526–1818—new orders emerge under Muslim Mughal rule

1818 onward—Jain teaching spreads out from India

1970s–80s—Jain monks establish centers outside India

REVIEW QUESTIONS

1   Explain how Jains practice ahimsa, how it has influenced the wider world, and your opinion of its origin and effectiveness.
2   Contrast Western consumerism with Jain asceticism and evaluate each.
3   Does the Jain principle of manifold aspects of the relativity of truths have a place in religion, which usually stresses orthodoxy?

DISCUSSION QUESTIONS

1   What do you think would motivate a person to become a Jain monk or nun?
2   What three different reactions to Jains do you think would come from people of three major different personality or social types?
3   Do you think that the Jain religion is too passive and individualistic, or that it does have an impact in changing society?

INFORMATION RESOURCES

De Bary, W. Theodore. *Sources of Indian Tradition*. New York: Columbia University Press, 1958.

Dundas, Paul. "Jainism," in *Encyclopedia of Religion*, ed. Lindsay Jones. 2nd ed. Vol. 7, pp. 4764–72. New York: Macmillan, 2005.

Introduction to Jainism
<http://www.cs.colostate.edu/~malaiya/jainhlinks.html>

Jain concepts and stories
<http://www.umich.edu/~umjains>

Jain photographs
<http://www.jainworld.com/photos/index.asp>

Jain, Surender K., ed. *Glimpses of Jainism*. Delhi: Motilal Banarsidass, 1997.

Jain texts
<http://www.sacred-texts.com/jai/index.htm>

Jain Words Glossary
<http://www.cs.colostate.edu/~malaiya/jaingloss.html>

Kund-Kund, Acharya. *Barasa Anuvekkha*. 2nd ed. Delhi: Kund-Kund Bharati, 2003.

Müller, F. Max, and **Hermann Jacobi**, eds. *Jaina Sutras in Two Volumes: Sacred Books of the East Volumes 22 and 45*. Delhi: Low Price Publications, 1996.

Sangave, Vilas A. *Aspects of Jaina Religion*. Delhi: Bharatiya Jnanpith, 1990.

Shah, Unmakant, and **G. Ralph Strohl**. "Jainism," in *Encyclopedia Britannica*. Vol. 22, pp. 247–53. London, 1997.

Tobias, Michael. *Life Force: The World of Jainism*. Berkeley, CA: Asian Humanities Press, 1991.

CHAPTER 5

BUDDHISM

Siddhartha Gautama, it is told, was born prince of the Sakya clan in northeastern India, and probably lived 563–483 BCE. He renounced his comfortable life to seek the solution to suffering. He first sat with famous gurus, and practiced severe austerities, almost starving himself to death. Unsatisfied, he meditated, awakened to his true nature, then taught a "middle way" between luxury and austerity.

Having become a **Buddha**, or Awakened One, he taught a practical way of escaping from suffering and achieving liberation. Monks and then nuns whom he trained were organized into orders, and the teachings spread throughout Asia, south into Sri Lanka and southeast Asia, north into Tibet and China, and east into Korea and Japan. Two major historical traditions developed: the **Theravada** and the **Mahayana**. As Mahayana Buddhism spread across Asia, it branched into **Vajrayana** in Tibet, Chan and Pure Land (also called Mindfulness or Amita Buddhism) in China, and Shingon and Nichiren in Japan. Chan and Pure Land Buddhism later spread to Japan as **Zen** and Jodo Shinshu respectively. Soka Gakkai developed from Nichiren in the twentieth century. Some branches of Buddhism, such as Vajrayana, Zen, and Pure Land are growing in North America. Contemporary Buddhism, as it spreads across the globe, is strengthening an earlier theme: Engaged Buddhism.

To become a Buddhist is to adopt the Three Refuges: "I take refuge in the Buddha, the **dharma**, and the sangha [community of practicing Buddhists]." It is not the Buddha who saves. It is by living by the dharma which the Buddha taught that one achieves liberation from the continual painful round of births and deaths into the blissful state known as **nirvana**. The techniques for becoming conscious of the workings of the mind and for bringing it under control have become highly appealing to contemporary citizens of industrial societies who are seeking peace of mind.

Buddha taught the Four Noble Truths: (1) Life inevitably involves suffering; (2) Suffering originates in desires for transient things; (3) Suffering can be ceased by the eradication of desires; (4) The path to liberation from desires is the Eightfold Path: (a) Right understanding, (b) Right thoughts or motives, (c) Right speech, (d) Right action, (e) Right livelihood, (f) Right effort, (g) Right mindfulness, and (h) Right meditation. Buddhists may undertake a further set of basic obligations or precepts (*sila*): (1) Not harming living beings; (2) Not taking anything not given; (3) Not misusing sensual pleasures; (4) Not speaking falsely or abusively; (5) Not taking intoxicating drinks or drugs; (6) Not eating solid food after midday; (7) Not engaging in frivolous amusements; (8) Not adorning one's body; (9) Not sleeping in a high or luxurious place; and (10) Not being involved with money.

The Awakened One

Several elaborated traditional texts about the Buddha's life have been preserved and revered, notably the account told by Asvaghosha, who lived during the second century CE. In his Sanskrit epic *Buddhacarita*, or *Acts of the Buddha*, Asvaghosha shows a deep reverence for the Buddha.

The Birth of the Holy One from the *Buddhacarita* by Asvaghosha

According to the legend of the birth of the Holy One (Pusya), as in birth legends of Hindu figures, he did not take birth through the birth canal, but rather from another place—in this case, from his mother's side. This was one of his many births on earth.

8. In that glorious grove the queen perceived that the time of her delivery was at hand and, amidst the welcome of thousands of waiting-women, proceeded to a couch overspread with an awning.
9. Then as soon as Puṣya became propitious, from the side of the queen, who was hallowed by their vows, a son was born for the weal of the world, without her suffering either pain, or illness.
10. As was the birth of Aurva from the thigh, or Pṛthu from the hand, of Māndhātṛ, the peer of Indra, from the head, of Kakṣīvat from the armpit, on such wise was his birth.
11. When in due course he had issued from the womb, he appeared as if he had descended from the sky, for he did not come into the world through the portal of life; and, since he had purified his being through many æons, he was born not ignorant but fully conscious.

SOURCE: Asvaghosha, the *Buddhacarita*, trans. E. H. Johnston. Delhi: Motilal Banarsidass, 1936, Part II, Canto i, p. 3

The Prince's Perturbation from the *Buddhacarita* by Asvaghosha

After marrying and fathering children, the Holy One was protected from the harsh realities of the world by his royal father. But, according to traditional legends, one day the Prince ordered his driver to take him out for a ride during which he encountered old age, sickness, and death. This disturbed him greatly. The following extract describes his encounter with death.

53. Then the royal highway was decorated and guarded with especial care; and the king changed the charioteer and chariot and sent the prince off outside.
54. Then as the king's son was going along, those same gods fashioned a

lifeless man, so that only the charioteer and the prince, and none other, saw the corpse being borne along.

55. Thereon the king's son asked the charioteer, "Who is being carried along yonder by four men and followed by a dejected company? He is dressed out gorgeously and yet they bewail him."

56. Then the driver's mind was overcome by the pure-natured Śuddhādhivāsa gods and, though it should not have been told, he explained this matter to the lord of mankind:—

57. "This is someone or other, lying bereft of intellect, senses, breath and qualities, unconscious and become like a mere log or bundle of grass. He was brought up and cherished most lovingly with every care and now he is being abandoned."

58. Hearing the driver's reply, he was slightly startled and said, "Is this law of being peculiar to this man, or is such the end of all creatures?"

59. Then the driver said to him, "This is the last act for all creatures. Destruction is inevitable for all in the world, be he of low or middle or high degree."

60. Then, steadfast-minded though he was, the king's son suddenly became faint on hearing of death and, leaning with his shoulder against the top of the chariot rail, he said in a melodious voice:—

61. "This is the end appointed for all creatures, and yet the world throws off fear and takes no heed. Hardened, I ween, are men's hearts; for they are in good cheer, as they fare along the road."

SOURCE: Asvaghosha, the *Buddhacarita*, trans. E. H. Johnston. Delhi: Motilal Banarsidass, 1936, Part II, Canto iii, pp. 41–2

The Middle Way

from the *Sermon at Benares*, in the *Buddhacarita* by Asvaghosha

Disturbed by life's suffering, the Holy One, here called **Tathāgata**[1] left the palace where he had a pleasurable life, and undertook austerities and severe self-mortifications, in search of the truth of existence. Then he renounced both extremes. He taught this principle to his **bhikkhus** (monks) as the path to nirvana (*Nibbana* in Pali), or awakening to ultimate reality.

"The Tathāgata," the Buddha continued, "does not seek salvation in austerities, but neither does he for that reason indulge in worldly pleasures, nor live in abundance. The Tathāgata has found the middle path.

"There are two extremes, O bhikkhus, which the man who has given up the world ought not to follow—the habitual practice, on the one hand, of self-indulgence which is unworthy, vain and fit only for the worldly-minded—and the habitual practice, on the other hand, of self-mortification, which is painful, useless and unprofitable.

1 Tathāgata—("thus come" or "transcendent one") one who has realized the truth.

"Neither abstinence from fish or flesh, nor going naked, nor shaving the head, not wearing matted hair, nor dressing in a rough garment, nor covering oneself with dirt, nor sacrificing to Agni, will cleanse a man who is not free from delusions.

"Reading the Vedas, making offerings to priests, or sacrifices to the gods, self-mortification by heat or cold, and many such penances performed for the sake of immortality, these do not cleanse the man who is not free from delusions.

"Anger, drunkenness, obstinacy, bigotry, deception, envy, self-praise, disparaging others, superciliousness and evil intentions constitute uncleanness; not verily the eating of flesh.

"A middle path, O bhikkhus, avoiding the two extremes, has been discovered by the Tathāgata—a path which opens the eyes, and bestows understanding, which leads to peace of mind, to the higher wisdom, to full enlightenment, to Nirvāna!

"What is the middle path, O bhikkhus, avoiding these two extremes, discovered by the Tathāgata—that path which opens the eyes, and bestows understanding, which leads to peace of mind, to the higher wisdom, to full enlightenment, to Nirvāna?

"Let me teach you, O bhikkhus, the middle path, which keeps aloof from both extremes. By suffering, the emaciated devotee produces confusion and sickly thoughts in his mind. Mortification is not conducive even to worldly knowledge; how much less to a triumph over the senses!

"He who fills his lamp with water will not dispel the darkness, and he who tries to light a fire with rotten wood will fail. And how can any one be free from self by leading a wretched life, if he does not succeed in quenching the fires of lust, if he still hankers after either worldly or heavenly pleasures. But he in whom self has become extinct is free from lust; he will desire neither worldly nor heavenly pleasures, and the satisfaction of his natural wants will not defile him. However, let him be moderate, let him eat and drink according to the needs of the body.

"Sensuality is enervating; the self-indulgent man is a slave to his passions, and pleasure-seeking is degrading and vulgar.

"But to satisfy the necessities of life is not evil. To keep the body in good health is a duty, for otherwise we shall not be able to trim the lamp of wisdom, and keep our mind strong and clear. Water surrounds the lotus-flower, but does not wet its petals.

"This is the middle path, O bhikkhus, that keeps aloof from both extremes."

SOURCE: Lin Yutang, ed. *The Wisdom of China and India*. New York: Modern Library, 1942, pp. 359–60

Speculations Undeclared from the *Culamalunkya Sutta*

One of the Buddha's most notable teachings was his practical rejection of most metaphysical speculation. In this passage from the *Culamalunkya Sutta*, he teaches

Mālunkyāputta, a disciple, that efforts to answer speculative questions such as whether the world is eternal are fruitless. They are like a man shot with an arrow who refuses to allow medical treatment until he is told the social caste of his attacker, his name, his size, his skin color, his home town, and the details of his weapon. Before he learned all this, he would die. The Buddha left such speculative metaphysics undeclared because they do not lead to the direct meditative experience of enlightenment that overcomes suffering.

Thus have I heard. On one occasion the Blessed One was living at Sāvatthī in Jeta's Grove, Anāthapindika's Park.

Then, while the venerable Mālunkyāputta was alone in meditation, the following thought arose in his mind:

"These speculative views have been undeclared by the Blessed One, set aside and rejected by him, namely: 'the world is eternal' and 'the world is not eternal'; 'the world is finite' and 'the world is infinite'; 'the soul is the same as the body' and 'the soul is one thing and the body another'; and 'after death a Tathāgata exists' and 'after death a Tathāgata does not exist' and 'after death a Tathāgata both exists and does not exist' and 'after death a Tathāgata neither exists nor does not exist.' The Blessed One does not declare these to me, and I do not approve of and accept the fact that he does not declare these to me, so I shall go to the Blessed One and ask him the meaning of this." ...

"Suppose, Mālunkyāputta, a man were wounded by an arrow thickly smeared with poison, and his friends and companions, his kinsmen and relatives, brought a surgeon to treat him. The man would say: 'I will not let the surgeon pull out this arrow until I know whether the man who wounded me was a noble or a brahmin or a merchant or a worker.' And he would say: 'I will not let the surgeon pull out this arrow until I know the name and clan of the man who wounded me; ... until I know whether the man who wounded me was tall or short or of middle height; ... until I know whether the man who wounded me was dark or brown or golden-skinned; ... until I know whether the man who wounded me lives in such a village or town or city; ... until I know whether the bow that wounded me was a long bow or a crossbow; ... until I know whether the bowstring that wounded me was fibre or reed or sinew or hemp or bark; ... until I know whether the shaft that wounded me was wild or cultivated; ... until I know with what kind of feathers the shaft that wounded me was fitted—whether those of a vulture or a crow or a hawk or a peacock or a stork; ...

"All this would still not be known to that man and meanwhile he would die. ...

"Mālunkyāputta, if there is the view 'the world is eternal,' the holy life cannot be lived; and if there is the view 'the world is not eternal,' the holy life cannot be lived. Whether there is the view 'the world is eternal' or the view 'the world is not eternal,' there is birth, there is ageing, there is death, there are sorrow, lamentation, pain, grief, and despair, the destruction of which I prescribe here and now. ...

"Therefore, Mālunkyāputta, remember what I have left undeclared as undeclared, and remember what I have declared as declared. And what have I left undeclared? 'The world is eternal'—I have left undeclared. 'The world is not eternal'—I have left undeclared. 'The world is finite'—I have left undeclared. 'The world is infinite'—I have left undeclared. 'The soul is the same as the body'—I have left undeclared. 'The soul is one thing and the body another'—I have left undeclared. 'After death a Tathāgata exists'—I have left undeclared. 'After death a Tathāgata does not exist'—I have left undeclared. 'After death a Tathāgata both exists and does not exist'—I have left undeclared. 'After death a Tathāgata neither exists nor does not exist'—I have left undeclared.

"Why have I left that undeclared? Because it is unbeneficial, it does not belong to the fundamentals of the holy life, it does not lead to disenchantment, to dispassion, to cessation, to peace, to direct knowledge, to enlightenment, to Nibbāna.[2] That is why I have left it undeclared.

"And what have I declared? 'This is suffering'—I have declared. 'This is the origin of suffering'—I have declared. 'This is the cessation of suffering'— I have declared. 'This is the way leading to the cessation of suffering'— I have declared.

"Why have I declared that? Because it is beneficial, it belongs to the fundamentals of the holy life, it leads to disenchantment, to dispassion, to cessation, to peace, to direct knowledge, to enlightenment, to Nibbāna. That is why I have declared it.

"Therefore, Mālunkyāputta, remember what I have left undeclared as undeclared, and remember what I have declared as declared."

That is what the Blessed One said. The venerable Mālunkyāputta was satisfied and delighted in the Blessed One's words.

SOURCE: *The Middle Length Discourses of the Buddha*, original translation by Bhikkhu Nānamoli, translation edited and revised by Bhikkhu Bodhi. Boston, MA: Wisdom Publications, 1995, pp. 533–6

Mindful Breathing   from the *Anapanasati Sutta* 118

In meditation a basic focus is on breathing. This helps free the mind from ordinary distractions and move the person meditating into a deeper awareness of existence, contemplating enlightening themes, such as impermanence and relinquishment.

(Mindfulness of breathing)

15. "Bhikkhus, when mindfulness of breathing is developed and cultivated, it is of great fruit and great benefits. When mindfulness of breathing is developed and cultivated, it fulfils the four foundations of mindfulness. When the four foundations of mindfulness are developed and cultivated, they fulfil the seven enlightenment factors. When the seven enlightenment factors are developed and cultivated, they fulfil true knowledge and deliverance.

2 Nibbāna—nirvana.

16. "And how, bhikkhus, is mindfulness of breathing developed and cultivated, so that it is of great fruit and great benefit?

17. "Here a bhikkhu, gone to the forest or to the root of a tree or to an empty hut, sits down; having folded his legs crosswise, set his body erect, and established mindfulness in front of him, ever mindful he breathes in, mindful he breathes out.

18. "... He trains thus: 'I shall breathe in tranquillising the bodily formation'; he trains thus, 'I shall breathe out tranquillising the bodily formation.'

19. "... He trains thus: 'I shall breathe in experiencing pleasure'; he trains thus: 'I shall breathe out experiencing pleasure.' He trains thus: 'I shall breathe in experiencing the mental formation'; he trains thus: 'I shall breathe out experiencing the mental formation.' He trains thus: 'I shall breathe in tranquillising the mental formation'; he trains thus: 'I shall breathe out transquillising the mental formation.'

20. "He trains thus: 'I shall breathe in experiencing the mind'; he trains thus, 'I shall breathe out experiencing the mind.' He trains thus: 'I shall breathe in gladdening the mind'; he trains thus: 'I shall breathe out gladdening the mind.' He trains thus: 'I shall breathe in concentrating the mind'; he trains thus: 'I shall breathe out concentrating the mind.'

21. "He trains thus: 'I shall breathe in contemplating impermanence'; he trains thus: 'I shall breathe out contemplating impermanence.' ...

22. "Bhikkhus, that is how mindfulness of breathing is developed and cultivated, so that is of great fruit and great benefit.'"

SOURCE: *The Middle Length Discourses of the Buddha*, original translation by Bhikkhu Nānamoli, translation edited and revised by Bhikkhu Bodhi. Boston, MA: Wisdom Publications, 1995, pp. 943–4

Theravada

The Theravada (Teaching of the Elders) traditions are the traditions of Buddhism as it spread south, to Sri Lanka (largely in the third century CE), then to southeast Asia, to regions now called Myanmar, Malaysia, Indonesia, and Cambodia (eleventh to fourteenth centuries). Theravada adheres to early scriptures (suttas) and monastic renunciation. Its texts are drawn from the Pali **Canon**, recorded in Sri Lanka as early as the first century BCE. Theravadan meditation emphasizes stages of attainment and mindfulness or **Vipassana** (insight) meditation. The ideal Buddhist is the arhat, a monk (*bhikkhu*) taking refuge in the Buddha, an accomplished ascetic who attains nirvana through self-effort.

The Dhammapada (verses by the Buddha)

The *Dhammapada* (Teaching of the Verses) is a collection of 423 key Buddhist verses of wide influence and importance. Teachers are often expected to conclude a discourse with a key verse (*gatha*), and this text is a collection of such verses.

It urges a life of peace and non-violence, and teaches that hatred can never be overcome by hatred, only by kindness. **Karmic** consequences follow from all actions, and actions follow naturally from thoughts. This extract emphasizes the importance of restraint and awakening to transcendence, rather than resorting simply to a life of seclusion. The texts are recorded in Pali, Tibetan, Chinese, and other languages.

Better than a thousand utterances, comprising useless words, is one
    single beneficial word, by hearing which, one attains peace. ...
Though one should conquer a thousand times a thousand men in battle,
    he who conquers his own self, is the greatest of all conquerors. ...
Ah, happily do we live without hate amongst the hateful; amidst
    hateful men we dwell unhating.
Ah, happily do we live in good health amongst the ailing; amidst
    ailing men we dwell in good health (free from the disease of
    passions).
Ah, happily do we live without yearning (for sensual pleasures)
    amongst those who yearn (for them); amidst those who yearn (for
    them) we dwell without yearning.
Ah, happily do we live, we who have no impediments. Feeders of joy
    shall we be even as the gods of the Radiant Realm.
Victory breeds hatred. The defeated live in pain. Happily the peaceful
    live, giving up victory and defeat.
There is no fire like lust, no crime like hate. There is no ill like the body,
    no bliss higher than Peace (Nibbana).
Hunger is the greatest disease. Aggregates are the greatest ill. Knowing
    this as it really is (the wise realize) Nibbana, bliss supreme.
Good health is the highest gain. Contentment is the greatest wealth.
    Trustworthy ones are the best kinsmen. Nibbana is the highest Bliss.
Having tasted the flavour of seclusion and the flavour of appeasement,
    free from anguish and stain becomes he, imbibing the taste of the
    joy of the Dhamma.
Happy is one, who beholds the holy ones. To live with the holy ones is
    ever pleasant. It would be pleasant if one never comes across a fool.
Truly, he who moves in company with fools grieves for a long time.
    Association with the foolish is ever painful as with a foe. Happy is
    association with the wise, even like meeting with kinsfolk.
Therefore: With the intelligent, the wise, the learned, the enduring,
    the dutiful and the Ariya[3]—with a man of such virtue and intellect
    should one associate, as the moon (follows) the starry path.

SOURCE: "The Thousands" and "Happiness," in *Dhammapada*, verses 100, 103, 197–208
<http://www.pathofdhamma.com/index.html>

3 Ariya Buddhism—a path of liberation from the human condition using spiritual concentration and intellectual catharsis, following the earliest teachings of the Buddha.

Rejection of Birth Castes   from the *Vasettha Sutta*

When the Buddha was living, there were several religious movements in India that arose out of dissatisfaction with the external religious formalities and the rigid social implications of the Hindu brahmanic caste system. Some protested against this system by becoming wandering ascetics. The Hindu Upanishads literature grew out of this movement, emphasizing renunciation and transcendental knowledge, rather than ritual and caste. In northeastern India, less influenced by the brahmanic traditions, arose several non-orthodox sects, including Buddhism. This extract, from the *Vasettha Sutta*, is a Buddhist statement rejecting the belief that one is born into one's social caste, and affirming that one's merit is determined by one's actions.

> One is not a brahmin by birth,
> Nor by birth a non-brahmin.
> By action is one a brahmin,
> By action is one a non-brahmin.
>
> For men are farmers by their acts,
> And by their acts are craftsmen too;
> And men are merchants by their acts,
> And by their acts are servants too.
>
> And men are robbers by their acts,
> And by their acts are soldiers too;
> And men are chaplains by their acts,
> And by their acts are rulers too.

SOURCE: *The Middle Length Discourses of the Buddha*, original translation by Bhikkhu Nānamoli, translation edited and revised by Bhikkhu Bodhi. Boston, MA: Wisdom Publications, 1995, p. 806

Mahayana

Mahayana (Large Vehicle) Buddhism is most prominent in Tibet, Mongolia, China, Korea, Vietnam, and Japan. The Mahayana dharma (teaching) emphasizes one's inherent wisdom and compassion for all sentient beings. The ideal practitioner (**bodhisattva**) honors the Pali Canon, yet delays his/her own nirvana in the effort to liberate other beings. Mahayana texts (**sutras**) emphasize the Buddha-nature (Buddhata) in all things and the importance of direct experience. The Buddha is not seen primarily as a historical person, as in Theravada, but is now conceived rather as a universal principle, a cosmic presence. Images of this Buddha-nature are common, although they are not to be conceived of as divinities. Two widespread bodhisattvas expressing compassion and mercy are Avalokiteshvara (masculine) and Guanyin (feminine). Mahayana dharma also teaches the emptiness of all things, in paradoxical language meant to take the mind beyond ordinary thought.

The Heart Sutra

The *Heart Sutra* comes from the Indian Prajnaparamita literature, about 350 CE, and is often chanted in Buddhist ceremonies. It distills the teachings on emptiness. The goal is to become a bodhisattva, seeking complete understanding, and dedicated to serving others by skillful means. Simultaneously, the realization is that there is no such thing as a bodhisattva, understanding, dedication, or attainment. To realize this emptiness is to approach perfection of wisdom.

Homage to the Perfection of Wisdom, the lovely, the holy!

Avalokita [Avalokiteshvara, a form of the Buddha emphasizing compassion], the holy Lord and Bodhisattva, was moving in the deep course of the wisdom which has gone beyond. He looked down from on high, he beheld but five heaps [aggregates], and he saw that in their own-being they were empty.

Here, O Sariputra [one of the Buddha's two principal followers], form is emptiness, and the very emptiness is form; emptiness does not differ from form, form does not differ from emptiness; whatever is form, that is emptiness, whatever is emptiness, that is form. The same is true of feelings, perceptions, impulses and consciousness.

Here, O Sariputra, all dharmas are marked with emptiness; they are not produced or stopped, not defiled or immaculate, not deficient or complete.

Therefore, O Sariputra, in emptiness there is no form, nor feeling, nor perception, nor impulse, nor consciousness; no eye, ear, nose, tongue, body, mind; no forms, sounds, smells, tastes, touchables or objects of mind; no sight-organ-element, and so forth until we come to: no mind-consciousness-element; there is no ignorance, no extinction of ignorance, and so forth until we come to: there is no decay and death, no extinction of decay and death; there is no suffering, no origination, no stopping, no path; there is no cognition, no attainment, and no non-attainment.

Therefore, O Sariputra, it is because of his indifference to any kind of personal attainment that a Bodhisattva, through having relied on the perfection of wisdom, dwells without thought-coverings. In the absence of thought-coverings he has not been made to tremble, he has overcome what can upset, and in the end he attains to Nirvana. All those who appear as Buddhas in the three periods of time fully awake to the utmost, right and perfect enlightenment because they have relied on the perfection of wisdom.

Therefore one should know the Prajnaparamita as the great spell, the spell of great knowledge, the utmost spell, the unequalled spell, allayer of all suffering, in truth—for what could go wrong? By the Prajnaparamita has this spell been delivered. It runs like this: *Gate! Gate! Paragate! Parasamgate! Bodhi Svaha!* (Gone! Gone! Gone beyond! Gone altogether beyond! O what an awakening!) All Hail! This completes the Heart of Perfect Wisdom.

SOURCE: *Buddhist Scriptures*, trans. Edward Conze. Harmondsworth, Middlesex: Penguin Books, 1986, pp. 162–4

Discovering Universal Emptiness by Dogen

Dogen was a major Japanese Buddhist Zen master who lived 1200–53 in Kyoto and had a major influence on Zen. Orphaned at age seven, he joined a monastery at thirteen, then traveled to China, where Chan is practiced (see page 175), returned to Japan and founded the Soto Zen sect and the still-active Eiheiji temple. He struggled with questions such as whether enlightenment is gradual or instantaneous, and concluded that in all zazen (sitting meditation) one is in the midst of realizing Buddha-nature. Some said all things have the Buddha-nature, but he said that all things are the Buddha-nature, although this realization remains dormant until awakened in Buddhist practice. Zazen is the practice of non-thinking, which goes beyond ideas of good or bad, enlightenment or illusion, because universal emptiness is as close as your nose.

When we reflect upon our experience and practice of zazen we actualize the life of the Buddhas and Patriarchs and receive their right transmission which has been handed down from generation to generation. Our subject today is universal emptiness—the universal emptiness that is in our entire body, skin, flesh, bones and marrow. Universal emptiness has numerous meanings and interpretations—the 20 kinds, the 84,000 kinds and so on—[and if you can define it properly you can be said to be a Buddha or Patriarch].

Zen Master Shakyō Ezō once asked Zen Master Seidō Chizō, who was Shakyō's senior, "Do you know how to comprehend universal emptiness?" "Of course," Seidō answered. "How?" Shakyō wanted to know. Seidō grasped a handful of air. "Aha! You don't know how to grasp it then!" Shakyō exclaimed. Seidō challenged Shakyō to show him universal emptiness. Shakyō grabbed Seidō's nose and yanked it until he cried out in pain. "Now I've got it!" Seidō said. "Yes, now you know what it is," Shakyō agreed.

The purpose of Shakyō's initial question was to find whether or not our entire body is hands and eyes [i.e., universal emptiness]. Seidō's "Of course" was a defilement of Buddhism. To say you understand universal emptiness is to defile the truth—universal emptiness falls to the earth. When Shakyō asked Seidō how he understood universal emptiness he was asking him to show the "suchness" of universal emptiness; that is, show the true state of reality. However, we must be careful about this since circumstances are constantly changing the form of "suchness." When Seidō grabbed a handful of air it revealed that he understood only the head, but not the tail, of universal emptiness. Shakyō then saw that Seidō's understanding was limited and he could not even dream about universal emptiness. It was too profound and absolute for him. Therefore, Seidō asked Shakyō to show him universal emptiness. Half of the answer was already contained in Seidō's request but he had to discover the rest by himself. Shakyō grabbed his nose; he hid in Seidō's nostril so to speak. At that time universal emptiness in the form of Seidō and universal emptiness in the form of Shakyō were united and only universal emptiness remained. Prior to having his nose yanked Seidō thought that universal emptiness existed outside himself, but now he has cast off body and mind. Yet you must be careful not to cling to such a discovery of universal emptiness—do not defile yourself but practice within your own universal emptiness. Shakyō confirmed Seidō's understanding but did not try to grasp universal emptiness with his hands—universal emptiness cannot be grasped with our hands. After all, the entire world is universal emptiness; there is absolutely no room for doubt. We can now see why this koan[4] is so famous.

SOURCE: Dogen Zenji, *Shobogenzo (The Eye and Treasury of the True Law)*, trans. Kosen Nishiyama and John Stevens. Sendai, Japan: Daihokkaikaku, 1975, vol. 1, pp. 130–1

Zen and Koans   by Daisetz T. Suzuki

D. T. Suzuki (1870–1966), a major early popularizer of Zen in the United States, taught Buddhist philosophy in Kyoto, Japan. He began Zen training at age 22, then spent 13 years in the United States, translating and writing about Zen. He spoke to Westerners in the language of ego ("we are too ego-centered"), love (which gives us "a glimpse into the infinity of things"), and tragedy ("God gives tragedies to perfect man"), as we can see in the first part of the extract below. In the second part, Suzuki discusses the classic method of learning by the Zen koan, a riddle given to a student by a Zen master. Classic koans are "What is the sound of one hand clapping?" or "Show me your face before you were born." Such a riddle may create a frustrating crisis for the student, but the Master strives to guide one past the merely intellectual answer into the Buddha-mind (see page 22).

We are too ego-centered. The ego-shell in which we live is the hardest thing to outgrow. We seem to carry it all the time from childhood up to the time we finally pass away. We are, however, given many chances to break through this shell, and the first and greatest of them is when we reach adolescence. This is the first time the ego really comes to recognize the "other." I mean the awakening of sexual love. An ego, entire and undivided, now begins to feel a sort of split in itself. Love hitherto dormant deep in his heart lifts its head and causes a great commotion in it. For the love now stirred demands at once the assertion of the ego and its annihilation. Love makes the ego lose itself in the object it loves, and yet at the same time it wants to have the object as its own. This is a contradiction, and a great tragedy of life. This elemental feeling must be one of the divine agencies whereby man is urged to advance in his upward walk. God gives tragedies to perfect man. The greatest bulk of literature ever produced in this world is but the harping on the same string of love, and we never seem to grow weary of it. But this is not the topic we are concerned with here. What I want to emphasize in this connection is this: that through the awakening of love we get a glimpse into the infinity of things, and that this glimpse urges

4 Koan—a paradoxical riddle in Zen training, challenging the student to break through conventional thought.

youth to Romanticism or to Rationalism according to his temperament and environment and education.

When the ego-shell is broken and the "other" is taken into its own body, we can say that the ego has denied itself or that the ego has taken its first steps towards the infinite. Religiously, here ensues an intense struggle between the finite and the infinite, between the intellect and a higher power, or, more plainly, between the flesh and the spirit. ...

What is a koan? A koan, according to one authority, means "a public document setting up a standard of judgment," whereby one's Zen understanding is tested as to its correctness. A koan is generally some statement made by an old Zen master, or some answer of his given to a questioner. The following are some that are commonly given to the uninitiated:

1   A monk asked Tung-shan [**Pinyin**, Dong Shan],[5] "Who is the Buddha?" "Three *chin* [Pinyin, *jin*] of flax."
2   Yun-men [Pinyin, Yunmen] was once asked, "When not a thought is stirring in one's mind, is there any error here?" "As much as Mount Sumeru."
3   Chao-chou [Pinyin, Zhaozhou] answered, "*Wu!*" (*mu* in Japanese) to a monk's question, "Is there Buddha-nature in a dog?" *Wu* literally means "not" or "none," but when this is ordinarily given as a koan, it has no reference to its literal signification; it is "*Wu*" pure and simple.
4   When Ming the monk overtook the fugitive Hui-neng [Pinyin, Huineng], he wanted Hui-neng to give up the secret of Zen. Hui-neng replied, "What are your original features which you have even prior to your birth?"
5   A monk asked Chao-chou, "What is the meaning of the First Patriarch's visit to China?" "The cypress tree in the front courtyard."
6   When Chao-chou came to study Zen under Nan-ch'uan [Pinyin, Nanquan], he asked, "What is the Tao [Pinyin, Dao] (or the Way)?" Nan-ch'uan replied, "Your everyday mind, that is the Tao."
7   A monk asked, "All things are said to be reducible to the One, but where is the One to be reduced?" Chao-chou answered, "When I was in the district of Ch'ing [Pinyin, Qing] I had a robe made that weighed seven *chin*."
8   When P'ang [Pinyin, Pang] the old Zen adept first came to Ma-tsu [Pinyin, Mazu] in order to master Zen, he asked, "Who is he who has no companion among the ten thousand things of the world?" Ma-tsu replied, "When you swallow up in one draught all the water in the Hsi Ch'iang [Pinyin, Xi Qiang], I will tell you."

---

5 Pinyin is the contemporary system of transliterating Chinese, replacing the earlier Wade-Giles system used in various extracts in this book. Within extracts we have indicated the Pinyin spelling in brackets at first occurrence; in other parts of the text Pinyin is used as the norm, with Wade-Giles shown once in parentheses so readers can recognize both forms of each word.

When such problems are given to the uninitiated for solution, what is the object of the master? The idea is to unfold the Zen psychology in the mind of the uninitiated, and to reproduce the state of consciousness, of which these statements are the expression. That is to say, when the koans are understood the master's state of mind is understood, which is *satori*[6] and without which Zen is a sealed book.

In the beginning of Zen history a question was brought up by the pupil to the notice of the master, who thereby gauged the mental state of the questioner and knew what necessary help to give him. The help thus given was sometimes enough to awaken him to realization, but more frequently than not puzzled and perplexed him beyond description, and the result was an ever-increasing mental strain or "searching and contriving" on the part of the pupil, of which we have already spoken in the foregoing pages. In actual cases, however, the master would have to wait for a long while for the pupil's first question, if it were coming at all. To ask the first question means more than half the way to its own solution, for it is the outcome of a most intense mental effort for the questioner to bring his mind to a crisis. The question indicates that the crisis is reached and the mind is ready to leave it behind. An experienced master often knows how to lead the pupil to a crisis and to make him successfully pass it. ...

The worst enemy of Zen experience, at least in the beginning, is the intellect, which consists and insists in discriminating subject from object. The discriminating intellect, therefore, must be cut short if Zen consciousness is to unfold itself, and the koan is constructed eminently to serve this end.

SOURCE: D. T. Suzuki, *Zen Buddhism*, ed. William Barrett. New York: Doubleday, 1956, pp. 6–7, 134–7

Nothing to Do with Rules by Bankei

In a radical form Buddhism challenges one to live so fully from the Buddha-mind that rules and precepts would not be necessary to guide behavior. A sense of rightness would so naturally flow that externally imposed rules would be superfluous. This is the view articulated here by the seventeenth-century Zen master Bankei (1622–93). Zen was becoming overly formalized in Japan in his time, so he insisted on spontaneity and such a clear everyday awareness of the Unborn Buddha Mind that precepts (the basic obligations undertaken by Buddhists) would be dispensable. In the West this view is echoed by Augustine's saying "Love and do what you will."

A certain master of the Precepts School asked: "Doesn't your Reverence observe the precepts?"

The Master said: "Originally, what people call the precepts were all for wicked monks who broke the rules; for the man who abides in the Unborn Buddha Mind, there's no need for precepts. The precepts were taught to help sentient beings—they weren't taught to help buddhas! What everyone has

6 *Satori*—awakening, or enlightenment.

from his parents innately is the Unborn Buddha Mind alone, so abide in the Unborn Buddha Mind. When you abide in the Unborn Buddha Mind, you're a living buddha here today, and that living buddha certainly isn't going to concoct anything like taking the precepts, so there aren't any precepts for him to take. To concoct anything like taking the precepts is not what's meant by the Unborn Buddha Mind. When you abide in the Unborn Buddha Mind, there's no way you can violate the precepts. From the standpoint of the Unborn, the precepts too are secondary, peripheral concerns; in the place of the Unborn, there's really no such thing as precepts."

SOURCE: *Bankei Zen: Translations from the Record of Bankei*, trans. Peter Haskel. New York: Grove Press, 1984, p. 7

Vajrayana

Vajrayana (Diamond Vehicle) Buddhism began in India, perhaps in Nagarjuna's time, and spread to Tibet. It encourages students to learn from both Theravada and Mahayana principles, then study Vajrayana. This school teaches that emptiness (**sunyata**) is complemented by the compassion of the bodhisattva (*karuna*), and also that the wisdom (prajna) of emptiness has an indestructible, diamond (vajra) quality that cuts through dualistic illusions. Compassion is the dynamic means (*upaya*) of acting in the world. Enlightenment emerges when wisdom and compassion are experientially discovered to be one. Further, physical-mental processes can also become vehicles for enlightenment. This approach is related to Hindu Tantric[7] ritual practices, and requires guidance from a compassionate teacher (lama). Rich in artistry, Vajrayana uses images of divinities, mudras (meditative gestures and postures), mantras (sacred syllables and phrases), and mandalas (sacred circular designs) as aids to meditation.

Love, Kindness, and Universal Responsibility
by the Dalai Lama

Many Tibetan Buddhists were forced into exile due to the communist Chinese takeover of Tibet in 1950. Some settled in Dharamsala, India, or Nepal. Others have spread Buddhism abroad with new monasteries in many countries. The current leader of Tibetan Buddhism, the Dalai Lama Tenzin Gyatso, has become a global spokesman for Vajrayana Buddhism. He has spoken with such peaceful integrity and wisdom that he was awarded a Nobel Peace Prize in 1989 for his adherence to Buddhist non-violence in the struggle with China. This is an extract from his Nobel Prize acceptance speech. He speaks of the dangers of the population and environmental crises, consumerism, religious intolerance, and the need for non-violence and compassion. In exile, he has attempted to shift his culture from a theocratic to a democratic government. A leader forcefully exiled from his country,

7 Tantra—esoteric spiritual practices of India, often involving emphasis on the feminine aspect of divinity.

still he inspires many by translating Buddhist principles of compassion and patience into contemporary application.

I believe that every individual has a responsibility to help guide our global family in the right direction. Good wishes alone are not enough; we have to assume responsibility. ...

[In our era] we find that the world has grown smaller and the world's people have become almost one community. Political and military alliances have created large multinational groups, industry and international trade have produced a global economy, and worldwide communications are eliminating ancient barriers of distance, language and race. We are also being drawn together by the grave problems we face: over-population, dwindling natural resources and an environmental crisis that threatens our air, water and trees, along with the vast number of beautiful life forms that are the very foundation of existence on this small planet we share.

I believe that to meet the challenge of our times, human beings will have to develop a greater sense of universal responsibility. Each of us must learn to work not just for his or her own self, family or nation, but for the benefit of all mankind. Universal responsibility is the real key to human survival. It is the best foundation for world peace, the equitable use of natural resources, and through concern for future generations, the proper care of the environment. ...

Whether we like it or not, we have all been born on this earth as part of one great human family. Rich or poor, educated or uneducated, belonging to one nation or another, to one religion or another, adhering to this ideology or that, ultimately each of us is just a human being like everyone else: we all desire happiness and do not want suffering. Furthermore, each of us has an equal right to pursue these goals.

Today's world requires that we accept the oneness of humanity. In the past, isolated communities could afford to think of one another as fundamentally separate and even existed in total isolation. Nowadays, however, events in one part of the world eventually affect the entire planet. Therefore we have to treat each major local problem as a global concern from the moment it begins. We can no longer invoke the national, racial or ideological barriers that separate us without destructive repercussion. In the context of our new interdependence, considering the interests of others is clearly the best form of self-interest.

I view this fact as a source of hope. The necessity for cooperation can only strengthen mankind, because it helps us recognize that the most secure foundation for the new world order is not simply broader political and economic alliances, but rather each individual's genuine practice of love and compassion. For a better, happier, more stable and civilized future, each of us must develop a sincere, warm-hearted feeling of brother- and sisterhood. ...

I believe that despite the rapid advances made by civilization in this century, the most immediate cause of our present dilemma is our undue emphasis on material development alone. We have become so engrossed in its pursuit that, without even knowing it, we have neglected to foster the most basic human needs of love, kindness, cooperation and caring. If we do not know someone or find another reason for not feeling connected with a particular individual or group, we simply ignore them. But the development of human society is based entirely on people helping each other. Once we have lost the essential humanity that is our foundation, what is the point of pursuing only material improvement?. ...

In particular, a tremendous effort will be required to bring compassion into the realm of international business. Economic inequality, especially that between developed and developing nations, remains the greatest source of suffering on this planet. Even though they will lose money in the short term, large multinational corporations must curtail their exploitation of poor nations. Tapping the few precious resources such countries possess simply to fuel consumerism in the developed world is disastrous; if it continues unchecked, eventually we shall all suffer. Strengthening weak, undiversified economies is a far wiser policy for promoting both political and economic stability. As idealistic as it may sound, altruism, not just competition and the desire for wealth, should be a driving force in business. ...

One religion, like a single type of food, cannot satisfy everybody. According to their varying mental dispositions, some people benefit from one kind of teaching, others from another. Each faith has the ability to produce fine, warmhearted people and all religions have succeeded in doing so, despite their espousal of often contradictory philosophies. Thus there is no reason to engage in divisive religious bigotry and intolerance and every reason to cherish and respect all forms of spiritual practice. ...

Throughout history, mankind has pursued peace one way or another. Is it too optimistic to imagine that world peace may finally be within our grasp? I do not believe that there has been an increase in the amount of people's hatred, only in their ability to manifest it in vastly destructive weapons. On the other hand, bearing witness to the tragic evidence of the mass slaughter caused by such weapons in our [era] has given us the opportunity to control war. To do so, it is clear we must disarm.

Disarmament can occur only within the context of new political and economic relationships. Before we consider this issue in detail, it is worth imagining the kind of peace process from which we would benefit most. This is fairly self-evident. First we should work on eliminating nuclear weapons, next, biological and chemical ones, then offensive arms, and, finally, defensive ones. At the same time, to safeguard the peace, we should start developing in one or more global regions an international police force made up of an equal number of members from each nation under a collective command. Eventually this force would cover the whole world. ...

Our planet is blessed with vast, natural treasures. If we use them properly, beginning with the elimination of militarism and war, truly, every human being will be able to live a wealthy, well-cared-for life. ...

I believe that the very process of dialogue, moderation and compromise involved in building a community of Asian states would itself give real hope of peaceful evolution to a new order in China. From the very start, the member states of such a community might agree to decide its defense and international relations policies together. There would be many opportunities for cooperation. The critical point is that we find a peaceful, nonviolent way for the forces of freedom, democracy and moderation to emerge successfully from the current atmosphere of unjust repression. ...

I see Tibet's role in such an Asian Community as what I have previously called a "Zone of Peace": a neutral, demilitarized sanctuary where weapons are forbidden and the people live in harmony with nature. This is not merely a dream—it is precisely the way Tibetans tried to live for over a thousand years before our country was invaded. ...

Another hopeful development is the growing compatibility between science and religion. Throughout the nineteenth century and for much of our [era], people have been profoundly confused by the conflict between these apparently contradictory world views. Today, physics, biology and psychology have reached such sophisticated levels that many researchers are starting to ask the most profound questions about the ultimate nature of the universe and life, the same questions that are of prime interest to religions. Thus there is real potential for a more unified view. In particular, it seems that a new concept of mind and matter is emerging. The East has been more concerned with understanding the mind, the West with understanding matter. Now that the two have met, these spiritual and material views of life may become more harmonized.

The rapid changes in our attitude towards the earth are also a source of hope. As recently as 10 or 15 years ago, we thoughtlessly consumed its resources, as if there was no end to them. Now, not only individuals but governments as well are seeking a new ecological order. ...

I think we can say that, because of the lessons we have begun to learn, the [new] century will be friendlier, more harmonious, and less harmful. Compassion, the seed of peace, will be able to flourish. I am very hopeful. At the same time, I believe that every individual has a responsibility to help guide our global family in the right direction. Good wishes alone are not enough; we have to assume responsibility. Large human movements spring from individual human initiatives.

SOURCE: Tenzin Gyatso, *Love, Kindness and Universal Responsibility*. Delhi: Paljor Publications, n.d., pp. 50–71

Living engaged Buddhism

How strong is the evidence that the Buddha fought for the common person against the establishment of his time, attempting to change society? He did oppose the birth caste system and the privileges of the brahmanic priestly caste. But his focus on individual consciousness does not seem like a direct critique of institutionalized social injustices. With the advent of modern technologies and increased resources far beyond those available during the Buddha's time, a renewed movement called Engaged Buddhism is emerging with a critique of social problems. The Dalai Lama is one leader critical of violence and consumerism, and others are applying Buddhist principles to rectify injustices in such areas as the environmental crisis and gender inequalities. Some of the traditional practices of Buddhism, such as monastic celibacy, are being called into question and modified in the global context of contemporary Buddhism.

Engaged Buddhism in Asia by Christopher Queen and Sallie King

Christopher Queen and Sallie King, in their book *Engaged Buddhism: Buddhist Liberation Movements in Asia* (1996), show the growing influence of social activism among Asian Buddhists. There is a debate about whether Buddhism is essentially a withdrawn, reflective spiritual practice, focusing on overcoming one's own desires and attachments, or whether it also authentically includes a movement into social and political arenas to improve the situation of poor, oppressed peoples and victims of war. Queen, King, and others argue that traditional Buddhist teachings and the modern situation do justify a Buddhist movement toward changing not only individual consciousness, but also oppressive social structures.

To most people in the West, the term "Buddhism" means a religion of introspective withdrawal. Yet the reality of contemporary Asian Buddhism is often something very different. "Buddhism" in contemporary Asia means energetic engagement with social and political issues and crises at least as much as it means monastic or meditative withdrawal. ...

In the socially engaged Buddhism of modern Asia, the liberation sought has been called a "mundane awakening" (*laukodaya*), which includes individuals, villages, nations, and ultimately all people (*sarvodaya*), and which focuses on objectives that may be achieved and recognized in this lifetime, in this world. George Bond has summarized the comprehensive nature of the liberative vision that inspires volunteers in the Sarvodaya Shramadana movement, including moral, cultural, spiritual, social, political, and economic dimensions. Thus, in addition to being a society based on the Buddhist precepts and offering opportunities for obtaining wisdom, happiness, and peace, Ariyaratna[8] and his colleagues have focused on the "ten basic human needs" that must be met for liberation to be possible: a clean and beautiful environment, an adequate and safe water supply, clothing, balanced diet, simple housing, basic health care, communication facilities, energy, education related to life and living, and free access to cultural and spiritual resources. The list is offered as a modern version of the Buddhist "middle way"—a balancing of the material and spiritual aspects of social change.

---

8 Ariyaratna—E. T. *Ariyaratna, Buddhism and Sarvodaya: The Sri Lankan Experience*. Delhi: Sri Satguru Publications, 1996.

We may conclude that a profound change in Buddhist soteriology[9]—from a highly personal and other-worldly notion of liberation to a social, economic, this-worldly liberation—distinguishes the Buddhist movements in our study. The traditional conceptions of karma and rebirth, the veneration of the *bhikkhu sangha*,[10] and the focus on ignorance and psychological attachment to account for suffering in the world (the second Noble Truth) have taken second place to the application of highly rationalized reflections on the institutional and political manifestations of greed, hatred, and delusion, and on new organizational strategies for addressing war and injustice, poverty and intolerance, and the prospects for "outer" as well as "inner" peace in the world. ...

Contemporary Buddhist liberation movements are as likely to apply their interpretive and organizational efforts to the critique and reform of social and political conditions as they are to propose and practice new spiritual exercises. The evils of war and genocide, of ethnic hatred and caste violence, and of economic disparity and degradation figure prominently in engaged Buddhist writings. On the other hand, the democratization, if not the transformation, of spiritual practices—for example, meditation and ritual initiations as now appropriated by lay practitioners—has been seen as an integral concomitant to the shift to mundane awakening.

To advance their vision of a new world, Buddhist liberation movements have harnessed modern methods of education, mass communication, political influence and activism, jurisprudence and litigation, and yes, even fund-raising and marketing. Many examples of these new "skillful means" may be cited.

If practical education is a basic human need, according to villagers in Sri Lanka, then the Buddhist liberation movements have concentrated major resources to this end. Among the first activities of the Buddhist women reformers in Sri Lanka at the turn of the century was the founding of primary schools for girls. ...

"Buddhism is based on service to others," wrote Walpola Rahula, the eminent Sinhalese scholar-monk and activist, in 1946. ...

Rahula's summary of the history of monastic engagement in the social and political life of Ceylon begins with a picture of the primitive sangha at the time of the Buddha. Here the founder and his followers are seen giving practical advice to villagers who were "poor, illiterate, not very clean, and not healthy ... [who] needed simple moral ideas conducive to their material well-being and happiness rather than deep and sublime discourses on philosophy, metaphysics, or psychology as taught in the *Abhidhamma*. Such ideas, taken from early Pali scriptures (*suttas*) Rahula was well-qualified to interpret, included the view that crime and immorality in society are rooted in poverty (*Cakkavatti-sihanada-sutta*), that employment opportunities must be provided to ensure the common wealth (*Kutadanta-sutta*), that merchants should be

9 Soteriology—doctrine of salvation from suffering.
10 *Bhikkhu sangha*—members of the Buddhist monastic communities.

diligent, savvy, and scrupulous in their dealings and that laypersons should seek economic security, freedom from debt, good health, and wholesome associations (*Sigala-sutta*; *Anguttara-nikaya*), and that political leaders should observe the Ten Duties of the King, including liberality, morality, self-sacrifice, integrity, nonviolence, and so on (*Dhammapadatthakatha*). In short, "the Buddha and the *bhikkhus* taught such important ideas pertaining to health, sanitation, earning wealth, mutual relationships, well-being of society, and righteous government—all for the good of the people." ...

In his introduction to the writings of contemporary engaged Buddhists, Kenneth Kraft has noted their agreement that "the principles and even some of the techniques of an engaged Buddhism have been latent in the tradition since the time of its founder. Qualities that were inhibited in pre-modern Asian settings ... can now be actualized through Buddhism's exposure to the West, where ethical sensitivity, social activism, and egalitarianism are emphasized." When these principles and techniques, regardless of their provenance, are proclaimed and practiced in the name of the Awakened One, in accord with the teachings of wisdom and compassion, and in the spirit of the unbroken community of those seeking human liberation—that is, in harmony with the ancient refuges of Buddha, Dharma, and Sangha— then we may regard the catechism as authentically Buddhist. ...

Simply put, in keeping with the Middle Path, Buddhist principles mandate that the poor need more attention given to the material dimension of life than do those who have enough; those who have more than enough need their attention turned to that fact. ...

Buddhist liberation movements, collectively, constitute a major turning point in the development of Buddhism and will continue to play a role of substantial importance in the evolution of Buddhism into the foreseeable future.

SOURCE: Christopher S. Queen and Sallie B. King, eds., *Engaged Buddhism: Buddhist Liberation Movements in Asia*. Albany, NY: State University of New York Press, 1996, pp. ix, 9–33, 411–35

North American Buddhism: Looking Forward

by Charles Prebish

The rapid recent rise and spread of Buddhism has encountered many new developments in North America. First-generation Asian immigrants are devoted to retaining their traditions, but American converts are quickly adapting Buddhism to modern culture. Democracy has overcome the Asian patriarchal authoritarianism and hierarchy of much of imported Buddhism. Women are now welcomed into positions of authority, more social engagement is encouraged, and many people active in Buddhist groups are also affiliated with other religions.

In this extract, Charles Prebish, the Charles Redd Chair in Religious Studies Emeritus, Utah State University and Professor Emeritus of Religious Studies, Penn State University, considers five important thematic issues in North American Buddhism. The author took refuge in the Buddha in 1965.

Buddhism's presence in North America, and its globalization in general, has become immense. Buddhism's growth to more than 2,500 communities on the continent doesn't begin to reflect the complexity of this expanding tradition. Now there are North American Buddhist titles on virtually every topic imaginable, and dozens of university courses devoted to North American Buddhism.

When Kenneth Tanaka and I edited *The Faces of Buddhism in America*, we settled on five major thematic issues: ethnicity, practice, democratization, engagement, and adaptation. I expanded a consideration of these topics in *Luminous Passage*, and framed the discussion between the two "bookends" of "Who is a Buddhist?" and "Ecumenicism." No matter where one goes, the discussion always focuses on these issues.

Who is a Buddhist?

Does "Taking Refuge" establish Buddhist identity? How about membership in a Buddhist community? Does attending meditation sessions, regularly or irregularly, make one a Buddhist? Does donating money to a Buddhist community give one Buddhist identity? What about regular attendance at temple services? The possible list could go on and on, and so could the various combinations. Yet no *one* standard, or combination, would work for everyone. A Buddhist is someone who says, "I am a Buddhist."

Boundaries

Can one maintain *multiple* affiliations? Can one be *both* a Buddhist *and* a Jew? Or Buddhist *and* Christian? Many people would clearly maintain they could! Read Rodger Kamenetz's *The Jew in the Lotus*. Jeff Wilson explores regionalism: "We need to be careful about allowing a handful of the largest metropolitan areas in North America to stand-in for the totality of Buddhist experience." But in an overall technological environment of increasing social networking, within a decade or two, regionalism may lose its punch as rural Buddhists in Nova Scotia pick up the urban savvy of Toronto.

Ethnicity

Probably no issue has been more divisive in the practice and study of North American Buddhism than ethnicity. To be sure, the problem goes back more than a century from the Helen Tworkov and *Tricycle* debacle ("Can Buddhism Survive America?") of the early 1990s. In the early 1970s, there were only two kinds of groups: communities of Asian immigrant Buddhists (and within these communities almost no white, black, or Hispanic faces were visible) and communities dominated by American convert Buddhists (and within these communities almost no Asian American, black or Hispanic faces could be found). That was why I coined the phrase "two Buddhisms" in 1979. The phrase was meant to delineate one form of Buddhism—now called Asian immigrant Buddhism—that placed primary emphasis on sound, basic doctrines, shared by all Buddhists, and on solid religious practice; and another form of Buddhism—now called American convert Buddhism—that seemed to emerge shortly after radical social movements, similar to those America had experienced in the 1950s and 1960s. I am concerned that North American Buddhism not promote racism.

Practice

"What's your practice?" The first time I asked that question was in a Buddhist Churches of America temple. The faithful and respectful Jodo Shinshu (Pure Land) practitioner looked at me like I was crazy. Her identity as a Buddhist and her identity as a person were inseparable. This immigrant Buddhist pattern persists.

Jack Kornfield[11], said "American lay people are not content to go and hear a sermon once a week or to make merit by leaving gifts at a meditation center. We, too, want to *live* the realizations of the Buddha and bring them into our hearts, our lives, and our times." A decade later when interviewed by *Time* magazine, Kornfield was far more direct: "American people don't want to be monks or nuns ... they want practices that transform the heart." Kornfield is certainly correct. North America has never been a monastic culture, but to focus exclusively on the lay Buddhist tradition overlooks the immensely critical role Buddhist monastics have played throughout Asia. But now an increasing number of American Buddhists—men and women—are choosing the monastic vocation as a means of making Buddhist practice the focal point of their lives.

Yet the monastic codes for monks and nuns, known as the *Vinaya*, are two millennia old, and no longer entirely applicable to our modern, and sometimes urban, lifestyle. So many Western Buddhist monastic centers have had to incorporate many exceptions into the detailed rules. As early as 1970, Suzuki Roshi[12] in San Francisco commented on the problematic choice between a lay or monastic life in America, noting that "American students are not priests yet not completely laymen."

I think it is important to understand that Asian immigrant Buddhists value ritual practices, chanting, and faith-based observances in quite the same way that convert communities emphasize sitting meditation. I think that the "precepts as practice" approach can additionally help bridge the gap, because all Buddhists are obliged to follow the five vows of the lay practitioner, all the time.

One cannot overestimate the importance of ethical concerns for the entire Buddhist community globally. In the more than 2,500 years since Buddha's ministry, the ethical concerns and challenges we face as global and American Buddhists have changed drastically. Look at issues never considered during Buddha's lifetime, like abortion, euthanasia, bio-ethics generally, sexual ethics, and the like. All of these increasingly complicated issues fall under the category called "practice."

11 Jack Kornfield—teacher of Mindfulness Meditation, clinical psychologist, and author of *Path with a Heart*.
12 Suzuki Roshi—leader of San Francisco Zen Center and author of *Zen Mind, Beginner's Mind*.

Rarely mentioned is Buddhist family life. Fortunately, we now have books like Sandy Eastoak's *Dharma Family Treasures: Sharing Mindfulness with Children,* and John and Myla Kabat-Zinn's *Everyday Blessings: The Inner Work of Mindful Parenting.* Buddhist parenting and family life cannot be overlooked because many of the young North American Buddhist converts and immigrant Buddhists now find themselves having given birth to a new generation of American Buddhists. One of these *"Dharma brats"* is Sumi Loundon Kim. In 2001 she edited *Blue Jean Buddha: Voices of Young Buddhists.* Buddhist communities need to create participatory roles designed to energize young people and to address their psychological needs.

Democratization

The ancient Buddhist tradition was hardly a democratic organization. But parts of it were. Nonetheless, the ancient Buddhist community was also primarily patriarchal, hierarchical, and highly authoritarian with respect to leadership roles; and that's what was transmitted to America. But now the leadership roles of male Asian masters with virtually unlimited authority are long gone. The White Plum Asanga, a consortium of Zen communities, lists nearly 100 teachers at www.whiteplum.org, and approximately 40 percent of those listed are female. More importantly, many North American Buddhist sanghas are now managed by a collective governing body. The San Francisco Zen Center, for example, has a governing "Board" of almost two dozen members.

Another item that has moved North American Buddhism safely forward in the aftermath of the well-publicized teacher-related scandals of the 1970s and 1980s is a much tighter regulation of the conduct allowed between teachers and students in North American Buddhist communities. Women now wield genuine authority in the North American Buddhist movement. And groups like the "Gay Buddhist Fellowship" provide resources that were totally absent just a generation earlier.

Engagement

The creator of socially engaged Buddhism is the Vietnamese monk Thich Nhat Hanh [see page 139]. This movement was contrary to the approach that many North American Buddhists had of Buddhism as a socially passive tradition, removed or withdrawn from the rigors of society. Now socially engaged Buddhists have combined Buddhist values with distinctly North American forms of social protest emphasizing peace issues, ecological and environmental concerns, hospice work, prison reforms, and a host of other concerns in an attempt to inject Buddhist inspired sanity into our dialog with the planet and each other. In North America, perhaps the greatest advocate of socially engaged Buddhism is the Buddhist Peace Fellowship.

Adaptation

American Zen has created, in addition to its distinct practices, a series of enterprises that Japanese Zen never imagined: residential communities, businesses, farms, hospices, publishing companies, Dharmacraft cottage industries, and the like. It is not unreasonable for some to wonder whether these innovations were a new and important kind of Zen practice or simply a distraction from it.

Diffuse affiliation accounts for the possibility of members maintaining concurrent affiliation in *more than one* Buddhist organization, or teachers having received training authorization in *more than one* tradition. The classic expression of diffuse affiliation can be witnessed in Rodger Kamenetz's popular book *The Jew in the Lotus*, in which he coined the term "JUBU," to describe individuals who maintained a Jewish-Buddhist dual affiliation. "Hybridity" is another trend, in which various Buddhist lineage groups work together. In the context of inter-religious and intra-religious hybridity, the issue of adaptation in North American Buddhism becomes not only significantly more complicated, but also more interesting.

Global Buddhist Dialog

Buddhist organizations such as the European Buddhist Union and the American Buddhist Congress can meaningfully see themselves as a part of worldwide Buddhist organizations like the World Buddhist Sangha Council or the World Fellowship of Buddhists. Professional and practical organizations like the Society for Buddhist-Christian Studies are cropping up and presenting an international framework of mutuality in which these organizations unite scholar-practitioners and practitioners from a variety of traditions.

Limping Toward Nirvana

There has been a huge development of Buddhist educational institutions on the continent—not only Naropa University, Nyingma Institute, University of the West, and Soka University of America, but also Buddhist high schools and elementary schools, such as the Developing Virtue Secondary Schools.

Perhaps the technological innovation that may have the biggest impact on the practice of North American Buddhism is the creation of "Blogs." One of the Buddhist blogs I visit regularly was established by Reverend Danny Fisher (at www.dannyfisher.org), and is one of the most inspiring and useful sites in cyberspace.

As Diana Eck[13] says: "It is not enough to preserve a religious or cultural heritage; that heritage must also nourish a new generation in a new environment."

SOURCE: Summarized from Charles Prebish's Keynote Address "Buddhism in Canada: Global Causes, Local Conditions" at the conference at the University of British Columbia, October 15–17, 2010. Full speech available online at <http://www.youtube.com/watch?v=RMk9z0baPRg>

---

13 Diana Eck—Director of The Pluralism Project at Harvard University and author of *New Religious America*.

Precepts for an Engaged Buddhism by Thich Nhat Hanh

After Vietnamese Zen master Thich Nhat Hanh's struggles against the 1960s war, he settled in exile in his "Plum Village" in France, where he teaches, writes, gardens, and helps other refugees. His several books have introduced many readers to a new brand of Buddhist activism. In his book *Being Peace* (1987) he outlines a number of new precepts for an Engaged Buddhism, "The Precepts of the Order of Interbeing." They clearly reflect careful study of both modern and ancient problems, such as religious intolerance, fanatical political ideology, and forceful indoctrination of children.

First: Do not be idolatrous about or bound to any doctrine, theory, or ideology, even Buddhist ones. All systems of thought are guiding means; they are not absolute truth. ...

Second: Do not think that the knowledge you presently possess is changeless, absolute truth. Avoid being narrow-minded and bound to present views. Learn and practice non-attachment from views in order to be open to receive others' viewpoints. Truth is found in life and not merely in conceptual knowledge. Be ready to learn throughout your entire life and to observe reality in yourself and in the world at times. ...

Third: Do not force others, including children, by any means whatsoever, to adopt your views, whether by authority, threat, money, propaganda, or even education. However, through compassionate dialogue, help others renounce fanaticism and narrowness. ...

Fourth: Do not avoid contact with suffering or close your eyes before suffering. Do not lose awareness of the existence of suffering in the life of the world. Find ways to be with those who are suffering by all means, including personal contact and visits, images, sound. By such means, awaken yourself and others to the reality of suffering in the world. ...

Fifth: Do not accumulate wealth while millions are hungry. Do not take as the aim of your life fame, profit, wealth, or sensual pleasure. Live simply and share time, energy, and material resources with those who are in need. ...

Sixth: Do not maintain anger or hatred. As soon as anger and hatred arise, practice the meditation on compassion in order to deeply understand the persons who have caused anger and hatred. Learn to look at other beings with the eyes of compassion. ...

Seventh: Do not lose yourself in dispersion and in your surroundings. Learn to practice breathing in order to regain composure of body and mind, to practice mindfulness, and to develop concentration and understanding. ...

Eighth: Do not utter words that can create discord and cause the community to break. Make every effort to reconcile and resolve all conflicts, however small. ...

Ninth: Do not say untruthful things for the sake of personal interest or to impress people. Do not utter words that cause division and hatred. Do not spread news that you do not know to be certain. Do not criticize or condemn things that you are not sure of. Always speak truthfully and constructively.

Have the courage to speak out about situations of injustice, even when doing so may threaten your own safety. ...

Tenth: Do not use the Buddhist community for personal gain or profit, or transform your community into a political party. A religious community should, however, take a clear stand against oppression and injustice, and should strive to change the situation without engaging in partisan conflicts. ...

Eleventh: Do not live with a vocation that is harmful to humans and nature. Do not invest in companies that deprive others of their chance to life. Select a vocation which helps realize your ideal of compassion. ...

Twelfth: Do not kill. Do not let others kill. Find whatever means possible to protect life and to prevent war. ...

Thirteenth: Possess nothing that should belong to others. Respect the property of others but prevent others from enriching themselves from human suffering or the suffering of other beings. ...

Fourteenth: Do not mistreat your body. Learn to handle it with respect. Do not look on your body as only an instrument. Preserve vital energies (sexual, breath, spirit) for the realization of the Way. Sexual expression should not happen without love and commitment. In sexual relationships be aware of future suffering that may be caused. To preserve the happiness of others, respect the rights and commitment of others. Be fully aware of the responsibility of bringing new lives into the world. Meditate on the world into which you are bringing new beings.

SOURCE: Thich Nhat Hanh, *Being Peace*. Berkeley, CA: Parallax Press, 1987, pp. 89–100

GLOSSARY

Bhikkhu (Pali) A Theravadin monk.

Bhikkhuni A Theravadin nun.

Bodhisattva (Sanskrit, Enlightenment Being; Pali, **Bodhisatta**) In Theravada, an historical Buddha before Buddhahood was attained; in Mahayana, a compassionate being who vows to become a Buddha for all sentient beings.

Buddha In Theravada, the historical persons who awaken to truth, such as Gautama; in Mahayana, an enlightened person and a universal principle of all beings.

Canon The official list of books with authority in a religion, either because they are believed to be inspired or revealed, or have been so designated.

Dharma (Sanskrit; Pali, **Dhamma**) In Buddhism, cosmic law, the teachings of the Buddha, and the realization and practice of truth (the second of the Three Jewels: Buddha, dharma, sangha); in Hinduism, the universal cosmic law, duty.

Karma In Buddhism, the cosmic moral law of consequences for ethical actions and their effects from prior incarnations; karma can be altered by good or bad intentions, is not fatalistic, and can be changed at any time by meditative insight.

Mahayana (Sanskrit, Large Vehicle) The form of Buddhism from northern Asia that teaches the effort to liberate other beings; it emphasizes the Buddha-nature in all things and the importance of direct experience.

Nirvana (Sanskrit; Pali, **Nibbana**) A heavenly realm discovered after death and, in Mahayana teaching, a state of awakening during life: the discovery of the path beyond ego's desires and passions, the realization of the union of opposites, the transcendence of mind's limits. It is peace and tranquillity on earth, coming from beyond the duality of ordinary life.

Pinyin New romanized transcription of Chinese adopted in 1979, replacing 1859 Wade-Giles system.

Sunyata (emptiness, or no-self; Sanskrit, **Anatman**) The lack of a permanent, self-existing soul in the *skandhas* and all reality.

Sutta (Theravada), **Sutra** (Mahayana) Sacred Buddhist texts.

Tathāgata "Thus-come," "Thus-arrived." Reincarnated Buddha.

Theravada (Pali, Teaching of the Elders) Form of Buddhism from southern Asia which adheres to early scriptures and monastic renunciation; its texts are the Pali Canon.

Vajrayana (Sanskrit, Diamond Vehicle) Form of Buddhism which teaches that emptiness is complemented by compassion and action. The Dalai Lama is its leader in the Tibetan tradition.

Vipassana (Pali, See Clearly) The central focus of meditation in Theravada practice, which stresses mindfulness and tranquillity, leading to liberation.

Zen A Chinese and Japanese form of Buddhism emphasizing immediate experience. Of the two main schools, Rinzai, influenced by Hakuin, uses the koan to promote satori (awakening), while Soto, influenced by Dogen, uses more "silent illumination."

HOLY DAYS

Celebrating the Buddha Buddhist cultures celebrate the events and the meaning of the life of the Buddha in several ways.

1 Buddha's Day, or Visaka Puja in Theravada, is often the most holy day of the year, commemorating the birth, life, and death of the Buddha. It is usually celebrated at a full moon. Devotees gather at monasteries, have processions, chant, listen to sermons, water local *bodhi* trees, serve the poor and sick, honor relics such as the Buddha's eyetooth, and bathe Buddha images.

2 Relics, such as teeth or bones supposedly preserved from the Buddha's body, are commemorated as a way of participating in the magical power of his divine presence with rituals such as a procession and sprinkling holy water. Sometimes kings attempt to legitimate their rule by using such relics to empower and bless their state.

3 Honoring the dharma is celebrated by chanting sacred texts. In Tibet the Feast of the First Discourse is held at a full moon. Thais celebrate the Buddha's teaching this to his mother, and his establishing the core of the monastic discipline.

4 The founding of the sangha/samgha, or gathering community, of Buddhists is celebrated annually. The miraculous, unannounced gathering of 1,250 arhats (in Theravada, highly evolved Buddhists) before the Buddha in Rajagrha is recalled as the founding time of the first sangha. In Sri Lanka, thousands celebrate the arrival of Buddhism on the island, brought by Mahind, son of King Ashoka, and his sister Sanghamitta, who brought a branch of Buddha's sacred *bodhi* tree.

The saints of Buddhism Saints are celebrated in annual festivals, honoring popular mythic events such as the Chinese Guanyin's birthday, enlightenment, and entry into nirvana. Holidays celebrate historical leaders such as Bodhidharma, the first Chinese Patriarch who brought Chan Buddhism to China, Hakuin, leader of the Rinzai Zen sect in Japan, and Padmasambhava, the leading missionary from India to Tibet.

Seasonal celebrations The Buddhist calendar incorporates festivals of seasonal changes, agricultural events, and human life and death rituals. New Year's Day is commonly celebrated, as are the origin of spring, the equinoxes, harvest thanksgiving, and festivals for the dead ancestors. These holidays are highly syncretic, blending Buddhist and ancient folk religion together. In Tibet, the New Year festival (Lo-gsar) combines the Buddhist miracle of Sravasti with the exorcism of the old year's evil and calling up good fortune for the new year. In Thailand the onset of the monsoon rains is the occasion of intensified monastic retreat activities, alongside New Year's sympathetic magic intended to ensure the new rains necessary for planting rice.

HISTORICAL OUTLINE

c. 563–483 BCE—life of Gautama Buddha

c. 258 BCE—King Ashoka spreads Buddhism outside India

200 BCE–200 CE—Theravada Buddhism develops

100 BCE—Theravada Pali Canon written down

c. 50 CE—Buddhism taken to China and East Asia

2nd century CE—Asvaghosha writes *Acts of the Buddha*

c. 100 ce—Mahayana Buddhism develops

c. 200 CE—Nagarjuna teaches emptiness

c. 500 CE—Buddhism taken to Japan

589–845 CE—peak of Chinese Buddhism

606 CE—Seng Can (Seng-tsan), third Buddhist Patriarch in China, dies

775 CE—Padmasambhava establishes first Buddhist monastery in Tibet

c. 1079–1153—Milarepa influences Tibetan Buddhism

13th century—Buddhism begins to lose influence in India

c. 13th century—Chan Buddhism taken from China to Japan, becomes Zen

c. 1250—Dogen founds Soto Zen Buddhism

c. 1750—Hakuin revitalizes Rinzai Zen Buddhism

1950—China annexes Tibet, Dalai Lama flees, Buddhism spreads to West

1966—Thich Nhat Hanh leaves Vietnam for the West

from 1970s—Dalai Lama teaches widely in the West

from 1980s—increased Eastern and Western Buddhist activities

REVIEW QUESTIONS

1   What are the "middle path," the Four Noble Truths, the Eightfold Path? What does it mean to be free from delusions? Why is this important to Buddhists?

2   What questions did the Buddha leave undeclared? Why?

3   Describe the similarities and contrast the differences of the Theravada, Mahayana, and Vajrayana traditions, naming and quoting classic texts in each tradition.

4   What is a koan? What is its purpose? Give an example.

DISCUSSION QUESTIONS

1   What are the major similarities and differences between Hinduism and Buddhism?

2   Why is meditation so important to Buddhism?

3   What reality do Buddhists constantly refer to as most important, and how is it different from theism?

4   How do changes made in Buddhism in North America illustrate the reasons why religions change?

INFORMATION RESOURCES

Buddhaghosha. *Buddhaghosha's Parables*, trans. T. Rogers. London, 1870.

Buddhism
<http://www.sacred-texts.com/bud/index.htm>

Buddhist studies
<http://www.dharmanet.org>

Buddhist temples
<http://www.sacred-destinations.com/categories/buddhist-temples>

Carter, Robert E. *The Nothingness Beyond God*. St. Paul, MN: Paragon House, 1997.

Chodron, Pema. *When Things Fall Apart*. Boston and London: Shambhala, 1997. <http://www.shambhala.org/teachers/pema> and <http://www.pemachodronfondation.org>

Conze, Edward, ed. *Buddhist Scriptures*. Harmondsworth, Middlesex: Penguin Books, 1986.

Cousins, L. S. "Buddhism," in *A New Handbook of Living Religions*, ed. John R. Hinnels. Oxford: Blackwell, 1997.

Goddard, Dwight, ed. *A Buddhist Bible*. Boston, MA: Beacon Press, 1966.

Gross, Rita M. *Buddhism After Patriarchy*. Albany, NY: State University of New York Press, 1993.

Juergensmeyer, Mark, ed. "Buddhist/Confucian Cultural Religions," *The Oxford Handbook of Global Religions*. Oxford: Oxford University Press, 2001.

Kapleau, Philip. *The Three Pillars of Zen*. Boston, MA: Beacon Press, 1965.

Loori, John Daido. "The Precepts and the Environment," in *Mountain Record*. Vol. 14, no. 3, pp. 12–17, 1996.

Macy, Joanna. *World as Lover, World as Self*. Berkeley, CA: Parallax Press, 1991. <http://www.joannamacy.net>

McGreal, Ian P. *Great Thinkers of the Eastern World*. New York: HarperCollins, 1995.

Naropa University
<http://www.naropa.edu>

Pilgrim, Richard. *Buddhism and the Arts of Japan*. Chambersburg, PA: Anima Press, 1993.

Powell, Andrew. *Living Buddhism*. Berkeley and Los Angeles, CA: University of California Press, 1989.

Prebish, Charles. *The Faces of Buddhism in America*. Berkeley and Los Angeles, CA: The University of California Press, 1998.

———. *Luminous Passages*. Berkeley and Los Angeles, CA: The University of California Press, 1999.

Ramanan, K. Venkata. *Nagarjuna's Philosophy*. Delhi: Motilal Banarsidass, 1966.

Reynolds, Frank, and **Charles Hallisey**, *et al*. "Buddhism," in *Encyclopedia of Religion*, ed. Lindsay Jones. Vol. 2, pp. 1087–316. New York: Macmillan, 2005.

Reynolds, Frank, *et al*. "The Buddha and Buddhism," in *Encyclopedia Britannica*. Vol. 15, pp. 263–305. London, 1997.

Thurman, Robert. *The Tibetan Book of the Dead*. New York: Bantam, 1994. <http://www.bobthurman.com>

Tricycle: The Buddhist Review
<http://www.tricycle.com>

Tworkov, Helen. *Zen in America*. New York: Kodansha International, 1994

World Buddhist Sangha Council
<http://www.wbsc886.org/Enlish/E-index2/E-index.html>

World Fellowship of Buddhists
<http://www.wfbhq.org>

Zen Mountain Monastery
<http://www.mro.org/zmm>

CHAPTER 6
CHINESE RELIGIONS

Chinese religions are today very syncretic, blending together major strands of ancient folk religions, Confucianism, Daoism (Taoism)[1], and Buddhism. People move from one tradition to another, and combine them easily. Temples commonly have various statues—a Buddha, a Daoist god, a Confucian figure, and a goddess.

The largest ancient layer of religion in China is folk religions, which encompass a vast array of *Shen*—ancient gods and goddesses. From earliest times, these folk religions have included rituals for ancestor worship, divination, and the placating of angry ghosts, as well as exorcism and healing practices.

Confucianism is considered a philosophy, the first major tradition in China that urged education, rather than inherited privilege, for leadership. It is now aimed at people who do not have religious beliefs. Its ancient principles pervade Chinese culture, stressing social ethics, personal integrity, family piety, ancestor veneration, education, and loyalty to rulers and friends. The Chinese hold these principles in high esteem, often practicing the goals of Confucianism without associating them with the tradition.

Daoism is more mystical and paradoxical than Confucianism, and includes ancient traditions such as **qi** (ch'i), energy in all things, the **yin/yang** modes of energy, and **Taijiquan** (*Tai-chi-ch'uan*), which are physical exercises practiced daily to enter into harmony with the universe. Over the years, Daoism developed alchemy, astrology, medicine, martial arts, feng shui, and qigong breathing. Daoism also cultivated monasteries, scriptures, vegetarianism, and the principle of emptiness.

Chinese Buddhism, the most popular spiritual tradition in recent times, now includes the Mahayana, Theravada, and Tibetan branches. Many people revere the Buddha **Amita** and his Pure Land paradise with chanting, incense, and pilgrimages to mountain shrines. **Chan** (Ch'an) Buddhism is a strong, but more monastic meditative Chinese development, influenced by Daoist distrust of scripture and

---

1 Chinese words are transliterated here using the contemporary **Pinyin** system, with the earlier Wade-Giles transliteration given in parenthesis at first occurrence; within extracts using Wade-Giles, the Pinyin version is shown in brackets.

embracing every moment. Buddhists borrowed many Daoist words and concepts in order to convey their teachings. Chan's silent meditation was exported to Japan in the thirteenth century, where it became Zen.

In the twentieth century, with the major shift in Chinese culture away from old feudal ways of aristocratic and imperial social structures reinforced by religions, atheistic Maoist Communism officially assumed that, as science developed, religions would fade away. During the Cultural Revolution of 1966–76, thousands of temples and religious images and texts were thus destroyed by those anxious to smash the religious support for rigid ancient traditions. Yet since the late 1980s, following Mao Zedong's (Mao Tse-tung, 1893–1976) death, the Communist Party has relaxed its opposition to religious practices. Many have been surprised at the resurgence of spiritual traditions, and the renovation of temples, taking place in the midst of expanding modernization, urbanization, and industrialization. The Chinese constitution now permits, but regulates, religions to make sure that they do not disturb communal harmony.

Chinese folk religions

Many ancient elements of Chinese religion concern the worship of the Shen, who can be nature, cultural or clan deities, city gods, demigods, or dragons. Popular female deities include Mazu (Ma-Tsu; Mother Ancestor, "Queen Mother," "Empress of Heaven" [Tianhou], or goddess of the sea) and Guanyin (Kwan-Yin, goddess of mercy and compassion).

Ancestor veneration (jingzu) is very important in folk religions and involves rituals to honor the spirits of the deceased. Such rituals are evident in household altars, where pictures and lists of ancestors are placed, daily prayers said, incense burnt, and food left for the comfort of the ancestors in the afterlife. Qingming (the third day of the third month) is a time for tidying the graves of ancestors, having a picnic, reciting memories, and leaving sacrifices such as food, wine, meat, and spirit money at the gravesite. This ancient support for the spirits reinforces the important Confucian respect for elders and obedience to social superiors. Some clans and towns have shrines to honor ancestors who have become Shen spirits.

Although suppressed between the Taiping Movement and the Cultural Revolution (1850–1976), folk religions are now being revived. However, many of the beliefs and practices are rejected by the Communist government as superstitious, drawing people away from socialist goals such as education.

The Great Goddesses of China by Lee Irwin

The goddesses of China are a major part of folk religions. Important expressions of the feminine principle, they are very popular. This study of goddesses indicates how they overlap in some ways with each other, and with other major religions.

Though Chinese mythology and religion have been dominated by male gods and masters, the presence of female divinities has always been a part of Chinese folk belief. These various divinities, usually identified with the feminine principle of moist, dark, receptive nature, constitute a somewhat obscure pantheon of water sprites, dragon ladies, snake queens, moon-goddesses, and rulers of heaven and earth. Among them may be recognized four divinities whose collective popularity extends from ancient times to the present. These four are Nügua, the ancient Zhou dynasty creatress; Xiwangmu, the Queen Mother of the West; Guanyin, the Goddess of Mercy; and Tianhou, the Empress of Heaven. These four divinities have an interesting and significant relationship with each other, indicative of the dynamic social and cultural history of China. Collectively, they represent the presence of the feminine element, divinized to the highest degree, in an almost unbroken continuity of spiritual potency and significance for both the masses of China, as well as for various religious and political groups. ...

Guanyin
This Buddhist divinity enjoyed great popularity in China as the Goddess of Mercy and Compassion. ... Taoism and Buddhism, which were able to maintain a degree of autonomy from the imperial hierarchy, both accepted the development of female divinities within the context of their religious ideals. ...

Guanyin thus appears as a shining example of a spiritualized feminine tendency that takes no interest in hierarchical order, but works for the salvation of all beings. This is a tendency she shared with the Queen Mother, who also granted health, long life and happiness, independent of the rank of the petitioners. ...

In 276 CE, the first translation of the Lotus Sutra was made by Dharmaraksa, the *Zhengfahuajing* which was quickly disseminated around Luoyang. As the 24th chapter of the Sutra deals with the saving power and grace of Avalokiteśvara (translated as Guanshiyin), the cult began to flourish by the end of the fourth century. In a second translation made by the Indian monk Kumārajīva (406 CE), Guanyin has thirty-three appearances, seven of which are female. This figure, as a celestial *bodhisattva* or *pusa*, who functioned autonomously and who was endowed with various miraculous powers, was distinguished as a great being of forgiveness, mercy, and compassion. In the Chinese context, these attributes came to be seen as primarily feminine characteristics and, by the Tang Dynasty, Guanyin was portrayed as a female goddess, companion to Amitabha or Emituofo, Lord of the Western Paradise. This association with the Western Paradise led inevitably to a certain sharing of characteristics with the Taoist Queen Mother of the West. By 828 CE there was a statue of Guanyin in most Buddhist monasteries in China, estimated at over 40,000 in all. Later conflation with the goddess Tianhou makes Guanyin also into a goddess of sailors and a protectoress of those at sea.

As a Goddess of Mercy, Guanyin receives the prayers of all those who are suffering or in danger. As an idealized woman of compassion and gentleness, she was believed to have manifested herself as Miaoshan. ... Being frugal in dress and appearance, she rejected marriage and, choosing to lead a life of religious devotion, was persecuted by her father. Fleeing her father, she lived in solitude for a number of years, most probably on Xiangshan, and having attained enlightenment, rescued her father from serious illness by giving up her arms and eyes for his recovery. Revealing herself to be none other than the celestial *bodhisattva* of 1,000 eyes and arms, she was miraculously healed and went on to become the great savioress, the Goddess of Mercy. This legend has its origins in a purely Chinese context and has been traced to the Xiangshan monastery in Northern China, where it was engraved on stone tablets in 1100 CE. ...

Thus, Guanyin came to embody an appeal to women through her association with the Miaoshan legend by which the renunciation of dominant male social values could be sanctioned. ...

In contrast to the more world-renouncing, celibate ideals expressed through the Miaoshan legend, Guanyin became a patroness of childbirth, Songzi Guanyin and is pictured as dressed in flowing garments holding a child in her arms, either seated or standing. This figure represents some synthesis with the Taoist goddess, Princess of the Flowery Clouds. ... In the Lotus Sutra, from which this image derives its sculptural origin, the desire for *female* children is sanctioned. Here again may be seen a confirmation of ideas associated with Guanyin that are in contrast to the dominant male desire for male children.

As a goddess associated with the sea and the dangers of the ocean, Putuo Guanyin was quite popular. This iconography refers to Putuo Island [in the bay south of Shanghai] and is usually represented as a female figure seated in Buddhist fashion where she receives the prayers of the distressed. Guanyin is believed to have practiced meditation for nine years on this island in the Chusan archipelago. As a sea-goddess, she also conveys souls in the "Ship of Salvation," which she pilots to the Western Paradise. ...

Tianhou, or Mazu

It is quite interesting to see how this goddess, styled the Empress of Heaven and popularly known as Mazu[2], received her officially sanctioned divine status, as well as both Taoist and Buddhist recognition. ... First and foremost, the Empress of Heaven is a patroness of the sea that protects all her devotees in ocean voyages, and, in general, responds to those in distress. Secondarily, she is also a goddess of procreation to whom prayers are addressed for conception. In this she shares definite associations with both Guanyin and Xiwangmu. ... As the Empress of Heaven [Tianhou], she appears seated upon waves or clouds, or often on a throne, clad in a long robe with an official girdle, wearing an imperial headdress. She holds an official tablet or a sceptre, as symbols of her imperial status. In rank, she is equal to all male emperors and subordinate only to the supreme (male) god. ...

2 Mazu—mother-ancestor.

On the popular level, these goddesses had a remarkable autonomy and stood out as distinct symbols of female virtue and potency. These qualities are fundamentally embodied in the virtues of love, compassion and forgiveness, and are infrequently manifest as powers of judgement or condemnation. They are qualities which celebrate life and promote both its continuity and its value in a world capable of being freed from suffering and sorrow. That these characteristics should be regarded as primarily feminine is a genuine testimony of the inherent life-giving potency of the female which seeks to promote growth and well-being. Furthermore, this power is not limited to a strictly controlled masculine hierarchy but represents an alternative means for Chinese women to recognize the value of their femininity as embodied by the highest celestial powers, a power that is both dynamic and creative. All these goddesses have shamanistic associations, as the *wu* class of female shamans was very popular and represented a recognized and legitimate means of expression by which women could manifest their spiritual abilities. In this sense, the non-familial and spiritual value of female power is associated with a free-flowing compassion, spontaneity and ability that was otherwise controlled and conditioned by gender and rank in the masculine social order.

SOURCE: Lee Irwin, condensation of "Divinity and Salvation: The Great Goddesses of China," in *Asian Folklore Studies*, Vol. 49, 1990, pp. 53–68. (Now published as *Asian Ethnology* by Nanzan University, Japan)

The Kitchen God by Clarence Day

In traditional pre-communist China, many versions of "paper horses" (paper representations of various gods), including a "Kitchen God," were popular in residential Chinese folk religions. The Kitchen God, fed a little food daily, watches over family activities and reports them regularly to Heaven. Part of the New Year festival is to ritually burn the old image of the Kitchen God and replace it with a new one, as a form of leaving behind old behavior and beginning a new, better life.

At the Chinese New Year season one is amazed at the immense variety of *chih-ma*, or "paper horses," which are used in the many religious observances in both urban and rural homes. These paper representations of various gods, though called "paper horses," do not usually portray a horse. According to ancient custom, real horses were required for sacrifice, but when the emperor saw that this practice would soon deplete the available supply of potential cavalry horses, he issued a decree that for burnt offerings only paper horses should be used. Since most of the New Year sacrifices involve the burning of the god, it has been found more economical to use the "paper horse" representation of the particular divinity being worshipped. The five indispensable articles associated with any kind of religious practice in China are the ubiquitous firecracker, incense sticks, candles, paper money of various sorts, and some form of the "paper horse." ...

The appearance and use of the kitchen god is fairly familiar to people in China, but a brief comparative description may be of further interest here. The common form of this picture used in East Central China is a red sheet about six-by-eleven inches, with a seated figure of the bearded Tsao-chün in clear black outline, filled in with green, yellow, and red coloring. Over his head is a palace roof marked with the characters for "Dispensing Happiness Palace" (Ting-fu Kung), with fish hanging as tassels from the roof corners—the fish being a symbol for wealth. Around the knees of the god may be a group of five or seven figures—either sons or devotees—all with faces expressive of happiness as a result of his protection and yearlong care. ...

In the ceremony in which the kitchen god ascends in smoke to make his annual report to the Pearly Emperor on the eve of the twenty-third of the twelfth month, his chair is usually made of split bamboo covered with colored paper. In Hangchow, it is quite ornate, standing about fourteen inches high, its framework being wrapped in red, pink, and green paper with a gilded crown on top. The carrying poles bear banners ... for the journey to the Taoist heaven.

... After the family has made its reverential bows, the old picture of the god is taken from its niche over the range, placed in his special chair, taken outdoors and, with some paper money, burned on a heap of cedar branches. As the fragrant smoke rises, Tsao-chün ascends to that celestial region where he is to make his report. On the last night of the year, he is expected to return before dawn, at which hour a new picture will be placed in the old niche. Again, in a brief ceremony, he will be welcomed back with lighted candles, bowings, and the burning of incense and *yüan-pao*[3].

This annual ceremonial is more elaborate at New Year, although the kitchen god reputedly makes monthly reports to heaven. It is therefore important for each household to make an offering of rice before each daily breakfast.

SOURCE: Clarence Day, *Popular Religion in Pre-Communist China*. San Francisco, CA: Chinese Materials Center, 1975

Confucianism

Confucianism has developed from the ancient emphasis on veneration of ancestors and maintenance of proper rituals, or **li**, in order to stay in harmony with Heaven. Kong Qiu (K'ung Ch'iu; c. 551–479 BCE), commonly known in the West by the latinized version of his name, Confucius, was an ardent proponent of the ancient rites as a practical base for an orderly and moral society. Born during a period of social chaos, he earnestly sought to advise rulers how to restore harmony. Failing to win their ear, he became a teacher of *li* and the arts of governance. The school

---

3 *Yüan-pao*—money.

of thought that he developed became the mainstream of Chinese philosophy for over two thousand years.

Confucius focuses much of his attention on the development of human virtues within relationships with others. A man or woman whom he calls "noble" or "superior" is not one of high birth but one who manifests such virtues as humanity, or **ren** (*jen*), filial regard for one's parents, reverence toward ancestors, and observance of proprieties in human relationships, including benevolence in rulers and loyalty in their subjects.

Whereas Confucius's ideas were not embraced by the rulers of his time, by the Han dynasty (206 BCE–220 CE) they were adopted as a way of uniting the people behind the ruler, who was portrayed as the link between Heaven and the populace. Study of the Confucian Classics became mandatory for public service. This requirement lasted until the twentieth century, when all religious practice was disrupted by Communism, but it has recently been revived, along with renewed interest in Confucian virtues as a guide to self-improvement.

THE CONFUCIAN CLASSICS

The heart of Confucian teachings is found in the "Four Books"—*The Analects of Confucius*, *The Book of Mencius*, and two extracts from the ritual collections: "The Doctrine of the Mean" and "The Great Learning."

The Analects of Confucius

The **Analects**, or *Lunyu* (*Lun-yu*), are terse sayings of Kong Qiu, as collected by his students, some of whom are named.

… Yü Tzu [Pinyin, Yuzi] said, "Few of those who are filial sons and respectful brothers will show disrespect to superiors, and there has never been a man who is not disrespectful to superiors and yet creates disorder. A superior man is devoted to the fundamentals [the root]. When the root is firmly established, the moral law [Dao] will grow. Filial piety and brotherly respect are the root of humanity."

Tseng-Tzu [Pinyin, Zengzi] said, "Every day I examine myself on three points: whether in counseling others I have not been loyal; whether in intercourse with my friends I have not been faithful; and whether I have not repeated again and again and practiced the instructions of my teacher."

Young men should be filial when at home and respectful to their elders when away from home. They should be earnest and faithful. They should love all extensively and be intimate with men of humanity. When they have any energy to spare after the performance of moral duties, they should use it to study literature and the arts. …

Yü Tzu said, "Among the functions of propriety [*li*] the most valuable is that it establishes harmony. The excellence of the ways of ancient kings consists of this. It is the guiding principle of all things great and small. If things go amiss, and you, understanding harmony, try to achieve it without regulating it by the rules of propriety, they will still go amiss."

Confucius said, "The superior man does not seek fulfillment of his appetite nor comfort in his lodging. He is diligent in his duties and careful in his speech. He associates with men of moral principles and thereby realizes himself. Such a person may be said to love learning."

Confucius said, "Lead the people with governmental measures and regulate them by law and punishment, and they will avoid wrongdoing but will have no sense of honor and shame. Lead them with virtue and regulate them by the rules of propriety, and they will have a sense of shame and, moreover, set themselves right." ...

When Confucius offered sacrifice to his ancestors, he felt as if his ancestral spirits were actually present. When he offered sacrifice to other spiritual beings, he felt as if they were actually present. He said, "If I do not participate in the sacrifice, it is as if I did not sacrifice at all."

Confucius said, "If you set your mind on humanity, you will be free from evil."

Confucius said, "Wealth and honor are what every man desires. But if they have been obtained in violation of moral principles, they must not be kept. Poverty and humble station are what every man dislikes. But if they can be avoided only in violation of moral principles, they must not be avoided. If a superior man departs from humanity, how can he fulfill that name? ...

Confucius said, "A superior man in dealing with the world is not for anything or against anything. He follows righteousness as the standard."

Confucius said, "If one's acts are motivated by profit, he will have many enemies."

Confucius said, "The superior man understands righteousness; the inferior man understands profit."

Confucius said, "I transmit but do not create. I believe in and love the ancients . . ."

Confucius said, "Set your will on the Way. Have a firm grasp on virtue. Rely on humanity. Find recreation in the arts."

Confucius said, "With coarse rice to eat, with water to drink, and with a bent arm for a pillow, there is still joy. Wealth and honor obtained through unrighteousness are but floating clouds to me." ...

Confucius said, "Have sincere faith and love learning. Be not afraid to die for pursuing the good Way. Do not enter a tottering state nor stay in a chaotic one. When the Way prevails in the empire, then show yourself; when it does not prevail, then hide. ...

Chi-lu [Pinyin, Jilu] asked about serving the spiritual beings. Confucius said, "If we are not yet able to serve man, how can we serve spiritual beings?" "I venture to ask about death." Confucius said, "If we do not yet know about life, how can we know about death?"

... Tzu-hsia [Pinyin, Zixia] said, "I have heard [from Confucius] this saying: 'Life and death are the decree of Heaven; wealth and honor depend on Heaven. If a superior man is reverential [or serious] without fail, and is respectful in dealing with others and follows the rules of propriety, then all within the four seas are brothers.' ...

Confucius said, "If a ruler sets himself right, he will be followed without his command. If he does not set himself right, even his commands will not be obeyed."

Confucius said, "A man who is strong, resolute, simple, and slow to speak is near to humanity."

Confucius said, "The superior man understands the higher things [moral principles]; the inferior man understands the lower things [profit]."

SOURCE: Wing-tsit Chan, trans. and compiled, *A Source Book in Chinese Philosophy*. Princeton, NJ: Princeton University Press, 1963, pp. 18–47

The Book of Mencius

Mengzi (Meng-tzu; c. 390–305 BCE), generally known in the West by the latinized version of his name, Mencius, was a major commentator on the teachings of Confucius. Living during a period of extreme chaos in China, he nonetheless maintained a basic belief in the goodness of humanity.

II.A.6 The Sprouts of Virtue Mencius said: "All persons have a heart which cannot bear to see the suffering of others. The Sage Kings had such a heart, and their governments did not permit the suffering of the people. In ruling the kingdom, if you manifest this heart to implement such a government, you can hold the world in the palm of your hand.

"What I mean by saying that 'all persons have a heart which cannot bear to see the suffering of others' is this: Anyone who suddenly came upon a toddler about to fall into a well would have a heart of alarm and concern. And we cannot say that this heart arises from wanting to be favored by the parents, or from seeking the praise of one's friends and community, or from hoping to avoid a reputation for callousness.

"Clearly, one who did not have the heart of concern would be inhuman. One who did not have the heart of shame for wrong-doing would be inhuman. One who did not have the heart which places others before oneself would be inhuman. And one who did not have the heart which distinguishes between right and wrong would be inhuman.

"The *heart of concern* is the sprout of *ren* (kindness). The *heart of shame* is the sprout of *yi* (morality). The *heart of yielding* is the sprout of *li* (propriety). The *heart of judgment* is the sprout of *zhi* (wisdom). ...

VI.A.6 Many Hearts from the Start ... Mencius said, "If he follows his natural inclinations, a man is capable of becoming good. That's what I mean by 'goodness.' Insofar as he does not do good, it is not a fault of his basic condition. All persons have the *heart of concern*. All persons have the *heart* *of shame.* All persons have the *heart of yielding.* All persons have the *heart of judgment.* . . . . *Ren, yi, li,* and *zhi* were not branded upon me from the outside; I possessed them from the start, even though I may not have known it. ... People who are less virtuous—even by a factor of two, five, or a hundred— are so simply because they have not realized their full potential."

SOURCE: Original translation for this book by Randall Nadeau, 2006

The Doctrine of the Mean

"The Doctrine of the Mean" (the middle way) emphasizes adherence to the **Dao** (Tao), or way. This word is central to both Confucianism and Daoism, but is given different emphasis in the two traditions. In Confucianism, the Dao is the way of natural human sincerity, which reflects the Way of Heaven.

What Heaven (*T'ien,* Nature; Pinyin, *Tian*) imparts to man is called human nature. To follow our nature is called the Way. Cultivating the Way is called education. The Way cannot be separated from us for a moment. What can be separated from us is not the Way. ...

... The Way of the superior man has its simple beginnings in the relation between man and woman, but in its utmost reaches, it is clearly seen in heaven and on earth. ...

... Conscientiousness (*chung*) and altruism (*shu*) are not far from the Way. What you do not wish others to do to you, do not do to them.

Only those who are absolutely sincere can fully develop their nature. If they can fully develop their nature, they can then fully develop the nature of others. If they can fully develop the nature of others, they can then fully develop the nature of things. If they can fully develop the nature of things, they can then assist in the transforming and nourishing process of Heaven and Earth. If they can assist in the transforming and nourishing process of Heaven and Earth, they can thus form a trinity with Heaven and Earth. . . .

The next in order are those who cultivate to the utmost a particular goodness. Having done this, they can attain to the possession of sincerity. As there is sincerity, there will be its expression. As it is expressed, it will become conspicuous. As it becomes conspicuous, it will become clear. As it becomes clear, it will move others. As it moves others, it changes them. As it changes them, it transforms them. Only those who are absolutely sincere can transform others.

It is characteristic of absolute sincerity to be able to foreknow. When a nation or family is about to flourish, there are sure to be lucky omens. When a nation or family is about to perish, there are sure to be unlucky omens. These omens are revealed in divination and in the movements of the four limbs. When calamity or blessing is about to come, it can surely know beforehand if it is good, and it can also surely know beforehand if it is evil. Therefore he who has absolute sincerity is like a spirit. ...

Therefore absolute sincerity is ceaseless. Being ceaseless, it is lasting. Being lasting, it is evident. Being evident, it is infinite. Being infinite, it is extensive and deep. Being extensive and deep, it is high and brilliant. It is because it is extensive and deep that it contains all things. It is because it is high and brilliant that it overshadows all things. It is because it is infinite and lasting that it can complete all things. In being extensive and deep, it is a counterpart of Earth. In being high and brilliant, it is a counterpart of Heaven. In being infinite and lasting, it is unlimited. Such being its nature, it becomes prominent without any display, produces changes without motion, and accomplishes its ends without action. ...

... The *Book of Odes* says, "The **Mandate of Heaven**, how beautiful and unceasing." This is to say, "This is what makes Heaven to be Heaven."

SOURCE: "The Doctrine of the Mean," from *The Book of Rites*, in *A Source Book in Chinese Philosophy*, trans. and compiled Wing-tsit Chan. Princeton, NJ: Princeton University Press, 1963, pp. 98–110

SCHOLARS' COMMENTARIES

Scholars were highly honored figures in traditional Confucianism. They assembled the teachings of Confucius, including his commentaries on ancient texts, and further developed his system of practical ethics.

Lessons for Women by Ban Zhao

Although the majority of Confucian scholars were men, there were also some female scholars. The most famous woman scholar was Ban Zhao (Pan Chao), who was historian for the imperial court of China in the first century CE. She accepted the Confucian ideals of gender and family roles, with the principle that a woman should modestly yield to others, putting others first and herself last. Marriage was conceived as a sacred duty, with husband and wife having children so that they could continue the rites for ancestors. Ban Zhao's essay about proper social roles, *Lessons for Women*, was adopted as a standard textbook for women.

Respect and Caution As *Yin* and *Yang* are not of the same nature, so man and woman have different characteristics. The distinctive quality of the *Yang* is rigidity; the function of the *Yin* is yielding. Man is honored for strength; a woman is beautiful on account of her gentleness. Hence there arose the common saying: "A man though born like a wolf may, it is feared, become a weak monstrosity: a woman though born like a mouse may, it is feared, become a tiger."

Now for self-culture nothing equals respect for others. To counteract firmness nothing equals compliance. Consequently it can be said that the Way of respect and acquiescence is woman's most important principle of conduct. So respect may be defined as nothing other than holding on to that which is permanent; and acquiescence nothing other than being liberal and generous. Those who are steadfast in devotion know that they should stay in their proper places; those who are liberal and generous esteem others, and honor and serve [them].

If husband and wife have the habit of staying together, never leaving one another, and following each other around within the limited space of their own rooms, then they will lust after and take liberties with one another. From such action improper language will arise between the two. This kind of discussion may lead to licentiousness. Out of licentiousness will be born a heart of disrespect to the husband. Such a result comes from not knowing that one should stay in one's proper place. ...

[If wives] suppress not contempt for husbands, then it follows [that such wives] rebuke and scold [their husbands]. [If husbands] stop not short of anger, then they are certain to beat [their wives]. The correct relationship between husband and wife is based upon harmony and intimacy, and [conjugal] love is grounded in proper union. Should actual blows be dealt, how could matrimonial relationship be preserved? Should sharp words be spoken, how could [conjugal] love exist? If love and proper relationship both be destroyed, then husband and wife are divided.

... With whole-hearted devotion to sew and to weave; to love not gossip and silly laughter; in cleanliness and order [to prepare] the wine and food for serving guests, may be called the characteristics of womanly work.

SOURCE: Pan Chao, "Lessons for Women," in *An Anthology of Sacred Texts by and about Women*, ed. Serinity Young. New York: Crossroad Publishing, 1995, p. 359

NEO-CONFUCIANISM

As Buddhism spread within China, Confucianism was also revived. This "Neo-Confucianism," which became dominant after the tenth century CE, was more metaphysical than classical Confucianism.

The Great Ultimate by Zhou Dunyi

The philosopher Zhou Dunyi (Chou Tun-i; 1017–73) is considered the pioneer of Neo-Confucianism. His "Explanation of the Diagram of the Great Ultimate," which follows, became the basic framework for Neo-Confucian metaphysics and cosmology.

The Great Ultimate through movement generates yang. When its activity reaches its limit, it becomes tranquil. Through tranquillity the Great Ultimate generates yin. When tranquillity reaches its limit, activity begins again. So movement and tranquillity alternate and become the root of each other, giving rise to the distinction of yin and yang, and the two modes are thus established.

By the transformation of yang and its union with yin, the Five Agents of Water, Fire, Wood, Metal, and Earth arise. When these five material forces (ch'i; Pinyin, qi) are distributed in harmonious order, the four seasons run their course.

The Five Agents constitute one system of yin and yang, and yin and yang constitute one Great Ultimate. The Great Ultimate is fundamentally the Non-ultimate. The Five Agents arise, each with its specific nature.

When the reality of the Ultimate of Non-being and the essence of yin, yang, and the Five Agents come into mysterious union, integration arises. *Ch'ien* (Pinyin, *Qian*; Heaven) constitutes the male element, and *K'un* (Pinyin, *Kun*; Earth) constitutes the female element. The interaction of these two material forces engenders and transforms the myriad things. The myriad things reproduce and reproduce, resulting in an unending transformation.

SOURCE: Chou Tun-i, "An Explanation of the Diagram of the Great Ultimate," in *A Source Book in Chinese Philosophy*, trans. and compiled Wing-tsit Chan. Princeton, NJ: Princeton University Press, 1963, pp. 463–5

The Western Inscription by Zhang Zai

Zhang Zai (Chang Tsai; 1020–77) was another of the leading developers of Neo-Confucian thought; his "Western Inscription" is one of its most famous treatises. It was inscribed on the west window of his lecture room.

Heaven is my father and Earth is my mother, and even such a small creature as I finds an intimate place in their midst.

Therefore that which fills the universe I regard as my body and that which directs the universe I consider as my nature.

All people are my brothers and sisters, and all things are my companions.

The greater ruler [the emperor] is the eldest son of my parents [Heaven and Earth], and the great ministers are his stewards. Respect the aged—this is the way to treat them as elders should be treated. Show deep love toward the orphaned and the weak—this is the way to treat them as the young should be treated. The sage identifies his character with that of Heaven and Earth, and the worthy is the most outstanding man. Even those who are tired, infirm, crippled, or sick; those who have no brothers or children, wives or husbands, are all my brothers who are in distress and have no one to turn to.

SOURCE: Chang Tsai, "The Western Inscription," in *A Source Book in Chinese Philosophy*, trans. and compiled Wing-tsit Chan. Princeton, NJ: Princeton University Press, 1963, pp. 497–8

LIVING CONFUCIANISM

During the twentieth century, Communism undercut the political, economic, and social base of Confucianism. However, Confucianism is not just a matter of past history, according to Confucian scholar Xinzhong Yao, Director of the King's China Institute at King's College London. He finds that even though Confucianism no longer molds Chinese social structure, its values continue to be significant in Chinese life.

Confucianism and the Twenty-first Century by Xinzhong Yao

Will Confucianism go into the twenty-first century merely as a remnant of history? Or will it have much to offer and to contribute to a meaningful life in a rapidly changing society? What elements or parts of the Confucian tradition enable it not to be a dead culture, nor to be a tradition of the past, but continually to be a living organism comprehensively functioning in a multi-cultural society, emotionally and rationally motivating the people, and naturally making contributions to world peace and prosperity?

The Modern Relevance of Confucianism With the Confucian retreat from political, social and economic stages in East Asia since the end of last century, the Confucian influence has been limited to a small area of learning, seeming to be alive only among tradition-minded people and merely as a social and psychological background of their activities. The political and religious role of Confucianism in Mainland China[4] changed from being the orthodox ideology to a "doctrinal furnishing" of feudalism and aristocracy, and its values and ideals were severely undermined or demolished both by radical revolutionaries and by radical liberals. For most academics and non-academic people, Confucianism represented the shadow of the past, the symbol and the reason of a backward, disadvantaged and powerless China. As a result three irreversible changes took place in relation to Confucianism: Confucian organizations and institutions disappeared, Confucians lost their social identity, and Confucian rituals no longer had spiritual values. Confucianism seemed to have been reduced to being merely a theory or a doctrine without practical meaning, an old image without effect on modern life.

However, this is only one side of the story of Confucianism in the twentieth century. … Communism inherited a great deal from the Confucian moral code, so much so that … Communist ethics and Confucianism were not very different in practice. …

It is agreed among the scholars in Confucian Studies that while the social structure of old Confucianism has gone, its doctrinal and idealistic values are inherent in Chinese psychology and underlie East Asian peoples' attitudes and behaviour. …

… For example, self-cultivation (*xiu shen*) as the basis for governing the state and bringing peace to the world has been partly accepted and deliberately adopted by this generation of students. The combination of Confucian values and modern qualities creates a new title for business leaders, "Confucian businessmen/women," praising the Confucian virtues of the industrial and commercial leaders, such as humaneness, trustfulness, sincerity and altruism in business dealings. Some people enthusiastically talk about "Marxist Confucianism" or "Confucian Marxism," while others

---

4 Mainland China—the current communist state of the People's Republic of China, as opposed to the Republic of China, which is the capitalist nationalist state in Taiwan.

see an opportunity in the economic experience of East Asia to merge Confucianism and the market economy, Capitalist Confucianism or Confucian Capitalism. ...

A Responsible Ethic Free choice is the foundation of modern society, and the pre-condition of market economy. However, freedom without responsibility would result in the collapse of the social network and in the conflict between individuals, and between individuals and society, and would lead to the sacrifice of the future in order to satisfy short-term needs. This has become a serious challenge to human wisdom and to human integrity. In this respect, Confucianism can make a contribution to a new moral sense, a new ecological view and a new code for the global village. Confucian ethics insists that the self be the centre of relationships, not in order to claim one's rights but to claim to be responsible; and that a sense of the community of trust must be modelled on the family, not in a way that excludes others but in a way that extends one's family affection to a wider world. According to a Confucian understanding, daily behaviour must be guided by an established ritual, not merely for restricting individuals, but more for cultivating the sense of holiness and mission in their heart. Education is essential for building up a good character, not primarily for building up one's physical power to conquer what is unknown, but for the ability to cooperate with others and to be in harmony with nature and the universe. ...

The purpose of education is not only to transmit knowledge. It is also to transmit and apply values. In this sense, all traditional forms of education are relevant, and Confucian education can be a useful and valuable supplement to modern school education. ... Confucian learning was never meant to be a merely scholarly exercise. It had practical extensions, one of which was to put into practice the doctrinal understanding of individual, family, community and society, the core of values fostering a spirit of self-discipline, family solidarity, public morality and social responsibility. Confucian education is fundamentally humanistic; its primary purpose is learning to be fully human and becoming a qualified member of the community of trust; and its primary tools are enhancing self-cultivation and developing one's inner strength of assuming responsibilities for oneself, for one's family and for society at large. ...

SOURCE: Xinzhong Yao, paper presented at First International Conference on Traditional Culture and Moral Education, Beijing, 1998

The Staying Power of Religion in China by Peng Liu

In contemporary China, there is considerable tension between the government and religions, because the Communist Party has long sought to eliminate any perceived threats to its ideological dominance. From the seventeenth century, the Confucian literati were opposed to Christianity, and even after the fall of the Manchu dynasty in 1911 and the resulting end of Confucianism as the state ideology, anti-Christian sentiments persisted in the form of nationalism and then communist atheism. Nevertheless, religions seem to be thriving in China today.

Peng Liu, a professor at the Institute of American Studies at the Chinese Academy of Social Sciences in Beijing, offers some observations about the government's pragmatic approach to this tension.

… The ruling Communist Party views religion as a "backward" or even "superstitious" idealist ideology, opposed to and incompatible with Marxist "scientific" materialism. A Marxist government should propagate an atheistic worldview and must not encourage religious belief. At best, the state will tolerate religious teachings that focus on ethics and social service, playing down supernatural elements. China's leaders also view religion as a tool used by foreign powers to exercise undue influence within China. The introduction of the Chinese people to Christianity—Protestant, Roman Catholic and Orthodox—was closely connected with the unequal treaties of the nineteenth and early twentieth centuries, through which China lost control of its sovereignty, owing to its humiliating military defeats by the Western imperialist powers.

China's rulers recognize, however, that religion cannot be ignored or excluded altogether. The history of religion in China is a long one. Many Chinese practice some form of religion, and in some areas of China, religion is an integral part of the people's daily lives and communities. The culture of nearly all of China's ethnic minorities is profoundly influenced by religion. Thus religious issues cannot be separated from ethnic issues. Given these concerns, the party-state cannot easily or quickly eliminate religious belief, regardless of the preferences of China's leaders. Even according to Marxist theory, the predicted gradual death of religion is a protracted process.

Finally, most of the world's population has some kind of religious belief, and China's leaders have been forced to recognize the role religion plays in shaping international affairs. Thus religion and religious freedom and tolerance continually arise as foreign affairs issues that China must address. The state focuses on the practical import of religious diplomacy in the interests of trade and national security.

Given the resilience of religion in China and the pervasiveness of religious concerns in international affairs, the only practical thing for China to do is to shape religious practice and diplomacy into vehicles that serve the political purpose of building a socialist China. Jiang Zemin, as president of the People's Republic of China and general secretary of the Chinese Communist Party, speaking at national religious affairs conferences in 1991 and 2001, stressed that an overriding goal of both religious policy and religious regulations was "to guide religion to adapt to socialism." This statement summarizes the Chinese government's approach to religion; it is a political strategy to unite religious believers at home and overseas behind the Chinese Communist Party.

China's approach to religion drives the structure of its regulation of religion. Government institutions manage religious affairs according to the policies of the party-state, and religious groups have the duty to cooperate and carry out these policies. ... The underlying premise of all the interaction and regulation is that the religious groups must accept the leadership of the government to the end of furthering the interests of the party-state. Foreign exchanges with religious groups are encouraged only when they are likely to serve this political purpose. . . .

Political elites in China are increasingly paying attention to and discussing religion, reversing their traditional tendency to ignore it altogether. In light of the party-state's continued fragmentation and weakening, coupled with the emergence of a more pluralistic society, there will most likely be increasing differences of approach to religion among the competing interest groups in society. ...

SOURCE: Peng Liu, "The Staying Power of Religion," in *God and Caesar in China*, eds. Jason Kindopp and Carol Lee Hamrin. Washington, DC: Brookings Institution Press, 2004, pp. 152–63

Daoism

In contrast to the pragmatic social ethics of Confucianism, the Daoist tradition is distinctly mystical. This mysticism actually had no name until scholars labeled it Daoism, lumping together ancient philosophical traditions and later religious sects which concentrate on the achievement of immortality.

Daoism is based on ancient Chinese ways and the teachings of **sages** whose remembrance is shrouded in the mists of time and legend. Most famous of these is Laozi (Lao-tzu), who is thought to have lived some time between 600 and 300 BCE. To him is attributed the central scripture of Daoism, the **Dao de jing** (*Tao-te Ching*), which proposes a philosophical detachment, allowing things to take their own natural course without interference. By remaining quiet and receptive, one lives in harmony with the natural flow of life, with the Dao, the unnamable eternal Reality. Everything is to be accepted with equanimity, without preferences. The sage is like flowing water, which naturally flows into a valley from higher regions, makes its way around obstacles, and gently wears them down. He or she "does nothing," for the Dao if left to its own ways will express the underlying harmony in the universe. Energy is not to be wasted in artificial action, but may be expressed spontaneously and creatively when the natural energy is flowing in that direction. Daoist sages have traditionally withdrawn into the mountains to live contemplatively in nature.

THE TRADITIONAL CANON

The Dao de jing has traditionally been attributed to Laozi, a curator of the royal library during the Zhou (Chou) dynasty. According to legend, he was leaving society to retire to the mountains at the age of 160, when a border guard requested him to share his wisdom. The terse five thousand characters thus inscribed have been translated more times than any book other than the Bible.

The Dao de jing by Laozi

The Dao

What we call "the Dao" is not the Dao forever.
Things named are not forever named.
"Non-being" is how we describe the origins of Heaven and Earth.
"Being" is how we describe the mother of the ten thousand things.
We employ "Eternal Non-Being" in observance of the subtleties of the Dao
And employ "Eternal Being" in observance of its fullest extent.
They are identical in origin, though differing in name.
But both may be called "mysterious,"
And in calling them mysterious they become even more mysterious—
The gate of all subtleties!

The Spirit of the Valley

The Spirit of the Valley is eternal; it is called "the mysterious female." The gateway of the mysterious female is called the root of Heaven and Earth. Though constantly flowing, it seems always to be present. Though used, it is never used up.

Water

The most marvelous things are like water. Water can benefit the ten thousand creatures without competing, and settle in places most people despise. In these ways it is like the Dao.

Embracing the One

Can you carry the soul and embrace the One without letting go?
Can you concentrate your qi and attain the weakness of an infant?
Can you polish the mirror of mystery so as to make it spotless?
Can you practice **wu-wei** in loving the nation and governing the people?
Can you adopt the role of the female when the gates of Heaven open and close?
    Can you abandon all knowing even as your insight penetrates the universe? To give birth and to rear, to give birth but not to possess, to act but not to depend on the outcome, to lead but not to command: this is called "mysterious power."

Emptiness

Thirty spokes share a single hub; by virtue of its **Emptiness**, the hub is useful to the cart. Clay is shaped to create a vessel; by virtue of its Emptiness, a vessel has its use. Doors and windows are cut out to make a room; by virtue of that Emptiness, a room has its use. So, to have something may be beneficial, but it is in its Emptiness that it has its use.

Anti-Confucianism

When the Great Dao declined, the doctrines of *ren* and *yi* appeared. When "knowledge" and "wisdom" emerged, there was great hypocrisy. It is only when relatives can't get along that they talk about "filial children" and "loving parents," only when the state is in disorder that there are "loyal ministers."

Su and Pu

Abandon "sageliness" and "wisdom," and the people will benefit a hundredfold. Abandon ren and yi, and the people will again be obedient to their parents and loving towards their children. Abandon clever words and profit, and there will be no more thieves or robbers. Those things [which should be abandoned] are good in appearance, but insubstantial. So, let the people have something they can follow:

> manifest simplicity (*su*);
> embrace the uncarved block (***pu***);
> reduce selfishness;
> have few desires.

The Daoist Sage

He is whole because he's crooked, straight because he's bent, full because he's hollow, new because he's worn; he has because he lacks, he is amazed because there is so much.

This is why the sage embraces the One and becomes the model of the universe. He does not show himself, and so he is luminous. He does not consider himself right, and so he is revered. He does not claim credit, and so he is rewarded. He does not boast, and so he endures.

It is because he does not compete with anyone that no one under Heaven competes with him. When the ancients said, "He is whole because he is crooked," those were not empty words. Truly, he is whole to the end.

Dao

There is a thing, shaped by chaos, born prior to Heaven and Earth, silent and shapeless! It stands alone, unchanged by exterior forces. Its motion is circular, and it never tires. It is capable of being the Mother of everything under Heaven. I do not know its name, but if forced to, I'll call it "Dao"; if forced to, I'll name it "Great."

> Great, it is flowing.
> Flowing, it becomes distant.
> Distant, it returns.

Thus, the Dao is great, Heaven is great, Earth is great, and humankind is great. Among the four great things in the universe, humankind is counted as one of them. Humankind models itself on Earth, Earth on Heaven, and Heaven on the Dao. The Dao models itself on spontaneity.

The Role of the Female

Understand the male but keep to the role of the female, and you will be the river of the world. As the river of the world, your energy will be unsapped, like returning to infancy.

Understand the white but keep to the role of the black, and you will be the model of the world. As the model of the world, your energy will be restored, like returning to the unbounded.

Understand the honored but keep to the role of the humble, and you will be the valley of the world. As the valley of the world, your energy will be abundant, like returning to the uncarved block.

Reversion

Reversion is the way the Dao moves.
Weakness is what the Dao employs.
The ten thousand creatures under Heaven were born from Being,
    and Being was born from Non-Being.

Weakness and Strength

The weakest things under Heaven ride like a stallion over the hardest.
The things which have no substance enter the places which have no space.
Because of this, I understand the advantage of *wu-wei*. Few have the capacity to reach an understanding of the wordless teaching or of the advantage of *wu-wei*.

Wu wei er wu bu wei

In study, one learns more every day. But in acting in accordance with the Dao, one does less every day. One does less and less until finally there is *wu-wei*, and *wu wei er wu bu wei* (with *wu-wei* there is nothing that remains undone).

Speaking and Knowing

One who knows does not speak; one who speaks does not know.

Block the opening;
Shut the door;
Blunt the sharpness;
Untie the knot;
Soften the brightness;
Become like dust.

This is what is meant by the "mysterious identity." So, it is impossible to be familiar with it, and yet it is also impossible to be separated from it. It is impossible to augment it, yet it is also impossible to diminish it. It is impossible to ennoble it, and yet it is also impossible to debase it. That is why it is valued throughout the world.

Water

Under Heaven, there is nothing softer or weaker than water. Yet, in attacking what is stubborn and strong, nothing can surpass it. That is why nothing can replace it. Everyone knows that the soft overcomes the stubborn, and the weak overcomes the strong, yet no one can put this into practice.

SOURCE: Original translation for this book by Randall Nadeau, 2006

The Great and Venerable Teacher by Zhuangzi

The second major book in the traditional Daoist canon is a compilation of the often humorous and ironic writings of the sage Zhuangzi (Chuang-tzu; c. 365–290 BCE). In the following passage, he refers to the ideal sage as the True Man.

He who knows what it is that Heaven does, and knows what it is that man does, has reached the peak. Knowing what it is that Heaven does, he lives with Heaven. Knowing what it is that man does, he uses the knowledge of what he knows to help out the knowledge of what he doesn't know, and lives out the years that Heaven gave him without being cut off midway—this is the perfection of knowledge.

However, there is a difficulty. Knowledge must wait for something to fix on to, and that which it waits for is never certain. How, then, can I know that what I call Heaven is not really man, and what I call man is not really Heaven? There must first be a True Man before there can be true knowledge.

What do I mean by a True Man? The True Man of ancient times did not rebel against want, did not grow proud in plenty, and did not plan his affairs. Being like this, he could commit an error and not regret it, could meet with success and not make a show. Being like this, he could climb the high places and not be frightened, could enter the water and not get wet, could enter the fire and not get burned. His knowledge was able to climb all the way up to the Way like this.

The True Man of ancient times slept without dreaming and woke without care; he ate without savoring and his breath came from deep inside. The True Man breathes with his heels; the mass of men breathe with their throats. Crushed and bound down, they gasp out their words as though they were retching. Deep in their passions and desires, they are shallow in the workings of Heaven.

The True Man of ancient times knew nothing of loving life, knew nothing of hating death. He emerged without delight; he went back in without a fuss. He came briskly, he went briskly, and that was all. He didn't forget where he began; he didn't try to find out where he would end. He received something and took pleasure in it; he forgot about it and handed it back again. This is what I call not using the mind to repel the Way, not using man to help out Heaven. This is what I call the True Man. . . .

You hide your boat in the ravine and your fish net in the swamp and tell yourself that they will be safe. But in the middle of the night a strong man shoulders them and carries them off, and in your stupidity you don't know why it happened. You think you do right to hide little things in big ones, and yet they get away from you. But if you were to hide the world in the world, so that nothing could get away, this would be the final reality of the constancy of things.

You have had the audacity to take on human form and you are delighted. But the human form has ten thousand changes that never come to an end.

Your joys, then, must be uncountable. Therefore, the sage wanders in the realm where things cannot get away from him, and all are preserved. He delights in early death; he delights in old age; he delights in the beginning; he delights in the end. If he can serve as a model for men, how much more so that which the ten thousand things are tied to and all changes alike wait upon!

The Way has its reality and its signs but is without action or form. You can hand it down but you cannot receive it; you can get it but you cannot see it. It is its own source, its own root. Before Heaven and earth existed it was there, firm from ancient times. It gave spirituality to the spirits and to God; it gave birth to Heaven and to earth. It exists beyond the highest point, and yet you cannot call it lofty; it exists beneath the limit of the six directions, and yet you cannot call it deep. It was born before Heaven and earth, and yet you cannot say it has been there for long; it is earlier than the earliest time, and yet you cannot call it old.

SOURCE: Chuang-tzu, *The Book of Chuang-tzu*, trans. Burton Watson. New York: Columbia University Press, 1968, pp. 77–83

LATER DEVELOPMENTS

In addition to the philosophical system known as Daoism, as expressed in the preceding texts, from the second century CE onward various religious sects developed that are often referred to as "Immortals Daoism" or "Religious Daoism." Their relationship to the philosophical tradition is a matter of debate. These sects tend to focus on gods, spirits, magic, ritual, and alchemical efforts to achieve physical immortality.

The Way of Perfect Truth by Wang Zhe

The new Daoist religious sects often freely mixed elements of Buddhism and Confucianism with Daoism, as these strands coexisted in Chinese culture without sharp demarcations. For example, the twelfth-century teacher Wang Zhe (Wang Che), also known as Wang Chongyang (Wang Ch'ung-yang, "Master Wang of Developed Yang"; 1112–70) had studied and practiced both Confucian and Buddhist ways before becoming a master of the Dao, living as a recluse in the mountains and attracting many followers to his "Perfect Truth" sect. He gave the sect these basic precepts for the spiritual life.

On Sitting in Meditation Sitting in meditation which consists only of the act of closing the eyes and seating oneself in an upright position is only a pretense. The true way of sitting in meditation is to have the mind as immovable as Mount T'ai [Pinyin, Mount Tai][5] all the hours of the day, whether walking, resting, sitting, or reclining. The four doors of the eyes,

---

5 Mount Tai—a particularly sacred Chinese mountain.

ears, mouth, and nose should be so pacified that no external sight can be let in to intrude upon the inner self. If ever an impure or wandering thought arises, it will no longer be true quiet sitting. For the person who is an accomplished meditator, even though his body may still reside within this dusty world, his name will already be registered in the ranks of the immortals or free spirits and there will be no need for him to travel to far-off places to seek them out; within his body the nature of the sage and the virtuous man will already be present. Through years of practice, a person by his own efforts can liberate his spirit from the shell of his body and send it soaring to the heights. A single session of meditation, when completed, will allow a person to rove through all the corners of the universe.

On Pacification of the Mind   There are two minds. One is quiet and unmoving, dark and silent, not reflecting on any of the myriad things. It is deep and subtle, makes no distinction between inner and outer, and contains not a single wandering thought. The other mind is that mind which, because it is in contact with external forms, will be dragged into all kinds of thoughts, pushed into seeking out beginnings and ends—a totally restless and confused mind. This confused mind must be eliminated. If one allows it to rule, then the Way and its power will be damaged, and one's Nature and Destiny will come to harm. Hearing, seeing, and conscious thoughts should be eliminated from all activities, from walking, resting, sitting, or reclining.

On Transcending the Three Realms   The Three Realms refer to the realms of desire, form, and formlessness. The mind that has freed itself from all impure or random thoughts will have transcended the first realm of desire. The mind that is no longer tied to the perception of objects in the object-realm will have transcended the realm of form. The mind that no longer is fixed upon emptiness will further transcend the realm of formlessness. The spirit of the man who transcends all three of these realms will be in the realm of the immortals. His Nature will abide forever in the realm of Jade-like Purity.

On Cultivating the Body of the Law   The Body of the Law is formless form. It is neither empty nor full. It has neither front nor back and is neither high nor low, long nor short. When it is functioning, there is nothing it does not penetrate. When it is withdrawn into itself, it is obscure and leaves no trace: it must be cultivated in order to attain the true Way. If the cultivation is great, the merit will be great: if the cultivation is small, the merit will be small. One should not wish to return to it, nor should one be attached to this world of things. One must allow Nature to follow its own course.

On Leaving the Mundane World   Leaving the mundane world is not leaving the body; it is leaving behind the mundane mind. Consider the analogy of the lotus: although rooted in the mud, it blossoms pure and white into the clean air. The man who attains the Way, although corporally abiding in the world, may flourish through his mind in the realm of sages. Those people who presently seek after non-death or escape from the world do not know this true principle and commit the greatest folly.

The words of these 15 precepts are for our disciples of aspiration. Examine them carefully!

SOURCE: Wang Che, "The Way of the Taoist Tradition of Perfect Truth," in *Chinese Religion: An Anthology of Sources*, ed. Deborah Sommer. New York and Oxford: Oxford University Press, 1995, pp. 200–3

The Story of He Xiangu, a Female Immortal

In popular Daoism, many stories are told of the Eight Immortals, some of whom may have been based on historical figures. One of the Immortals is a female: He Xiangu (Ho Hsien Ku). The following story illustrates how her selfless virtue, as well as her asceticism, won her a place among the **Immortals**.

An old woman owned a small farm at the foot of Mi-Lo Shan [Pinyin, Milo Shan; Mount Milo]. She had never completed a full day's work and had no intention of doing so. As the years progressed she had become lazier and lazier, spending most of the day maliciously gossiping with her neighbours or giving abrupt orders to her servant.

Her latest servant was a young, beautiful and generous hearted girl called Ho Hsien Ku [Pinyin, He Xiangu]. However hard she worked the old woman was never satisfied. She continually harangued, scolded and punished the helpless girl. Ho Hsien Ku's day began at five o'clock in the morning and rarely finished before midnight.

Besides clearing the house and preparing the food she had to plant and reap the crops and feed and care for the animals. Ho Hsien Ku did this without complaint in return for food and lodgings, but at night, when she fell exhausted onto her straw mattress, she silently wept herself to sleep.

One day the old woman set off to visit her cousin, leaving the young girl to guard the house. Ho Hsien Ku placed a small wicker chair outside the front door and sat down with her sewing basket to repair the old woman's clothes.

Through the haze of the hot afternoon sun, she saw seven figures moving slowly towards her. As they drew closer, she saw their ragged clothes, gaunt faces and downcast eyes. The beggars eventually gathered around her. One stepped forward and in pleading tones addressed Ho Hsien Ku. "Could you please help us? We have not eaten a morsel of food in five days and now we are starving. Could you spare us a bowl of rice?"

Ho Hsien Ku was moved by their distress. If she had had the choice, she would have given the beggars all the food in the house but she was hesitant. The old woman meticulously checked the amount of food in the house each day. If a handful of rice or a spoonful of oil was missing, she would beat the girl mercilessly. But Ho Hsien Ku could not turn the beggars away. She would rather be beaten black and blue than let these unfortunate ragged men starve by the roadside.

She beckoned the beggars to rest on the straw mats in front of the house then went into the kitchen to boil a pan of rice [noodles]. Ten minutes later each beggar had a bowl of rice in his hands which he devoured eagerly and gratefully. The rice gave them renewed strength and after thanking Ho Hsien Ku profusely, the beggars wandered in the direction of the nearest town.
No sooner had they disappeared from view, when the old woman returned home. Without acknowledging Ho Hsien Ku, she marched straight into the kitchen to check the rice, noodles, eggs, fish, oil and wood. Ho Hsien Ku sat trembling outside the door and within a few minutes a piercing scream of anger came from the kitchen. The old woman ran from the kitchen brandishing a wooden broom.

"You thief, you ungrateful wretch! What have you done with my rice? Have you eaten it or sold it?" she demanded as she held the girl's arm with a vise-like grip.

Holding back her tears, Ho Hsien Ku recounted the whole story but the old woman had a heart like iron. "I have no pity for these dirty beggars. You either find them and bring them back to me or I will beat your legs till you can no longer walk."

The old woman loosened her grip on Ho Hsien Ku's arm, just enough for Ho Hsien Ku to break free and dash after the beggars. She eventually caught up with them as they were resting by the dusty road-side. Standing breathlessly before them she pleaded desperately.

"I am sorry to ask you this, but could you return with me to prove to my mistress that you ate the rice. If you do not come she will beat me black and blue."

The beggars were only too willing to help the girl who had taken pity on them and they returned home with her. The old woman was still in a furious temper when they arrived.

"How dare you eat the food that belongs to a poor old woman," she screamed. "I demand that you vomit every morsel on the floor in front of me. If you don't, I will make sure that nobody in this district offers you food or water. You deserve to starve."

The beggars had no choice but to do as they were told. One by one they vomited the noodles on to the packed earth floor in front of the house. The old woman then turned to Ho Hsien Ku and demanded vehemently, "Eat every single noodle that has been vomited. This is the price you have to pay for feeding dirty beggars."

She pushed the tearful and frightened Ho Hsien Ku to the floor and the helpless girl was forced to put a handful of the vomited noodles into her mouth. As soon as the noodles touched her tongue she felt her body become lighter and lighter. She felt her legs rise from the ground and her body began to float away from the spiteful old woman, away from the home where she had suffered so miserably.

The old woman began to panic and turned round to demand an explanation from the beggars, but they too had risen high above the house.

She caught a last glimpse of the beggars before they disappeared into the clouds and her servant, Ho Hsien Ku, was in their midst.

The Seven Immortals had come to earth to test the young girl's character and she had proved herself worthy of immortality. Because she had endured suffering without complaint and given to the poor without thought for herself, she could work alongside the Immortals for eternity.

SOURCE: "The Story of Ho Hsien Ku," from Kwok Man Ho and Joanne O'Brien, *The Eight Immortals of Taoism*, in *An Anthology of Sacred Texts by and about Women*, ed. Serinity Young. New York: Crossroad, 1995, pp. 394–5

The Essence of Tai Ji by Al Chung-liang Huang

Today there is considerable global interest in Daoism, with many translations of the ancient texts being undertaken and some of the spiritual practices being taught to people from other societies. Even under atheistic communist rule, decades of Chinese have begun their days with Taijiquan exercises for the sake of health and longevity. These slow, graceful movements were developed over two thousand years ago as a spiritual means of mental discipline and a physical aid to allowing the vital breath (qi) to flow freely through the body. In addition to the millions of people in East Asia who practice Taijiquan, Daoist masters such as Al Huang are teaching the practice to Westerners.

The yin/yang symbol is the interlocking, melting together of the flow of movement within a circle. The similar—and at the same time obviously contrasting—energies are moving *together*. Within the black area there is a white dot and within the white fish shape, there is a black dot. The whole idea of a circle divided in this way is to show that within a unity there is duality and polarity and contrast. The only way to find real balance without losing the centering feeling of the circle is to think of the contrasting energies moving together and in union, in harmony, interlocking. In a sense this is really like a white fish and a black fish mating. It's a union and flowing interaction. It's a kind of consummation between two forces, male and female, mind and body, good and bad. It's a very important way of living. People identify with this kind of concept in [Asia] much more than in our Western culture, where the tendency is to identify with one force and to reject the contrasting element. If you identify with only one side of the duality, then you become unbalanced. T'ai chi [Pinyin, **Tai Ji**] can help you to realize how you are unbalanced and help you to become centered again as you re-establish a flow between the two sides. So don't get stuck in a corner, because a circle has no corners. If you think in this way, you open up more, and you don't feel like you have to catch up with anything.

Someone said that the difference between an [Asian] man and a Western man is this: The [Asian] man is very empty and light up here in the head and very heavy down here in the belly and he feels very secure. The Western man is light in the belly and very heavy up here in the head, so he topples over. In our Western society so much is in the head, so much is in talking and thinking about things, that we can analyze everything to pieces and it's still distant from us, still not really understood. We have so many mechanical gadgets to do our work for us that our bodies are underemphasized. In order to regain balance we have to emphasize the body and we must work with the mind-body together. ...

In t'ai chi practice, you move very slowly. By moving very slowly you have time to be aware of all the subtle details of your movement and your relationship to your surroundings. It's so slow that you really have no way of saying this is slower than that or faster than that. You reach a level of speed that is like slow motion, in which everything is just happening. You slow it to the point that you are fully involved in the process of each moment as it happens. ...

Wherever you are, whatever you do, you can always come back to this marvelous sense of stillness, the feeling of yourself, very, very much *here*. This is your reference point; this is your stability. This is your life force that gives you balance. This is your home you carry around with you wherever you are. This is your powerhouse, your reservoir, your endless inexhaustible resource, that center you. ... And the movement goes on and on and on.

SOURCE: Al Chung-liang Huang, *Embrace Tiger, Return to Mountain: The Essence of Tai Chi*. Moab, UT: Real People Press, 1973, pp. 12–19, 182–5

The Significance of Daoist Ethical Thought in the Building of a Harmonious Society by Zhou Zhongzhi

Although Daoism is an ancient spiritual way, practice of Daoist ideals may be of great relevance in contemporary China, according to Zhou Zhongzhi. He teaches Law, Economics, and Politics at Shanghai Normal University, is chief editor of the textbook *Ethics*, and has been deeply engaged in research pertaining to ethics in business, consumption, economics, globalization, and values education.

Daoism is an indigenous religion of China which has had a profound influence on Chinese traditional culture for thousands of years. Although what has prevailed in traditional China is Confucianism, Daoism nonetheless has its unique value that cannot be underestimated in that, as the whole society is concerned, Daoism and Confucianism complement each other. As China enters the twenty-first century, it enters an era calling to build a harmonious society. The author argues that the ethical thought of Daoism may play an important role in the building of a harmonious society in contemporary China. This will be shown in three ways, as follows.

1. According to the idea of the unification between man and universe, Daoism believes that man, as the organic part of nature, is inalienable from it, and emphasizes that "Dao follows the laws of its intrinsic nature." That is to say, man should act in accordance with the laws of nature, or he will be punished by nature. As a result of China's rapid economic growth, the ecological environment in China is now at risk.

China's present effort in enhancing harmony between man and nature should absorb the ethical nourishment of Chinese Daoist ecological wisdom. Moreover, the Daoist School advocates avoiding selfishness and limiting desire, and calls for upholding thriftiness and restraining sumptuousness, which is evidently beneficial to the society of China in refraining from consumerism and becoming environment-friendly with lower consumption of resources.

2. In the Daoist opinion, the value of life is constituted not in the pursuit of material benefit or personal fame, but in the respect for Dao—the only thing to be desired to pursue—and the prize of virtue. People should therefore have the sentiment of being content with their lot and keep in good psychological condition. The development of a market economy in contemporary China, on the one hand, can improve people's living standards; while on the other hand, it may result in the fact that most people, who are fickle and uneasy, will take maximizing utility as the supreme aim of life. According to a survey conducted in China, more than 70 percent of respondents say that their biggest desire is to "get more money." The Daoist view on the value of life may urge these people to reflect imperturbably upon what the worth of life is, to maintain a harmony between material and spiritual life, and to seek the equilibrium in their mind.

3. Aiming to build a perfect world of peace and tranquillity, Daoism advocates loving others as well as loving oneself and encourages everyone to accumulate merits and become a virtuous man. The Daoists attach great importance to beneficence, which is regarded as critical to the realization of the perfect world. In their opinion, beneficence is not something for which people gain another's compliment but a duty they should assume. In contemporary China, the gap between the rich and the poor is widening, but the involvement in domestic charity is not as one would wish because most of the rich are indifferent to it. To change this situation, and hence to make different social classes get on well with each other, the Daoist ethic of encouraging beneficence is of course helpful.

SOURCE: Zhou Zhongzhi, abstract of paper presented at Metanexus conference on Continuity and Change: Perspectives on Science and Religion, Philadelphia, PA, June 3–7, 2006

Chinese Buddhism

Buddhism was introduced into China from India, traditionally in the first century CE. Two types became most prominent: Amita Buddhism (Amita-fo, Amitabha, or Pure Land), that emphasizes chanting and gaining merit to go to the Pure Land after death, and Chan Buddhism, which is more focused on silent meditation, being in the moment. Tibetan Buddhism was also practiced by some. In China, Buddhism took on some typically Chinese characteristics, notably in the form of the female Bodhisattva Guanyin, who in Buddhist tradition is the Chinese version of the Buddha of Compassion, Avalokiteshvara, usually portrayed as male. Guanyin overlaps with figures in folk religions (see pages 145–149), granting female babies to women, for example.

For centuries the upper classes did not like Buddhism, preferring humanistic Confucian social stability, strong families, and practical values. They did not see how monasticism and personal nirvana for anyone could help the empire. But after centuries of conflict and assimilation, the two eventually reconciled. Then Communist rule banned Buddhism and destroyed many temples and monasteries. But after Mao Zedong's death in 1976, Buddhism slowly returned to become the largest organized religion in China.

The Larger Sukhavativyuha Sutra or The Sutra on the Buddha of Eternal Life

Pure Land Amita Buddhism is the major form of Buddhism in China. In this passage from a main sutra of Pure Land Buddhism, as described in the narrative by Ananda, in the Presence of the Buddha (Bhagavat), the Bhikkhu[6] Dharmakara (once a king, who has just become the Amita Buddha), vows to fulfill his tasks in the Pure Land, or else not achieve the highest knowledge. The text entered China about the first century CE and has been translated many times.

Bhikku Dharmakara thus spoke at that time to the Bhagavat: "May the Bhagavat thus listen to me, to what my own prayers are and how, after I shall have obtained the highest perfect knowledge, my own Buddha country will then be endowed with all inconceivable excellences and good qualities.

1. "O Bhagavat, if in that Buddha country of mine there should be either hell, animals, the realm of departed spirits, or the body of fighting spirits, then may I not obtain the highest perfect knowledge.

2. "O Bhagavat, if in that Buddha country of mine the beings who are born there should die and fall into hell, the animal realm, the realm of departed spirits, or into the body of fighting spirits, then may I not obtain the highest perfect knowledge.

3. "O Bhagavat, if in that Buddha country of mine the beings who are born there should not all be of one color, that is, a golden color, then may I not obtain the highest perfect knowledge.

4. "O Bhagavat, if in that Buddha country of mine there should be perceived any difference between gods and men, except when people count and tell, saying: 'These are gods and men, but only in ordinary and imperfect parlance,' then may I not obtain the highest perfect knowledge.

6 Bhikkhu—a Theravadin monk.

5. "O Bhagavat, if in that Buddha country of mine the beings who are born there should not be possessed of the highest perfections of miraculous power and self-control, so that they could at least in the shortest moment of one thought step over a hundred thousand nayutas of kotis[7] of Buddha countries, then may I not obtain the highest perfect knowledge.

6. "O Bhagavat, if in that Buddha country of mine the beings who are born there should not all be possessed of the recollection of their former births, so as at least to remember a hundred thousand nayutas of kotis of kalpas,[8] then may I not obtain the highest perfect knowledge.

7. "O Bhagavat, if in that Buddha country of mine the beings who are born there should not all acquire the divine eye, so as at least to be able to see a hundred thousand nayutas of kotis of worlds, then may I not obtain the highest perfect knowledge.

8. "O Bhagavat, if in that Buddha country of mine the beings who are born there should not all acquire the divine ear, so as at least to be able to hear at the same time the good Dharma from a hundred thousand nayutas of kotis of Buddha countries, then may I not obtain the highest perfect knowledge."

SOURCE: Translated from the Sanskrit by F. Max Müller, edited by Richard St. Clair
<http://web.mit.edu/stclair/www/larger.html>

Pure Land, Pure Mind by Zhu Hong and Cong Ben

Amita Buddhism emphasizes the achievement of the Pure Land paradise afterlife by chanting "Namo Amita-fo" or "Praise Amita Buddha," and meritorious living. This emphasis on an afterlife paradise earned by merit is different from the Chan and Zen Buddhist goals of avoiding reincarnation in this suffering world by reaching nirvana through meditative self-awakening.

The authors, Zhu Hong (Chu-hung) and Cong Ben (Tsung-pen) were responsible for the revival of Pure Land Buddhism in the sixteenth century.

Main Characteristics of Pure Land

i)   Its teachings are based on *compassion*, on faith in the compassionate Vows of Amitabha Buddha to welcome and guide all sentient beings to His Pure Land;

ii) It is an *easy* method, in terms of both goal (rebirth in the Western Pure Land as a stepping-stone toward Buddhahood) and form of cultivation (can be practiced anywhere, any time with no special liturgy, accoutrements or guidance);

iii) It is a *panacea* for the diseases of the mind, unlike other methods or meditations which are directed to specific illnesses (e.g., meditation on the corpse is designed to sever lust, counting the breath is meant to rein in the wandering mind);

7 Nayutas of kotis—multitudes.
8 Kalpas—sacred precepts.

iv) It is a *democratic* method that empowers its adherents, freeing them from arcane metaphysics as well as dependence on teachers, gurus, roshis and other mediating authority figures.

For these reasons, since the thirteenth century, Pure Land has been the dominant tradition in East Asia, playing a crucial role in the democratization of Buddhism and the rise of the lay movement. Honen Shonin (1133–1212), the Patriarch of the Jodo (Pure Land) school in Japan, expressed the very essence of Pure Land teaching when he wrote:

> There shall be no distinction, no regard to male or female, good or bad, exalted or lowly; none shall fail to be in his Land of Purity after having called, with complete faith, on Amida.

Making a vow to attain birth in the Pure Land signifies a fundamental reorientation of the believer's motivations and will. No longer is the purpose of life brute survival, or fulfillment of a social role, or the struggle to wrest some satisfaction from a frustrating, taxing environment. By vowing to be reborn in the Pure Land, believers shift their focus. The joys and sorrows of this world become incidental, inconsequential. The present life takes on value chiefly as an opportunity to concentrate one's awareness on Amitabha, and purify one's mind accordingly.

The hallmark of Pure Land Buddhism is reciting the buddha-name, invoking Amitabha Buddha by chanting his name. Through reciting the buddha-name, people focus their attention on Amitabha Buddha. This promotes mindfulness of buddha, otherwise known as *buddha-remembrance* [buddha recitation].

In what sense is buddha "remembered"? "Buddha" is the name for the one reality that underlies all forms of being, as well as an epithet for those who witness and express this reality. According to the Buddhist Teaching, all people possess an inherently enlightened true nature that is their real identity. By becoming mindful of buddha, therefore, people are just regaining their own real identity. They are remembering their own buddha-nature.

Buddha as such is a concept that transcends any particular embodiment, such as Shakyamuni Buddha (the historical buddha born in India), or Maitreya Buddha (the future buddha), or Vairocana Buddha (the cosmic buddha) or Amitabha Buddha (the buddha of the western paradise). Buddha exists in many forms, but all share the same "body of reality," the same **Dharmakaya**, which is formless, omnipresent, all-pervading, indescribable, infinite—the everywhere-equal essence of all things, the one reality within-and-beyond all appearance.

Dharmakaya Buddha is utterly abstract and in fact inconceivable, so buddha takes on particular forms to communicate with living beings by coming within their range of perception. For most people, this is the only way that buddha can become comprehensible and of practical use. The particular embodiments of buddha, known as Nirmanakaya, are supreme examples of compassionate skill-in-means.

Pure Land people focus on Buddha in the form of Amitabha, the buddha of infinite life and infinite light. Believers put their faith in Amitabha Buddha and recite his name, confident in the promises he has given to deliver all who invoke his name. All classes of people, whatever their other characteristics or shortcomings, are guaranteed rebirth in the Pure Land and ultimate salvation, if only they invoke Amitabha's name with singleminded concentration and sincere faith.

SOURCE: *Pure Land, Pure Mind: The Buddhism of Masters Chu-hung and Tsung-pen*, trans. J. C. Cleary. New York, San Francisco, and Toronto: Sutra Translation Committee of the United States and Canada, 1994, pp. iv, 4, and 5

The Gates of Chan by Venerable Jing Hui

Chan is the other major form of Chinese Buddhism. Bodhidharma was the first Patriarch of Chan in the sixth century CE. The teaching of Chan is that words and scriptures are not the gate to the dharma, but that enlightenment must be experienced directly without relying on ritual, morality, discipline, and philosophy. Of course this is a paradox, since we cannot avoid these things, but Chan lets wisdom be passed on wordlessly from the master and in meditation so that enlightenment may come through the "gateless gate" in a flash. This extract is from a text by Venerable Jing Hui, a Chan master and a vice-president of the Buddhist Association of China.

We have to use language and words as the finger that points to the moon. "We see the moon because of the finger, whereas we forget the finger because we have seen the moon." That is the function of language and words. ... In India, as we all know, Chan's beginning is recounted as follows: one day on Mount Gridhrakuta the Buddha, realizing that his end was at hand, addressed an assembly of thousands; holding up a flower he blinked his eyes. Nobody amongst the audience recognized the true significance of what was happening yet there was one exception. At that very moment the only one who understood the message was Mahakashyapa, who smiled. The Buddha then said: "I have the Treasury of the True Dharma Eye, the serene Mind of Nirvana, the formless form of the Absolute Existence and the marvelous Path of Teachings. It does not rely on letters and it is transmitted outside the scriptures. I now hand it over to Mahakashyapa." This is the origin of Chan that the Chan School upholds. ...

Bodhidharma (?–628 or 536), the 28th Patriarch in India and also the First Patriarch in China, came to China to proclaim the Dharma. ...

He ... finally reached Mount Song in Henan. There he spent nine years sitting facing a wall in the Shaolin temple, waiting for a man to come. From this simple fact we can imagine how difficult it was to proclaim the Chan tradition at that time. It took him a full nine years before the Second Patriarch Shen Guang (487–593) came to Mount Song to be his disciple, and to seek for the path that could pacify the Mind.

He encountered and overcame all kinds of hardships. The time of his arrival in China coincided with the period of doctrinism that was then prospering throughout the country; dogma and intellect knowledge was also being stressed to a certain extent. In such circumstances, it was very difficult for him to disseminate the Chan tradition, that is, a "special transmission outside the scriptures, with no dependence on words or letters ..."

What is Chan? Firstly, Chan is a state. There is a saying in the Chan School that: "When drinking water, the drinker knows how hot or how cold the water is." What kind of a state is this? It is the state in which an enlightened person lives. The enlightened one is the Buddha, who was always in the state of Chan, whose every single act or every single word was nothing other than Chan. Hence the saying "hold on to the state of Chan in walking or sitting, enjoying the wholeness at depth of one's being no matter whether giving a speech or keeping silent." ...

It is the same with a monk registered in a temple. If he comes and is led to a room where he feels at ease he is able to sleep soundly throughout the night. The next day, someone informs him that it was in that very room that a person died of a terrible illness or that a person hung himself the day before. After hearing the shocking news he does not dare to stay in that room again for fear of ghosts. Where are the ghosts? They are in his mind, in the mind of separation. ...

That is what the message means and entails. "Seeing into one's own nature and the attainment of Buddhahood," in this context, means to forcefully drive this message home, to work on it and to realize it in one step. ...

Chan is also a path one seeks for emancipation. The shackles of convention are fetters and handcuffs. If one breaks them apart, he becomes emancipated right at that very moment. This is what Chan offers. In terms of the ultimate end, Chan is a path that leads to a perfect life. Now, we are living a life full of self-made and self-inflicted faults and defects, yet this does not reflect our primordial state or nature. We are actually perfect, enlightened beings in nature, living a perfect and enlightened life. The reason why we are so full of faults and defects is that we can barely gain the slightest awareness of our own self-nature, can barely fathom the deepest recesses of our being; instead we are constantly driven outwards to seek the Dharma, or driven outwards by our enormous and utterly insatiable desires. ...

Chan is an eternal happiness, a true blissfulness. The ultimate end of Chan is to reach the state of eternal happiness and attain the state of true bliss. It could be said that Chan is a serene and relaxed enjoyment, the perfection out of all separations, a great freedom beyond life and death, and the ultimate freedom that abides neither in life-death nor in Nirvana. As such, Chan can enable us to release all our intrinsic potentials. ...

The ultimate goal of the Chan School is the same as that of all scriptural Schools. The only difference is that they do not take the same kind of path. The scriptural teachings are not direct, but indirect through a continuous process. The Chan approach is immediate, straightaway. It is a bursting into enlightenment in one step. This is how the Chan approach differs from others. ...

Chan (Zen) in fact is an "impregnable fortress," without a gate to enter. Suppose there is really a gate, that gate would simply be a method of training to be taken up in the Chan tradition. That is why when a monk asked Master Zhao Zhou (778–897): "Has a dog Buddha-nature or not?" Master Zhao Zhou retorted: "Wu." Later on, this Gongan (koan) formed part of a specific approach in the Chan School. During the Song Dynasty (960–1279), Master Wumen Huikai (1183–1260) wrote a book entitled "Wumenguan" (the Gateless Barrier) based on this specific word "Wu." The very first sentence in the "Wumenguan" states that: "Mind is the essence of the Buddha's teachings, while the gateless gate is the gate." This is the gate we must use to enter. "Mind is the essence of the Buddha's teachings"… .

SOURCE: <http://www.buddhanet.net/pdf_file/gates_of_chan.pdf>

GLOSSARY

Amita-fo The major Chinese Buddha of Infinite Light and Pure Land paradise this side of nirvana. Associated with Guanyin.

Analects of Confucius The most revered Confucian scripture, a collection of the sayings of Confucius, probably compiled by the second generation of his disciples.

Chan Branch of Chinese Buddhism that emphasizes meditative direct experience of the Buddha, awakening to nirvana, not just from books or conventional ritual. In Japan it became Zen.

Dao (the Way) A term used by all Chinese schools of thought. The Daoist path of self-directing righteousness and harmony, the ineffable, ultimate, universal reality, hidden behind existence.

Dao de jing (The Classic of the Way of Power) The primary text of Daoism, in condensed paradoxical poetry.

Dharmakaya The formless, all present, indescribable, infinite essence of all things.

Emptiness The imperceptible, undifferentiated void giving birth to all existence, not-being, nothingness. Central in both Daoism and Buddhism.

Immortals Eight Daoist legendary perfected persons.

Li The largely Confucian guides to ritual, propriety, etiquette, and social norms.

Mandate of Heaven Confucian sense of transcendent rightness of the state, closer to religion than most Confucian ideas; may or may not be present in a ruler or state.

Pinyin New Romanized transcription of Chinese adopted in 1979, replacing 1859 Wade-Giles system.

Pu Uncarved block, uncut tree, a Daoist and Chan image of ultimate reality.

Qi Vital energy in the universe and in our bodies; union of yin and yang. A theme of folk religions and Daoism, and synthesized with other traditions.

Ren Benevolence, human-heartedness, humanistic love toward others; the highest Confucian virtue.

Sage An educated, sensible, wise man.

Tai Ji (Great Ultimate Reality) Creates yin and yang, drawn in a circle.

Taijiquan (Power of the Great Ultimate) Stylized, graceful physical exercises practiced daily to enter into harmony with the universe, the Dao.

Wu-wei Non-purposeful action, non-assertive flowing with the Dao.

Yang The bright, assertive, "masculine" cosmic energy of qi, like a mountain.

Yin The dark, receptive, "feminine" cosmic energy of qi, like a lake.

HOLY DAYS

Many Chinese holy days are syncretic blends of various traditions, and some are distinct to one tradition.

Buddha's birthday The eighth day of the fourth lunar month is a celebration of the birth, enlightenment, and passing away of the Buddha. Some monks stay up all night in shifts reading sutras; people take flowers, incense, and candles to Buddhist teachers, avoid killing, and liberate animals. Laughing Buddha's birthday is January 1, also celebrated by Daoists.

Chun Jie, New Year's Festival The most important celebration of the year, the Spring Festival, during the first 15 days of the first lunar month, early February. The purpose is to leave behind bad spirits and welcome a fresh, positive new year. Each year is named after an animal, such as the rabbit. Rituals include family and business reunion meals, dragon street parades, exploding firecrackers to scare off demons, and eating symbolic foods such as dumplings (symbolizing wealth). People send cards to friends, clean their houses, burn old pictures of gods (such as the "Kitchen God") and put up new ones. They also give gifts, light lanterns, forgive grudges, and wish happiness to all.

Duanwu, Dragon Boat Festival Celebrated on the fifth day of the fifth new moon when colorful long boats with dragon's heads are raced.

Guanyin's birthday Celebrated on the nineteenth day of the second, sixth, and ninth lunar months. Women eat a vegetarian diet, and young men and women gather to worship the goddess in the temple. They may offer incense, flowers, oil for her lamp, silk scrolls if they are hoping to bear a child, and they also pray for health and peace.

Gui Jie (Kui Chieh), Ghost Festival Celebrated on July 1 when ghosts and spirits of ancestors are allowed to come from the lower realm for 15 days, and people visit graves and burn imitation money for them.

Mazu's birthday Celebrated on the third day of the third lunar month, especially along China's southeast seacoast where fishermen and sailors revere the goddess for protection on the dangerous sea. At her temples, or in a parade, her statue wears a dragon robe and a crown. Older women dress in traditional style and burn incense.

Mountain pilgrimages China has several sacred mountains, in tradition holding up the heavens. People make arduous pilgrimages up these mountains to temples of various traditions, where they praise and pray for blessings. There are four traditional Daoist mountains, and five Buddhist ones.

Qingming, Grave Sweeping Day An ancient folk tradition as well as one of Confucian ancestor veneration, this takes place on the fifteenth day after Spring Equinox. It is a time for people to enjoy springtime with walks and picnics, and also a time to unite the family and tend to the graves of departed ones.

Yuan Xiao (Yuan Hsiao), Lantern Festival People eat round sticky rice balls, symbolizing the family's getting together in harmony. In the evening they carry lanterns, attend temple, where they enjoy plays, acrobats, food, and lantern puzzles.

Zhai (Chai) Festival A major Daoist rite of Cosmic Renewal to purify and renew the community by acts of repentance and purification, such as bathing, almsgiving, and abstinence from meat. Statues of "Heavenly Worthies" from other temples are brought in and people light lanterns, have parades, and a huge feast for the spirits.

Zhongqiu Moon, Mid-Autumn Festival Celebrated on the fifteenth day of the eighth lunar month. People eat mooncakes under the full moon, give gifts, carry lanterns, burn incense, and celebrate the Moon Goddess of Immortality.

HISTORICAL OUTLINE

c.1500–1040 BCE—Shang dynasty; bone and shell divination with writing, huge royal tombs

c. 1040–256 BCE—Zhou dynasty; Mandate of Heaven as source of king's authority; ancient folk religions

c. 551–479 BCE—Confucius advocates moral reform of society by opposing leadership by inherited privilege, advocating education instead

c. 300 BCE—*Dao de jing* text, traditionally ascribed to Laozi

210 BCE—Terracotta Army of 8,000 buried with Emperor in Xi'an

1st to 3rd centuries CE—Buddhism spreads from India to China

25–220 CE—later Eastern Han Dynasty Emperor Wu adopts Confucianism

2nd to 4th centuries CE—institutionalized Daoism develops

c. 500 CE—Chan Buddhism founded

562–645 CE—Amita-fo Buddhism becomes more accessible to common people

618–907 CE—Tang Dynasty and Daoism in peak development

635 CE—first Christian missionaries arrive in China

800s CE—Confucians react against new religions, Buddhists persecuted

1115–1234—Jin dynasty unifies China after chaos; Confucianism and Buddhism revive, Chan develops into major monastic tradition

1241—Neo-Confucianism, with more transcendence

1300s—Christians increase missions in China

1721—Christian teaching banned in China, but Christians return later

1850–1911—period of conflict and turmoil between invading Western traders and Chinese

1911–49—war between Kuomintang nationalists and Maoist communists; invasion by Japanese

1949— Mao Zedong and communists win control; Kuomintang nationalists go to Taiwan

1966–76—Cultural Revolution against ancient feudal class traditions, including religions; many temples destroyed, priests killed

1980s–2010—after death of Mao Zedong in 1976, Confucianism, Daoism, Buddhism, and folk religions increase, and Western religions allowed

REVIEW QUESTIONS

1   Do various Chinese religions see humans as basically good or evil? What are the social implications of this belief?
2   What is Laozi's idea of "emptiness"? Illustrate.
3   Explain the meaning of the yin/yang circle.
4   What are the differences between Pure Land Amita and Chan Buddhism?
5   Describe what the goddesses Guanyin and Mazu represent.

DISCUSSION QUESTIONS

1   Does ethical behavior need transcendent sources such as gods, goddesses, or a Mandate of Heaven to give it a strong enough motivating force?
2   Do you think the moderation and harmony of Confucianism and Daoism stifle or encourage progressive new ideas and corrections of social injustices?
3   Why do Daoists speak in paradoxical riddles? Explain some.
4   What do you think Confucianism and Daoism have to offer Western culture?
5   Why do you think Buddhism is flourishing today amid a Marxist-educated Chinese population?
6   What do the various Chinese folk religions discussed in this book offer that the major Chinese philosophies and religions do not?

INFORMATION RESOURCES

GENERAL

China books and periodicals
<http://www.chinabooks.com>

Ching, Julia. *Chinese Religions*. Maryknoll, New York: Orbis Books, 1993.

Confucian, Daoist, and Buddhist texts
<http://www.sacred-texts.com/cfu/index.htm>

MacInnis, Donald. *Religion in China Today*. Maryknoll, New York: Orbis Books, 1989.

Nadeau, Randall. *Confucianism and Taoism*, Vol. 2 in *Introduction to the World's Major Religions*. Westport, CT: Greenwood Press, 2006.

Overmeyer, Daniel. *Religions of China*. Prospect Hts. IL: Waveland Press, 1986.

Photographs of Chinese gods and goddesses
Guanyin: <http://www.theworldgeography.com/2011/03/top-10-tallest-monuments-around-world.html>

Mazu: <en.wikipedia.org/wiki/File:Statue_of_Mazu.jpg>

Yang, C. K. "Communism as a New Faith," in *Religion in Chinese Society*. pp. 378–404. Berkeley, CA: University of California Press, 1961.

Zhufang, Luo, ed. *Religion Under Socialism in China*. Armonk, NY: M. E. Sharpe, 1991.

FOLK RELIGIONS

Cheng Machao and **Feng Huaxi**. *The Origin of Chinese Deities*, trans. Fang Zhiyun and Chen Dezhen. Beijing, China: Foreign Languages Press, 1995.

Cultural China
<http://traditions.cultural-china.com/14two.html>

Day, Clarence B. *Popular Religion in Pre-Communist China*. San Francisco, CA: Chinese Materials Center, 1975.

DeGroot, J. J. M. *The Religious System of China*. 6 Vols. Rpt. Taipei, Taiwan: Ch'eng-wen Publishing, 1976.

Paper, Jordan. "Female Spirits and Spirituality in Chinese Religion," in *The Spirits are Drunk:*

Comparative Approaches to Chinese Religion. pp. 217–43. Albany, NY: State University of New York Press, 1995.

Wang, Minqin and **Lee W. Bailey**. "Guan Yin" in *Encyclopedia of Psychology and Religion*. pp. 368–73. New York: Springer, 2010.

Yü, Chün-fang. "Kuan-yin Devotion in China," in *Dharma World Magazine*, April–June 2008. <http://www.kosei-shuppan.co.jp/english/text/mag/2008/08_456_3.html>

CONFUCIANISM

Csikszentmihalyi, Mark, *et al.* "Confucianism," in *Encyclopedia of Religion*, ed. Lindsay Jones. 2nd ed. Vol. 3, pp. 1890–937. New York: Macmillan, 2005.

Lau, D.C., trans. *Confucius: The Analects*. London: Penguin Books, 1979.

Ross, Kelley. "Confucius." <http://www.friesian.com/confuci.htm>

Taylor, Rodney. *The Religious Dimensions of Confucianism*. Albany, NY: State University of New York Press, 1990.

DAOISM

Bokenkamp, Stephen, *et al.* "Daoism," in *Encyclopedia of Religion*, ed. Lindsay Jones. 2nd ed. Vol. 4, pp. 2175–216, New York: Macmillan, 2005.

The Daoist Foundation <http://www.daoistfoundation.org/ritual.html>

Johnson, Ian. "The Rise of the Tao," in the *New York Times*, Nov. 5, 2010. <http://www.nytimes.com/2010/11/07/magazine/07religion-t.html?nl=todaysheadlines&emc=tha29>

Kohn, Livia. *The Taoist Experience: An Anthology*. Albany, NY: State University of New York Press, 1993.

Lao-Tsu. *Tao te Ching*, trans. Gia-Fu Feng and Jane English. New York: Vintage Books, 1989.

Saso, Michael. *Taoism and [Chiao] the Rite of Cosmic Renewal*. Pullman, WA: Washington State University Press, 1990.

BUDDHISM

Chu-hung and Tsung-pen. *Pure Land, Pure Mind: The Buddhism of Masters Chu-hung and Tsung-pen*, trans. J. C. Cleary. New York: Sutra Translation Committee of the United States and Canada, 1994.

Hershock, Peter. *Chan Buddhism*. Honolulu, HI: University of Hawai'i Press, 2005.

Wang, Minqin and **Lee W. Bailey**. "Amita Buddha" in *Encyclopedia of Psychology and Religion*. pp. 25–28. New York: Springer, 2010.

Yü, Chün-fang. *Kuan-Yin: The Chinese Transformation of Avalokiteshvara*. New York: Columbia University Press, 2000.

CHAPTER 7

SHINTO

The ancient indigenous traditions of Japan are referred to as Shinto. Over time, Japanese people have adopted global religions as well, including Buddhism, Confucianism, and Christianity, and mixed them with their native ways. Contemporary scholars feel that Shinto is not a single religious tradition, but rather a general label that has been applied to ways that revere the **kami**, or spirits, present in the cosmos and in the natural environment.

From the seventh century CE onward, the kami have also been linked with rulers, giving the stamp of divine authority to their power, with the emperors said to be offspring of the sun goddess, Amaterasu. From 1868 to the end of World War II, the Meiji monarchy officially promoted Shinto as a **state cult**, with the last emperor regarded as a god whom ordinary people could not touch or even see.

The term "**sect Shinto**" has been applied to various sects derived from personal communications with the kami by seers and shamans. Many of these new religious movements appeared during the nineteenth and twentieth century and continue today.

Scriptural sources

The *Kojiki* (712 CE) and *Nihongi* (720 CE) are the central scriptures that were compiled from ancient regional and family myths starting in the seventh century CE as part of a political effort to bring national unity. The *Kojiki*, "Record of Ancient Matters," includes myths about the origin of the islands of Japan, and links the kami with imperial genealogies. It starts with the "beginning of heaven and earth," with deities coming into existence in heaven.

The Kojiki, Chapter 3

Chapter 3 of the *Kojiki* is the story of the divine creation of the first island of Japan from its primeval form as something "resembling floating oil and drifting like a jellyfish" (*Kojiki* 1:2), by the two important deities Izanagi and Izanami, standing on the bridge which deities used for traveling between heaven and earth.

At this time the heavenly deities, all with one command, said to the two deities Izanagi-nö-mikötö and Izanami-nö-mikötö:

"Complete and solidify this drifting land!"

Giving them the Heavenly Jeweled Spear, they entrusted the mission to them.

Thereupon, the two deities stood on the Heavenly Floating Bridge and, lowering the jeweled spear, stirred with it. They stirred the brine with a churning-churning sound; and when they lifted up [the spear] again, the brine dripping down from the tip of the spear piled up and became an island. This was the island of Onögörö.

SOURCE: The *Kojiki*, Book 1, Chapter 3, trans. Donald L. Philippi. Tokyo: University of Tokyo Press, 1968, p. 49

The Kojiki, Chapter 11

After Izanagi and Izanami gave birth to eight islands and many deities, Izanami died in childbirth. Grief-stricken, Izanagi tried to bring her back from the underworld. Emerging from that polluted place, he tried to purify himself. Purification still plays a major role in Shinto rituals. And as Izanagi shed his possessions and washed himself, ancestral deities belonging to various influential families were said to be born, thus bringing all aristocratic families into one mythological lineage. Most significant was the kami Amaterasu, who came from the washing of his left eye (linked in legend with the sun), and to whom the emperors traced their ancestry.

Hereupon, Izanagi-nö-opo-kamï said: "I have been to a most unpleasant land, a horrible, unclean land. Therefore I shall purify myself."

Arriving at [the plain] Apaki-para by the river-mouth of Tatibana in Pimuka in Tukusi, he purified and exorcised himself.

When he flung down his stick, there came into existence a deity named Tuki-tatu-puna-to-nö-kamï.

Next, when he flung down his sash, there came into existence a deity named Miti-nö-naga-ti-pa-nö-kamï.

Next, when he flung down his bag, there came into existence a deity named Töki-pakasi-nö-kamï.

Next, when he flung down his cloak, there came into existence a deity named Wadurapi-nö-usi-nö-kamï.

Next, when he flung down his trousers, there came into existence a deity named Ti-mata-nö-kamï. ...

The twelve deities in the above section ... all were born from his taking off the articles worn on his body.

Then he said: "The current of the upper stream is a current too swift; the current of the lower stream is a current too weak."

Then, when he went down and dived into the middle stream and bathed, there came into existence a deity named Yaso-maga-tu-pi-nö-kamï, next Opo-maga-tu-pi-nö-kamï.

These two deities came into existence from the pollution which he took on when he went to that unclean land.

Next, in order to rectify these evils, there came into existence the deity Kamu-napobi-nö-kamï; next, Opo-napobi-nö-kamï; next, Idu-nö-me-nö-kamï.

Next, when he bathed at the bottom of the water, there came into existence the deity named Sökö-tu-wata-tu-mi-nö-kamï; next Sökö-dutu-nö-wo-nö-mikötö.

When he bathed in the middle [of the water], there came into existence the deity named Naka-tu-wata-tu-nö-kamï; next Naka-dutu-nö-wo-nö-mikötö.

When he bathed on the surface of the water, there came into existence the deity named Upa-tu-wata-tu-mi-nö-mikötö; next, Upa-dutu-nö-wo-nö-mikötö.

These three Wata-tu-mi deities are the deities worshipped by the murazi of the Adumi as their ancestral deities. The murazi of the Adumi are the descendants of Utusi-pi-gana-saku-nö-mikötö, the child of these Wata-tu-mi deities.

The three deities Sökö-dutu-nö-wo-nö-mikötö, Naka-dutu-nö-wo-nö-mikötö, and Upa-dutu-nö-wo-nö-mikötö are the three great deities of Sumi-nö-ye.

Then when he washed his left eye, there came into existence a deity named Ama-terasu-opo-mi-kamï.

Next, when he washed his right eye, there came into existence a deity named Tuku-yömi-nö-mikötö.

Next, when he washed his nose, there came into existence a deity named Take-paya-susa-nö-wo-nö-mikötö.

The fourteen deities in the above section, from Ya-so-maga-tu-pi-nö-kamï through Paya-susa-nö-wo-nö-mikötö, are deities born from bathing his body.

SOURCE: The *Kojiki*, Book 1, Chapter 11, trans. Donald L. Philippi. Tokyo: University of Tokyo Press, 1968, pp. 68–70

Purification

Traditional purification litanies conducted by shrine priests continue to form an essential part of Shinto worship, to keep the places of the kami and the hearts of worshipers clean, bright, and "straight." Sources of pollution range from natural catastrophes, leprosy, and eating dead flesh to malicious thinking and crude language.

Purification Ritual from the *Engishiki*

The *Engishiki*, completed in 927 CE, is a 50-volume compilation of seasonal festivals, governmental procedures, and rituals for the kami, all to ensure the well-being of the nation. This is an excerpt from a major purification litany, of which the original is written in beautiful classic language. It is especially poignant in the wake of the catastrophic earthquake, tsunami, and threat of nuclear contamination that shook Japan in 2011.

> Thus hearing the litany,
> And that there be no blot of sin in the court or the country,
> May the deities bestow their purification that no offense remain,
> And as the wind blows from its origin to carry away the clouds of
>   heaven,
> Even as the wind of morning and the wind of evening
> Clear away the morning and evening mists,
> As the ship in harbor casts off its moorings stem and stern
> To be borne out onto the great plain of the sea,
> And as the rank grasses beyond the river
> Are swept away with the clean stroke of the scythe—
> Even so, may the deity Seoritshumie-no-kami,
> Dwelling in the swift-flowing stream
> That falls from the high mountains and low hills
> Carry away these sins and pollutions without remain, to the wide
>   sea plain.
> Our sins thus swept away,
> May the goddess Hayaakitsuhimi-no-kami,
> Who lives in the stream of the sea plain,
> Open wide her great mouth
> To engulf those sins and impurities,
> And when they are thus imbibed,
> May the god Ibukidonushi-no-kami
> Dwelling in the place where breath is breathed,
> Blow them out with a great rushing breath.
> And when he has thus banished them to the underworld,
> May the goddess Hayasasurahime-no-kami disperse them one and all.
> Even in this way, may the sins of all in the realm,
> From officials of the court on down,
> Every transgression in the land be washed away.

SOURCE: *Engishiki*, 8, in *The World of Shinto*, trans. Norman Havens. Tokyo: Bukkyo Dendo Kyokai, 1985, p. 372

Shrine worship

"Shinto" shrine worship is thought to have begun after the introduction of Buddhism to Japan in the sixth century CE. Now there are over one hundred thousand shrines in Japan to honor the kami and to serve as their dwelling place, or *jinja*. Shinto master Motohisa Yamakage explains the spiritual process by which a site may become a *jinja*.

After the Spirit of Kami Descends, a Place Becomes Jinja

by Motohisa Yamakage

For a *jinja*, one must choose a suitable place and then create an appropriate setting for a sacred space. Then it is necessary to ask Kami to descend upon it and make its presence felt. In other words, *jinja* need not be a place where Kami have dwelled eternally, or will always live. ...

The ancients believed that it did not matter if a shrine were small and simple, because there is a huge shrine much higher in the world of the spirit of Kami where many Kami (*kamigami*) reside. ...

It is also said that the Kami itself does not reside in the shrine. Rather, the guardian spirit is said to reside there. The guardian spirit protects *kamizane*, which literally means "Kami's core," acting as a substitute or *katashiro* for Kami. This guardian spirit is active in the world of spirit (*reikai*), which is at a lower level than the world of Kami (*shinkai*). The role of this guardian spirit is to connect this earthly world with the higher world of Kami. We are told that when believers practice morning and evening worship, this guardian spirit from the world of spirit worships the great Kami in the world of Kami in order to convey the believers' prayers. ...

As for the proper attitude for welcoming Kami, it is vital for the *kannushi* [priest] to have a reverential attitude with a feeling of awe and to prostrate himself in front of Kami. This reverential attitude, combined with a feeling of awe, can probably be described in the broadest sense as "an apologetic attitude." The *kannushi* must have an awe-inspired and humble attitude, which will make him feel like saying, "I am not worthy of evoking Kami and of being in front of the presence. I have much pollution within me and I am an unclean person. I beg forgiveness from the bottom of my heart and pray you will purify me."

To give deeper meaning to this attitude, we need correct behaviour and manners. A *kannushi* must therefore carefully practice the conduct of his ritual services. ...

With each movement of the body one must contain and reflect reverence and respect toward Kami. If people deepen this reverential attitude, then not only by the way they carry the body but also by the integrity of their daily character will they naturally reveal their cleanness and brightness and humility. Being around that person, others will be able to appreciate the outer and inner qualities—which we often call fragrance—worthy of one who serves Kami. I know many *kannushi* who are men and women of such noble character. When a *kannushi* of this caliber holds a ritual ceremony at his shrine, the service reaches a true level of solemnity. We feel awe-struck in front of the shrine and we feel that Kami is truly present. A refreshing sense of tranquility pervades such shrines, and a spirit of benign humility is transmitted from older to younger generations of *kannushi*. In fact, the *kannushi*, serving in a shrine, should be sincere, otherwise the act of reverence cannot become truly pure, and the shrine cannot become a suitable *yuniwa*. Therefore, whether or not the spirit of Kami descends to the festival site depends upon how well the *kannushi* cultivates his moral character on a daily basis. ...

The body of Kami called *katashiro* is usually represented by the mirror, but this mirror itself is not Kami. When a mirror is put in the right place and is revered, the spirit of Kami descends upon the mirror, through which its spiritual vibration permeates the surrounding area. Only then does the mirror become *kamizane*. And if the spirit of Kami always visits this site, only then does it become the shrine where Kami is present.

In order for this to happen, the body of Kami and the place dedicated to it must be very clean and pure. ...

The body of Kami is often enveloped and folded many times and put in the clean box. It is then enshrined in the *kamidoko* (Kami's floor), which is called *naijin*, the sanctuary of the main shrine. This *naijin* is surrounded by its outer enclosure called *gejin*. This *gejin* is the inner wall of the main shrine and is made of wood. The main shrine is also surrounded with another outer enclosure, which is in turn surrounded by fences—first the *mizugaki* then the *uchitamagaki* and finally the *sototamagaki*. The inside of these areas are called *kinsokuchi*, meaning "an area not allowed for feet to step on." People are prohibited from entering there.

Why is the cleanness of the shrine protected many times over? The body of Kami and the place for the descent of the spirit of Kami are still of physical matter itself, and matter can be easily contaminated. ...

When the sacred area is contaminated, the spiritual vibration of the spirit of Kami cannot permeate. This is because the spiritual light is cut off, in much the same way that a dirty, clouded mirror does not reflect objects well. The spirit of Kami does not clean the impurity by itself. It simply turns off the source switch of spiritual vibration and light.

SOURCE: Motohisa Yamakage, *The Essence of Shinto*. Tokyo/New York/London: Kodansha International, 2006, pp. 72–9

Sect Shinto

Ancient practices of communicating with the kami led many people—often women—to act as shamans, with the kami speaking through them while they were in trance. Some of these women had devotees who eventually developed movements around them. During the Meiji regime, these movements were labeled "Sect Shinto." They have evolved somewhat separately from mainstream shrine Shinto.

The Origin of Oomoto by Sahae Oishi

One such continuing movement is Oomoto, which developed around Deguchi Nao (1836–1918). The name "Oomoto" means "The great origin," referring to the movement's attempts to return to ancient Shinto ways. Nao was an extremely poor and self-sacrificing mother of eight who at the age of 56 began to be possessed by the kami Ushitora no Konjin. According to her biography written by a follower, at first the kami spoke in a roaring voice from within terrified Nao. Thinking her mad and blaming her for arson, the local people put her in jail.

While still in detention, Nao appealed to the spirit …, "Would it not be possible to make your august will known in some other way?" The voice in reply commanded her to take up a writing brush. However there was no writing brush in the cell, and even if there were, unlettered as she was, Nao could not have written even a single word.

Nao hesitated, but the voice spoke again: "It is not you who will do the writing. I will make you write, so take up the brush and forget your doubts." Nao looked around. Her eyes fell on a nail and she picked it up. To her amazement, her hand began to move of its own accord and scratched some words on a pillar—words which the illiterate Nao could not read.

This was the beginning of the scriptures of Oomoto, to be called the *Ofodesaki* meaning "from the tip of the writing brush." Later, Nao was to write in profusion on proper paper with brush and ink, reaching, by her passing in 1918, approximately two hundred thousand pages of which she was never able to read any part.

The following are some sentences from the opening of the work:

The Greater World shall burst into bloom as plum blossoms at winter's end. I, Ushitora no Konjin, have come to reign at last. … Know ye, this present world is a world of beasts, the stronger preying upon the weaker, the work of the devil. Alas, ye world of beasts! Evil holds you in such thrall that your eyes are blinded to its wickedness—a dark age, indeed. If allowed to go on in this way, society will soon lose the last vestiges of harmony and order. Therefore, by a manifestation of Divine Power, the Greater World shall undergo reconstruction, and change into an entirely new creation. The old world shall suffer a most rigorous purification that it may become the Kingdom of Heaven where peace will reign through all ages to come. Prepare yourselves for the Age of Peace! Ye sons of men, hold yourselves in readiness! For the world of God is never-failing. …

On April 19, 1901, Nao wrote the following in the Ofudesaki: "There is no water in the world to compare with the pure crystal water of the door of the Celestial Rock Cave at Moto-Ise. Go there and bring back some of the water."

The Celestial Rock Cave is the scene of the ancient Shinto myth of the Sun-Goddess Amaterasu, who, upset by the wild behaviour of her younger brother, the deity Susanoo no Mikoto, hid herself in the Rock Cave so that the world was plunged into darkness. This cave is said to be at Moto-Ise, north of Ayabe, where the Sun Goddess was originally enshrined before the present Grand Shrine of Ise was established on the Pacific Coast. The Ofudesaki continues: "If this were not the command of Ushitora no Konjin, you would not be able to get this precious water. Ushitora no Konjin has given his permission, so you will not be hindered."

Keitarô Kinoshita went to Moto-Ise to reconnoitre. When he got back he reported that the drawing of this water had been prohibited from time immemorial, and it was said that should anyone defy this ban, there would be devastating hurricanes and great floods. There was a priest on guard to see that no one touched the sacred water, and to get to the place where the water could be drawn it was necessary to cross a fast-flowing river some twelve feet wide.

Six days later, on April 26, 1901, Nao, now sixty-four years old, left Ayabe with Onisaburo, Sumiko and thirty-nine followers, most of whom had no knowledge of what the mission was about. With them they took two segments of green bamboo to carry the water.

Arriving at Moto-Ise, they stopped to rest at a tea shop. Unknown to the other followers, one of the party, a man by the name of Yoshimatsu Moritsu, slipped away to the shrine while Kinoshota waited at the entrance of the tea shop for word that the coast was clear. ... As the sun was beginning to set, Moritsu came back and reported that the priest on guard had gone back to his house, probably for his supper. Kinoshita, realizing it was now or never, ran off as fast as his legs could carry him. Arriving at the rock cave, he could dimly make out in the fading twilight an old tree trunk lying across the river, an access which had not been there six days before. Using the tree trunk as a bridge, he crossed the river, filled the bamboo joints with the sacred water, and returned to the tea shop.

Nao was overjoyed, and when Kinoshita told her about the tree trunk, she said, "That was no ordinary tree trunk. That was surely the Dragon God himself coming to our help." ...

The holy water which they had brought back was first offered on the altar of Ushitora no Konjin. One cylinder was set aside, and the other the followers passed around, taking a sip each, before pouring the remainder into the Oomoto well, to be designated as Kimmeisui [golden bright water]. ... The remaining cylinder of water they mixed with the water of Kimmeisui, and in May, Nao, accompanied by thirty-five followers, took this water to the island of Meshima, climbed to the summit of the rock where they had landed the previous year, and poured the water into the sea, praying:

"Oh, Ushitora no Konjin, we humbly beseech you, with your power, wide as the Pacific Ocean and deep as the Sea of Japan, to make this pure water from Moto-Ise circle the seas of the world, turning to clouds, turning to rain, snow and hail, watering the five continents, cleansing corrupt spirits, washing away impurities, and building a paradise on earth."

Concerning this ritual decantation, Nao remarked, "In three years this water will go around the whole world, and then the world will begin to move. Meanwhile people whose destiny it is to serve the divine plan will begin to gather here."

SOURCE: *Nao Deguchi—A Biography of the Foundress of Oomoto*, based on *Kaiso-den* by Sahae Oishi, pp. 11–13, 19–21
<http://www.oomoto.or.jp>

Shinto today

Although Shinto is thoroughly Japanese in orientation, even to the point of being used in the past as a nationalistic imperial state cult, few Japanese today identify themselves as Shintoists. On the other hand, there have been some contemporary attempts to export the teachings of Shinto. In the United States, a natural setting in Washington State has become home to a transplanted branch of the Tsubaki Grand Shrine. It is dedicated primarily to the deity Sarutahiko-no-o-kami, who according to the *Kojiki* was born when Izanagi threw down his staff in the process of purifying himself. Tsubaki Grand Shrine of America is run by Japanese Shinto priests as teachers to Western devotees. It emphasizes the purification ritual of *misogi*, with devotees bathing every morning in the "sacred Pilchuck River." The following is a translation of the purification ritual and an explanation of the origin and purpose of *misogi* in terms that transcend identification with Japan.

Misogi Shuho   by Tsubaki Grand Shrine of America

We will be able to recognize [see] the Kami [truth] only after we purify ourselves of all negativity, impurities, faults and restore ourselves to what we are meant to be (natural brightness). ...

Izanagi-no-Okami [Kami who created the solar system and ancestor Kami of all on earth] conducted the first *Misogi-Shuho* following his visit to the ... world of death. His purpose was to "wash away defilement," "cleanse his body from pollutants," and to "perform the purification of his august person." Prior to entering the Tachibana River to cleanse completely, Izanagi-no-Mikoto rid himself of all his possessions. As he was being pursued by elements of impurity from the Underworld he first threw his staff. From that staff Sarutahiko-no-o-kami was born. This is why Sarutahikono-o-Kami is also known as Kami to protect the path, Kami to protect crossroads, Mai to ward off misfortune.

Then Izanagi-no-Okami threw away all his jewelry and clothing into the river as they were also contaminated by impurities. These articles became the twelve Kami who protect the directions in which people live, travel, work, and conduct business.

Then after finding the spot in the river not too swift and not too slow, Izanagi-no-Okami entered the river to purify himself. Many Kami were created from this act—many Kami of wrongdoing as well as Kami to rectify wrongdoing originated from this first Misogi. Then when Izanagi-no-Okami washed his face Amaterasu-Omikami [Heaven Shining Great August Deity, Sun Kami] was born from his left eye. From his right eye was created Tsukiyomi-no-Mikoto [Augustness Moon Night Possessor, Moon Kami] and from his nose appeared Susa-no-Mikoto [Brave Swift Impetuous male Deity, Kami of Stars]. ...

Amaterasu-Omikami is responsible for the Sun, the source of our life power, Tsukiyomi-no-Mikoto is responsible for night and quietness and growth, and Susa-no-Mikoto is responsible for rhythmic movement of earth as Kami of Stars. These Kami, born through the first Misogi are responsible for the three heavenly light sources: sun, moon, and stars.

Before the first Misogi, Izanagi-no-Mikoto rid himself of possessions and attachments. To purify from attachment is the 1st element of Misogi. Self reflection is the 2nd element. In order to do Misogi, Izanagi-no-Mikoto chose the part of the stream that was not too swift and not too sluggish. The "Middle Way" is the 3rd aspect of purification. The 4th element is to check constantly and correct thoroughly. The 5th element is inner willingness and sincere effort. The 6th element is completeness. …

Misogi Shuho is the sacred activity meant to teach us: to live every day fully, how to pray sincerely to fulfill our wishes, how to choose the most correct life path, how to work for the benefit of humanity and the world, how to help assist in purifying *tsumi/kegare* [negativity and lack of vital energy], how to pray for health of our family, how to find right livelihood, how to pass through critical junctures, how to solve problems.

Through Misogi we can learn to harmonize with the Ki [vital energy] of Heaven and Earth and the Ki of protection.

SOURCE: "Misogi Shuho," Tsubaki Grand Shrine of America
<http://www.tsubskishrine.org/misogishuho/index.html>

GLOSSARY

Kami The invisible spirits in nature and deities of the cosmos.

Sect Shinto New religious movements springing from Shinto roots in the nineteenth and twentieth century.

State Shinto During the Meiji Regime, the cult of the emperor as a descendant of the sun goddess.

REVIEW QUESTIONS

1 Summarize the tradition and symbolism of Izanagi and Izanami.
2 What are the kami? What powers do they represent?
3 Describe the various ways in which the themes of pollution and purification take form.

DISCUSSION QUESTIONS

1 What is a *jinja*? What effects might a *jinja* have on Shinto believers?
2 Why do you think that the theme of purification and washing away sins is so strong in Shinto?
3 How would you compare Shinto to another religion, such as Buddhism?

INFORMATION RESOURCES

Bocking, Brian. *A Popular Dictionary of Shinto*. Richmond, UK: Curzon Press, 1996.

Breen, John and **Mark Teeuwen**. *A New History of Shinto*. Chichester, UK: Wiley-Blackwell, 2010.

Carter, Robert E. *The Japanese Arts and Self-Cultivation*. Albany, NY: State University of New York Press, 2008.

Kojiki text
<http://www.sacred-texts.com/shi/kj/index.htm>

Nelson, John K. *A Year in the Life of a Shinto Shrine*. Seattle, WA: University of Washington Press, 1995.

Oomoto Foundation
<http://www.oomoto.or.jp>

Shinto practices in the United States
<http://www.tsubakishrine.org>

Shinto shrines
<http://www.sacred-destinations.com/sacred-sites/shinto-shrines.htm>

Swanson, Paul L. and **Clark Chilson**. *Nanzan Guide to Japanese Religions*. Honolulu, HI: University of Hawai'i Press, 2006.

Yamakage, Motohisa. *The Essence of Shinto: Japan's Spiritual Heart*. Tokyo/New York: Kodansha International, 2006.

Yusa, Michiko. *Japanese Religious Traditions*. Upper Saddle River, NJ: Prentice Hall, 2002.

ZOROASTRIANISM

In approximately 1800 to 1500 BCE, a great reformer and prophet named Zarathushtra (Zoroaster) took birth in Central Asia. At that time, many Indo-Iranian deities were being worshipped, but his visionary experience with the Wise Lord, Ahura Mazda, led him to ardently preach more monotheistic beliefs centered on Ahura Mazda. Zarathushtra perceived a cosmic battle between good and evil both in the human mind and in the cosmos. The antidote he preached was good thoughts, good words, and good deeds. The forces of good are understood as a means of approaching Ahura Mazda, such as Asha (righteousness, truth, divine law). In later theology, these forces were personified as heavenly beings. This faith, known as Mazdayasna in Iran, eventually became the official religion of the Iranian Empire. It is historically related to Hinduism through Indo-Iranian traditions and, as one of the major religions of the ancient Western world, may have influenced Judaism, Christianity, and Islam. Remnants of the ancient faith survive in a few places, including the Parsi community in India, to which Zoroastrians migrated to escape persecution.

The Gathas by Zarathushtra

Of all Zoroastrian scriptures, the *Gathas* are the only words directly attributed to Zarathushtra. They are 17 hymns that were memorized and thus preserved in their original language and poetic form. When the destruction of the Sassanian Empire in 630 CE brought hard times to Zoroastrians and extensive damage to their sacred texts, the *Gathas* survived because the priests remembered them from their liturgies. The succinct verses invoke spiritual blessings and lead the faithful toward Ahura Mazda by stimulating good thoughts, good words, and good deeds.

Ahunuvaiti Gatha: Yasna 28

I pray to Thee, O Mazda, with uplifted hands, and to thy Holy Spirit, first of all and hope that through truths and righteousness I would enjoy the light of wisdom and a clean conscience, thus bringing solace to the Soul of [Mother Earth] Creation.

I shall, verily, approach and succeed in seeing Thee, O Mazda Ahura [Lord of Wisdom and Creator of Life] through pure mind and enlightened heart. O, Creator, do grant me in both worlds, corporeal as well as spiritual, the recompense which can be achieved only through truthfulness and would make happy the faithful ones.

O, Mazda, O, Asha and Vohuman [good thought and love towards humanity], I shall now sing songs which have not so far been heard by anyone. I hope that through Asha, Vohuman and ever-lasting Kshashathra [symbol of strength and will of the Almighty], the faith and self-sacrifice would increase in our hearts. O, Almighty God, please accept our wishes, come at our call and grant us bliss.

I shall lead my soul towards heaven by pure thought, and being well aware of the blessings which the Almighty, Ahura, shall pour down upon good deeds, I shall teach the people to strive for truth and follow righteousness.

SOURCE: *Ahunuvaita Gatha*, Yasna 28, 1-4, trans. Mobed Firouz Azargoshasb
http://zarathushtra.com/z/gatha/az/gathtml.htm

Ushtavad Gatha: Yasna 43

Mazda Ahura, the Absolute Ruler, has specified that good fortune is for him who makes others happy. O, my Lord, to remain steadfast in truth, I want from Thee the strength of body and soul. O, Armaiti, the symbol of faith and love, do grant me that power which is the reward for a life lived with good thought.

In truth, such a person shall enjoy the best gifts of God. The person who desires inner light and tries to achieve it, O, Mazda, do bestow upon him the same, through Thy holy and bright wisdom. Through Asha, the Eternal Law of Truth and Purity, O my Lord, grant us wisdom and knowledge which are the gifts of Vohuman, so that we may enjoy happiness through our lengthy lives. …

I recognize Thee, O Mazda Ahura, as pure and holy when good thought entered my mind and asked me, "Who art Thou, to which family do Thou belong? Which path would you choose when you are in doubt? The path which leads to the benefit of your brothers and relatives, or the one which is to your own benefit?"

I replied thus: "I am Zoroaster, the staunch enemy of liars and falsehood. I shall fight against liars as long as I have strength and shall uphold truth and righteous people whole-heartedly. May I enjoy Thy spiritual and endless strength, O my Lord, and may I be Thy worshipper and devotee for ever, O Mazda." …

Guide me towards truth and purity for which I have ever yearned, O, my Lord. By following Armaiti, symbol of faith and love, I hope to achieve perfection. Do Thou test us, O my Lord, so that we may prove our faith. Thy testing shall give spiritual strength to humans, particularly the leaders, who are inspired by Thee, O Mazda, [and who] shall guide the people with power and heroism and shall fulfill Thy plan.

As Divine and Sacred have I recognized Thee, O Lord of Life and Wisdom, when Vohuman entered within me and through Thy inspiring words I grew wise and far-sighted. Although I have realized that creating of faith in the hearts of people is very hard, nevertheless I shall accomplish, my Lord, whatever is realized by Thee as the best action, with self-sacrifice and great attempt. ...

As Divine and Sacred have I recognized Thee, O Ahura Mazda, when Vohuman entered within me and light of Truth and knowledge brightened my heart. Do grant me a long life, O my Lord, so that I may achieve my best wishes and desires, the gift which no one else, except Thee, can grant: A life full of service to humanity and activity for the progress of the world which depends upon Thy Khashathra [bodily strength, willpower and spiritually helping the people].

Just as a brave and strong man loves his friend and brings solace to him, so also do grant excessive happiness to my followers. Do Thou grant that joy and happiness which are achieved only by truth and is in your power alone to grant. I shall protect, O my Lord, the religion of truth and all who sing the song sung by Thy heavenly Messenger.

SOURCE: *Ushtavad Gatha*, Yasna 43, 1–2, 4, 7–8, 10–11, 14, trans. Mobed Firouz Azargoshasb <http://zarathushtra.com/z/gatha/az/gathtml.htm>

The Zoroastrian Creed

This creed is thought to have originated in the early days of the Zoroastrian faith, perhaps for communal recitation. The last paragraphs are included in the oft-repeated kusti ritual, in which the faithful wind a sacred thread-girdle around their waists and declare themselves staunch followers of Ahura Mazda and staunch enemies of Ahriman (the false, evil, destructive spirit, or evil tendency in humans) and of the Daevas (gods worshipped by polytheists).

I curse the Daevas. I declare myself a Mazda-worshipper, a supporter of Zarathushtra, hostile to the Daevas, fond of Ahura's teaching, a praiser of the Amesha Spentas [heavenly forces]. I ascribe all good to Ahura Mazda, "and all the best," Asha-endowed, splendid, ... whose is the cow, whose is Asha, whose is the light, "may whose blissful areas be filled with light." ...

I reject the authority of the Daevas, the wicked, no-good, lawless, evil-knowing, the most *druj*-like of beings, the foulest of beings, the most damaging of beings. I reject the Daevas and their comrades; I reject the demons and their comrades; I reject any who harm beings. I reject them with my thoughts, words, and deeds. I reject them publicly.

Even as I reject the head [authorities] so too do I reject the hostile followers of the druj. ...

I profess myself a Mazda-worshipper, a Zoroastrian, having vowed it and professed it. I pledge myself to the well-thought thought, I pledge myself to the well-spoken word, I pledge myself to the well-done action.

I pledge myself to the Mazdayasnian religion, which causes the attack to be put off and weapons put down, Asha-endowed, which of all religions that exist or shall be, is the greatest, the best, and the most beautiful: Ahuric, Zoroastrian. I ascribe all good to Ahura Mazda. This is the creed of the Mazdayasnian religion.

SOURCE: *The Zoroastrian Creed*, trans. Joseph H. Peterson, copyright 1997 by Joseph H. Peterson <http://www.avesta.org/yasna/yasna.htm>

The Towers of Silence by Tina Mehta

In an autobiographical novel, Tina Mehta of India recalls the Zoroastrian traditions in which she was raised. Her grandfather's death was prefaced by his teachings pertaining to the soul, proper disposal of the body, and respect for the deities of earth and sky. In her account, one senses the importance which the elders attached to maintaining the remnants of their ancient faith.

My Grandpa took pride in his once strong and handsome body. But now, as he lay ill, he demanded the quick disposal of his mortal remains when the time came. He could already see the action of *Nasu*, the fiend of decomposition and decay, taking place on his now frail frame. He abhorred anything ugly and the degeneration of his own body clearly disturbed him more than his debilitating cough. Over and over again he drew the attention of his family to the lower drawer of his almirah where he had stored the clean but old garments and worn sheets that must be used to wrap the contemptible *Nasu* which would ultimately destroy his body. ...

Once a month on *Fravardin Roz*, the day dedicated to the *fravashis* [heavenly selves], Grandpa would go to the grounds of the Towers of Silence, the repository of the dead, to offer prayers to those who had made the journey back to spirit before him. And once, before he was confined to his bed, he asked me to accompany him. ...

I will never forget the surprising sense of peace that greeted us once we entered the extensive wooded grounds. ... The gardeners were working silently and the sounds of the city receded as we drew closer to one of the roofless round-walled structures which had some steps leading up to a single door. That the building was roofless to allow the entry of sunlight and the scavenger birds I could understand, but the huge lock on the door seemed incongruous. Who but the insane would want to enter a place reserved for the dead? ...

A vulture, disturbed by our presence, flew lethargically past us and I caught a glimpse of its ugliness. I drew closer to Grandpa who, sensing my discomfort, said, "A beautiful creature, especially fashioned by the wise Creator to clean up quickly and efficiently *Ahriman's* [the destructive Spirit, Evil One] filthy corruption. ... Perhaps you still think going underground is better?" he asked.

"Going underground?" Before I could ask what he meant, I realized that he was referring to burial. ... "*Khorshed najarashni, dokhmanashini* [exposure to sun and carrion-eaters in towers] is *our* way, and would be adopted by everyone if people stopped to give some serious thought to the fact that even if the good birds are scarce, the sun's rays have the power to arrest the spread of disease. ..."

We had dwelt long enough on the subject of the swift consuming of corpses by birds inside the sunlit Towers of Silence as against the slow process of worms devouring decomposing bodies in dark graves. ... As for cremation, the subject was most abhorrent to Grandpa for reasons doctrinal first and secondly because the very thought of little bits of *Nasu* matter floating into the air and then into our lungs via the crematoria smoke was enough to set off a coughing fit, even when his asthma was under control.

"Except for the smoke which rises out of burning herbs and incense which is pleasant and harmless to us and unpleasant only to *khrafsthras* [agents of evil], all other smoke is *ahrimanic*. ... Aside from the disrespect we show to *atash* [fire] when we even suggest *that* method. ..." Grandpa would avoid even mentioning the word cremation, "isn't it folly to disregard one's own precious body by inhaling the filth of *Ahriman*?"

And whenever we passed the local crematoria, out would come his eau-de-cologne scented handkerchief which he would place, with a flourish for all of us to notice, over his nose and mouth and then looking heavenward, he would apologise to Khshathra Vairya for his fellow-beings' disrespect for the Spirit of the Sky. A similar apology was made to Spenta Armaiti, the Spirit of the Earth, whenever we passed by a cemetery. ... "Instead of housing the dead we could use all that space to house our homeless poor or grow food here for the hungry. And look!" he would say, pointing to a particularly elaborate gravestone, "even in death the rich are made to appear more exalted than the poor. ... The departing souls, bless them, if they could speak would have cried out for equality in death and escape from the darkness of graves."

With *dokhmanashini* all Zarathushtrians were equal at death and their *urvans* [souls] could take their own time to gently ascend into the light. This is what Grandpa believed and this is how he would have it be. In ancient times, in the wide open spaces of Inner Asia, or in sparsely populated hills of Iran, our ancestors simply left the corpse to be quickly devoured by wild animals. This could be a last act of charity considering all the meat one consumes through one's lifetime. ...

Grandpa, who had lived only in India and followed the customs adhered to here, did not want to think about what his people, the Parsis abroad, would have to resort to in their worship and at the time of one's death. ... Of course, he realized the impracticality of sky burial for his kith and kin in foreign lands and felt saddened by this forced breach of tradition. ... He was no less concerned about living as pure a life as he humanly could, as he was about maintaining the laws of purity at death.

SOURCE: Tina Mehta, *The Zarathustran Saga*. Calcutta: Writers' Workshop, 1998, pp. 120–6

CHAPTER 8

JUDAISM

In the West, the oldest of the major global religions is Judaism. It is in fact the seminal tradition for the two largest existing world religions: Christianity and Islam. They all share a central belief in **monotheism**; all also refer back to the first Hebrew patriarch: Abraham. It is thought that he lived some time between 1900 and 1700 BCE. God is said to have called him to Canaan and made a **covenant** with him that he would be the father of a great nation. In addition, his first son, Ishmael, is considered the progenitor of the Muslim lineage.

Jewish tradition recognizes many later patriarchs and prophets. Moses is believed to have led the Israelites out of bondage in Egypt, to have spoken directly to God, and to have received God's commandments for the people. The revered King David united the kingdoms of Judah and Israel and established his capital in Jerusalem. His son Solomon (r. c. 967–928 BCE) increased the extent, wealth, and power of the kingdom of Israel and built the great Temple in Jerusalem for the priests to strengthen Hebrew piety. But the power of the nation diminished compared to surrounding empires until 586 BCE, when Babylonia captured Jerusalem, destroyed the Temple, and took many Jews into exile. Fifty years later some were allowed to return and rebuild the Temple, but the Hebrew kingdom had by then become a dispersed people (the **Diaspora**).

After the Second Temple was destroyed by the Roman occupiers in 70 CE, Judaism was maintained and shaped primarily by **rabbis**: teachers, decision-makers, and interpreters of the written and oral traditions. Outside Israel, Babylon became a center of Jewish theological activity; Jewish intellectual life also flourished in Spain, France, and Germany, and under Muslim rule in Baghdad. Despite their growing cultural and financial power, Jewish people were eventually oppressed by certain Christians in Western Europe, which led to large-scale massacres, ultimately including the murder of over a third of the world's Jews by Nazi Germany during World War II. In 1948 a special "homeland" for Jews was established in Palestine and given the ancient name of Israel, but it has never been free from tensions with the earlier and surrounding inhabitants of that area.

Today many people who are Jewish by birth do not practice the **Orthodox** tradition. Nevertheless, there is a renewal of interest in Judaism today, among **Conservatives**, **Reform**, and **Reconstructionist** Jews who are re-interpreting their traditions to find their relevance to contemporary life.

The Jewish Bible: Tanakh

The Jewish Bible, written in the Hebrew language, is called the **Tanakh**, an acronym for its three parts:

1. The **Torah** ("teaching" or "law"), which is the first five books: Genesis, Exodus, Leviticus, Numbers, Deuteronomy. These are traditionally believed to have been given by God and written by Moses, they are also known as the **Pentateuch**, or "five scrolls." They contain the major founding traditions of the faith and the establishment of the Law.
2. The **Prophets** (Nevi'im) are a group of books ascribed to leading reformers such as Isaiah. The prophets spoke boldly and critically of the flaws in their society, but also promised a **Messiah** to free them and lead them to power.
3. The Wisdom Literature, or Writings (*Kethuvim*), is a diverse collection of texts, ranging from poetic Psalms to the nearly tragic drama of Job.

With many parts originating as oral tradition, the Tanakh was slowly written down over hundreds of years, particularly during the Babylonian Exile, 586–535 BCE. It was translated into Greek from about 200 BCE. Following the destruction of Jerusalem in 70 CE the Hebrew **canon** was gradually collected and finalized by rabbis.

TORAH

The Five Books of Moses start with Genesis, which includes two stories of God's creation, Adam and Eve's disobedience, Noah's flood, and the lives of the patriarchs Abraham, Isaac, Jacob, and matriarchs Sarah, Rebekah, Leah, and Rachel, their wives. Exodus tells of God's liberation of the Hebrews from Egyptian slavery, led by Moses, his reception of the Torah's first Ten Commandments at the holy Mount Sinai, many later laws, and some historical accounts. Leviticus is a manual of rules for the ancient Hebrews. The movement of the tribes from Sinai to Canaan is recorded in Numbers. Deuteronomy includes a long farewell address from Moses and his death.

Since the nineteenth century, scholars have made historical and literary analyses of the Torah. They have found evidence that the Pentateuch is woven like a rope from strands of four different texts from different historical periods: the **Yahwist**, the **Elohist**, the **Priestly**, and the **Deuteronomic**.

In the Beginning from Genesis

The first book of the Torah begins with creation, which scholars divide into two sections. The first (a "Priestly" text) is the account of God's cosmic creation (Genesis 1:1–2:4). In six days, God created the universe from a void, the earth, vegetation, and humans, male and female in the divine image, giving humans responsibility for creation. On the seventh day he rested, which is why the Sabbath is kept as a holy day each week.

In the second creation account (Genesis 2:4–3:24, a "Yahwist" text), God first created one human, *ha'adam* ("earthling," from *ha'adamah*, "earth"). Later he made a second person, as the first one was lonely, and thus created *ish* and *ishshah*, man and woman (Adam and Eve). This is why "a man leaves his parents and cleaves to the woman and the two become one flesh." God then created vegetation and animals in the Garden of Eden. Eve, tempted by the serpent, took the fruit of the tree of knowledge of good and bad. She gave some to Adam; both ate. Their punishment was to labor—Eve in childbirth, Adam in the fields—and ultimately to die. This creation account is markedly different from the neighboring Babylonian *Enuma Elish*, in which many gods fight with each other until chaotic Tiamat is killed by heroic Marduk. However, the Genesis 6 flood story is very similar to the Babylonian *Epic of Gilgamesh* and Noah compares with Utnapishtim.

The First Creation Account in Genesis   When God began to create heaven and earth—the earth being unformed and void, with darkness over the surface of the deep and a wind from God sweeping over the water—God said, "Let there be light"; and there was light. God saw that the light was good, and God separated the light from the darkness. God called the light Day, and the darkness He called Night. And there was evening and there was morning, a first day.

God said, "Let there be an expanse in the midst of the water, that it may separate water from water." God made the expanse, and it separated the water which was below the expanse from the water which was above the expanse. And it was so. God called the expanse Sky. And there was evening and there was morning, a second day.

God said, "Let the water below the sky be gathered into one area, that the dry land may appear." And it was so. God called the dry land Earth, and the gathering of waters He called Seas. And God saw that this was good. And God said, "Let the earth sprout vegetation: seed-bearing plants, fruit trees of every kind on earth that bear fruit with the seed in it." And it was so. The earth brought forth vegetation: seed-bearing plants of every kind, and trees of every kind bearing fruit with the seed in it. And God saw that this was good. And there was evening and there was morning, a third day.

God said, "Let there be lights in the expanse of the sky to separate day from night; they shall serve as signs for the set times—the days and the years; and they shall serve as lights in the expanse of the sky to shine upon the earth." And it was so. God made two great lights, the greater light to dominate the day and the lesser light to dominate the night, and the stars. And God set them in the expanse of the sky to shine upon the earth, to dominate the day and the night, and to separate light from darkness. And God saw that this was good. And there was evening and there was morning, a fourth day.

God said, "Let the waters bring forth swarms of living creatures, and birds that fly above the earth across the expanse of the sky." God created the great sea monsters, and all the living creatures of every kind that creep, which the waters brought forth in swarms, and all the winged birds of every kind. And God saw that this was good. God blessed them, saying, "Be fertile and increase, fill the waters in the seas, and let the birds increase on the earth." And there was evening and there was morning, a fifth day.

God said, "Let the earth bring forth every kind of living creature: cattle, creeping things, and wild beasts of every kind." And it was so. God made wild beasts of every kind and cattle of every kind, and all kinds of creeping things of the earth. And God saw that this was good. And God said, "Let us make man in our image, after our likeness. They shall rule the fish of the sea, the birds of the sky, the cattle, the whole earth, and all the creeping things that creep on earth." And God created man in His image, in the image of God He created him; male and female He created them. God blessed them and God said to them, "Be fertile and increase, fill the earth and master it; and rule the fish of the sea, the birds of the sky, and all the living things that creep on earth."

God said, "See, I give you every seed-bearing plant that is upon all the earth, and every tree that has seed-bearing fruit; they shall be yours for food. And to all the animals on land, to all the birds of the sky, and to everything that creeps on earth, in which there is the breath of life, [I give] all the green plants for food." And it was so. And God saw all that He had made, and found it very good. And there was evening and there was morning, the sixth day.

The heaven and the earth were finished, and all their array. On the seventh day God finished the work that He had been doing, and He ceased on the seventh day from all the work that He had done. And God blessed the seventh day and declared it holy, because on it God ceased from all the work of creation that He had done. Such is the story of heaven and earth when they were created. (Genesis 1:1–2:4)

The Second Creation Account in Genesis   When the Lord God made earth and heaven—when no shrub of the field was yet on earth and no grasses of the field had yet sprouted, because the Lord God had not sent rain upon the earth and there was no man to till the soil, but a flow would well up from the ground and water the whole surface of the earth—the Lord God formed man from the dust of the earth. He blew into his nostrils the breath of life, and man became a living being.

The Lord God planted a garden in Eden, in the east, and placed there the man whom He had formed. And from the ground the Lord God caused to grow every tree that was pleasing to the sight and good for food, with the tree of life in the middle of the garden, and the tree of knowledge of good and bad.

A river issues from Eden to water the garden, and it then divides and becomes four branches. The name of the first is Pishon, the one that winds through the whole land of Havilah, where the gold is. (The gold of that land is good; bdellium[1] is there, and lapis lazuli.[2]) The name of the second river is

---

1 Bdellium—a tree whose resin is the basis for perfume.
2 Lapis lazuli—a deep blue semi-precious stone.

Gihon, the one that winds through the whole land of Cush. The name of the third river is Tigris, the one that flows east of Asshur. And the fourth river is the Euphrates.

The Lord God took the man and placed him in the garden of Eden, to till it and tend it. And the Lord God commanded the man, saying, "Of every tree of the garden you are free to eat; but as for the tree of knowledge of good and bad, you must not eat of it; for as soon as you eat of it, you shall die."

The Lord God said, "It is not good for man to be alone; I will make a fitting helper for him." And the Lord God formed out of the earth all the wild beasts and all the birds of the sky, and brought them to the man to see what he would call them; and whatever the man called each living creature, that would be its name. And the man gave names to all the cattle and to the birds of the sky and to all the wild beasts; but for Adam no fitting helper was found. So the Lord God cast a deep sleep upon the man; and, while he slept, He took one of his ribs and closed up the flesh at that spot. And the Lord God fashioned the rib that He had taken from the man into a woman; and He brought her to the man. Then the man said, "This one at last is bone of my bones and flesh of my flesh. This one shall be called Woman, for from man was she taken." Hence a man leaves his father and mother and clings to his wife, so that they become one flesh.

The two of them were naked, the man and his wife, yet they felt no shame. Now the serpent was the shrewdest of all the wild beasts that the Lord God had made. He said to the woman, "Did God really say: You shall not eat of any tree of the garden?" The woman replied to the serpent, "We may eat of the fruit of the other trees of the garden. It is only about fruit of the tree in the middle of the garden that God said: 'You shall not eat of it or touch it, lest you die.'" And the serpent said to the woman, "You are not going to die, but God knows that as soon as you eat of it your eyes will be opened and you will be like divine beings who know good and bad." When the woman saw that the tree was good for eating and a delight to the eyes, and that the tree was desirable as a source of wisdom, she took of its fruit and ate. She also gave some to her husband, and he ate. Then the eyes of both of them were opened and they perceived that they were naked; and they sewed together fig leaves and made themselves loincloths.

They heard the sound of the Lord God moving about in the garden at the breezy time of day; and the man and his wife hid from the Lord God among the trees of the garden. The Lord God called out to the man and said to him, "Where are you?" He replied, "I heard the sound of You in the garden, and I was afraid because I was naked, so I hid." Then He asked, "Who told you that you were naked? Did you eat of the tree from which I had forbidden you to eat?" The man said, "The woman You put at my side— she gave me of the tree, and I ate." And the Lord God said to the woman, "What is this you have done!" The woman replied, "The serpent duped me, and I ate." Then the Lord God said to the serpent, "Because you did this, more cursed shall you be than all cattle and all the wild beasts: on your belly shall you crawl and dirt shall you eat all the days of your life. I will put enmity between you and the woman, and between your offspring and hers; they shall strike at your head, and you shall strike at their heel." And to the woman, He said, "I will make most severe your pangs in childbearing; in pain shall you bear children, yet your urge shall be for your husband, and he shall rule over you." To Adam He said, "Because you did as your wife said and ate of the tree about which I commanded you, 'You shall not eat of it,' cursed be the ground because of you; by toil shall you eat of it all the days of your life: thorns and thistles shall it sprout for you. But your food shall be the grasses of the field; by the sweat of your brow shall you get bread to eat, until you return to the ground—for from it you were taken. For dust you are, and to dust you shall return."

The man named his wife Eve, because she was the mother of all the living. And the Lord God made garments of skins for Adam and his wife, and clothed them.

And the Lord God said, "Now that the man has become like one of us, knowing good and bad, what if he should stretch out his hand and take also from the tree of life and eat, and live forever!" So the Lord God banished him from the garden of Eden, to till the soil from which he was taken. He drove the man out, and stationed east of the garden of Eden the cherubim and the fiery ever-turning sword, to guard the way to the tree of life. (Genesis 2:4–3.24)

Abraham's Covenant from Genesis

Essential to Judaism is the covenant. Like contracts made between individuals, states, and kings with their subjects, God made numerous covenants with Israel, such as "I shall be your God and you shall be my people" (Leviticus 26:12). Most notable are the covenants with:

1. Noah, signified by the rainbow, that God would never again destroy humanity with a flood (Genesis 9:8–17)
2. Abraham, signified by male circumcision, that God had chosen Israel as his people and that they would have the land that they "sojourn in" and be numerous (Genesis 17:1–21)
3. Moses, signified by the laws of the Torah, that, if Israel obeyed God's Law, they would be God's treasured "kingdom of priests and a holy nation" (Exodus 19:5–6)
4. King David, that he should build a temple in Jerusalem, and that his "throne shall be established forever" (II Samuel 7:5–16).

When Abram was ninety-nine years old, the Lord appeared to Abram and said to him, "I am El Shaddai. Walk in My ways and be blameless. I will establish My covenant between Me and you, and I will make you exceedingly numerous."

Abram threw himself on his face; and God spoke to him further, "As for Me, this is My covenant with you: You shall be the father of a multitude of nations. And you shall no longer be called Abram, but your name shall be Abraham, for I make you the father of a multitude of nations. I will make you exceedingly fertile, and make nations of you; and kings shall come forth from you. I will maintain My covenant between Me and you, and your offspring to come, as an everlasting covenant throughout the ages, to be God to you and to your offspring to come. I assign the land you sojourn in to you and your offspring to come, all the land of Canaan, as an everlasting holding. I will be their God." (Genesis 17:1–8)

The Mosaic Covenant from Exodus

Exodus records the heart of much of Jewish tradition, focusing on God's power to liberate the chosen people from unjust suffering. The Hebrews were slaves in Egypt, and the infant Moses was saved from Pharaoh's destruction to grow up a prince in Pharaoh's household. But he ran away, then returned to lead his people out of slavery after a great struggle with Pharaoh around 1250 BCE. At Sinai, the Hebrews were given the Ten Commandments, the first of the 613 laws of the Torah, when Moses ascended the holy mountain. In this extract from Exodus, notice that God says that the Commandments must be kept in order for Him to show kindness.

Moses led the people out of the camp toward God, and they took their places at the foot of the mountain. Now Mount Sinai was all in smoke, for the Lord had come down upon it in fire; the smoke rose like the smoke of a kiln, and the whole mountain trembled violently. …

God spoke all these words, saying:

I the Lord am your God who brought you out of the land of Egypt, the house of bondage: You shall have no other gods besides Me.

You shall not make for yourself a sculptured image, or any likeness of what is in the heavens above, or on the earth below, or in the waters under the earth. You shall not bow down to them or serve them. For I the Lord your God am an impassioned God, visiting the guilt of the parents upon the children, upon the third and upon the fourth generations of those who reject Me, but showing kindness to the thousandth generation of those who love Me and keep My commandments.

You shall not swear falsely by the name of the Lord your God; for the Lord will not clear one who swears falsely by His name.

Remember the sabbath day and keep it holy. Six days you shall labor and do all your work, but the seventh day is a sabbath of the Lord your God: you shall not do any work—you, your son or daughter, your male or female slave, or your cattle, or the stranger who is within your settlements. For in six days the Lord made heaven and earth and sea, and all that is in them, and He rested on the seventh day; therefore the Lord blessed the sabbath day and hallowed it.

Honor your father and your mother, that you may long endure on the land that the Lord your God is assigning to you.

You shall not murder.

You shall not commit adultery.

You shall not steal.

You shall not bear false witness against your neighbor.

You shall not covet your neighbor's house: you shall not covet your neighbor's wife, or his male or female slave, or his ox or his ass, or anything that is your neighbor's. (Exodus 19:17–18, 20:1–14)

An Eye for an Eye   from Leviticus

For millennia the typical form of justice was clan vengeance. If someone killed a member of your clan, you were justified in killing a member of that clan. Rare was a sense of fair punishment for a crime. So the Torah, along with other cultures' earlier legal documents, such as Hammurabi's Code in Babylon (1792–1750 BCE), attempted to set up fair punishment systems enacted by judges in court. Hammurabi's Code, inscribed on a stone pillar, listed among its laws "If a son has struck his father, his hands shall be cut off," and "If a man had destroyed the eye of another free man, his own eye shall be destroyed." This selection from Leviticus also shows the "eye for an eye" law. It represents an effort to limit excessive retaliation and revenge, which was a refinement of justice.

And to the Israelite people speak thus: Anyone who blasphemes his God shall bear his guilt; if he also pronounces the name Lord, he shall be put to death. The whole community shall stone him; stranger or citizen, if he has thus pronounced the Name, he shall be put to death.

If anyone kills any human being, he shall be put to death. One who kills a beast shall make restitution for it: life for life. If anyone maims his fellow, as he has done so shall it be done to him: fracture for fracture, eye for eye, tooth for tooth. The injury he inflicted on another shall be inflicted on him. (Leviticus 24:15–20)

The Davidic Covenant   from II Samuel

"Further, say thus to My servant David: Thus said the Lord of Hosts: I took you from the pasture, from following the flock, to be ruler of My people Israel, and I have been with you wherever you went, and have cut down all your enemies before you. Moreover, I will give you great renown like that of the greatest men on earth. I will establish a home for My people Israel and will plant them firm, so that they shall dwell secure and shall tremble no more. Evil men shall not oppress them any more as in the past, ever since I appointed chieftains over My people Israel. I will give you safety from all your enemies.

"The Lord declares to you that He, the Lord, will establish a house for you. When your days are done and you lie with your fathers, I will raise up your offspring after you, one of your own issue, and I will establish his kingship. He shall build a house for My name, and I will establish his royal throne forever. I will be a father to him, and he shall be a son to Me. When he does wrong, I will chastise him with the rod of men and the affliction of mortals; but I will never withdraw My favor from him as I withdrew it from Saul, whom I removed to make room for you. Your house and your kingship shall ever be secure before you; your throne shall be established forever." (II Samuel 7:8–16)

PROPHETS

In the Ancient Near East, prophets were well-known cultic revealers of divine will. Known for their states of trance and ecstatic speaking, they performed miracles and symbolic actions. The biblical pre-classical prophets— Samuel, Nathan, Elijah, and Elisha—were renowned for foretelling events and working miracles, and were consulted by kings. The classical prophets—Isaiah, Jeremiah, Ezekiel, and the 12 minor prophets—also spoke in the name of God, beginning around 750 BCE. They emphasized ethical monotheism rather than cult activities and foretelling the future, criticizing their society's injustices and pleading with Israel to repent. They promised God's forgiveness and the coming of the Messiah.

The Prophecies of Isaiah

The Hebrew prophet Isaiah (c. 740–701 BCE) wrote during the difficult times when the great empires of Assyria and Babylonia (now Iraq) were attacking Israel and slowly conquering it. His text, chapters 1–35, is supplemented by two later writers in chapters 36–9 and 40–66. The people were extremely distressed and, since they believed in the Davidic Covenant in which God promised the land to them forever, they questioned how God could allow this. Prophets such as Isaiah spoke up and said that God was punishing the nation for insincere worship, belief in other gods, and social injustice. He compared it to the corrupt cities of Sodom and Gomorrah, whose destruction is described in Genesis 18–19. Isaiah said that God was even repulsed by the ancient rituals of sacrificial offerings of rams, bulls, lambs, and goats, and astrological calculations of new moons. This was a radical precursor to the abandonment of Temple sacrifices in favor of rabbinical teaching and learning. But, Isaiah assured the people, God promised that He would send a great leader, a Messiah, to save them later.

Ah, sinful nation! People laden with iniquity! Brood of evildoers! Depraved children! They have forsaken the Lord, spurned the Holy One of Israel, turned their backs [on Him].

Why do you seek further beatings, that you continue to offend? Every head is ailing, and every heart is sick. From head to foot no spot is sound: all bruises, and welts, and festering sores—not pressed out, not bound up, not softened with oil. Your land is a waste, your cities burnt down; before your eye, the yield of your soil is consumed by strangers—a wasteland as overthrown by strangers! ...

... "What need have I of all your sacrifices?" says the Lord. "I am sated with burnt offerings of rams, and suet of fatlings, and blood of bulls; and I have no delight in lambs and he-goats. That you come to appear before Me—who asked that of you? Trample my courts no more; bringing oblations is futile, incense is offensive to Me. New moon and sabbath, proclaiming of solemnities, assemblies with iniquity, I cannot abide. Your new moons and fixed seasons fill Me with loathing; they are become a burden to Me, I cannot endure them. And when you lift up your hands, I will turn My eyes away from you; though you pray at length, I will not listen. Your hands are stained with crime—wash yourselves clean; put your evil doings away from My sight. Cease to do evil; learn to do good. Devote yourselves to justice; aid the wronged. Uphold the rights of the orphan; defend the cause of the widow.

"Come, let us reach an understanding,—says the Lord. Be your sins like crimson, they can turn snow-white; be they red as dyed wool, they can become like fleece." If, then, you agree and give heed, you will eat the good things of the earth; but if you refuse and disobey, you will be devoured [by] the sword. For it was the Lord who spoke. (Isaiah 1:4–20)

The people that walked in darkness have seen a brilliant light, on those who dwelt in a land of gloom light has dawned. You have magnified that nation, have given it great joy; they have rejoiced before You as they rejoice at reaping time, as they exult when dividing spoil. ... For a child has been born to us, a son has been given us. And authority has settled on his shoulders. He has been named "The Mighty God is planning grace; The Eternal Father, a peaceable ruler"—In token of abundant authority and of peace without limit upon David's throne and kingdom, that it may be firmly established in justice and in equity now and evermore. The zeal of the Lord of Hosts shall bring this to pass. (Isaiah 9:1–2, 5–6)

WISDOM LITERATURE

Wisdom Literature was common in Ancient Near Eastern cultures. In the Tanakh it includes a diverse collection of texts, from songs sung in the Temple to the story of Job and the Song of Solomon. Proverbs is a collection of short oral sayings, while Ecclesiastes is a book skeptical of religion, raising many doubts. Job is a drama adapted from a Babylonian source in which Job's faith is tested by terrible suffering when he loses all his wealth and children and is stricken with illness. Here Psalm 23 and two quotes from Job have been selected, one showing a sense of ecological harmony with nature demonstrating God behind it all, and one showing God's grand cosmic answer to Job's suffering. The Psalms were songs sung in worship services in Jerusalem's Temple.

Psalm 23

A Psalm of David

The Lord is my shepherd; I lack nothing. He makes me lie down in green pastures; He leads me to water in places of repose; He renews my life; He guides me in right paths as befits His name.

Though I walk through a valley of deepest darkness, I fear no harm, for You are with me; Your rod and Your staff—they comfort me.

You spread a table for me in full view of my enemies; You anoint my head with oil; my drink is abundant. Only goodness and steadfast love shall pursue me all the days of my life, and I shall dwell in the house of the Lord for many long years.

The Earth Will Teach You from Job

But ask the beasts, and they will teach you; the birds of the sky, they will tell you, or speak to the earth, it will teach you; the fish of the sea, they will inform you. Who among all these does not know that the hand of the Lord has done this? In His hand is every living soul and the breath of all mankind. (Job 12:7–10)

Where Were You When I Laid the Earth's Foundations?

from Job

When, in his suffering, Job considered doubting God's justice, God replied:

Who is this who darkens counsel, speaking without knowledge? Gird your loins like a man; I will ask and you will inform Me.

Where were you when I laid the earth's foundations? Speak if you have understanding. Do you know who fixed its dimensions or who measured it with a line? Onto what were its bases sunk? Who set its cornerstone when the morning stars sang together and all the divine beings shouted for joy? …

Have you ever commanded the day to break, assigned the dawn its place, so that it seizes the corners of the earth and shakes the wicked out of it? …

Have the gates of death been disclosed to you? Have you seen the gates of deep darkness? Have you surveyed the expanses of the earth? If you know of these—tell Me. (Job 38:1–7, 12–13, 17–18)

SOURCE: Bible excerpts in this chapter are taken from *Tanakh: A New Translation of the Holy Scriptures*. Philadelphia, PA: Jewish Publication Society, 1985

Commentaries on the Tanakh

Over many centuries rabbis collected numerous interpretations and extrapolations of Jewish Law, adapting them to the era in which they lived. The **Midrash** are folklore elaborations, mainly concerned with interpreting Tanakh texts. The earliest

Midrash may well be the Passover ritual **Haggadah**, now preserved in many versions. The **Mishnah** is a collection of laws originally handed down orally on festivals, marriage, damages, holy things, and purities, while the **Talmud** is the body of teachings commenting on earlier Mishnah.

Midrash

The first brief midrash below describes how God told Adam not to corrupt the world. The second demonstrates a strict versus a freer way of understanding the Tanakh: an unbeliever approached the influential rabbi Shammai (c. 50 BCE–30 CE), a strict interpreter of Torah, and then the sage Hillel, who lived at about the same time. He was a less rigorous interpreter of Torah who became president of the Sanhedrin, the supreme religious, political, and judiciary body of Israel.

Your World

In the hour when the Holy One, blessed be he, created the first man,
 he took him and let him pass before all the trees of the garden of
 Eden, and said to him:
See my works, how fine and excellent they are!
Now all that I have created for you have I created.
Think upon this, and do not corrupt and desolate my world;
 for if you corrupt it, there is no one to set it right after you.

The Rest is Commentary

Once a heathen came before Shammai. He said to him:
 I will be converted, if you can teach me all the Torah while I stand
 on one leg.
Shammai pushed him away with the builder's measure he had in
 his hand.
The man came before Hillel. He converted him.
He said to him:
What is hateful to you, do not do to your fellow.
That is all the Torah. The rest is commentary—go and study.

SOURCE: Nahum N. Glatzer, ed., *Hammer on the Rock*. New York: Schocken, 1962, pp. 13, 80

Talmud

The Talmud is the large commentary on the Mishnah's oral traditions. The Jerusalem Talmud dates from about 500 CE, and the Babylonian Talmud was completed about 600 CE. The contents of the Talmud are historical, containing folklore, manners, customs, proverbs, prayers, ritual, and medical advice. The literary style is that of a discussion in an academy (yeshivah), led by scholars such as Ben Zoma. The visual format places a text in the middle of the page, and commentaries (Gemara) are written around it. One third of the Talmud's two and a half million words is commentary on **Halakhah** (written, oral, and customary laws) and the rest Haggadah, including the Passover Seder ritual.

Ben Zoma says: Who is a wise man? He that learns from all men, as it is said, *From all my teachers have I got understanding* (Psalm 119:99).

Who is a mighty man? He that subdues his evil impulse, as it is said, *He that is slow to anger is better than the mighty, and he that ruleth his spirit than him that taketh a city* (Proverbs 16:32).

Who is a rich man? He that is content with his portion, as it is said, *When thou eatest the labor of thy hands happy shalt thou be and it shall be well with thee* (Psalm 128:2): *Happy shalt thou be* in this world, *and it shall be well with thee* in the world to come.

Who is an honorable man? He that honors mankind, as it is said, *For them that honor me I will honor and they that despise me shall be lightly esteemed* (I Samuel 2:30).

A Wise Man: It is he who is ready to learn even from his inferiors. With such readiness, if his inferior should present him with a wise view, he will not be ashamed to accept it and will not treat his words with contempt. This was characteristic of David, King of Israel, who said, "I would pay attention to any man who came to teach me something."

The Gentile philosophers say that even if a person were to know everything [as it were], if he does not want to increase his knowledge, he is not a wise man but a fool. ... On the other hand, one who passionately loves to increase his wisdom may be called a wise man even if he were to know nothing. Only this way can you attain true wisdom and discover the will of God.

SOURCE: Judah Goldin, ed. and trans., *The Living Talmud*. New Haven, CT: Yale University Press, 1957, p. 153

Prayer and ceremony

Prayer: Shema

Most important ancient instructions for prayer are spoken by Moses in the Torah. The first sentence is called the Shema after its opening Hebrew word, "*Shema Ysrael Adonai Elohainu Adonai Echad.*" Included is the important theme of the "chosen people" ("He chose you"), the idea that God chose one ethnic group to be his "light unto the world," showing the true religion and thus granting his people a sense of the ultimate rightness of their religion, and justifying more authority and rights.

Hear O Israel! The Lord is our God, the Lord Alone. You shall love the Lord your God with all your heart and with all your soul and with all your might. Take to heart these instructions with which I charge you this day. Impress them upon your children. Recite them when you stay at home and when you are away, when you lie down and when you get up. Bind them as a sign on your hand and let them serve as a symbol on your forehead, inscribe them on the doorposts of your home and on your gates. (Deuteronomy 6:4–9)

And now O Israel, what does the Lord your God demand of you? Only this: to revere the Lord your God, to walk only in His paths, to love him and to serve the Lord your God with all your heart and soul, keeping the Lord's commandments and laws, which I enjoin upon you today, for your good. Mark, the heavens to their uttermost reaches belong to the Lord your God, the earth and all that is on it! Yet it was to your fathers that the Lord was drawn in His love for them, so that He chose you, their lineal descendants, from among all peoples—as is now the case. Cut away, therefore, the thickening about your hearts and stiffen your necks no more. For the Lord your God is God supreme and Lord supreme, the great, the mighty, and the awesome God, who shows no favor and takes no bribe, but upholds the cause of the fatherless and the widow, and befriends the stranger, providing him with food and clothing.—You too must befriend the stranger, for you were strangers in the land of Egypt. You must revere the Lord your God: only Him shall you worship, to him shall you hold fast, and by His name shall you swear. He is your glory and He is your God, who wrought for you these marvelous, awesome deeds that you saw with your own eyes. (Deuteronomy 10:12–21)

The Passover Story from the Seder Meal Ceremony

The Jewish Passover Seder Meal is a major annual celebration of liberation from slavery in Egypt. "Passover" refers to God's angel of death coming to Egypt but passing over the Hebrew homes, thus freeing them. Unleavened matzah bread must be eaten, since the Hebrews escaping Egypt had no time to let their bread rise; it is called "the bread of affliction." The ceremonial plate at home always includes a bone (symbol of the sacrificial lamb), bitter herbs (*maror*), and a blend of fruit, spices, wine, and matzah meal (*charoset*) to symbolize the mortar made while slaves. Seder includes special prayers, reading the Haggadah text, from which we excerpt below, eating a festive meal, drinking wine, singing Passover songs, and finally saying "Next year in Jerusalem!"

The Four Questions How different is this night from all other nights? On all other nights we may eat either leavened or unleavened bread; on this night, only unleavened bread. On all other nights we may eat any vegetable; on this night we are required to eat bitter herbs. On all other nights we are not bidden to dip our vegetables even once; on this night we dip them twice. On all other nights we eat our meals in any manner; on this night, why do we sit around the table together in a ceremonial fashion?

Uncover the Matzah *and begin the reply.*

The Answer "We were slaves of Pharaoh in Egypt," and the Lord our God brought us forth from there "with a strong hand and an outstretched arm." If the Holy One, blessed be He, had not brought forth our ancestors from Egypt, then we and our children, and our children's children, would still be enslaved to Pharaoh in Egypt. Therefore, even if we are all learned and wise, all elders and fully versed in the Torah, it is our duty nonetheless to retell the story of the Exodus from Egypt. And the more one dwells on the Exodus from Egypt, the more is one to be praised.

Point to the shank bone: The Passover offering which our ancestors ate in Temple days, what was the reason for it? It was because the Holy One, blessed be He, passed over the houses of our ancestors in Egypt, as it is written: "And you shall say, 'It is the Passover offering to the Lord, Who passed over the houses of the children of Israel in Egypt, when He smote the Egyptians, and spared our houses.' And the people bowed their heads and worshipped."

Point to the Matzah: This *Matzah* which we eat, what is the reason for it? It is because there was not enough time for the dough of our ancestors to rise when the King of all kings, the Holy One, blessed be He, revealed Himself to them and redeemed them, as it is written: "And they baked the dough which they had brought out from Egypt into cakes of unleavened bread; for it had not leavened, because they were driven out of Egypt and they could not tarry; nor had they prepared any provisions for themselves."

Point to the bitter herbs: These bitter herbs which we eat—what is their meaning? It is because the Egyptians embittered the lives of our ancestors in Egypt, as it is written: "And they embittered their lives with hard labor, with mortar and bricks, and with every kind of work in the fields; all the work which they made them do was cruel."

In every generation one must see oneself as though having personally come forth from Egypt, as it is written: "And you shall tell your child on that day, 'This is done because of what the Lord did for me when I came forth, from Egypt.'" It was not our ancestors alone whom the Holy One, blessed be He, redeemed; He redeemed us too, with them, as it is written: "He brought us out from there that He might lead us to, and give us, the land which He had promised to our ancestors."

SOURCE: *Passover Haggadah*, trans. Nathan Goldberg. Hoboken, NJ: Ktav Publishing, 1949/1993, pp. 8–24

Evolving theology and spirituality

Jewish theology has continually elaborated and interpreted the principles of the faith in the light of contemporary life and thought. The philosopher Maimonides (c. 1135–1204), who was born in Spain and migrated to Egypt, blended Jewish theology with Greek and Muslim philosophy. His "Thirteen Principles of Faith" affirms his interpretation of the Creator, the Law, and the Messiah.

Thirteen Principles of Faith by Maimonides

1. I believe with perfect faith that the Creator, blessed be his name, is the Author and Guide of everything that has been created, and that he alone has made, does make, and will make all things.

2. I believe with perfect faith that the Creator, blessed be his name, is a Unity, and that there is no unity in any manner like unto his, and that he alone is our God, who was, is, and will be.

3. I believe with perfect faith that the Creator, blessed be his name, is not a body, and that he is free from all the accidents of matter, and that he has not any form whatsoever.

4. I believe with perfect faith that the Creator, blessed be his name, is the first and the last.

5. I believe with perfect faith that to the Creator, blessed be his name, and to him alone, it is right to pray, and that it is not right to pray to any being besides him.

6. I believe with perfect faith that all the words of the prophets are true.

7. I believe with perfect faith that the prophecy of Moses our teacher, peace be unto him, was true, and that he was the chief of the prophets, both of those that preceded and of those that followed him.

8. I believe with perfect faith that the whole Law, now in our possession, is the same that was given to Moses our teacher, peace be unto him.

9. I believe with perfect faith that this Law will not be changed, and that there will never be any other law from the Creator, blessed be his name.

10. I believe with perfect faith that the Creator, blessed be his name, knows every deed of the children of men, and all their thoughts, as it is said, It is he that fashioneth the hearts of them all, that giveth heed to all their deeds.

11. I believe with perfect faith that the Creator, blessed be his name, rewards those that keep his commandments and punishes those that transgress them.

12. I believe with perfect faith in the coming of the Messiah, and, though he tarry, I will wait daily for his coming.

13. I believe with perfect faith that there will be a resurrection of the dead at the time when it shall please the Creator, blessed be his name, and exalted be the remembrance of him for ever and ever.

SOURCE: Maimonides, "Thirteen Principles of Faith," trans. S. Singer, in *The Authorized Daily Prayer Book of the United Hebrew Congregations of the British Empire*. London: Eyre and Spottiswoode, 1912, pp. 89–90

The Baal Shem Tov and the Doctor   by Doug Lipman

Baal Shem Tov ("Master of the Good Name") was founder of mystical eighteenth-century Hasidism in Eastern Europe, a form of Judaism that emphasizes study of the mystical **Kabbalah** texts. Hasidism's main theological principle is "panentheism," the belief that the entire universe, mind and matter, is a manifestation of Divine Being. Worship is energetic, with song and dance (men are separated from women). Ultra-Orthodox Hasidism emphasizes prayer, study, and good deeds. Men wear nineteenth-century clothes and beards, and look for a messiah. Most of the half a million (approx.) Hasidic Jews live in the United States or Israel.

This story shows how the Baal Shem Tov taught using his remarkable insight into the body and soul, for he strove to see the divine in all.

Once, a famous doctor met one of his patients on the street. Without a word of greeting, the doctor said, "I told you not to walk on that leg until it heals!"

"But it IS healed," said the man.

"Impossible! I saw the wound in that leg. It will take months!"

"I went to another kind of healer, doctor. I went to a mystical rabbi, the one they call the Baal Shem Tov."

The doctor narrowed his eyes, then simply walked away.

A week later, the doctor rapped loudly on the Baal Shem Tov's door. When the door opened, he said, "I hear you claim to be a healer!"

The Baal Shem Tov looked at his visitor. "God is the healer, my friend. Come in!"

The doctor did not move. "Let us examine each other," he said. "Whoever best diagnoses the sickness of the other will be proved the better doctor."

The Baal Shem Tov smiled. "As you wish. But please do me the favor of coming in!"

Once inside, the doctor began his examination of the Baal Shem Tov. The doctor poked him, pinched him, gazed in his ears, and tapped on his knees. After an hour, the doctor said, "You have no sickness that I can find."

"I am not surprised that you could not find it," said the Baal Shem Tov. "I so desire the presence of God that my heart cries out in pain when I cannot feel it. My sickness is this constant yearning for God." The Baal Shem Tov looked at the doctor a long while. "Let me now examine you."

The Baal Shem Tov took the doctor's hands and gazed into his eyes. At last the rabbi said, "Have you ever lost anything very valuable?"

"As a matter of fact," said the doctor, "I once had a large jewel, but it was stolen from me."

"Ah! That is your sickness!" said the Baal Shem Tov.

"What? Missing my diamond?"

"No. My sickness is yearning after God. *Your* sickness is that you have forgotten that you ever had that desire."

The doctor sucked in a breath. In a moment, a tear flowed down his cheek. One tear turned into many. Still holding the hands of the Baal Shem Tov, he began to sob. "Please," he said. "Teach me how to yearn!"

"With God's help," said the Baal Shem Tov, "your healing has already begun."

SOURCE: <http://www.hasidicstories.com/Stories/The_Baal_Shem_Tov/doctor.html>

Branches of Judaism

There are several branches of modern Judaism, since there is no central authority. The majority of Jews form four major groups: the Orthodox, Conservative, Reform, and Reconstructionist.

Most non-assimilated Jews light candles on Sabbath (Shabbat) evening before dinner, participate in the Passover Seder, light Hanukkah candles, and celebrate high holidays: Rosh Hashanah and Yom Kippur. Many Jews have **Bar Mitzvahs** and Jewish weddings, go to summer camps, and support the nation of Israel.

More divisive are questions such as: should the Tanakh be read literally, or it is subject to scientific and historical criticism? Should Jews seek to maintain centuries-old traditions, such as speaking Yiddish and wearing a particular era's clothing, keep kosher food rules including avoiding pork, prohibit all work on the Sabbath, keep women separate in **synagogue**, and ordain only men to be rabbis? Should Jews have to marry only other Jews? Today such issues divide Jews into groups on a continuum, from strict Orthodox, through middle-ground Conservativism, to liberal Reform and Reconstructionism. One writer saw this process of questioning as the "de-ghettoization" of Judaism.

ORTHODOX

Many Orthodox Jews today are really Neo-Orthodox, holding mostly to nineteenth-century interpretations of literal reading of the Torah, speaking German-related Yiddish, requiring men to wear beards and nineteenth-century Eastern European clothing, keeping women separate in synagogue and out of the rabbinate, eating strictly kosher meals, observing rigorous Sabbath practices, and requiring marriage to other Jews. Ultra-Orthodox Jews dominate Israel's politics and reject the validity of non-Orthodox rabbis and converts.

The Orthodox movement originated in a reaction against reformers in Germany, led notably by Rabbi Samson Raphael Hirsch (1808–88), a founder of modern Orthodoxy, who wrote the following.

Religion Allied to Progress by Samson Hirsch

Now what is it that we want? Are the only alternatives either to abandon religion or to renounce all progress with all the glorious and noble gifts which civilisation and education offer mankind? Is the Jewish religion really of such a nature that its faithful adherents must be the enemies of civilisation and progress? … We declare before heaven and earth that if our religion demanded that we should renounce what is called civilisation and progress we would obey unquestioningly, because our religion is for us truly religion, the word of God before which every other consideration has to give way. We declare, equally, that we would prefer to be branded as fools and do without all the honour and glory that civilisation and progress might confer on us rather than be guilty of the conceited mock-wisdom which the spokesman of a religion allied to progress here displays.

For behold whither a religion allied to progress leads! Behold how void it is of all piety and humanity and into what blunders the conceited, Torah-criticising spirit leads. Here you have a protagonist of this religion of progress. See how he dances on the graves of your forefathers, how he drags out their corpses from their graves, laughs in their faces and exclaims to you: "Your fathers were crude and uncivilised; they deserved the contempt in which they were held. Follow me, so that you may become civilised and deserve respect!" Such is the craziness which grows on the tree of knowledge of this "religion allied to progress"!

SOURCE: <http://www.ucalgary.ca/~elsegal/363_Transp/Orthodoxy/SRHirsch.html>

CONSERVATIVE

Middle-ground Conservative Jews embrace a wide range of practices, some close to Orthodoxy, some close to Reform. Most accept scientific study of the Tanakh and see it as written by inspired human hands, thus fallible and subject to interpretation as history progresses. But changes come through communal decision-making, not completely individual free choice.

Shabbat and high holidays are celebrated, conversions are accepted, kosher food preparation is not required, dress rules are minimally decorous, some Hebrew is spoken in synagogue (and some Yiddish from Eastern Europe) and is encouraged, but it is not required. Support for Israel as a nation is strong, but criticism of its politics may be heard. Women sit with men in synagogue and take synagogue leadership roles, including being counted in the minyan (minimum number required for worship). In 1983, New York's Jewish Theological Seminary opened its doors to women, allowing them to become Conservative rabbis. They are often active in community reform movements. This passage illustrates the Conservative view of revelation.

The Conservative Jewish Doctrine of Revelation
by Seymour Siegel

The basic question concerning Jewish law involves a doctrine of Revelation. All forms of Judaism accept the notion of God's communicating with man [sic] in general and the Jewish people in particular. Most Orthodox thinkers argue that the traditional doctrine of Torah MiSinai (the Torah coming from Sinai) posits that God literally commanded everything written in the Torah. This, in their view, makes Jewish law immutable, and change can take place only within the most narrow limits. The Reform thinkers believed that the moral and ethical demands of Judaism were revealed, and that the ritual laws (which means most of the corpus of Jewish law) were the products of human legislation, reflecting various social conditions of the time. This means that *halachah* [Jewish law] is not binding today.

In recent times, Conservative Judaism has tried to find a third way in which revelation could be taken seriously but not literally. Most thinkers have relied on the thinking of Franz Rosenzweig. Rosenzweig argued that revelation is not the transmittal of concrete directives. Revelation means that man and God have met each other. Revelation means the self-uncovering of the Divine in relation to man. It is the transmission to man of God's love and concern. It is a miracle that God does reveal Himself to man. ...

Scripture and its interpretation in the rabbinic writings are not literally revelation. They are the human recordings of the experience of revelation. Therefore, Scripture is both divine and human. The words contain the divine initiative and the human response to it. In each word the two—the divine and the human—are joined and cannot be separated. Therefore, Scripture and Talmud are infinitely precious—for through them the divine is revealed. Scripture and Talmud contain the human response—and therefore are not infallible. ... The history of Judaism is the history of the interpretation of revelation. In [Abraham] Heschel's striking sentence: "Judaism is a minimum of revelation and a maximum of interpretation." ...

This, of course, means that there will be change and modification. It is true, for example, that God countenanced slavery, as is evident in Scripture, when there was no possibility of abolishing the institution. The aim of Jewish law was to humanize the institution until it could be abolished. Though God may have wanted slavery in antiquity, He certainly does not want it now. It is true that God once wanted the law of an "eye for an eye" to be applied literally. He certainly does not want it now. It is possible that God once wanted women to limit themselves to their roles as princesses whose grandeur consisted of being concealed. He probably does not want it now. Total subjectivity is avoided because of the presence of the community and because of the character of Catholic [the practicing community] Israel. The concrete laws are not to be viewed as if they were Platonic Ideas eternally residing in the world of Forms. They are dynamic concepts—subject to the dynamic voice of God, which encounters us anew at all times.

SOURCE: Seymour Siegel, ed., *Conservative Judaism and Jewish Law*. New York: The Rabbinical Assembly, 1978, pp. xx–xxi

REFORM

The Reform branch of Judaism developed in the nineteenth century, beginning in Germany, as the strongest movement to adapt to modern times. Reform Jews are more assimilated into their surrounding culture than Orthodox or Conservative. While honoring the Torah and much Jewish tradition, they seek to reconcile religion with science. Torah is interpreted using historical criticism, which sees many texts as humanly influenced by ancient times, and thus subject to being neglected or changed. They may or may not practice kosher dietary rules. While supporting Israel as a nation, Reform Jews respect voices of dissent about Israel's politics. They have been the leaders in opening doors for women in the synagogue and home, encouraging higher education, careers, equality with men, and ordination as rabbis. In 1972 the first American Jewish woman to be ordained was Sally Preisand, a Reform Jew. Members of this branch of Judaism are often active in social reform movements, as may be seen in Michael Lerner's *Tikkun* magazine.

The fundamental principles of today's Reform Judaism are captured in the Statement of Principles which was adopted in 1999 by the Central Conference of American Rabbis.

Principles of Reform Judaism

G-d[3] Reform Jews affirm the reality and oneness of G-d, even as we may differ in our understanding of the Divine presence.

Reform Jews affirm that the Jewish people is bound to G-d by an eternal b'rit, covenant, as reflected in our varied understandings of Creation, Revelation, and Redemption.

Reform Jews affirm that every human being is created b'tzelem Elohim, in the image of G-d, and that therefore every human life is sacred.

Reform Jews regard with reverence all of G-d's creation and recognize our human responsibility for its preservation and protection.

Reform Jews encounter G-d's presence in moments of awe and wonder, in acts of justice and compassion, in loving relationships and in the experiences of everyday life.

Reform Jews respond to G-d daily: through public and private prayer, through study and through the performance of other **mitzvot**, sacred obligations—*bein adam la Makom*, to G-d, and *bein adam la-chaveiro*, to other human beings.

Reform Jews strive for a faith that fortifies us through the vicissitudes of our lives—illness and healing, transgression and repentance, bereavement and consolation, despair and hope.

Reform Jews continue to have faith that, in spite of the unspeakable evils committed against our people and the sufferings endured by others, the partnership of G-d and humanity will ultimately prevail.

Reform Jews trust in our tradition's promise that, although G-d created us as finite beings, the spirit within us is eternal.

Torah   Reform Jews affirm that Torah is the foundation of Jewish life.

Reform Jews cherish the truths revealed in Torah, G-d's ongoing revelation to our people and the record of our people's ongoing relationship with G-d.

Reform Jews affirm that Torah is a manifestation of *ahavat olam*, G-d's eternal love for the Jewish people and for all humanity.

Reform Jews affirm the importance of studying Hebrew, the language of Torah and Jewish liturgy, that we may draw closer to our people's sacred texts.

Reform Jews are called by Torah to lifelong study in the home, in the synagogue and in every place where Jews gather to learn and teach. Through

---

3 G-d—the term G-d is used to indicate that the name of the Holy One is too sacred to pronounce or write, since the reality is beyond human language.

Torah study Reform Jews are called to mitzvot, the means by which we make our lives holy.

Reform Jews are committed to the ongoing study of the whole array of mitzvot and to the fulfillment of those that address us as individuals and as a community. Some of these mitzvot, sacred obligations, have long been observed by Reform Jews; others, both ancient and modern, demand renewed attention as the result of the unique context of our own times.

Reform Jews bring Torah into the world when we seek to sanctify the times and places of our lives through regular home and congregational observance. Shabbat calls us to bring the highest moral values to our daily labor and to culminate the workweek with *kedushah*, holiness, *menuchah*, rest and *oneg*, joy. The High Holy Days call us to account for our deeds. The Festivals enable us to celebrate with joy our people's religious journey in the context of the changing seasons. The days of remembrance remind us of the tragedies and the triumphs that have shaped our people's historical experience both in ancient and modern times. And we mark the milestones of our personal journeys with traditional and creative rites that reveal the holiness in each stage of life.

Reform Jews bring Torah into the world when we strive to fulfill the highest ethical mandates in our relationships with others and with all of G-d's creation. Partners with G-d in *tikkun olam*, repairing the world, we are called to help bring nearer the messianic age. We seek dialogue and joint action with people of other faiths in the hope that together we can bring peace, freedom and justice to our world. We are obligated to pursue *tzedek*, justice and righteousness, and to narrow the gap between the affluent and the poor, to act against discrimination and oppression, to pursue peace, to welcome the stranger, to protect the earth's biodiversity and natural resources, and to redeem those in physical, economic, and spiritual bondage. In so doing, we reaffirm social action and social justice as a central prophetic focus of traditional Reform Jewish belief and practice. We affirm the mitzvah of *tzedakah*, setting aside portions of our earnings and our time to provide for those in need. These acts bring us closer to fulfilling the prophetic call to translate the words of Torah into the works of our hands.

Israel ... Reform Jews embrace religious and cultural pluralism as an expression of the vitality of Jewish communal life in Israel and in the Diaspora.

Reform Jews pledge to fulfill Reform Judaism's historic commitment to the complete equality of women and men in Jewish life.

Reform Jews are an inclusive community, opening doors to Jewish life to people of all ages, to varied kinds of families, to all regardless of their sexual orientation, to *gerim*, those who have converted to Judaism, and to all individuals and families, including the intermarried, who strive to create a Jewish home.

Reform Jews believe that we must not only open doors for those ready to enter our faith, but also to actively encourage those who are seeking a spiritual home to find it in Judaism. ...

Reform Jews are committed to *Medinat Yisrael*, the State of Israel, and rejoice in its accomplishments. We affirm the unique qualities of living in *Eretz Yisrael*, the land of Israel, and encourage *aliyah*, immigration to Israel.

Reform Jews are committed to a vision of the State of Israel that promotes full civil, human and religious rights for all its inhabitants and that strives for a lasting peace between Israel and its neighbors.

Reform Jews are committed to promoting and strengthening Progressive Judaism in Israel, which will enrich the spiritual life of the Jewish state and its people.

Reform Jews affirm that both Israeli and Diaspora Jewry should remain vibrant and interdependent communities. As we urge Jews who reside outside Israel to learn Hebrew as a living language and to make periodic visits to Israel in order to study and to deepen their relationship to the Land and its people, so do we affirm that Israeli Jews have much to learn from the religious life of Diaspora Jewish communities.

Reform Jews are committed to furthering Progressive Judaism throughout the world as a meaningful religious way of life for the Jewish people.

SOURCE: <http://www.scjfaq.org/faq/18-01-02.html>

RECONSTRUCTIONIST

Reconstructionism is a twentieth-century American liberal Jewish movement that honors individual choice over strict legalism and dogma. It originated with Rabbi Mordecai Kaplan (1881–1983), and formally became a distinct denomination within Judaism with the foundation of the Reconstructionist Rabbinical College, in Wyncote, Pennsylvania in 1968. Religion, Rabbi Kaplan believed, should seek to help humans rise above brutality and oppose violence. It should not offer a set of beliefs that one must accept, but individuals should be able to choose how to honor Jewish law and theology. Kaplan's theology borders on "naturalism" (the idea that religion is a natural cultural construct, with no transcendent origin) and a belief in God as an ultimate, absolute cosmic reality—an abstract principle, independent of human beliefs. He rejected "theism," the language of God as if divinity were a human figure (anthropomorphism), though members are free to refer to God as "He."

Reconstructionists believe that much of Jewish tradition is non-binding folkways, not law, so individual Jews can choose various ways of being Jewish— using Hebrew, studying Torah, keeping commandments (*mitzvot*), or celebrating Jewish holidays. The Reconstructionist Jewish community is democratic and rejects the notion of the "chosen people" that implies any superiority. They also reject traditional divine revelation and believe that humans can extract valid permanent principles from archaic cultural additions. Women are treated as equal to men, and may be ordained as rabbis.

Reconstructionism on One Foot by Rabbi Les Bronstein

... I try to show people how Reconstructionist Jews (and, truth be told, a myriad of Jews around the world) view these matters in a way that is different from traditional Judaism, but surprisingly close to the spirit of that tradition. My three litmus topics are Torah, prayer and ritual, and mitzvot. Here are my few words on each:

Torah: Tradition tells us that the Torah was dictated by God to Moses, and then transmitted through the generations. Reconstructionist Jews see the Torah as the Jewish people's response to God's presence in the world (and not God's gift to us). That is to say, the Jews wrote the Torah. But that is not to say that the Torah is merely a human creation. It is a response to the sacred. It is an attempt to convince an entire people to view everyday life in a sacred way.

Yes, it is intriguing to apply the tools of history, science, and chronology to the Torah. These vehicles give us the historical and natural context of the Torah. But they don't give us the essence of the Torah. The essential Torah is neither the tidal explanation for the parting of the sea, nor the geological definition of the primordial flood nor the cosmological identification of "let there be light." The essential Torah consists in the truth deep within these stories, a truth that radiates a picture of a society based on courts of justice and on social empathy. God didn't write that Torah, since God does not write per se. But God is everywhere in the details of it.

Prayer and Ritual: On the face of it, the text of the *siddur* [Prayer Book] suggests that our prayers are direct recitations and petitions to a God who is "other" and who, we hope, is listening and contemplating a favorable response. Reconstructionist Jews retain the traditional language of Jewish prayer, but not the obvious understanding of its meaning and function.

Rather, we understand prayer to help us perform the task of awakening. We need to awaken ourselves to the miracle that is life and to the obligations that inhere in that life. We believe that we are the primary respondents to our own prayers, and that we need prayer to remind us of the Godly values behind our benevolent actions in the world. We also understand prayer as a way of calling out to others in the world, in the hope that they, too, would sign on to the Godly enterprise of healing, caring, and righting injustice.

In sum, prayer and ritual are the Jewish people's way of heightening our awareness of the sacredness of life, of clarifying and reiterating our moral values and of marking time and space in a sacred way.

Mitzvot: The word mitzvah means "commandment," and tradition literally understands mitzvot to be direct commandments from God, via the Torah. As such, we might utilize a mitzvah as an opportunity for meaningful relationship with God or our own souls, but we are obligated to perform the deed in any case, regardless of any spiritual uplift it may or may not provide.

As you would expect, Reconstructionist Judaism teaches that the mitzvot are our own invention. Mitzvot are our particularly Jewish ways of responding to the universal God. We perceive God as demanding sacredness in general, and the Jewish mitzvot are our people's way of bringing that universal sacredness to the minutiae of daily life in our own specifically Jewish context.

In this system, God does not choose the Jews to be performers of the commandments. Rather, the Jews choose to be called by God by means of a vast network of sacred acts (mitzvot) ranging from balancing work and rest (Shabbat), to establishing courts and laws, to sexual fidelity, filial respect, medical ethics and the rhythms of the seasons. (Hence, *asher ker'vanu la'avodato*, "who has called us to your service.") Paradoxically, it is the mitzvot that keep us Jewish, but which simultaneously attune us to the greater universe of which we are a tiny part.

SOURCE: Jewish Reconstruction Federation Archives
<http://jrf.org/showres&rid=728>, October 16, 2007

Living Judaism

Contemporary Jewish culture has been haunted by the question of how to respond to the Nazi **Holocaust**, challenged by the new women rabbis, and enlivened by revival movements.

The Perils of Indifference by Elie Wiesel

During World War II in Europe, the right-wing German Nazis believed in the racist myth of the white Aryans, and sought to "purify" their race by exterminating people they designated as "undesirable," including six million Jews. They forced these undesirables into numerous prison camps, such as Buchenwald, Auschwitz, and Treblinka, and then denied the existence of the camps. The scars and collective grief caused by the Holocaust have been expressed by Elie Wiesel who, as a boy, was a prisoner at Auschwitz. Born in an Orthodox Jewish family in Romania, Wiesel studied in Paris and, in 1955, moved to New York City, where he wrote many books including *Night* (1960). He is Mellen Professor of the Humanities at Boston University and won a Nobel Prize in 1986 for speaking out against racism, violence, and oppression. In this extract he speaks out against indifference.

Fifty-four years ago to the day, a young Jewish boy from a small town in the Carpathian Mountains woke up, not far from Goethe's[4] beloved Weimar[5], in a place of eternal infamy called Buchenwald. He was finally free, but there was no joy in his heart. He thought there never would be again. Liberated a day earlier by American soldiers, he remembers their rage at what they saw.

---

4 Goethe—Johann W. von Goethe (1749–1832) was a writer of German Enlightenment and Romantic literature, notably *Faust* (1808), about the selling of one's soul to the Devil in exchange for worldly power.
5 Weimar—a city in eastern Germany and a major center of political and artistic creativity.

And even if he lives to be a very old man, he will always be grateful to them for that rage, and also for their compassion. Though he did not understand their language, their eyes told him what he needed to know that they, too, would remember, and bear witness. ...

What will the legacy of this vanishing century be? How will it be remembered in the new millennium? Surely it will be judged, and judged severely, in both moral and metaphysical terms. These failures have cast a dark shadow over humanity: two World Wars, countless civil wars, the senseless chain of assassinations (Gandhi, the Kennedys, Martin Luther King, Sadat, Rabin), bloodbaths in Cambodia and Algeria, India and Pakistan, Ireland and Rwanda, Eritrea and Ethiopia, Sarajevo and Kosovo; the inhumanity in the gulag[6] and the tragedy of Hiroshima[7]. And, on a different level, of course, Auschwitz and Treblinka. So much violence; so much indifference.

Of course, indifference can be tempting, more than that, seductive. It is so much easier to look away from victims. It is so much easier to avoid such rude interruptions to our work, our dreams, our hopes. It is, after all, awkward, troublesome, to be involved in another person's pain and despair. Yet, for the person who is indifferent, his or her neighbor are of no consequence. And, therefore, their lives are meaningless. Their hidden or even visible anguish is of no interest. Indifference reduces the Other to an abstraction.

Over there, behind the black gates of Auschwitz, the most tragic of all prisoners were the "Muselmanner," as they were called. Wrapped in their torn blankets, they would sit or lie on the ground, staring vacantly into space, unaware of who or where they were, strangers to their surroundings. They no longer felt pain, hunger, thirst. They feared nothing. They felt nothing. They were dead and did not know it.

Rooted in our tradition, some of us felt that to be abandoned by God was worse than to be punished by Him. Better an unjust God than an indifferent one. For us to be ignored by God was a harsher punishment than to be a victim of His anger. Man can live far from God, not outside God. God is wherever we are. Even in suffering? Even in suffering.

Indifference elicits no response. Indifference is not a response. Indifference is not a beginning; it is an end. And, therefore, indifference is always the friend of the enemy, for it benefits the aggressor never his victim, whose pain is magnified when he or she feels forgotten. The political prisoner in his cell, the hungry children, the homeless refugees not to respond to their plight, not to relieve their solitude by offering them a spark of hope is to exile them from human memory. And in denying their humanity, we betray our own.

Indifference, then, is not only a sin, it is a punishment. And this is one of the most important lessons of this outgoing century's wide-ranging experiments in good and evil. ...

---

6 Gulag—the chain of remote Soviet work camps, many in freezing Siberia, where dissidents and criminals were sent.

7 Hiroshima—a city in southern Japan destroyed by the first atomic bomb in 1945.

And our only miserable consolation was that we believed that Auschwitz and Treblinka were closely guarded secrets; that the leaders of the free world did not know what was going on behind those black gates and barbed wire; that they had no knowledge of the war against the Jews that Hitler's armies and their accomplices waged as part of the war against the Allies.
If they knew, we thought, surely those leaders would have moved heaven and earth to intervene. They would have spoken out with great outrage and conviction. They would have bombed the railways leading to Birkenau[8], just the railways, just once.

And now we knew, we learned, we discovered that the Pentagon knew, the State Department knew. … Why did some of America's largest corporations continue to do business with Hitler's Germany until 1942? It has been suggested, and it was documented, that the Wehrmacht[9] could not have conducted its invasion of France without oil obtained from American sources. How is one to explain their indifference?

SOURCE: From a speech delivered April 12, 1999, Washington, D.C. Transcription by Michael E. Eidenmuller. <http://www.americanrhetoric.com/speeches/PDFFiles/Elie%20Wiesel%20-%20Indifference.pdf>

Women in Jewish Life by Ellen M. Umansky

The changing roles of Jewish women are described by Ellen M. Umansky of Fairfield University, Connecticut. Increasing numbers of educated Jewish women, women's rights, and persuasive feminist texts are dissolving many of the limits of ancient traditions.

The past hundred years have witnessed a tremendous change in the role of women in Jewish communal life. Up through the early nineteenth century, with generations of rabbis developing expectations and norms for Judaism as a way of life, women's religious roles were largely relegated to the home. To the rabbis, the destruction of the Second Temple in 70 CE led to the creation of two religious centers: the synagogue, which was largely the domain of men; and the home, largely the domain of women.

In addition to following most of the commandments encumbent upon men, women were seen as having three special commandments: baking *challah*, the braided loaf eaten on the Sabbath and holidays, in a ritually prescribed way; lighting the Sabbath candles (thereby ushering in the Sabbath); and following the laws of ritual purity, biblically based laws that regulated the times during which sexual relations between married couples were permitted. Today, many Jewish women continue to bake (or buy) ritually prepared *challah* and light candles on Friday night. Only the traditionally observant follow the laws of *niddah* (ritual purity). From the contemporary perspective of most non-Orthodox Jewish women, the laws of *niddah* are antiquated and thus rarely, if ever, followed. To Orthodox

8 Birkenau—an expansion of Auschwitz Nazi prison camp, built for extermination of "undesirables."
9 Wehrmacht—the Nazi military army, navy, and air force.

women, however, these laws, whether literally mandated by God or not, remain *halakhically* (legally) binding upon them. Indeed, some traditionally observant women today see these laws, which include immersing oneself in a ritual bath or *mikvah* after a set number of days following one's menstrual period or giving birth to a child, as a source of power. It is only when a woman has immersed herself in a *mikvah* that she and her husband can resume having sexual intercourse, thus enabling her husband to fulfill the obligation to be "fruitful and multiply."

Prior to the seventeenth century and the advent of modernity, Jewish women received a minimal religious education because of their exemption from the obligation to study. Consequently the Hebrew prayer book was inaccessible to most of them. While there were Jewish women throughout the Middle Ages who attended synagogue services, following the Hebrew or, by the sixteenth century, reading prayers in the vernacular written especially for them, most Jewish women cultivated a more private sense of spirituality. Those who became scholars were few and far between, always viewed as exceptions that proved the rule. Indeed, recognizing the fact that much of Jewish religious life is home-centered and well aware of the extent to which the continuation of Jewish life depended on them, it seems that prior to the nineteenth century, most Jewish women thought of their religious world as one which primarily, though again, not exclusively, centered around and within the home.

Since the end of the nineteenth century, and even more so, during the second half of the twentieth, women's roles in Jewish life have greatly expanded. In Europe and the United States, these changes have reflected the leadership roles assumed by women in many Protestant denominations and new nineteenth-century religious movements, including Christian Science, the Salvation Army, and the Seventh Day Adventists, founded, or co-founded by women; the creation of liberal or progressive Jewish religious movements, particularly Reform Judaism, founded in Germany in the early nineteenth century; Conservative Judaism, founded in the United States in 1886 with the opening of the Jewish Theological Seminary of America; and Reconstructionist Judaism, founded in New York in 1922 by Conservative rabbi Mordecai Kaplan. The expansion of Jewish women's roles within the synagogue and Jewish communal life have also been influenced by the second wave of American feminism, which began in the late 1960s, and has greatly, and perhaps irrevocably, changed women's expectations of what they want to achieve, and increasingly have achieved, not just in the United States but throughout the modern, largely Western world.

The first woman ordained as a rabbi was Regina Jonas. She was privately granted a rabbinic diploma in 1935 by Reform rabbi Max Dienemann of Offenbach, Germany, after the Talmud professor empowered with ordaining her from the Berlin Academy for the Scientific Study of Judaism, where she had studied, refused to do so on the grounds that she was a woman. Yet it wasn't until 1972 that Sally Preisand became the first woman ordained from a rabbinical seminary. Ordained in Cincinnati, Ohio, from the Reform movement's Hebrew Union College—Jewish Institute of Religion, she became the first of hundreds of women who have since been ordained in the United States, England, and Israel. While in 1985 the historic ordination of Amy Eilberg from the Jewish Theological Seminary of America led to a split in the Conservative movement, with some more traditional members arguing that women's ordination could not be justified within the framework of *halakhah* (rabbinic law), these traditionalists have since left the Conservative movement, which has increasingly followed Reform in investing women as cantors [Jews trained to lead the prayer service, noted for their musical and chanting skills], and, as in all of Judaism's more liberal branches, and some more traditionally religious congregations, encouraging them to serve as officers of congregations, including assuming the role of synagogue president.

For the past few decades, in Reform, Conservative, and Reconstructionist synagogues in the United States and in liberal synagogues throughout the world, women have been counted in the *minyan* (the quorum necessary for public worship), called to the Torah to recite the blessings before and after the Torah reading, and invited to read from the Torah itself. Women's increased educational and religious opportunities within these movements, including being called to the Torah as a **Bat Mitzvah**, at the age of 12 or 13 or, especially in the United States, as an adult Bat Mitzvah following a specific period of study, have helped facilitate such participation. Within many Conservative and Reconstructionist synagogues, and some Reform congregations as well, women have begun to wear *kippot* (skull caps) and *tallitot* (prayer shawls), traditionally worn only by Jewish men, and some women have begun to lay *tefillin* (leather straps wrapped around the arm, hand, and forehead during morning prayer) as well. These innovations have been influenced by Jewish feminism, which first arose in the United States as a short-lived national organization and has since led to the creation of smaller interest-based feminist groups that have called for, and in many cases helped institute, change.

Particularly noteworthy have been the creation of gender inclusive prayers in liberal congregations throughout the world, in which God is addressed "You" rather than "He" and invoked not only as the God of "our [biblical] fathers, Abraham, Isaac, and Jacob," but of "our [biblical] mothers, Sarah, Rebekah, Leah, and Rachel" as well. Equally significant have been the creation in all branches of Judaism of naming ceremonies for girls, frequently called a "Simchat Bat" (rejoicing in the birth of a daughter) or a "B'rit B'not" (covenant of the daughters, paralleling the term "B'rit Milah" which refers to the covenant of ritual circumcision of boys), and of *Rosh Chodesh* (New Moon) rituals created by and for women.

For several decades, women's Passover seders (ritual meals) have become communal gatherings of women that relive slavery and liberation through the lens of women's experiences. At these and family and synagogue *sedarim*, an increasing number of Jews, especially in the United States and Canada, have begun to place a "Miriam's Cup" of water on the table, along with the traditional Elijah's Cup of wine. Some have also begun to place an orange on the *seder* plate. According to Reconstructionist rabbi Rebecca Alpert, legend has it that this was instigated in the early 1980s by a group of Jewish feminists in response to a Hasidic (ultra-Orthodox) rabbi who declared that there was as much room for lesbians in Judaism as there was for leavened bread on the *seder* table. That is, no place at all. Initially these feminists placed bread on the table in protest. Moved by the ritual but uncomfortable with the bread, they soon substituted an orange which, like bread, traditionally has no place on a *seder* table but which, unlike bread, can be eaten during Passover. By the early 1990s, the story was retold as one in which a Jewish feminist was rebuked by a man who said that women rabbis had as much of a role in Judaism (or alternately, that women had as much of a place on the *bimah*, the stage or platform from which synagogue services are led) as oranges on a *seder* plate (Rebecca Alpert, *Like Bread on the Seder Plate*, pp. 2–3). Since then, many feminists have added an orange to their seder plates, to emphasize women's place in every facet of Jewish life.

Women's opportunities for full participation in the synagogue and greater roles of religious and communal leadership remain more limited in Orthodox Judaism. Nonetheless, modern Orthodox women are taking on new roles of public religious and communal leadership. In 2009, following his conferring the title "Mahara't," an acronym for a teacher of Jewish law and spirituality, upon Sara Hurvitz (he has since given her the title of "Rabba"), Rabbi Avi Weiss of the Hebrew Institute of Riverdale, New York, founded Yeshivat Maharat as the "first institution in Jewish history to train women to be fully integrated into the Orthodox community as spiritual leaders and *halakhic* authorities" (<http://yeshivatmaharat.org/>). The creation of the Jewish Orthodox Feminist Alliance (JOFA) in 1999 provided a forum for Orthodox feminists worldwide to voice concerns and suggested courses of action. By 2006, JOFA began to compile information about practices in Orthodox synagogues related to women. Believing that women's equality and, thus, inclusivity, are overarching Jewish values, it hopes to serve as a resource for those seeking to join a synagogue and a reference for Orthodox congregations considering innovations that would create a more "welcoming environment for women in *shul* [synagogue]" (*JOFA Journal*, Summer 2006, p. 21).

Religious and political activism have come together in the actions of Women of the Wall, a group of Jewish women who since 1988 have gathered together in prayer at the *Kotel* (Western Wall) in Jerusalem on *Rosh Chodesh* and other holidays. Long facing opposition from Orthodox Israeli men who strenuously object to women's praying as a group at the wall, wearing *tallitot*, and holding and reading from the Torah, these women have faced several ongoing legal battles, arguing before the Israeli Supreme Court with varying degrees of success for women's religious rights at the *Kotel*.

Other Jewish women's groups, including synagogue auxiliary organizations throughout the world and such independent national or international organizations as the National Council of Jewish Women (in the United States), Hadassah, and Jewish Women International (formerly known as B'nai Brith women), have long fought for women's political, religious, and economic rights. Women continue to take an active role in Jewish philanthropy, through combined efforts with men and through separate women's divisions of such organizations as the United Jewish Appeal, the largest Jewish fund raising agency in the world. Some argue that a glass ceiling still exists for women at the top levels of Jewish organizational life. Yet if such a ceiling exists, it is on the verge of collapsing. Through the ongoing efforts of women and their male supporters and the growing impact of feminism on Judaism, equal access to roles within congregational and communal life, and with it the transformation of those roles by women, are increasingly becoming a reality, for as I have written elsewhere (see Arvind Sharma and Katherine Young, *Feminism and World Religions*, p. 208), "despite the fact that increasing opportunities and expectations undoubtedly create new internal and external conflicts, having tasted the fruit of the tree of knowledge, Jewish women are discovering that there is no road back to Eden."

SOURCE: Original article for this book by Ellen M. Umansky, 2011.

Ten Commitments, Not Commandments by Michael Lerner

Rabbi Michael Lerner is the editor of *Tikkun* magazine. *Tikkun* means "repair" in the cosmic sense. A philosopher and psychologist, he is an outspoken leader of a liberal Jewish renewal movement in our times. Advocating a sweeping renewal of Judaism rooted in Torah, he calls for a strong social conscience, a genuine sense of transcendence, and a vital Jewish community. He urges release from the silent pain inherited from the Holocaust and from a sense of victimization. He stands for liberation from sexism, homophobia, and ecological harm. Here he writes an interpretation of the traditional Ten Commandments in the biblical book of Exodus 20, generalizing so they make sense today.

Many of us find the notion of "commandments" oppressive and hierarchical. Yet we know that a community cannot be built on the principle of only doing what feels right at the moment—it requires a sense of responsibility to each other. So, we encourage our community to take on the following ten commitments, based roughly on a rereading of the Torah's ten commandments (and incorporating the framework and many specific ideas articulated by Rami Shapiro in his book *Minyan*).

Ten Commitments
1. *YHVH, the Power of Transformation and Healing, is the Ultimate Reality of the Universe and the Source of Transcendent Unity* Aware of the suffering caused by not acknowledging the ultimate Unity of All Being, I vow to recognize every human being as a manifestation of the Divine and to spend more time each day in awe and wonder at the grandeur of Creation.

Aware of the suffering that is caused when we unconsciously pass on to others the pain, cruelty, depression, and despair that has been inflicted upon us, I vow to become conscious and then act upon all the possibilities for healing and transforming my own life and being involved in healing and transforming the larger world.

2. *Idolatry* Aware of the suffering caused by taking existing social realities, economic security, ideologies, religious beliefs, national commitments, or the gratification of our current desires as the highest value, I vow to recognize only God as the ultimate, and to look at the universe and each part of my life as an evolving part of a larger Totality whose ultimate worth is measured by how close it brings us to God and to love of each other. To stay in touch with this reality, I vow to meditate each day for at least ten minutes and to contemplate the totality of the universe and my humble place in it.

3. *Do not take God in Vain* Aware of the suffering caused by religious or spiritual fanaticism, I vow to be respectful of all religious traditions which preach love and respect for the Other, and to recognize that there are many possible paths to God. I vow to acknowledge that we as Jews are not better than others and our path is only one of the many ways that people have heard God's voice. I vow to remain aware of the distortions in our own traditions, and the ways that I myself necessarily bring my own limitations to every encounter with the Divine. So I will practice spiritual humility. Yet I will enthusiastically advocate for what I find compelling in the Jewish tradition and encourage others to explore that which has moved me.

4. *Observe the Sabbath* Aware of the suffering produced by excessive focus on "making it" and obtaining material satisfactions, I vow to regularly observe Shabbat as a day in which I focus on celebrating the world rather than trying to control it or maximize my own advantage within it. I will build Shabbat with the Beyt Tikkun[10] community and enjoy loving connection with others. I will use some Shabbat time to renew my commitment to social justice and healing. I will also set aside significant amounts of time for inner spiritual development, personal renewal, reflection, and pleasure.

5. *Honor your Mother and Father* Aware of the suffering caused by aging, disease, and death, I vow to provide care and support for my parents. Aware that every parent has faults and has inflicted pain on their children, I vow to forgive my parents and to allow myself to see them as human beings with the same kinds of limitations as every other human being on the planet. And I vow to remember the moments of kindness and nurturance, and to let them play a larger role in my memory as I develop a sense of compassion for them and for myself.

6. *Do not Murder* Aware of the suffering caused by wars, environmental irresponsibility, and eruptions of violence, I vow to recognize the sanctity of life and not to passively participate in social practices that are destructive of the lives of others. I will resist the perpetrators of violence and oppression of others, the poisoners of our environment, and those who demean others

10 Beyt Tikkun—the Tikkun school of interpretation of Jewish tradition.

or encourage acts of violence. Aware that much violence is the irrational and often self-destructive response to the absence of love and caring, I vow to show more loving and caring energy to everyone around me, to take the time to know others more deeply, and to struggle for a world which provides everyone with recognition and spiritual nourishment.

7. *Do not Engage in Sexual Exploitation* Aware of the suffering caused when people break their commitments of sexual loyalty to each other, and the suffering caused by using other people for our own sexual purposes, I vow to keep my commitments and to be fully honest and open in my sexual dealings with others, avoiding deceit or manipulation to obtain my own ends. I will rejoice in my body and the bodies of others, will treat them as embodiments of Divine energy, and will seek to enhance my own pleasure and the pleasure of others around me, joyfully celebrating sex as an opportunity for encounter with the holy. I will do all I can to prevent sexual abuse in adults and children, the spreading of sexually transmitted diseases, and the misuse of sexuality to further domination or control of others. I will respect the diversity of non-exploitative sexual expression and lifestyles and will not seek to impose sexual orthodoxies on others.

8. *Do not Steal* Aware of the suffering caused by an unjust distribution of the world's resources, exploitation, and theft, I vow to practice generosity, to share what I have, and to not keep anything that should belong to others while working for a wise use of the goods and services that are available. I will not [hoard] what I have, and especially will not [hoard] love. I will support a fairer redistribution of the wealth of the planet so that everyone has adequate material well-being, recognizing that contemporary global inequalities in wealth are often the resultant of colonialism, genocide, slavery, theft, and the imposition of monetary and trade policies by the powerful on the powerless. In the meantime, I will do my best to support the homeless and others who are in need.

   Aware that others sometimes contribute much energy to keeping this community functioning, I will give time and energy to the tasks of building the Beyt Tikkun community, and, when possible, will donate generously of my financial resources and my talents and time.

9. *Do not Lie* Aware of the suffering caused by wrongful speech, I vow to cultivate a practice of holy speech in which my words are directed to increasing the love and caring in the world. I vow to avoid words that are misleading or manipulative, and avoid spreading stories that I do not know to be true, or which might cause unnecessary divisiveness or harm, and instead will use my speech to increase harmony, social justice, kindness, hopefulness, trust, and solidarity. I will be generous in praise and support for others. To heighten my awareness of this commitment, I will dedicate one day a week to full and total holiness of words, refraining from any speech that day which does not hallow God's name or bring joy to others.

10. *Do not Covet* Aware of the suffering caused by excessive consumption of the world's resources, I vow to rejoice in what I have and to live a life of ethical consumption governed by a recognition that the world's resources are already strained and by a desire to promote ecological sustainability and material modesty. I vow to see the success of others as an inspiration rather than as detracting from my own sufficiency and to cultivate in myself and others the sense that I have enough and that I am enough and that there is enough for everyone.

SOURCE: *Tikkun* magazine, October 11, 2005
<http://www.tikkun.org>

GLOSSARY

Bar Mitzvah (son of the Commandment) An initiation for Jewish boys about 13 who have studied Judaism and ritually become responsible adults.

Bat Mitzvah (daughter of the Commandment) An initiation for Jewish girls about 13 who have studied Judaism and ritually become responsible adults.

Canon The official list of books with authority in a religion, believed to be either inspired or revealed.

Conservative A moderate branch of modern Judaism, between Orthodox and Reform traditions.

Covenant A sacred contract between God and Israel, stipulating obligations such as circumcision and obedience to Torah and God's promise of a great nation in Israel.

Deuteronomic One of four strands of the Pentateuch, primarily Deuteronomy.

Diaspora (dispersion, exile) Jewish communities outside the land of Israel.

Elohist One of four strands of the Pentateuch, using "Elohim" to name God.

Haggadah The order of service for the Jewish Passover Seder.

Halakhah The written and oral Jewish Law.

Holocaust The destruction of many Jews in Germany, Poland, and other European countries by the Nazis before and during World War II.

Kabbalah The Jewish mystical tradition.

Messiah (the anointed one) Descendant of King David expected to restore the kingdom promised by the prophets; blended with apocalyptic expectations.

Midrash Interpretations of scriptures, the basis of much of the Talmud.

Mishnah A legal code based on the Torah, in oral traditions from around 200 CE.

Mitzvot Sacred obligations to God and humans.

Monotheism Belief in one supreme god only, in contrast with polytheism.

Orthodox The branch of a religious tradition that seeks to practice the original religion in its strictest form, in contrast with reform movements; a Jewish group, strong in Israel since 1948.

Pentateuch The first five books of the Hebrew Bible, also called "Torah": Genesis, Exodus, Leviticus, Numbers, and Deuteronomy.

Priestly One of four strands of the Pentateuch, written late, with ritual concerns.

Prophets Oracular seers in many religions, believed to channel divine messages; in Judaism, a group of such seers recorded in books such as Isaiah and Jeremiah who emphasized social injustices and promised the Messiah.

Rabbi (teacher) The Jewish leader of a congregation; the local synagogue leaders who replaced the priests of the old central Temple in Jerusalem.

Reconstructionism A radical branch of Judaism that rejects theism and its anthropomorphic language as metaphors and sees the Law as evolving flexibly with modern autonomy of the individual and science.

Reform Progressive Jewish movement from the nineteenth century in Europe and the United States; accepts moral laws, rejects ritual laws inconsistent with modernity.

Synagogue A local center of worship, community and teaching that replaces the central Temple in Jerusalem.

Talmud Body of commentary and discussion of interpretations of tradition.

Tanakh The complete Jewish scriptures: Torah, Prophets, and Writings.

Torah (teaching) Variously used to mean the first five scrolls of the Hebrew Scriptures (Pentateuch), all the Laws of Israel.

Yahwist (or Jahwist) One of four strands of the Pentateuch, using "YaHWeH" to name God.

HOLY DAYS

Shabbat (Sabbath) The seventh day of the week, when Jews abstain from work. It begins after dark on Friday. Synagogue services are held Friday nights and Saturdays.

Rosh Hashanah (New Year) Around the fall equinox, the spiritual year begins with the blowing of a ram's horn and prayers.

Yom Kippur (Day of Atonement) To renew God's covenant, a time of inner spiritual cleansing, forgiveness, and reconciliation.

Sukkot (Feast of Tabernacles) A fall harvest festival.

Hanukkah (Feast of Dedication) Around the winter solstice, eight candles are lit on a candle-holder (menorah), one each night, to commemorate two miracles.

Purim (Feast of Lots) A joyous remembrance of Esther and Mordecai's saving of Jews from destruction by Persians.

Pesach (Passover) The spring celebration of the liberation of Jews from Egyptian slavery by Moses; opens with an instructional, symbolic Seder meal.

Yom Hashoah Holocaust memorial day, honoring the victims.

Yom Haatzuma-ut Israel Independence Day, celebrating May 14, 1948, when Israel again became a sovereign state, after centuries of the Diaspora.

HISTORICAL OUTLINE

c. 1900–1700 BCE?—Abraham, the first patriarch

c. 1250 BCE—Exodus from Egypt led by Moses through Sinai to the promised land

c. 1010–970 BCE—King David unites northern and southern Israel in Jerusalem

c. 950 BCE—First Temple built by David's son, King Solomon

c. 750–250 BCE—age of classical prophets: Isaiah, Jeremiah, Ezekiel, and 12 minor prophets

722 BCE—fall of Northern Kingdom (Israel) to Assyria

586 BCE—fall of Southern Kingdom (Judah) to Babylon; First Temple destroyed; Jews taken into slavery

c. 535 BCE—exiles return from Babylon and rebuild Temple; Ezra and Nehemiah lead

168 BCE—successful Jewish Maccabean Revolt against Hellenistic rulers

70 CE—Romans destroy Jerusalem and Second Temple; end of sacrifices and priests at Temple, beginning of Diaspora and rabbinic leadership in synagogues

c. 90 CE—canon of Tanakh agreed by consensus

c. 200 CE—compilation of Mishnah

c. 1135–1204—Maimonides adapts Jewish theology to philosophy

c. 1200–1300—Zohar appears in Spain, contributes to Kabbalah

1470—Spanish Inquisition begins to purge Muslims, Jews, other non-Christians

1492—mass expulsion of Jews from Spain

c. 1555—ghettos built in Italy and Germany

c. 1700–60—Baal-Shem Tov in Eastern Europe begins Hasidism

1933–1945—Nazi Holocaust, reaching its climax during World War II

1948—state of Israel re-established after British rule

1950—Law of Return allows Jews to emigrate to Israel; beginning of rebuilding of culture, industry, and agriculture

1967–70—conflicts with Palestinians, Jordan, and Egypt erupt into war

1972—ordination of first Jewish (Reform) woman in U.S., Sally Preisand

1982—United Nations supports independent Palestinian state

1994—Vatican and Israel establish first diplomatic relations

2005—Israel evacuates Jewish settlements in Gaza, conflicts continue

2010—Direct Israeli–Palestinian talks open in Washington

REVIEW QUESTIONS

1   What is a Jewish covenant? Describe three major covenants.
2   What major themes did Maimonides see as central to Jewish faith?
3   Contrast the Ten Commandments of the Mosaic Covenant in Exodus with Michael Lerner's "Ten Commitments, Not Commandments." What do you think about this?

DISCUSSION QUESTIONS

1   What are the two different creation stories in Genesis? Discuss major themes, different sequences of events (especially plant/human creation), mastery of nature, and gender issues. What do these differences in creation accounts tell us about how to interpret the Torah?
2   What are the important differences among the four major branches of contemporary Judaism? Which make most sense to you and why?
3   What do you think should be proper responses to the Holocaust? Discuss Holocaust literature, Holocaust museums, Holocaust Remembrance Day, American government financial support for Israel, and Jewish settlements in Israel and Palestine.

INFORMATION RESOURCES

Berenbaum, Michael and **Fred Skolnik**, eds. *Encyclopedia Judaica*, 2nd ed. 22 vols. Detroit, MI: Macmillan Reference USA, 2007. Also online at libraries.

Bernstein, Ellen, ed. *Ecology and the Jewish Spirit*. Woodstock, VT: Jewish Lights Publishing, 1998.

Coalition on the Environment and Jewish Life
<http://www.coejl.org/index.php>

Cohen, Arthur, and **Paul Mendes-Flohr**, eds. *Contemporary Jewish Religious Thought*. New York: Free Press/Macmillan, 1987.

Commentary Magazine
<http://www.Commentarymagazine.com>

Fackenheim, Emil. *God's Presence in History*. New York: New York University Press, 1970.

Gillman, Neil. *The Death of Death*. Woodstock, VT: Jewish Lights Publishing, 2000.

Glatzer, Nahum. *Hammer on the Rock: A Short Midrash Reader*, trans. Jacob Sloan. New York: Schocken, 1987.

Goodstein, Laurie. "Conservative Jews Allow Gay Rabbis and Union."
<http://www.nytimes.com/2006/12/07/us/07jews.html>

Heschel, Abraham. *The Prophets*. New York: Harper and Row, 1962.

Holz, Barry. *The Schocken Guide to Jewish Books*. New York: Schocken, 1992.

Israel-Palestine conflict timeline
<http://www.mideastweb.org/timeline.htm>

Jewish Film Archive Online
<http://www.Jewishfilm.com>

Jewish links on the web
<http://www.adath-shalom.ca/jewish_links.htm>

Jewish Virtual Library
<http://www.jewishvirtuallibrary.org>

Jewishnet
<http://www.Jewishnet.net>

Jewish Women's Archive
"Jewish Women: A Comprehensive Historical Encyclopedia"
<http://jwa.org/encylopedia>

Kaplan, Dana E. *The Cambridge Companion to American Judaism*. Cambridge, UK: Cambridge University Press, 2005.

Kaplan, Mordecai. *Judaism as a Civilization: Toward a Reconstruction of Jewish Life*. Philadelphia, PA: Jewish Publication Society, 1934/1994.

Neusner, Jacob. *The Way of Torah: An Introduction to Judaism*. Belmont, CA: Wadsworth/Thomson, 2004.

Onishi, Norimitsu. "Reading Torah Women's Group Tests Tradition," in *The New York Times*, Feb. 16, 1997, Metro Section, pp. 43, 49.

Rubenstein, Richard. *After Auschwitz*, 2nd ed. Baltimore, MD: Johns Hopkins University Press, 1992.

Schäfer, Peter. *Gershom Scholem's Major Trends in Jewish Mysticism 50 Years After*. Tübingen, Germany: Mohr, 1993.

Silverman, Lou H., *et al.* "Judaism," in *Encyclopedia Britannica*. Vol. 22, pp. 379–456. London, 1997.

Swartz, Michael, *et al.* "Judaism," in *Encyclopedia of Religion*, ed. Lindsay Jones. 2nd ed. Vol. 7, pp. 4968–5022. New York: Macmillan, 2005.

CHAPTER 9

CHRISTIANITY

Christianity is such a widespread and influential religion that, around the world, dates are now commonly measured from the approximate birth date of Jesus, probably a few years before 1 CE. According to Christian tradition, he was born in Israel to a poor family under lowly circumstances, and his spiritual help was often offered to those who were neglected or rejected by society. When he began preaching openly at the age of about 30, he was sharply critical of religious hypocrisy. Himself a Jew, he upheld the spirit of the teachings of the Torah while pointing out their abuses by religious authorities. To his followers, however, he was not just a reformer. He was known as a miracle worker; many who came to him were healed. Some became convinced that Jesus was the Messiah for whom they had long been waiting.

Jesus spoke often about the kingdom of God, but it seems that he was referring to a spiritual rather than a political realm. Nonetheless, the religious authorities and the Roman rulers of the region ultimately had him crucified in Jerusalem. Three days later, according to varied accounts in the Bible, he was miraculously resurrected and appeared again in the flesh to his closest disciples, charging them to carry on his work. They, too, became great healers and preachers, despite persecution. One of the persecutors was reportedly transformed by a vision of Jesus, becoming the Apostle Paul. His extensive travels and writings were extremely influential in shaping Christianity as an organized religion and theology.

According to the biblical accounts, Jesus brought a message of love for all, especially the weak. He urged radical inner transformation and promised that God was forgiving to sinners who sincerely repented and turned toward him. Paul's teachings brought the additional beliefs that Jesus was the incarnation of God and that Jesus' death offered atonement for the sins of a believer of any nationality. With this understanding, many Christians feel that, while other religions may have their saints and prophets, only Jesus offers the way to receiving God's **grace**.

Christian belief is not unitary; on the contrary, those professing belief in Jesus have over time separated into some 21,000 different denominations in three major divisions: **Eastern Orthodox**, **Roman Catholic**, and **Protestant**. Today there are lively conservative and liberal movements throughout Christianity.

Jesus the Christ

Stories of the life and teachings of Jesus and their theological interpretation appear in the New Testament of the Christian Bible, written in Greek and some Aramaic (spoken by Jesus). The Christian Bible also includes a version of the Hebrew Bible, or Tanakh, labeled as the Old Testament. The New Testament begins with the four Gospels—Matthew, Mark, Luke, and John—and writings about Jesus' followers after his death, including letters from Paul to the new Christian congregations.

The first three Gospels were written down between 70 and 90 CE. Mark is the oldest, and they all show evidence of earlier sources, oral and written. They are similar, and are thus called the **Synoptic** Gospels. But they also differ: Matthew has a genealogy of Jesus' family line, Mark has no appearances of the resurrected Christ, and Luke has a long birth narrative. The fourth Gospel, John (c. 95 CE), shows a more mystical and Greek influence (the Light, the Word). Paul's letters, or Epistles, were written between 48 and 64 CE, before the Gospels took their present form. Other New Testament books were written down as late as 150 CE. The following selections are taken from a mid-twentieth-century translation of the Bible, the **RSV**.

The Annunciation   from Luke

In the sixth month the angel Gabriel was sent from God to a city of Galilee named Nazareth, to a virgin betrothed to a man whose name was Joseph, of the house of David; and the virgin's name was Mary. And he came to her and said, "Hail, O favored one, the Lord is with you!" But she was greatly troubled at the saying, and considered in her mind what sort of greeting this might be. And the angel said to her, "Do not be afraid, Mary, for you have found favor with God. And behold, you will conceive in your womb and bear a son, and you shall call his name Jesus.

> He will be great, and will be called the Son of the Most High;
> and the Lord God will give to him the throne of his father David,
> and he will reign over the house of Jacob for ever;
> and of his kingdom there will be no end."

And Mary said to the angel, "How shall this be, since I have no husband?" And the angel said to her,

> "The Holy Spirit will come upon you,
> and the power of the Most High will overshadow you;
> therefore the child to be born will be called holy,
> the Son of God." (Luke 1:26–35)

The Magnificat   from Luke

And Mary said, "My soul magnifies the Lord, and my spirit rejoices in God my Savior, for he has regarded the low estate of his handmaiden. For behold, henceforth all generations will call me blessed; for he who is mighty has done great things for me, and holy is his name. And his mercy is on those who fear him from generation to generation. He has shown strength with his arm, he has scattered the proud in the imagination of their hearts, he has put down the mighty from their thrones, and exalted those of low degree; he has filled the hungry with good things, and the rich he has sent empty away. He has helped his servant Israel, in remembrance of his mercy, as he spoke to our fathers, to Abraham and to his posterity for ever." (Luke 1:46–55)

Jesus's Birth   from Luke

In those days a decree went out from Caesar Augustus that all the world should be enrolled. This was the first enrollment, when Quirinius was governor of Syria. And all went to be enrolled, each to his own city. And Joseph also went up from Galilee, from the city of Nazareth, to Judea, to the city of David, which is called Bethlehem, because he was of the house and lineage of David, to be enrolled with Mary, his betrothed, who was with child. And while they were there, the time came for her to be delivered. And she gave birth to her first-born son and wrapped him in swaddling cloths, and laid him in a manger, because there was no place for them in the inn.

And in that region there were shepherds out in the field, keeping watch over their flock by night. And an angel of the Lord appeared to them, and the glory of the Lord shone around them, and they were filled with fear. And the angel said to them, "Be not afraid; for behold, I bring you good news of a great joy which will come to all the people; for to you is born this day in the city of David a **Savior**, who is Christ the Lord. And this will be a sign for you: you will find a babe wrapped in swaddling cloths and lying in a manger." And suddenly there was with the angel a multitude of the heavenly host praising God and saying, "Glory to God in the highest, and on earth peace among men with whom he is pleased!" (Luke 2:1–14)

Jesus's Ministry Begins   from Matthew

And he went about all Galilee, teaching in their synagogues and preaching the gospel of the kingdom and healing every disease and every infirmity among the people. So his fame spread throughout all Syria, and they brought him all the sick, those afflicted with various diseases and pains, demoniacs,[1] epileptics, and paralytics, and he healed them. And great crowds followed him from Galilee and the Decapolis[2] and Jerusalem and Judea and from beyond the Jordan. (Matthew 4:23–5)

---

1 Demoniac—person possessed by a demon.
2 Decapolis—Greek for "ten towns," a confederation of ten cities near the Sea of Galilee.

The Beatitudes   from Matthew

Seeing the crowds, he went up on the mountain, and when he sat down his **disciples** came to him. And he opened his mouth and taught them, saying:

"Blessed are the poor in spirit, for theirs is the kingdom of heaven.

"Blessed are those who mourn, for they shall be comforted.

"Blessed are the meek, for they shall inherit the earth.

"Blessed are those who hunger and thirst for righteousness, for they shall be satisfied.

"Blessed are the merciful, for they shall obtain mercy.

"Blessed are the pure in heart, for they shall see God.

"Blessed are the peacemakers, for they shall be called sons of God.

"Blessed are those who are persecuted for righteousness' sake, for theirs is the kingdom of heaven.

"Blessed are you when men revile you and persecute you and utter all kinds of evil against you falsely on my account. Rejoice and be glad, for your reward is great in heaven, for so men persecuted the prophets who were before you." (Matthew 5:1–12)

Sincerely Motivated Faith and Works   from Matthew

"You have heard that it was said to the men of old, 'You shall not kill; and whoever kills shall be liable to judgment.' But I say to you that every one who is angry with his brother shall be liable to judgment; whoever insults his brother shall be liable to the council, and whoever says, 'You fool!' shall be liable to the hell of fire. So if you are offering your gift at the altar, and there remember that your brother has something against you, leave your gift there before the altar and go; first be reconciled to your brother, and then come and offer your gift." (Matthew 5:21–4)

True Treasures   from Matthew

"Do not lay up for yourselves treasures on earth, where moth and rust consume and where thieves break in and steal, but lay up for yourselves treasures in heaven, where neither moth nor rust consumes and where thieves do not break in and steal. For where your treasure is, there will your heart be also." (Matthew 6:19–21)

Healing the Blind   from Matthew

And as Jesus passed on from there, two blind men followed him, crying aloud, "Have mercy on us, Son of David." When he entered the house, the blind men came to him; and Jesus said to them, "Do you believe that I am able to do this?" They said to him, "Yes, Lord." Then he touched their eyes, saying, "According to your faith be it done to you." And their eyes

were opened. And Jesus sternly charged them, "See that no one knows it."
(Matthew 9:27–30)

The Light of the World   from John

In the beginning was the Word, and the Word was with God, and the Word
was God. He was in the beginning with God; all things were made through
him, and without him was not anything made that was made. In him was
life, and the life was the light of men. The light shines in the darkness, and
the darkness has not overcome it. (John 1:1–5)

The Word (Logos)   from John

And the Word became flesh and dwelt among us, full of grace and truth; we
have beheld his glory, glory as of the only Son from the Father. (John 1:14)

The Last Supper   from Mark

Then Judas Iscariot, who was one of the twelve [disciples], went to the chief
priests in order to betray him to them. And when they heard it they were
glad, and promised to give him money. And he sought an opportunity to
betray him.

And on the first day of Unleavened Bread, when they sacrificed the
passover lamb, his disciples said to him, "Where will you have us go and
prepare for you to eat the passover?" ... And the disciples set out and went to
the city, and found it as he had told them; and they prepared the passover.

And when it was evening he came with the twelve. And as they were at
table eating, Jesus said, "Truly, I say to you, one of you will betray me, one
who is eating with me." They began to be sorrowful, and to say to him one
after another, "Is it I?" He said to them, "It is one of the twelve, one who is
dipping bread into the dish with me. For the Son of man goes as it is written
of him, but woe to that man by whom the Son of man is betrayed! It would
have been better for that man if he had not been born."

And as they were eating, he took bread, and blessed, and broke it, and
gave it to them, and said, "Take; this is my body." And he took a cup, and
when he had given thanks he gave it to them, and they all drank of it. And
he said to them, "This is my blood of the covenant, which is poured out
for many. Truly, I say to you, I shall not drink again of the fruit of the vine
until that day when I drink it new in the kingdom of God." (Mark 14:10–12,
16–25)

The Crucifixion   from Mark

And Pilate again said to them, "Then what shall I do with the man whom
you call the King of the Jews?" And they cried out again, "Crucify him."
And Pilate said to them, "Why, what evil has he done?" But they shouted all

the more, "Crucify him." So Pilate, wishing to satisfy the crowd, released for them Barabbas; and having scourged Jesus, he delivered him to be crucified.

And the soldiers led him away inside the palace (that is, the praetorium[3]); and they called together the whole battalion. And they clothed him in a purple cloak, and plaiting a crown of thorns they put it on him. And they began to salute him, "Hail, King of the Jews!" And they struck his head with a reed, and spat upon him, and they knelt down in homage to him. And when they had mocked him, they stripped him of the purple cloak, and put his own clothes on him. And they led him out to crucify him.

And they compelled a passer-by, Simon of Cyrene, who was coming in from the country, the father of Alexander and Rufus, to carry his cross. And they brought him to the place called Golgotha (which means the place of a skull). And they offered him wine mingled with myrrh; but he did not take it. And they crucified him, and divided his garments among them, casting lots for them, to decide what each should take. ... So also the chief priests mocked him to one another with the scribes, saying, "He saved others; he cannot save himself. Let the Christ, the King of Israel, come down now from the cross, that we may see and believe." Those who were crucified with him also reviled him.

And when the sixth hour had come, there was darkness over the whole land until the ninth hour. And at the ninth hour Jesus cried with a loud voice, *"Elo-i, Elo-i, lama sabach-thani?"* which means, "My God, my God, why hast thou forsaken me?" And some of the bystanders hearing it said, "Behold, he is calling Elijah." And one ran and, filling a sponge full of vinegar, put it on a reed and gave it to him to drink, saying, "Wait, let us see whether Elijah will come to take him down." And Jesus uttered a loud cry, and breathed his last. And the curtain of the temple was torn in two, from top to bottom. ...

... Joseph of Arimathea, a respected member of the council, who was also himself looking for the kingdom of God, took courage and went to Pilate, and asked for the body of Jesus. And Pilate wondered if he were already dead; and summoning the centurion, he asked him whether he was already dead. And when he learned from the centurion that he was dead, he granted the body to Joseph. And he bought a linen shroud, and taking him down, wrapped him in the linen shroud, and laid him in a tomb which had been hewn out of the rock; and he rolled a stone against the door of the tomb. (Mark 15:12–24, 31–8, 43–6)

The Resurrection   from Mark

And when the sabbath was past, Mary Magdalene, and Mary the mother of James, and Salome, bought spices, so that they might go and anoint him. And very early on the first day of the week they went to the tomb when

---

3 Praetorium—the official residence of the governor of the Roman province.

the sun had risen. And they were saying to one another, "Who will roll away the stone for us from the door of the tomb?" And looking up, they saw that the stone was rolled back—it was very large. And entering the tomb, they saw a young man sitting on the right side, dressed in a white robe; and they were amazed. And he said to them, "Do not be amazed; you seek Jesus of Nazareth, who was crucified. He has risen, he is not here; see the place where they laid him. But go, tell his disciples and Peter that he is going before you to Galilee; there you will see him, as he told you." And they went out and fled from the tomb; for trembling and astonishment had come upon them; and they said nothing to any one, for they were afraid. (Mark 16:1–8)

Paul's Conversion from Acts

But Saul, still breathing threats and murder against the disciples of the Lord, went to the high priest and asked him for letters to the synagogues at Damascus, so that if he found any belonging to the Way,[4] men or women, he might bring them bound to Jerusalem. Now as he journeyed he approached Damascus, and suddenly a light from heaven flashed about him. And he fell to the ground and heard a voice saying to him, "Saul, Saul, why do you persecute me?" And he said, "Who are you, Lord?" And he said, "I am Jesus, whom you are persecuting; but rise and enter the city, and you will be told what you are to do." The men who were traveling with him stood speechless, hearing the voice but seeing no one. Saul arose from the ground; and when his eyes were opened, he could see nothing; so they led him by the hand and brought him into Damascus. And for three days he was without sight, and neither ate nor drank.

... So Ananias departed and entered the house. And laying his hands on him he said, "Brother Saul, the Lord Jesus who appeared to you on the road by which you came, has sent me that you may regain your sight and be filled with the Holy Spirit." And immediately something like scales fell from his eyes and he regained his sight. Then he rose and was baptized, and took food and was strengthened.

For several days he was with the disciples at Damascus. And in the synagogues immediately he proclaimed Jesus, saying, "He is the Son of God." (Acts 9:1–9, 17–20)

Paul's letters to the new Christian churches

Paul traveled and wrote to the new Christian communities, helping interpret the meaning of Jesus for them. His writings show the universalizing of the new faith, by taking it outside the Jewish Law and opening it to any believers.

---

4 The Way—an early understanding of followers of Jesus, not yet called "Christians."

Paul on Faith and Works from Romans

For we hold that a man is justified by faith apart from works of law. Or is God the God of Jews only? Is he not the God of Gentiles also? Yes, of Gentiles also, since God is one; and he will justify the circumcised on the ground of their faith and the uncircumcised through their faith. Do we then overthrow the law by this faith? By no means! On the contrary, we uphold the law. (Romans 3:28–31)

Paul on Faith, Hope, and Love from I Corinthians

If I speak in the tongues of men and of angels, but have not love, I am a noisy gong or a clanging cymbal. And if I have prophetic powers, and understand all mysteries and all knowledge, and if I have all faith, so as to remove mountains, but have not love, I am nothing. If I give away all I have, and if I deliver my body to be burned, but have not love, I gain nothing.

Love is patient and kind; love is not jealous or boastful; it is not arrogant or rude. Love does not insist on its own way; it is not irritable or resentful; it does not rejoice at wrong, but rejoices in the right. Love bears all things, believes all things, hopes all things, endures all things.

Love never ends; as for prophecies, they will pass away; as for tongues, they will cease; as for knowledge, it will pass away. For our knowledge is imperfect and our prophecy is imperfect; but when the perfect comes, the imperfect will pass away. When I was a child, I spoke like a child, I thought like a child, I reasoned like a child; when I became a man, I gave up childish ways. For now we see in a mirror dimly, but then face to face. Now I know in part; then I shall understand fully, even as I have been fully understood. So faith, hope, love abide, these three; but the greatest of these is love. (I Corinthians 13:1–13)

SOURCE: Bible excerpts in this chapter are taken from the Revised Standard Version. New York: Thomas Nelson, 1952.

History and literature

A major biblical interpretive problem is how to differentiate between historical facts and literary images. When Jesus was healing two blind men he asked, "Do you believe that I am able to do this?" The history of Christianity has echoed with this question. What does it mean to believe that Christ was the Son of God on earth who can transform history? Does it mean that we are to interpret scripture as literally, factually true? Or, at the other extreme, should we read many biblical passages symbolically, understanding Jesus as healing the blindness of despair or bigotry? Or both? Christians have discussed these issues for two millennia.

The emphasis on the historical, factual side has been strengthened by ancient texts. The Jewish historian Josephus (c. 37–100 CE) wrote, "At about this time lived Jesus, a wise man … He performed astonishing feats … He attracted many Jews and many of the Greeks … Upon an indictment brought by leading members of our society, Pilate sentenced him to the cross." In two Jewish commentaries, supplements to the Mishnah (compiled before 200 CE), are several references to Jesus, including: "It has been taught: On the even of Passover they hanged Yeshu … because he practiced sorcery and enticed and led Israel astray" (Ian Wilson, *Jesus: the Evidence*. New York: Harper and Row, 1984, pp. 44–5).

But twentieth-century discoveries of other texts from biblical times have raised controversial and fascinating questions. The problem of how to interpret scripture is renewed by these religious texts, because they raise the question of the **canon**: how did the Bible come into history? Books not selected for the canon are called the **Apocrypha**. Protestants list many, but Roman Catholics and Eastern Orthodox Christians accept more as canonical.

EARLY NON-CANONICAL TEXTS

A number of spiritual writings were circulating among Jews and Christians in New Testament times; some are preserved in the Dead Sea Scrolls and the Nag Hammadi Library. However, they were not selected for inclusion in the biblical canon.

In 1945 Egyptian peasants discovered the first of many jars with scrolls, buried about 400 CE, written in the Coptic language and translated from Greek. These scrolls have given us a much better understanding of Gnosticism—a religious complex with roots in several faiths that blended with Christianity from the first century CE. Some Gnostics postulated a remote supreme divinity and an inferior, imperfect creator god. They stressed mystical, experiential gnosis (knowledge) as opposed to faith, and saw Jesus as more human than other Christians did. In the second and third centuries, Gnostics were rejected by the church as **heretics** on account of their theology, alleged elitism, opposition to church authority, and egalitarian view of women. However, as the following selections show, they were capable of highly poetic, paradoxical, and mystical insights.

The Gospel of Mary from the Nag Hammadi Library

The figure of Mary Magdalene in the Gospels has been a fascinating character in Christianity. She suffered the criticism of being called a prostitute by a medieval pope, with no biblical evidence. The discovery of the Nag Hammadi scrolls added fuel to this debate with the "Gospel of Mary" text. It does not use the word "Magdalene," but many take it to be she who saw a vision of the risen Christ and conveyed it to the Apostles, as indicated in this extract.

Peter said to Mary, "Sister, We know that the Savior loved you more than the rest of women. Tell us the words of the Savior which you remember— which you know (but) we do not nor have we heard them." Mary answered and said, "What is hidden from you I will proclaim to you." And she began to speak to them these words: "I," she said, "saw the Lord in a vision and I said to him, 'Lord, I saw you today in a vision.' He answered and said to me, 'Blessed are you, that you did not waver at the sight of me. For where the mind is, there is the treasure.' I said to him, 'Lord, now does he who sees the vision see it <through>[5] the soul <or> through the spirit?' The Savior answered and said, 'He does not see through the soul nor through the spirit, but the mind which [is] between the two—that is [what] sees the vision and it is [...].' (pp. 11–14 missing)

"The soul answered and said, 'What binds me has been slain, and what turns me about has been overcome, and my desire has been ended, and ignorance has died. In a [world] I was released from a world, [and] in a type from a heavenly type, and (from) the fetter of oblivion which is transient. From this time on I will attain to the rest of the time, of the season, of the aeon, in silence.'"

When Mary had said this, she fell silent, since it was to this point that the Savior had spoken with her.

SOURCE: "The Gospel of Mary," trans. George W. MacRae, in *The Nag Hammadi Library*, ed. James M. Robinson. San Francisco, CA: Harper and Row, 1977, pp. 472–3

The Thunder, Perfect Mind from the Nag Hammadi Library

This text, in the voice of a woman, is similar in tone and style to some earlier Jewish Wisdom Literature and to Egyptian Isis goddess texts. Its antithetical character uses paradox to proclaim the absolute transcendence of its source, prior to opposites, whose greatness is unfathomable.

I was sent forth from the power, and I have come to those who reflect
    upon me, and I have been found among those who seek after me.
Look upon me, you who reflect upon me, and you hearers, hear me.
You who are waiting for me, take me to yourselves.
And do not banish me from your sight. ...

I am the wife and the virgin. I am [the mother] and the daughter.
I am the members of my mother.
I am the barren one and many are her sons.
I am she whose wedding is great, and I have not taken a husband. ...

I am the silence that is incomprehensible
    and the idea whose remembrance is frequent.
I am the voice whose sound is manifold
    and the word whose appearance is multiple.
I am the utterance of my name.
Why, you who hate me, do you love me, and hate those who love me?
You who deny me, confess me, and you who confess me, deny me. ...

---

5 < > pointed brackets indicate a corrected scribal omission or error in the original manuscript; [ ] square brackets indicate a gap; ( ) parentheses indicate material supplied by modern editor or translator to clarify meaning.

But I am she who exists in all fears and strength in trembling.
I am she who is weak, and I am well in a pleasant place.
I am senseless and I am wise.
Why have you hated me in your counsels?
For I shall be silent among those who are silent,
and I shall appear and speak. ...

I am the one whose image is great in Egypt
and the one who has no image among the barbarians.
I am the one who has been hated everywhere
and who has been loved everywhere.
I am the one whom they call Life, and you have called Death.
I am the one whom they call Law, and you have called Lawlessness. ...

I am she who does not keep festival,
and I am she whose festivals are many.
I, I am godless, and I am the one whose God is great. ...
Come forward to childhood,
and do not despise it because it is small and it is little. ...
For what is inside of you is what is outside of you,
and the one who fashions you on the outside
is the one who shaped the inside of you.
And what you see outside of you, you see inside of you;
it is visible and it is your garment. ...

SOURCE: "The Thunder, Perfect Mind," trans. George W. MacRae, in *The Nag Hammadi Library*, ed. James M. Robinson. Rev. ed. San Francisco, CA: HarperCollins, 1990, pp. 272–7

Eastern Orthodox Church

As the church developed historically, three major branches emerged that answered questions of theology and spirituality, sometimes in quite different ways. The Eastern Orthodox is the oldest, most Greek, and mystical, while the Western Roman Catholics worshipped in Latin and developed more legalistic traditions under the pope; conflicts led to a mutual separation in the year 1054. The most democratic branch—the Protestants—broke away in 1517.

The Eastern Orthodox Church, which numbers about 240 million members today, focuses on the earliest days of Christianity. It held seven major councils that decided basic beliefs, such as the divinity of Jesus. Its theologians, among them Origen, wrote about how to interpret the Bible; its mystical monks include such figures as Gregory of Sinai.

How to Interpret Scripture by Origen

Jesus was known for stilling storms, feeding the hungry, healing the sick and blind, and raising the dead. From the beginning of the Christian faith, thinkers questioned the proper ways to interpret these reports. Here Origen, an Egyptian theologian

(c. 185–254 CE), makes the important distinction between a literal, historical, factual ("bodily") reading and a symbolic, metaphoric, spiritual interpretation.

The right way, as it appears to us, of approaching the scriptures and gathering their meaning, is the following, which is extracted from the writings themselves. We find some such rule as this laid down by Solomon in the Proverbs concerning the divine doctrines written therein: "Do thou portray them threefold in counsel and knowledge, that thou mayest answer words of truth to those who question thee" (Proverbs 22:20–21).

One must therefore portray the meaning of the sacred writings in a threefold way upon one's own soul, so that the simple man may be edified by what we may call the flesh of the scripture, this name being given to the obvious interpretation; while the man who has made some progress may be edified by its soul, as it were; and the man who is perfect and like those mentioned by the apostle: "We speak wisdom among the perfect; yet a wisdom not of this world, nor of the rulers of this world, which are coming to naught; but we speak God's wisdom in a mystery, even the wisdom that hath been hidden, which God foreordained before the worlds unto our glory" (I Corinthians 2:6–7)—this man may be edified by the spiritual law (Romans 7:14), which has "a shadow of the good things to come" (Hebrews 10:1). For just as man consists of body, soul, and spirit, so in the same way does the scripture, which has been prepared by God to be given for man's salvation.

But since there are certain passages of scripture which, as we shall show in what follows, have no bodily [literal] sense at all, there are occasions when we must seek only for the soul and the spirit, as it were, of the passage.

That it is possible to derive benefit from the first, and to this extent helpful meaning, is witnessed by the multitudes of sincere and simple believers.

But if the usefulness of the law and the sequence and ease of the narrative were at first sight clearly discernible throughout, we should be unaware that there was anything beyond the obvious meaning for us to understand in the scriptures.

Now what man of intelligence will believe that the first and the second and the third day, and the evening and the morning existed without the sun and the moon and stars? And that the first day, if we may so call it, was even without a heaven (Genesis 1:5–13)? And who is so silly as to believe that God, after the manner of a farmer, "planted a paradise eastward in Eden," and set in it a visible and palpable "tree of life," of such a sort that anyone who tasted its fruit with his bodily teeth would gain life; and again that one could partake of "good and evil" by masticating the fruit taken from the tree of that name (Genesis 2:8–9)? And when God is said to "walk in the paradise in the cool of the day" and Adam to hide himself behind a tree, I do not think anyone will doubt that these are figurative expressions which indicate certain mysteries through a semblance of history and not through actual events (Genesis 3:8).

The aim of the divine power which bestowed on us the holy scriptures is not that we should accept only what is found in the letter; for occasionally the records taken in a literal sense are not true, but actually absurd and impossible, and even with the history that actually happened and the legislation that is in its literal sense useful there are other matters interwoven.

But someone may suppose that the former statement refers to all the scriptures, and may suspect us of saying that because some of the history did not happen, therefore none of it happened; and because a certain law is irrational or impossible when taken literally, therefore no laws ought to be kept to the letter; or that the records of the Savior's life are not true in a physical sense; or that no law or commandment of his ought to be obeyed. We must assert, therefore, that in regard to some things we are clearly aware that the historical fact is true ... [e.g.] that Jerusalem is the chief city of Judea, in which a temple of God was built by Solomon; and thousands of other facts.

For our contention with regard to the whole of divine scripture is, that it all has a spiritual meaning, but not all a bodily [literal] meaning; for the bodily meaning is often proved to be an impossibility. Consequently the man who reads the divine books reverently, believing them to be divine writings, must exercise great care.

SOURCE: "Origen on First Principles," in *Readings in Christian Thought*, ed. Hugh T. Kerr. Nashville, TN: Abingdon Press, 1966, pp. 45–7

The Nicene Creed

This is the ancient creed that is thought to have been worked out at the Council of Nicaea, organized by the Byzantine emperor Constantine in 325 CE. Its main purpose was to unify the emerging church and oppose the Arian belief that Jesus was not the divine Son of God, but was human only. This is the English version said in many Eastern Orthodox churches' Divine Liturgy. It omits the phrase in brackets below—[and the Son]—which was not in the original version, but was added by the Roman Church later. Eastern Orthodox and Roman Catholic Christians generally recite it each Sunday, many Protestants less often.

I believe in one God, the Father, the Almighty, Creator of heaven and earth, and of all things visible and invisible.

And in one Lord, Jesus Christ, the only begotten Son of God, begotten of the Father before all ages. Light of Light, true God of true God, begotten, not created, of one essence with the Father, through whom all things were made. For us and our salvation, He came down from heaven and was incarnate by the Holy Spirit and the Virgin Mary and became man. He was crucified for us under Pontius Pilate, and He suffered and was buried. On the third day He rose according to the Scriptures. He ascended into heaven and is seated at the right hand of the Father. He will come again in glory to judge the living and the dead. His kingdom will have no end.

And in the Holy Spirit, the Lord, the Giver of Life, who proceeds from the Father [and the Son], who together with the Father and the Son is worshiped and glorified, who spoke through the prophets.

In one holy, catholic, and apostolic Church.

I acknowledge one baptism for the forgiveness of sins. I expect the resurrection of the dead. And the life of the age to come. Amen.

SOURCE: *The Divine Liturgy of Saint John Chrysostom*. Brookline, MA: Holy Cross Orthodox Press, 1985, pp. 18–19

Grief and Joy by Gregory of Sinai

The *Philokalia* (love of what is beautiful) is an ancient collection of Orthodox writings, ascetic and mystical, reflecting the monastic life of the Eastern Church. It has a wide influence on the modern Orthodox world, and new editions still add texts. This selection is from Gregory of Sinai, one of the bright lights of fourteenth-century Christianity. Born around 1265, he entered the monastic life at Sinai, then spent years at the famous Mount Athos monastery complex, perched precariously atop a remote mountain in Greece. Like other Orthodox Christians, he practiced repetition of the "Jesus Prayer"—"Jesus Christ, Son of God, have mercy on me"—to bring God into his heart. Here he discusses the depths of grief and the heights of joy in meditation.

Unless your life and actions are accompanied by a sense of inner grief you cannot endure the incandescence of stillness. If with this sense of grief you meditate—before they come to pass—on the many terrors that await us prior to and after death you will achieve both patience and humility, the twin foundations of stillness. Without them your efforts to attain stillness will always be accompanied by apathy and self-conceit. From these will arise a host of distractions and day-dreams, all inducing sluggishness. In their wake comes dissipation, daughter of indolence, making the body sluggish and slack and the intellect benighted and callous. Then Jesus is hidden, concealed by the throng of thoughts and images that crowd the mind. …

For beginners prayer is like a joyous fire kindled in the heart; for the perfect is like a vigorous sweet-scented light. Or again, prayer is the preaching of the Apostles, an action of faith or, rather, faith itself, "that makes real for us the things for which we hope," active love, angelic impulse, the power of the bodiless spirits, their work and delight, the Gospel of God, the heart's assurance, hope of salvation, a sign of purity, a token of holiness, knowledge of God, baptism made manifest, purification in the water of regeneration, a pledge of the Holy Spirit, the exultation of Jesus, the soul's delight, God's mercy, a sign of reconciliation, the seal of Christ, a ray of the noetic[6] sun, the heart's dawn star.

SOURCE: Gregory of Sinai, *The Philokalia*, ed. G. E. H. Palmer, *et al.* London: Faber and Faber, 1995, vol. 4, pp. 236–7

6 Noetic—intellectual or abstract.

Roman Catholic Church

The Roman Catholic Church, which has about one billion members worldwide today, is centered in Rome and is hierarchically organized under the pope, and his cardinals, whose offices are at the Vatican. The largest branch of Christianity, Catholics are diverse worldwide, characterized by a strong celibate male priesthood. Mary, mother of Jesus, is greatly honored, as in the many French "Our Lady" cathedrals, such as Notre Dame in Paris. Roman Catholics emphasize the Eucharist in Mass, understanding it as Christ's saving grace coming through both the priest and the congregation.

The Eucharistic Prayer from the Roman Catholic Mass

The Eucharist is the high point of Christian liturgies, especially in the Orthodox and Catholic churches. Most Protestants celebrate Communion less often and stress the Word, or sermon. What follows is a prayer said by English-speaking priests during the Roman Catholic Mass as part of the Eucharist, when bread and wine are shared as Jesus' body and blood.

Bless and approve our offering; make it acceptable to you, an offering in spirit and in truth. Let it become for us the body and blood of Jesus Christ, your only Son, our Lord. [Through Christ our Lord, Amen.]

The day before he suffered he took bread in his sacred hands and looking up to heaven to you, his almighty father, he gave you thanks and praise. He broke the bread, gave it to his disciples, and said:
Take this, all of you, and eat it: this is my body which will be given up for you.

When supper was ended, he took the cup. Again he gave you thanks and praise, gave the cup to his disciples, and said:
Take this, all of you, and drink from it; this is the cup of my blood, the blood of the new and everlasting covenant. It will be shed for you and for all so that sins may be forgiven. Do this in memory of me.

SOURCE: *Today's Missal Large Print Ordinary*. Portland, OR: Oregon Catholic Press, 2004, vol. 71, no. 4, p. 94

The Confessions of Augustine by Augustine of Hippo

Augustine (354–430 CE), Bishop of Hippo in North Africa, wrote the first surviving Western autobiography showing an intense self-awareness. It describes in detail his transformation from a pleasure-enjoying youth, who fathered a child outside marriage, to a man awakened to deep spiritual realities. He struggled with the question of the nature of evil: is it a second cosmic force like God, as the **Manichaeans** believed (he was once a Manichaean), or is it a lack of God's goodness (*privatio boni*)? Augustine was persuaded by the Neoplatonists of a heavenly hierarchy, descending from an immaterial, eternal, and intelligible God down to earth. He wrote several influential books, including *The City of God*

(426 CE), which criticizes "pagan" civic religions[7] as bankrupt. He wrote on the divine illumination of the intellect, the importance of introspection, and the need for God's grace to motivate morality.

My sins were being multiplied, and my concubine being torn from my side as a hindrance to my marriage, my heart which clave unto her was torn and wounded and bleeding. And she returned to Afric,[8] vowing unto Thee never to know any other man, leaving with me my son by her. But unhappy I, who could not imitate a very woman, impatient of delay, inasmuch as not till after two years was I to obtain her I sought, not being so much a lover of marriage as a slave to lust, procured another, though no wife, that so by the servitude of an enduring custom, the disease of my soul might be kept up and carried on in its vigour, or even augmented, into the dominion of marriage. Nor was that my wound cured, which had been made by the cutting away of the former, but after inflammation and most acute pain, it mortified, and my pains became less acute, but more desperate. …

And to Thee is nothing whatsoever evil: yea, not only to Thee, but also to Thy creation as a whole, because there is nothing without, which may break in, and corrupt that order which Thou hast appointed it. But in the parts thereof some things, because unharmonizing with other some, are accounted evil: whereas those very things harmonize with others, and are good; and in themselves are good. And all these things which harmonize not together, do yet with the inferior part, which we call Earth, having its own cloudy and windy sky harmonizing with it. …

But after Thou hadst soothed my head, unknown to me, and closed mine eyes that they should not behold vanity, I ceased somewhat of my former self, and my frenzy was lulled to sleep; and I awoke in Thee, and saw Thee infinite, but in another way, and this sight was not derived from the flesh.

And I looked back on other things; and I saw that they owed their being to Thee; and were all bounded in Thee: but in a different way; not as being in space; but because Thou containest all things in Thine hand in Thy Truth; and all things are true so far as they be; nor is there any falsehood, unless when that is thought to be, which is not. And I saw that all things did harmonize, not with their places only, but with their seasons. … And I enquired what iniquity was, and found it to be no substance, but the perversion of the will, turned aside from Thee, O God, the Supreme, towards these lower things, and casting out its bowels, and puffed up outwardly. …

I had found the unchangeable and true Eternity of Truth above my changeable mind. And thus by degrees I passed from bodies to the soul, which through the bodily senses perceives; and thence to its inward faculty, to which the bodily senses represent things external, whitherto reach the

---

7 Civic religion—a semi-religious nationalist cult of patriotism, pride, and identity with several qualities of traditional religions.
8 Afric—Africa, then referring only to the area of present-day Egypt, Libya, Algeria, and Morocco, as the rest of the continent was unknown to the Romans.

faculties of beasts; and thence again to the reasoning faculty, to which what is received from the senses of the body is referred to be judged. ...

Then I sought a way of obtaining strength sufficient to enjoy Thee; and found it not, until I embraced that Mediator betwixt God and men, the Man Christ Jesus, who is over all, God blessed for evermore, calling unto me, and saying, I am the way, the truth, and the life, and mingling that food which I was unable to receive, with our flesh. For, the Word was made flesh, that Thy wisdom, whereby Thou createdst all things, might provide milk for our infant state. For I did not hold to my Lord Jesus Christ, I, humbled, to the Humble; nor knew I yet whereto His infirmity would guide us. For Thy Word, the Eternal Truth, far above the higher parts of Thy Creation, raises up the subdued unto Itself.

SOURCE: Augustine of Hippo, *The Confessions of Saint Augustine*, trans. Edward B. Pusey. New York: Washington Square Press, 1960, pp. 101, 119–22

Everything Lives in God by Hildegard of Bingen

Hildegard (1098–1179) was a German nun of rare intelligence and originality. Beginning in childhood she had visions of God's light and angels and developed a spiritual wisdom based on her view that the Word of God is present in every living thing, expressed in its beauty. She pressed forward her conviction of the spiritual equality of men and women, and was able to establish an independent Benedictine convent. A popular public speaker in an age when women seldom preached, she gave sermons to crowds at cathedrals. Her wisdom was sought by many for personal counsel and healing.

Your eyes are not strong enough to look at God. Your mind is not strong enough to comprehend his mysteries. You can only see and know what God allows. Yet in your desire to see and know more, you engage in all manner of foolish speculations, which cause your soul to stagger. Just as water is absorbed by the heat of a burning forge, so your soul is absorbed by the restlessness of your thoughts, as you try to grasp what is beyond your grasp.

The Word of God regulates the movements of the sun, the moon and the stars. The Word of God gives the light which shines from the heavenly bodies. He makes the wind blow, the rivers run and the rain fall. He makes trees burst into blossom, and the crops bring forth the harvest.

The sky above us imitates God. Just as the sky has no beginning and no end, so God has no beginning and end. Just as the stars sparkle, so spiritual stars emanate from the throne of God, to sparkle within people's souls.

The Word of God spoke, and brought all creatures into being. God and his Word are one. As the Word spoke, so God's eternal will was fulfilled. The echo of the Word awakened life from inanimate dust.

When the Word of God spoke at the moment of creation, his sound was implanted in every creature, and gave life to every creature.

The love of God is symbolized by a leaping fountain. All who come near to it are showered by its sparkling waters. And they can see their own image in the pool below.

Everything lives in God, and hence nothing can truly die, since God is life itself. God is the wisdom that brought all things into being. He breathes life into all things.

In all creation—in trees, plants, animals and stones—there are hidden secret powers which no one can discern unless they are revealed by God.

SOURCE: Robert Van de Weyer, ed., *Hildegard*. London: Hodder and Stoughton, 1997, pp. 32–4

Protestant Churches

The Protestant Churches, beginning with Martin Luther in 1517, emphasize the priesthood of all believers, meaning that God's presence can be experienced directly by all believers, with no priest in between. Born in a time of growing literacy, they emphasize the authority of the Bible. Most allowed any Protestant to start a church, so numerous branches of Protestantism grew. All emphasize democratic governance, sermons, and congregational singing in varying degrees. They range from the Anglican, with King/Queen as leader of the state Church of England, with a fairly strong priesthood and Catholic-like liturgy, through mainstream Reformed Churches—Presbyterians, Methodists, Congregationalists, and Baptists— to more radical Free Churches—Mennonite, Quaker, Amish—which usually reject government affiliation, military service, and any formal priesthood. Today, the Protestant Churches have about four hundred million members worldwide.

Baptism from the Episcopal Church's *Book of Common Prayer*

This rite of initiation can be performed on infants or adults. Orthodox, Catholic, and Anglican churches prefer that a bishop administers baptisms, but sometimes a priest must do it and a deacon or lay leader may assist. For an infant the parents and possibly godparents are involved, as are the congregation ("people"). Adults being baptized speak for themselves. This selection combines both possibilities.

Celebrant [to parents and godparents, for a child] Will you be responsible for seeing that the child you present is brought up in the Christian faith and life? *Parents and godparents* I will, with God's help.

Question [to candidates who can speak for themselves] Do you renounce Satan and all the spiritual forces of wickedness that rebel against God? *Answer* I renounce them. …
Question Do you turn to Jesus Christ and accept him as your Savior? *Answer* I do. …

Leader [to the congregation, about those being baptized] Deliver them, O Lord, from the ways of sin and death.
People Lord, hear our prayer.
Leader Open their hearts to your grace and truth.

People Lord, hear our prayer.
Leader Teach them to love others in the power of the Spirit.
People Lord, hear our prayer.

Celebrant [praying to God] Now sanctify this water, we pray you, by the power of your Holy Spirit, that those who here are cleansed from sin and born again may continue forever in the risen life of Jesus Christ our Savior. ...

Each candidate is presented by name to the Celebrant, or to an assisting priest or deacon, who then immerses, or pours water upon, the candidate, saying
[Name], I baptize you in the Name of the Father, and of the Son, and of the Holy Spirit. Amen.

SOURCE: *The Book of Common Prayer, The Episcopal Church.* New York: Seabury Press, 1977, pp. 302–7

LUTHERAN CHURCH

The Protestant Reformation began with Martin Luther (1483–1546) in 1517. He argued for certain theological principles, most importantly **justification** by faith and the priesthood of all believers. These code phrases unraveled a number of the church's structures, and it was Luther who unintentionally splintered the church.

Some social factors which contributed to religious reform in the sixteenth century were the new printing press and spreading literacy, growth of the middle classes, expanding democracy, capitalism, European nationalism, and global exploration.

Faith Can Rule Only in the Inward Man by Martin Luther

Luther was a German priest who taught at Wittenberg University. He proclaimed many of the principles of the Protestant Reformation, beginning with his "95 Theses"—his 1517 denunciation of the sale of indulgences (releases from spiritual punishment for sins). His inflammatory tracts resulted in his excommunication in 1521. In the following "Treatise on Christian Liberty" (1520) he argues for justification by faith rather than just by works. Luther said that God's grace and faith should lead to ethical action, but "religious" behavior alone is not sufficient to determine righteousness. Most basic was the priesthood of all believers, meaning that everyone has direct access to God, with no need for ecclesiastical intermediaries. Along with others, Luther proclaimed the Bible to be the authority in faith, and translated it into German (1534/45). He also opposed priestly celibacy, in 1525 marrying Catharine von Bora, a former nun.

One thing and one only is necessary for Christian life, righteousness and liberty. That one thing is the most holy Word of God, the Gospel of Christ. ... The Word of God cannot be received and cherished by any works whatever, but only by faith. ... When you have learned this, you will know that you need Christ, Who suffered and rose again for you, that, believing in Him, you may through this faith become a new man, in that all your sins are forgiven, and you are justified by the merits of another, namely, of Christ alone.

Since, therefore, this faith can rule only in the inward man, as Romans 10 says, "With the heart we believe unto righteousness"; and since faith alone justifies, it is clear that the inward man cannot be justified, made free and be saved by any outward work or dealing whatsoever, and that works, whatever their character, have nothing to do with this inward man. … yet he remains in this mortal life on earth, and in this life he must needs govern his own body and have dealings with men. Here the works begin; here a man cannot take his ease; here he must, indeed, take care to discipline his body by fastings, watchings, labors and other reasonable discipline, and to make it subject to the spirit so that it will obey and conform to the inward man and to faith, and not revolt against faith and hinder the inward man, as it is the body's nature to do if it be not held in check.

SOURCE: Martin Luther, "Treatise on Christian Liberty," letter to Pope Leo X, in *A History of Christianity*, ed. Clyde L. Manschreck. Englewood Cliffs, NJ: Prentice-Hall, 1964. Reprinted from *Works of Martin Luther, II*, trans. W. A. Lambert. Philadelphia, PA: Muhlenburg Press, 1943, pp. 25–7

ANGLICAN CHURCH

The Protestant Church of England began when King Henry VIII of England (r. 1509–47) rejected the rule of the pope in 1533, 16 years after Luther's revolt. Adopting some of Luther's principles, he made the Church of England independent from Rome. The Anglican Church today is a worldwide communion, with a strong priesthood and formal liturgy. Despite some opposition from conservative Anglicans, women priests have been ordained into the Church since 1992.

In local churches today, the Church of England is promoting the wide-reaching *UN Millennium Project*, a United Nations' program that provides a platform for the Church's ethics and urges specific actions "for the world to reverse the grinding poverty, hunger and disease affecting billions of people."

This section from a 2008 Church report summarizes its support for this challenging global project.

The Link Between the Environment and the Millennium Development Goals

1. Eradicate extreme poverty and hunger
The livelihood strategies of 2 billion poor people, and the food security of most poor people, depend on ecosystems sustaining diverse goods and services. Good management of environmental and natural resources is often essential for economic growth.

2. Achieve universal primary education
Children, especially girls, collect water and fuel wood, reducing school attendance. Better school sanitation increases attendance by girls.

3. Promote gender equality and empower women

Poor women suffer indoor air pollution, the burden of collecting water and fuel wood, and unequal access to land and natural resources.

4. Reduce child mortality

Diarrhoea and respiratory infections are the main killers of children under five. These are strongly linked to unclean water, inadequate sanitation, and air pollution.

5. Improve maternal health

Indoor air pollution and the burden of carrying water and fuel wood affect women's health and fitness for safe childbirth.

6. Combat major diseases

Up to 20% of disease burdens in developing countries are associated with environmental factors. Preventive environmental health measures are as important as health treatment.

7. Ensure environmental sustainability

About half of the world's poor live in environmentally fragile rural areas. Environmental degradation must be reversed to sustain environmental services such as water, carbon, nitrogen and nutrient cycling.

8. Develop a global partnership for development

Many international environmental problems—such as climate change and depletion of major fisheries—can only be solved through partnerships between rich and poor countries.

SOURCE: World Bank, EC, DFID, UNDP (2002) *Linking Poverty Reduction and Environmental Management; UN Millennium Project* (2004) Report of Task Force 6 on Environmental Sustainability

REFORMED CHURCH

John Calvin (1509–64) welcomed Luther's new principles and his theology led to the Reformed Church, the Churches of Christ, Presbyterian, Congregational, and other churches. John Knox (c. 1513–72) led the founding of the Presbyterian Church in Scotland in 1690. In the United States, Presbyterians have supported the abolition of slavery, temperance, and women's rights.

The following is a portion of a sermon by Christine Chakoian, minister at the Presbyterian Church in Lake Forest, Illinois, the largest Presbyterian congregation in America led by a woman. Women now make up about 27% of Presbyterian ministers in the United States.

Essential Things by Christine Chakoian

Massive change challenges everything we find secure in life. ... Maybe you saw the article in Friday's *Wall Street Journal*. "Where Have All the Presbyterians Gone?" The author, Russell Moore, is dean of the Southern Baptist Seminary in Louisville, but he's not picking on our sort. Behind him is study after study indicating that we are "witnessing the death of America's Christian denominations." His evidence?

> Fewer and fewer American Christians ... strongly identify with a particular religious communion—Methodist, Baptist, Presbyterian, Pentecostal, etc. ... More and more choose a church not on the basis of its denomination, but on the basis of more practical matters. Is the nursery easy to find? Do I like the music? Are there support groups for those grappling with addiction?

For those of us who are "in the biz," this is hardly news. Nor is it necessarily *bad* news. As Moore himself says, "If denominationalism simply denotes a 'brand' vying for market share, then let denominationalism fall." I agree. It's my conviction that our congregation's "competition" isn't Church of the Holy Spirit or Christ Church of Lake Forest—may their tribes prosper. In fact, [Episcopal] Rector Jay Sidebotham and I joke that our congregations are so much alike, we ought to consider a merger. Our *competition* is New Hope-of-Sleeping In, Our Lady of the *New York Times,* and in the summer, the Temple of the Golf Course. At least there, no doubt, many prayers are offered.

It's a real question: do we need denominations? Some today argue that denominations *get in the way* of our Christian witness. This is the stance theologian Jung Rhee takes. We ought, he says, to focus on the essentials of our faith that we share in common, and worry less about the odds and ends of our differences that don't really matter. In a remarkable lecture, "Reclaiming *adiaphora* in Postmodern Times," he reminds us of three categories Christians have long used to sort things out in times of massive change: when Reformers like Luther and Calvin were picking and choosing what to keep and what to throw from Roman Catholicism; when St. Paul and even Jesus himself were sorting through Jewish law and Greco-Roman culture at the dawn of Christianity. People of faith have always found help in these three categories: the technical Latin terms are "*Adiaphora*," things that are indifferent; "*esse*," things that are essential; and an in-between category: "*bene esse*," things that are good but not essential. Sorting out what's essential, what's indifferent, and what's good—it's a sorting method that has stood the test of the most challenging upheavals in human thought. And it is the sorting method I believe we must use today.

SOURCE: "Essential Things," portion of a sermon given on February 6, 2011 by Rev. Christine Chakoian, First Presbyterian Church, Lake Forest, Illinois
<http://www.firstchurchlf.org/>

FREE CHURCHES

Some Protestant groups that were outlawed by the Church of England and persecuted in Europe emigrated to new colonies in North America. These churches are known as "Free Churches" because they reject government affiliation and refuse military service. They also reject priests, formal worship, church buildings, and infant baptism. One of the largest Free Church groups is the Baptists, a denomination in which people are baptized as conscious adults rather than as infants. Most Quakers, a Free Church group dating from the seventeenth century, still worship without any liturgy or minister, while the Amish, another group who fled persecution, withdraw from mainstream society. Today, the Pentecostal and Evangelical Free Churches are both expanding globally and have given rise to many megachurches (see page 263).

The Fire Falls in Los Angeles by Harvey Cox

Pentecostalism is an evangelical Free Church movement that began with the African American preacher William Joseph Seymour (1870–1912) in 1906 in Los Angeles. Today it numbers about 105 million members worldwide and emphasizes direct, personal experience of the divine. In Pentecostal worship services, music and prayer help to shift the consciousness of worshippers into an ecstatic state, enabling some to speak in strange languages.

The fire from heaven descended on April 9, 1906, on a small band of black domestic servants and custodial employees gathered for prayer in a wooden bungalow at 214 North Bonnie Brae Avenue in Los Angeles, California. Their leader, a self-educated traveling preacher named William Joseph Seymour, had been assuring them for weeks that if they prayed with sufficient earnestness, God was ready to send a new Pentecost. Like the miraculous event described in the Acts of the Apostles, this latter-day outpouring of the Spirit would be demonstrated with tongues of flame, healing, speaking in strange tongues, and other signs and wonders. Many scoffed and doubted. Because of his controversial teaching, Seymour—from Louisiana by way of Houston—had been locked out of one church by an irate pastor and denied access to others. But he and his tiny company continued to meet in kitchens and parlors, praying that God would renew and purify a Christianity they believed was crippled by empty rituals, dried-up creeds, and the sin of racial bigotry.

When the fire finally did fall, shouts of joy and rapturous dancing before the Spirit resounded throughout the neighborhood. The word got out. Night after night, people crowded into the little house, stood on the porch, and stopped in the street to listen and catch a glimpse. White people began to come, and Mexicans. Soon the crowds grew too large, so Seymour and his friends rented a small abandoned church on nearby Azusa Street. ...

The Azusa Street revival itself continued day after day, month after month for three years...when the flames came, they would purge and purify as well as enliven and inspire. The proud would be brought low and the humble exalted. ...It would be the fearful as well as the wonderful day of the Lord.

SOURCE: Harvey Cox, *Fire from Heaven: The Rise of Pentecostal Spirituality and the Reshaping of Religion in the Twenty-First Century*. New York: Addison-Wesley Publishing, 1994, pp.45–6

Why the Amish Forgave a Killer by Steven M. Nolt

The Amish are a surviving branch of the Mennonites, who fled persecution in Europe and settled in Pennsylvania. Influenced by memories of persecution, one of their teachings is forgiveness. Following the attack in 2006, in which an armed man entered a small Amish school and shot the young girls, the Amish community drew on this teaching for their response. The following report about the tragedy is by Steven Nolt, Professor at Goshen College, also co-author of *Amish Grace* (2007).

It turns out that the Amish have a far from simplistic understanding of forgiveness. True, some things were clear from the start: The decision to forgive came quickly, instinctively. The Amish knew they wanted to forgive, knew it so clearly that they could express it immediately and publicly, even if and when they didn't feel that way. One Amish grandmother laughed when we asked if there had been a meeting to decide if the gunman should be forgiven. No, she and others said, forgiveness was a decided matter—decided long before October 2 ever raised the occasion for forgiveness.

At the same time, this grandmother and others made clear that forgiving is hard work, emotionally, and that deciding to forgive and expressing that desire with words and actions are only a first step. Many of those close to the tragedy made use of professional counselors and, a year later, continue to work with their grief. Although the Amish drew on the resources of professionals, they often explained that forgiveness was a long process by citing biblical language: Jesus had said that even small offenses need to be forgiven seventy times seven, they note, suggesting that forgiving takes time and is not a simple once-and-done event. It's important here to clarify what the Amish believe forgiveness is and is not:

* It's not pretending that nothing happened or that the offense wasn't so bad.
* It's not pardon; it's not saying there should be no consequences for actions. Had Charles Roberts lived, the Amish no doubt would have supported his prosecution and imprisonment for the sake of everyone's safety.
* Instead, forgiveness is about giving up: giving up your right to revenge. And giving up feelings of resentment, bitterness and hatred, replacing them with compassion toward the offender. And treating the offender as a fellow human being.

This is hard work, even if the decision to forgive is settled. When a grieving grandfather, asked by reporters less than 48 hours after two of his granddaughters had been slain, if he had forgiven the killer, responded, "In my heart, yes," his words conveyed a commitment to move toward forgiveness, offered with the faith that loving feelings would eventually replace distraught and angry ones.

Speaking the folk wisdom of experience, Amish people told us, "The acid of hate destroys the container that holds it." And "It's not good to hold grudges. Why not let go, give it up and not let the person [who wronged you] have power over you." Forgiving may be about self-denial, but it is not self-loathing. In fact, forgiving, the Amish affirm, is good for you, not just for the person forgiven.

If the Amish explanation of forgiveness is more complicated than many of the popular presentations of Amish forgiveness that suggested they stoically stuffed their feelings in a box, it still begs the question of why? Why and how could the Amish forgive in the way that they did, in the way that they understand forgiveness?

1. The first thing they cite when explaining their understanding of forgiveness, perhaps not surprisingly, is theological: Jesus tells us to forgive and God expects us to forgive, they say.

They immediately point to Jesus' parables on forgiveness and especially to the Lord's Prayer, with its key line: "Forgive us as we forgive others."

This phrase rings loudly in Amish ears, because they pray the Lord's Prayer frequently. It's not uncommon in the Lancaster, Pennsylvania settlement for Amish people to recite the Lord's Prayer eight times a day, and ten times on Sundays. The Amish there discourage composing original prayers and use the Lord's Prayer routinely and liturgically.

As well, they point out that the line "forgive us as we forgive others," is the only part of the Lord's Prayer that Jesus underscores. Immediately following the Prayer, Jesus says: "For if you forgive others their trespasses your heavenly Father will also forgive you; but if you do not forgive others, neither will your heavenly Father forgive your trespasses," adding emphasis to what the Amish see as a key theological truth.

Indeed, the Amish believe that God's forgiveness of them is dependent in some way on their forgiving others. Not that they are trying to manipulate God into forgiving them, but they see their relationship with God and their relations with other people as so closely bound together that they cannot be separated. Forgiveness becomes a religious obligation.

2. But if forgiveness is a duty, it does not stand alone as a cold command to be born in isolation. Amish forgiveness is supported by hundreds of years of Amish history and culture, hundreds of years' worth of storytelling and cultivating habits that celebrate forgiveness and make the terribly difficult responses at Nickel Mines nonetheless seem normal.

And to the degree that forgiveness involves giving up, forgiveness is central to Amish life every day, even when there is no criminal offense to forgive. In many ways, the essence of Amish life is giving up. Giving up self to the group, to God. From how one dresses to the kind of work one does, Amish life is shaped by rituals and routines of self-surrender.

So if forgiveness is about giving up one's right to revenge, or giving up grudges, Amish culture has primed its members to give up in a host of daily practices. That doesn't make forgiving easy for the Amish. But it does make it something that is part of the rest of life, and not an unnatural act—as it seemed to appear to outsiders whose culture resists giving up and celebrates getting one's due.

This cultural context also means that for the Amish, forgiveness is not an individual matter. It was not the job of the wounded girls or shell-shocked boys to forgive. (Their parents say they hope someday those children will feel compassion for Charles Roberts, but they have not pressed the children on this point.) Amish forgiveness is collective. There was not just one victim, but many; many people can forgive. And so the Amish do not have to puzzle over whether it is right for them to forgive on behalf of someone else—an ethical dilemma that has confounded ethicists in individualistically-oriented societies. The Amish forgive on their own behalf because they see the emotional pain as broadly shared, and not the sole burden of those the rest of the world would call "primary victims." Although the Amish never anticipated the horror of Nickel Mines, they were prepared to respond long before they needed to.

SOURCE: "Why the Amish Forgave a Killer," speech by Professor of History Steven M. Nolt on Monday, October 1, 2007 at Goshen College Convocation, Church-Chapel <http://www.goshen.edu/news/pressarchive/10-02-07-nolt-convo/speech.html>

Living Christianity

Christianity is facing some challenging issues in the twenty-first century. The struggle for social justice continues, inspired still by leaders such as Martin Luther King, Jr. and carried out by religious servants such as Mother Teresa's Missionaries of Charity in India. The globalization of the faith has also exploded to the extent that there are now more Christians in Africa, South America, and Asia than in Europe and the United States, where it took shape. Megachurches, mostly full of Evangelical and Pentecostal Christians taught by missionaries, are also on the rise across the globe.

Gender issues too have become increasingly important, particularly with conservative African Anglicans who are trying to hold on to the patriarchal strand in historical Christianity. The sweeping ecological crisis is also of concern and more Christians are acknowledging it as "the moral assignment of our time" (as called by the National Council of Churches of the USA) and responding with a new theological sensibility that sees nature as sacred.

Letter from the Birmingham Jail by Martin Luther King, Jr.

Rev. Dr. Martin Luther King, Jr. was a Baptist minister and the outstanding African-American leader of the American Civil Rights non-violent movement from 1955 until 1968, when he was assassinated. He inspired many with his charismatic speeches, notably his "I Have a Dream" speech in Washington in 1963. The following extracts are from a letter written while in jail, and convey well his firm determination and influential thinking.

April 16, 1963

My Dear Fellow Clergymen:

While confined here in the Birmingham city jail, I came across your recent statement calling my present activities "unwise and untimely." ...

We know through painful experience that freedom is never voluntarily given by the oppressor; it must be demanded by the oppressed. Frankly, I have yet to engage in a direct-action campaign that was "well timed" in the view of those who have not suffered unduly from the disease of segregation. For years now I have heard the word "Wait!" It rings in the ear of every Negro with piercing familiarity. This "Wait" has almost always meant "Never." We must come to see, with one of our distinguished jurists, that "justice too long delayed is justice denied." ...

But when you have seen vicious mobs lynch your mothers and fathers at will and drown your sisters and brothers at whim; when you have seen hate-filled policemen curse, kick and even kill your black brothers and sisters; when you see the vast majority of your twenty million Negro brothers smothering in an airtight cage of poverty in the midst of an affluent society. ... when you are forever fighting a degenerating sense of "nobodiness" then you will understand why we find it difficult to wait. There comes a time when the cup of endurance runs over, and men are no longer willing to be plunged into the abyss of despair....

How does one determine whether a law is just or unjust? A just law is a man-made code that squares with the moral law or the law of God. An unjust law is a code that is out of harmony with the moral law. To put it in the terms of St. Thomas Aquinas:[9] An unjust law is a human law that is not rooted in eternal law and natural law. Any law that uplifts human personality is just. Any law that degrades human personality is unjust. All segregation statutes are unjust because segregation distorts the soul and damages the personality. It gives the segregator a false sense of superiority and the segregated a false sense of inferiority. Segregation, to use the terminology of the Jewish philosopher Martin Buber, substitutes an "I-it" relationship for an "I-thou" relationship and ends up relegating persons to the status of things. Hence segregation is not only politically, economically and sociologically unsound, it is morally wrong and awful. Paul Tillich said that sin is separation. Is not segregation an existential expression of man's tragic separation, his awful estrangement, his terrible sinfulness? Thus it is that I can urge men to obey the 1954 decision of the Supreme Court, for it is morally right; and I can urge them to disobey segregation ordinances, for they are morally wrong. ...

Of course, there is nothing new about this kind of civil disobedience. ... It was practiced superbly by the early Christians, who were willing to face hungry lions and the excruciating pain of chopping blocks rather than submit

9 Thomas Aquinas (1225–74)—medieval theologian who proposed five arguments that he thought could prove the existence of God by reason alone.

to certain unjust laws of the Roman Empire. …We should never forget that everything Adolf Hitler did in Germany was "legal" and everything the Hungarian freedom fighters did in Hungary was "illegal." It was "illegal" to aid and comfort a Jew in Hitler's Germany. Even so, I am sure that, had I lived in Germany at the time, I would have aided and comforted my Jewish brothers. …

But the judgment of God is upon the church as never before. If today's church does not recapture the sacrificial spirit of the early church, it will lose its authenticity, forfeit the loyalty of millions, and be dismissed as an irrelevant social club with no meaning for the twentieth century. Every day I meet young people whose disappointment with the church has turned into outright disgust. ….

I hope the church as a whole will meet the challenge of this decisive hour. But even if the church does not come to the aid of justice, I have no despair about the future. I have no fear about the outcome of our struggle in Birmingham, even if our motives are at present misunderstood. We will reach the goal of freedom in Birmingham, and all over the nation, because the goal of America is freedom. … We will win our freedom because the sacred heritage of our nation and the eternal will of God are embodied in our echoing demands.

Yours for the cause of Peace and Brotherhood,
Martin Luther King, Jr.

SOURCE: <http://www.law.umkc.edu/faculty/projects/ftrials/conlaw/mlkjail.html>

I Don't Want to Eat Any Sugar by Mother Teresa

Mother Teresa's life (1910–97) and work were exemplary. This Albanian Catholic nun in Calcutta picked up off the street and cared for thousands of dying people; she wore a sari worth about a dollar. She crawled past piles of manure into caves to help frightened people with leprosy. What gave her strength was faith and love. This is an extract from her 1979 Nobel Prize acceptance speech.

Jesus too suffered in order to love us. He still suffers. To be sure that we might remember his great love he became our bread of life to satisfy our hunger for his love, our hunger for God, because it was for this love that we were created. We were created to love and to be loved, and he became man to enable us to love him as he loves us. He has become one with the hungry, the naked, the homeless, the sick, the persecuted, the lonely, the abandoned ones. …

I was amazed when I learned that in the West so many young people are on drugs. I tried to understand the reason for this. Why? The answer is, "because in the family there is nobody who cares for them." Fathers and mothers are so busy they have no time. Young parents work, and the child lives in the street, and goes his own way. …

The poor are good people. They can teach us much. One day a man came to thank us: "You who practice chastity have taught us very well how to plan

our family, because self-control is nothing but love of one for the other."
I think he was right. And many times these are people who have nothing
to eat, nor a house to live in, yet they know how to be great.

The poor are wonderful people. One evening we picked up four in the
street; one was in a pitiful condition. I told the other Sisters: "You take
care of the other three; I will see about this weakest one." I did all that my
love enabled me to do: I put her in a bed, and on her face there appeared
a marvelous smile. She took my hand, and after saying just one word:
"Thanks!" she died. ...

That is why we believe what Jesus said: "I was hungry, naked, homeless,
unwanted, hated, nobody cared about me ... And you did this for me!" ...

There was a time in Calcutta when it was very difficult for us to get any
sugar. I don't know how this came to the ears of the children, but a little
four-year-old went home and said to his parents: "I don't want to eat any
sugar for three days; I want to give it to Mother Teresa." Three days later his
father and mother came to our house with the little fellow. I had never seen
them before, and the child could hardly pronounce my name. But he knew
very well why he had come: to share his love with others.

SOURCE: Lush Gjergji, *Mother Teresa: Her Life, Her Works*. New Rochelle, NY: New City Press, 1991, pp. 137–41

Megachurches by Lee W. Bailey

The megachurch phenomenon features a number of large churches with
distinctly contemporary style that draw in many young and un-churched people.
In sports arenas, on television, and the internet, megachurches preach a
conservative Gospel in modern dress. Evangelical, Pentecostal, Southern Baptist or
independent, they typically advocate a strong uplifting self-confidence psychology
and a "prosperity gospel," which means support for the American-style "dream"
of raising oneself out of poverty into the modern middle class—being "victors"
not "victims."

If you walk into a typical megachurch on a Sunday, it will seem large
compared to most churches—the service may be taking place in a football
stadium. It will seem modern in architecture, TV and computer use. A
megachurch may have mall-like cafés, schools, stores, fitness centers, medical
clinics, and support groups. There will be many young single people in the
congregation. There will likely be a mix of ethnic groups—African, Asian,
Latino, Caucasian. You will see thousands of people dressed casually. You
will hear a large choir, rock band, or an orchestra. You will see large video
projection screens. You will hear an enthusiastic preacher and a pumped-
up congregation, lifting their arms, and singing praise to God. What is
happening within Christianity here?

Megachurch participants would say that the Lord is raising their
spirits, healing their hearts, and spreading the Gospel to those bored
with old traditions. They see themselves as a new Great Awakening.

Some are more oriented to traditional Evangelical personal salvation and oppose homosexuality and abortion; others include more social activism. Critics would say it is conservative theology in modern high-tech dress, superficial, market-driven, and riding the coat-tails of middle-class suburban materialism. Either way, megachurches are attracting huge crowds, while older Protestant churches are shrinking.

The megachurch is largely a Protestant movement. It is an outgrowth of the independent Free Church branch, free of a strong denominational organization. Only about 40 percent of the ministers have the educational requirements for ordination that traditional churches require (a college education and study at a theological seminary), but they are charismatic and have the "calling." In the United States, megachurches are strong in the South. The largest one, Lakewood, is in Houston in a former sports arena, and the second largest, Second Baptist Church of Houston, recently baptized 668 teenagers at a beach retreat. They flourish in Georgia, Illinois, Oklahoma, Los Angeles, California, and Florida.

Five of the world's largest megachurches are in South Korea, where a quarter of the population is now Christian. The largest in that country is the Yoido Full Gospel Church in Seoul, a Pentecostal-style Protestant Church of the Pentecostal Assembly, founded in 1958, and which now has about half a million members. The senior pastor says they are successful because, in a hierarchical Confucian culture, being a Christian will give spiritual blessing, health, and prosperity (<http://news.bbc.co.uk/1/hi/world/asia-pacific/8322072.stm>). In Africa, megachurches such as the Deliverance Church, Umoja in Nairobi, Kenya (<http://www.dcumoja.org>), are growing, providing needed schools, social services, and support groups. In Bogatá, Colombia, and several other cities worldwide, the Misión Carismática Internacional, like many megachurches, provides media programs on radio, CD, DVD, and e-mail. Whether they provide an unchallenging "feel-good" ministry or an uplifting, purposeful faith, the megachurches are blossoming.

SOURCE: Original article for this book by Lee W. Bailey, 2011.

Rising Protestant Tide Sweeps Catholic Brazil   by Todd Benson

Brazil is the largest Roman Catholic country in the world, but now it is being challenged by the Protestants, mainly evangelical missionaries, who lead about 25 percent of Brazil's churches. Some argue that this is because the Protestants allow more lay leadership, others that the Catholic Church has long been too close to the ruling elite.

CARAPICUIBA, Brazil (Reuters)—For years, Ronaldo da Silva's daily routine consisted of drinking himself into a stupor until he passed out on a sidewalk. Now he spends his days praying and singing with hundreds of fellow Christians at the Universal Church of the Kingdom of God in Carapicuiba, a sprawling shantytown on the outskirts of Sao Paulo where Pentecostal congregations are found on just about every block. "I'd probably be dead or in jail if it weren't for this church," said da Silva, a 38-year-old former Catholic who claims God cured him of epilepsy and helped him straighten out his life when he converted to Pentecostalism a decade ago.

Conversions like da Silva's are increasingly common all over Brazil, where a boom in evangelical Protestantism is steadily chipping away at the supremacy of the Roman Catholic Church. The trend, which is playing out all across Latin America, poses a major challenge for Pope Benedict, who arrives in Brazil on May 9 for a five-day visit largely aimed at blunting the decline of Catholicism in this continent-sized nation.

Although Brazil still has more Catholics than any other country in the world, with about 125 million, the percentage of believers that practice the Vatican's brand of Christianity has been dropping rapidly in the last three decades. When the late Pope John Paul II visited Brazil in 1980, 89 percent of Brazilians identified themselves as Catholic. By 2000, when the last census was taken, the share of Catholics in the population had fallen to 74 percent.

The number of evangelical Protestants nearly tripled in the same period to 26 million, or about 15 percent of the population. That growth, which is expected to continue, is dramatically altering the religious landscape of a country where the national identity has been intertwined with Catholicism since the Portuguese landed 500 years ago. "The face of Christianity in Brazil, and all over the developing world, is increasingly Pentecostal," said Luis Lugo, director of the Pew Forum on Religion and Public Life, a research group in Washington.

Reaching the masses

Pentecostals are not Brazil's only "evangelicos," as Protestants are called here. Mainstream churches such as Presbyterian and Lutheran are also present, but Pentecostalism is by far the fastest growing kind of Protestantism.

More than other Christians, Pentecostals believe that God, acting through the Holy Spirit, plays an active role in everyday life. They belong to denominations such as the Assemblies of God and the Universal Church, which was started in a Rio de Janeiro funeral home in 1977 and now has more than 2 million members.

Pentecostalism is especially strong in poor urban areas, where the precariousness of daily life—blackouts, violent crime, high unemployment—can make people seek divine intervention. Many converts are also attracted to the pop-style music and dynamic liturgies, which resonate with contemporary tastes more than the traditional Catholic Mass.

At the Universal Church in Carapicuiba, the weekly Saturday night service at times looks more like a dance hall than a religious temple, with worshippers flailing their arms in the air and singing in unison. Some, like the former alcoholic da Silva, frequently break into tears as they look to the sky and thank God for their good fortune.

SOURCE: © Thomson Reuters 2011
<http://www.reuters.com/article/2007/05/03/us-brazil-pope-religion-idUSN3023920920070503>

African Christian Communities   by David Chidester

Today, Christianity is the major religion in most of sub-Saharan Africa, with about 380 million members. Islam dominates North Africa, while north-eastern Ethiopia and Egypt are home to ancient Oriental Orthodox Christians. The largest recent increase in Christians, mainly Pentecostal and Charismatic, has been due to African and not European missionaries. African Instituted Religions—new blends of Christianity with indigenous African elements—are also growing.

As a global religion, Christianity is also an African religion, and increasingly so. During the twentieth century, the number of Christians in Africa rose from an estimated 10 million to 350 million, a dramatic increase from less than 10 percent to nearly 50 percent of the continent's population. It is likely that at some point during the twenty-first century, more Christians will be living in Africa than on any other continent. Both ancient and modern, African Christian communities have given global Christianity a distinctively local character in Africa. While ancient churches maintain forms of Christian Orthodoxy in North Africa, a rich, complex variety of Christian communities in sub-Saharan Africa emerged out of the contacts, relations, and exchanges of five hundred years of European colonialism. The majority of African Christians belong to churches, whether Catholic or Protestant, with historical roots in Europe. During the twentieth century, however, substantial and widespread Christian commitment was generated by new forms of African Christianity that have been variously identified as African independent, indigenous, or initiated churches. Revitalizing traditional African culture, these local innovations in Christianity have also responded to global forces— conquest, colonization, capitalism, and urbanization—while participating actively in the twentieth-century transatlantic expansion of intensely experiential forms of Christianity. …

Within the predominantly Muslim region of North Africa, ancient Christian communities survive. The Coptic Church, which traces its origin back to the first-century mission of Mark the Evangelist, has preserved an ancient orthodoxy in Egypt. The Ethiopian Church, once the state religion of the ancient African kingdom of Abyssinia, maintains a distinctive form of African Christianity that features certain religious practices, such as circumcision, dietary regulations, and observance of Saturday as Sabbath, that Ethiopian Christians regard as signs of their authentic roots in ancient Israel. In Sudan traces remain of the once powerful Nubian Church, although Sudanese Christians have struggled to maintain their religious identity within an Islamic State. ...

In sub-Saharan Africa, Christian communities emerged out of the more recent history of European interventions in the Atlantic world. The historical formation of African Christianity involved two processes—translation and exchange—that reveal important facets of Christianity as a global religion in the modern world. Although Christian missionaries from Europe insisted that they were bringing light into a region of darkness, their gospel of sin and salvation was experienced by Africans as a local problem of translation. When the Portuguese Catholic missionaries succeeded in converting the ruler of the BaKongo in central Africa in the 1480s, they set out to destroy the power of traditional religious leaders, the diviners and healers known as *nganga*, and to abolish the use of ritual objects known as *nkisi*. In the local idiom, however, BaKongo Christians referred to the missionaries as nganga, the crucifix as an nkisi, and the Bible as *mukanda nkisi*, the most powerful ritual object. From the fifteenth century, therefore, African Christian communities have been engaged in an ongoing process of intercultural translation, moving back and forth between indigenous religious knowledge and the terms of Christian doctrine, practice, and authority. ...

During the twentieth century, the formation of new African Christian movements was particularly revealing about the ways in which Christianity has operated as a global religion with local effects in Africa. Through local African initiatives in dealing with the problems of intercultural translation and economic exchange raised by Christianity, African initiated churches developed different strategies for engaging indigenous African structures of religious, cultural, and social authority. On the one hand, some African initiated churches have adopted the stance of opposition to traditional religion and culture. For example, the Harrist churches of West Africa, inspired by the early twentieth-century work of the prophet William Wade Harris, embraced and extended the missionary rejection of the entire indigenous religious heritage. As the prophet Harris insisted, all traces of indigenous religion, the ancestral shrines, sacrificial altars, ritual masks, and ceremonial objects, had to be destroyed to make way for Christianity. At the same time, Harris rejected the authority of the European Christian missionaries who had failed to protect Africans from military conquest, political oppression, and economic exploitation. Although independent of foreign missionary control, Harrist churches nevertheless continued the missionary strategy of forming African Christian communities in strict opposition to traditional African religion.

On the other hand, some African initiated churches have actively sought to weave together the resources of Christianity and African heritage in a new synthesis. Also in West Africa, for example, the Aladura movement, a constellation of new Yoruba Christian churches that began to emerge during the 1920s, consciously sought to draw elements of local indigenous religion, such as Yoruba proverbial wisdom, an indigenous understanding of the soul's destiny, respect for ancestors, divination, healing, and protection from the evil forces of witchcraft, into a dynamic Christian context. Meaning "owners of the prayer," Aladura represented a strategy for building religious communities by affirming the sacred power of both African ritual speech and Christian prayer. Rejecting both foreign missions and traditional structures of religious authority, such independent Christian communities have forged new forms of African Christianity by appropriating the religious resources of both. Although Christian theologians have accused them of the heresy of syncreticism, the illicit mixing of "pure" Christianity with African indigenous religion, the Aladura Christians have used the term "struggle" for the spiritual and practical work of prayer through which they have made Christianity an indigenous African religion.

In over 8,000 denominations, with perhaps as many as 50 million members, these independent churches have often been regarded from the outside as if they were distinctively, perhaps even strangely, African in character. More recently, however, African initiated churches have been recognized as part of the most significant demographic development in twentieth-century Christianity, the global expansion of pentecostalism. In southern Africa, for example, the largest African initiated church is the Zion Christian Church (ZCC), founded in 1910 by the prophet Ignatius Lekganyane, with its headquarters at Moriah, the mountain of God, that represents the sacred center of the Christian world for over three million members who meet weekly in local house churches throughout southern Africa. ...

During the last decade of the twentieth century, the link between Christianity and economic activity was explicitly advanced by conservative evangelical or fundamentalist missions, usually from the United States, that proclaimed a "gospel of prosperity" for Africa. Rather than stressing the self-discipline and self-denial of the Protestant work ethic, many of these missions promised miraculous wealth by the grace of God. ...

By the end of the twentieth century, African leaders continued to assume that Christianity was an integral part of sub-Saharan African political culture. In the last African nation to achieve liberation with its first democratic elections of 1994, South Africa instituted a Truth and Reconciliation Commission (TRC), under the leadership of the Anglican Archbishop Desmond Tutu, to forge national unity out of the conflicts and divisions of the past. At the opening of the commission, Archbishop Tutu explicitly drew upon the resources of the Christian tradition by proclaiming the TRC as a process of national contrition, confession, and forgiveness. As a pervasive system of symbols, myths, and rituals, therefore, Christianity has been integrated into African political culture. ...

SOURCE: David Chidester, "African Christian Communities,' in *The Oxford Handbook of Global Religions*, ed. Mark Juergensmeyer. Oxford: Oxford University Press, 2006, pp. 349–55

God's Earth is Sacred by the National Council of Churches USA

Leading representatives of Christian Churches have called urgent attention to the worldwide ecology crisis. The National Council of Churches USA released the call below to the theologically new perception that the earth is sacred, and that humans have the "the moral assignment of our time," to halt the devastating pollution, materialistic overconsumption, and unjust suffering of the most vulnerable members of God's creation.

God's creation delivers unsettling news. Earth's climate is warming to dangerous levels; 90 percent of the world's fisheries have been depleted; coastal development and pollution are causing a sharp decline in ocean health; shrinking habitat threatens to extinguish thousands of species; over 95 percent of the contiguous United States forests have been lost; and almost half of the population in the United States lives in areas that do not meet national air quality standards. In recent years, the profound danger has grown, requiring us as theologians, pastors, and religious leaders to speak out and act with new urgency.

We are obliged to relate to Earth as God's creation "in ways that sustain life on the planet, provide for the [basic] needs of all humankind, and increase justice." ... While we honor the efforts in our churches, we have clearly failed to communicate the full measure and magnitude of Earth's environmental crisis—religiously, morally, or politically. It is painfully clear from the verifiable testimony of the world's scientists that our response has been inadequate to the scale and pace of Earth's degradation.

To continue to walk the current path of ecological destruction is not only folly; it is sin. As voiced by Ecumenical Patriarch Bartholomew, who has taken the lead among senior religious leaders in his concern for creation: "To commit a crime against the natural world is a sin. For humans to cause species to become extinct and to destroy the biological diversity of God's creation ... for humans to degrade the integrity of Earth by causing changes in its climate, by stripping the Earth of its natural forests, or destroying its wetlands ... for humans to injure other humans with disease ... for humans to contaminate the Earth's waters, its land, its air, and its life, with poisonous substances ... these are sins." We have become un-Creators. Earth is in jeopardy at our hands. ...

The imperative first step is to repent of our sins, in the presence of God and one another. This repentance of our social and ecological sins will acknowledge the special responsibility that falls to those of us who are citizens of the United States. Though only five percent of the planet's human population, we produce one-quarter of the world's carbon emissions, consume a quarter of its natural riches, and perpetuate scandalous inequities at home and abroad. We are a precious part of Earth's web of life, but we do not own the planet and we cannot transcend its requirements for regeneration on its own terms. We have not listened well to the Maker of Heaven and Earth. ...

We believe that the created world is sacred—a revelation of God's power and gracious presence filling all things. This sacred quality of creation demands moderation and sharing, urgent antidotes for our excess in consumption and waste. ...

Guiding Norms for Church and Society ... We affirm the following norms of social and environmental responsibility: ...

Humility—recognizing, as an antidote to arrogance, the limits of human knowledge, technological ingenuity, and moral character. We are not the masters of creation. ...

Generosity—... A measure of a good society is not whether it privileges those who already have much, but rather whether it privileges the most vulnerable members of creation. ...

Frugality—restraining economic production and consumption for the sake of eco-justice. Living lives filled with God's Spirit liberates us from the illusion of finding wholeness in the accumulation of material things ... It demands the careful conservation of Earth's riches, comprehensive recycling, minimal harm to other species, material efficiency and the elimination of waste, and product durability. ...

Solidarity—...The social and environmental problems of the age must be addressed with cooperative action at all levels—local, regional, national and international. ...

Compassion—... Members of the body of Christ see the face of Christ in the vulnerable and excluded.

A Call to Action: Healing the Earth and Providing a Just and Sustainable Society—For too long, we, our Christian brothers and sisters, and many people of good will have relegated care and justice for the Earth to the periphery of our concerns. This is *not* a competing "program alternative," one "issue" among many. In this most critical moment in Earth's history, we are convinced that *the central moral imperative* of our time is the care for Earth as God's creation. Churches, as communities of God's people in the world, are called to exist as representatives of the loving Creator, Sustainer, and Restorer of all creation. We are called to worship God with all our being and actions, and to treat creation as sacred. ... We are convinced that it is no longer acceptable to claim to be "church" while continuing to perpetuate, or even permit, the abuse of Earth as God's creation. Nor is it acceptable for our corporate and political leaders to engage in "business as usual" as if the very future of life-support systems were not at stake. ...

SOURCE: <http://www.ncccusa.org/news/godsearthissacred.html>

GLOSSARY

Apocrypha (hidden things) Non-canonical books associated with the Bible.

Canon The official list of books with authority in a religion, either because they are believed to be inspired or revealed, or have been so designated.

Disciples The 12 companions of Christ, the first followers of his teachings.

Eastern Orthodox Branch of Christianity, once Church of the Byzantine Empire; broke with Roman Church in 1054; especially strong in Russia and Greece.

Grace God's freely given, unmerited love and forgiveness.

Heresy, heretic Belief contrary to the orthodox doctrines of Christianity; a follower of such beliefs.

Justification God's saving of humans from sin by grace through sacraments (Catholic) or faith (Protestant).

Manichaeism Third-century Iranian religion founded by Mani, with a dualistic faith opposing God and matter; apostles of light fight powers of darkness.

Orthodox The branch of a religious tradition that seeks to practice the original religion in its strictest form, in contrast with reform movements.

Protestant Branch of Christianity that began with Martin Luther in 1500s; stresses authority of Bible, priesthood of all believers, justification by faith; many denominations.

Roman Catholic Branch of Christianity centered in Rome, led by pope; priests officially male and celibate, Mary honored, opposed to abortion.

RSV Revised Standard Version of the Bible: American English translation, using twentieth-century language (1946/52); the New RSV is more gender-inclusive (1989/95).

Savior Christians focus on Jesus as the Messiah or *Christos* (Greek), a human appearance of God who brings salvation; some hoped for political leadership, but Jesus stressed spirituality.

Synoptic The similar gospels of Matthew, Mark, and Luke, whose contents can be compared side-by-side in synopsis fashion.

HOLY DAYS

Epiphany January 6, celebration of the three kings' visit to the baby Jesus.

Ash Wednesday The beginning of Lent; ashes on the forehead initiate a 40-day period of self-restraint and reflection before Easter.

Palm Sunday The Sunday before Easter; begins Holy Week, commemorating Christ's ride into Jerusalem.

Maundy Thursday The Thursday before Easter; remembering the Last Supper and the betrayal of Christ by Judas.

Good Friday Christ's crucifixion.

Easter Sunday Christ's resurrection; Catholic and Protestant date is the Sunday after the full moon after the spring equinox; Orthodox celebrate later.

Ascension Christ's withdrawal into Heaven 40 days after his resurrection.

Pentecost or **Whitsun** The Holy Spirit descends on the Apostles.

The Assumption August 15; Roman Catholic feast, Virgin Mary taken body and soul into Heaven when she died; declared dogma by Pope Pius XII in 1950.

All Saints' Day November 1; memorial for all saints and deceased, with requiem masses in Roman Catholic Church.

Immaculate Conception December 8; Roman Catholic celebration of dogma of Mary's freedom from original sin.

Christmas December 25, celebration of Christ's birth; absorbed festive atmosphere of Roman Saturnalia; Eastern Orthodox date is January 6.

HISTORICAL OUTLINE

c. 4 BCE–0 CE—Jesus born

c. 27–33 CE—Jesus crucified

c. 37–100 CE—Josephus wrote about "Yeshu"

c. 48–64 CE—letters of Paul

c. 70–95 CE—Gospels written down

c. 150 CE—last of New Testament writings; Gnostic syncretism of Jewish, Iranian, and Platonic mysticism emerges

c. 185–254 CE—Origen

325 CE—Nicene Creed; Council of Nicaea affirms divinity of Jesus

354–430 CE—Augustine

392 CE—Roman Empire adopts Christianity as official religion

c. 400 CE—canon of Bible set

800–1300—consolidation of papal power

950–1350—Crusades

1054—division between Western Roman Catholic and Eastern Orthodox churches

1098–1179—Hildegard of Bingen

1182–1226—Francis of Assisi

1225–74—Thomas Aquinas

1412–31—Joan of Arc

1453—Gutenberg Bible published

1478—Spanish Inquisition established

1491–1547—King Henry VIII, English founder of Anglican Church

1505–72—John Knox, Scottish leader in Presbyterian tradition

1509–64—John Calvin, French founder of "Reformed" traditions

1517—Protestantism begins with Martin Luther's "95 Theses"; Luther excommunicated four years later

1527—Free Church *Schleitheim* Confession

1545–63—Council of Trent: Roman Catholic Reformation; rejection of sale of indulgences

1624–91—George Fox, English founder of Quakers (Friends)

1707–88—John Wesley, founder of Methodism

1825–1921—Antoinette Brown Blackwell, first Christian woman ordained

1906—Pentecostal Church founded

1910–97—Mother Teresa in India

1929–68—Martin Luther King, Jr.

1945—Nag Hammadi Library discovered

1947—first of Dead Sea Scrolls found

1962—Vatican II brings more democracy to Catholic Church

2002—seven women claim ordination as Roman Catholic priests

2003—priestly child abuse conflicts expand; U.S. Episcopalians ordain Gene Robinson

2005—Pope John Paul II dies; Joseph Ratzinger elected Pope Benedict XVI

2008—Megachurches continue to increase

2010—Church globalization continues; more Christians now in southern hemisphere than in northern

REVIEW QUESTIONS

1 What is the significance of the Resurrection?
2 Contrast the ideas of Augustine of Hippo and Hildegarde of Bingen.
3 How is globalization affecting the church?

DISCUSSION QUESTIONS

1 Outline the main themes of Jesus' teachings. How are they similar to and different from those of other major religions?
2 What were the main principles of the Protestant Reformation? Why did they stimulate such a violent reaction?
3 Discuss what you consider to be the major strengths and weaknesses in Christianity today. How do you think Christianity might develop in the future?

INFORMATION RESOURCES

Barrett, David, George Kurian, and **Todd M. Johnson**, eds. *World Christian Encyclopedia*. 2 vols. Oxford: Oxford University Press, 2001.

Cone, James, and **Gayraud Wilmore**, eds. *Black Theology: A Documentary History*. 2 vols. Maryknoll, NY: Orbis, 1993.

Cox, Harvey. *Fire From Heaven: The Rise of Pentecostal Spirituality and the Reshaping of Religion in the Twenty-First Century*. New York: Addison-Wesley, 1995.

Cross, F. L., ed. *The Oxford Dictionary of the Christian Church*. Oxford: Oxford University Press, 1997.

Dictionary of African Christianity
<http://www.dacb.org/index.html>

Dillenberger, John, ed. *Martin Luther*. Garden City, NY: Anchor Doubleday, 1961.

Esposito, John, Darrell Fasching, and **Todd Lewis**, eds. *Religion and Globalization*. Oxford: Oxford University Press, 1998.

Ferme, Deane W., ed. *Third World Liberation Theologies: A Primer*. Maryknoll, NY: Orbis, 1986.

Fox, Matthew. *The Coming of the Cosmic Christ*. San Francisco, CA: Harper and Row, 1988.

Freedman, David N., ed. *The Anchor Bible Dictionary*. 6 vols. Garden City, NY: Doubleday, 1992.

Furlong, Monica. *Visions and Longings: Medieval Women Mystics*. Boston: Shambhala, 1996.

Global Anabaptist Mennonite Encyclopedia Online
<http://www.gameo.org>

Gottlieb, Roger. *The Oxford Handbook of Religion and Ecology*. Oxford: Oxford University Press, 2006.

Harrington, Daniel. "Introduction to the Canon," in *The New Interpreter's Bible*. Vol. 1, pp. 7–21. Nashville, TN: Abingdon Press, 1994.

Hartford Seminary for Religion Research
<http://hirr.hartsem.edu/megachurch/research.html>

Juergensmeyer, Mark, ed. *The Oxford Handbook of Global Religions*. Oxford: Oxford University Press, 2006.

Keck, Leander, ed. *The New Interpreter's Bible*. 12 vols. Nashville, TN: Abingdon Press, 1994.

Kraybill, Donald, Steven Nolt, and **David Weaver-Zercher**. *Amish Grace: How Forgiveness Transcended Tragedy*. San Francisco, CA: John Wiley, 2007.

Kraybill, Donald. *Conscise Encyclopedia of Amish, Brethren, Hutterites, and Mennonites*. Baltimore, MD: Johns Hopkins University Press, 2010.

Küng, Hans, *et al. Christianity and the World Religions*. Garden City, NY: Doubleday, 1986.

Lampman, Jane. "Megachurches' way of worship is on the rise," in the *Christian Science Monitor*, Feb. 6, 2006. <http://www.csmonitor.com/2006/0206/p13s01-lire.html>

Leith, John. *Creeds of the Churches*. Louisville, KY: John Knox Press, 1963.

Lindler, Eileen. "Megachurches: How Do they Count?" in her *Yearbook of American and Canadian Churches 2003*. Nashville, TN: Abingdon Press, 2003.

Lossky, Vladimir. *The Mystical Theology of the Eastern Church*. Crestwood, NY: St. Vladimir's Seminary Press, 1976.

Marty, Martin, *et al*. "Christianity," in *Encyclopedia Britannica*. Vol. 16, pp. 251–366. London, 1997.

McGrath, Alister, ed. *The Blackwell Encyclopedia of Modern Christian Thought*. Oxford: Blackwell, 1993.

Pagels, Elaine. *The Gnostic Gospels*. New York: Random House, 1979.

Pelikan, Jaroslav, *et al*. "Christianity," in *Encyclopedia of Religion,* ed. Lindsay Jones. 2nd ed. Vol. 3, pp. 1661–756. New York: Macmillan, 2005.

Penyak, Lee, and **Walter J. Petry**, eds. *Religion and Society in Latin America: Interpretive Essays from Conquest to Present*. Maryknoll, NY: Orbis Books, 2009.

Photographs of sacred buildings <http://www.sacred-destinations.com/categories/cathedrals> <http://www.sacred-destinations.com/categories/protestant-sites> <http://www.sacred-destinations.com/categories/eastern-orthodox>

Ruether, Rosemary, and **Rosemary Keller**, eds. *Women and Religion in America*. 3 vols. San Francisco: Harper and Row, 1981.

Scalon, Maria. "Catholics and Protestants in Brazil," in *America: The National Catholic Weekly*. August 18, 2003. <http://www.americanmagazine.org>

Taylor, Bron, **Jeffrey Kaplan**, **Laura Hobgood-Oster**, **Adrian Ivakhiv**, and **Michael York**, eds. *The Encyclopedia of Religion and Nature*. London: Thoemmes Continuum, 2005.

Thumma, Scott, and **Dave Travis**. *Beyond Megachurch Myths*. San Francisco, CA: John Wiley & Sons, Inc: 2007.

Tillich, Paul. *A History of Christian Thought*. New York: Harper and Row, 1968.

Walker, Williston, **Richard Norris**, **Robert Handy**, and **David Lotz**. *A History of the Christian Church*. New York: Scribner, 1985.

Wilson, Ian. *Jesus: the Evidence*. New York: Harper and Row, 1984.

Zefferelli, Franco, dir. *Jesus of Nazareth*. DVD. Artisan Entertainment, 2000.

CHAPTER 10

ISLAM

الله

In the sixth century CE, another great spiritual messenger appeared: the Prophet Muhammad. Although illiterate, he said he received revelations from an angel of God, and recited them in language so beautiful that to this day people weep when they hear it. Many of the revelations concern the absolute oneness of the deity, who has many names according to his attributes (such as the Merciful, the All-Knowing) but who is generally referred to with love and awe by the name of Allah. The most important virtue is submission to the will of Allah. This is one derivation of the word "Islam," which also means "peace."

The Prophet Muhammad is not considered divine, for in Islam worship is to be directed only toward Allah. Nevertheless, his life is considered a beautiful model for humanity, and his sayings and doings have been lovingly recorded. Muslims consider him the last in a series of great prophets of monotheism, beginning with Abraham and the other Jewish patriarchs, and including Jesus. They thus tend to regard Judaism, Christianity, and Islam as a single evolving tradition which was renewed, corrected of historical distortions, and sealed by the Prophet Muhammad.

After early opposition in **Mecca** and subsequent migration to **Medina** in 622 CE (1 AH),[1] the Prophet Muhammad became a strong political leader, returned triumphantly to Mecca, and made it a great center of monotheistic worship—which it remains to this day. Pilgrimage to Mecca's holy sites at least once in one's life is incumbent upon all Muslims, even though today they are spread around the world, forming the second largest and fastest-growing of all world religions. They are expected to regard all humanity as a single family, without racial distinctions, and to share the Prophet's message in a non-coercive way with non-Muslims so that they, too, may embark upon the straight path that leads to heavenly bliss, rather than the path of non-believers, which leads to hellish torments.

After Muhammad's death, conflicts over leadership divided Muslims into major groups. The **Sunni** (at present about 80 percent of all Muslims) elect their caliph leaders. The **Shi'a** (adj. Shi'ite) recognize not elected Sunni caliphs, but a series of 12 hereditary **Imams** (leaders, guides) following Muhammad.

---

1 The Muslim (AH) calendar is based on lunar years starting from the **Hijrah** (migration to Medina). Compared to the solar calendar used for calculating Common Era (CE) dates, which are based on the approximate birth year of Jesus, there are 11 days fewer in a lunar calendar, so the difference between CE dates and AH dates is continually changing.

Islamism is an attempt to create Muslim-dominated societies ruled by Muslim law, a desire which has spawned passionate revolutionary movements in various parts of the world. However, Islam has also given birth to great mystics and great intellectuals over the centuries, and its rich spirituality continues to coexist today with more politicized versions of the faith.

The Prophet Muhammad

The Prophet Muhammad was born in 570 CE into an Arabic culture of clans who lived by farming, herding, and camel caravan trade between Asia and the Mediterranean. Their religions were polytheistic and nature-oriented; their ethics were tribally centered, the societies largely patriarchal. Prophecy was often practiced, involving trance visions and behavioral guidelines. Contact with nearby Jews and Christians was commonplace. Many traditions of the actions and words of the Prophet, outside the Qur'an, were collected in **Hadith** (reports of the Prophet's actions). Two of the most important Hadith concerning the faith tell of the Prophet's first revelations around 610 CE, and his **Night Journey** to the seventh heaven. **'A'isha**, the Prophet's youngest wife, was the source for many Hadith.

The Beginning of Muhammad's Revelation
from *Sahih Muslim*, Chapter 74

'A'isha, the wife of the Apostle of Allah (may peace be upon him), reported: The first (form) with which was started the revelation to the Messenger of Allah was the true vision in sleep. And he did not see any vision but it came like the bright gleam of dawn. Thenceforth solitude became dear to him and he used to seclude himself in the cave of Hira', where he would engage in *tahannuth* (and that is a worship for a number of nights) before returning to his family and getting provisions again for this purpose. He would then return to **Khadija** [revered first wife of the Prophet] and take provisions for a like period, till Truth came upon him while he was in the cave of Hira'. There came to him the angel and said: Recite, to which he replied: I am not lettered. He took hold of me [the Apostle said] and pressed me, till I was hard pressed; thereafter he let me off and said: Recite. I said: I am not lettered. He then again took hold of me and pressed me for the second time till I was hard pressed and then let me off and said: Recite, to which I replied: I am not lettered. He took hold of me and pressed me for the third time, till I was hard pressed and then let me go and said: Recite in the name of your Lord Who created, created man from a clot of blood. Recite. And your most bountiful Lord is He Who taught the use of pen, taught man what he knew not (Qur'an 96:1–4). Then the Prophet returned therewith, his heart was trembling, and he went to Khadija and said: Wrap me up, wrap me up! So they wrapped him till the fear had left him. He then said to Khadija: O Khadija! what has happened to me?—and he informed her of the happening, saying: I fear for myself. She replied: It can't be. Be happy. I swear by Allah that He shall never humiliate you. By Allah, you join ties of relationship, you speak the truth, you bear people's burden, you help the destitute, you entertain guests, and you help against the vicissitudes which affect people. Khadija then took him to Waraqa b. Naufal b. Asad b. 'Abd al-'Uzza, and he was the son of Khadija's uncle, i.e. the brother of her father. And he was the man who had embraced Christianity in the Days of Ignorance [i.e. before Islam] and he used to write books in Arabic and, therefore, wrote Injil in Arabic as God willed that he should write. He was very old and had become blind. Khadija said to him: O uncle! listen to the son of your brother. Waraqa b. Naufal said: O my nephew! what did you see? The Messenger of Allah (may peace be upon him), then, informed him what he had seen, and Waraqa said to him: It is *namus*[2] that God sent down to Musa. Would that I were then (during your prophetic career) a young man. Would that I might be alive when your people would expel you! The Messenger of Allah (may peace be upon him) said: Will they drive me out? Waraqa said: Yes. Never came a man with a like of what you have brought but met hostilities. If I see your day I shall help you wholeheartedly.

SOURCE: *Sahih Muslim,* trans. 'Abdul Hamid Siddiqi. Lahore, Pakistan: Sh. Muhammad Ashraf, 1973, vol. 1, pp. 96–8

The Night Journey from *Sahih Muslim*

It is narrated on the authority of Anas b. Malik that the Messenger of Allah (may peace be upon him) said: I was brought al-Buraq who is an animal white and long, larger than a donkey but smaller than a mule, who would place his hoof at a distance equal to the range of vision. I mounted it and came to the Temple (Bait-ul-Maqdis[3] in Jerusalem), then tethered it to the ring used by the prophets. I entered the mosque and prayed two **rak'ahs** in it, and then came out and Gabriel brought me a vessel of wine and a vessel of milk. I chose the milk, and Gabriel said: You have chosen the natural thing. Then he took me to heaven.

Gabriel then asked the (gate of the heaven) to be opened and he was asked who he was. He replied: Gabriel. He was again asked: Who is with you? He (Gabriel) said: Muhammad. It was said: Has he been sent for? Gabriel replied: He has indeed been sent for. And (the door of the heaven) was opened for us and lo! we saw Adam. He welcomed me and prayed for my good. Then we ascended to the second heaven. Gabriel (peace be upon him) asked the door of the heaven to be opened, and he was asked who he was. He answered: Gabriel; and he was again asked: Who is with you? He replied: Muhammad. It was said: Has he been sent for? He replied: He has indeed been sent for. The gate was opened. When I entered Isa b. Maryam [mother of Jesus] and Yahya b. Zakariya (peace be upon both of them),

---

2 *Namus*—the angel entrusted with divine secrets.
3 Bait-ul-Maqdis—"The Much Frequented House"; the Dome of the Rock.

cousins from the maternal side, welcomed me and prayed for my good.
Then I was taken to the third heaven and Gabriel asked for the opening (of
the door). He was asked: Who are you? He replied: Gabriel. He was (again)
asked: Who is with you? He replied: Muhammad (may peace be upon him).
It was said: Has he been sent for? He replied: He has indeed been sent for.
(The gate) was opened for us and I saw Yusuf [Joseph] (peace of Allah be
upon him) who had been given half of (world) beauty. He welcomed me and
prayed for my well-being. Then he ascended with us to the fourth heaven.
Gabriel (peace be upon him) asked for the (gate) to be opened, and it was
said: Who is he? He replied: Gabriel. It was (again) said: Who is with you?
He said: Muhammad. It was said: Has he been sent for? He replied: He has
indeed been sent for. The (gate) was opened for us, and lo! Idris was there.
He welcomed me and prayed for my well-being. (About him) Allah, the
Exalted and the Glorious, has said: "We elevated him (Idris) to the exalted
position" (Qur'an 19:57).

Then he ascended with us to the fifth heaven and Gabriel asked for
the (gate) to be opened. It was said: Who is he? He replied: Gabriel. It was
(again) said: Who is with thee? He replied: Muhammad. It was said: Has
he been sent for? He replied: He has indeed been sent for. (The gate) was
opened for us and then I was with Harun (Aaron—peace of Allah be upon
him). He welcomed me and prayed for my well-being. Then I was taken
to the sixth heaven. Gabriel (peace be upon him) asked for the door to be
opened. It was said: Who is he? He replied: Gabriel. It was said: Who is
with thee? He replied: Muhammad. It was said: Has he been sent for? He
replied: He has indeed been sent for. (The gate) was opened for us and there
I was with Musa (Moses—peace be upon him). He welcomed me and
prayed for my well-being. Then I was taken up to the seventh heaven.
Gabriel asked the (gate) to be opened. It was said: Who is he? He said:
Gabriel. It was said: Who is with thee? He replied: Muhammad (may peace
be upon him). It was said: Has he been sent for? He replied: He has indeed
been sent for. (The gate) was opened for us and there I found Ibrahim
(Abraham—peace be upon him) reclining against the Bait-ul-Ma'mur and
there enter into it seventy thousand angels every day, never to visit (this
place) again.

Then I was taken to Sidrat-ul-Muntaha[4] whose leaves were like elephant
ears and its fruit like big earthenware vessels. And when it was covered by
the Command of Allah, it underwent such a change that none amongst the
creation has the power to praise its beauty. Then Allah revealed to me a
revelation and He made obligatory for me fifty prayers every day and night.
Then I went down to Moses (peace be upon him) and he said: What has your
Lord enjoined upon your **Ummah** [community]? I said: Fifty prayers. He
said: Return to thy Lord and beg for reduction (in the number of prayers),
for your community shall not be able to bear this burden, as I have put to

---

4 The Sidr is the Arabian lote tree, known for its abundant shade.

test the children of Isra'il and tried them (and found them too weak to bear such a heavy burden). He (the Holy Prophet) said: I went back to my Lord and said: My Lord, make things lighter for my Ummah. (The Lord) reduced five prayers for me. I went down to Moses and said: (The Lord) reduced five (prayers) for me. He said: Verily thy Ummah shall not be able to bear this burden, return to thy Lord and ask Him to make things lighter. I then kept going back and forth between my Lord Blessed and Exalted and Moses, till He said: There are five prayers every day and night, O Muhammad, each being credited as ten, so that makes fifty prayers. He who intends to do a good deed and does not do it will have a good deed recorded for him; and if he does it, it will be recorded for him as ten; whereas he who intends to do an evil deed and does not do, it will not be recorded for him; and if he does it, only one evil deed will be recorded. I then came down and when I came to Moses and informed him, he said: Go back to thy Lord and ask Him to make things lighter. Upon this the Messenger of Allah remarked: I returned to my Lord until I felt ashamed before Him.

It is narrated on the authority of Anas b. Malik that the Messenger of Allah (may peace be upon him) said: (The angels) came to me and took me to the Zamzam[5] and my heart was opened and washed with the water of Zamzam and then I was left (at my place).

Anas b. Malik reported that Gabriel came to the Messenger of Allah (may peace be upon him) while he was playing with his playmates. He took hold of him and lay him prostrate on the ground and tore open his breast and took out the heart from it and then extracted a blood-clot out of it and said: That was the part of Satan in thee. And then he washed it with the water of Zamzam in a golden basin and then it was joined together and restored to its place. The boys came running to his mother, i.e. his nurse, and said: Verily Muhammad has been murdered. They all rushed towards him (and found him all right). His colour was changed. Anas said: I myself saw the marks of needle on his breast.

SOURCE: *Sahih Muslim*, trans. 'Abdul Hamid Siddiqi. Lahore, Pakistan: Sh. Muhammad Ashraf, 1973, vol. 1, pp. 100–3

Islamic scripture: The Qur'an

The Holy Book of Islam, the Qur'an (Koran), was revealed to Muhammad and was written down by aides. Unlike the Jewish Tanakh, which was assembled over a thousand-year period, the Qur'an was recorded by the year 650 CE, a scant 18 years after Muhammad died. It has a stronger historical basis than many sacred texts of world religions, since it was written down more recently than most. Its original language—Arabic—has been carefully preserved, and it is felt that the Holy Qur'an cannot be translated properly from Arabic into any other language.

5 Zamzam or Zumzum—("abundant water") the legendary sacred spring at Mecca near the Ka'ba stone, opened by Gabriel to save Hajira [Hagar] and Ismail from dying of thirst.

Nonetheless, English translations have been attempted for the sake of those who do not understand Arabic. None of them is able to capture the musical, soulful quality of the Arabic, or the full meanings of its images, rhetorical devices, and contexts without extensive footnotes, but they give some idea of the scripture's content. There follows a selection of passages, beginning with the **Fatiha** or opening chapter, and covering topics such as right behavior, the family, and **jihad** as well as figures familiar from other religions—Adam, Mary, and Jesus.

The Outward and Inward Aspects of the Qur'an
by Sayyid Muhammad Husayn Tabatabai

Over the centuries and across cultures, many different schools of interpretation of the Qur'an have developed. One basic difference among interpretations involves literal versus allegorical and spiritual understandings of its meanings. Shi'ites have taken a path of clerical authority in such matters. Their **ulama**, the spiritual and intellectual elite, are thought to have enlightened understanding that allows them to grasp inner truths that are not apparent to common people. A prominent Iranian Shi'ite scholar, Muhammad Husayn Tabatabai (1892–1981), explained that there are inner as well as outer meanings in the Qur'an:

It has been explained that the Holy Quran elucidates religious aims through its own words and gives commands to mankind in matters of doctrine and action. But the meaning of the Quran is not limited to this level. Rather, behind these same expressions and within these same meanings there are deeper and wider levels of meaning which only the spiritual elite who possess pure hearts can comprehend.

The Prophet, who is the divinely appointed teacher of the Quran, says: "The Quran has a beautiful exterior and a profound interior." ...

The capacity for comprehension of divine sciences, which are the source of man's inner life, differs among people. There are those for whom there is no reality beyond physical existence and the material life of this world which lasts but a few days. Such people are attached to material appetites and physical desires alone and fear nothing but the loss of material benefits and sensory enjoyment. Such people, taking into consideration the differences of degree among them, can at best accept the divine sciences on the level of believing in a summary fashion in the doctrines and performing the practical commands of Islam in purely outward manner without any comprehension. They worship God with the hope of recompense or fear of punishment in the next world.

There are also those who, because of the purity of their nature, do not consider their well-being to lie in attachment to the transient pleasures of the fleeting life of this world. ... Such men [sic] who possess pure hearts are naturally attracted to the world of eternity. They view the different phenomena of this passing world as symbols and portents of the higher world, not as persisting and independent realities. ...

When they hear from the Quran that God has forbidden the worship of idols, which outwardly means bowing down before an idol, they understand this command to mean that they should not obey other than God, for to obey means to bow down before someone and to serve him. Beyond that meaning they understand that they should not have hope or fear of other than God; beyond that, they should not surrender to their selfish appetites, and beyond that, they should not concentrate on anything except God, May His Name be Glorified.

Likewise when they hear from the Quran that they should pray, the external meaning of which is to perform the particular rites of prayers, through its inner meaning they comprehend that they must worship and obey God with all their hearts and souls. Beyond that they comprehend that before God they must consider themselves as nothing, must forget themselves and remember only God. ...

The inner meaning of the Quran does not eradicate or invalidate its outward meaning. Rather, it is like the soul which gives life to the body. Islam, which is a universal and eternal religion and places the greatest emphasis upon the "reformation" of mankind, can never dispense with its external laws which are for the benefit of society, nor with its simple doctrines which are the guardians and preservers of these laws. ...

Tawil or hermeneutic interpretation of the Holy Quran is not concerned simply with the demonstration of words. Rather it is concerned with certain truths and realities that transcend the comprehension of the common run of men; yet it is from these truths and realities that the principles of doctrine and the practical injunctions of the Quran issue forth.

The whole of the Quran possesses the sense of *tawil*, of esoteric meaning, which cannot be comprehended directly through human thought alone. Only the Prophets and the pure among the Saints of God who are free from the dross of human imperfection can contemplate these meanings while living on the present plane of existence. On the Day of Resurrection the *tawil* of the Quran will be revealed to everyone.

SOURCE: Sayyid Muhammad Husayn Tabatabai, *Shi'ite Islam,* trans. S. H. Nasr. Albany, NY: State University of New York Press, 1979
<http://www.ummah.net/khoei/shia/part1.htm>

Faith in Allah

The Holy Qur'an is replete with professions of faith in the divine powers of **Allah** (God, known by the names of many qualities, of which Allah is the most comprehensive). The first, and most important, of these professions of faith is the Fatiha. It is the first **Sura,** or chapter, of the Qur'an. Some other expressions of faith in Allah from other parts of the Qur'an are also given below. In his widely-used English translation of, and commentary on, the Qur'an, the Indian Sunni scholar Abdullah Yusuf Ali (1872–1953) noted that in the Fatiha the reference to the wrath of God is expressed impersonally, as the result of our own actions, whereas all other references in the Fatiha are expressed as active signs of God's grace. In the last passage quoted here, "His Servant" is a reference to the Prophet.

The Fatiha

In the name of Allah, Most Gracious, Most Merciful.
Praise be to Allah, the Cherisher and Sustainer of the Worlds:
Most Gracious, Most Merciful;
Master of the Day of Judgment.
Thee do we worship, and Thine aid we seek.
The way of those on whom Thou has bestowed Thy Grace,
Those whose (portion) is not wrath, and who go not astray. (Sura 1: 1–7)

Allah

There is no god but He; That is the witness of Allah, His angels, and those endued with knowledge, standing firm on justice. There is no god but He, the Exalted in Power, the Wise. (3:18)

He it is Who created the heavens and the earth in Six Days, and is moreover firmly established on the Throne (of Authority). He knows what enters within the earth and what comes forth out of it, what comes down from heaven and what mounts up to it. And He is with you wheresoever ye may be. And Allah sees well all that ye do. (57:4)

To Allah belongeth all that is in the heavens and on earth. Whether ye show what is in your minds or conceal it, Allah calleth you to account for it. He forgiveth whom He pleaseth, and punisheth whom he pleaseth, for Allah hath power over all things. (2:284)

To Allah belong the East and the West: Whithersoever ye turn, there is the presence of Allah. For Allah is all-Pervading, all-Knowing. (2:115)

He is the First and the Last, and the Outward and the Inward; and He is Knower of all things. (57:3)

He is the One Who sends to His Servant Manifest Signs, that He may lead you from the depths of Darkness into the Light and verily Allah is to you most kind and Merciful. (57:9)

Messengers

The Qur'an does not hold up the Prophet Muhammad to be worshipped. Only Allah is worthy of worship, and the Prophet Muhammad is only the last in a series of prophets sent to guide humanity on the true monotheistic path.

Muhammad is no more than a Messenger:

Many were the Messengers that passed away before Him. (Sura 3: 144)

We have sent thee inspiration, as We sent it to Noah and the Messengers after him: We sent inspiration to Abraham, Isma'il, Isaac, Jacob, and the Tribes, to Jesus, Job, Jonah, Aaron, and Solomon, and to David We gave the Psalms. (4:163)

Say: "We believe in Allah, and in what has been revealed to us and what was revealed to Abraham, Isma'il, Isaac, Jacob, and the Tribes, and in (the Books) given to Moses, Jesus, and the prophets, from their Lord: We make no distinction between one and another among them, and to Allah do we bow our will (in Islam)." (3:84)

People of the Book

Special respect is given in Muslim thought and law to people of other religions who have received scripture thought to be divinely revealed—primarily Jews and Christians. These are "People of the Book." To ascribe divinity to any but the one God is *shirk*, considered one of the greatest human sins.

Say: "O People of the Book! come to common terms as between us and you: That we worship none but Allah; that we associate no partners with him; that we erect not, from among ourselves, Lords and patrons other than Allah." If then they turn back, say ye: "Bear witness that we (at least) are Muslims (bowing to Allah's Will)." (3:64)

Those who believe (in the Qur'an), and those who follow the Jewish (scriptures), and the Christians and the Sabians,[6] any who believe in Allah and the Last Day, and work righteousness, shall have their reward with their Lord; on them shall be no fear, nor shall they grieve. (2:62)

Unity of Humanity

From warring tribes, the Prophet Muhammad fashioned a single egalitarian society with bonds of fraternity which, it was hoped, would eventually encompass all of humankind.

And hold fast, all together, by the Rope which God stretches out for you, and be not divided among yourselves; and remember with gratitude God's favor on you; for ye were enemies and He joined your hearts in love, so that by His Grace, ye became brethren. (3:103)

Righteousness

Muslims are enjoined to live virtuous lives, for which they will receive their reward in paradise. Sinners and nonbelievers will be consigned to hell until the Last Judgment.

---

6 Sabians (or Mandaeans)—a small monotheistic sect from southern Iraq with ancient roots which practices baptism and Babylonian astrology; their holy book is the *Ginza Rba*.

Those who believe, and do deeds of righteousness, and establish regular prayers and regular charity, will have their reward with their Lord: on them shall be no fear, nor shall they grieve. (2:277)

Allah hath promised to Believers, men and women, gardens under which rivers flow, to dwell therein, and beautiful mansions in gardens of everlasting bliss. But the greatest bliss is the good pleasure of Allah: that is the supreme felicity. (9:72)

Mecca

The revelations of the Qur'an advised Muslims to change the direction of their prayer (Qibla) from the Temple of Jerusalem to Mecca, site of the Holy Ka'bah. Around the world, all Muslims are facing that same spiritual center when they pray. And once in their lifetime, all Muslims who are capable of doing so are expected to make the holy pilgrimage to Mecca (**hajj**).

We see the turning of thy face (for guidance) to the heavens: now shall We turn thee to a Qibla[7] that shall please thee. Turn then thy face in the direction of the sacred Mosque: wherever ye are, turn your faces in that direction. (2:144)

For Hajj are the months well known. If any one undertakes that duty therein, Let there be no obscenity, nor wickedness, nor wrangling in the Hajj. And whatever good ye do, (be sure) Allah knoweth it. And take a provision (with you) for the journey, but the best of provisions is right conduct. So fear Me, o ye that are wise. (2:197)

Jihad

Jihad means striving. According to the Prophet Muhammad, the greater jihad is to struggle against one's own evils. The lesser jihad is to struggle against those who oppose the religion of Allah. Strict rules have been laid down for the latter, as we will see later (pages 304–313).

Not equal are those believers who sit (at home) and receive no hurt, and those who strive and fight in the cause of God with their goods and their persons. God hath granted a grade higher to those who strive and fight. (4:95)

Fight in the cause of God those who fight you, but do not transgress limits; for God loveth not transgressors. (2:190)

And fight them on until there is no more tumult or oppression, and there prevail justice and faith in God; but if they cease, let there be no hostility except to those who practice oppression. (2:193)

---

7 Qibla—the direction faced in prayer (toward Mecca).

Let there be no compulsion in religion: Truth stands out clear from Error: whoever rejects evil and believes in Allah hath grasped the most trustworthy hand-hold, that never breaks. And Allah heareth and knoweth all things. (2:256)

Family Relationships

The Qur'an deals at length with proper relationships among men and women. Some of the injunctions are related to the culture of pre-Islamic Arabia. The interpretation and current relevance of such passages is a matter of considerable scholarly debate today.

Say to the believing men that they should lower their gaze and guard their modesty: that will make for greater purity for them: And Allah is well acquainted with all that they do.
    And say to the believing women that they should lower their gaze and guard their modesty; that they should not display their beauty and ornaments except what (ordinarily) appears thereof; that they should draw their veils over their bosoms and not display their beauty except to their husbands, their fathers, their husbands' fathers, their sons, their husbands' sons, their brothers or their brothers' sons, or their sisters' sons, or their women, or the slaves whom their right hands possess, or male attendants free of sexual desires, or small children who have no carnal knowledge of women. (24: 30–31)

Men are the protectors and maintainers of women, because God has given the one more (strength) than the other, and because they support them from their means. Therefore the righteous women are devoutly obedient, and guard in (the husband's) absence what God would have them guard. As to those women on whose part ye fear disloyalty and ill-conduct, admonish them (first), (next), refuse to share their beds, (and last) beat them (lightly); but if they return to obedience, seek not against them means (of annoyance): For God is Most High, Great (above you all). (4:34)

If ye fear that ye shall not be able to deal justly with the orphans, marry women of your choice, two or three or four; but if ye fear that ye shall not be able to deal justly (with them), then only one, or (a captive) that your right hands possess, that will be more suitable, to prevent you from doing injustice. (4:3)

If a wife fears cruelty or desertion on her husband's part, there is no blame on them if they arrange an amicable settlement between themselves; and such settlement is best; even though men's souls are swayed by greed. But if ye do good and practice self-restraint, Allah is well-acquainted with all that ye do. (4:128)

So if a husband divorces his wife (irrevocably), he cannot, after that, remarry her until after she has married another husband and he has divorced her.

In that case there is no blame on either of them if they re-unite, provided they feel that they can keep the limits ordained by Allah. (2:23)

Self-restraint

O ye who believe! Fasting is prescribed to you as it was prescribed to those before you, that ye may (learn) self-restraint. … Ramadan is the (month) in which was sent down the Qur'an, as a guide to mankind, also clear (signs) for guidance and judgment (between right and wrong). So every one of you who is present (at his home) during that month should spend it in fasting, but if any one is ill, or on a journey, the prescribed period (should be made up) by days later. (2:183, 185)

Adam

We said: "O Adam! dwell thou and thy wife in the Garden; and eat of the bountiful things therein as (where and when) ye will; but approach not this tree, or ye run in harm and transgression."

Then did Satan make them slip from the (garden), and get them out of the state (of felicity) in which they had been. We said: "Get ye down, all (ye people), with enmity between yourselves. On earth will be your dwelling-place and your means of livelihood—for a time."

Then learnt Adam from his Lord words of inspiration and his Lord turned towards him; for He is Oft-Returning, Most Merciful. (2:33–7)

Mary and Jesus

Behold! the angels said: "O Mary! Allah hath chosen thee and purified thee—chosen thee above the women of all nations. … Behold! the angels said: "O Mary! Allah giveth thee glad tidings of a Word from Him: his name will be Christ Jesus, the son of Mary, held in honour in the world and the Hereafter and of (the company of) those nearest to Allah; He shall speak to the people in childhood and in maturity. And he shall be (of the company) of the righteous." (3:42–7)

Then will Allah say: "O Jesus the son of Mary! Recount My favour to thee and to thy mother. Behold! I strengthened thee with the holy spirit, so that thou didst speak to the people in childhood and in maturity. Behold! I taught thee the Book and Wisdom, the Law and the Gospel and behold! thou makest out of clay, as it were, the figure of a bird, by My leave, and thou breathest into it and it becometh a bird by My leave, and thou healest those born blind, and the lepers, by My leave. And behold! thou bringest forth the dead by My leave. And behold! I did restrain the Children of Israel from (violence to) thee when thou didst show them the clear Signs, and the unbelievers among them said: 'This is nothing but evident magic.'" (5:110)

Christ the son of Mary was no more than a messenger; many were the messengers that passed away before him. His mother was a woman of truth. They had both to eat their (daily) food. (5:75)

They say: "Allah hath begotten a son." Glory be to Him.—Nay, to Him belongs all that is in the heavens and on earth: everything renders worship to Him. (2:116)

If only they had stood fast by the Law, the Gospel, and all the revelation that was sent to them from their Lord, they would have enjoyed happiness from every side. There is from among them a party on the right course: but many of them follow a course that is evil. (5:66)

The Day of Judgment

Then, on the Day of Judgment, He will cover them with shame, and say: "Where are My 'partners' concerning whom ye used to dispute (with the godly)?" Those endued with knowledge will say: "This Day, indeed, are the Unbelievers covered with shame and misery (namely) those whose lives the angels take in a state of wrong-doing to their own souls." Then would they offer submission (with the pretence), "We did no evil (knowingly)." (The angels will reply), "Nay, but verily Allah knoweth all that ye did; So enter the gates of Hell, to dwell therein. Thus evil indeed is the abode of the arrogant." To the righteous (when) it is said, "What is it that your Lord has revealed?" they say, "All that is good." To those who do good, there is good in this world, and the Home of the Hereafter is even better and excellent indeed is the Home of the righteous, Gardens of Eternity which they will enter: beneath them flow (pleasant) rivers: they will have therein all that they wish: thus doth Allah reward the righteous, (namely) those whose lives the angels take in a state of purity, saying (to them), "Peace be on you; enter ye the Garden, because of (the good) which ye did (in the world)." (16:27–32)

SOURCE: Excerpts adapted from *The Holy Quran: Text, Translation, and Commentary*, by Abdullah Yusuf Ali. Durban, South Africa: Kamil Muslim Trust for the Islamic Propagation Centre International, 1934,1946

Hadith

"Hadith," as we have seen, means "report" on the actions and words of the Prophet, outside the Qur'an, as told by his companions. Hadith range from grand revelations from Allah to descriptions of the Prophet's life, rules of war, marriage, **mosque** conduct, and personal behavior. Like all religious guidelines, they reflect their cultural environment. They are the second basis, after the Qur'an, for Islamic law, or **Shari'ah**. They contain references to their sources and seek to establish an authoritative chain (*isnah*) of transmission. Traditionally, the most authoritative and famous Hadith collections are the *Sahih* ("the Authentic") *of Muhammad Ibn Ismail* *al-Bukhari* (d. 870 CE, called "Bukhari") and the *Sahih of Abu-l-Husayn Muslim ibn al-Hajjaj* (d. 875 CE, called "Muslim"). The following are from *Sahih Muslim*.

Allah's Mercy

Allah's Messenger (may peace be upon him) said: When Allah created the creation He put down in his Book, which is with Him upon the Throne: Verily, My mercy predominates My wrath. (Arabic 4939)

SOURCE: *Sahih Muslim*
<http://hadith.al-islam.com/Bayan/Display.asp?Lang=eng&ID=1571>

Allah is a Light

It is narrated on the authority of Abu Dharr: I asked the Messenger of Allah (may peace be upon him): Did you see thy Lord? He said: He is a Light: how could I see Him?

Abu Musa reported: The Messenger of Allah (may peace be upon him): was standing among us and he told us five things. He said: Verily, the Exalted and Mighty God does not sleep, and it does not befit him. He lowers the scale and lifts it. The deeds of the day are taken up to Him before the deeds of the night. His veil is the light. In the Hadith narrated by Abu Akr (instead of the word "light") it is fire. If he withdraws it (the veil) the splendour of His countenance would consume His creation so far as His sight reaches. (I:341, 343)

Seeking Consent for Marriage

Abu Huraira (Allah be pleased with him) reported Allah's Messenger (may peace be upon him) as having said: A woman without a husband (or divorced or a widow) must not be married until she is consulted, and a virgin must not be married until her permission is sought. They asked the Prophet of Allah (may peace be upon him): How her (virgin's) consent can be solicited? He (the Holy Prophet) said: That she keeps silent. (II:714)

Prohibition of Killing Women and Children in War

It is narrated on the authority of 'Abdullah that a woman was found killed in one of the battles fought by the Messenger of Allah (may peace be upon him). He disapproved of the killing of women and children.

It is narrated by Ibn 'Umar that a woman was found killed in one of these battles; so the Messenger of Allah (may peace be upon him) forbade the killing of women and children. (IV:946)

Removal of the Idols from the Vicinity of the Ka'ba

It has been narrated by Ibn 'Abdullah who said: The Holy Prophet (may peace be upon him) entered Mecca. There were three hundred and sixty idols around the Ka'ba. He began to thrust them with the stick that was in his hand saying: "Truth has come and falsehood has vanished. Lo! falsehood was destined to vanish" (xvii:8). Truth has arrived, and falsehood can neither create anything from the beginning nor can it restore to life. (III:978)

The Merits of Jesus Christ (Peace Be Upon Him)

Abu Huraira reported Allah's Messenger (may peace be upon him) as saying: I am most akin to the son of Mary among the whole of mankind and the Prophets are of different mothers, but of one religion, and no Prophet was raised between me and him (Jesus Christ). (IV:1260)

It is Forbidden to Commit Oppression

Abu Dharr reported Allah's Messenger (may peace be upon him) as saying that Allah, the Exalted and Glorious, said: My servants, I have made oppression unlawful for Me and unlawful for you, so do not commit oppression against one another. (IV:1365)

SOURCE: *Sahih Muslim*, trans. 'Abdul Hamid Siddiqi. Lahore, Pakistan: Sh. Muhammad Ashraf, 1973–5, vol. 1, p. 113, to vol. 4, p. 1555

Shari'ah

Muslim law is called Shari'ah ("the path leading to the watering place"). Since the Qur'an could not be a guide for all future developments, the Hadith were collected to help prescribe behavior. But even more guidelines were needed. The third source of sacred authority in Islam is Shari'ah, or the law. Its roots, in declining order of importance, are the Qur'an, the Sunna of the Prophet as compiled in the Hadith, consensus, and analogical reasoning. Fundamental to Shari'ah are the Five Pillars of Islam: (1) Pronouncing the confession of faith, (2) Performing salaat prayers, (3) Fasting during the month of Ramadan, (4) *Zakat*, or charity, and (5) Hajj, or spiritual pilgrimage to Mecca. There are five types of law: (1) obligatory, (2) meritorious, (3) indifferent, (4) reprehensible, and (5) forbidden. Shari'ah includes dietary prohibitions (such as pork and alcohol) and guidelines for dress (no sexually provocative clothing); it also commands further legal rights for women (divorce, owning property, making a will). In medieval times, when tribal loyalty and customs were uppermost, Shari'ah began to restrict destructive practices such as infanticide, drunkenness, and gambling. But some legal experts feel that the traditional principles by which Muslim laws have been derived are not being sincerely followed today, particularly in the case of laws regarding women.

Hajj: Asceticism and Social Leveling   by Maulana Muhammad Ali

Hajj, the fifth Pillar of Islam's primary prescriptions, is centered on the revered Ka'ba, which is traditionally considered to date from the time of Abraham and his son Ishmael. Under the guidance of the Qur'an, the pilgrimage became a means of ascetic practice and social equality. This explanation was provided by the founder of the Pakistan-based missionary society Ahmadiyya Anjuman Isha'at Islam.

Islam discourages asceticism in all its aspects. ... Yet Islam lays the greatest stress upon the spiritual development of man [sic], and in its four main institutions—prayer, *zakat* [charity], fasting, and hajj—introduces workable ascetic formulae into the daily life of man—an asceticism which is quite in keeping with the secular side of life. The five daily prayers require the sacrifice of a small part of his time and, without in any way interfering with his everyday life, enable him to realize the Divine that is within him. The institution of *zakat* demands the giving up of a small portion of his wealth without interfering with his right to property. Fasting requires the giving up of food and drink but not in such a manner as to make him unfit for carrying on his regular work or business. It is only in hajj that asceticism assumes a marked form, for the pilgrim is required not only to give up his regular work for a number of days for the sake of the journey of Makkah [Mecca], but he must, in addition, give up many other amenities of life, and live, more or less, the life of an ascetic. The hajj is, however, a function which generally comes only once in a lifetime, and, therefore, while leading a man through the highest spiritual experience, it does not interfere in any appreciable degree with the regular course of his life. ...

No other institution in the world has the wonderful influence of the hajj in leveling all distinctions of race, colour and rank. Not only do people of all races and all countries meet together before the Holy House of God as His servants, as members of one Divine family, but they are clad in one dress—in two white sheets—and there remains nothing to distinguish the high from the low. There is a vast concourse of human beings, all clad in one dress, all moving in one way, all having but one word to speak, *labbaika Allah-umma labbaika*, meaning "here are we, O Allah! Here are we in Thy Presence." It is hajj alone that brings into the domain of practicality what would otherwise seem impossible, namely, that all people, to whatever class or country they belong, should speak one language and wear one dress. Thus is every Muslim made to pass once in his life through that narrow gate of equality which leads to broad brotherhood. All men are equal in birth and death; they come into life and pass out of it in the same way, but hajj is the only occasion on which they are taught how to live alike, how to act alike and how to feel alike.

SOURCE: Maulana Muhammad Ali, *The Religion of Islam*. 6th ed. Delhi: Motilal Banarsidass, 1994, pp. 386–7

Legal Dictates in Saudi Arabia by Khaled Abou El Fadl

The traditional ways in which Shari'ah was established used to be a dynamic and subtle process, according to Khaled Abou El Fadl from Kuwait, an international expert in Islamic Law now teaching at the University of California, Los Angeles.

El Fadl argues that this process has been stultified by authoritarian approaches, including that of the Orthodox Hanbali school of thought which currently predominates in Saudi Arabia as the basis for secular law in personal matters. The Taliban also follow Hanbali thought. In Saudi Arabia, women are not allowed to travel without a male relative, are not allowed to drive cars, and are required to wear a full burqa in public. As an example of contemporary thinking by these jurists, El Fadl explores the ruling concerning whether a woman can visit a grave.

The case studies discussed below are focused on *responsa* issued by jurists who claim to represent the law of God. Most of the *responsa* are taken from The Permanent Council For Scientific Research and Legal Opinions (hereinafter C.R.L.O.), the official institution in Saudi Arabia entrusted with issuing Islamic legal opinions. Other *responsa* are taken from jurists issuing legal opinions in a private capacity. All the jurists discussed are well-known in the Arabic-speaking world both at the juristic and popular level. The questions presented to these jurists arrive from different parts of the Muslim world ...

Typically, a person submits a written question, and either a council of jurists or individual jurists issue a written response. ... The legal *responsa* issued by the *Saudi Permanent Council* often serve as the basis for official state law—the Saudi government often adopts the legal opinions of the Council as the law of the land. Otherwise, the *responsa* of the jurists have persuasive authority for those who consider the opinions authoritative. ...

One notices that the earmark of contemporary approaches to Islamic law, whether Wahhābī[8] or anti-Wahhābī, is the certainty of results, incontrovertibility of conclusions, and the unequivocalness of the asserted determinations. The end result is that the subtlety and richness of the Islamic legal heritage is largely absent in the contemporary age.

With this background in mind, we can analyze a group of *responsa* dealing with the legality of women visiting graves. 'Abd Allāh b. Qa'ūd, 'Abd Allāh b. Ghidyān, 'Abd al-Razzāq 'Afīfī, 'Abd al-'Azīz b. 'Abd Allīh b. Bīz, Muḥammad al-Ṣāliḥ al-'Uthaymīn, and Ṣāliḥ b. Fawzān, are asked if it is lawful for Muslims to visit the graves of deceased relatives or non-relatives, including the grave of the Prophet. Among the *responsa*, a woman states that out of love and respect for her deceased husband, she visits his grave every Thursday and performs certain religious supplications. She insists that she does not perform any of the prohibited acts such as wailing or the ripping of cloth. Again, the virtue of the jurists' response is its straightforwardness and clarity. They determine that visiting graves for men is lawful, and, in fact, encouraged. In this context, they cite a *ḥadīth* attributed to the Prophet that states, "Visit the graves for it will remind you of the Hereafter.." However, the same rule does not apply to women. The Prophet, they assert, stated, "May God curse women who visit the graves." Regardless of the reason or motive, women are not allowed to visit the graves of relatives or

8 Wahhābī—one of the primary schools of contemporary Islamic thought, founded in the eighteenth century. It discards all practices that are not specifically approved by the Qur'an and Sunnah.

non-relatives. The jurists then offer speculations as to the reason for this prohibition: they argue that women are intellectually meek and emotionally weak; if they visit the graves they are prone to commit reprehensible acts such as screaming, wailing, and beating their chests in grief. Furthermore, due to their fragile state, the visitation of graves is bound to damage and endanger their psychology. Importantly, the jurists contend, if women are allowed to visit graves, increasing numbers will do so until cemeteries become points for female congregation. This is only bound to attract immoral men who will head to the cemeteries to look at women or, worse, to molest them. In summary, the visitation of graves by women is bound to be a source of *fitnah* (calamity, corruption, civil discord).

Importantly, the determination of the jurists mentioned above is the minority view in the Islamic legal tradition, including in the Ḥanbalī school of thought. Nevertheless, the jurists do not mention any disagreements of this matter although some of their language indicates that they are well aware of its existence. To summarize the juristic tradition on this matter, there are three distinct points of view. A minority view held that the visitation of graves by women is always prohibited for men and women, and then was permitted both for men and women. They relied on several traditions, one in which 'Ā'isha, the Prophet's wife, confirms that the abrogation of the prohibition against visiting graves included men and women. 'Ā'ishah, herself, is reported to have visited the graves of her relatives. Furthermore, various traditions report that the Prophet encountered women visiting the cemeteries, and did not advise them against doing so. Another minority view, argued that whether it is unlawful for men or women to visit graves depends entirely on the conduct and customary practices of the time and place in question. If individuals, within a particular society, tend to commit prohibited acts such as wailing or self-beating while visiting graveyards, then it is unlawful for those individuals to do so. But if a man or woman adheres to proper Islamic conduct in graveyards, their visitations are lawful, and, in fact, recommended. Some jurists, for instance, argued that the prevailing practice of women in Egypt is to engage in un-Islamic conduct, and therefore, it is unlawful for women in that country to visit graveyards unless they can exercise the requisite degree of self-control.

There is another issue that warrants a comment. The tradition relied on by the modern jurists which states, "May God curse women who visit graves," is problematic at several levels. In numerous traditions, the Prophet is reported to have said that he is not a curser (*la'ān*) or that it is not consistent with proper Islamic character to curse even one's enemies (*al-la'n*). This blanket curse hurled at women who visit graves is not consistent with reports in which the Prophet affirmatively refused to curse individuals or groups. A comprehensive response would evaluate and assess the impact of this inconsistency. This is important in light of the fact of the doubts raised about the authenticity of the cursing tradition. In addition, there are different versions of the cursing *ḥadīth*. One version, which is mentioned above, condemns women who visit graves (*zā'irāt al-qubūr*), but another, condemns women who frequent the graveyard or those who repeatedly visit cemeteries (*zawwārāt al-qubūr*). This is significant because it raises the issue of the socio-historical context of the tradition. As is the practice in some countries today, there were women who mourned the dead for a living. As such, the mourning of the dead and the visitation of graveyards becomes a professional activity. The common practice of these women was to wail, beat their chests, and rip their cloth in return for compensation. This was done because of the belief that the louder and more vigorous the mourning, the higher the social position of the deceased. Many jurists condemned this practice, and argued that the cursing tradition is directed at those individuals, and not directed at women in general. In other words, the term *zawwārāt* referred to a specific social practice by a particular guild of professional mourners.

None of these subtleties emerge in the *responsa* of the modern jurists, but as stated above, it is unlikely that this is the result of a lack of knowledge or sloppy investigation. Rather, what is more likely is that the authors of the *responsa*, because of their value-based assumptions about the role of women, selectively disclosed the evidence to their audience. The net result was to misrepresent the efforts of the interpretive communities of Islamic law, and to create the impression that the determination is far more closed than the evidence, itself, admits. Accordingly, the roles of the author and the text become far more limited and diminished while the reader (special agent) stands supreme and uncontested in the determinative process. Most importantly, unless the common agents have a faith-based belief that those particular special agents are divinely guided or inspired, the trust that the common agents have placed in the special agents has been violated.

SOURCE: Khaled Abou El Fadl, *Speaking in God's Name: Islamic Law, Authority, and Women*. Oxford: Oneworld Publications, 2001, pp. 173–83.

Reason and revelation

The Qur'an serves as the basis of the Muslim's search for truth that guides the actions of believers. Thus the theological debates that developed are concerned with establishing with certainty the moral and ethical responsibility of the individual in relation to Allah.

The rationalist Mu'tazilah school (ninth century CE) emphasized the capacity, when aided by reason, to act in accordance with God's unity and justice. In response the more spiritual Ash'arites (tenth century CE), in asserting the omnipotence of Allah, attempted to shift the focus back to the Qur'an as the starting point of all ethical knowledge. The incorporation and translation of inspiring Greek ideas into Muslim ideals by subsequent philosophers refined Muslim philosophy. Logic, reason's tool, became instrumental in developing the moral and ethical system of Islamic law.

Rationalism by Ibn Sina (Avicenna)

Ibn Sina (980–1037 CE), the Persian philosopher, followed others such as al-Kindi (b. 800 CE?) and al-Razi (d. 926 CE). But it was the theories of logic, metaphysics, and politics of al-Farabi (d. 950 CE) that set the foundations for Ibn Sina's causal scheme. In Ibn Sina's Neoplatonist system, God's self-knowledge evokes a First Intelligence, then successive intelligences.

That person upon whom the First Intelligence gazes, so that he or she becomes refined, cultivated, subtle, beautiful, brave, and perfect in intellect, becomes a prophet. The First Intelligence becomes for this person as our intellect (is for us). And intellect for him or her is on the level of our soul. Just as the soul that grasps a truth from the intellect is learned, the intellect that grasps from the First Intelligence is a prophet.

But this state varies. Either it occurs in sleep, since in wakefulness the preoccupations of the senses and the multitude of activities become a hindrance; or it occurs in wakefulness, since in sleep the imaginative faculty predominates; or in each it is full and true. The motion and repose of this person is pure in legislative function. It never admits abrogation or distortion. This person is free of worldly distractions and secular controls and is devoted to the affairs of the Necessary Existent. The First Intelligence nourishes his or her soul from itself. This nourishing is called sanctification. As the Qur'an states, "We have supported him with the Holy Spirit." (The First Intelligence) reveals itself to this person so that through (its) good auspices he or she comprehends. ... Thus (Muhammad) said, "My Lord instructed me; and how well was my instruction; and I instructed 'Ali, and I instructed him well." Similarly (the Qur'an) said, "And We taught him knowledge from Us." ... That which becomes clear from this summons is religion. And the law of that religion is religious creed. The acceptance of all this is faith. The name of that which prophets receive is revelation. When it is united with a human, and the Holy Spirit opens his or her way to itself and becomes governor of that disposition, it makes (that person) lofty in aspiration, and slight in greed, rancourless, without envy. Whatever this person does is through that Holy Power. Just as is (found) in the (prophetic) tradition, "I ask of you a faith that my heart touches."

Thus the Holy Spirit is the noblest of all souls, for all (other) souls are subordinate to the Universal Intelligence. The Holy Spirit, however, is that which is the intermediary between the Necessary Existent and the First Intelligence. The faith of that Power is the prophet, who is the messenger and bearer of the Holy Emanation. That Power is the fruit of proximity to the First Intelligence. ...

Reason comprehends truth through itself, while prophethood comprehends truths through Holy Support. Just as speech is not reason, reason is not summons, and summons is not prophethood. Recollection[9]

---

9 Recollection—a Platonic concept: the eternal soul's recalling universals known in Heaven.

stands between speech and reason, and apostleship between prophethood and summons.

Hence, whatever rational concepts that the intellect wishes to convey to the senses, it does so by means of recollection. (The latter then) formulates it in sensible sounds and unites (it) with speech, so that hearing apprehends.

SOURCE: Peter Heath, *Allegory and Philosophy in Avicenna (Ibn Sina)*. Philadelphia, PA: University of Pennsylvania Press, 1992, pp. 118–19

Mysticism by al-Ghazali

Al-Ghazali (1058–1111) was an Ash'ari theologian, jurist, and mystic who criticized the rationalism of al-Farabi and Ibn Sina. Following a spiritual crisis, al-Ghazali concluded that systematic reasoning could not yield the insights of mysticism.

When I had finished with these sciences, I next turned with set purpose to the method of mysticism (or Sufism). I knew that the complete mystic 'way' includes both intellectual belief and practical activity; the latter consists in getting rid of the obstacles in the self and in stripping off its base characteristics and vicious morals, so that the heart may attain to freedom from what is not God and to constant recollection of Him. . . .

I apprehended clearly that the mystics were men [sic] who had real experiences, not men of words, and that I had already progressed as far as was possible by way of intellectual apprehension. What remained for me was not to be attained by oral instruction and study but only by immediate experience and by walking in the mystic way. ...

Next I considered the circumstances of my life, and realized that I was caught in a veritable thicket of attachments. I also considered my activities, of which the best was my teaching and lecturing, and realized that in them I was dealing with sciences that were unimportant and contributed nothing to the attainment of eternal life.

After that I examined my motive in my work of teaching, and realized that it was not a pure desire for the things of God, but that the impulse moving me was the desire for an influential position and public recognition. I saw for certain that I was on the brink of a crumbling bank of sand and in imminent danger of hell-fire unless I set about to mend my ways. ...

For nearly six months beginning with Rajab[10] 488 AH [July 1095 CE], I was continuously tossed about between the attractions of worldly desires and the impulses towards eternal life. In that month the matter ceased to be one of choice and became one of compulsion. God caused my tongue to dry up so that I was prevented from lecturing. One particular day I would make an effort to lecture in order to gratify the hearts of my following, but my tongue would not utter a single word nor could I accomplish anything at all.

This impediment in my speech produced grief in my heart, and at the same time my power to digest and assimilate food and drink was impaired;

10 Rajab—the month during which Muhammad ascended to Heaven.

I could hardly swallow or digest a single mouthful of food. My powers became so weakened that the doctors gave up all hope of successful treatment. "This trouble arises from the heart," they said, "and from there it has spread through the constitution; the only method of treatment is that the anxiety which has come over the heart should be allayed."

Thereupon, perceiving my impotence and having altogether lost my power of choice, I sought refuge with God most high as one who is driven to Him, because he is without further resources of his own. He answered me, He who "answers him who is driven (to Him by affliction) when he calls upon Him" (Qur'an 27:63). He made it easy for my heart to turn away from position and wealth, from children and friends. ...

I learnt with certainty that it is above all the mystics who walk on the road of God; their life is the best life, their method the soundest method, their character the purest character; indeed, were the intellect of the intellectuals and the learning of the learned and the scholarship of the scholars, who are versed in the profundities of revealed truth, brought together in the attempt to improve the life and character of the mystics, they would find no way of doing so; for to the mystics all movement and all rest, whether external or internal, brings illumination from the light of the lamp of prophetic revelation; and behind the light of prophetic revelation there is no other light on the face of the earth from which illumination may be received.

SOURCE: W. Montgomery Watt, *The Faith and Practice of Al-Ghazali*. London: George Allen and Unwin, 1953, pp. 54–61.

Sufism

Muslims who seek direct mystical experiences of Allah are known as **Sufis**. Initially Sufis lived simply, wore a coarse woolen garment, and practiced asceticism. Today many Muslims are associated with variations of Sufism, some emphasizing its uniquely Muslim quality, some its universalism. Techniques such as *dhikr* (prayer), *sama* (music), or dance (the "Whirling Dervishes") are customs used to induce trance states and thus refine spiritual awareness of Allah.

One notable Sufi, Ibn 'Arabi, perceived that in the world there is actually nothing but God, transcendent yet manifested on earth. Two other great Sufis, quoted below, were Rabi'a and Rumi.

The Rarest Treasure by Rabi'a

Rabi'a al-Adawiyya (713–801 CE) was born into a poor family and sold into slavery, but later freed. She devoted herself to a life of prayer, poverty, and seclusion. Her asceticism and pure love of God banished hatred and inspired many Sufis thereafter. She believed that one should not love out of desire for paradise or fear of hell, but for love of God alone.

"Doorkeeper of the Heart"

Your hope in my heart is the rarest treasure
Your Name on my tongue is the sweetest word
My choicest hours
Are the hours I spend with You—

O God, I can't live in this world
Without remembering You—
How can I endure the next world
Without seeing Your face?

I am a stranger in Your country
And lonely among Your worshippers:
This is the substance of my complaint.

"One who Tastes, Knows"

In love, nothing exists between breast and Breast.
Speech is born out of longing,
True description from the real taste.
The one who tastes, knows;
The one who explains, lies.
How can you describe the true form of Something
In whose presence you are blotted out?
And in whose being you still exist?
And who lives as a sign for your journey?

SOURCE: *Rabi'a*, trans. Charles Upton. Brattleboro, VT: Threshold Books, 1988.

The Sound of Love by Rumi

Jalal ad-Din ar-Rumi (1207–73) was one of the greatest of Muslim mystics. Living in Persia and Turkey, he founded the order of the Mevlevi—the "Whirling Dervishes"—known for their spinning, ecstatic dances. His belief in reincarnation, his universalism, and his Platonic influence went beyond Islamic orthodoxy, but have been neglected in view of his strong influence otherwise.

With every breath the sound
of love surrounds us,
and we are bound for the depths
of space, without sightseeing.
We've been in orbit before
and know the angels there.
Let's go there again, Master,
for that is our land.
Yet we are beyond all that
and something more than angels.
Out beyond duality,
we have a home, and it is Glory.

That pure substance is
different from this dusty world.
What kind of place is this?
We once came down, soon we'll return.
A new happiness befriends us
as we work at offering our lives.
Muhammad, an ornament to the world,
is our caravan's chosen guide.
The sweetness we breathe on the wind
is from the scent of his hair,
and the radiance of this thought
is from the light of his day.
His face once split the moon in two—
she couldn't endure the sight of him.
Yet how lucky she was,
she who humbly received him.
Look into our hearts and see
the splitting moon in each breath.
Having seen that vision,
how can you still dream?
When the wave of *Am I not?* struck,
it wrecked the body's ship;
when the ship wrecks once more,
it will be the time of union.

SOURCE: William C. Chittick, *The Sufi Path of Love: The Spiritual Teachings of Rumi*. Albany, NY: State University of New York Press, 1983, pp. 36–7

Between the Yea and the Nay   by Ibn 'Arabi

Ibn 'Arabi Muhyi al-Din (1165–1240) was born in Spain. As a young man at a party in Seville, he heard a strange voice say: "O Muhammad, it was not for this that you were created." Disturbed, he retreated and had a vision in which he saw Moses, Jesus, and Muhammad. He studied with several spiritual masters, began traveling, and eventually wrote over 700 books, influencing many Sufis. He considered all prophets to be teachers of a primordial religion: "There is no knowledge except that taken from God." He taught a **monism** in which Being is essentially one: "There is nothing in Being but God." Ibn 'Arabi performed the pilgrimage to Mecca in 1202, then settled in Damascus in 1223 until his death. In this passage he tells of his meeting with the great philosopher Ibn Rushd.

I spent the day in Cordoba at the house of Abu al-Walid Ibn Rushd. He had expressed a desire to meet me in person, since he had heard of certain revelations I had received while in retreat and had shown considerable astonishment concerning them. In consequence my father, who was one of his closest friends, took me with him on the pretext of business, in order to give Ibn Rushd the opportunity of making my acquaintance. I was at

the time a beardless youth. As I entered the house, the philosopher rose
to greet me with all the signs of friendliness and affection, and embraced
me. Then he said to me "Yes," and showed pleasure on seeing that I had
understood him. I, on the other hand, being aware of the motive for his
pleasure, replied "No." Upon this Ibn Rushd drew back from me, his colour
changed and he seemed to doubt what he had thought of me. He then put
to me the following question, "What solution have you found as a result of
mystical illumination and divine inspiration? Does it coincide with what is
arrived at by speculative thought?" I replied, "Yes and no. Between the Yea
and the Nay the spirits take their flight beyond matter, and the necks detach
themselves from their bodies."

At this Ibn Rushd became pale, and I saw him tremble as he muttered
the formula "there is no power save from God." This was because he
understood my allusion ... After that he sought from my father to meet
me in order to present what he himself had understood: he wanted to
know if it conformed with or was different from what I had. He was one
of the great masters of reflection and rational consideration. He thanked
God that in his own time he had seen someone who had entered into the
retreat ignorant and had come out like this—without study, discussion,
investigation or reading.

SOURCE: Muhyi al-Din Muhammad ibn 'Ali Ibn al-'Arabi, *Sufis of Andalusia*. London: George Allen and
Unwin, 1971/Northleach, Gloucestershire: Beshara Publications, 1988, p. 23

Teachings of the Sufi Masters: Nizam Ad Din Awliya
by Amir Hasan

In the Indian sub-continent, Islam was spread primarily through the Sufi masters.
Their path of intense love for God was part of the great bhakti movement that
swept medieval India, cutting across all distinctions between high and low caste,
educated and illiterate, and men and women. There were various Sufi lineages
in which spiritual teachings and blessings were transmitted directly from master
to disciple. In the great Chisti lineage of spiritual masters, the renowned ascetic
Shaykh Farid was teacher of Shaykh Nizam Ad-Din Awliya (1242–1325) of Delhi.
The latter's informal conversations with his followers were recorded by his disciple,
Amir Hasan, and published as Fawa-id al-Fu'ad, "Morals for the Heart." This story
concerns the Sufi ideal of *fana*, annihilation of the ego, so that nothing remains
except God.

Friday, the 28th of Dhu'l-Qa'da, AH 711 (6 April 1312)
I obtained the benefit of kissing his feet [an Indian expression of devotion] in
the house which faces the Friday Congregational mosque of Kilogarhi. Before
the time of Friday prayer conversation focused on THE WORLD OF SUFISM.
Mention was made of those men who truly immerse themselves in remembering God, and the contrast between them and those who, just because they
engage in research and study, want others to consider them as men of God.

In this connection the master told a story about a very bright student named Sharaf ad-din. "One day this Sharaf ad-din came into the presence of the Great Shaykh Farid ad-din—may God sanctify his lofty secret. The Shaykh asked him: 'How do you fare in your studies?' 'For the moment I have forgotten all about them!' was his reply. The Shaykh was unhappy with what he said. After he left, the Shaykh turned to those present and remarked: 'This man thinks he has the power to fly!'"

As he concluded telling this story, the master—may God remember him with favor—became teary-eyed. "There was once a spiritual master," he recalled. "One of his sons, named Muhammad, became extremely learned and was highly accomplished. He then resolved to pursue the path of Sufism. Coming to his father, he said: 'I want to become a dervish.' 'Fine,' said his father. 'First go and spend forty days and nights in ascetical devotion (*chilla*).' That son went and observed a *chilla*. When he had passed his fortieth night in prayer and solitude, he came back to his father. His father proceeded to ask him questions about what he had studied. The son answered all of them. 'Alas, Muhammad,' said his father, 'your *chilla* seems to have been useless. Go and spend another forty days and nights in ascetical devotion.' He went and did as he had been told. After the fortieth in prayer and solitude, he came back to his father. The father again asked him some questions. This time he began to stumble here and there in the answers that he gave. 'Go and perform one more *chilla*,' exhorted his father. When he had completed his third consecutive period of secluded immersion in prayer and meditation for forty days, he returned to his father. The father again put some questions to him, but this time he had become so immersed in God that he could give no reply!"

SOURCE: Amir Hasan Sijzi, *Nizam Ad-Din Awliya: Morals for the Heart*, trans. Bruce B. Lawrence. New York: Paulist Press, 1992, pp. 173–4

Living Islam

In Islam's encounter with contemporary secular materialistic cultures it is challenged to adapt or defend its traditional ways. Among the issues being raised are the rights of women, the desirability of combining religion and government in Islamist states, and whether terrorism in the name of Islam is justified by Muslim traditions.

Rights of Women: Qur'anic Ideals Versus Muslim Practice
by Riffat Hassan

Extensive research is currently being done to determine the legal position of women according to Muslim tradition. There are many sources of the tradition, the most important of which is the Qur'an. It is considered the Word of God, as transmitted to the Prophet Muhammad through the angel Gabriel. Other sources include sayings attributed to the Prophet, decisions of schools of law, and the Shari'ah, or code of law. Feminist scholar Riffat Hassan, at the University of Louisville, has carefully researched the rights of women granted by the Qur'an but notes that these are not necessarily upheld.

Muslim men never tire of repeating that Islam has given more rights to women than has any other religion. Certainly, if by "Islam" is meant "Qur'anic Islam" the rights that it has given to women are, indeed, impressive. Not only do women partake of all the "General Rights" mentioned in the foregoing pages [rights to life, respect, justice, freedom, knowledge, sustenance, work, privacy, protection from slander and ridicule, development of one's aesthetic sensibilities and enjoyment of God's bounties, leaving one's homeland when there is oppression, and the "good life"], they are also the subject of much particular concern in the Qur'an. Underlying much of the Qur'an's legislation on women-related issues is the recognition that women have been disadvantaged persons in history to whom justice needs to be done by the Muslim Ummah. Unfortunately, however, the cumulative (Jewish, Christian, Hellenistic, Bedouin, and other) biases which existed in the Arab-Islamic culture of the early centuries of Islam infiltrated the Islamic tradition and undermined the intent of the Qur'an to liberate women from the status of chattels or inferior creatures and make them free and equal to men.

A review of Muslim history and culture brings to light many areas in which—Qur'anic teaching notwithstanding—women continued to be subjected to diverse forms of oppression and injustice, often in the name of Islam. While the Qur'an, because of its protective attitude toward all downtrodden and oppressed classes of people, appears to be weighted in many ways in favor of women, many of its women-related teachings have been used in patriarchal Muslim societies against, rather than for, women. Muslim societies, in general, appear to be far more concerned with trying to control women's bodies and sexuality than with their human rights. Many Muslims, when they speak of human rights, either do not speak of women's rights at all,[11] or are mainly concerned with how a woman's chastity may be protected.[12] (They are apparently not worried about protecting men's chastity.)

Women are the targets of the most serious violations of human rights which occur in Muslim societies in general. Muslims say with great pride that Islam abolished female infanticide; true, but it must also be mentioned that one of the most common crimes in a number of Muslim countries (e.g., in Pakistan) is the murder of women by their husbands. These so-called "honor-killings" are, in fact, extremely dishonorable and are frequently used to camouflage other kinds of crimes.

Female children are discriminated against from the moment of birth, for it is customary in Muslim societies to regard a son as a gift, and a daughter as

---

11 For example, R. A. Jullundhri, "Human Rights in Islam," in *Understanding Human Rights*, ed. A. D. Falconer. Dublin: Irish School of Ecumenics, 1980.
12 For example, A. A. Maududi, *Human Rights in Islam*. Lahore, Pakistan: Islamic Publications, 1977.

a trial, from God. Therefore, the birth of a son is an occasion for celebration while the birth of a daughter calls for commiseration, if not lamentation. Many girls are married when they are still minors, even though marriage in Islam is a contract and presupposes that the contracting parties are both consenting adults. Even though so much Qur'anic legislation is aimed at protecting the rights of women in the context of marriage,[13] women cannot claim equality with their husbands. The husband, in fact, is regarded as his wife's gateway to heaven or hell and the arbiter of her final destiny. That such an idea can exist within the framework of Islam—which, in theory, rejects the idea of there being any intermediary between a believer and God—represents both a profound irony and a great tragedy.

Although the Qur'an presents the idea of what we today call a "no-fault" divorce and does not make any adverse judgments about divorce,[14] Muslim societies have made divorce extremely difficult for women, both legally and through social penalties. Although the Qur'an states clearly that the divorced parents of a minor child must decide by mutual consultation how the child is to be raised and that they must not use the child to hurt or exploit each other,[15] in most Muslim societies, women are deprived both of their sons (generally at age 7) and their daughters (generally at age 12). It is difficult to imagine an act of greater cruelty than depriving a mother of her children simply because she is divorced. Although polygamy was intended by the Qur'an to be for the protection of orphans and widows,[16] in practice Muslims have made it the Sword of Damocles which keeps women under constant threat. Although the Qur'an gave women the right to receive an inheritance not only on the death of a close relative, but also to receive other bequests or gifts during the lifetime of a benevolent caretaker, Muslim societies have disapproved greatly of the idea of giving wealth to a woman in preference to a man, even when her need or circumstances warrant it. Although the purpose of the Qur'anic legislation dealing with women's dress and conduct[17] was to make it safe for women to go about their daily business (since they have the right to engage in gainful activity as witnessed by Surah 4: An-Nisa':32 without fear of sexual harassment or molestation), Muslim societies have put many of them behind veils and shrouds and locked doors on the pretext of protecting their chastity, forgetting that according to the Qur'an,[18] confinement to their homes was not a normal way of life for chaste women but a punishment for "unchastity."

Woman and man, created equal by God and standing equal in the sight of God, have become very unequal in Muslim societies. The Qur'anic

---

13 For instance, see Surah 4: An-Nisa':4, 19; Surah 24: An-Nur:33; Surah 2: Al-Baqarah:187; Surah 9: At-Tawbah:71; Surah 7: Al-A'raf:189; Surah 30: Ar-rum:21.
14 For instance, see Surah 2: Al-Baqarah:231, 241.
15 The reference here is to Surah 2: Al-Baqarah:233.
16 The reference here is to Surah 4: An-Nisa':2–3.
17 For instance, see Surah 24: An-Nur:30–1; Surah 33: Al-Ahzab:59.
18 The reference here is to Surah 4: An-Nisa':15.

description of man and woman in marriage: "They are your garments/ And you are their garments" (Surah 2: Al-Baqarah:187), implies closeness, mutuality, and equality. However, Muslim culture has reduced many, if not most, women to the position of puppets on a string, to slave-like creatures whose only purpose in life is to cater to the needs and pleasures of men. Not only this, it has also had the audacity and the arrogance to deny women direct access to God. It is one of Islam's cardinal beliefs that each person— man or woman—is responsible and accountable for his or her individual actions. How, then, can the husband become the wife's gateway to heaven or hell? How, then, can he become the arbiter not only of what happens to her in this world but also of her ultimate destiny? Such questions are now being articulated by an increasing number of Muslim women and they are bound to threaten the existing balance of power in the domain of family relationships in most Muslim societies.

However, despite everything that has gone wrong with the lives of countless Muslim women down the ages due to patriarchal Muslim culture, there is hope for the future. There are indications from across the world of Islam that a growing number of Muslims are beginning to reflect seriously upon the teachings of the Qur'an as they become disenchanted with capitalism, communism, and western democracy. As this reflection deepens, it is likely to lead to the realization that the supreme task entrusted to human beings by God, of being God's deputies on earth, can only be accomplished by establishing justice which the Qur'an regards as a prerequisite for authentic peace. Without the elimination of the inequities, inequalities, and injustices that pervade the personal and collective lives of human beings, it is not possible to talk about peace in Qur'anic terms. Here, it is of importance to note that there is more Qur'anic legislation pertaining to the establishment of justice in the context of family relationships than on any other subject. This points to the assumption implicit in much Qur'anic learning, namely, that if human beings can learn to order their homes justly so that the human rights of all within its jurisdiction—children, women, and men—are safeguarded, then they can also order their society and the world at large justly. In other words, the Qur'an regards the home as a microcosm of the Ummah and the world community, and emphasizes the importance of making it "the abode of peace" through just living.

SOURCE: Excerpted from Riffat Hassan, "Are Human Rights Compatible with Islam?" <http://religiousconsultation.org/hassan2.htm>

Islamic Governance by Ayatollah Khomeini

Arguments in favor of running governments according to Shari'ah, traditional Islamic law, were advanced in the twentieth century by the cleric Ayatollah Khomeini (c. 1900–89) in Iran. After helping to overthrow the Shah of Iran in 1979, he became the "guardian" or Supreme Leader of Iran and tried to export his Islamist revolution to other Shi'ite areas.

The wisdom of the Creator has decreed that men should live in accordance with justice and act within the limits set by divine law. This wisdom is eternal and immutable, and constitutes one of the norms of God Almighty. Today and always, therefore, the existence of a holder of authority, a ruler who acts as trustee and maintains the institutions and laws of Islam, is a necessity—a ruler who prevents cruelty, oppression, and violation of the rights of others; who is a trustworthy and vigilant guardian of God's creatures; who guides men to the teachings, doctrines, laws and institutions of Islam; and who prevents the undesirable changes that atheists and the enemies of religion wish to introduce in the laws and institutions of Islam. ...

If the ordinances of Islam are to remain in effect, then, if encroachment by oppressive ruling classes on the rights of the weak is to be prevented, if ruling minorities are not to be permitted to plunder and corrupt the people for the sake of pleasure and material interest, if the Islamic order is to be preserved and all individuals are to pursue the just path of Islam without any deviation, if innovation and the approval of anti-Islamic laws by sham parliaments are to be prevented, if the influence of foreign powers in the Islamic lands is to be destroyed—government is necessary. None of these aims can be achieved without government and the organs of the state. It is a righteous government, of course, that is needed, one presided over by a ruler who will be a trustworthy and righteous trustee. Those who presently govern us are of no use at all for they are tyrannical, corrupt, and highly incompetent.

In the past we did not act in concern and unanimity in order to establish proper government and overthrow treacherous and corrupt rulers. Some people were apathetic and reluctant even to discuss the theory of Islamic government, and some went so far as to praise oppressive rulers. It is for this reason that we find ourselves in the present state. The influence and sovereignty of Islam in society have declined; the nation of Islam has fallen victim to division and weakness; the laws of Islam have remained in abeyance and been subjected to change and modification; and the imperialists have propagated foreign laws and alien culture among the Muslims through their agents for the sake of their evil purposes, causing people to be infatuated with the West. It was our lack of a leader, a guardian, and our lack of institutions of leadership that made all this possible. We need righteous and proper organs of government; that much is self-evident.

SOURCE: Imam Khomeini, *Islam and Revolution: Writings and Declarations of Imam Khomeini*, trans. Hamid Algar. Berkeley, CA: Mizan Press, 1981, pp. 53–4

Rules Concerning the Aspect of War in Jihad   by Hamza Aktan

According to most contemporary scholars, Islam has no tradition that can condone acts of terror and suicide attacks. The following analysis by the Turkish scholar Hamza Aktan looks at traditional restrictions on the conduct of war.

The rules concerning the aspect of jihad that is concerned with war in Islam can be summarized under the following headings that are based on the Sunna of the Prophet and taken in the light of the Qur'an:

1. Treating the enemy with mercy

The Prophet never intended to crush the enemy, neither physically nor psychologically, under any circumstances, even in a time of war. We have learned from the Prophet that we have to show mercy to people when they are in a state that invokes our mercy and that calls for our pity, even if these people are our enemies. In AH 8 (629), in the month of Shawwal in the lunar calendar, the Prophet sent Khalid ibn Walid to fight the tribe of the Bani Jazima with a force of 300 men. He told Khalid ibn Walid not to wage war against them unless they were attacked first. When the Bani Jazima saw the forces of Khalid ibn Walid, they took up arms. During battle, a young man from a good family was killed in front of the woman he loved by the Muslim forces. The woman collapsed upon the man and she sobbed twice. Her heart stopped beating due to the deep sorrow she felt and she died, holding the dead man. This incident was later recounted to the Prophet. The Prophet was saddened and he said, "Was there no one who had mercy among you?" When he was informed that Khalid had killed some of the prisoners of war he raised his two hands to the sky and pleaded, "Dear God! I swear to you that I am in no way involved in what Khalid has done. I did not order him to do so!" (Ibn Kathir 1976, 3/591). …

2. The ban on torture

The Prophet did not allow the enemy to be tortured in any way. Suhayl ibn 'Amr was one of the prominent individuals of Makkan pagans. He was among those who had insulted and oppressed the Prophet before his Emigration to Madina. He was taken as a prisoner of war in the Battle of Badr. At one point he tried to escape, but was caught and taken back. Suhayl was a good speaker. He was capable of influencing people with his words. 'Umar said to the Prophet: "O, Messenger of God! Allow me to take out his two front teeth so that he will not be able to speak against you again." To which the Prophet replied: "No, I will not have him tortured. If I did, God would punish me. Moreover, we should always have the hope that one day he will act in a way that will not seem unsympathetic to you." Indeed, after the death of the Prophet, when there were cases of apostasy in Makka, Suhayl ibn 'Amr called out to the Makkans, "O, Makkans! You were the last to accept the religion of God. Do not let yourselves be among the first to leave it." and thus prevented many people of Makka from leaving Islam. …

3. Respecting the enemy's dead

Pagans at the time of the Prophet had the habit of mutilating the bodies of the people they killed in battle, and disemboweling them for revenge. This act was known as *musla*. When the Prophet saw the disemboweled and defiled body of his uncle Hamza during the Battle of Uhud, he was deeply saddened. He said, "If God allows me victory, I will do the same to thirty pagans in return for what they have done to Hamza." Upon this the following verse was revealed:

> And if you have to respond to any wrong, respond to the extent done to you; but if you endure patiently this is indeed better for he who endures. (Nahl 16:126).

The Prophet renounced his oath and paid the appropriate amount for atonement as set down by Islamic law. To Abu Qatada, enraged by the *musla* carried out on Hamza and who was about to perform the same to the bodies of the pagans, the Prophet said: "Sit down! Wish for the reward you will get from God! The dead of the Qurayshi pagans are entrusted to our care … Would you rather your name was remembered with what you did and resented along with what they have done?" …

4. Not attacking civilians and innocent targets

The fact that the Prophet warned his friends and followers many times about sparing the lives of those who were not involved in a war has often been cited in the literature of both *tabaqat* [books which study contemporaneous scholars] and *maghazi* [books on the military campaigns of the Prophet].

After the conquest of Makka, and the Quraysh's submission to Islam, the Hawazin, especially Bani Hanifa, who regarded themselves as the greatest tribe after Quraysh, called for war against Muslims, and they were supported by the tribe of Thaqif. At the end of the battle which was joined at Hunayn, the Prophet saw the body of a dead woman among the dead of the pagans. "What is this that I see?" he asked. Those who were present answered: "This is a woman, killed by the forces of Khalid bin Walid." The Prophet said to one of them, "Run to Khalid! Tell him that the Messenger of God forbids him to kill children, women, and servants." One of those present said, "Dear Messenger of God! But are they not the children of the pagans?" The Prophet answered: "Were not the best of you, too, once the children of pagans? All children are born with their true nature and are innocent." …

5. Not targeting Muslims

Having established that it is forbidden to kill innocent non-Muslims, even during war, it is inconceivable to think that it would be permissible to kill innocent Muslims under any circumstances. Whether Muslims can fire against the enemy who are shielding themselves with Muslim captives is still a topic of debate among scholars of Islamic law—even if not shooting means defeat and the utmost care is taken not to hit the Muslim captives. …

6. Acting within the hierarchy of order and command

Another very important principle concerning the aspect of war in jihad is to act according to a centralized plan accepted by all Muslims. If individuals or groups should act without taking orders from a central authority, if they should act according to their own discretion, the fact that they are not responsible to anyone for their actions will result in chaos. Even if central authority has been lost, this cannot justify acting in a disparate or irresponsible manner. Chaos cannot possibly be condoned in the name of jihad. In these situations, it is highly probable that any movement will degenerate, become diverted from its original goal, and cause more harm than good.

In the Age of Happiness, no act of jihad, in terms of armed struggle, occurred without the Prophet's order or permission. There have only ever been a few incidents of this kind where conflicts arose due to misunderstanding. These incidents grieved the Prophet, and their perpetrators were warned. He chided 'Abd Allah ibn Jahsh for doing something that he was not ordered to do; Khalid ibn Walid was warned against killing women and children; 'Amr ibn Umayya paid the blood money of the Muslims that he killed. ...

7. Humanitarian aid to the enemy

Jihad does not always mean that the enemy must be harmed. Helping the enemy in moments of dire need is within the scope of jihad. Such behavior can also lessen enmity, and break down the resolve of the enemy.

In the years of draught and famine in Makka after the Muslims left for Madina, the Prophet sent gold to Makka so that they could buy wheat, dates, and animal feed; these contributions helped them to make up the cash shortage. Even though the leading pagans of the Quraysh, like Umayya ibn Halaf and Safwan ibn Umayya, did not want to accept this aid, Abu Sufyan voiced his gratitude in the following manner: "May God reward the son of my brother with favors, for he has taken into consideration the dues of kinship" (Köksai 1981, 14/304). ...

8. War as the last resort

Using force in the context of jihad is not always the right thing to do. The fact that armed conflict was not allowed until the Battle of Badr attests to this fact. In the second 'Aqaba Pledge, which took place three months before the Prophet's emigration to Madina, Abbas ibn Ubada said, "O, the Prophet of God! I swear by God who sent you with the true faith and the Book, if you should ask me, we shall put all the people in Mina to the sword." Although the Prophet had suffered at the hands of the people of Makka who came to 'Aqaba for the fair, he answered: "This is not what we have been ordered to do; now return to your goods." This should be sufficient to make it clear that the response to oppression, insult, and torture need not always be crude force. ...

The Prophet abandoned the siege of Taif, which promised to be a long one, to prevent the deaths of women and children, who would be at the receiving end of the blind shots of the catapults; he wanted to prevent many deaths on both sides. This was a wise policy and strategy that allowed for the goal to be reached with no battle being engaged; the result was that the people of Taif—people who realized their homeland had become an isolated island of unbelievers in the Arabian peninsula—came to Madina before the end of the same year, saying that they had converted to Islam.

In short, the acts of those who kill civilians, women, children and the elderly on crowded streets of our cities, those who burn or bomb vehicles and buildings, those who torture and kill people that they have kidnapped or taken as hostage, the acts of suicide bombers who kill themselves and innocent people with explosives placed on their persons or in automobiles— all of these acts, for which no legal authority is responsible—cannot be seen as being jihad and these people cannot be seen as being *mujahids*. There is no foundation for these acts in either the Qur'an or the Sunna. What is important is the structure and character of a thing; it does not matter what people call it. There is no way that Muslims could have come up with such a bloody and contaminated form of struggle in order to make their voices heard. Rather, this is a method that was principally adopted by non-Muslim anarchist terrorist groups. These acts have not helped Muslims in any way to date. On the contrary, they have destroyed the good image of Islam—an image which is founded on science and knowledge, rights and justice, love and peace. At the same time, these acts have led people to postulate a connection between Islam, Muslims, and terrorism. These actions, known as jihad, have done more harm to Islam than anything else could have done.

SOURCE: Hamza Aktan, "Acts of Terror and Suicide Attacks in the Light of the Qur'an and the Sunna," in Ergun Capan, ed., *Terror and Suicide Attacks: An Islamic Perspective*. Somerset, NJ: The Light, 2006, pp. 29–42

Jihad and Just War   by James Turner Johnson

Osama bin Laden claimed to be basing his terrorist campaign on Muslim tradition. James Turner Johnson, Professor of Religion at Rutgers University, analyzes this claim in historic context.

In February 1998, long before the September 11 terrorist attacks on America, Osama bin Laden and four other leaders of radical Islamist groups in various countries issued a **fatwa**, or religious ruling, calling for jihad against "the crusader–Zionist alliance" in the following language:

In compliance with God's order, we issue the following fatwa to all Muslims: the ruling to kill the Americans and their allies—civilians and military—is an individual duty for every Muslim who can do it in any country in which it is possible to do it, in order to liberate the al-Aqsa Mosque [Jerusalem] and the holy mosque [Mecca] from their grip, and in order for their armies to move out of the lands of Islam. ... This is in accordance with the words of Almighty God, "and fight the pagans all together as they fight you all together," and "fight them until there is no more tumult or oppression, and there prevail justice and faith in God."

While more examples of bin Laden's thinking emerged after the September 11 attacks, this fatwa stands as a fundamental statement of his rationale for a campaign of violence against America and the West: an appeal to the Islamic tradition of defensive jihad by which every Muslim is obligated, as an individual duty, to take up arms against invaders. It lays out the justification not only for the attacks of September 11 but also for other terrorist attacks linked to bin Laden's al-Qaeda group. ... It also provides a warrant for future attacks by "every Muslim who can do it in any country in which it is possible to do it" —in short, for a continuing war by terrorist and other means by Muslims against "Americans and their allies," an ongoing clash of civilizations. How should this call be understood in relation to the Islamic tradition? And how does it compare to the just war tradition of Western culture?

The classical Islamic conception of jihad in the sense of warfare comes not from the Qur'an directly, where the term jihad is used to refer to the believer's inner struggle for righteousness, but from the jurists of the early Abbasid period (the late eighth and early ninth centuries A.D.), who developed it in the context of a general effort to clarify the nature of the Islamic community, the proper leadership of that community, and the community's relations with the non-Islamic world. Central to this conception was a legal division of the world into two realms: the *dar al-Islam* or abode of Islam, and the remainder of the world, defined as the *dar al-harb* or abode of war.

The *dar al-Islam*, as the jurists understood it, had existed since its creation by the Prophet Muhammad himself, who had been its first head. It is a community at once religious and political, and thus its ruler, like the Prophet, was understood to be supreme in both spheres. There could be at any time only one right ruler, understood to be the successor of the Prophet and inheritor of his authority. Because of its character—its essential unity, its rule by a successor of the Prophet, its governance according to divinely given law—the *dar al-Islam* is fundamentally different from the rest of the world, which is torn by perpetual conflict and is a constant threat to the peace of the *dar al-Islam*. A general, lasting, universal peace is impossible until the *dar al-harb* is no more, when the whole world has become the *dar al-Islam*, a place within which submission (*islam*) to God is the law of the land. Until then war between the two realms is the normal state. Yet at the same time extended periods of peace are possible by means of treaties between the *dar al-Islam* and non-Islamic societies.

This conception formed the background for the jurists' conception of the idea of jihad as warfare. As they described it, this warfare could take two forms: that of the *dar al-Islam* as a body under the authority of its legitimate ruler, the caliph for the Sunni tradition, the imam for the Shiite—a conception that encompassed offensive war against the general threat and organized collective defense against attack—and an emergency form of defensive jihad against a direct attack on the *dar al-Islam* by a force from some part of the *dar al-harb*. In the former case the duty to take part in jihad was conceived as a collective one, with some Muslims fighting and others playing other roles, including simply going about their normal lives;

in the latter case, though, to fight was an individual duty, incumbent on all Muslims who were able to do so in the immediate area of the aggression.

These were significantly different forms of warfare. The collective jihad was a thoroughly rule-governed activity, from the requirement of the caliph/ imam's authority to that of a declaration of hostilities and a call for peace to a form of combatant–noncombatant distinction to extensive discussion of the disposition of spoils by the ruling authority. The jurists clearly understood this as the norm for the warfare of the *dar al-Islam*. This form of jihad drew upon the religious unity of the Islamic community even as it depended on the social and institutional relationships that comprised the Islamic state; the proper exercise of jihad on this model strengthened the *dar al-Islam* and the role of its ruler both religiously and politically.

The jihad of emergency defense was another matter entirely. It assumed an acute emergency in which normal religiously and socially prescribed relationships and structures were erased. The model the jurists had in mind was simple: a direct attack across the border of the *dar al-Islam* by a force from the *dar al-harb* in some particular place remote from the *dar al-Islam*'s center of authority and power. Against this attack Muslims in the area were to rise up in arms, on their own authority, as a kind of *levée en masse*. The individual duty to take up arms crossed and eliminated all the usual divisions: not only healthy men of fighting age but women, children, the aged, and the infirm were to fight to the limit of their ability to do so. Correspondingly, the rules of collective jihad did not apply: the enemy was the invading army, so noncombatants were not present and thus played no part in the conflict. While the jurists admitted this form of jihad in time of dire emergency caused by overt aggression, there was an inherent tension between it and the collective jihad of the *dar al-Islam* under the authority of the caliph/imam. In practical terms, local leaders on the frontiers might (and did) use the excuse of the jihad of emergency to challenge the legitimacy of the central authority. However, this form of jihad was originally meant to be an exceptional response to an exceptional circumstance, not the norm for Muslim warfare.

It is generally agreed within Islam that jihad of the first sort is impossible today, as there is no central caliph or imam. This gives new importance to what was originally considered to be an exceptional case: the idea of jihad as an individual duty in the face of external aggression. In the Islamic mainstream this conception has developed along lines compatible with international law to allow Muslim heads of state to organize and execute defense collectively, though on the juristic model they do so on the basis of the individual responsibility of all their people to respond to aggression. The historical model for such action is the medieval hero Saladin, who though only a regional commander (not the caliph) organized and led a successful defense against the armies of the second Crusade. In theory, this mainstream conception of defense respects the patterns of relationships within the society as well as the limits to be observed in fighting, the most important of which are understood to come from the Prophet Muhammad himself.

However, the last hundred years or so have seen the development of another line of interpretation of jihad. First appearing in North Africa as an ideology for resistance against colonialism, by 1960 it was being used as a justification for terrorist attacks against Israel, and in the 1970s and 1980s it was adapted to justify armed struggle by terror and assassination in such states as Iran, Egypt, and Algeria against rulers who were nominally Muslim but were judged to be tools of the West. It is out of this tradition that bin Laden's fatwa has emerged.

This radical form of jihad makes several critical assumptions not found in the traditional conception or in the mainstream theory. First, the *dar al-Islam* is conceived as any territory whose population is mainly Muslim and which was once part of the historical *dar al-Islam*. By this reasoning any non-Islamic state existing within the territory of the historical *dar al-Islam*, as well as all non-Islamic presence within that space, must be resisted and subdued or eliminated. Further, the "aggressors" are deemed to be all those who support such states or non-Islamic presence, so that the usual lines of distinction between combatants and noncombatants are erased, with the result that all individuals are considered acceptable targets. Further, because of its origins in an "emergency," there are no limits on means in this struggle. Finally, all Muslims are faced with the duty to take part in this struggle, so that it ultimately becomes one involving individuals rather than politically organized communities; anyone who accepts this duty—men of fighting age, women, children, or the aged or infirm—becomes a combatant in the war

This extreme interpretation of the idea of defensive jihad implicitly rejects much of the actual history of Muslim societies and the Muslim faith. It leaves scant room for toleration of "people of the book," as prescribed in the Qur'an, because it treats the simple presence of Christians and Jews in dominantly Muslim societies as an act of aggression. It also leaves no room for differences of interpretation as to what Islam requires; its reading of Islamic law is narrow and unyielding on doctrine and behavior alike. Social developments identified with modernity are rejected as un-Islamic, even if large numbers of Muslims have accepted them without losing their faith.

Bin Laden's fatwa reflects all these assumptions. The United States is deemed an aggressor against all Islam because of the presence of U.S. troops in Saudi Arabia, despite the fact that they are there by agreement, and despite the fact that their purpose is to protect Saudi Arabia, not to dominate it. Likewise, the "protracted blockade" against Iraq is viewed as an assault on the Iraqi people, despite the fact that Saddam Hussein's diversion of resources for his own purposes is the real cause of their suffering. The same could be said of bin Laden's hostility to U.S. support for "the Jews' petty state" and "its occupation of Jerusalem and murder of Muslims." In other words, the United States has become the embodiment of the *dar al-harb*, engaged in aggression against Islam, despite the fact that millions of Muslims live and enjoy freedom of religion within its borders. But bin Laden's fatwa takes the radical line of jihad to new extremes when it calls for any and all Muslims to kill any and all Americans—"civilians and military" alike—"in any country in which it is possible to do it." No longer a defensive war, this is jihad on the offensive.

Bin Laden and his associates in the fatwa of course lack the religiously mandated authority to wage such war, as they do not bear the mantle of succession to the Prophet. That is why they try to describe the war against America as a defensive one. By painting the entire nation of America as guilty of "aggression," the fatwa can set aside the limits imposed on warfare by normative Islamic tradition, which includes no direct, intended killing of noncombatants and no use of fire, which is prohibited among Muslims because it is the weapon God will use in the last days. Bin Laden's jihad not only pits Islam against America, the West as a whole, and ultimately the rest of the non-Islamic world; it also seeks to overthrow the contemporary Muslim states and mainstream views of Islamic tradition among the great majority of contemporary Muslims.

To be sure, the early Abbasid jurists also thought the relation of the Islamic and non-Islamic worlds to be one of inherent conflict, and their notion of the collective warfare aimed at ensuring the eventual submission of the entire world to God reflected this. Yet they never defined this eschatological goal as one that could be achieved only by war or even primarily by war. And in the absence of any universal Muslim ruler bearing the mantle of authority of the Prophet, Muslim tradition and Muslim life have found ways of pursuing this goal by other, nonmilitary means. The radical ideology of jihad changes this, making the use of violent means, indiscriminately and without principled limits, a binding obligation for all Muslims.

While the idea of just war is deeply rooted in Western culture, it is perhaps more strongly institutionalized today in international law, in American military doctrine and practice, and even in political culture than at any time since the age of Victoria. Though the just war tradition has important Christian roots, it differs from the Islamic juristic tradition in that it can be employed without explicitly religious premises. Similarly, in Western political thought and theology more generally, the nature of the political community, the role of government, and the use of armed force are conceived in secular rather than religious terms. All these features differentiate just war tradition from the juristic tradition of jihad by the *dar al-Islam* on the authority of the caliph/imam.

Yet there are also significant points of contact, which reveal important common interests. I have already suggested this by noting that mainstream Islamic thought and political practice have developed in a way compatible with international law and orderly, peaceful interaction with non-Muslim nations. More specifically, both traditions link the right to use armed force to the exercise of legitimate governing authority for the protection and common good of the governed community. That common good, moreover, is defined normatively in terms of high ideals of value and behavior, not in terms of repression and intolerance. Both traditions recognize that even the use of force justified in this way is not without limits when it comes to the question of who may be targeted and the means that may be used against aggressors. These are all matters on which there can and should be a pursuit of common cause. The radical doctrine of jihad advanced as the justification for contemporary terrorism is a challenge to both of these traditions, and people of good will from both communities have reason to reject it.

SOURCE: James Turner Johnson, "Jihad and Just War," from *First Things* 124 (June/July 2002): 12–14. Used by permission of First Things: www.firstthings.com <http://www.leaderu.com/ftissues/ft0206/opinion/johnson.html>

GLOSSARY

'A'isha Muhammad's youngest wife, who was the source of many Hadith.

Allah The most inclusive form of God.

Fatiha The first Sura of the Qur'an.

Fatwa Legal opinion by an authority in a school of Islamic law.

Hadith A traditional report about the Prophet's sayings or actions.

Hajj The holy pilgrimage to Mecca, taken at least once in a lifetime if affordable.

Hijrah (or **Heqira**) The journey of the Prophet from Mecca to Medina in 622 CE.

Imam A Muslim prayer leader, and a Shi'ite religious leader.

Islamism Movement for establishment of Muslim states governed by Shari'ah.

Jihad The Muslim term for struggle, with two meanings: an inner struggle against evil, and an outer struggle for a Muslim social order.

Khadija Muhammad's first wife, who supported him when he received prophecies.

Mecca The holy city of Islam whose Ka'ba is the goal of Hajj pilgrimages.

Medina City where organized Islam began.

Monism The philosophy that ultimately only one substance exists underneath the multiplicity of appearances.

Mosque Sacred building for Muslim worship, usually an open-roofed rectangle with towers (minarets) for calling to prayer.

Night Journey Muhammad's visionary journey to Jerusalem and up through seven heavens to Allah to receive revelations.

Rak'ah Unit of prayer.

Shari'ah The divine law, as interpreted by judges, based on Qur'an and Hadith.

Shi'a Minority branch of Islam, believing in a series of imams as successors to the Prophet.

Sufi Muslim mystical tradition; some say Islamic only, some say universal.

Sunni Majority branch of Islam, in which successors to the Prophet were to be chosen by the Muslim community.

Sura A chapter in the Qur'an.

Ulama Educated clerics who are considered authorities in matters of Islamic law and theology.

Ummah The Muslim community as a whole.

HOLY DAYS

Friday Mosque worship

10th of Muharram New Year

12th of Rabi'al-Awwai The Prophet's Birthday

27th of Rajab Muhammad's Ascension

Ramadan Month of Fasting

27th of Ramadan Night of Power

1st of Shawwal Breaking of the Fast; Pilgrimage Season

Dhu al-Qa'da Pilgrimage season

8th–13th of Dhu al-Hihha Hajj: Pilgrimage to Mecca

HISTORICAL OUTLINE

570 CE—birth of Muhammad

c. 610 CE—revelations of Qur'an begin

622 CE—migration from Mecca to Medina (Hijrah)

c. 630 CE—Muhammad converts southern Arabian tribes

632 CE—death of Muhammad; election of Abu Bakr as first caliph

633 CE—spread of Islam begins, expanding to northern Egypt, Palestine, Iran

650 CE—canon of the Qur'an set

691 CE—Dome of the Rock in Jerusalem completed

750 CE—Islam spreads to Spain, southern Russia, Afghanistan

750–1258—Islam reaches its peak under Abbasid caliphs: control of Indonesia, India, Middle East, Egypt, Turkey, Balkans, Spain; much cultural development

by 870 CE—Muhammad Ibn Ismail al-Bukhari writes authoritative Hadith (*Sahih Bukhari*)

by 875 CE—Abu-l-Husayn Muslim writes authoritative Hadith (*Sahih Muslim*)

980–1037—Ibn Sina (Avicenna), major rationalist philosopher

1058–1111—Al-Ghazali, leading mystical philosopher

1126–98—Ibn Rushd (Averroes), important philosopher of "two truths"—revelation and reason

1165–1240—Ibn 'Arabi, influential mystical philosopher

1171—Salah-al-Din recaptures Jerusalem from Crusaders

1300–1400s—Christians fight to retake Spain using Inquisition

1453—Turks conquer Constantinople, renaming it Istanbul

1556—Akbar becomes the Muslim Mughal emperor in India

1800–1900s—many Muslim colonies come under European control

1947—Muslim-majority Pakistan separates from Hindu-majority India

1970s—oil-wealthy Muslim nations start OPEC; Muslim resurgence begins

2001—September 11 attacks in United States

2003—United States and allies invade Iraq

2011—Pro-democracy movements begin in Arab countries

2011—Osama bin Laden killed by U.S. commandos

REVIEW QUESTIONS

1   Based on the readings, what kind of society did Muhammad encounter?
2   What views of women, children, and divorce does the Qur'an teach?
3   Describe how three major Islamic philosophers saw the relation between reason and revelation.
4   What is Sufism? Describe the thoughts of three major Sufis.

DISCUSSION QUESTIONS

1   Why do you think that of all possibilities, "submission" is the major theme of Islam? What various forms does it take?
2   Do you think that Islam promotes violence more or less than any other religion?
3   How has Islam shaped its place in geography and history, and how has it been shaped by these factors?

INFORMATION RESOURCES

Ahmed, Leila. *Women and Gender in Islam*. New Haven, CT: Yale University Press, 1992.

Ask, Karen, and **Marit Tjomsland**, eds. *What is Islam*? New York: Oxford University Press, 1998.

Athar, Shahid. *What is Islam*? <www.islam-usa.com>

Bayat, Mojedh, and **Mohammad Ali Jamnia**. *Tales from the Land of the Sufis*. Boston and London: Shambhala, 1994.

Beck, Lois, and **Nikki Deddie**, eds. *Women in the Muslim World*. Cambridge, MA: Harvard University Press, 1982.

Capan, Ergun, ed. *An Islamic Perspective: Terror and Suicide Attacks*. Somerset, NJ: The Light, 2006.

Delong-Bas, Natana J. *Wahhabi Islam: From Revival and Reform to Global Jihad*. Oxford and New York: Oxford University Press, 2004.

El Fadl, Khaled Abou. *Speaking in God's Name: Islamic Law, Authority and Women*. Oxford: OneWorld Publications, 2001.

Ernst, Carl W. *The Shambhala Guide to Sufism*. Boston and London: Shambhala, 1997.

Fakhry, Majid. *A History of Islamic Philosophy*. 3rd ed. New York: Columbia University Press, 2004.

Holy Qur'an English translation <http://www.quran4u.com/quran_english_yep.htm>

Jomier, Jacques. *How to Understand Islam*. New York: Crossroad, 1991.

Lawrence, Bruce B. *Defenders of God: The Fundamentalist Revolt Against the Modern Age*. San Francisco: Harper and Row, 1989.

Martin, Richard C. *Islamic Studies: A History of Religions Approach*. Upper Saddle River, NJ: Prentice-Hall, 1982/1996.

Mevlevi Order <http://www.hayatidede.org>

Mosques <http://www.sacred-destinations.com/categories/mosques>

Nasr, Seyyed Hossein. *Ideals and Realities of Islam*. London: George Allen and Unwin/Harper, 1966.

Rahman, Fazlur, *et al.* "Islam," in *Encyclopedia of Religion*, ed. Lindsay Jones. 2nd ed. Vol. 7, pp. 4560–726. New York: Macmillan, 2005.

Ruthven, Malise. *Islam: A Very Short Introduction*. Oxford and New York: Oxford University Press, 2001.

———. *Islam in the World*, 3rd edition. Oxford and New York: Oxford University Press, 2006.

Schimmel, Annemarie. *Islam: An Introduction*. Albany, NY: State University of New York Press, 1992.

Shah, Idries. *The Way of the Sufi*. New York: Dutton, 1970.

Sijzi, Amir Hasan. *Nizam Ad-Din Awliya: Morals for the Heart*, trans. Bruce B. Lawrence. New York: Paulist Press, 1992.

Stern, S. M., **Albert Hourani**, and **Vivian Brown**, eds. *Islamic Philosophy and the Classical Tradition*. Columbia, SC: University of South Carolina Press, 1972.

Wadud-Muhsin, Amina. *Qur'an and Woman*. Kuala Lumpur: Penerbit Fajar Bakti Sdn. Bhd, 1992.

CHAPTER 11

SIKHISM

ੴ

From 1469 to 1708, not one but a continuous series of ten prophets appeared in North India, developing a tradition that has come to be known as Sikhism. In the Punjabi language of the founders, *sikh* means "student." And according to contemporary understanding of the religion, those who are known as Sikhs are students not only of the Ten Sikh **Gurus** but also of the founders and saints of other traditions. Even more so, Sikhs are those who love God, try to remember God in everyday life, and attempt to serve God in the world.

The first of the Sikh Gurus became known as Guru Nanak (1469–1539). He was born into a Hindu family but in his eleventh year, when the time came for him to be invested with the traditional sacred thread, he refused. He explained in inspired verse that the thread would wear out, in contrast to eternal spiritual virtues which should be inwardly cultivated. This preference for inward transformation and closeness to God rather than outward rituals is evident in many stories told about his life. Guru Nanak spent much of his adult life on long journeys, preaching to Hindus and Muslims alike about spiritual truth. During his last 20 years, he developed a unique village in which land was owned in common, people pooled their labor, and the food was offered to everyone freely in a **langar**—a communal kitchen. He praised women, cut through the caste system, and declared manual work holy, thereby challenging prejudices that had developed within Hindu society. He offered a straightforward path to God-realization: work hard to support yourself by honest means, share with others, and always recite the Name of God.

The mystical teachings, new social order, and practicality of Guru Nanak's path were continued and developed by his nine successors. Their spiritual power and the devotion of their followers were construed as threatening by the Mughal rulers, as well as the Hindu hill chiefs, and from time to time the Gurus and their Sikhs had to face armed attacks. The saintly Fifth and Ninth Gurus were martyred. Ultimately, the powerful Guru Gobind Singh (1666–1708), tenth of the Sikh masters, transformed his intimidated people into **Khalsa**, extraordinarily courageous warrior-saints pledged to protect people of all religions and castes from oppression. Sacrificing his entire family and ultimately himself, Guru Gobind Singh instructed his followers thenceforth to regard as their master the sacred scriptures compiled by the Gurus: the **Guru Granth Sahib**.

Guru Nanak at Mecca

Many stories are told about miracles said to have occurred in the Gurus' lives. This one concerns Guru Nanak's journey to Mecca, the holy city to which only Muslims are allowed to travel.

The Guru after a fairly long sojourn at Kapurthala started for Mecca and joined a party of faqirs.[1] The Guru wore a long yellow robe on which were impressed some words and carried a staff such as a Haji[2] carried.

The faqirs watched him and one day asked, "What is your religion?"

"I belong to the religion of those who follow the path of God," replied the Guru.

The faqirs pressed him to confess that he was a Muslim but the Guru refused to do so. The faqirs were greatly troubled. They were not sure whether they were right in having with them a man who was an infidel. The Guru read their hearts and disappeared from amongst them with his two attendants. They noticed that a cloud that used to protect them from the scorching rays of the sun also disappeared with him.

The faqirs thought that travelling by himself he would never reach Mecca. They were astonished when they found that the Guru had already arrived with his two attendants. They were even more puzzled when they were told that the Guru had been there for several days. They were convinced that he was some great soul and begged him to forgive them for their suspicions about him.

The keeper of the Kaaba[3] one night discovered that he was sleeping with his feet towards the Kaaba. It was time for prayers so he informed the priest that a pilgrim was committing a great sacrilege by turning his feet towards the house of God. The priest in high dudgeon rushed to where the Guru was sleeping.

"Wake up, you stupid fool," he exclaimed, "and rub your face on the ground and beg to be forgiven for turning your feet towards the house of God."

The Guru did not move, but said, "Turn my feet towards the place where God does not dwell."

The priest could no more control himself and ordered the keeper to take him by the feet and turn him right about in the other direction. The door keeper obeyed but whichever direction they turned the Guru's feet they say that the Kaaba turned with them. The priest stood spell-bound. He saw that the house of God was in all directions.

The Guru rose and looked at the priest with eyes full of compassion. "Your eyes have been opened just for a moment," he said. "Don't forget what you have seen. The entire space is nothing but God's dwelling place."

SOURCE: Jogendra Singh and Daljit Singh, *The Great Humanist Guru Nanak*. Patiala, Punjab: Languages Department Punjab, 1970, pp. 52–3

1 Faqir—Muslim ascetic.
2 Haji—a pilgrim to Mecca.
3 Kaaba—the revered central cubic stone structure of the great mosque in Mecca.

Daily prayers

Traditional Sikhs spend several hours each day in reciting prayers composed under inspiration by the Gurus, in addition to trying always to recite the Name of God inwardly. The day begins early in the morning with prayer and recitation of five hymns. Another long prayer is recited at dusk, and another at bedtime. Repeated recitation of the prayers is a way of training the mind in thinking spiritually, and of increasing one's faith in and awareness of God. Excerpts from two of these prayers are offered here.

JapJi Sahib by Guru Nanak

JapJi (a title based on the verb meaning "to recite") sets forth the essence of Sikh philosophy. It is the first of the morning prayers. Of many translations, this excerpt is from a rare out of print English translation by the great Sikh poet, scientist, and philosopher, Professor Puran Singh (d. 1931).

> He is One. He is the First. He is all that is.
> His name is Truth.
> He is the Creator of all.
> Fearing naught, striking fear in naught;
> His Form, on lands and waters, is Eternity;
> The One Self-existent.
> Through the Grace of His true servant,
> Continually repeat His Name.
>
> He was in the beginning;
> He is through all ages,
> He shall be the One who lives forever.
> Beyond thought, no thinking can conceive Him,
> Not even if the minds of men should think for ages and ages.
> Nor silence can see him,
> Even if the minds of men meditate on Him for ages and ages.
> Nor can He be known by gaining the worlds:
> For man's desire is never satiated,
> Even though all the worlds laden with gold fall to his share.
> Nor human thoughts can carry man far.
> The moments of his mind, the thousand acts of wisdom of the world,
> Leave him dark; nothing avails.
> Vain are the ways of men.
> How then to find Him?
> How then to get rid of the dark pall?
> One way there is,—to make His Will our own.
> No other way, naught else.

SOURCE: Guru Nanak, *JapJi Sahib*, trans. Professor Puran Singh, 4th ed. Lahore, Pakistan: Lahore Book Shop, 1945

Jaap Sahib by Guru Gobind Singh

Jaap Sahib is the second morning prayer. In wave after wave of negative and positive epithets, it paints a vast picture of the Formless God.

> Salutations to the Eternal, Salutations to the Merciful.
> Salutations to the Formless, Salutations to the Peerless. ...
>
> Salutations to the One beyond deeds,
> Salutations to the One beyond creeds.
> Salutations to the One beyond names,
> Salutations to the One beyond any fixed locale.
>
> Salutations to the Unconquerable,
> Salutations to the Fearless.
> Salutations to the Unshakeable,
> Salutations to the Invincible.
>
> Salutations to the One without colour or hue,
> Salutations to the One who hath no beginning.
> Salutations to the One who is impenetrable,
> Salutations to the One who is unfathomable. ...
>
> Salutations to the One who is ever steady,
> Salutations to the One beyond physical elements.
> Salutations to the One who cannot be seen,
> Salutations to the One beyond sorrow or grief. ...
>
> Salutations to the One who hath no caste,
> Salutations to the One who hath no lineage.
> Salutations to the One beyond confines of religions,
> Salutations to the One who is wonderful. ...
>
> Salutations to the Destroyer of all,
> Salutations to the Creator of all.
> Salutations to the Annihilator of all,
> Salutations to the Preserver of all. ...
>
> Salutations to the Lord, immanent everywhere,
> Salutations to the Lord, who pervades everything.
> Salutations to the Lord, manifest in all colours,
> Salutations to the Lord, who destroys everything. ...
>
> O Lord,
> Having Thy domain in all quarters,
> Thou art the Reveller everywhere.
> Self-created, compassionate and auspicious,
> Thou art ever united with everyone.
> Destroyer of bad times,
> Thou art the Embodiment of Compassion.

Ever so close to everyone,
Everlasting is the treasure of Thy glory and power.

SOURCE: Guru Gobind Singh, *Jaap Sahib*, trans. Surendra Nath. Delhi: Gobind Sadan, 1991, rev. 1996, pp. 20–33, 174

Sikh scripture: The Guru Granth Sahib

Sikhs treat their scripture with great reverence. It is a vast collection of mystical devotional poetry—some 5,867 hymns sung in classical musical forms. They were composed by seven of the Sikh Gurus and also by numerous Hindu and Muslim saints of all castes. The overarching theme is devotion to God and inner detachment from worldly concerns. Living by the instructions of the Guru and remembering God's Holy Name are prescribed as antidotes to worldliness. A few selections from this unique inter-religious scripture are given here, after an introduction to the Guru Granth Sahib.

One Reality Is by Nikky Gunninder Kaur Singh

The Guru Granth Sahib, the Sikh holy book, contains no historical narratives, no biographical details and no obligatory rituals. It is a collection of spiritually exalted poetry carrying only intimations. The theme running throughout is that of the individual's longing to experience the Transcendent Reality, moulded into poetic symbolism of great delicacy and beauty.

Granth means "book" and, since the Tenth and last human Guru declared it so in 1708, this collection of poetic revelations by the Sikh Gurus and by Hindu and Muslim saints has been treated by Sikhs as their personal Guru. The epithet *Sahib* is often added to the title as a sign of respect. It is also known as the *Adi Granth* or the "Primal Book." It is the sole visual and aural icon for the Sikhs and main source of their daily prayers. All rites of passage take place in the sound and sight of this text: the new-born baby is named in its presence, the marriage ceremony entails walking around it four times, death in a home is followed by a reading, often continuous, of its 1430 pages. In times of uncertainty and difficulty, or of joy and celebration, different types of recitations are the prescribed religious observance: *saptah* (seven-day), *akhand* (non-stop for forty-eight hours) or *sampat* (one particular hymn repeated after each different hymn). ...

The Guru Granth begins with the Jap, the most famous of the divinely-inspired poems, or *bani* of Guru Nanak (1469–1539 CE), the founder of Sikhism. It is chanted daily by Sikhs and its first line, *Ikk Oan Kar*, literally "One Reality Is," is the cornerstone of the faith. The Guru Granth and the Dasam Granth are an exposition of that One Reality, Its relation with our world, Its relation with each of us personally.

At the core of Guru Nanak's message is the understanding that all forms (*saguna*) are informed by the Formless (*nirguna*). Infinite and formless, the Ultimate Being is inherent within all forms and yet remains transcendent.

Whichever way we turn, we see our Source,
Says Nanak, the One has form, and yet the One is formless.

You are the ocean and all are within You,
Without You, there is no other.

The Gurus use an endless variety of images to evoke our connection
with the Divine Reality: the potter with his clay, the blacksmith with
his anvil, the mother nursing her child, the lady churning her pot of
yogurt, the flowers in the garden, the animals of the earth. The entire
world pulsates with divine potentiality, every atom vibrates with ultimate
possibility. The Sikh understanding of Ultimate Reality is a dynamic and
joyous experience.

Among the most beautiful ways by which the Gurus describe the special
relationship between the Ultimate Reality and humanity is through the
language of intimate human relationships. The words of Guru Arjan, "You
are my father, You are my mother, You are my brother, You are my friend,"
are regularly recited by the Sikhs. Images of conception, the growth of the
unborn child in its mother's womb, and birth express the creative force of
the Ultimate. "From mother's blood and father's semen, the human form is
created," says the Guru Granth. In the warmth of the mother's womb are we
first formed.

Marriage, the highest experience of human love, is a particular form of
this universal and formless love. It expresses the longing for union with the
Ultimate Reality. The Gurus often speak from the point of view of a woman,
a bride awaiting her divine Groom, who addresses the Formless One as
"Beloved."

My mind and body yearns
but my Lover is far away in foreign lands.
The Beloved does not come home, I am sighing to death,
and the lightning strikes fear in me.

I lie alone on the bed, tormented;
mother, the pain is like death to me.
Without the Divine One, how can there be sleep or hunger?
What clothing can soothe the skin?
Nanak says, the bride is truly wed
when she is embraced by her Beloved.

In giving these yearnings a female voice which speaks for all humanity,
Sikh scripture opens out the definition of "man." The Sikh view is that a
separation between male and female denies the wholeness of human nature.
The Guru Granth emphasizes instead the significance of being human. In it,
men and women share human suffering and hope. The explicit male and
female imagery in the Guru Granth does not contradict the formless nature
of the Ultimate One. Rather, it suggests a vast inclusiveness. The Ultimate

Reality is above all and includes all. Whatever human beings can experience in their world is a part of the Metaphysical One.

SOURCE: Nikky Gunninder Kaur Singh, "One Reality Is," in *The Name of My Beloved: Verses of the Sikh Gurus*. San Francisco, CA: HarperSanFrancisco, 1995, pp. 1–4

HYMNS OF THE SIKH GURUS

"Oh honey-bee, thou art lost in worldly flowers"
by Guru Nanak (the First Guru)

… O my soul, thou honey-bee,
Buzzing around the blossoms to rifle their sweets,
Hear me, thy sorrow is great:
I asked the Guru in so many words
"What is the true path?"
And the Guru in so many words answered me:
O honey-bee, thou art lost in worldly flowers,
When the sun rises after death,
Thy soul will suffer as a body scalded by oil.

Without the Word of the Guru
Man is stupid and cannot find his way,
He dieth and forever suffereth agony.
Forget not God, O heart of a fool, O honey-bee:
On the other road lieth death,
On the other road lieth destruction, saith Nānak.

My soul thou art not a native of this world,
Wherefore then get caught in the net?
Entertain within thyself the Holy Name of God.
The fish like the human soul is ensnared in the net of death,
It weeps and gasps in agony,
And now she knows that life ever pleasant was a delusion.
Adore and cherish the Lord
And cast out baseless fears.
Pay heed, O my soul, to this admonition of Nānak:
My soul, thou art not native to this place,
In thine inner depths cherish the true Lord.

As streaming rivers that start from the same source
Are separated but meet in the Ocean,
So do souls meet in the Infinite,
One in a million knows
That age upon age
The world's illusions enchant and poison the soul.
Those that contemplate the Guru
Learn easily and realize God.

"Oh my mind, remember the Holy Name"

by Guru Amar Das (the Third Guru)

> If the mind is unclean, all else is unclean;
> And ceremonial washings cannot wash the mind.
> This world is the realm of illusion:
> There are few who grasp the Real.
> O my mind, remember the Holy Name![4]
> That is the precious gift of the Guru to men.
> Were a man to learn all the postures of the most austere Yogis,
> And mortify all his senses,
> Not so would he cleanse the mind, or discard self-will.
> There is no cure for the mind's sickness
> But taking shelter at the Guru's feet.
> To meet the Guru is to experience
> A change of outlook that cannot be described.
> Saith Nānak: From the mind of him who dies to self
> Through meeting the Guru, and is reborn through the Guru's Word,
> All uncleanness is removed.

"The true Guru is an ocean of pearls"

by Guru Arjun Dev (the Fifth Guru)

> That man is blind within and blind without,
> Though he pretendeth to sing of the Lord
> And performeth ritual washings and puts on caste-marks,
> If in his heart he runneth after Mammon.
> He cannot remove his inner dirt of self-sense.
> In births he comes and goes,
> Overwhelmed by sleep, played by lust,
> And uttereth the name of God.
> Though he call himself a Vaishnav,[5]
> Since self-will is the goad of his actions
> What can he hope to gain?
> Pretended holiness is like thrashing empty husks,
> Or like the crane who sits among the swans,
> Is still on the watch for fish. The swans find him an intruder.
> They live upon pearls and precious stones, the crane on frogs,
> And finally the poor crane flies away
> In fear that the swans might spot his true nature.
> Men do as God wills. Why should we blame anyone?
> When anything happens, God wills that it should.

---

4 Holy Name—nam, remembrance of God by inner or outer recitation of one of God's names, a central Sikh practice.
5 Vaishnav—an ascetic devoted to some form of Lord Vishnu, such as Krishna.

The True Guru is an ocean-wide lake of pearls:
The sincere seeker after his pearls shall find them.
The True Guru is the holy lake of Mansrover,[6]
And his Sikhs are there gathered like his swans.
The lake is full of pearls and precious stones;
However many the swans eat, they will not be exhausted.
The Sikhs are like swans who remain at the lake for ever
And banquet for ever on jewels. God has so willed it.
Nānak, blessed is the disciple who comes to the Guru:
The Guru will save him, save his family,
Nay, in the end he will save the whole world!

"The one who mingles with God"

by Guru Tegh Bahadur (the Ninth Guru)

That man who in the midst of grief is free from grieving,
And free from fear, and free from the snare of delight,
Nor is covetous of gold that he knows to be dust,
Who is neither a backbiter nor a flatterer,
Nor has greed in his heart, nor vanity, nor any worldly attachment,
Who remains at his centre unmoved by good and ill fortune,
Who is indifferent to the world's praise and blame
And discards every wishful fantasy
Accepting his lot in a disinterested fashion,
Not worked upon by lust or by wrath,
In such a man God dwelleth.
The man on whom the Grace of the Guru alights
Understands the way of conduct:
His soul, O Nānak, is mingled with the Lord
As water mingles with water!

HYMNS OF THE HINDU AND MUSLIM SAINTS

In addition to hymns of the Sikh Gurus, the Guru Granth Sahib includes compositions by numerous Hindu and Muslim saints and musicians who lived before the Sikh Gurus. Many were of a low caste, illustrating the Sikh conviction that the heights of spiritual realization transcend caste distinctions. Nam Dev (1270–1350) was a low-caste Hindu tailor.

"God is the object of the yearning of my soul" by Nam Dev

As water is precious
To the traveller in Marwar,
As the hungry camel

---

6 Lake Mansrover—a holy lake high in the Himalayas.

Yearns for the creeper,
As the wild deer at night
Hearken enrapt
To the hunter's bell,
So God is the object
Of the yearning of my soul!

Thy Name is beauty,
Thy Form is beauty,
Thy Hues are beauty,
O my living Lord!

As the dry earth yearneth
In thirst for the raindrops,
As the honey-bee yearneth
For the scent of the flowers,
As the kokil[7] loves the mango-tree,
So I long for the God.

As the sheldrake
Longs for sunrise,
As the swan yearneth
For Mansrover Lake,
As the wife pines
For her husband,
So God is the object
Of the yearning of my soul!

As the babe yearneth
For his mother's breast-milk,
As the chatrik[8] who drinketh
Only the raindrops
Yearneth for the rain,
As the stranded fish
Yearneth after water,
So God is the object
Of the yearning of my soul!

"How can there be any difference between me and Thee?"
by Ravi Das

Ravi Das was a fourteenth- to fifteenth-century Hindu saint who was an extremely low-caste hide-tanner and shoemaker.

---

7 Kokil—a type of bird.
8 Chatrik—a type of bird, said to drink only raindrops.

Between Thee and me, between me and Thee,
How can there be likeness or difference?
Likeness or difference as between gold
And a bracelet made of it, as between water
And the waves that move on its surface!
Were I not a sinner, O Eternal Lord,
How couldst Thou have the title of Redeemer of Sinners?
Thou, O Lord, art the Searcher of hearts.
Through God, the Master, we know the saints, His Servants:
Through the servants of God, we know God.
Grant me O Lord that my body may be Thy shrine.
Few, O Ravi Das, see God in everything.

SOURCE: Hymns from the Guru Granth Sahib are taken from *Selections from the Sacred Writings of the Sikhs*, trans. Trilochan Singh et al. New York: Samuel Weiser, 1973, standard pagination pp. 438, 558, 960, 633, 393, 93

"Pray crow, peck not these eyes, so that I may see the Beloved"   by Sheikh Farid, with commentary by Guru Nanak

The mystical poetry of several Muslim saints is lovingly included in the Guru Granth Sahib. One is the great Sufi dervish, Sheikh Farid (1175–1265). His burning ardor for his Beloved is tempered by a later commentary from Guru Nanak. A number of such "conversations" across the centuries appear in Guru Granth Sahib.

Thou crow pecking at my emaciated body, eating away its flesh,
Pray touch not these two eyes, so I have sight of the Beloved.
Pray crow, peck not at my body; fly off from where thou art settled.
Swallow not the flesh of this body wherein is lodged the Beloved.
Farid, the lowly grave makes call to homeless man to come to his real
    abode—
Saying, come to me thou must; fear not death.
With these eyes have I beheld the vast world vanish into eternity.
Each in his own trials is caught;
Nor am I free from mine.

In separation from God my body burns like the oven;
My bones flame like firewood;
To find union with the Beloved
Could I walk till my feet be tired,
Would walk on my head.

Theme continued by Guru Nanak
Thou needst not burn thyself like the oven nor put in flames thy bones:
Why torture thy poor limbs? Behold the Beloved in thy own heart.

SOURCE: Sheikh Farid, with commentary from Guru Nanak, *Sri Guru Granth Sahib*, trans. Gurbachan Singh Talib. Patiala, Punjab: Punjabi University Publication Bureau, 1990, pp. 2761–4

Writings of the Tenth Guru: Dasam Granth

When Guru Gobind Singh undertook the final compilation of the Guru Granth Sahib, including in it the poetry of his father, the martyred Guru Tegh Bahadur (1621–75), he included only one of his own compositions. However, the literature attributed to Guru Gobind Singh is vast and complex. It includes lengthy descriptions of "Hindu" deities, discipline for the Khalsa, a powerful letter to the tyrannical Muslim ruler Aurangzeb (r. 1658–1707), his spiritual autobiography (*Bacchitar Natak*), and *Akal Ustat*, assertions of the oneness of all religions and the unity of humankind. The authorship of certain compositions in the Dasam Granth is contested by some contemporary scholars.

"This is the purpose for which God sent me"
by Guru Gobind Singh

> I now relate my own story,
> How while doing "Tapasya"[9] I had to come to earth.
> There is a mountain by the name of Hemkund,
> Which is adorned by seven peaks.
>
> There I remained in deep meditation and performed "Tapasya"
> worshipping the timeless and mighty God who transcends death.
> In consequence of this "Tapasya,"
> from the dual state, I became One with God.
>
> Then under command of God,
> I took birth in Kali Yug,[10]
> My heart did not really wish to come down,
> because I was totally immersed in meditation at the feet of the Lord.
> He then explained to me His purpose,
> and sent me here with His command.
>
> Lord (Akal Purukh) said:
> "You are my chosen and cherished son
> whom I have installed for strengthening faith and religion.
> Go down to earth and propagate righteousness
> and guide mankind away from wickedness."
>
> This is the purpose for which Lord sent me
> and in consequence I took birth on this earth.
> I shall speak (and act) as directed by Lord
> and shall not bear enmity to anyone.
> But any people who address me as God,

---

9 Tapasya—austere meditation.
10 Kali Yug, or Kali Yuga—the last and darkest of the four ages which continually recur, according to Indian thought.

will be consigned to the cauldron of hell.
Regard me only as the humble servant of God.
Let there be no doubt or mystery on this score.
I am the servant of the Supreme Lord,
come to earth to watch His play.
I shall utter on earth the word of Lord,
and shall not remain silent in this mortal world.

SOURCE: Guru Gobind Singh, *Bacchitar Natak*, in *Jap*, trans. Surendra Nath. Delhi: Gobind Sadan, n.d., pp. xv–xvi

"Let all humanity be recognized as one" by Guru Gobind Singh

There are monks with shaven heads; there are many kinds of yogis, celibates, and ascetics, Hindus, Turks, Shi'ite Muslims, and Sunni Muslims.
But know that all of humanity is recognized as one race.
The Creator and the Beneficent One are the same; the Provider and the Merciful One are the same;
Let no one make the mistake of thinking there is a difference.
There is not one God for Hindus and another for Muslims.
Worship the one God who is the divine Preceptor for all, the One Form whose Light suffuses all.
Temples and mosques are the same,
Hindu worship and Muslim prayer are the same,
All people are the same.
It is only through erroneous thinking that they appear different.
Deities and demons, Muslims and Hindus wear their regional garb,
But all people have the same eyes, the same ears, the same body, the same composition of earth, air, fire, and water.
Allah and Abekh[11] are the same, the messages of the Puranas[12] and Qur'an are the same.
All are alike; one God created all.
As from one fire millions of sparks arise separately and then unite again in the fire,
As from one dustheap many dust particles fill the air and then resettle, blending with the dust,
As in one stream millions of waves are produced, but being made of water, become water again,
So from God's Form all non-sentient and sentient things are manifested, and springing from God, all shall be united in God again.

SOURCE: Guru Gobind Singh, *Manas ki jaat*, from *Akal Ustat*, trans. Gobind Sadan, Delhi (unpublished)

11 Abekh—a Name of God, meaning "without garb."
12 Puranas—Sanskrit sacred writings.

Living Sikhism

In 1999, Sikhs around the world jubilantly celebrated the three-hundredth anniversary of Guru Gobind Singh's creation of the Khalsa. In the process, many people proclaimed the idealistic and universalist nature of the Gurus' mission.

The Sikh Gurus' Vision of an Ideal Society   by Dharam Singh

Dharam Singh, who teaches at Punjabi University in Patiala and specializes in Guru Gobind Singh's social philosophy, asserts that the Sikh Gurus' mission included measures designed to develop an ideal classless society.

Besides caste which is peculiar to Indian society, the economic factor is equally responsible for stratification of society into different classes all over the world. In such a set-up, the affluent and the haves generally adopt an oppressive and exploitative attitude towards the poor and the have-nots: this is equally true in the case of individuals as well as nations. This gulf between the two classes widens further as a result of the pace of social, material progress being different for these different classes. Since the economic factor comes to determine human social relations, man [sic] becomes unduly more unmindful of moral and ethical values in this struggle for economic betterment. Sikhism, however, believes in the universal brotherhood of mankind, and therefore holds everyone an equal claimant to the natural resources provided them by the universal Father. Any attempt to deny one's share in that heritage would amount to sacrilege against God. The ethics of the kingdom of God as taught in the Sikh scripture are the ethics of a classless society.

An important socio-religious directive for the Sikhs is to earmark a tithe[13] of their income for philanthropic purposes. Every Sikh, when he visits a *gurdwara*[14] to pay obeisance to the Guru Granth Sahib, offers some cash. There is no lower or higher limit on this offer and, in fact, it is not even obligatory if one is not in a position to offer any. This offer of cash, though made with religious faithfulness, is not to please the Guru or God: it is an individual's modest contribution towards general, communal purposes. ...

Besides caste and class, religion is another very potent factor which divides mankind into diverse groups of different religious denomination. At the time Sikhism was born and during the period of its ascendancy, persecution of man in the name of religion was quite common. The Sikh Gurus felt it an insult to the divine essence in man, and declared that all human beings, irrespective of their religious denominations, are one. Guru Gobind Singh in his *Akal Ustat* refers to the diversity of religions followed by people of the world, and declares emphatically that followers of diverse religions are one. Religious labels are temporary and wither away with the

---

13 Tithe—a proportion, originally a tenth.
14 *Gurdwara*—a Sikh temple.

bodily vesture whereas it is the worth of deeds done by man that is the criterion of judgment both in this world and the Divine Court. Guru Amar Das confers equal validity on all religions in helping man realize the ultimate end of life. The role of religion is not that of scissors that tears asunder but that of a needle that sews together the torn fabric of human society. ...

The concept of the equality of mankind includes the womenfolk as well. Woman occupies a subordinate position in the patriarchal society, but her position becomes worse in the poor societies, especially in India where she suffers oppression as a woman and as a member of the oppressed caste or class. The Indian woman of Guru Nanak's time was a victim of this sexist discrimination and oppression, and was completely denied an independent personality of her own. Infanticide, child marriage, malnutrition and *sati*[15] were some of the evils resulting from this *Weltanschauung*.[16] Sikhism makes no distinction between man and woman, and considers both as the equal manifestation of the Divine. Man and woman are equal but distinct because of the functional distinction they have in the historical order. Even if none of the Gurus was a woman, there is no inferiority for woman in the orthodox Sikh ecclesiology. Guru Nanak was perhaps the first personage in the religious history of mankind to raise his voice against her discrimination.

The Sikh Gurus not only provided ideational basis in their hymns for the socio-religious rehabilitation of women but also undertook and advised to undertake some widespread and practical steps in this direction. As a result of this, she came to occupy a place equal to man and play an active role in the socio-religious life. That the women were quite active as missionaries of Sikh faith during the Guru-period is confirmed by a *hukumnama*[17] issued by Guru Tegh Bahadur to the *sangat*[18] of Patna wherein he refers among others to one Bebe Peri Bai. The role played by Mai Bhago[19] during the pontificate of Guru Gobind Singh is common knowledge. Sikh tradition, supported by the *Rahitnama*[20] literature, lays injunctions against female infanticide, *purdah*[21] and *sati*. It also permits widow remarriage for her rehabilitation in social life. The *Rahitnamas* denounce any kind of marginalization of woman. Chastity and fidelity, two important constituents of the sanctity of the family life as well as of social relations, are no more the virtues expected of woman alone: they apply to women as much as they apply to men and even to the rulers. ... The Sikhs in their daily supplication (*ardas*) seek the welfare of all—*sarbat da bhala*. ...

There is no priestly class as such in Sikhism and anybody can lead the congregation. ... In the appointment of leaders of congregation, caste, class

---

15 *Sati, suttee*—the Hindu custom of a widow's self-immolation on her husband's funeral pyre.
16 *Weltanschauung*—philosophy, literally "world view" (German).
17 *Hukumnama*—spiritual instructions taken from opening the Guru Granth Sahib at random.
18 *Sangat*—Sikh congregation.
19 Mai Bhago—great female warrior and martyr in Sikh history.
20 *Rahitnama*—disciplines prescribed for Sikhs.
21 *Purdah*—veiling and separation of women.

and status are given no consideration, and the only criterion of merit is the incumbent's spiritual and moral state. ...

In the *gurdwara*, everybody is welcome irrespective of his social or economic status, and none is favoured or discriminated against on any count. Here the prince and the pauper sit together and pray.

When membership of the *sangats* and the frequency of their visits to the *dharamsalas*[22] increased, it was considered imperative to arrange food for the devotees. The institution of *langar* or *Guru-ka-Langar* (free community kitchen) started with a view to meeting this requirement. The institution became popular during the pontificate of Guru Angad Dev. ... Guru Amar Das further consolidated the institution and made it mandatory for every visitor, high or low, to partake of food in the *langar* before seeing the Guru. Each successive Guru contributed to the consolidation of this institution, and today we find *langar* an integral part of almost every *gurdwara* or the Sikh place of worship the world over.

In the *langar*, the food is prepared communally, without anybody asking for the caste or class of the volunteer lending a helping hand. *Seva*[23] or service in the *langar* has been accepted as highly meritorious. All the visitors sit in *pangat* (row) without any distinction of caste, class or creed, and take their food. There is an injunction against providing a special seat or special food for anyone whosoever. The Sikh history stands witness that here princes have sat alongside peasants. This has been a very important step in translating the principle of equality into practice—more so, in a society where rigidity of casteism and sectarianism segregated people from one another. It has also served as a medium of social integration between the king and the commoner, the prince and the peasant. ...

The desire for *seva* is born of the feeling of love for others. Love is, as we have said earlier, the natural corollary of the Sikh precept of the universal brotherhood of mankind and universal fatherhood of God. All men, whatever their caste, clan or creed, are the children of God and all are spiritually united to each other and to the Creator-Lord. That is why, like *seva*, love has also been declared a very potent means of reaching God. ...

Love for all as equal members of the universal brotherhood of mankind and social service and other altruistic deeds done with humility and with absolutely no selfish motives naturally lead to the establishment of a social order which is marked by justice, communal harmony and peaceful co-existence. These social conditions are all the more needed in the modern social phenomena which are experiencing rapid socio-cultural transformations that do not, however, occur at a uniform pace. Consequently, the economically poor and the socially backward are in the world today at odds with the affluent and the socially and politically advanced. These inequalities cause personal and social insecurity, distrust

---

22 *Dharamsala*—holy place.
23 *Seva*—voluntary service in devotion to God.

and hatred in personal and social relations and gross violation of human rights and a widespread sense of fear and frustration. … It was to overcome these and such other negative tendencies that the Sikh Gurus preached a distinct metaphysical theory and then made it the *vis-a-tergo*[24] of their vision of an ideal social structure marked by humanitarian outlook.

According to the Sikh thought, *kirt karna* (to earn one's bread with the sweat of one's brow), *nam japna* (remember the Divine Name; … feeling and realizing His presence in all beings and at all places), and *wand chhakna* (to share with others what one earns through honest means) are the three cardinal values in the Sikh vision of an ideal society.

SOURCE: Dharam Singh, *Sikhism: Norm and Form*. Patiala, Punjab, and Delhi: Vision and Venture, 1997, pp. 120–9

GLOSSARY

Guru A teacher of religious knowledge and spiritual insight, a channel of divine understanding.

Guru Granth Sahib The Sikh holy scripture, now regarded as the Guru.

Khalsa Sikh warrior-saints pledged to protect people of all religions and castes from oppression.

Langar Free community kitchen.

HOLY DAYS

Sikh celebrations usually include continuous reading of the entire Guru Granth Sahib over a period of 48 hours, followed by offering of a large communal meal. Dating of holy days has traditionally followed the lunar calendar, but now some organizations are attempting to fix the dates according to the solar calendar.

January 14 Maghi, celebration of the martyrdom of 40 Immortals at Muktsar in Guru Gobind Singh's last battle against the Mughal forces.

April 13 or 14 Baisakhi, anniversary of the creation of the Khalsa, often including initiation of new members of the Khalsa with amrit (holy water stirred with a double-edged sword as the Sikh prayers are recited).

[June] 4th day of the lunar month of Jeth Martyrdom of Guru Arjun Dev by heat torture, commemorated by offering of a cooling drink to all passers-by.

[October–November] Full moon of the lunar month of Kartik Traditional celebration of Guru Nanak's birthday (although scholarship has placed the true date at April 15).

[November] 5th light part of the lunar month of Maghar Martyrdom of Guru Tegh Bahadur.

[December–January] 7th light part of the lunar month of Poh Birthday of Guru Gobind Singh.

---

24 *Vis-a-tergo*—(Latin) literally "push from behind."

HISTORICAL OUTLINE

1469–1539—life of Guru Nanak, the first Sikh Prophet

1563–1606—life of the Fifth Guru, Arjun Dev, tortured to death by the Mughal emperor Jahangir

1621–75—life of the Ninth Guru, Tegh Bahadur, who offered his life to protect Hindus' freedom of religion

1666–1708—life of Guru Gobind Singh, the Tenth Guru, who turned his followers into courageous saint-soldiers

1699—Guru Gobind Singh initiates the order of Khalsa

1708—at his death, Guru Gobind Singh installs the Guru Granth Sahib as the Guru

1780–1839—Maharaja Ranjit Singh rules

a strong Sikh kingdom with regard for all religions

1848—British move into Punjab, Sikh rule falls

1919—bloody massacre by the British in Amritsar

1947—in India/Pakistan partition, two and a half million Sikhs are compelled to leave Pakistan for India

1984—Indian army storms the Golden Temple to dislodge Sikh separatists; prime minister Indira Gandhi assassinated by Sikh bodyguards, starting widespread Hindu violence against Sikhs

1999—millions of Sikhs converge on Anandpur Sahib to celebrate the 300th anniversary of the Khalsa

REVIEW QUESTIONS

1   What are the three cardinal values in the Sikh vision of an ideal society?
2   How does Sikh theology reflect its environment? Discuss, for example, karma, caste, one formless God. How is Sikh theology and practice different from its environment?
3   Is Sikh faith focused on monastic retreats or active work? What view of society does this reflect?

DISCUSSION QUESTIONS

1   What does Sikh history illustrate about reforming religions?
2   How do Sikh Gurus differ from rabbis, priests, ministers, caliphs, or imams?
3   What do you think of the problem seen by some Sikhs that a majority of Sikhs are so by birth only and lack the commitment of conversion by choice?

INFORMATION RESOURCES

Cole, W. Owen, and **Piara Singh Sambhi**. *The Sikhs: Their Religious Beliefs and Practices*, 2nd ed. Brighton, UK: Sussex Academic Press, 1995.

———. *A Popular Dictionary of Sikhism*. Richmond, Surrey: Curzon Press, 1990.

Duggal, K. S. *Sikh Gurus: Their Lives and Teachings*. Delhi: UBS Publishers' Distributors, 1993.

Gateway to Sikhism
<http://www.allaboutsikhs.com>

Gobind Sadan
<http://www.gobindsadan.org>

Institute of Sikh Studies
<http://www.sikhinstitute.org>

Kohli, Surindar Singh. *The Life and Ideals of Guru Gobind Singh*. Delhi: Munshiram Manoharlal Publishers Pvt., 1986.

Macauliffe, Max Arthur. *The Sikh Religion: Its Gurus, Sacred Writings, and Authors*. Oxford: Oxford University Press/Delhi: S. Chand and Company, 1963.

Mann, Gurinder Singh. *The Making of Sikh Scripture*. New Delhi: Oxford University Press, 2001.

McLeod, W. H. *Sikhs and Sikhism*. Oxford and New York: Oxford University Press, 1999.

Nesbitt, Eleanor. *Sikhism: A Very Short Introduction*. Oxford and New York: Oxford University Press, 2005.

Sikhism
<http://www.srigurugranthsahib.org>

SikhiWiki
<http://www.sikhiwiki.org>

Singh, Harbans, ed. *The Encyclopedia of Sikhism*. Patiala, Punjab: Punjabi University, 1992–99.

Singh, Nikky-Guninder Kaur. *The Feminine Principle in the Sikh Vision of the Transcendent*. Cambridge: Cambridge University Press, 1993.

———. "Sikhism," in *Encyclopedia of Religion*, ed. Lindsay Jones. 2nd ed. Vol. 12, pp. 8393–8. New York: Macmillan, 2005.

CHAPTER 12
NEW RELIGIOUS MOVEMENTS

From time immemorial, there have been many visionaries and philosophers proclaiming spiritual truth. Some with particular abilities of leadership and spiritual qualities have attracted followers; those who have been especially successful in doing so are still honored today as the founders of the world's major living religions. Others are now forgotten. This process continues in the present, with thousands of new religious movements emerging since World War II and others withering away.

New religious movements have always been regarded skeptically by previously established religions. In general, most religions claim to be the best, perhaps the exclusive carriers of authentic spiritual truth. Whether institutionalization or human waywardness is the cause, people may drift away from the initial fervor of their religion. Spiritual renewal may then arise either within the religion as a reform movement or without, as a new religious movement which nonetheless is likely to have some links with past tradition.

New religious movements may be perceived not only as threats to earlier movements, but also as threats to their followers' mental health and personal safety. In our times, there have been group suicides by members of movements anticipating doomsday or even trying to be picked up by unidentified flying objects. Some groups have encouraged their followers to withdraw from their communities and families to develop a non-worldly lifestyle. Such behaviors have led to negative branding of new religious movements as **cults** or **sects**, and have led to vigorous anti-cult organizations in some parts of the world. However, the word "cult" is value-neutral and could be applied to some existing religions; it connotes a religion that is centered upon devotion to a single person or deity. Similarly, "sect" connotes a branch of a larger tradition. The term "new religious movements" is preferred today by scholars of religion.

Following a charismatic leader

Charismatic leadership often attracts converts to new religious movements. During the twentieth century, many young people were drawn to give up their possessions and adopt a self-sacrificing lifestyle for the sake of others, while regarding Rev. Dr. Sun Myung Moon of Korea as the promised second coming of Christ. He teaches that Jesus' mission was incomplete, and that he and his wife have come to fulfill God's original plan as the "True Parents" of humankind.

God's Model Ideal Family and Nation, and the Peace Kingdom by Rev. Dr. Sun Myung Moon

As you may know, this year marks the eighty-seventh year since my birth. On this remarkable occasion, as the founder of the Universal Peace Federation, which is to open wide the era after the coming of heaven, I would like to convey to you the essence of the truth of Heaven that I have taught throughout my life. This message is entitled, "God's Model Ideal Family and Nation, and the Peace Kingdom."

Ladies and gentlemen, on looking back, my life has indeed been like a dream. At the young age of sixteen, with nothing but the buoyant spirit and aspirations of youth, I was called by Heaven and began to live for the will of God. This left no room in my heart for any worldly ambitions I may have cherished. It has never been an easy path, but I have followed it for more than eighty years, looking nowhere but straight ahead. This was the life I was fated to lead, with no choice but to shake off the embrace of my beloved parents, and brothers and sisters, who clung to me, wanting me to stay with them. They endured great self sacrifice and walked a thorny path of sorrowful suffering for my sake.

It has been a journey through the wilderness that no one among the 6.5 billion people living on earth could ever comprehend. Even when I persevered through the hardships of prison life six times, I never let go of the key to the providence, such has been my life.

This was all because I came to know only too well how anguished, aggrieved and full of bitter sorrow was the heart of God as He waited for thousands of years to find us. I realized that if God, who is the origin of billions of people and the Creator of everything in the universe, was not relieved from His sorrow, human life would remain completely without value.

When, where and how did God come to carry such agonizing sorrow in His heart? Who on earth could inflict this grief upon Him, the absolute and omnipotent Being?

God created Adam and Eve and established them as the first ancestors of humankind. He invested His whole being in raising them as His son and daughter, and they were connected to Him through love, life and lineage. The parent-child relationship is the highest and most important of all relationships, and the only way through which His lineage can be bequeathed and made to last forever.

However, this parent-child relationship, more precious and important than life itself, was severed through the Fall of Adam and Eve. As God's own flesh and blood, and as His eternal, only-begotten son and daughter, Adam and Eve formed a blood relationship with His enemy Satan, and became Satan's children instead. In the face of this, God's heart has been crushed and wounded with grief and sorrow throughout history. This still remains the most mortifying and harrowing anguish, which no one before in history could either know or resolve.

In this way God's ideal of creation to establish a true family in that first generation through Adam and Eve, a family through which He could eternally pass on His lineage, was frustrated. The only way to relieve His sorrow is to restore and establish a true family unrelated to the lineage of Satan. Herein lies the reason why all of us need to establish true families, which is God's ideal of creation. Herein also lies the fundamental object and purpose of the founding of the Universal Peace Federation. ...

The family sets the pattern for living together in harmony. The family wherein parents and children love and respect each other, husband and wife are grounded in mutual trust and love, and brothers and sisters trust and rely on each other, and all live together as one, is the model ideal family. This means that you need to establish a true family wherein the stem of true love emerges from the root of true love and bears the fruit of true love.

Such families contain the living root of history and the roots of the kingdom of heaven. In such families, the kingdom of heaven on earth takes root. They are the soil in which God's everlasting kingship is firmly planted. The grandparents, parents, and children represent the roots of the past, present and future, respectively. The root of the past represents the spirit world, the root of the present is the palace representing the world today, and the root of the future establishes the grandsons and granddaughters as princes and princesses. Through such a family we erect the palace of peace, representing the harmony of the two worlds, the spirit world and the physical world.

In this manner, the three generations of grandparents, parents, and grandchildren should live together as one family, serving the eternally existent God. You should know that to seek after and establish such a family of Cheon Il Guk—God's kingdom—is the responsibility of tribal messiahs, the mission of the Ambassadors for Peace, and the desire of God.

You should form families that God will miss and yearn to return to after He has been away. You should raise families to which He can come freely as a parent visiting His children. This is what it means to live in service to God. To such a family, God becomes the subject of our conscience, acting vertically. Following that vertical subject, your mind stands in the position of the vertical subject of yourself, and brings your mind and body into unity. That is where parental love, conjugal love, children's love, and siblings' love—in short, the four realms of love or the four realms of heart—are perfected. Only in such a family can the upper and lower, front and back, left and right be connected as one and spherical motion ensue. This leads to God's everlasting, model ideal families and nations, and His peace kingdom.

SOURCE: Excerpted from "God's Model Ideal Family and Nation, and the Peace Kingdom," speech by Rev. Dr. Sun Myung Moon during a series of assemblies for Ambassadors for Peace and rallies for the Return of the Homeland to God held in 180 nations during 2006
<http://www.familyfed.org/trueparents/chapter.php?id+11&page=1&chapter=pyungwhat>

Offshoots of older religions

Not infrequently a new religion is an offshoot that claims to return to an earlier, purer version of an old tradition, but is not recognized as part of the mainstream by that tradition, and thus continues to evolve independently.

One such new religious movement is the Mormon Church—The Church of Jesus Christ of Latter-day Saints. It is an American offshoot of Christianity that originated in the nineteenth century near Palmyra, New York, and is now centered in Salt Lake City, Utah. It recognizes not only the Old and New Testaments of the Bible but also other books which its members regard as authoritative scriptures: *The Book of Mormon* (the "restored gospel" which is said to have been written on brass plates discovered in 1827 in New York State, describing nations who reportedly came to the Americas before the time of Jesus, and who also received revelations from Jesus after his crucifixion), *The Doctrine and Covenants* (revelations to Joseph Smith, who is said to have found the brass plates), *The Pearl of Great Price* (more revelations and stories from Joseph Smith), and *Pronouncements by the President*. Mormons' belief in continuing revelation is one of the characteristics which distinguish The Church of Jesus Christ of Latter-day Saints from Christianity as a whole. With a strong emphasis on spiritual renewal, family life, and missionary outreach, the Church continues to grow rapidly, with members in over 170 countries.

The Re-appearance of Jesus from *The Book of Mormon*

The Book of Mormon describes an apocalyptic destruction of many cities in the Americas because of their evil ways, from which only a righteous remnant of "the seed of Joseph" are saved. It was to this remnant that Jesus is said to have reappeared.

And now it came to pass that there were a great multitude gathered together, of the people of Nephi, round about the temple which was in the land Bountiful; and they were marveling and wondering one with another, and were showing one to another the greatest and marvelous change which had taken place.

And it came to pass, as they understood they cast their eyes up again towards heaven' and behold, they saw a Man descending out of heaven; and he was clothed in a white robe; and he came down and stood in the midst of them; and the eyes of the whole multitude were turned upon him, and they durst not open their mouths, even one to another, and wist not what it meant, for they thought it was an angel that had appeared unto them.

And it came to pass that he stretched forth his hand and spake unto the people, saying:

Behold, I am Jesus Christ, whom the prophets testified shall come into the world.

And behold, I am the light and the life of the world; and I have drunk out of that bitter cup which the Father hath given me, and have glorified the Father, in taking upon me the sins of the world, in the which I have suffered the will of the Father in all things from the beginning.

And it came to pass that when Jesus had spoken these words the whole multitude fell to the earth; for they remembered that it had been prophesied among them that Christ should show himself unto them after his ascension into heaven.

And it came to pass that the Lord spake unto them saying:

Arise and come forth unto me, that ye may thrust your hands into my side, and also that ye may feel the prints of the nails in my hands and in my feet, that ye may know that I am the God of Israel, and the God of the whole earth, and have been slain for the sins of the world. ...

And the Lord said unto him: I give unto you power that ye shall baptize this people when I am again ascended into heaven.

And again the Lord called others, and said unto them likewise; and he gave unto them power to baptize. And he said unto them: On this wise shall ye baptize; and there shall be no disputations among you.

Verily I say unto you, that whoso repenteth of his sins through your words, and desireth to be baptized in my name, on this wise shall ye baptize them—Behold, ye shall go down and stand in the water, and in my name shall ye baptize them.

And now behold, these are the words which ye shall say, calling them by name, saying:

Having authority given me of Jesus Christ, I baptize you in the name of the Father, and of the Son, and of the Holy Ghost. Amen.

And then shall ye immerse them in the water, and come forth again out of the water.

And after this manner shall ye baptize in my name; for behold, verily I say unto you, that the Father, and the Son, and the Holy Ghost are one; and I am in the Father, and the Father in me, and the Father and I are one.

SOURCE: *The Book of Mormon*, 3 Nephi 11: 1–27. Salt Lake City, UT: Corporation of the President of The Church of Jesus Christ of Latter-day Saints, 1981

Continuing Revelation

from the official website of The Church of Jesus Christ of Latter-day Saints

Mormons believe that God continues to speak today to those who sincerely seek to know his will. Individuals can receive personal revelations through visions, prophetic dreams, visitations of angels, and inspiration by the Holy Spirit. The Quorum of the Twelve Apostles are specially blessed as prophets and seers, and the President of the Church has the authority to receive revelations for the entire Church. This piece from the Church's website explains the official position.

As members of The Church of Jesus Christ of Latter-day Saints, we are blessed to be led by living prophets—inspired men called to speak for the Lord, as did Moses, Isaiah, Peter, Paul, Nephi, Mormon, and other prophets of the scriptures. We sustain the President of the Church as prophet, seer, and revelator—the only person on the earth who received revelation to guide the entire Church. We also sustain the counselors in the First Presidency and the members of the Quorum of the Twelve Apostles as prophets, seers, and revelators.

Like the prophets of old, prophets today testify of Jesus Christ and teach His gospel. They make known God's will and true character. They speak boldly and clearly, denouncing sin and warning of its consequences. At times, they may be inspired to prophesy of future events for our benefit.

We can always trust the living prophets. Their teachings reflect the will of the Lord, who declared: "What I the Lord have spoken, I have spoken, and I excuse not myself; and though the heavens and the earth pass away, my world shall not pass away, but shall all be fulfilled, whether by mine own voice or by the voice of my servants, it is the same" (Doctrines and Covenants 1:38).

Our greatest safety lies in strictly following the word of the Lord given through His prophets, particularly the current President of the Church. The Lord warns that those who ignore the words of the living prophets will fall (see Doctrines and Covenants 1:14–16). He promises great blessings to those who follow the President of the Church:

"Thou shalt give heed unto all his words and commandments which he shall give unto you as he receiveth them, walking in all holiness before me;

"For his word ye shall receive, as if from mine own mouth, in all patience and faith.

"For by doing these things the gates of hell shall not prevail against you; yea, and the Lord God will disperse the powers of darkness before you, and cause the heavens to shake for your good, and his name's glory" (Doctrines and Covenants 21:4–6).

SOURCE: "Prophets"
<http://lds.org/study/topics/prophets?lang=eng>

Combinations of older religions

New religious movements may also arise as mixtures of older religions. When two religions are mixed which are normally considered quite different, the process is called **syncretism**. Boundaries between religions become rather porous when they appear in the same culture. In the Americas, slaves from Africa carried their indigenous religions but were not allowed to practice them openly, so in some cases they adopted the Christian religion of their masters as an overlay to their traditional ways, producing various syncretic hybrids in which Christian saints are merged with African deities. In Vietnam, Daoism, Confucianism, and Buddhism were joined in 1926 in a new religious movement called **CaoDai** (short for Dai Dao Tam Ky Pho Do: Great Religion of the Third Period of Revelation and Salvation). In predominantly Muslim Iran, a prophetic voice announced the oneness of all religions, and developed the new religious movement known as Baha'i.

The Religious Constitution of Caodaism by His Saintness Ho Phap

Members of CaoDai worship under a symbol of the Divine Eye in the sky, and venerate figures representing the "Five Branches and Three Anchors": Guanyin, Laozi, Buddha, Confucius, Guan Yu (Kwan Yu, a deified Chinese general), Li Bai (alternatively pronounced Li Po, a Chinese poet), Jesus Christ, and Jiang Ziya (Chiang Tseya, a Chinese sage). They are taught that God is not taking a human form now, but rather is communicating teachings through sacred séances. According to the movement's website, <http://www.caodai.org>, "CaoDai is a universal faith with the principle that all religions have one same divine origin, which is God, or Allah, or the Tao, or the Nothingness, one same ethic based on LOVE and JUSTICE, and are just different manifestations of the same TRUTH." Members believe that Caodaism was revealed by God, who instructed the first disciples to establish a new religion, superceding older ones, for the "Third Era of Religious Amnesty." Revelations and poems continue to be received.

The following extract is from a book explaining the laws of CaoDai, as reportedly revealed by God, with commentary from Ho Phap Pham Cong Tac, Chief of the Hiep Thien Dai (Heavenly Union Palace). Here we can see a new religious movement organizing and distinguishing itself from older religions: the top levels of CaoDai's religious hierarchy are spelled out, and the amalgamation of three existing religions into an allegedly more valid new religion is explicitly stated.

I. Power of the Giao Tong (Pope)

Divine text: The Giao Tong is your eldest brother.

Commentary: The Giao Tong represents the Master preserving religion on earth. He is the elder brother responsible for the guidance of all God's children, young and old, for their spiritual well-being.

Although the CaoDai church is formed of two temporal parts, the "Cuu Trung Dai" [Nine Sphere Palace] and the "Hiep Thien Dai" [Heavenly Union Palace], the Ho Phap, who is the chief of the Hiep Thien Dai, is of lesser power than the Giao Tong in the temporal aspect. However, they are both equal spiritually.

Divine text: The Giao Tong has the power to represent Me in the guidance of My children in their spiritual and temporal life.

Commentary: … He cares for each and every one of them, guides them and helps them avoid any infraction of the divine law. He obliges them to conform strictly to the requirements of the New Code. …

Divine text: He has the authority to communicate spiritually with the thirty-six Heavens, the three-thousand Worlds, the sixty-seven Earths and the Ten Courts of Hell to ask for the salvation of your souls.

Commentary: … How can the Giao Tong communicate with the thirty-six Heavens, the three-thousand Worlds, the sixty-seven Earths and the Ten Courts of Hell? He must go to the sanctuary of the Hiep Thien Dai and engage the miraculous power of spiritism. … Even his requests addressed to the Bat Quai Dai [Council of Gods] must pass through the Hiep Thien Dai. The Hiep Thien Dai is consequently the intermediary between the Giao Tong and the Superior Spirits: Than [Genies, Angels]; Thanh [Saints]; Tien [Immortals]; Phat (Buddhas).

II. Powers of the Chuong Phap [Censor Cardinals]

Divine text: There are three Chuong Phap [Dharma Holders] for three branches: Taoist, Confucianist, and Buddhist.

Commentary: There is only one Chuong Phap per branch. The three branches differ from each other internally and externally. The doctrinal principles are different. They are united only by the New Code. Thus the Master adds:

Divine text: Although the Laws and Principles of these three doctrines are different, I consider them as one.

Commentary: … When humans were coerced by law into virtue, they found the way difficult. But now that the Great Spirits themselves help them, they may be virtuous more freely and more spontaneously, and thus the path to salvation becomes easier. This is natural.

Moreover, at the present time, we have passed the "Cycle of Progress" and attained the greatest dignity. The ancient laws no longer have enough moral authority to maintain faith. And when men [sic] lose their faith, the tendency toward self destruction increases, with disorder the inevitable consequence. …

The New Code, established according to the master's instructions, may be modified in the future to adapt to the ever evolving human mind. The temporal and the spiritual must unite to guide humanity on the eternal way.

For example, some may ask: "Why is the Master not using the ancient laws already established for the three existing religions? Why did he create the New Code, asking men [sic] to abandon the old for the new?" We would answer: "Precisely, the master has given us a spiritual message: The Jade Court [The Court of Gods] has rejected the ancient laws and the Temple of

Thunder [Celestial Sanctuary] has destroyed the ancient principles. Thus, the ancient laws and principles have no longer applied. ..."

Divine text: Thus one becomes three and three is nothing else than one.

Commentary: Thus, the New Code is the synthesis of the three religions—which makes one embracing three, and the three old religions become one code, the New Code.

SOURCE: *Phap-Chanh-Truyen, The Religious Constitution of Caodaism*, explained and commented by His Saintness Ho Phap, trans. Bui Dac Hum. Redlands, CA: Chân Tâm, 1992
<http://www.caodai.org>

A New Revelation from the Unifier   by Baha'u'llah

Baha'i was founded by Baha'u'llah (1817–92) from Iran. It appeared in a predominantly Muslim culture, but emphasized the harmony of all religions. It therefore supports appreciation of major religious prophets from the Abrahamic religions, such as Moses, Jesus, and Muhammad, but also messengers from other religious streams such as Krishna and Buddha. Despite persecution, the movement has spread globally and claims five million members from many and varied cultures. Its central beliefs include the oneness of religions and of the human family, equality of men and women, opposition to all forms of prejudice, independent search for truth, the harmony of science and religion, linkage of economic problems to spiritual problems, and the need for world peace. Baha'u'llah proclaimed:

This is the Day in which God's most excellent favors have been poured out upon men, the Day in which His most mighty grace hath been infused into all created things. It is incumbent upon all peoples of the world to reconcile their differences, and, with perfect unity and peace, abide beneath the shadow of the Tree of His care and loving-kindness. It behoveth them to cleave to whatsoever will, in this Day, be conducive to the exaltation of their stations, and to the promotion of their best interests. ...

Beseech ye the one true God to grant that all men [sic] may be graciously assisted to fulfil that which is acceptable in Our sight. Soon will the present-day order be rolled up, and a new one spread out in its stead. Verily, thy Lord speaketh the truth, and is the Knower of things unseen.

This is the Day whereon the Ocean of God's mercy hath been manifested unto men, the Day in which the Day Star of His loving-kindness hath shed its radiance upon them, the Day in which the clouds of His bountiful favor have overshadowed the whole of mankind. Now is the time to cheer and refresh the down-cast through the invigorating breeze of love and fellowship, and the living waters of friendliness and charity.

They who are the beloved of God, in whatever place they gather and whomsoever they may meet, must evince, in their attitude towards God, and in the manner of their celebration of His praise and glory, such humility and submissiveness that every atom of the dust beneath their feet may attest the depth of their devotion. ...

It is incumbent upon every man, in this Day, to hold fast unto whatsoever will promote the interests, and exalt the station, of all nations and just governments. Through each and every one of the verses which the Pen of the Most High hath revealed, the doors of love and unity have been unlocked and flung open to the face of men. We have erewhile declared— and Our Word is the truth—: "Consort with the followers of all religions in a spirit of friendliness and fellowship." Whatsoever hath led the children of men to shun one another, and hath caused dissensions and divisions amongst them, hath, through the revelation of these words, been nullified and abolished. From the heaven of God's Will, and for the purpose of ennobling the world of being and of elevating the minds and souls of men, hath been sent down that which is the most effective instrument for the education of the whole human race. The highest essence and most perfect expression of whatsoever the peoples of old have either said or written hath, through this most potent Revelation, been sent down from the heaven of the Will of the All-Possessing, the Ever-Abiding God. Of old it hath been revealed: "Love of one's country is an element of the Faith of God." The Tongue of Grandeur hath, however, in the day of His manifestation proclaimed: "It is not his to boast who loveth his country, but it is his who loveth the world." Through the power released by these exalted words He hath lent a fresh impulse, and set a new direction, to the birds of men's hearts, and hath obliterated every trace of restriction and limitation from God's holy Book.

SOURCE: Bahá'u'lláh, *Gleanings from the Writings of Bahá'u'lláh*, trans. Shoghi Effendi. 2nd ed. Wilmette, IL: Baha'i Publishing Trust, 1976, pp. 6–7, 94–6

Social trends

New religious movements also arise as expressions of contemporary social trends, with many and varying manifestations. Two such trends that began during the twentieth century are interest in nature as a spiritual path and worship of goddesses. These ways have arisen primarily in urbanized, industrialized cultures as new forms that refer to, but are not historically connected with, ancient traditions, such as those practiced by some indigenous or now-extinct societies. Not being directly connected with such cultures, some are now freely adapting spiritual practices that regard the cosmos as sentient and sacred, forming a movement often known as **Neo-paganism**.

The Goddess and Women's Spirituality by Charlene Spretnak

Charlene Spretnak teaches at the California Institute for Integral Studies in San Francisco. In this selection from her first book, *The Politics of Women's Spirituality* (1982), she criticizes patriarchal religions as beyond reform and calls for a reawakening of the goddess tradition as the best path to the divine for women.

The underlying rationale for patriarchal societies is patriarchal religion. Christianity, Judaism, Islam, and Hinduism all combine male godheads with proscriptions against woman as temptress, as unclean, as evil. We were all made to understand that Eve's act of heeding the word of the serpent caused the expulsion of the human race from the Garden of Eden. We were made to understand that, as a result of her act, it was decreed by God that woman must submit to the dominance of man. We were all raised in cultures that reflect this decree: men enjoy the secular and spiritual positions of power; women cook and clean for them and supply them with heirs.

Most of the four billion people currently living in accordance with the patriarchal order do not question it: things have been this way for a long time; it must be the natural order. But what if the patriarchy is only a few thousand years old? What if, for tens of thousands of years before that, societies were built around the concept of the Great Goddess? If this is the case, our entire overview of history is altered: We once passed through a very long phase of matrifocal[1] culture; we are now passing through a phase of patriarchal culture (which appears to be self-destructing after a relatively brief run); and the future phase is ours to design.

Manifestations of our reclaimed spirituality Anat, Aphrodite, Artemis, Asherah, Astarte, Athena, Attor, Au Set, Blodeuwedd, Britannia, Britomaris, Changing Woman, Demeter, Dictynna, Gaia, Hathor, Hecate, Hera, Ananna, Ishtar, Isis, Ix Chel, Kali, Kuan Yin, Magna Mater, Nut, Pandora, Persephone, Rhea, Rhiannon, Saraswati, Selene, Tara, Themis, White Goddess.

Ours is the oldest spiritual tradition on Earth. Now we understand the symbolism in patriarchal myths wherein Apollo slays the python at Delphi, wherein evil comes to weak-willed Eve in the form of a snake, wherein Saint George fiercely slays the giant snake-like dragon, wherein Saint Patrick rids Ireland of the snakes—for in matrifocal spirituality snakes were a widespread symbol of cyclical renewal and regeneration, continually growing and shedding their skins. We understand why the animal declared unclean by the Judaic fathers was the pig, which had long been held sacred to Demeter[2] and other Mediterranean forms of the Goddess for its prolificacy.

The great silence has been broken at last. Women are coming together to cultivate the powers that can result from exploring matrifocal heritage, personal and collective mythology, natural healing, meditation, dreamwork, celebrating the cycles of nature (i.e., our surroundings and our own bodies), and ritual. As we all bear scars from having been raised under patriarchy, the ability to heal ourselves and each other psychically and physically is essential to the growth of women's culture. Ritual can generate and transform tremendous fields of force. That energy is always there for us to tap and manifest. Rituals created within a framework of women's spirituality differ in form and content from the empty, hierarchically imposed, patriarchal

1 Matrifocal—focused on women as the leaders of society.
2 Demeter—Greek goddess of fecundity and plenty.

observances with which most of us grew up. They involve healing, strengthening, creative energy that expands with spontaneity from a meaningful core of values. ...

SOURCE: Charlene Spretnak, ed., *The Politics of Women's Spirituality*. New York: Anchor/Doubleday, 1982, pp. 394–5. Reprinted from *Chrysalis: A Magazine of Women's Culture*, no. 6, November 1978

Principles of Wiccan Belief by The American Council of Witches

In the United States, Canada, and Europe, interest in **Wicca**—a major form of Neo-paganism—continues to grow. There are many versions of this trend, which can perhaps be traced to a Witchcraft movement started in the United Kingdom in the 1940s that referred back to ancient Celtic spiritual ways. In 1974, 73 witches organized The American Council of Witches and tried to define the general characteristics that Wiccans have in common.

In seeking to be inclusive, we do not wish to open ourselves to the destruction of our group by those on self-serving power trips, or to philosophies and practices contradictory to those principles. In seeking to exclude those whose ways are contradictory to ours, we do not want to deny participation with us to any who are sincerely interested in our knowledge and beliefs, regardless of race, color, sex, age, national or cultural origins, or sexual preference.

Principles of the Wiccan Belief:

1. We practice rites to attune ourselves with the natural rhythm of life forces marked by the phases of the Moon and the seasonal Quarters and Cross Quarters.

2. We recognize that our intelligence gives us a unique responsibility towards our environment. We seek to live in harmony with Nature, in ecological balance offering fulfillment to life and consciousness within an evolutionary concept.

3. We acknowledge a depth of power far greater than that is apparent to the average person. Because it is far greater than ordinary it is sometimes called *"supernatural,"* but we see it as lying within that which is naturally potential to all.

4. We conceive of the Creative Power in the universe as manifesting through polarity—as masculine and feminine—and that this same Creative Power lies in all people, and functions through the interaction of the masculine and feminine. We value neither above the other, knowing each to be supportive of the other. We value sex as pleasure, as the symbol and embodiment of life, and as one of the sources of energies used in magickal practice and religious worship.

5. We recognize both outer and inner, or psychological, worlds—sometimes known as the Spiritual World, the Collective Unconscious, Inner Planes,

etc.—and we see in the interaction of these two dimensions the basis for paranormal phenomena and magickal exercises. We neglect neither dimension for the other, seeing both as necessary for our fulfillment.

6. We do not recognize any authoritarian hierarchy, but do honor those who teach, respect those who share their greater knowledge and wisdom, and acknowledge those who have courageously given of themselves in leadership.

7. We see religion, magick and wisdom-in-living as being united in the way one views the world and lives within it—a world view and philosophy of life which we identify as *Witchcraft, the Wiccan Way*.

8. Calling oneself "Witch" does not make a Witch—but neither does heredity itself, nor the collecting of titles, degrees and initiations. A Witch seeks to control the forces within her/himself that make life possible in order to live wisely and well without harm to others and in harmony with Nature.

9. We believe in the affirmation and fulfillment of life in a continuation of evolution and development of consciousness, that gives meaning to the Universe we know, and our personal role within it.

10. Our only animosity towards Christianity, or toward any other religion or philosophy of life, is to the extent that its institutions have claimed to be *"the only way,"* and have sought to deny freedom to others and to suppress other ways of religious practice and belief.

11. As American Witches, we are not threatened by debates on the history of the Craft, the origins of various terms, the origins of various aspects of different traditions. We are concerned with our present and our future.

12. We do not accept the concept of absolute evil, nor do we worship any entity known as "Satan": or "the Devil," as defined by Christian tradition. We do not seek power through the suffering of others, nor do we accept that personal benefit can be derived only by denial to another.

13. We believe that we should seek within Nature that which is contributory to our health and well-being.

SOURCE: Principles of Wiccan Belief, The American Council of Witches, 1974
<http://www.religioustolerance.org/wic_stat1.htm>

The fate of new religious movements

No matter how successfully a new prophet has gathered followers, the continuation of his or her mission depends upon what happens after he or she dies. J. Gordon Melton, co-founder of the Center for Studies on New Religions, director of the Institute for the Study of American Religion, and one-time United Methodist pastor, discusses the organizational matters that come into play after the prophet's death.

After the Founder's Death   by J. Gordon Melton

In simple terms, the average founder of a new religion, especially one that shows some success during the first generation, is obviously an important factor in the growth and development of his/her movement. The movement is initially an extension of the founder's ideas, dreams, and emotional make-up. The leader may be valued as a teacher and/or venerated as a cosmic being or even divine entity. However, once the founder articulates the group's teachings and practices, they exist independently of him/her and can and do develop a life of their own. Once the follower experiences the truth of the religion, that experience also exists independently. Once a single spokesperson for the founder arises, the possibility of transmitting the truth of the religion independently of the founder has been posited. If a leader has developed a religious vision with the depth to gain a significant following during his/her lifetime, it will be a religion in which the role of the individual who created the religion, however important, will be but one element, not the overwhelming reality. Just as the disconfirmation of a prophecy rarely alters the direction of a group, so the death of the founder rarely proves fatal or leads to drastic alteration in the group's life. But what does happen when the founder dies? Generally the same thing that happens in other types of organizations, that is, very simply, power passes to new leadership with more or less smoothness depending upon the extent and thoroughness of the preparation that has been made ahead of time.

... When a new religion dies, it usually has nothing to do with the demise of the founder; it is from lack of response of the public to the founder's ideas or the incompetence of the founder in organizing the followers into a strong group. Most new religions will die in the first decade, if they are going to die.

In the overwhelming majority of cases, however, if a new religion finds some response and survives its initial phases of organization to attain a relative stability (the more so if it becomes fairly successful, with multiple centers and a mature leadership), the death of the founder will be experienced as a sad event but not a fatal or even traumatic one. In years past, the passing of a founder has often led to a power struggle, with the loser breaking away and taking some supporters to establish a rival organization. Such power struggles are a clear sign that leadership was allowed to develop in the group, though the final choice among several possible successors was postponed until after the founder's death.

Such power struggles, while momentarily important, are no more significant than any other issues that threaten schism. The more preparation is made for a smooth transition, the more likely an orderly succession is to occur. ...

One important factor that has served to further lessen the impact of succession problems on new religions is the control of property. In past years, the single leader of a group could have complete control of the group's assets. If no clear successor was named, the property was the bounty to be won by rivals. However, that concern has increasingly become a non-issue. … In the United States, almost all new religions are organized as corporations under the leadership of boards of directors who have formal legal control of the corporate assets. … Given the collective nature of the board leadership, it is not subject to the disturbances caused by the death of any single person, including a founder, in a leadership position. Imposed for tax purposes, the corporate structure has as a by-product given new religious groups an additional stability that no single leader could bequeath.

In Conclusion As we rid ourselves of the myths about new religions, we lose our naïveté about their seriousness and the fullness of their religious life. We also can discard the inappropriate list of superlatives frequently used to describe new religions as totalistic societies under the absolute control of their charismatic leaders. Such talk is more rhetoric than reality and more polemic than analysis. While we observe the adulation of religious leaders in ritual setting, we also experience the ability of members to distance themselves emotionally when away from the presence of the guru. As the myths drop away, we become free to explore the rich storehouse of data available to us in the experience and operation of first-generation religion. Normal, creative people form new religious structures, and the continued generation of new religions is to be expected as a sign of health in any open society.

New religions as first-generation religions, whether a new orthodox Christian movement such as eighteenth-century Methodism, or a new Hindu group built around a recently arrived guru, share many characteristics. During the first generation, the founder, whose new ideas led to the formation of the group, places a definitive stamp upon it. The first members are self-selected because of their initial confidence in the leader and/or their agreement with the leader's program. The first generation is also a time of experimentation and rapid change. The leader must discover the right elements to combine in a workable program, generate solutions to unexpected obstacles, choose and train capable leaders, and elaborate upon the initial ideas or vision that motivated the founding of the group in order to create a more complete theology. The group formally or informally gives feedback in the form of approval or disapproval of the leader's actions. The most successful leaders are continually adjusting and reacting to that feedback.

Over time, the choices open to the leader are narrowed. Structures (and expectations) develop. As the movement grows, and especially as branches are established, the leader has to work through intermediaries, and the lines of authority and communication become more impersonal. The leader's real ability to change structures, should s/he desire such adjustments, meets greater and greater resistance. Though the leader may retain some important pieces of control, the real task of managing the organization and administering the organization's affairs increasingly passes to the second and third echelon [of] leadership. The analogy between religious and secular corporations, however much it offends religious sensibilities, is both appropriate to and informative of religious group dynamics.

Just as different religious groups will believe and act differently when their founders are alive, different groups will bring all of their unique experiences as new religions to bear in their responses to the leaders' deaths and to filling the vacuums created by those losses. ... The problem of succession is not the determinative trauma it has often been considered to be and it in no way cuts off options limiting the group's determination of its own future course. Groups will tend to react to their leaders' deaths as they have previously reacted to other situations, and will make the necessary decisions in much the same way they have made decisions in the past.

SOURCE: J. Gordon Melton, Introduction to *When Prophets Die: The Postcharismatic Fate of New Religious Movements*, ed. Timothy Miller. New York: State University of New York Press, 1991, pp. 8–12

GLOSSARY

Baha'i A universalist religion which began in nineteenth-century Iran and now has followers in most countries.

CaoDai A syncretic new religious movement from Vietnam.

Charismatic Extraordinary personal magnetic appeal of a person, or speaking in a strange language.

Cult A religious group devoted to a single person or deity.

Neo-paganism A variety of religions reawakening ancient nature mysticism.

Sect A religious group different from an orthodox tradition, with a charismatic leader, strict rules of conduct, a sense of elite privilege, and restrictions on individuality.

Syncretism Combination of various religions' beliefs and practices.

Wicca Neo-pagan movement of witches traced to the writings of Gerald Gardner in England in the 1940s.

REVIEW QUESTIONS

1   What themes in Asian cultures are echoed in Sun Myung Moon's writings?
2   Do your own research and identify the major strands of traditional religions syncretized in CaoDai.
3   How do the new Wiccan movement themes differ from traditional stereotypes of witches? How do you evaluate these themes—positively or negatively?

DISCUSSION QUESTIONS

1   Do you think that offshoots of traditional religions, or syncretic blends of traditional religions, have the authenticity of the originals?
2   Should any legal limits be placed on new religions? If so, by what criteria? If not, why not?
3   Which qualities and beliefs do you believe would constitute a positive new religion? Why?

INFORMATION RESOURCES

The Baha'i Faith
<http://www.bahai.org>

Bowker, John, ed. "New Religious Movements," in *Oxford Dictionary of World Religions*. Oxford: Oxford University Press, 1997.

CSUS Library: Religion in America
<http://library.csus.edu/guides/warej/religionamerica.html#top>

Fisher, Mary Pat. *Religion in the Twenty-first Century*. Upper Saddle River, NJ: Prentice-Hall, 1999.

Introductions to New Religious Movements
<http://www.religioustolerance.org>

Religion Facts
<http://www.religionfacts.com/>

Wessinger, Catherine, *et al*. "New Religious Movements," in *Encyclopedia of Religion*, ed. Lindsay Jones. 2nd ed. Vol. 10, pp. 6513–82. New York: Macmillan, 2005.

CHAPTER 13

RELIGION IN A NEW ERA

In the twenty-first century, processes of urbanization, globalization, and industrialization are leaving no area of the world untouched. Traditional religious cultures are being challenged to respond to the fast-changing social scene. These responses take many forms. This final chapter will explore various facets of religions' engagement with a changing world, including globalization, secularism, exclusivism, interfaith initiatives, and concern about issues such as environmental destruction and poverty. The chapter ends with a piece on spirituality in general, in contrast with the organized religions that have been examined throughout the book.

Globalization and religions

Globalization is an old process now moving at warp speed. When it spreads from major industrial nations, it sends global capitalism—jobs, products, television shows, technology—but also ideas about human rights, democracy, the role of women, and environmental concerns. When it spreads to Western industrial nations from other cultures, it results in products such as oil and coffee, and introduces new languages, food, music, and practices such as yoga, martial arts, and meditation.

The irony is that globalization is not all homogenized. Pluralism (the diversity of cultures in one society) shapes moving forces to local forms, so ancient-type despots use modern weaponry to enforce old tribal rules. Migrants flock to rich countries to earn money, much of which is used to build temples in their home style, or is sent home. Globalization is welcomed by some, and furiously opposed by others. Wars are fought to control resources such as oil. Terrorism spreads devastation to oppose modern imperialistic hegemony and maintain local culture.

The Global Village by Lester Kurtz

Religions, too, have become global. Hindus build temples abroad, Buddhists establish monasteries, and Christians send missionaries—each tradition gaining converts. Interfaith initiatives seek dialogue among them all. The challenge is for people of conscience to find common spiritual and ethical principles. In the following extract Professor Lester Kurtz, of University of Texas at Austin, contributes some thoughts to this conversation.

The global village is becoming a reality economically and socially, if not politically, as every isolated corner of the planet is being knit together into a world system. This global order, emerging for several centuries, [became] a reality in the twentieth century as all humans increasingly participate in a "shared fate". ... Our economic and social institutions, our culture, art, music, and many of our aspirations, are now tied together around the world. But the human race is constructing a multicultural global village full of conflict and violence as well as promise.

Just as the Cold War between the United States and the Soviet Union ended in the 1990s and we made astounding progress in solving old conflicts, ethnic and religious nationalism exploded in violence around the world. Mark Juergensmeyer[1] contends that rather than witnessing the "end of history" ... and the emergence of a worldwide consensus in favor of secular liberal democracy, we may see the coming of a new Cold War, one between the secular West and numerous new religious nationalisms. "Like the old Cold War," says Juergensmeyer, "The confrontation between these new forms of culture-based politics and the secular state is global in its scope, binary in its opposition, occasionally violent, and essentially a difference of ideologies."

Social life may be fundamentally different in the [twenty-first] century, although many features of today's life will persist, just as there was much continuity between pre-agricultural and agricultural eras, premodern and modern times. A major task ... will be to order our lives together and to create an ethos, or style of life, with a moral basis. The ethos must include sufficient agreement about common norms to facilitate cross-cultural interactions, international commerce, and conflict resolution while permitting considerable cultural diversity on the planet. The process of coming together, however, will not be an easy one. Religious traditions are central to that process because of their role in defining norms, values, and meaning; in providing the ethical underpinning for collective life; and in forging the cultural tools for cooperation and conflict.

Much of the best and worst of human history is in the name of its Gods, and religious traditions continue to provide both an ethical critique of, as well as a justification for, much bloodletting. ... The sociological study of religion has important insights into the central issues of how we can live together in our multicultural global village as well as helpful tools for investigating the problems created by our newly created common life with its diverse norms and values. ... Whether or not we can discover a means for sustaining a diversity of religious traditions and a wide range of ethical values and still live together remains an unanswered question.

The world's religions will be an integral part of the process, for better

---

1 Mark Juergensmeyer—noted professor of sociology and global religions.

or for worse. Faith traditions "work" because they answer fundamental questions in a comprehensive way. That very strength, however, sometimes results in exclusivistic claims to a monopoly on the "Truth," which, in a multicultural global village, often precipitates fatal conflicts among competing religious claims and the people who make them. The very things that hold a community together can also tear it apart. ...

Our ancient ancestors sat around the fire and heard stories about their forebears—about the time when life first emerged in the universe, about lessons for living their lives. When people gather today, the flickering light comes from a television rather than a fire, but we still hear stories about the nature of reality as it is perceived in our own cultures. Many of Earth's previous inhabitants heard only one story about creation during their lifetime, but today most people hear more than one as the various religious traditions of the world—as well as newer scientific ones—diffuse widely through modern means of mass communication. We are surrounded not only by our own cultures but those of countless other peoples. Encountering these different perspectives on life is stimulating and enticing, but the overall process of cross-cultural contact is highly complicated because meaningful differences do exist among religions and sometimes provide the basis or excuse for confrontation.

Historically, religious ideas have provided the major organizing principles for explaining the world and defining ethical life for elites and masses alike, and they continue to do so, but modern critiques of religion have shaken them to the root. The globalization of our "lifeworlds" ... will have as great an impact on religious life as industrialization did. Just when humanity most needs an ethical system that enables diverse peoples to coexist peacefully and justly, the traditional sources of such guidelines are being daily undermined by the challenge of modern science and the increased cross-cultural contact.

Many conflicts occurred through the history of Christianity, of course, but none so radical as those precipitated by the crisis of modernism in the last two centuries. Scientific arguments called into question not just specific dogmas but the very notion of dogma. As the Roman Catholic Pope put it in 1907, modernism lays "the axe not to the branches and shoots, but to the very root" of the faith. ... Cross-culturally, meanwhile, competing religious traditions were offering alternative religious explanations to fundamental questions about life and how it should be lived.

Even before the changes in society and culture associated with industrialization had time to become fully absorbed, however, the world changed again—just as profoundly—when the various human communities were thrust into intimate contact by late twentieth-century communications and transportation technologies and the globalization of an advanced capitalist economy that relies on far-flung networks of production and consumption. Most scholars in the nineteenth century predicted a new era of peace and prosperity, yet the twentieth century brought bloodshed on a scale never before experienced and prosperity for a privileged few, accompanied by mass starvation and misery for many more.

The communications and transportation revolutions of the twentieth century took off in the post-World War II era. By the time Marshall McLuhan (1960)[2] introduced the term "global village" into our vocabulary, a new awareness of the interconnectedness of our lives was emerging. In the 1960s and 1970s, a massive increase in international trade transformed the nature of economic processes. Capital from the industrialized countries, in search of cheap labor, was shifted to so-called "less developed" nations so that much of the actual production process moved outside the United States and Western Europe and into Third World countries. By the early 1970s, the 500 U.S. major corporations were making 40 percent of their profits abroad. ...

Cultural diffusion, driven in part by economic developments, has resulted in a global greed for consumer goods among those people who can afford to participate in the system (and often a hope for participating among those who cannot afford to do so). In addition to nation-states, regional and international political alliances and institutions are playing an increasingly important role, right up to the United Nations, which functions as something of a quasistate at the global level.

At the close of the nineteenth century, the sociologist Emile Durkheim ([1893] 1933) observed that the emerging world system of his day showed two separate and contradictory trends: increasing unity and increasing diversity. This insight proved to be an enduring one. Even as our lives are becoming ever more intertwined, the people who exist in our everyday world are more and more diverse. Most people do not live in isolated homogeneous villages but in heterogeneous cities. International trade, global social networks, and telecommunications locate us all in the same shared space. Even rural villagers are linked in an unprecedented way to the world economy as they send and receive goods around the globe.

Most people are ambivalent about the new world order. Many enjoy the material benefits, but they have come at a high price—including the destruction of many of the world's indigenous cultures and radical transformations of other societies as well as widespread ecological devastation. The last two centuries have seen violence and misery on an unprecedented scale, but a portion of the world is healthier, eats better, and lives longer than the royalty of past civilizations. In the nineteenth century, the people with the most advanced technology, Western Europeans, subjugated most of the rest of the world; in the twentieth century they began slaughtering one another at an unprecedented rate as militarized conflict was industrialized and the technology of war created "total war," in which—for the first time in history—all humanity is involved and all are potential victims.

SOURCE: Lester R. Kurtz, *Gods in the Global Village: The World's Religions in Sociological Perspective*, 2nd ed. Thousand Oaks, CA: Pine Forge Press, 2007, pp. 2–5

2 Marshall McLuhan (1911–1980)—was Director for the Center of Technology and Culture at the University of Toronto and wrote the influential *Understanding Media: The Extensions of Man* (1964).

Secularism versus exclusivism

In contrast to the modernist assumption that religion would quietly fade into the background as rationality and secularism took front stage, quite the opposite is happening in many places: some forms of religions are experiencing rapid growth. Among these, some exclusivist movements have become influential in the contemporary world.

The Battle for God   by Karen Armstrong

One of the most startling developments of the late twentieth century has been the emergence within every major religious tradition of a militant piety popularly known as "fundamentalism." Its manifestations are sometimes shocking. Fundamentalists have gunned down worshippers in a mosque, have killed doctors and nurses who work in abortion clinics, have shot their presidents, and have even toppled a powerful government. It is only a small minority of fundamentalists who commit such acts of terror, but even the most peaceful and law-abiding are perplexing, because they seem so adamantly opposed to many of the most positive values of modern society. Fundamentalists have no time for democracy, pluralism, religious toleration, peacekeeping, free speech, or the separation of church and state. Christian fundamentalists reject the discoveries of biology and physics about the origins of life and insist that the Book of Genesis is scientifically sound in every detail. At a time when many are throwing off the shackles of the past, Jewish fundamentalists observe their revealed Law more stringently than ever before, and Muslim women, repudiating the freedoms of Western women, shroud themselves in veils and *chadors*. Muslim and Jewish fundamentalists both interpret the Arab–Israeli conflict, which began as defiantly secularist, in an exclusively religious way. Fundamentalism, moreover, is not confined to the great monotheisms. There are Buddhist, Hindu, and even Confucian fundamentalisms, which also cast aside many of the painfully acquired insights of liberal culture, which fight and kill in the name of religion and strive to bring the sacred into the realm of politics and national struggle.

   This religious resurgence has taken many observers by surprise. In the middle years of the twentieth century, it was generally taken for granted that secularism was an irreversible trend and that faith would never again play a major part in world events. It was assumed that as human beings became more rational, they either would have no further need for religion or would be content to confine it to the immediately personal and private areas of their lives. But in the late 1970s, fundamentalists began to rebel against this secularist hegemony[3] and started to wrest religion out of its marginal position and back to center stage. In this, at least, they have enjoyed remarkable success. Religion has once again become a force that no government can

---

3 Hegemony—the dominating influence of one group's worldview over another.

safely ignore. Fundamentalism has suffered defeats, but it is by no means quiescent. It is now an essential part of the modern scene and will certainly play an important role in the domestic and international affairs of the future. It is crucial, therefore, that we try to understand what this type of religiosity means, how and for what reasons it has developed, what it can tell us about our culture, and how best we should deal with it.

SOURCE: Karen Armstrong, *The Battle for God: A History of Fundamentalism.* New York: Ballantine Books, 2001, pp. xi–xii

Demonizing the "Other"—A Self-Critique from Islam

by Farish A. Noor

Throughout history, religious fanatics from all religions have often swayed public opinion by painting those they regard as their opponents in the battle for God as demonic figures. Such negative images have been so powerful that they have been used to justify violence against the "Other," in contradiction to the central messages of love and peace that are taught by all religions. Farish Ahmad Noor, a Malaysian political scientist and human rights activist, who has taught in Malaysia, Berlin, and the Netherlands, attempts to trace some of the threads of dualistic thinking that have distorted views of Islam and Muslims' perceptions of other religions in our times. Such self-critiques could well be forthcoming from all religions if we are to move toward a more harmonious world.

Walking in the streets of London in the early 1990s, I came across a poster that bore the slogan *"The Islamic State Coming soon to a country near you."* The poster was put up by the radical Islamist group *Hizb al-Tahrir*, which was originally formed in Palestine in the early 1950s and had spread its branches all over the world, extending as far as Western Europe. For decades groups like *al-Muhajirun* and *Hizb al-Tahrir* have been pre-occupied with the single-minded task of projecting themselves as the sole and exclusive voice of "pure Islam" in the West, confronting not only their respective Western governments but also other Islamic groups and movements that they regard as un-Islamic and "contaminated" by the evils of the Western environment.

Marginalized though they were groups such as these were propelled to the forefront of European Muslim politics thanks to the machinations of the Western media (perpetually working on the basis of a "take me to your leader" mentality) and variable factors that were beyond the control of anyone. Events such as the *Satanic Verses* controversy, the Gulf War of 1990–1, the military coup in Algeria after the elections of 1992, and the Bosnian crisis contributed to a growing sense of insecurity and persecution among Muslims the world over. For Muslims living in Europe, the fear of being engulfed by "the Other" and losing one's identity seemed even more acute.

In time, a host of radical Islamist groups began to appear on local university campuses in Britain and other Western countries. Many of these were made up of young, angry, and frustrated Muslim youths who were desperate for change in their own societies. Fed up with what they saw as the passivity of their elders and weakness of their community, these groups began to mobilize themselves and demand their rights on a communitarian basis. The groups themselves were a myriad assembly of different movements with radically different beliefs and orientations. While some adopted the politics of communitarianism (fighting for Muslim rights on the basis of democratic pluralism and democracy), others opted for a more radical approach by directly challenging the law of the land. Groups like *Hizb al-Tahrir* organized numerous "worldwide" rallies in cities like London which managed to attract mainly local participants and a number of foreign dissidents who graced their events. In many of their rallies and campaigns, talk was rife of the "second coming of Islam" and Islam's "final victory" over Western hegemony. Another common theme that was often brought up was the final victory over Israel and "international Jewry," calling on Muslims to unite and rise up against a common foe.

It struck me that what actually united these Muslims were the common negative tropes of the malevolent Other. On the many occasions when I attended these rallies, I was struck by the number of books and leaflets that were being distributed which spoke of the so-called "Western/Jewish/Zionist/ Christian/communist conspiracy against Islam and Muslims." There were books about how AIDS was a plot to destroy the *umma*, how population control was a Zionist/Vatican plot to stop the growth of Islam, and how young Muslims were being corrupted by the secular education they were being given in Western schools. There were also the usual sensational revelations that insults to Islam could be read in Coca Cola labels, provided one looked at them upside-down and reflected backwards in a mirror, and so on.

Here the unity of the *umma* was based on a simplistic form of dialectical opposition which invariably pitted Muslims against the non-Muslim Other. Two neat chains of equivalences were formed: Islam was equated with Muslim needs and concerns, ethics, morality, spirituality, and justice. By default, everything un-Islamic was portrayed as immoral, secular, worldly, and corrupt. A Hegelian dialectic follows suit: Islam is presented as an oppositional force that has to propel itself towards confrontation and conflict, in order to overcome obstacles placed before it before achieving its final and ultimate triumph.

Another recurrent theme that struck me was the millenarian idea of the victory of Islam over the West and the forces of *kufr* (unbelief). A harrowing image was being painted through the discourses that were circulating in these meetings. The propagandists of groups like *Hizb al-Tahrir* and *al-Muhajirun* spoke of a glorious age yet to come when Islam would reign triumphant over the West, and the flags and banners of Islam would flutter over the gilded towers and parapets of Western capitals. ...

This state of affairs was allowed to go unchecked and to fester for years. During the 1990s the fortunes of many of these radical groups improved markedly as their leaders were quick to hog the limelight and grab the headlines with their fiery rhetoric and combustible speeches. Calls for the creation of an Islamic state in Britain, the imposition of *Hudud* law in the West, the formation of separate Islamic communes with legislatures, courts, and councils of their own—all reinforced the popular Western prejudice of Islam as a religion of exclusivism, intolerance, and dogmatism, unable to cope with the demands of the present and unwilling to live with the realities of a multicultural world.

Then came September 11, 2001, and in a flash the paranoia of the West took on a life of its own. The nightmare of a resurgent militant Islam growing in the very heart of the Western world seemed to many a reality, and there were just as many at hand to support the claim that Islam was indeed a religion of violence, conflict, and terror. ...

The net result of years of radical thinking among some Islamist movements in the West and elsewhere was the reinforcement and perpetuation of the myth of Islam as a threat to the West. By living up to the stereotype of Muslims as intolerant fanatics, these radical movements had given additional support to the claim that Islam was indeed an enemy and threat to the world. A monumental own-goal had been scored by the radicals against not only themselves, but the Muslim community as a whole.

Caught as Muslims are in this mess that is partly of our own making, the question remains: how do we extricate ourselves from this impasse while maintaining our identity and right to speak about matters that are of pivotal concern for the Muslim community? How can we defend our rights, articulate our demands, communicate our anxieties, and aspire to success in a way that is inclusive and non-confrontational? In short, how do we work towards a new understanding of the *umma* (and its relationship with the Other) and political success in the contemporary world? ...

One of the key features of many contemporary Islamist movements is their reliance on a form of simplistic oppositional dialectics which requires the creation of a negative Other as the constitutive alterative to the Islamist project. Such dialectical opposition rests upon a neat and clear division, usually constructed along a strictly policed boundary line that demarcates the differences between the self ("us") and the other ("them"). ...

Such a dialectical approach is certainly not unique to Islamist movements. It was, after all, derived from the Western political tradition and experience of Western societies and the Islamists merely took up a strategy that had worked elsewhere. The problem with such a dialectical approach, however, is that it also introduces internal boundaries and strategies of differentiation that contribute to the bifurcation of society and the distortion of social relations. It introduced a movement of internal division and potential conflict that is necessary for the dialectic to get off the ground in the first place. Indeed, such a dialectical approach cannot possibly work without first introducing tension and division within society and, after doing so, emphasizing such divisions.

Over the past few decades we have seen how such a dialectical approach has been normalized and generalized across the board among Islamist movements worldwide. In fact one of the defining features of the current Islamist resurgence worldwide is that it requires the presence of the trope of the negative Other, which manifests itself in a number of forms: secularism, the West, international Jewry/Zionism, capitalism, etc. ...

If a political project begins with the premise that opposition and confrontation are the engines of change, then one cannot simply discard confrontation and conflict as redundant once the initial revolutionary moment is enacted. Dialectical movements tend to be on the lookout for new enemies all the time, as an opponent is required to give the revolution its identity. This in turn means that the constitutive Other will also remain as a perpetual presence, like a ghost that does not abandon its victim. The Islamist project (like many other religious and secular dialectical projects) has been haunted by ghosts from the beginning.

The second problem relates to the relationship between ethics and politics in Islam. Islam, as we all know, places ethics at the forefront of all human relations. ... We are told that Muslims do not have the right to torture their victims, kill their prisoners, destroy their property, do harm to civilians, and so on. What is more, so great is this moral imperative that Muslims are not even allowed to slander their opponents lest this diminishes their human identity and status as fellow creatures in the eyes of God. It is for this reason that racist caricatures and dehumanizing propaganda against the enemy are frowned upon. Muslims need to remember that even their mortal enemies are fellow human beings, the creation of the same God. This reminds us of the fundamental unity of all things, a principle emphasized time and again in the notion of *tawhid* (unity of God).

Dialectical opposition flies in the face of Islamic ethics and undermines the universal basis of Islam by creating and perpetuating not only false dichotomies but also violent hierarchies between the self and other. It dehumanizes the other, reducing the other to a subject whose human potential and status are diminished in our eyes. Islamic ethics, on the other hand, reminds us of the need to recognize the subjectivity of the other all the time. It is also there to remind us that the other can and should be seen as our friends and potential ally as soon as hostilities cease. It is often stated that Islam is a religion of peace, and this is true, but only if we realize that this peace can only be realized when Muslims acknowledge the fundamental humanity they share with others. ... No amount of sincerity and conviction on our part will help us communicate the message and values of Islam to the world as long as we view the rest of the world as alien and antithetical to us.

... Despite the painfully and brutally obvious suffering that has been inflicted upon us, Muslims have not been able to communicate our pain and anxieties to the outside world (which at times may even be the neighbor next door), for the simple reason that we think of them as the *outside* world. The division between inside and outside, in-group and out-group, has been so forcibly enforced by this dialectical outlook which we have foisted upon ourselves that we have effectively exiled ourselves from the rest of humanity. When the Palestinian mother cries amidst the rubble of her home, searching for the bodies of her children buried underneath, her pain is seen as somewhat "exotic" and "incomprehensible" by some. When the Bosnian son bares his heart and vows to avenge the death of his siblings who were killed by some murderous mercenaries, his cry for justice is seen instead as an irrational cry for blood. Somehow the agony of Muslims is presented as being somewhat less than human, or beyond the frontiers of intelligibility. Less than, or more than, or other than human, Muslims are often seen as being radically different. Much of this is due to our own introvertedness, born and bred in a climate of suspicion and frustration.

There is not much that we can do about the deliberate falsification and re-construction of the image of Islam and Muslims in the mainstream global media. Despite protests of the contrary, the world is still being fed a stream of instrumental fictions about Islam and Muslims that continue to frame us as being radically "Other." But we can—and I would argue, must—take the first step by abandoning such a dialectical approach ourselves in order to extricate ourselves from this hopeless impasse. The Muslim world has every right and duty to communicate its anger, pain, frustration, and fears to the rest of the world. But it must do so with intelligence, with honesty, and with compassion not just for Muslims, but for all of humanity.

The first thing that has to be attempted is a self critique of ourselves and our own notions of identity and difference. For so long the Muslim world has been trapped in a dialectical impasse of its own making. The time has come for us to utilize the tools of contemporary social science and critical theory to interrogate some of the fundamental notions of identity and belonging which have shaped and colored Muslim politics for so long. The Muslim world needs to recognize, accept, and even celebrate the internal differences and plurality within itself. The myth of a homogeneous and static Muslim world, forever paralyzed in frozen time, must be exposed for what it is: a discursive strategy and little else. ...

Pluralism in Islam has been frowned upon, suppressed, denied, and even hounded on the grounds that it would undermine the unity of the [community] itself. ... But progressive Muslims would argue that pluralism is a fact of life and a feature that is found in all civilizations, cultures, and belief systems, and is certainly not unique to Islam. ...

Recognizing the multiplicity within ourselves opens the way for us to recognize the multiplicity of the other as well. It would mean that we would be able to look at the West (and the rest) for what it truly is: a complex assembly of actors and agents, interests, beliefs, values, and ideas that may not be completely in harmony with each other. It may also help us realize that in the midst of that confusing and complex heterogeneity that is the other are also values, beliefs, and ideas that are common to ours. The poor in the Muslim world may come to realize that their poverty is shared by others beyond their faith community as well. Muslim women will come to realize that their lot is a common one, shared by women outside the frontier of *dar al-Islam* (Abode of Islam).

The recognition of the other as similar to the self is the first step toward building effective collaborative coalitions and alliances that may actually help us Muslims get our point of view across and to understand the point of view of the Other. Only then will the moment arrive when Muslims can work hand in hand with non-Muslims on matters that affect all of humanity as a whole, and not the *umma* exclusively. ...

What progressive Muslims are calling for here is, in a sense, an *Islam bi la Hudud*—an Islam without borders—that locates itself in the present realities of the borderless, plural, multicultural, complex, unequal, and unjust world that we live in today. We call for the rejection of the narrow and exclusive mindset and siege mentality that have robbed us of the channels of communication and cooperation that we desperately need. We call for the rejection of a dialectical approach to the Other which can only frame the other in negative terms as the enemy (or potential enemy) that has to be greeted with suspicion and fear. We also call for an introspection and self-critique that will help disabuse us of some of the myths of our own making, such as the myth of a "pure," "authentic," and "uncontaminated" *umma* that appears *ex nihilo*. ...

Universalism, which rests at the heart of Islam and the Islamic message, needs to be reactivated and made an article of faith among Muslims living in the world today. Our concerns for justice, equity, rights, and freedom need to be articulated in the context of a borderless world where our audience is not only ourselves but the world as a whole, both now and in the future. We need to take up, defend, and promote this form of universalism as part of our identity as Muslims. There has to come a time when being a Muslim means living not only for oneself but for a multitude of others as well. That time is now.

SOURCE: Farish A. Noor, "What is the Victory of Islam? Towards a different understanding of the Ummah and political success in the contemporary world," in *Progressive Muslims: On Justice, Gender, and Pluralism*, Omid Safi, ed. Oxford: OneWorld Publications, 2003, pp. 320–32

Interfaith movement

Religious pluralism as cultures mix has the potential for either struggles for dominance or the opposite: attempts to understand and appreciate each others' religious ways. The two excerpts below are examples of the latter impulse, as expressed by two great religious leaders. Interfaith appreciation has become formalized as the "interfaith movement," with conferences and organizations of scholars and leaders from all religions proliferating everywhere.

The Essential Truth is One   by Hazrat Inayat Khan

Mystics of all religions find underlying unity in their spirituality, which transcends the externals of religions. The following passage is from a great Sufi mystic from India who brought a universal spiritual message to the West early in the twentieth century.

Perhaps a person belongs to the best religion in the world. He does not live it, belongs to it. He says that he is a Muslim, or a Christian, or a Jew. He is sure it is the best religion, but at the same time he does not care to live it—he just belongs to it, and thinks that belonging to a certain religion, which is an accepted religion, is all that is needed. And people of all different religions have made it appear so, owing to their enthusiasm, and forced by their mission in life. For they have made facilities for those who belong to their particular religion, saying that by the very fact of their belonging to that particular religion they will be saved on the Day of Judgment, while others, with all their good actions, will not be saved, because they do not belong to that particular religion. This is a man-made idea, not God-made. God is not the Father of one sect; God is the Father of the whole world, and all are entitled to be called His children, whether worthy or unworthy. And in fact it is man's [sic] attitude toward God and Truth which can bring him closer to God, who is the idea of every soul. And if this attitude is not developed, then, whatever a man's religion be, he has failed to live it. Therefore, what is important in life is to try and live the religion to which one belongs, or that one esteems, or that one believes to be one's religion.

But one must always know that religion has a body and has a soul. Whatever body of religion you may touch, you touch the soul; but if you touch the soul, you touch all its bodies, which are like its organs. And all the organs constitute one body, which is the body of *the* religion, the religion which is the religion of Alpha and Omega, which was and which is and which will always be. Therefore the dispute, "I am right and you are wrong," in the path of religion is not necessary. We do not know what is the heart of man. If outwardly he seems to be a Jew, a Christian, a Muslim, or a Buddhist, we are not the judge of his religion, for every soul has a religion peculiar to itself, and no one else is entitled to judge its religion. There may be a person in a very humble garb, without any appearance of belief in God, or of piety or orthodoxy, and he may have a religion hidden in his heart which not everybody can understand. And there may be a person who is highly evolved, and his outward conduct, which alone manifests to people's views, may appear to be altogether contrary to their own way of looking at things, and they may accuse him of being a materialist or an unbeliever, or someone who is far from God and Truth. And yet we do not know; sometimes appearances are merely illusions; behind them there may be the deepest religious devotion or the highest ideal hidden, of which we know very little.

… Those who, with the excuse of their great faith in their own religion, hurt the feeling of another and divide humanity, whose Source and Goal is the same, abuse religion, whatever be their faith. The Message, whenever, at whatever period it came to the world, did not come to a certain section of humanity; it did not come to raise only some few people who perhaps accepted the faith, the Message, or a particular organized Church. No, all these things came afterwards. The rain does not fall in a certain land only; the sun does not shine upon a certain country only. All that is from God is for all souls. If they are worthy, they deserve it; it is their reward; if they are unworthy, they are the more entitled to it. Verily, blessing is for every soul; for every soul, whatever be his faith or belief, belongs to God. ...

Every child is born in life a pupil, one who is willing to learn and willing to believe. As the Prophet Muhammad says: "Every soul is born on earth a believer; it is only afterwards that he turns into an unbeliever." It is certain that if one had not been born a believer one would never have learned the language of one's country, because if anyone had tried to teach the words and one had refused to accept the teachings as true, one would never have learned the names and character of things. For instance, if it were said, "This is water," and one had not believed it, and had thought, "It is fruit," then one would never really have known what was water and what fruit. A child is born with the tendency to believe and learn what it is taught.

The divine life has a certain capability to give life, and it gives this life as teaching to the children of earth, and this teaching is called *Dharma*, religion. Religions are many and different from one another, but only in form. Water is one and the same element, and formless, only it takes the shape of the channel which holds it and which it uses for its accommodation; and so the name water is changed into river, lake, sea, stream, pond, etc. So it is with religion; the essential truth is one, but the aspects are different. Those who fight about external forms will always fight, those who recognize the inner truth will not disagree, and thus will be able to harmonize the people of all religions.

Dharma has been given from time to time to the world, at times quietly, and sometimes with a loud voice; but it is a continual outpouring of the inner knowledge, of life, and of divine blessing.

SOURCE: Hazrat Inayat Khan, *The Unity of Religious Ideals.* New Lebanon, NY: Sufi Order Publications, 1979, pp. 5–8.

God Will Break All the Barriers! by Baba Virsa Singh

Baba Virsa Singh (1934–2007) was a revered teacher from Sikh tradition. Under his inspiration, celebrations of the major holy days of all religions have long been held in his communities in India and the United States, known as Gobind Sadan. As Sikhs, Hindus, Muslims, and Christians gathered joyously on December 28, 1996 at his community outside Delhi to celebrate the birthdays of both Jesus and Guru Gobind Singh, Baba Virsa Singh made the following prophetic statement.

One day, when Gobind Sadan was facing many problems, I was sitting on a sofa, feeling very serene and joyous. My mind was neither asleep nor awake. Great rays of light awoke me and in a vision drew my attention to this very place where we are sitting. Jesus was standing right here [a place near the dairy where now a statue of Jesus has been erected], with his arms outspread. Speaking as loud as thunder, he said, "Blesssss!" His voice seemed to echo through the cosmos. For an hour and a quarter, Jesus kept blessing and speaking about the things which were weighing on my mind. Just by his words, they were all resolved.

Even before that, I did not think that Jesus was separate from other prophets. Whatever slight sectarian boundary that existed in my mind was completely demolished then. It was not a matter of faith or pride on my part. It was by his wish that I saw him standing here in vision. I fully believe that after this happened, indescribable blessings came to Gobind Sadan.

These spiritual Powers are not only for one country, one community, one fortified institution. I feel that they are meant to bring enlightenment to the whole cosmos. Their light spreads everywhere. Our attempts to divide the Light into different countries and sects have caused us great trouble. The Light cannot be broken into pieces. It is everyone's right to celebrate whenever the holy day of any prophet, messiah, or messenger of God occurs. It is our right to welcome them in all places. I feel that if we all mold our minds like this, the light of the prophets will manifest in everyone's minds, throughout the world.

Guru Gobind Singh said, "Listen everyone, for I speak the truth: Only those who have deeply loved God have realized God." What is God? Love. Guru Gobind Singh, who called God his Father, said, "My Father is spreading light throughout the cosmos, giving blessings to the entire Creation." Jesus likewise said, "If you want to see the Power of my Father, the Creation of my Father, look at the flowers, the rivers, the trees, the animals. There is no place where my Father's light is not doing its work of blessing."

At present, our problem is that we take the name of religion without having faith in religion. Love is one, truth is one, and God is one. Then why are there divisions? If a person speaks ill of one messenger and praises another, he can never receive enlightenment. We must believe that light appeared when they came, that they were bestowing light, and that their light is here even today.

Today you yourself may be feeling inexplicable happiness, inexplicable peace. Why? Because we have been celebrating both Jesus' birthday and Guru Gobind Singh's birthday. Our feeling is that we have been moving through light all day, with light falling all around us. My firm faith is that God has filled each one with love, each to his own mind's capacity for love. Those who have come here have learned something new: that Jesus has come to a gurdwara [Sikh temple]. What is a gurdwara? The house of God. And Jesus is His son; he must come to his house. And we are loving him—what else?

Don't go near people who are critical of such things, for they are far from the Light. All of us should come beneath the Light. When you shall see one Form in all the prophets, your mind's tendency to hate will turn into kindness. Your mind will rise above the tendency to create boundaries.

I can say from full inner wisdom that these boundaries will be broken, that all these barriers will be removed, because God wants it so. He has been looking at these barriers, confined within these boundaries for a very long time, and now He feels, "I can no longer live within these boundaries." God wants to enjoy Himself, and God wants you to enjoy yourselves. Now you will see: God will break all these forts. We will all be happy, for then His blessings will fall upon us all. When a person breaks out of confinement, he breathes fresh air and moves freely through nature. When he remains in confinement, he feels suffocated.

We have been in confinement for a long time, but God now wants to break the barriers. At last He will now manifest His Light. I have full faith that the minds of the whole world will change. The public will be happy, but the religious authorities may experience some difficulties. They may be disappointed with God: "We were enjoying ourselves—What have You done now? We have concealed You until now, but now You are in the open." God will laugh: "I waited for a very long time, but you did not allow Me to come out of the boundaries, so now I am going to manifest Myself." He will say, "Let the Light go forth! Such a long time has passed while you 'authorities' were keeping a curtain between the Light and the people. ..."

I pray, "Oh God, please make Your priests understand, for they have become very rigid and exclusive. You are the King of the Spirit. Please refresh their minds and make them understand. The public is very good; they will follow whatever they are told." Today our prayer has reached God, and now He will send a bit of His Love to His priests. He can make them understand through their dreams, through visions. We leave it to God to decide how to make them understand, but He will surely do so.

Today is a day of great happiness, of great blessings, of great mercy. I have never spoken like this in the past, but today He has said, "Speak!" and I have done so. Today is a day of great celebration. It is a day for dancing. All of you dance!

SOURCE: Baba Virsa Singh, "God Will Break All the Barriers!" Talk given at Gobind Sadan, Delhi, on December 28, 1996

Religion and social issues

Religions do not exist in a rarefied space. They are imbedded in human communities and affect, and are affected by, all that goes on therein. Dire poverty, an increasing gap between rich and poor, environmental destruction, earthquakes, tsunamis, nuclear radiation, gender oppression, AIDS, crime, violence, and such are concerns of people from all faiths. The following extract illustrates the role that compassion—a value taught by all religions—may play in countering the grave threat of environmental destruction.

Sacred Whispers in the World by Lee W. Bailey

Of all the recent books about religion and nature, the most striking to me is *The Hand of God*, a picture book showing stunning photographs of deep space taken from satellite cameras. They have shown us the incredible vastness of the universe, the awesome immensity of about 150 billion visible galaxies—150 billion!—colorful nebulae clouds, rings around planets, huge balls of nuclear fire, and enough dazzling visions of outer space to awaken a newfound wonder at this astonishing spectacle. Our planet is just a tiny blue dot in the disk of the Milky Way galaxy, one hundred thousand light years across (590,000 trillion miles—6,400,000 trips from earth to the sun), with 100 to 200 billion stars.

All this new scientific awareness is shaping a new cosmology, broadening our sense of who we are in the cosmos. We inhabit a precious planet gifted with the right conditions for life—just the right temperatures, gravity, oxygen, water, that seem to be rare. Our neighbor planets are deadly cold or hot, with toxic atmospheres or oceans. Mercury's day can rise to 873°F hot and sink to −303°F cold at night. Jupiter, which could be filled with a thousand earths, is covered with a vast ocean of liquid hydrogen. Venus has a dense atmosphere of carbon dioxide and sulfuric acid that traps heat in a greenhouse effect of about 900°F—hot enough to melt lead.

All this could make us feel incredibly blessed to be given life on such a rarely fruitful planet in such a huge universe. But do we look up at the stars and thank the mysterious power that created us and turn back to earth with great respect and careful stewardship of our resources? Or do we carelessly poison the waters, overfish the oceans, overheat the atmosphere, drive species to extinction, pollute the air we breathe, and exploit our resources as fast as we can? You know. But why? If our instincts for power and pleasure are released in the frenzy to conquer the planet, don't our religions urge restraint and care of nature? They offer guidance for social justice and moral behavior, spiritual peace in troubled times, and life after death. But even though they may also have embedded messages about respect for all life, these have had precious little actual impact on the way we relate to nature.

Western religions have almost totally left nature out of their theologies and ethics, and are seeing ecological devastation as a result. Western-invented nuclear energy is spreading cancerous radiation across the globe. Hinduism, which sees Brahman in all the world, still cannot control the overpopulation of its land and the accompanying ecological disaster. The sacred Ganges, a holy place for bathing, is terribly polluted. Japan has a beautiful sense of preserving nature expressed in its mountain pilgrimages and gardens, but its industrial development is having harsh effects. Its huge fishing fleets are overfishing oceans and ignoring world calls for restraint in whaling. Earthquakes threaten confidence in nuclear power.

We are all ignoring global warming when we refuse to give up our fossil-fuel electric generation plants and smoky transportation systems that daily send tons of dangerous gases into the atmosphere. The damaging march of technological "progress" listens to precious few calls for restraint, and not many of them are from religions. The worldviews and cosmologies of our traditional religions are not being called upon to deal with the ecological crisis, and some cling fiercely to archaic creation myths and familiar but old traditions that ignore our urgent environmental predicament. We desperately need a new sense of the sacred in nature and our holy obligations to live in harmony with our environment. We urgently need to hear and attend to the ecological implications of the sacred whispers that fill the cosmos.

Ancient religions (and their surviving indigenous peoples) saw sacred spirits in nature. Some were ancestor spirits, others spirits of vegetation, birth, and death, and they were all respected. The numerous southwestern American Pueblo *kachinas*, for example, are ritual images of supernatural beings between humans and gods, both helpful and harmful. Some are believed to be spirits of departed ancestors. *Kachina* dolls are very popular gifts for Pueblo children and are sold to tourists. Hopi *kachinas* represent the spirits behind nature and society: the solstice, cactus, flowers, eagles, bears, buffalo, sheep, snow, rain, thunder, corn, and an earth god, as well as brides, chiefs, mothers, clowns, and warriors. Each has its sacred ways and requires respect for them. Men wear *kachina* masks and dance in ceremonies at *mesa* villages (villages on level desert mountaintops) several times a year, such as for the solstices. Have you seen the sacredness in the rain, the thunder, the solstice, the flowers, the animals, the stars?

Major world religions retain remnants of ancient beliefs about nature. In the biblical book of Job the question is asked, who made the world, and answered:

> But ask the beasts, and they will teach you,
> Ask the birds of the air to inform you,
> or tell the creatures that crawl to inform you,
> and the fish of the sea to instruct you.
> Who does not come to know from all these
> that the hand of the Lord has done this?
> In his hand are the souls of all that live,
> The spirits of every human being. (Job 12:7–10)

This nature spirituality has come to mean a sense of God as the remote creator, rather than the sacred spirit always present in the "Book of Nature." Nature theology is part of Western religions, but it plays a minor role. Humanity instead dwells on the outdated Genesis command to "fill the earth and subdue it, have dominion over the fish in the sea, the birds of the air, and every living thing that moves on the earth" (Genesis 1:28).

Western science of course assumes the metaphysical desacralization of the world in order to analyze it fearlessly. Humans need little encouragement to dominate, but religion and science have combined to permit a massive project of domination. During the long dawn of human history, when people suffered greatly from hunger, wild animals, cold, and hard work, domination made sense. But now we are coming to the end of the era when careless, unrestrained domination over nature, irrational and immoral, can continue, given the massively destructive weapons available and the widespread pollution poisoning our nest. We need a major shift in consciousness and priorities to take us away from thoughtless domination and bring us into careful harmony with our delicate home.

The first step in this urgently needed shift in awareness can arrive with a spiritual opening to sacred whispers from the world. The world is not overtly sacred, since it contains suffering and evil, and is not eternal. But there are quiet moments and glorious spectacles when the sense of sacredness floats forth. We need to discern these.

First we must differentiate the sacred in nature from technological wonders. Space rockets thundering aloft are awesome human accomplishments, but are only tiny bursts of power compared to the cosmic gravitation of the sun that holds our planet in its annual cycle around the sun. Computers are wonderful accomplishments of human reasoning, but are merely partial, artificial extensions of the incredible brains that we are given at birth, perhaps the most complex organs in the known universe. Cell phones are delightful ways to communicate wirelessly, but they pale in comparison to the very existence of the organic ear itself, the language we share, and the electromagnetic radio waves that we have learned to use. There are large natural and cultural phenomena of great antiquity and wide power that our clever technologies simply share.

We can think of ourselves as "taking advantage" of natural phenomena like these, or gratefully, thankfully sharing in their wonders harmoniously and respectfully, remembering our place in the grand sacred scheme, rather than grabbing for all the power we can get and running from the consequences. Our technologies are enchanting and exciting, powerful and welcome reliefs from suffering. But they simply rest upon the vast store of water, oil, steel, silicon, electricity, and other resources that make them possible—the cosmic furnaces that generated the atoms, the oceans that nourished the molecules and cells, the species that evolved into life's wondrous variations. This all has a sacred dimension, not just for human use, but in itself. We are not atop a hierarchy of beings that we should dominate. We depend on a vast network of subatomic forces, electromagnetic fields, gravitational pulls, life-supporting air, earth, water, food, and endless reproducing species of plants and animals. The mystery of the origin and finely tuned structure of all this has an incredible sacredness. A new consciousness would say "thank you" instead of "gimme"—thanks to our home universe, galaxy, sun, planet, oceans, atmosphere, foods, medicines, fellow creatures on earth, our inner feelings, and our varieties of social developments.

Our spirituality and traditional religions have a great task, the challenge of developing ways to experience the sacredness in nature, to honor it, and to work out the many ethical implications for living sustainably on earth—reducing resource consumption, pollution, and population growth as well as social injustice. We can and must shift our spiritual beliefs and practices so that they inspire not the vision of humans standing above nature, exploiting it just for the ego's pride, power, and pleasures. Promoting the "prosperity gospel" and ethnic-group population growth, for example, are not consistent with sacred whispers in the world. Sharing the sacred wonders of the sunrise and sunset, the seasonal round, the powers of life's sustaining reproduction patterns, and the beautiful gifts of our home planet's land, plants, animals, and fellow humans living around the globe—this is feeling the sacred whispers in the world. Our eco-spirituality goal is to learn to live in tune with the sacredness inherent around us and within us. This would be the start of a truly significant sacred earth ethic, a new dimension that we urgently need to cultivate.

SOURCE: Original article for this book by Lee W. Bailey, 2011

Spirituality

"I'm not religious, I'm spiritual." This is a comment often heard in personal discussions of religion. The heart longs for authentic glimmers of the sacred, in love, peace, healing, community, nature, and social justice—the great mysterious powers of the universe that we sense behind the stars and feel deep in the soul.

We can differentiate between the core essential elements of a religion, such as compassion, and the inevitable changing additions, such as ritual and politics. Traditions tend to make institutional practices seem unchangeable. But, like an underground river bubbling up in new places, sacred powers emerge in new ways, as in the deep ecology movement. Then the question arises as to whether these new experiences are authentic. This is where those seeking a new spirituality have to understand the core, so they do not fall into problems such as culturally limited ideas. The study of world religions helps with this task.

Authentic Spirituality   by David Elkins

In this extract, David Elkins, of Pepperdine University, explores core signs of authentic spirituality. Based on a survey, Elkins concludes that a universal pattern of spirituality, as distinct from institutional religion, would contain the following components:

1. Transcendent dimension. The spiritual person has an experientially based belief that there is a transcendent dimension to life. The content of this belief may range from the traditional view of a personal God to a psychological view that the transcendent dimension is simply a natural extension of the conscious self into the regions of the unconscious or Greater Self. But whatever the content, typology, metaphors, or models used to describe the transcendent dimension, the spiritual person believes in the "more," that what is seen is not all there is. She believes in an unseen dimension and believes that harmonious contact with and adjustment to this unseen dimension is beneficial. The spiritual person is one who has experienced the transcendent dimension, often through what Maslow[4] referred to as peak experiences, and she draws personal power through contact with this dimension.

2. Meaning and purpose in life. The spiritual person has known the quest for meaning and purpose and has emerged from this quest with confidence that life is deeply meaningful and that his own existence has purpose. The actual ground and content of this meaning vary from person to person, but the common factor is that each person has filled the existential vacuum with an authentic sense that life has meaning and purpose.

3. Mission in life. The spiritual person has a sense of vocation. She feels a sense of responsibility to life, a calling to answer, a mission to accomplish, even a destiny to fulfill. The spiritual person is "metamotivated" and understands that it is in losing one's life that one finds it.

4. Sacredness of life. The spiritual person believes life is infused with sacredness and often experiences a sense of awe, reverence, and wonder in nonreligious settings. He does not dichotomize life into sacred and secular, but believes all of life is holy and that the sacred is in the ordinary.

5. Spiritual vs. material values. The spiritual person may appreciate material goods such as money and possessions but does not seek ultimate satisfaction from them nor attempt to use them as substitutes for frustrated spiritual needs. The spiritual person knows that ontological thirst can only be quenched by the spiritual and that ultimate satisfaction is found in spiritual, not material, things.

6. Altruism. The spiritual person believes we are our brother's keeper and is touched by the pain and suffering of others. She has a strong sense of social justice and is committed to altruistic love and action. The spiritual person knows that no man is an island—rather, that we are all part of the continent of humanity.

7. Idealism. The spiritual person is a visionary committed to the betterment of the world. He loves things for what they are, yet also for what they can become. The spiritual person is committed to high ideals and to the actualization of positive potential in all aspects of life.

8. Awareness of the tragic. The spiritual person is solemnly conscious of the tragic realities of human existence. Deep awareness of human pain, suffering, and death gives depth to the spiritual person and provides her with an existential seriousness toward life. Somewhat paradoxically, however,

4 Abraham Maslow—scholar who wrote *Religions, Values and Peak Experiences* (1970).

awareness of the tragic enhances the spiritual person's joy, appreciation, and valuing of life.

9. Fruits of spirituality. The spiritual person is one whose spirituality has borne fruit in her life. True spirituality has a discernible effect upon one's relation to self, others, nature, life, and whatever one considers to be the Ultimate.

As we move into the postmodern age, we can no longer afford the luxury of tribal gods and narrow spiritual views. We simply must see that God is everywhere, that artesian wells of spirituality exist across the land. We must recognize that spirituality is universal and that the spiritual blood, as it were, that flows in our own veins is no different from that which flows in the veins of every other man and woman. To develop a new, universal vision of spirituality, we must be willing to open our hearts and let go of narrow religious views. We must be willing to join hands with others and work toward a common faith. As the Dalai Lama said, "We must find, all of us together, a new spirituality."

source: David N. Elkins, *Beyond Religion*. Wheaton, IL: Quest Books, 1998, pp. 34–6

REVIEW QUESTIONS

1   How is globalization stimulating a reaction? Why?
2   What is meant by "demonizing the other?" Is this an ancient or modern way of thinking? Is it central or peripheral to religion?
3   What major ideas are being offered in this chapter to overcome global conflict?

DISCUSSION QUESTIONS

1   What elements of secular modernism deserve your criticism? Why? What elements of opposition to modernism deserve your agreement? Why?
2   Do you think spirituality and religions have something to offer in solving the ecological crisis?
3   Looking over what you have learned from this book, how have your ideas about religion changed?

INFORMATION RESOURCES

Abdul-Matin, Ibrahim. *Green Deen: What Islam Teaches About Protecting the Environment.* San Francisco, CA: Berrett-Koehler Publishers, 2010.

Bailey, Lee W. and **Jenny Yates**, eds. *The Near-Death Experience: A Reader.* New York: Routledge, 1996.

BBC Globalisation News
<http://news.bbc.co.uk/2/hi/in_depth/business/2007/globalisation/default.stm>

Beyer, Peter. "Globalization and Religion," in *Encyclopedia of Religion*, ed. Lindsay Jones. 2nd ed. Vol. 5, pp. 3497–504. New York: Macmillan, 2005.

Bowker, John, ed. "Dialogue," in *The Oxford Dictionary of World Religions.* Oxford: Oxford University Press, 1997.

Brasher, Brenda. *The Encyclopedia of Fundamentalism.* New York: Routledge, 2001.

Braybrooke, Marcus. *Pilgrimage of Hope: One Hundred Years of Global Interfaith Dialogue.* New York: Crossroad, 1992.

Council for a Parliament for the World's Religions
<http://www.cpwr.org/index.html>

Debold, Elizabeth. "Spiritual but not Religious."
<http://www.enlightennext.org/magazine/j31/spiritual-not-religious.asp>

Ellens, Harold, ed. *The Destructive Power of Religion: Violence in Judaism, Christianity, and Islam.* 4 vols. Westport, CT: Greenwood Press, 2004.

Emerging Earth Community
<http://www.emergingearthcommunity.org>

Evans, Donald. *Spirituality and Human Nature.* Albany, NY: State University of New York Press, 1993.

The Forum on Religion and Ecology
<http://fore.research.yale.edu/>

Fox, Matthew. *Creation Spirituality.* San Francisco: HarperSanFrancisco, 1991.

———. *One River, Many Wells.* New York: Tarcher/Putnam, 2000.

Fuller, Robert C. *Spiritual but not Religious.* Oxford: Oxford University Press, 2001.

Gibson, James W. *A Reenchanted World.* New York: Metropolitan Books/Henry Holt, 2009.

The Globalist
<http://www.theglobalist.com>

Globalization, Stanford Encyclopedia of Philosophy
<http://plato.stanford.edu/entries/globalization/>

The Globalization Website
<http://www.sociology.emory.edu/globalization>

The globalization of religion
<http://www.units.muohio.edu/aisorg/syllabi/McCormack%20Simulation%201.pdf>

Gobind Sadan
<http://www.gobindsadan.org>

Gottlieb, Roger, ed. *This Sacred Earth: Religion, Nature, and Environment.* New York and London: Routledge, 1996.

———. *The Oxford Handbook of Religion and Ecology.* Oxford: Oxford University Press, 2006.

International Interfaith Centre, U.K.
<http://interfaith-centre.org>

Islamic Fundamentalism
<http://www.brucegourley.com/fundamentalism/islamicfundamentalismintro.htm>

Juergensmeyer, Mark. *The Oxford Handbook of Global Religions.* Oxford: Oxford University Press, 2006.

Maguire, Daniel and **Larry Rasmussen**. *Ethics for a Small Planet.* Albany, NY: State University of New York Press, 2001.

Marty, Martin, and **Scott Appleby**, eds. *The Fundamentalism Project.* 5 vols. Chicago, IL: University of Chicago Press, 1991–5.

National Council for Churches Eco-Justice Programs
<http://nccecojustice.org>

Palmer, Martin with **Victoria Finlay**. *Faith in Conversation: New Approaches to Religion and the Environment.* Washington DC: The World Bank, 2003.

Selig, Jennifer L. *Thinking Outside the Church.* Kansas City, KS: McMeel Publishing, 2004.

Spiritual Beliefnet
<http://www.beliefnet.com>

Swatos, William. "Globalization," in *Encyclopedia of Religion and Society*. Alta Mira Press.
<http://hirr.hartsem.edu/ency/globa.htm>

Taylor, Bron. *Dark Green Religion*. Berkeley, CA: University of California Press, 2010.

———, ed. *Encyclopedia of Religion and Nature*. 2 vols. London and New York: Continuum Publishers, 2006.
<http://www.religionandnature.com>

Thich Nhat Hanh. *Living Buddha, Living Christ*. New York: Riverhead/Putnam, 1995.

Thurow, Lester. *Fortune Favors the Bold: What We Must Do to Build a New and Lasting Global Prosperity*. New York: HarperCollins, 2003.

Tucker, Mary E., and **John Grim**. "Ecology and Religion," in *Encyclopedia of Religion*, ed. Lindsay Jones. 2nd ed. Vol. 4, pp. 2605–68. New York: Macmillan, 2005.

———, eds. *Worldviews and Ecology*, Maryknoll, NY: Orbis Books, 1994.

Walsh, Roger. *Essential Spirituality*. New York: John Wiley, 1999.

Wenz, Peter. *Environmental Ethics Today*. Oxford: Oxford University Press, 2001.

LITERARY ACKNOWLEDGMENTS

Laurence King Publishing wish to thank those who have kindly allowed their copyright material to be reproduced in this book, as listed below. Every effort has been made to contact or trace copyright holders prior to publication, but should there be any errors or omissions, the publishers would be pleased to insert the appropriate acknowledgment at the earliest opportunity.

CHAPTER 1
pp.3–8 Original article for this book by Lee W. Bailey © 2005, 2011.
pp.8–9 Harcourt, Inc.: From *The Sacred and the Profane: The Nature of Religion* by Mircea Eliade, translated by Willard R. Trask (New York: Harcourt Brace Jovanovich, 1959) © 1959 by Harcourt Brace Jovanovich, Inc.
pp.10–11 Ninian Smart, *Dimensions of the Sacred: An Anatomy of the World's Beliefs.* ©1997 by Ninian Smart. Published by the University of California Press. Reprinted by permission.
pp.11–12 *The Future of an Illusion* from Volume 21 of *The Standard Edition of the Complete Psychological Works of Sigmund Freud* translated and edited by James Strachey, published by The Hogarth Press. Reprinted by permission of The Random House Group Ltd.
p.13 International Publishers, Inc.: From *On Religion* by Karl Marx and Friedrich Engels (Moscow: Foreign Languages Publishing House, 1955).
p.14 *The Gay Science* from *The Portable Nietzsche*, by Friedrich Nietzsche, edited by Walter Kaufmann, translated by Walter Kaufmann, copyright 1954 by The Viking Press, renewed © 1982 by Viking Penguin Inc. Used by permission of Viking Penguin, a division of Penguin Group (USA) Inc.
pp.16–18 Jung, C. G., *The Archetypes and the Collective Unconscious* © 1959 Bollingen. Reprinted by permission of Princeton University Press.
pp.18–21 Princeton University Press: From *The Hero with a Thousand Faces* by Joseph Campbell (Princeton, NJ: Princeton University Press, 1949; 2nd edition, 1968).
p.23 *Zen Flesh, Zen Bones: A Collection of Zen and Pre-Zen Writings* compiled by Paul Reps. New York: Doubleday & Company Inc., 1957, pp.24–6. © Estate of Paul Reps.
pp.24–25 Abraham Heschel, *Between God and Man: An Interpretation of Judaism.* New York and London: Simon and Schuster, 1998. © Abraham Heschel. Reprinted with permission of Professor Susannah Heschel.
pp.25–27 © David L. Miller.
pp.27–32 Dharma Publishing: From *Openness Mind* by Tarthang Tulku (Berkeley, CA: Dharma Publishing, 1978).
pp.28–30 From *The Blind Watchmaker: Why the Evidence of Evolution Reveals a Universe Without Design* by Richard Dawkins. Copyright © 1996, 1987, 1986 by Richard Dawkins. Used by permission of W.W. Norton & Company, Inc.
pp.31–32 Copyright © 2004 John Haught. Reprinted by permission of Westview Press, a member of the Perseus Books Group.
pp.32–34 The publisher acknowledges the Indian Institute of Advanced Study (IIAS), Shimla for granting permission to reproduce extracts from the book *Walking Naked: Women, Society, Spirituality in South India* by Vijaya Ramaswamy, published by the IIAS.
pp.34–36 From Paul Tillich, "The Lost Dimension in Religion," in *The Essential Tillich.* New York: Macmillan 1987. © SEPS. Licensed by Curtis Licensing, Indianapolis, IN. All rights reserved.

CHAPTER 2
pp.40–41 Rev. Dr. Harvey J. Sindima, "Mysticism and Spirituality in African Tradition" for Mysticism in World Religions conference, 17–18 Feb 2010, co-convened by Jamia Milia University and Gobind Sadan Institute for the Advanced Study of Comparative Religion, New Delhi.
pp.41–43 Georges Niangoran-Bouah: "The Talking Drum: A Traditional African Instrument of Liturgy and of Mediation with the Sacred," from *African Traditional Religions in Contemporary Society*, Jacob Olupona, ed., Paragon House, 1991. Used with permission.
p.45 Stephen Trimble, ed., *Our Voices, Our Land*, based on an audio-visual show created for the Heard Museum, Phoenix, Arizona. Flagstaff, Ariz.: Northland Press © 1986, pp. 24–47.
pp.45–46 Shambhala Publications, Inc.: From *Oya: In Praise of the Goddess* by Judith Gleason (Boston: Shambhala Publications, 1987).
pp.47–49 From John Grim, ed., *Indigenous Traditions and Ecology: The Interbeing of Cosmology and Community*, Center for the Study of World Religions, Harvard University Press, 2001.
pp.49–51 *The Shaman: Patterns of Siberian and Ojibway Healing* by Grim, John A. Copyright © 1983. Reproduced with permission of University of Oklahoma Press.
pp.51–55 Penguin Books: From *Of Water and Spirit: Ritual, Magic, and*

Initiation in the Life of an African Shaman by Malidoma Patrice Somé (New York: G. P. Putnam's Sons, 1994) © Malidoma Patrice Somé, 1994.
pp.56–57 Copyright © 1993 by Diane Bell.
pp.57–58 <http://www.alphacdc.com/banyacya/un92.html>: From "The Hopi Message to the United Nations General Assembly" by Thomas Banyacya, Kykyotsmovi, Arizona (December 10, 1992).
pp.58–60 From John Grim, ed., *Indigenous Traditions and Ecology: The Interbeing of Cosmology and Community*, Center for the Study of World Religions, Harvard University Press, 2001.

CHAPTER 3
pp.65–66 Motilal Banarsidass: From *The Hymns of the Rigveda*, new revised edition, translated by Ralph T. H. Griffith (Delhi: Motilal Banarsidass, 1976, 1986) © Motilal Banarsidass.
pp.66–67 "Married Life," from the Rig Veda and Atharvaveda, in *Thus Spake The Vedas.* Published by Sri Ramakrishna Math, Mylapore, Chennai-600004, India.
pp.67–68 Svetasvatara Upanishad 1, trans. Swami Nikhilananda, *The Upanishads: A New Translation.* From www.sankaracharya.org.
pp.68–69 Mundaka Upanishad in *The Upanishads*, 2nd edition, translated by Bibek Debroy and Dipavali Debroy, 1995. Pradeep Mittal, Books For All, Delhi (India).
pp.69–70 Brihadaranyaka Upanishad 4, English translation of Holy Upanishads by Swami Nikhilananda. From www.ishwar.com/hinduism.
pp.70–71; 71–72 *The Bhagavad Gita*, translated by Eknath Easwaran, founder of the Blue Mountain Center of Meditation, copyright © 1985, 2007; reprinted by permission of Nilgiri Press, P. O. Box 256, Tomales, CA 94971, www.easwaran.org.
pp.72–74 Bharatiya Vidya Bhavan: From *Ramayana*, 27th edition, by C. Rajagopalachari (Mumbai: Bharatiya Vidya Bhavan, 1990) © Bharatiya Vidya Bhavan.
pp.74–75 From *Sources of Indian Tradition*, Volume 1, edited by William Theodore de Bary. Copyright © 1958 Columbia University Press. Reprinted with permission of the publisher.
pp.75–76 *An Anthology of Sacred Texts by and about Women*, ed. Serinity Young, 1995. Published by The Crossroad Publishing Company. © 1993 by Serinity Young.
pp.76–77 "A Method of Enlightening the Disciple" from *Upadesa Sahasri (A Thousand Teachings)*, Chapter 1, by Adi Sankaracharya, trans. Swami Jagananda. Published by Sri Ramakrishna Math, Mylapore, Chennai-600004, India.
pp.77–78 "Yoga Sutras" by Patanjali, from Swami Venkatesananda © 2009 CYT. http://swamivenkatesananda.org/
pp.78–79 Motilal Banarsidass: From the *Siva Purana*, edited and translated by Prof. Jagdish Lal Shastri (Delhi: Motilal Banarsidass, 1970) © Motilal Banarsidass.
p.80 From *Sources of Indian Tradition*, Volume 1, edited by William Theodore de Bary. Copyright © 1958 Columbia University Press. Reprinted with permission of the publisher.
pp.81–82 Shiromani Gurdwara Parbandhak Committee: From *Guru Granth Sahib*, 3rd edition, adapted from English translation of Manmohan Singh (Amritsar, Punjab: Shiromani Gurdwara Parbandhak Committee, 1989).
pp.82–83 Motilal Banarsidass: From *The Devotional Poems of Mirabai*, translated by A. J. Alston (Delhi: Motilal Banarsidass, 1980) © Motilal Banarsidass.
pp.83–84 From *Songs of Kabir*, trans. Rabindranath Tagore. New York: Samuel Weiser, 1977.
pp.84–85 *Autobiography of a Yogi*, 2nd edition, by Paramahansa Yogananda (Mumbai: Jaico Publishing House, 1975/Los Angeles: Self-Realization Fellowship, 1998) © 1946 Paramahansa Yogananda, © renewed 1974 Self-Realization Fellowship.
pp.85–87 From *Religion in India*, eg. T. N. Madan. Delhi: Oxford University Press, 1991–92.
pp.87–88 Navajivan Trust: From *The Message of Mahatma Gandhi* by Mahatma Gandhi, edited by U. S. Mohan Rao (Delhi: Publications Division, Ministry of Information and Broadcasting, Government of India, 1968).
pp.88–89 From *Sources of Indian Tradition*, Volume 2, edited by S. Hay. Copyright © 1988 Columbia University Press. Reprinted with permission of the publisher.
pp.90–91 *Vidyajyoti Journal*: "The Secular Face of Hinduism" by Joseph Vellaringatt, from *Vidyajyoti Journal*, volume 65, no. 9 (September 2001), 4/A, Raj Niwas Marg, Delhi 110054.
pp.91–92 Mata Amritanandamayi: From "The Awakening of Universal Motherhood," an address to A Global Peace Initiative of Women Religious and Spiritual Leaders, Geneva (October 7, 2002).

CHAPTER 4

pp.97–99 Manas Publications: From *Spiritual Masters from India* by Shashi Ahluwalia (Delhi: Manas Publications, 1987).

pp.99–100 "Jain Sutras," trans. Dr. Jyoti Prasad Jain, in *Religion and Culture of the Jains*, 3rd ed., 1983. Courtesy Bharatiya Jnanpith.

pp.100–101 From *Sources of Indian Tradition*, Volume 1, edited by William Theodore de Bary. Copyright © 1958 Columbia University Press. Reprinted with permission of the publisher.

pp.101–103 "Akaranga Sutra," Book II, trans. Hermann Jacobi in *The Sacred Books of the East*, ed. F. Max Müller, 1964, vol. 22. (Delhi: Motilal Banarsidass, 1964.)

pp.103 L.M.Singhvi, *The Jain Declaration on Nature*, published privately, 1990.

pp.105–106 Kund-Kund Bharati: From *Barasa Anuvekkha by* Acharya Kund-Kund (Delhi: Kund-Kund Bharati, 1990).

pp.107–109 Indian Books Center: From "The Renunciate Life of *Sādhvi* Vicakṣaṇa," in *The Unknown Pilgrims: The Voice of the Sādhvis* by N. Shanta, translated by Mary Rogers (Delhi: Sri Satguru Publications, 1997). All rights reserved.

pp.109–111 Jain Publishing Company: From *Life Force: The World of Jainism* by Michael Tobias (Berkeley, CA: Asian Humanities Press, 1991). www.jainpub.com.

CHAPTER 5

pp.115; 115–116 Motilal Banarsidass: From *Buddhacarita, or Acts of the Buddha* by Asvaghosha, new enlarged edition, translated by E. H. Johnson (Delhi: Motilal Banarsidass, 1984).

pp.116–117 From *The Wisdom of China and India*, ed. Lin Yutang. New York: Modern Library, 1942.

pp.118–119; 119–120 © Bhikkhu Bodhi, 1995. Reprinted from *The Middle Length Discourses of the Buddha: A Translation of the Majjhima Nikaya* with permission from Wisdom Publications, 199 Elm Street, Somerville, MA 02144 USA. www.wisdompubs.org.

p.121 www.pathofdhamma.com/index.html, "The Thousands" and "Happiness," in *Dhammapada*.

p.122 © Bhikkhu Bodhi, 1995. Reprinted from *The Middle Length Discourses of the Buddha: A Translation of the Majjhima Nikaya* with permission from Wisdom Publications, 199 Elm Street, Somerville, MA 02144 USA. www.wisdompubs.org.

p.123 Penguin Group (UK): From *Buddhist Scriptures,* translated by Edward Conze (London: Penguin Classics, 1959) © Edward Conze 1959.

pp.124–125 Daihokkaikaku Publishing Company: From *Shobogenzo*, volume 1, by Dogen Zenji, translated by Kosen Nishiyama and John Stevens (Sendai, Japan: Daihokkaikaku, 1975) © 1975 by Kosen Nishiyama and John Stevens.

pp.125–127 Doubleday Broadway Publishing Group: From *Zen Buddhism* by D. T. Suzuki, edited by William Barrett (New York: Doubleday, 1956).

pp.127–128 Grove/Atlantic, Inc.: From *Bankei Zen: Translations from the Record of Bankei* by Peter Haskel (New York: Grove Press, 1984) © 1984 by Peter Haskel and Yoshito Hakeda.

pp.128–131 Courtesy Office of His Holiness the Dalai Lama.

pp.132–134 Reprinted by permission from *Engaged Buddhism: Buddhist Liberation Movements in Asia*, edited by Christopher S. Queen and Sallie B. King, the State University of New York Press © 1996, State University of New York. All rights reserved.

pp.135–138 Courtesy Charles S. Prebish, Charles Redd Endowed Chair Emeritus, Utah State University.

pp.139–140 Reprinted from *Being Peace* (1987, 2005) by Thich Nhat Hanh with permission of Parallax Press, Berkeley, California. www.parallax.org.

CHAPTER 6

pp.145–148 "Divinity and Salvation: The Great Goddesses of China" by Lee Irwin. *Asian Folklore Studies* (now *Asian Ethnology*) is an open access journal.

pp.148–149 Chinese Materials Center. From *Popular Religion in Pre-Communist China* by Clarence Day, 1975.

pp.150–152 Chan, Wang-tsit: *A Source Book in Chinese Philosophy.* © 1963 Princeton University Press, 1991 renewed PUP. Reprinted by permission of Princeton University Press.

pp.152–153 Courtesy Randall L. Nadeau, Trinity University.

pp.153–154 Chan, Wang-tsit: *A Source Book in Chinese Philosophy.* © 1963 Princeton University Press, 1991 renewed PUP. Reprinted by permission of Princeton University Press.

pp.154–155 From "Lessons for Women" by Pan Chao, in *An Anthology of Sacred Texts by and about Women*, edited by Serinity Young (New York: The Crossroad Publishing Company, 1995) © 1993 by Serinity Young.

pp.155–156; p.156 Chan, Wang-tsit: *A Source Book in Chinese Philosophy.* © 1963 Princeton University Press, 1991 renewed PUP. Reprinted by permission of Princeton University Press.

pp.157–158 Courtesy Professor Xinzhong Yao.

pp.159–160 Peng Liu: "The Staying Power of Religion," from *God and Caesar in China*, edited by Jason Kindopp and Carol Lee Hamrin (Washington, DC: Brookings Institution Press, 2004).

pp.161–163 Courtesy Randall L. Nadeau, Trinity University.

pp.164–165 From *The Book of Chuang-tzu*, translated by Burton Watson. Copyright © 1968 Columbia University Press. Reprinted with permission of the publisher.

pp.165–167 Simon and Schuster, Inc.: "The Way of the Taoist Tradition of Perfect Truth" by Wang Che, from *Chinese Civilization and Society: A Sourcebook* by Patricia Buckley Ebrey (New York: The Free Press, 1981) © 1981 The Free Press, a division of Macmillan, Inc.; reprinted in *Chinese Religion: An Anthology of Sources*, edited by Deborah Sommer (New York: Oxford University Press, 1995).

pp.167–169 From "The Story of Ho Hsien Ku," from Kwok Man Ho and Joanne O'Brien, "The Eight Immortals of Taoism," in *An Anthology of Sacred Texts by and about Women*, edited by Serinity Young (New York: The Crossroad Publishing Company, 1995) © 1993 by Serinity Young.

pp.169–170 Huang (2011) *Embrace Tiger, Return to Mountain: The Essence of Tai Chi*, Singing Dragon, London and Philadelphia. Reproduced with permission of Singing Dragon.

pp.170–171 Zhou Zhongzhi, abstract of paper delivered at the conference "Continuity and Change: Perspectives on Science and Religion," Philadelphia (June 3–7, 2006), a program of the Metanexus Institute. www.metanexus.net.

pp.172–173 Translated from the Sanskrit by F. Max Müller, edited by Richard St. Clair. http://web.mit.edu/stclair/www/larger.html.

pp.173–175 Sutra Translation Committee of the United States and Canada: From *Pure Land, Pure Mind, the Buddhism of Masters Chu-hung and Tsung-pen*, trans. J.C.Cleary, 1994.

pp.175–177 Buddha Dharma Education Association Inc.: From "The Gates of Chan," by Venerable Jing Hui. www.buddhanet.net.

CHAPTER 7

pp.182–183; pp.183–184 The University of Tokyo Press: From *The Kojiki*, Book 1, trans. Donald L. Philippi, 1968.

pp.184–185 Bukkyo Dendo Kyokai, Tokyo: From *The World of Shinto*, trans. Norman Havens, 1985.

pp.186–187 Courtesy Kodansha International.

pp.187–189 *Nao Deguchi—A Biography of the Foundress of Oomoto*, based on *Kaiso-den* by Sahae Oishi.

pp.190–191 *Misogi Shuho*, courtesy of Tsubaki Grand Shine of America. www.tsubakishrine.org.

ZOROASTRIANISM

pp.193–194; pp.194–195 http://zarathushtra.com. Translated by Mobed Firouz Azargoshasb.

pp.195–196 Translation of the Zoroastrian Creed by Joseph Peterson, reprinted with permission.

pp.196–197 The Writer's Workshop, Calcutta: From *The Towers of Silence* by Tina Mehta, 1998.

CHAPTER 8

pp.199–208 Reprinted from *Tanakh: The Holy Scriptures* © 1985 by The Jewish Publication Society, with the permission of the publisher.

p.209 Judith Glatzer Wechsler: From *Hammer on the Rock*, edited by Nahum N. Glatzer, translated by Jacob Sloan (New York: Schocken Books, 1962).

p.210 Yale University Press: From *The Living Talmud*, edited and translated by Judah Goldin (New Haven, CT: Yale University Press, 1957).

pp.211–212 Ktav Publishing House: From *Passover Haggadah*, translated by Nathan Goldberg 1949, 1993. Used with permission.

pp.213–214 www.hasidicstories.com: From *The Baal Shem Tov and the Doctor* by Doug Lipman.

pp.216–217 *Conservative Judaism and Jewish Law*, pp. xx-xxi © The Rabbinical Assembly, 1978, reprinted with permission.

pp.218–220 www.scjfaq.org: From *Principles of Reform Judaism*.

pp.221–222 Jewish Reconstruction Federation Archives: From *Reconstructionism on One Foot*, by Rabbi Les Bronstein, Oct 16, 2007. © Rabbi Les Bronstein.

pp.222–224 Elie Wiesel Foundation: From *The Perils of Indifference*, by Elie Wiesel from speech delivered 12 April 1999, Washington DC, transcription by Michael E. Eidenmuller.

pp.224–228 Original article for second edition of this book, by Ellen M. Umansky © 2006. Revised 2011.

pp. 228–231 Reprinted from *Tikkun: A Bimonthly Interfaith Critique of Politics, Culture, & Society*. www.tikkun.org.

CHAPTER 9

pp.243–244; pp.244–245 *The Nag Hammadi Library in English*, third completely revised edition, by James M. Robinson, general editor. Copyright © 1978, 1988 by E. J. Brill, Leiden, The Netherlands. Reprinted by permission of HarperCollins Publishers.

pp.245–247 From "Origen on First Principles" in *Readings in Christian Thought*, ed. Hugh T. Kerr, Abingdon Press, 1966. By permission of The Society for Promoting Christian Knowledge.

pp.251–252 Hodder and Stoughton Ltd.: From *Hildegard*, edited by Robert Van de Weyer (London: Hodder and Stoughton, 1997) © 1997 Robert Van de Weyer.

pp.254–255 UN Millennium Project: From *The Link Between the Environment and the Millennium Development Goals*, Church of England report, 2004.

pp.255–256 From a sermon by Rev. Christine Chakoian, February 6 2011, First Presbyterian Church, Lake Forest, Illinois.

p.257 Copyright © 1995 by Harvey Cox. Reprinted by permission of the author.

pp.258–260 Courtesy Steven M. M. Nolt, Professor of History, Goshen College, Goshen, Indiana, U.S.A.

pp.260–262 Writers House: From *Letter from the Birmingham Jail* by Martin Luther King. © Estate of Martin Luther King.

pp.262–263 New City Press: From *Mother Teresa: Her Life, Her Works* by Lush Gjergji (New Rochelle, NY: New City Press, 1991).

pp.263–264 Original article for this book by Lee W. Bailey © 2011.

pp.265–266 From *Rising Protestant Tide Sweeps Catholic Brazil*, by Todd Benson, 3 May 2007. All rights reserved. Republication or redistribution of Thomson Reuters content, including by framing or similar means, is expressly prohibited without the prior written consent of Thomson Reuters. © Thomson Reuters 2007. Thomson Reuters journalists are subject to an Editorial Handbook which requires fair presentation and disclosure of relevant interests.

pp.266–268 Oxford University Press: From "African Christian Communities," by David Chidester in *The Oxford Handbook of Global Religions*, ed. Mark Juergensmeyer, 2006.

pp.269–270 Courtesy National Council of Churches USA. www.ncccusa. org.

CHAPTER 10

pp.276–277, 277–279 Sh. Muhammad Ashraf: From *Sahih Muslim*, volume 1, translated by 'Abdul Hamid Siddiqi (Lahore, Pakistan: Sh. Muhammad Ashraf, 1973) © Sh. Muhammad Ashraf, Lahore.

pp.280–281 Reprinted by permission from *Shi'ite Islam* edited by Seyyed Hossein Nasr, the State University of New York Press. © 1980 State University of New York. All rights reserved.

p.288 http://hadith.al-islam.com.

pp.288–289 From Sahih Muslim, trans. 'Abdul Hamid Siddiqi. Lahore: Sh. Muhammad Ashraf 1973.

pp.289–290 Ahmadiyya Anjuman Isha'at Islam: From *The Religion of Islam*, 6th edition, by Maulana Muhammad Ali (Delhi: Motilal Banarsidass, 1994) © Ahmadiyya Anjuman Isha'at Islam.

pp.291–293 From *Speaking in God's Name: Islamic Law, Authority, and Women* by Khaled Abou El Fadl. Oxford: OneWorld Publications, 2001.

pp.294–295 From *Allegory and Philosophy in Avicenna (Ibn Sina)* by Peter Heath (Philadelphia, PA: University of Pennsylvania Press, 1992) © 1992 by the University of Pennsylvania Press.

pp.295–296 W. Montgomery Watt: From *The Faith and Practice of Al-Ghazali* by W. Montgomery Watt (London: George Allen and Unwin, 1953).

p.297 The Threshold Society: from *Rahi'a* translated by Charles Upton (Brattleboro, VT: Threshold Books, 1988).

pp.297–298 Reprinted by permission from *The Sufi Path of Love: The Spiritual Teachings of Rumi* edited by William C.Chittick, the State University of New York Press © 1983 State University of New York. All rights reserved.

pp.298–299 From *Sufis of Andalusia: The Ruh Al-Quds and 'Al-Durrat al-Fakhirah* by Muhyi al-Din Muhammad ibn al-'Arabi (London: George Allen and Unwin, 1971).

pp.299–300 From *Nizam Ad-Din Awliya: Morals for the Heart*, trans. Bruce B. Lawrence. Copyright © 1992 by The Missionary Society of St. Paul the Apostle in the State of New York, Paulist Press, Inc., Mahwah, NY. Reprinted by permission of the Paulist Press, Inc., www. paulistpress.com.

pp.301–303 Riffat Hassan: From "Are Human Rights Compatible with Islam?" <http://religiousconsultation.org/hassan2.htm>.

p.304 Imam Khomeini: *Islam and Revolution: Writings and Declarations of Imam Khomeini*, trans. Hamid Algar. Berkeley, CA: Mizan Press 1981.

pp.305–308 Ergun Capan, ed., *Terror and Suicide Attacks: An Islamic Perspective*. Somerset, NJ: The Light, 2006.

pp.308–313 James Turner Johnson, "Jihad and Just War" from *First Things* 124. Used by permission of First Things www.firstthings.com.

CHAPTER 11

p.317 Languages Department Punjab: From *The Great Humanist Guru Nanak* by Sir Jogendra Singh and Raja Sir Daljit Singh (Patiala, Punjab:

Languages Department Punjab, 1970).

p.318 *JapJi Sahib*, trans. Professor Puran Singh, 4th ed. Lahore: Lahore Book Shop, 1945.

pp.319–320 *Jaap Sahib*, trans. Surendra Nath. Delhi: Gobind Sadan, 1991, 1996.

pp.320–322 © International Sacred Literature Trust, 22 Northumberland Avenue, London WC2N 5AP.

pp.322–326 George Allen and Unwin Ltd.: Hymns from the Guru Granth Sahib, in *Selections from the Sacred Writings of the Sikhs*, translated by Trilochan Singh *et al.* (London: George Allen and Unwin, 1960/New York: Samuel Weiser, 1973).

p.326 Punjabi University: "Pray crow, peck not these eyes, so that I may see the Beloved" by Sheikh Farid, with commentary by Guru Nanak, in *Sri Guru Granth Sahib*, translated by Gurbachan Singh Talib (Patiala, Punjab: Punjabi University Publication Bureau, 1990) © Punjabi University, Patiala.

pp.327–328, 328 Gobind Sadan Institute: From *Bacchitar Natak* by Guru Gobind Singh, in *Jap*, translated by Surendra Nath (Delhi: Gobind Sadan, n.d.); from *Manas ki jaat* by Guru Gobind Singh, from *Akal Ustat*, translated by Gobind Sadan Institute, previously unpublished.

pp.329–332 Vision and Venture: From *Sikhism: Norm and Form* by Dharam Singh (Patiala, Punjab, and Delhi: Vision and Venture, 1997) © 1997, The Author.

CHAPTER 12

pp.336–338 Speech by Rev. Dr. Sun Myung Moon, 2006, http://www.familyfed.org/trueparents/main.php?chapter=pyungwha.

pp.338–339 From *The Book of Mormon* by Joseph Smith (Salt Lake City, UT: The Church of Jesus Christ of Latter-day Saints, 1830/1963).

p.340 From the official website of The Church of Jesus Christ of Latter-day Saints, http://lds.org/?lang=eng.

pp.341–343 From *The Religious Constitution of Caodaoism*, explained and commented by His Saintness Ho Pháp, trans. Bui Dac Hum. Redlands, CA: Chân Tâm, 1992.

pp.343–344 Baha'i Publishing Trust: From *Gleanings from the Writings of Bahá'u'lláh*, 2nd edition, translated by Shoghi Effendi (Wilmette, IL: Baha'i Publishing Trust, 1976), copyright 1939, 1952 © 1976 by the National Spiritual Assembly of the Baha'is of the United States. All rights reserved.

pp.344–346 Charlene Spretnak: From "The Politics of Women's Spirituality," from *Chrysalis: A Magazine of Women's Culture*, no. 6 (November 1978).

pp.346–347 From the website of The American Council of Witches, 1974, http://www.religioustolerance.org/wic_stat1.htm.

pp.348–350 Reprinted by permission from *When Prophets Die: The Postcharismatic Fate of New Religious Movements* edited by Timothy Miller, the State University of New York Press © 1991 State University of New York. All rights reserved.

CHAPTER 13

pp.353–355 Lester R. Kurtz, *Gods in the Global Village: The World's Religions in Sociological Perspective* 2nd edition. Thousand Oaks, CA: Pine Forge Press, 2007.

pp.356–357 Random House, Inc.: From *The Battle for God: A History of Fundamentalism* by Karen Armstrong (New York: Ballantine Books, 2001).

pp.357–362 From *Progressive Muslims: On Justice, Gender, and Pluralism*, ed. Omid Safi. Oxford: OneWorld Publications, 2003.

pp.363–364 Sufi Order Publications: From *The Unity of Religious Ideals* by Hazrat Inayat Khan (New Lebanon, NY: Sufi Order Publications, 1979), © 1979 by Sufi Order. All rights reserved.

pp.364–366 Gobind Sadan Institute: "God Will Break All the Barriers!" by Baba Virsa Singh, talk given at Gobind Sadan, Delhi (December 28, 1996).

pp.367–370 Original article for this book by Lee W. Bailey © 2006, 2011.

pp.370–372 David N. Elkins, *Beyond Religions* © 1998. This material was reproduced by permission of Quest Books, the imprint of The Theosophical Publishing House (www.questbooks.net).

INDEX